The Cistercians

The Cistercians

Ideals and Reality

Louis J. Lekai

The Kent State University Press

Imprimi potest:
   +Anselm A. Nagy, O. Cist.
   Abbot of O.L. of Dallas
   March 19, 1977

Nihil obstat:
   Fr. Bede Lackner, O. Cist.
   censor deputatus

Imprimatur:
   +Thomas Tschoepe
   Bishop of Dallas
   March 15, 1977

Library of Congress Cataloging in Publication Data

Lekai, Louis Julius, 1916-
   The Cistercians.

   Bibliography: p.
   Includes index.
   1. Cistercians. I. Title.
BX3402.2.L44   271'.12   77-3692
ISBN 0-87338-201-3

Library of Congress Catalog Card Number: 77-3692
ISBN: 0-87338-201-3
Printed in the United States of America

Table of Contents

List of Plates
Section one (following p. 148)
1. Cîteaux about 1670.
2. A pair of windows of the church of Obazine, France.
3. Initial from the *Moralia in Job* (by Pope Gregory the Great) copied in Cîteaux in 1111.
4. The chapter hall of Ossegg (Osek), Czechoslovakia.
5. The cloister of Fontfoide, France, end of 12th century.
6. The cloister of the nunnery of Las Huelgas, Burgos, Spain.
7. The refectory of Poblet, Spain.
8. The monks' dormitory at Eberbach, Germany.
9. The washing fountain at Maulbronn, Germany.
10. The monks' choir (stalls) at Maulbronn, Germany.
11. The monumental grange barn (Lissewege) of Ter Doest, Flanders.
12. Nave of the Church of Alcobaça, Portugal.
13. The ruins of the church of Rievaulx, England.
14. The Gothic interior of the church at Neuberg, Austria, 14th century, with Baroque furnishings.
15. Interior of the shrine of Vierzehnheiligen, Germany, designed by Balthasar Neumann, 1743.
16. The interior of the new church of Mehrerau, Austria.

Section two (following p. 308)
1. The façade of the church at Fontenay, France.
2. The church of Fossanova, Italy.
3. The ruins of Fountains Abbey, England.
4. Fontfroide, France.
5. The façade of the church of Heiligenkreuz, Austria.
6. Cloister and church of Noirlac, France.
7. The church of Pontigny, France.

TABLE OF CONTENTS

Acknowledgments

The task of presenting in one volume the history of a religious institution, as ancient, influential and widely extended as the Cistercian Order is a challenging one. Nevertheless, my first such attempt, *The White Monks* (1953), together with its slightly updated versions in French (*Les moines blancs,* 1957) and German (*Geschichte und Wirken der Weissen Mönche,* 1958), were well received. The last quarter of a century, however, has revolutionalized our traditional views on Cistercian beginnings and a large number of recent studies have modified and greatly widened our knowledge of the rest of Cistercian history.

Since my original work in English has been out of print for some years, I first considered the publication of a second, revised edition. The sheer bulk of the new material, however, soon convinced me that the writing of a new survey was a better and easier solution. Here, then, is a new history of the Cistercian Order, related to *The White Monks* through its structure and basically narrative character, but, except for some scattered paragraphs, textually independent and substantially enlarged. The complete recasting of the seventeenth and eighteenth centuries was based largely on my studies published previously in the *Analecta Cisterciensia*; a particular aspect of it, *The Rise of the Cistercian Strict Observance,* appeared in a separate volume.

Among the many confreres and colleagues who have followed the progress of my work with keen interest, special thanks are due to Professor Polycarpe Zakar, editor of the *Analecta Cisterciensia,* for his reading and constructive suggestions regarding the chapters dealing with Cistercian beginnings; to Father Chrysogonus Waddell of Gethsemani Abbey, for his generous assistance in the presentation of recent Trappist developments; to Dom Jean Leclercq, our own *doctor universalis* of monastic studies, for his most valued comments on the chapter "Spirituality and Learning;" to Professor Meredith Lillich of Syracuse University, for her expert observations on the chapter "Art;" to my fellow-monk at Our Lady of Dallas, Professor Bede K. Lackner of the University of Texas at Arlington, for his generous consent to publish for the first time his new translations of early Cistercian documents as an appendix to this book; to Father Maur Cocheril of Port-du-Salut, for the professionally drawn set of maps, designed specially for the present volume; and to my old friend and classmate at the Cistercian *gymnasium* of Budapest, Dr. Dezsö Kassay, who expertly redrew and redesigned several of my charts and tabulations.

Those, however, to whom I owe most are Dr. Rozanne Elder and Professor John Sommerfeldt, both of Western Michigan University. Both have read the whole manuscript, corrected most charitably countless stylistic infelicities and called my attention to many errors and omissions. I owe the same degree of gratitude, and for the same reason, to Professor Giles Constable of Harvard University, who reviewed most constructively the whole manuscript at the final stage of its completion. Needless to say, for all possible errors of this work I am solely responsible.

May this be the opportunity to recognize my indebtedness to Professor Coburn V. Graves of Kent State University, the first American reviewer of *The White Monks,* friend and fellow-student in the field of Cistercian studies. His warm interest and encouragement have been instrumental in the completion of the present work. His mastery of medieval Latin has helped in the elimination of several imperfections in the translation of the appended documents.

The contributors to the illustrations will be recognized on the printed reproductions, although I wish to point out that a number of fine photographs of German Cistercian abbeys reached me through the courtesy of Father Hermann Josef Roth, O. Cist. of the abbey of Marienstatt.

Finally, a word of sincere appreciation is the well-earned due of the dedicated officers and staff of The Kent State University Press, particularly of Mr. Paul H. Rohmann, Director, and Mr. Michael A. DiBattista, Editor. Their warm support of the project from its inception and the countless hours of hard work they invested in all details of the process of publication have exceeded the highest standards of professional services. May the success of this book be their most appropriate reward.

L. J. Lekai

PART I

Cistercian Centuries

I

The Eleventh-Century Monastic Reforms

 The year 1000 can justly be considered a turning point in the history of Christian Europe for weightier reasons than its conveniently round figure. The first attempt to establish peace, prosperity and civilized order on the ruins of the Roman Empire, the so-called Carolingian Renaissance, had failed. The proud empire of Charlemagne fell apart under his feuding grandchildren, and the flickering lights of monastic learning and piety were snuffed out by a new storm of barbarian invasions. The Vikings attacked from the north, the Saracens from the south, the Hungarians from the east. By the end of the ninth century the question was no longer the preservation of Christian civilization but the survival of Christianity itself. The barbarians again rode or sailed at will throughout the continent. Rome and Paris became as unsafe as Bordeaux, Marseilles or Naples. Smoking ruins of once mighty abbeys dotted the devastated landscape, while the papacy sank to the level of a degraded institution of purely local significance.

By the middle of the tenth century, however, hopeful signs began to multiply. The fury of invading barbarians abated. Both the Northmen and the Hungarians settled down in their newly acquired lands, embraced Christianity and turned out to be constructive partners in the slow process of recovery. The Saxon Otto I created a semblance of order in the German lands, renewed the Empire and rescued the papacy from the clutches of powerful and perpetually feuding Roman families. Meanwhile the rapidly expanding Cluny restored confidence and respect for monasticism in western Europe.

As the turn of the century approached, an elementary degree of order and security from invasion was achieved. This modest success set the stage for the spectacular outburst of creative energies behind the rise of the new civilization of the High Middle Ages. In the eleventh century the institutions of feudalism reached full development. The same era witnessed the emergence of medieval cities and a remarkable revival of international trade and commerce. The new cathedral and municipal schools soon outshone the earlier monastic centers of learning, and prepared the way for the universities. The laity eagerly seized the new

1

opportunities, and professionally trained bureaucrats began to replace bishops and abbots in governmental administrative positions. Artists, scholars and poets remained humble admirers and imitators of classical antiquity no longer. The new Romanesque architecture exhibited amazing originality in both engineering and decorative details. Saint Anselm, Archbishop of Canterbury, can justly be considered the father of scholasticism and his contemporary, Duke William IX of Aquitaine, a pioneer of courtly (troubadour) poetry. In Lombardy the study of Roman law was resumed, and this, in turn, inspired the rise of canon law. But there is no more dramatic an illustration and proof of the enormous vigor and self-confidence of this new Europe than the successful counterattack against the infidels: the heroic *reconquista* in Spain, and the First Crusade, which took French knights thousands of miles away to the recapture of Jerusalem.

The reason, however, that modern historians unhesitatingly call the eleventh century an era of revolution, comparable in its impact to the Reformation or the French Revolution, is the sudden reversal, commonly known as the Gregorian Reform, that took place in the field of Church-State relations. But "reform" is not quite the appropriate term. This was not a simple effort to eradicate abuses and return to some earlier pattern of Church life, but a violent demand for drastic change. It was, in fact, an ideological struggle aiming to shake off age-old traditions and to establish in the world a new order, better suited to changed circumstances.

After the short-lived Carolingian experiment, a seemingly lasting equilibrium in Church-State relations had been achieved in the Ottonian and early Salian Empires, a balance characterized by an interpenetration of *ecclesia* and *mundus*. The emperor was not merely a secular ruler, but *rex et sacerdos,* with dual obligations to protect and propagate the Church with broad authority over ecclesiastical appointments and functions. Similarly, the hierarchy was fully integrated with the emerging feudal society, and in addition to administering the sacraments, bore a variety of governmental, judicial and even military duties. Over a large area the authorities of pope and emperor overlapped, and the emperor's mild tutorship over the papacy was not only condoned but often expected. This state of affairs was never more conspicuous than under Henry III (1039-1056), a stern and pious ascetic, a monk in worldly garb. At the synod of Sutri (1046) he settled a scandalous schism. He deposed three competitors for the papal throne (Benedict IX, Sylvester III, and Gregory VI) and arranged the successive elections of three popes, the third his own uncle, Leo IX (1049-1054), the first "Gregorian" reformer.

A drastic change in attitudes manifested itself suddenly in 1059 in the famous papal election decree, and in the publication of the equally epoch-making *Three Books Against the Simoniacs* by Cardinal Humbert of Silva Candida. Under the banner of "freedom of the Church" began the fight against secular influence in ecclesiastical administration and clerical involvement in wordly affairs. The first can be conveniently simplified as the Investiture Conflict, the second as measures against buying and selling Church positions (simony) and clerical marriage (nicolaitism). Both phases of the struggle reached a dramatic climax under the pontificate of Gregory VII (1073-1085), whose goal evidently included the total readjustment of Christian society, leading to an institutional separation of Church and State. This objective entailed stripping the emperor of quasi-sacerdotal powers, securing for the pope extensive and effective jurisdiction over the whole Church, setting a morally purified clergy sharply apart from the world, and, in the case of secular and ecclesiastical conflicts, insuring a decisive role for the pope. The revolutionary program could not be entirely executed either by Gregory or by his successors, but during the course of fifty years of incessant debate every facet of Christian life, including monasticism, came under critical re-examination.

Monastic renewal in the eleventh century, then, can be properly understood only as an integral component of the Gregorian Reform. Renewal became inevitable not because of declining morals or lax discipline, but because monks were forced to find a new place in a rapidly changing society. Events resembled the optical magic of an old-fashioned kaleidoscope. When the viewer turns the tube all particles are bound to move, assuming each time a different pattern of colors in perfect balance and harmony. Those who try to justify any significant monastic reform by piling up incidents of abuses and misdeeds are banging on the wrong door. Unfortunately, human failings have always been in evidence even in the most perfect monasteries, but the eleventh century showed no conspicuous signs of monastic "decline." On the contrary, under Abbot Hugh the Great (1049-1109), the empire of Cluny, with its countless direct or indirect affiliations, reached its apogee. The swelling wave of criticism directed against Benedictine monasticism in the eleventh century can be explained largely by the fact that Cluny and its affiliations were dilatory in noticing changes around them and even tardier to adapt themselves to new conditions. In fact, contrary to an often expressed belief, Cluniac spirituality had no direct role in launching the Gergorian Reform. Abbot Hugh was less than enthusiastic about Gregory's extreme ideas and, instead of supporting them, tried to mediate between the Pope and Henry IV. This great Abbot's instrumental role in the outcome of the famous confrontation at Canossa has received due attention.

Criticism of traditional forms of monasticism had come from various sources, but most often from the monks themselves. The best known and certainly the most influential of the critics was Saint Peter Damian who, in spite of his high position in the Curia, referred to himself as "sinful monk" (*peccator monachus*). He accused many abbots of his time of worldly display: they spent more time at royal courts than in their monasteries; they were better versed in politics than in matters pertaining to their office; they were constantly involved in litigations over property and income. He nourished no admiration for the great builders who embellished their churches and enlarged their abbeys. He could not resist recounting a vision of the famous Abbot Richard of Saint-Vanne in hell, condemned to erect scaffoldings forever in punishment for his extravagant taste for fine architecture. Cardinal Peter had no appreciation for liturgical splendor, and criticised "the unnecessary sounding of bells, the protracted chanting of hymns and the conspicuous use of ornament." On his memorable visit to Cluny in 1063, he observed that various offices were so prolonged that in a day's routine there was scarcely half an hour left to engage the monks in conversation. At the same time he deplored the lack of penance and mortification, particularly in food and drink.

Other critics of monasticism, whose numbers could be multiplied at will, spoke out against seculars living among monks under various pretexts; against the disturbing presence of children and other unwanted individuals; against monasteries built so close to cities that their solitude was endangered; and against unnecessary travelling and widespread vagrancy among monks. They pointed out that the clerical status of most monks served merely as an excuse for the abandonment of manual labor, and that the assumption of pastoral duties led to undesirable competition with the secular clergy. In fact, the critics continued, many abbots usurped episcopal authority and eagerly acquired churches and a variety of other profitable benefices, the holding of which was improper for monks.

The secular clergy's dissatisfaction with monastic standards became evident at a number of provincial synods held in France throughout the eleventh century. In 1031 the Synod of Bourges stressed the virtues of obedience and stability, and threatened vagrant monks with excommunication. The Council of Toulouse in 1056 attacked abbots who disregarded their duties, and emphasized the neglected virtue of poverty. In 1059 a similar gathering at Rouen chided monks for the vanity of pursuing exalted positions and lofty dignities. At subsequent synods at Toulouse (1068) and Rouen (1074), the clergy enjoined the monks to adhere to the strict observance of the Rule of Saint Benedict without relaxing its prescriptions concerning silence, vigils, fasting and clothing.

In the eyes of many contemporaries, it seems, the root of such abuses was the monk's disregard for their divinely ordained role and place in the

Church. This conviction was expressed in the writings of William of Volpiano (d. 1031), the reformer of St. Bénigne in Dijon, who deplored that in their conduct there was no distinction either between clergy and people, or between priests and monks. His nephew, John of Fécamp, placed the same issue in an even sharper light when, following Gregory the Great, he insisted that there must be a clear line separating the laity from the clergy and an equally distinct place for monks, who should spend their lives in penance and solitude.

In spite of their many failings, the monks of the time must be credited with manful efforts to reform themselves along the lines suggested by their critics. Zealous new foundations multiplied from Calabria to Brittany, while practically all older abbeys of any reputation undertook the arduous work of mending their practices.

The three basic ideas that seem to have guided eleventh-century monastic renewal were poverty, eremitism and apostolic life. The three concepts overlapped and all had been, to some extent, already integrated with the Rule of Saint Benedict: their reappearance, therefore, resulted in the revival of older forms of monasticism. The originality of new establishments consisted largely in the peculiar blend of the three basic elements.

Contemporary critics singled out riches and luxury as their prime targets, while reformers urged the strictest poverty as a first step toward meaningful renewal. A new stress on poverty emerged as a spontaneous reaction to prosperity. The problem was so keenly felt in the eleventh century that, in search of a solution, the reformers bypassed the Rule of Saint Benedict and reached back to the poverty of Christ on the Cross, and to the poverty of the apostles and their first disciples. The movement apparently started early in the century in Italy and spread quickly throughout the rest of Europe. The re-emerging dualistic heresies, disdaining material things and condemning wealth and possessions, added to the impact of half-naked, weird-looking preachers of poverty roaming the countryside in increasing numbers. Not only priests and monks but also the laity became fascinated by the idea of absolute poverty, as the example of the much-researched *Patarini* of northern Italy clearly indicates.

In this light the teaching of Saint Peter Damian, strict as it was, cannot be regarded as extreme. He replaced Benedictine moderation (*sufficientia*) with harshness (*extremitas*) and destitution (*penuria*) and encouraged his followers to go barefoot, sleep on hard beds and be satisfied with minimal necessities in clothing, food and drink. Contending that God must be the monk's sole property, he considered the holding of money outrightly sinful and a violation of the contract made by the monk when he signed his profession. "Therefore, let us turn back, beloved, to the innocence of the primitive Church, so that we may learn to relinquish possessions and enjoy the simplicity of regal poverty," Damian exhorted his disciples.

No religious body could escape the impact of the trend. The "poor of Christ" (*Pauperes Christi*) became the customary reference to both monks and canons regular and was a phrase often repeated in the correspondence of Gregory VII. Nothing can attest better to the idea's overwhelming power than the strange attempt of Paschal II, a former monk of Vallombrosa, to reach a solution in the Investiture Conflict. In 1111, to the amazement of Europe, he proposed that, in exchange for the total preclusion of secular interference in church matters, the imperial hierarchy should surrender its landed possessions once granted by the crown.

As an idea as well as a historical phenomenon, the revival of eremitism was closely linked with the new concept of poverty. The hermit not only withdrew from society, he lived in total renunciation, in total poverty, both internal and external. As Saint Jerome put it: "the desert loves the naked" (*nudos amat eremus*). The roots of the movement reached back to the deserts of Egypt and Syria in the early Christian centuries. As a form of religious life it survived, particularly in the East, in spite of the increased popularity of cenobitism. It seems, moreover, that the continuity of eremitism remained unbroken to the eleventh century even in the West. What appears to be new in the epoch under examination is its enormous popularity, its rapid geographic spread and its penetration to all strata of existing society. In attempts to explain the obvious facts, various links have been proposed between the movement and social and economic problems of the eleventh century. Such conditions were, however, very different from place to place, while the appeal of eremitism seems to have been universal: any suspected causal link between the two remains, therefore, ambiguous. Since the revival of eremitism first became visible in Italy, the movement is often thought to have been inspired by eastern anchorites who settled down in the peninsula after they had been forced out from their homeland by the advance of Islam. Religious contacts between Italy and the Byzantine Empire had never been entirely broken, however, and a few hermits could hardly have imported novelties of consequence. Furthermore, even if the local influence of some Byzantine hermits, like Saint Nilus of Calabria, was significant, such isolated incidents cannot adequately explain the spread of eremitism north of the Alps. It is probably safer to state that eremitism, like the new and strict interpretation of poverty, emerged as a reaction to the prevailing standards of monastic life, a spontaneous protest against the comfort and quiet daily routine of the monks of great abbeys, which no longer presented sufficient challenge to souls yearning for the heroic life of the Desert Fathers.

This attitude clearly implied that to the eyes of the new generation of reformers eremitic life appeared higher than life spent under the Rule of Saint Benedict. The monastery was conceived, accordingly, merely as a training ground for future hermits. As Peter Damian put it: "As the priesthood is the goal of clerical education, proficiency in the arts is the purpose of attending the schools of the grammarians, and as brilliant pleading at law is the culmination of dreary hours of legal study, so monastic life with all its observances is but a preparation for that higher goal, the solitude of the hermitage." The monastery, he contended, was acceptable for the sick and infirm; those who chose to stay there permanently could only be tolerated.

The lasting influence of individual hermits, as long as they truly remained in solitude and isolation, poses a peculiar problem. Obviously such people, no matter how deep or rich their spirituality, would pass away without having made any specific impression on others. On the other hand, the presence of disciples might facilitate the transmission of spiritual values, but would destroy the solitude and involve the hermit in some sort of organization, the very thing he was trying to escape. Individuals are ephemeral; only institutions have enduring existence. Most great hermits of the eleventh century solved the dilemma by concessions, and wound up as founders of religious communities where solitude was blended with cenobitic elements. Camaldoli, Fonte Avellana, Vallombrosa, Fontevrault, Savigny, Grandmont, Grand Chartreuse and Obazine are only the best known of many similar eremitical foundations, where institutional frameworks guaranteed the survival of a peculiar spirituality long after the disappearance of the founding hermits and the decline of eremitism as a popular movement.

The third incentive for monastic renewal was the drive to imitate the life of the apostles, or, more specifically, the life of the apostolic community in Jerusalem, in poverty, simplicity and mutual charity. It must be emphasized, however, that in the eleventh century the world "apostolic" carried no connotation of preaching the Gospel or discharging other duties of the "care of souls" (*cura animarum*); the following of the apostles could well be within the program of contemplatives or even hermits. On the other hand, the appeal of the "apostolic life" extended far beyond monastic circles. It inspired canons regular, itinerant preachers, lay poverty movements and many features of the Gregorian Reform. Nothing more eloquently demonstrates the movement's elementary force than the difficulty Church authorities experienced in trying to contain the

7

growing number of itinerant preachers within the bonds of moderation and orthodoxy. Even so renowned a person as Robert of Arbrissel, the founder of Fontevrault, was severely reprimanded by the Bishop of Rennes for his bizarre appearance and extravagant behavior.

The influence of the primitive Church over monasticism is as ancient as monasticism itself. The novelty consisted in the urgent and extensive demand to reform religious communities in the light of the New Testament. Peter Damian obliged his followers to "return to the innocence of the primitive Church." At the Council of Rome in 1059, Hildebrand used virtually the same phrases, demanding the restoration of the common life of the first century. According to Stephen of Muret, a prominent "poor man of Christ" in the next generation, rules written by men are of secondary importance; therefore, "if anyone should ask you to what religious order you belong, tell him the order of the Gospel, which is the basis of all rules." A treatise of the early twelfth century "On the Truly Apostolic Life" (*De vita vere apostolica*), attributed to Rupert, abbot of Deutz, went even further: "If you wish to consult the relevant passages of Scripture, you will find that they all seem to say plainly that the Church originated in the monastic life." Saint Benedict's Rule was in fact the adaptation of the "apostolic rule" (*regula apostolica*). Therefore, he continued, the apostles had been monks, and thus the monks were the apostles' authentic successors.

The implications of such interpretations were plain enough. Monks must free themselves from the entanglements of feudal society; they must abandon their splendid surroundings, their elaborate ceremonials, the ease and comfort which the work of their predecessors made possible. Monks worthy of their apostolic heritage should turn their backs to the world and seek a renewed life in simplicity, poverty, manual labor and charity.

In addition to the three motives for monastic renewal just discussed, many authors refer to another related movement: "back to the sources" of Christian monasticism. While it is undeniable that all reformers attempted to justify their demands by references to the Bible, the Desert Fathers or the Rule of Saint Benedict, it remains doubtful that such manifestations amounted to a "movement" characteristic of the eleventh century. Reformers of all times and every designation have employed the same tactics to vindicate novel approaches. Changes, innovations, breaks with the past, have rarely generated universal enthusiasm among monks. Those who proposed such moves felt compelled to disguise their intentions as attempts to return to ancient and hallowed traditions. At the same time, radical alterations in the fabric of society necessitate institutional reforms. The initiation of corresponding institutional changes manifests a healthy instinct of survival. In such circumstances a traditional organization cannot ensure its own sufficient readjustment simply by turning back to observances and procedures which are admittedly old. The problem can be solved by accommodations faithful to genuine traditions, but it is doubtful how far the eleventh-century monastic reformers were aware of the nature of their task or how sincerely they were devoted to the past. To be sure, they were scarcely in a position to interpret their sources authentically, for the simple reason that they remained unaware of the fundamental differences separating the mentality of the late Roman world from their own.

In their use of available sources the reformers followed their instincts. This amazing liberty can be observed in the variety of contradictory interpretations to which the Rule of Saint Benedict was subjected. Its text, in virtually identical form, was certainly available to all monks from Benedict of Aniane to Robert of Molesme. None dared to reject its authority. A few, such as Stephen of Muret, practically ignored it; others like Saint Bruno, embraced only certain elements of it. The majority of reformers, while professing utmost devotion to the Rule, interpreted it with less than hermeneutic scrupulosity. This made possible a wide range of foundations: the Roman "basilica abbeys," the Anglo-Saxon "mission abbeys" and "culture abbeys," the Carolingian "prayer abbeys" and "pilgrimage abbeys," the Cluniac "cult abbeys," and the eleventh-century "solitude abbeys."

The most articulate spokesman of "solitude abbeys" was certainly Peter Damian who, while paying homage to the Rule of Saint Benedict, managed to read into it his own peculiar idea on mortification. He saw no incompatibility between the monastic concepts of Saint Benedict and those of his desert predecessors, for he urged his followers to abide by "whatever is found in the Rule of Saint Benedict or in the Institutes or Collations of the Fathers." Encountering Benedict's manifest moderation he argued that the Rule had been written for the guidance of innocent souls, that Saint Benedict had had no intention of supplanting the penitential canons applying to sinners, and that therefore "the Rule did not avoid the precepts of the Fathers who had gone before." He himself, however, was quite willing to void in practice seventy-two chapters of the Rule in order to live up to the full extent of the seventy-third, which, indeed, referred to the example of the Desert Fathers.

Reformers of the younger generation quite possibly realized the inner contradiction of such approaches and reacted by drawing sincerely closer to the Rule. Not only was Vallombrosa "founded on the authority of

Saint Benedict," but John Gualbert "diligently began to discern the meaning of the Rule and intended to observe it with all his strength," while urging his disciples to follow it "in everything." Bernard of Tiron and Vitalis of Mortain (in Savigny) adopted similar attitudes, while zeal for a still more exact observance of the Rule was the very reason for the foundation of Cîteaux.

The common denominator of all eleventh-century reforming efforts was the desire to establish a life of heroic mortifications spent in retirement from all worldly entanglements. In this the founders of new monastic institutions were eminently successful. But the very success of the reformers carried the germ of another epoch of relative decline. Peter Damian and his heirs did establish a life of heroic asceticism and raised their new abbeys to never before experienced heights of monastic perfection, but such standards could not be maintained indefinitely. While insisting on the meticulous observance of certain passages of the Rule, they overlooked its governing spirit of moderation. Saint Benedict was willing to offer compromises to human frailty, but many of the new reformers were not. They refused to recognize the truth that institutions to endure must take into account the limitations of average men, not the ambitions of saintly and heroic men. Once again, the wisdom of Saint Benedict proved far more enduring than the zeal of unworldly enthusiasts. Most eremitical or semi-eremitical foundations disintegrated, were absorbed by successive reforms, or slipped into insignificance. Of the new crop of monks, the Cistercians remained in the forefront of religious history for centuries to come.

II

From Molesme to Cîteaux

 The story of the foundation of Cîteaux cannot be told without an account of a previous attempt at monastic reform, the establishment of Molesme in 1075 by Saint Robert. It was at Molesme that a group of disillusioned monks conceived the idea of still another foundation to be executed after better planning and with better results in the forests of Cîteaux.

The early life of Robert is shrouded in obscurity, and the meager details given in his thirteenth-century *Vita* appear to be much colored by his later roles at Molesme and Cîteaux. Robert was born about 1028 somewhere in Champagne. His noble parents, Theodoric and Ermengarde, were probably related to the counts of Tonnerre and to the house of Raynald, viscount of Beaune. Robert, in his early youth, joined the abbey of Montier-la-Celle near Troyes, where, some time after 1053, he became prior. Between 1068 and 1072 he served as abbot at Saint-Michel-de-Tonnerre, an abbey under Cluniac discipline in the diocese of Langres. For some reason his term as abbot ended abruptly and Robert returned to Troyes as a simple monk. His stay at the abbey of his profession was short, however; after a few months he was appointed or elected prior at Saint-Ayoul, a dependent priory of Montier-la-Celle at Provins in the diocese of Sens. But this place proved to be even less congenial to him than Saint-Michel had been and in 1074 he joined a group of hermits in the forests of Collan. It was with the participation of these hermits that Robert founded in 1075 the monastery of Molesme in the diocese of Langres on a suitable piece of land donated for the purpose by Hugh, lord of Maligny.

Robert had had considerable experience with monastic life. Though dissatisfied with the standards of Cluniac discipline and attracted to the solitary life, as his enterprise at Molesme indicated, he stood firm in his belief that the ascetic standards of the desert practiced within a monastic community came closest to an ideal religious life. His obvious sincerity soon attracted a number of followers and, with the material support of the local nobility, Molesme turned out to be one of the more successful reform-abbeys of the late eleventh century. In fact, the influx of new vocations and generous donations made possible a number of new foundations. Some were only small cells, others dependent priories or abbeys. Numbering about forty by 1100, these foundations had spread to twelve dioceses.

The rapid growth of this new monastic congregation clearly attested to the soundness of Robert's original ideas, but the mounting problems of organization and control far surpassed the saintly founder's talents. In 1082 Molesme attracted Saint Bruno and his companions, who spent some time there before they departed for the mountains of Grenoble, the cradle of the Carthusian Order. But by 1090 Robert himself had come to the conclusion that his place was no longer in his abbey and he joined a group of hermits at Aux near Riel-les-Eaux. The embarrassed monks of Molesme soon prevailed upon him and Robert consented to return to his abbey, but, if credence can be given to the *Vita,* before long four of Robert's closest adherents, among them Alberic and Stephen, staged another escape, abiding "for some time" at Vivicus, an otherwise unknown location.

These unhappy incidents do not necessarily imply Molesme's moral decadence; unabated public esteem and the expansion of the abbey seem to militate against such a supposition. The fundamental problem lay in the fact that the small group of founding hermits had become so outnumbered by new vocations that they lost control over discipline, and Molesme consequently began to resemble more and more the other prosperous abbeys of the neighborhood, all under the irresistible influence of Cluny, which Abbot Robert had specifically tried to escape. By the 1090s Molesme had accumulated ecclesiastical benefices and tithes, revenues of churches, villages and serfs, and the abbey itself was swarming with lay servants (*famuli*), brothers (*conversi*), children (*oblati*) and *praebendarii,* that is, people who offered their goods to the abbey in exchange for room and board for life. All this fell well within standard monastic traditions, but it was a far cry from Robert's dream of seclusion and poverty, a life unhampered by worldly cares and dedicated to God's service alone.

Quarrels rose over such issues and acrimonious debates fought with all the bitterness of religious controversies continued for years. If the famous chroniclers of the next generation, Ordericus Vitalis and William of Malmesbury, can be trusted, Robert found it convenient to bolster the weight of his argument by frequent allusions to the Rule of Saint Benedict, while the hostile majority insisted on the legitimacy of Cluniac customs and rejected the Abbot's proposals as dangerous and impractical novelties. A meaningful compromise seemed out of the question, but the polarization of the issues helped reshape a reform program to be carried out in the future with better results than those at Molesme. In this way utter dedication to the Rule sank deeply into the minds of the future founders of Cîteaux, and it was joined by deep-seated suspicion toward Cluny and an acute awareness of the unhappy consequences of too close a relation with feudal society.

Some of the hermit-monks tired of the continuous wrangle. They left Molesme for the foundation of Aulps, a small cell in the diocese of Geneva, which, late in 1096 or early in 1097, was raised to an abbey. Significantly the document of this latter event emphasized the monks' dedication to the strict observance of the Rule of Saint Benedict; even more importantly, the hand which penned this document was Stephen's, the English secretary of Abbot Robert, and the event was legally witnessed by Alberic, the prior of Molesme, both future abbots of Cîteaux.

It was perhaps in the fall of 1097 that Abbot Robert, accompanied by a number of his monks, among them again Alberic and Stephen, visited Archbishop Hugh de Die of Lyons, papal legate in France and a stalwart promoter of Gregorian Reform. Robert presented to the sympathetic prelate his plan for a new foundation, giving as his chief reason the "lukewarm and negligent" observance of the Rule at Molesme, which he vowed to follow "henceforth more strictly and more perfectly." Hugh was obviously impressed, gave his blessing to the project, encouraged the petitioners "to persevere in their holy endeavor" and, since such a move seemed to serve the interests of both parties at Molesme, authorized Robert and his followers to leave the abbey and retire "to another place," where they would be able "to serve the Lord undisturbedly in a more wholesome manner." Robert, bishop of Langres, in whose diocese Molesme was located, seems not to have been involved in the action. He was, perhaps, not particularly anxious to meddle in an affair of potentially embarrassing implications, nor did Abbot Robert consider his permission necessary. The monks of Molesme watched the dissidents' preparations with a sigh of relief, and after their departure promptly elected as their new abbot a certain Geoffrey, who was invested in due course by the Bishop of Langres.

Early in 1098 twenty-one monks made themselves ready to follow Robert to the site of a "new monastery," donated for the purpose by Raynald, viscount of Beaune, the Abbot's old kinsman and benefactor. Although he was a vassal of Odo, duke of Burgundy, the land Raynald granted was his allod, land not burdened by feudal taxes or services due a third party. It was located some twenty kilometers south of Dijon, in a heavily wooded area that the author of the *Exordium Cistercii,* borrowing a picturesque phrase from Deuteronomy (XXXII,10), characterized as "a place of horror and vast solitude." No doubt the small band of hermit-monks had searched for such a site, but in fact the land, within the diocese of Chalon-sur-Saône, included a few peasant dwellings and most likely even an old chapel, where the new arrivals held their first services. The place even had a name: Cîteaux (in Latin, *Cistercium*), the etymology of which was variously explained; the most probable was a reference to its position, being "on this side of the third milestone" (*cis tertium lapidem miliarium*) on the old Roman road between Langres and Chalon-sur-Saône. For a number of years, however, the new foundation was not called by this name, but was simply known as the New Monastery (*Novum monasterium*). The traditional foundation date, given in later documents, was March 21, 1098. Palm Sunday of that year and the feast of Saint Benedict, it was chosen more for its symbolic significance than for any particular external event that took place in the hard daily life of the new settlers, who had certainly arrived there earlier. The canonical erection of the primitive facilities to an abbey, Abbot Robert's oath of obedience to Bishop Walter of Chalon-sur-Saône, or the monks' vow of stability to the New Monastery, all mentioned in the *Exordium Cistercii,* might have happened on that date, but it is more logical to assume that these momentous legal acts took place during the course of the summer of 1098.

Robert and his companions yearned to live an ascetic life in poverty and perfect solitude, providing for themselves, like the Apostles of Christ, through their own labor. In this they were not disappointed, for their survival in the forest must have been hard indeed. The first months were doubtless spent in clearing woods, erecting some temporary shelters and planting for the autumn harvest. The routine of prayers and manual labor, however, was soon disturbed by news from Molesme. Monks of the abbey who had taken their restless Abbot's departure complacently had begun to have second thoughts. The nobility of the neighborhood, whose members populated the abbey, had been scandalized over the turbulent events in the community. They suspected grave abuses among the monks, and Molesme began to feel the consequences of hostile public opinion. From the point of view of those who had remained in the abbey, the easiest way out of the predicament, as past experience had proven, was to return Robert to Molesme. Since there was no hope that Robert would come back voluntarily, the monks sent a delegation to Rome asking Pope Urban II to order the Abbot back to Molesme. It was probably then that the legality of the secession to Cîteaux was first questioned. The Pope did

14

not wish to decide the issue on the testimony of one side only, and he entrusted the thorny problem to his legate in France, Hugh of Lyons, merely suggesting that "if possible, the Abbot be brought from solitude back to the abbey." The legate demonstrated equal reluctance in passing final judgment in the matter alone and called for consultation several bishops and "many other honorable and esteemed men." The "synod" took place probably late in June 1099, at Port-d'Anselle where the Bishop of Langres took the side of the monks of Molesme. At issue was not the forcible return to Molesme of all dissidents, but only Robert. In order to facilitate his return, Geoffrey, his successor, offered his resignation, whereupon Archbishop Hugh declared that Abbot Robert must indeed return to Molesme. Permission to return to Molesme was simultaneously given to all those in the New Monastery who chose to follow Robert, provided that in the future no attempt would be made to lure monks from one community to the other. Should Robert "in his usual fickleness leave the same community," continued the document, Geoffrey was to succeed him without new election. The New Monastery was permitted to keep the "chapel" of Abbot Robert, that is, church furnishings and liturgical books, except a precious breviary, but even this they were allowed to keep until the feast of the Passion of St. John the Baptist (August 29), so that in the meantime they could copy it.

Robert accepted the legate's verdict without apparent resentment and, followed by the monks who were more attached to him than to Cîteaux, he returned to Molesme, where he resumed his abbatial duties and governed the abbey until his death in 1111. His popular veneration as a saint was officially recognized by his canonization in 1220, and in 1222 the Cistercian calendar designated April 29 as his feastday. Robert's sudden change of heart and willing return to Molesme, however, puzzled contemporaries as much as it baffles modern historians. He was, to be sure, an elderly man in his seventies, therefore the hardships of the first year at Cîteaux must have afflicted him more than his younger companions. On the other hand, he should have realized that his defection would endanger the survival of the New Monastery, the foundation that he himself had planned with care and devotion. The danger was made more acute by the number of monks who followed his example, perhaps a majority of the twenty-one founders. This latter opinion is substantiated by the report of William of Malmesbury, who, only some twenty-five years after the event, asserted in his chronicle (*Gesta regum Anglorum*) that after the exodus-in-reverse only eight monks remained at Cîteaux. The same author, leaning evidently on Cistercian sources, was the first to voice the suspicion that Robert had a secret understanding with his subjects at Molesme, and that the delegates sent to the Pope demanding his return had acted with his previous consent. The subsequent order of the authorities had therefore found him willing indeed (*volentem cogentes*). Cistercian resentment toward Robert was still in evidence as late as about 1190, when Conrad, monk of Clairvaux and later abbot of Eberbach, composed his *Exordium magnum,* in which he berated Robert for his inexcusable desertion. The first lists of the abbots of Cîteaux do not even mention his name. This attitude, however, became a source of such embarrassment after Robert's canonization that strenuous efforts were made to rewrite or delete the incriminating passages. The restoration of the original text of the *Exordium magnum* was made possible only after the chance discovery of an unretouched manuscript in 1908.

Shortly after the departure of Abbot Robert and his adherents, very likely in July 1099, the small community of the New Monastery elected in his stead Alberic, who had served as prior under Robert, and had probably been one of the founders of Molesme. He must have been a man of ability and firm character, for the consolidation of Cîteaux both materially and morally should be ascribed to him. After the initial donation of the site for the new settlement, it was not the Viscount of Beaune, but rather Odo, duke of Burgundy, and after his death in the Holy Land in 1102, his son, Hugh, who came to the monks' material aid. Odo assured the monks the use of the surrounding forests and donated Meursault, the first of many vineyards Cîteaux came eventually to possess. When, for lack of sufficient water, Alberic found the site of the first settlement inadequate and moved about a kilometer northward, Hugh probably furnished material for the construction of the first stone church of Cîteaux, consecrated by Bishop Walter of Chalon on November 16, 1106, and dedicated to the Blessed Virgin Mary, the beginning of an unbroken Cistercian tradition.

Even more significant was the bull of papal protection that Alberic obtained from Paschal II, as soon as he succeeded Urban II. In view of the much weakened position of Cîteaux and in the expectation of further pressure from Molesme and other unfriendly abbeys, the procurement of such a document was a vital necessity. In order to insure success, Alberic solicited letters of recommendation from the new papal legates, Cardinals John of Gubbio and Benedict, who, in passing through Burgundy happened to visit Cîteaux. The same favor was granted by the ex-legate, Hugh de Die, and Bishop Walter of Chalon. These three documents, as published in the *Exordium parvum,* do not seem to be the genuine ones, but the Roman mission of the two delegated monks, John and Ilbodus, certainly succeeded. The bull of Paschal II, issued on October 19, 1100, and known in Cistercian history as the "Roman privilege," ordained that the inhabitants of the New Monastery "be secure and free from any annoyance . . . under the special protection of the Apostolic See, . . . save the canonical reverence due to the church of Chalon." Although the document cannot be construed as the beginning of Cistercian "exemption," it confirmed the decision of Port-d'Anselle and the legal existence and independence of the abbey, it approved, at least implicitly, the particular discipline the monks followed, and it assured their freedom and security indispensable to future expansion.

That the rest of Alberic's term was spent in a tranquil atmosphere of modest prosperity seems indicated by an exchange of letters between Alberic and Lambert, abbot of Saint-Pierre de Pothières. Alberic asked for the benefit of the *scriptorium* of Cîteaux about the proper accent and meaning of certain Latin words, and Lambert answered in an elaborate scholarly essay on the subject. According to immemorial tradition it was under Alberic that the monks adopted the white, or rather unbleached, habit under a black scapular, which accounts for their popular name: White Monks. According to the *Exordium parvum,* Alberic issued the first "institutes" for the New Monastery. This regulation, the much debated fifteenth chapter of that famous narrative, seems, however, to be merely the conjecture of the author, a member of the second Cistercian generation.

After the death of Alberic on January 26, 1109, the monks elected as abbot the prior, Stephen Harding, an Englishman, the first person in the Order's history who can unmistakably be recognized as a creative genius. He inherited only one of countless reform-abbeys of some notoriety; he left behind the first "order" in monastic history, possessing a clearly formulated program, held together by a firm legal framework and in the process of an unprecedented expansion.

Stephen was born to noble Anglo-Saxon parents about 1060 and as a youth he had spent some time in the Benedictine abbey of Sherborne in Dorsetshire. But the Norman conquest had ruined his family and he himself had had to flee to Scotland and from there to France. He completed his education probably in Paris, and then, with a fellow-refugee from England, Peter, he undertook a long pilgrimage to Rome, where he became assured of his monastic vocation. On their way back, their attention was called to the promising new venture of Molesme. They were impressed, and both decided to join the community. By this time, about 1085, Stephen was a young man of great promise. As a boy he had been exposed to the rich traditions of Celtic and Anglo-Saxon monasticism, reformed by Saint Dunstan (d. 988) according to Cluniac and

Lotharingian models. France offered him the latest scholarship and acquainted him with contemporary problems of monastic and ecclesiastical reform. During his Italian journey, he must have been greatly influenced by the prevailing spirit of Saint Peter Damian and impressed by the examples of Camaldoli and Vallombrosa. At Molesme he had an opportunity to observe the process as well as the causes of the corruption of a noble project through poor internal organization and external intervention. As abbot of Cîteaux, Stephen was ready to employ his erudition, his experiences and his abilities as an organizer to insure the success of Cîteaux, which until then had merely been trying to find a safe place within a revolutionized monastic society.

Attesting to Stephen's excellent relation with his noble neighbors, the fast expansion of Cîteaux's estates began early in his administration. Within five or six years the monks had established their first "granges," Gergueil, Bretigny and Gremigny, on land donated mostly by the family of Countess Elizabeth de Vergy, who proved to be a generous friend of Abbot Stephen and his monks. Gilly-les-Vougeot, the site of the summer residence of abbots of a later age, was granted by Aimon de Marigny. To this the monks managed about 1115 to attach the famous vineyards later known as Clos-de-Vougeot, which turned out to be perhaps the most valuable piece of real estate in Burgundy. Many donations were made as "free alms." Any rights over tithes held by the donor were either entirely remitted, or converted to a nominal annual gift of crops from the land.

At heart Abbot Stephen was far more a scholar than an economist. His erudition enabled him to undertake tasks that would test the talents of the best modern researchers. Mindful of the Rule's references to hymns attributed to Saint Ambrose, Stephen attempted to verify that both in texts and melodies, all hymns sung by his monks were genuinely "Ambrosian." Furthermore, examining the textual variants of the Old Testament codices at his disposal, he made up his mind to restore the original Vulgate of Saint Jerome. In order to clarify such problems he had recourse to the Hebrew and Aramaic versions, consulted with the help of some erudite Jewish rabbis. Through the highly competent *scriptorium* of Cîteaux he not only produced works of great care and accuracy, but also of outstanding beauty. The illuminations of his Bible and the *Moralia in Job*, both produced during the first three years of his administration, were the most original achievements of the whole epoch, proving that in those years Cîteaux harbored some of the greatest artistic talents of France.

Undoubtedly, Cîteaux's rise from obscurity to prominence and Stephen's engaging personality attracted numerous disciples, and by 1112 there emerged the plan for a new foundation, which materialized when in May

FROM MOLESME TO CÎTEAUX

1113, a group of monks set out to La Ferté, south of Cîteaux, but still within the diocese of Chalon-sur-Saône. By then a second house had become all but inevitable, because, as the foundation document stated joyfully, "there was such a number of brethren at Cîteaux that neither the existing estates were sufficient to support them, nor could the place where they lived conveniently accommodate them."

This picture of growth and prosperity is, of course, vastly different from the one that the author of the *Exordium parvum* tried to convey to posterity. Toward the end of this narrative, just before recording the arrival of the youthful Bernard and his companions, the writer referred to Stephen and his monks as "praying, crying and weeping before [God], groaning and sighing deep and long, day and night, all but verging on complete despair, because they had scarcely any successors." The writer of these lines had obviously been blinded by the later fame of Saint Bernard and did his best to show that Cîteaux could not possibly have survived without his dramatic arrival on the desperate scene. Subsequent tampering with the date of Bernard's entry to Cîteaux was done with the same intention and with such success that, until the publication of the studies of A.H. Bredero in 1961, most modern scholars believed that Bernard was admitted in April 1112, whereas the first manuscripts of the *Vita prima* clearly give 1113 for this momentous event. This pious fraud was intended to demonstrate that the foundation of La Ferté had been made possible only by Bernard's arrival. It is conceivable that the settlement of La Ferté was accelerated in anticipation of the new candidates' arrival. That further foundations were indeed made under the impact of the mass movement toward Cîteaux and Clairvaux, initiated by Bernard, remains, of course, uncontested.

La Ferté was followed in 1114 by Pontigny in the diocese of Auxerre; Clairvaux was settled by the twenty-five year old Bernard in 1115, and in the same year Morimond came to life in the diocese of Langres. A pause of three years was followed in quick succession by Preuilly in 1118, then La Cour Dieu, Bouras, Cadouin and Fontenay, all in 1119. It was in this same year that Abbot Stephen found it advisable to turn to the newly elected Pope Callistus II to ask him for a new bull in behalf of Cîteaux and its affiliated houses. The Pope, formerly archbishop of Vienne, knew Cîteaux well, and he had, moreover, actively supported the foundation of Bonneval in the face of Benedictine opposition. In the new document, issued on December 23, 1119, he congratulated Stephen and his monks and "put the seal of confirmation to the work of God they had initiated." The text specifically refers to certain "capitula" and "constitutions" passed after due "deliberation and consent of the abbots and brethren of your monasteries," all aiming at the "observance of the Rule of Blessed Benedict." "We, therefore," concluded the Pope, "rejoicing in the Lord over your progress, confirm by apostolic authority those capitula and constitutions, and decree that all remain forever binding."

This second bull in the history of Cîteaux is another milestone on the road from hard beginning to eventual success. By 1119 the existence of a number of affiliated houses called for certain measures to safeguard the cohesion of the new "order," including the formulation of rules and regulations to be observed by all communities. These goals were achieved after repeated consultations among the abbots and the monks, and took the shape of a constitution and a set of regulations subsequently presented to, and approved by, the Pope. Had the bull preserved the texts presented to the Pontiff's inspection, the historian's assignment of reconstructing the image of early Cîteaux would be infinitely simpler than it is. Not only do the substance of the earliest Cistercian regulations and constitution remain debatable but the stages of their development also continue to puzzle scholars dedicated to scrutinizing the available manuscripts.

III

The Fundamentals of Cistercian Reform

The Cistercian reform was, above all, a movement of spiritual renewal, and a factual recital of its origins must therefore be followed by an analysis of the ideals which inspired the small band of monks who founded Cîteaux. The first stage in this ideological development took place at Molesme. During prolonged and occasionally heated debates the future founders of Cîteaux had ample opportunity to clarify their intentions and to reduce them to a simple practical formula: return to the Rule of Saint Benedict. The application of such principles to everyday conditions took place at Cîteaux during Alberic's administration, although the process probably more resembled day-to-day improvisation than conscious legislation. In fact, there is no indication that either Robert or Alberic intended to do anything more than secure the life of the reform-minded community by the same means countless similar monasteries had taken to survive. The movement's expansion through new foundations induced Stephen Harding to commit to writing the basic elements of observances at Cîteaux and to insure the cohesion of the expanding monastic congregation by devising the nucleus of a constitutional framework. The unexpected success of Cîteaux aroused the jealousy not only of Molesme, but also of the mighty Cluny, and a debate with widespread publicity followed, which covered every facet of the fledgling organization. A clear-cut program, able leadership, cohesion and a sense of victory scored over strong opposition became the elements which constituted the first medieval "order," an organization, visibly distinct among the many autonomous or loosely affiliated conglomeration of Benedictine houses.

To historians writing about thirty years ago the task of telling this story appeared simple. It was universally believed that the basic narrative of Cistercian beginnings, the *Exordium parvum,* not only presented the facts and fundamental doctrines with unquestionable accuracy, but had, in fact, issued from the pen of one of the founders, Saint Stephen Harding. Similarly, the *Charter of Charity,* the constitution of the nascent Order, was regarded as the embodiment of the principles that had enabled the same Abbot Stephen to carry out his program with enduring success. In this traditional view, the true *raison d'être* of Cîteaux, lay in the strict, possibly literal, observance of the Rule of Saint Benedict. The *Charter of Charity* had served as a practical guide toward the reconstruction of a monastic life along the same ideological lines.

Since the early 1930s, however, a re-examination of the manuscript tradition has led to a thorough reappraisal of everything previously written about Cistercian beginnings. The discovery of the *Exordium Cistercii,* a shorter but earlier and more factual narrative than the *Exordium parvum,* cast serious doubt on the reliability of the better known document. Its author turned out not to have been Abbot Stephen, but a member of Saint Bernard's generation who had published it some time after Stephen's death in 1134. It was written as a Cistercian "white paper" to defend the legitimate nature of Cîteaux's foundation against the charges of the Cluniac "Black Monks," who had argued that the New Monastery had been established without due canonical formalities. With the intention of proving "how canonically" the disputed action had been carried out, the author assembled and transcribed a number of documents, but several of these, including the crucial "institutes" of Alberic, lack the marks of authenticity. Constant references to the Rule of Saint Benedict, particularly in the "institutes," were made with the obvious purpose of creating an illusion of rigid legality. The anonymous author's contention that Saint Bernard's timely arrival had saved Cîteaux from extinction tends to corroborate the contention that the author was indeed a younger man, drawn to the Order by the Saint's magnetic personality.

In a similar manner, the latest research on the *Charter of Charity* reveals that it was not the fruit of the earliest abbatial conventions, but had come into being after decades of evolution. Its text had been initiated by Stephen Harding, but the exact nature of this as yet undiscovered "primitive" text as well as the date and extent of its amplifications remain contested. Since the presently available manuscripts do not suffice to clarify the many questions raised during the course of the last decades, it is still impossible to replace the old, traditional image of early Cîteaux with a similarly neat and clear picture sketched with the assistance of modern scholarship. Compensating for such disappointments, however, recent research has managed to throw more light on contemporary monastic movements in general and on the impact of eremitism in particular. It has increased our appreciation of non-Cistercian sources, re-emphasized the importance of the conflict between Cîteaux and Cluny, and placed the juridical problems of the new foundation into the context of twelfth-century canon law.

After we have made allowance for all such considerations, however, it remains true that the founders of Cîteaux intended to return to a stricter interpretation of the Rule. Their efforts resulted not in the restoration of the monastic life of the sixth century, but in the introduction of a life strongly influenced by the ideals of pre-Benedictine monasticism. The search for greater solitude, poverty and austerity certainly acted as powerful incentives for Robert and his companions as they had in countless other abbeys of the late eleventh century. The peculiarity of the case of Cîteaux resulted largely from its immediate proximity to Cluny. In Burgundy the advocacy of eremitical discipline within a monastic community was taken as a challenge to the mode of life accepted everywhere in the heartland of the Cluniac "empire." The founding fathers of Cîteaux were forced at the outset into a defensive posture. The most effective tactic against the accusation that they were introducing unwelcome novelties was to hold up the Rule as a shield. Robert and his monks insisted that they had intended no novelties, only a return to the strict observance of Saint Benedict's venerable code for monks. In doing so the first Cistercians instinctively emphasized those elements of the Rule which fitted their eremitical lifestyle, particularly the seventy-third chapter, where the author stated modestly that his rule was intended for beginners; those aspiring to a higher perfection of religious life should consult the teachings of the "Holy Fathers," particularly the works of Saint Basil (d. 379) and John Cassian (d. 435), rich in references to the heroic lives of eastern anchorites.

Because reconciliation of the Rule with eremitical asceticism seemed not only impossible but undesirable to the monks of Molesme, heated disputes ensued between the two groups. The two sources which give surprisingly detailed information about the nature of the argument are the chronicles of William of Malmesbury and Ordericus Vitalis, both Benedictines, both keen observers of their times and both informed historians. The pertinent passage in William of Malmesbury's *Gesta regum Anglorum,* composed in 1122-1123, was based in all likelihood on Cistercian sources and focused attention on Stephen Harding. The corresponding chapter in the *Historia ecclesiastica* of Ordericus Vitalis was written about ten years later, and featured the exhortations of Saint Robert, as they were remembered at Molesme. There is no need to believe that either Stephen or Robert spoke exactly the way they are quoted in these sources; on the other hand, there is no reason to doubt that the issues discussed in them were indeed the real issues.

According to William of Malmesbury, Stephen, still at Molesme, vigorously attacked the way of life based on Cluniac customs. He found tradition alone insufficient to justify them. He insisted that permissible usages must be founded on a rule and supported by both reason and authority, and he added that all these requirements were embodied in the

23

Rule of Saint Benedict. When his opponents persistently "refused the new things because they loved the old ways," the future Cistercians redoubled their efforts to show that in fact all their proposals were taken from a source older than the Cluniac usages, and that this was why they were "watching over the Rule so carefully that they would not miss a single jot or point."

Ordericus Vitalis also reported the same crucial debates, but he featured the Abbot of Molesme and his reluctant monks. He had Robert strongly criticize the violations of poverty, the abandonment of manual labor, the acceptance of tithes and other ecclesiastical revenues, and urge his subjects to "observe the Rule of Saint Benedict in everything . . . [so that] in the footsteps of the Fathers we might fervently follow Christ." Robert made no clear distinction between the observances of the Desert Fathers and those demanded by the Rule, and he seasoned his exhortations with frequent references to "the imitable lives of Egyptian Fathers." His opponents took pains to prove that the standards of the desert were no longer applicable in their circumstances and they declared their intention of adhering to the well-established customs of Cluny, "lest they be condemned by the brethren far and wide as inventors of temerarious novelties." The debate ended in the same way as that related by William of Malmesbury: in order to avoid the opprobrium of being innovators, the founders of Cîteaux "resolved to observe the Rule of Benedict to the letter, as much as the Jews observe the laws of Moses."

Dispute over monastic observances flared up much higher after 1124, when Saint Bernard launched a full-scale attack against Cluny in his first widely distributed work, the *Apology* (*Apologia ad Guillelmum*). By then Cistercians had gained general popularity, while Cluny, under the turbulent administration of Pons de Melgueil (1109-1122), had suffered embarrassing reverses. The time was therefore ripe for a spirited counteroffensive, not only against Cluny, but also against the "old and outdated monastic establishment," conveniently symbolized by Cluny. The *Apology* is the best proof that after a quarter century many Cistercians had come to believe that, in the words of an unnamed monk quoted by Bernard, they were "the only ones with any virtue, holier than everyone else, and the only monks who lived according to the Rule; as far as [they] were concerned, other monks were simply transgressors." Somewhat later in the text Saint Bernard quoted the same unnamed Cistercian as asserting that "all those who make profession of the Rule are obliged to keep it literally without any possible dispensation." It was obvious, however, that the strict observance of the Rule was only one of many distinctive features the new Order could be proud of. In his masterful style, Saint Bernard contrasted with devastating directness the rich, pompous and comfortable Black Monks and the Cistercians, heralds of a new monasticism, thoroughly reformed along Gregorian ideals: poor with the poor Christ; living from the fruits of their own manual labor, like the Apostles, secluded from the world and having no interest in it; parsimonious in clothing and everything else they use; abstemious in food and drink; unpretentious in their dwellings; simple and austere even in their liturgical services; approaching excess only in asceticism.

Peter the Venerable, the new abbot of Cluny (1122-1156), whose first task was to repair the damage caused by his predecessor, replied with measured dignity. He blunted the charge that Cluniacs had discarded certain precepts of the Rule by stressing that the essence of Saint Benedict's teaching consisted in charity and moderation. He readily acknowledged the splendid virtues of his Cistercian opponents, who, he wryly remarked, lacked only humility. The debate continued for decades and produced nearly a dozen still extant pamphlets. One of the last, the *Dialogue of Two Monks* (*Dialogus duorum monachorum*), written about 1155 by Idung of Prüfening, a Benedictine turned Cistercian, was the most detailed, and made ample use of two great novelties: canon law and scholasticism. The *Dialogue* is a long disputation between a Cistercian and a Cluniac, in which the naive questions and inept answers of the latter merely present opportunities for the Cistercian to discourse with remarkable erudition on issues which proved that the White Monks excelled Benedictines. The Cluniac repeated the old charges of "instability," alluding to Robert and his followers who had left the "old and discrete" Molesme for the "indiscrete novelties" of Cîteaux. The Cistercian labeled the accusations calumnious and insisted on the "old, discrete and regular" features of Cistercian life, to the detriment of Cluniac customs which were "largely superstitious, contrary to [Church] decrees, synodal sanctions, even to the Holy Rule." The Cistercians, on the other hand, "live according to the Rule of Saint Benedict which they vow to observe, the law given to monks by God through Saint Benedict, a legislator, like Moses."

The merits of the debated issues could scarcely be decided in verbal battles, but the protracted engagement boosted the *esprit de corps* enormously in the Cistercian camp. The White Monks certainly enjoyed a taste of victory when Peter the Venerable advocated many features of the Cistercian reform and toward the end of his administration managed to introduce them at his own Cluny.

The earliest tangible evidence of Cistercian efforts to convert ideals into practical regulations comes in a set of twenty paragraphs, the *capitula*.

25

Some of these were very probably attached to an early version of the *Charter of Charity* and the *Exordium Cistercii* at the time they were presented to Callistus II for his approval in 1119. In these paragraphs the first reference was made to the admission of lay-brothers, who were to assist the monks in agricultural labor. They were received, like the monks, with the permission of their bishops "as our necessary helpers and brethren, as much partakers in our spiritual and temporal benefits as the monks." After a year of probation they took profession in the chapter hall, but they could never hope for admission to the ranks of choir monks.

Other paragraphs dealt with the circumstances of new foundations. Each new abbey was to have in addition to some lay-brothers, at least twelve monks under an abbot and to be well furnished with the necessary liturgical books. All houses were to be dedicated to the Blessed Virgin Mary and located far away from villages or towns. After the construction of the "regular places" no monk was to stay outside of the cloister. Most importantly, stated the text, "in order to preserve forever among our abbeys an indissoluble union, it is resolved first of all that all brethren follow the Rule of Saint Benedict in the same way, from which they are not to deviate even in the smallest matter. It follows from this that they must use the same books for the divine office, wear the same garments, eat the same food; in a word, the same usages and customs should prevail everywhere." The kind and quality of clothing was described with great care, as was the monks' simple diet, which excluded meat and meat products. The monks' livelihood was to be derived exclusively from "manual labor, from the cultivation of land and from raising animals." It was clearly stated that such lands should not be too close to the possessions of seculars, although the rules set no limit to the extension of the monks' possessions, and, in fact, approved the establishment of granges under the care of lay-brothers. Churches, burial dues, tithes, villages, serfs, taxes, dues from ovens or mills and "other such things contrary to monastic purity," were strictly excluded as sources of revenue. To preclude such temptations the monks were not to engage in parochial or pastoral services of any kind, but were to live in perfect seclusion from the world. Unavoidable business with outsiders was to be conducted by lay-brothers. All ostentation of wealth was to be avoided, even in the design and construction of churches, and in their interior decoration and furnishing.

From 1119 to 1151 the annual convention of abbots, the "general chapter," specified these regulations still further, added a number of new points and finally edited a collection of ninety-two paragraphs as the *Institutes of the General Chapter (Instituta generalis capituli).* Unique to it was its clarification of procedural and other purely legal questions: the conduct of general chapters, the acquisition of privileges; the formalities of annual visitation; punishments for various delinquents; procedures for abbatial elections; relationships with bishops; the conduct of abbots who became bishops; the reception of guests, work in the *scriptorium,* the administration of granges; rules concerning buying and selling, the behavior of traveling monks, and the care of the sick. Finally a number of liturgical matters were decided and, significantly, children were excluded from monastic precincts.

At about the same time two other closely related sets of directives came into existence. One, the *Ecclesiastica officia,* dealt with the pervasive liturgical matters; the other concerned itself with the conduct of lay-brothers, the *Usus conversorum.* These, together with the *Instituta,* formed the basic manual of everyday life for individuals and communities, the *Consuetudines,* the "Book of Customs." There was nothing radically new in these collections; they drew their material heavily from monastic sources of the preceding century and a half, particularly from the usages of Cluny and Molesme. However, their relative simplicity and brevity, their universal application, and their concise legal terminology can be considered characteristically Cistercian.

Elaborate designs for uniform observances would have remained ineffective without a firm constitutional framework to hold the growing number of Cistercian abbeys together. This purpose was served by the *Charter of Charity,* a document traditionally attributed to Stephen Harding. As we have stated above, the third Abbot of Cîteaux should indeed be regarded as the initiator of the scheme, but some fifty years passed before it received its final features. The first reference to such a charter comes in the undated foundation document of Pontigny, drawn up shortly after Bishop Humbald of Auxerre invited "the lovers of the Holy Rule" to settle down in his diocese. At the same time (1114?), as the document states, "the same Bishop, together with the convent of his canons, accepted in everything the validity of the charter of charity and unanimity, [already] composed and corroborated between the New Monastery and the abbeys founded by it." The text of this "primitive" *Charter of Charity* has not been found, however, so its contents cannot be safely established. The next reference to a "constitution" occurs in the Bull of Callistus II of 1119, which poses a problem of a different nature: recent research has unearthed two actual versions of the Charter, both apparently amplifications of the "primitive" text, and both written probably shortly before or after 1119. One bears the title *Summa cartae Caritatis,* the other came to be known as the *Carta caritatis prior.* It

27

remains equally uncertain which version of this famous document was approved in still another Bull, issued by Eugenius III in 1152. We can safely assume only that after repeated changes, the final Charter, the *Carta caritatis posterior*, emerged some time between 1165 and 1190.

The chief significance of the *Charter of Charity* in its final form, as it has been known for centuries, lies in the happy balance it achieved between central authority and local autonomy, thus avoiding the twin pitfalls of extremely tight Cluniac controls and insufficient cohesion that had been the undoing of many promising reform congregations. Cîteaux remained the heart and center of the new Order and its abbot the living symbol of unity. But, in sharp contrast to Cluny, Cîteaux's abbot could not exercise unlimited governmental powers. Ultimate authority resided in the annual convention of all Cistercian abbots, the General Chapter, convened traditionally at Cîteaux on September 14, the feast of the Exaltation of the Holy Cross. Under the presidency of the abbot of Cîteaux, the Chapter's primary duty was to maintain a uniform monastic discipline on the highest possible level, so that "all may live together in the bond of charity under one rule and in the practice of the same observances." Accordingly, the Chapter was expected to curb abuses, punish delinquents, and make occasional adjustments by new legislation or timely modification of established customs. The means of execution and local control was the annual visitation of each abbey by the abbot of the founding house. The visiting "father abbots" were to effect corrections, or, in extreme cases, to report their findings to the Chapter, which authorized further measures to be carried out by them. Cîteaux, having no "mother house," was to be visited simultaneously by the abbots of her first four "daughters," the abbots of La Ferté, Pontigny, Clairvaux and Morimond, known later collectively as "proto-abbots." In spite of multiple controls, however, each abbot was free to govern his community without undue external interference, as long as his monastery remained within the fixed regulations. Besides these constitutional arrangements, the Charter called for mutual aid in time of material need or emergency, encouraged hospitality, regulated precedence among the abbots, established procedures for abbatial elections and specified precautionary or punitive measures against negligent or unworthy abbots.

It must be emphasized, however, that the features just discussed pertain properly only to the final version of the Charter, while earlier versions exhibited significantly different characteristics. Thus, diocesan bishops initially enjoyed considerable authority over Cistercian establishments. Such episcopal privileges as canonical visitation, supervision of abbatial elections, punitive powers, and the right to demand an oath of obedience from the newly elected abbot, were gradually reduced and eventually eliminated as the Order approached total exemption from diocesan jurisdiction, thanks to a steady flow of highly favorable papal privileges. Similarly, at an early stage the abbot of Cîteaux enjoyed prominent power, while the first sessions of the General Chapter seemed scarcely more than expanded chapters of the mother-house or annual "chapters of faults" for abbots. In about 1135, the Abbot of Cîteaux still appeared to Ordericus Vitalis to be the "chief" (*archimandrita*) over the sixty-five other abbots of the Order. The gradual increase in the number of participants resulted in the growing authority of the General Chapter, although its legislative role did not become conspicuous before the 1180s. The stature of Saint Bernard and the others heading the first foundations from Cîteaux accounted for the rising influence of the "proto-abbots" who could act collectively as a counterweight against an ambitious abbot at Cîteaux.

As is true of the Cistercian reform in general, none of the component elements of the *Charter of Charity* was entirely new. Efforts at maintaining uniform discipline through visitation and occasional abbatial conventions had been in evidence in the monastic world long before the foundation of Cîteaux. Such trends were visible in a reform organized by Richard of Saint-Vanne (d. 1046) in eastern France, and even more conspicuous in the congregation of Vallombrosa, well known to Stephen Harding. The initiator of the latter, Saint John Gualbert (d. 1073), left behind as a "bond of charity" a set of regulations to be followed by his foundations. It granted pre-eminence to his successors at Vallombrosa, called for abbatial conventions endowed with extensive legislative powers, introduced a system of visitations, and insisted on the maintenance of a uniform discipline, all features of the Cistercian *Charter of Charity*. In 1110, just before the first draft of the Cistercian Charter, a somewhat similar document was composed regulating the relationship of Aulps with its new foundation, Balerne. Both were members of the congregation of Molesme, and both eventually joined the Cistercians. This act, the so-called "Accord of Molesme," also stipulated visitation by the founding house, mutual assistance "for the sake of charity," and a measure of supervision over both houses by Molesme.

In spite of heavy borrowing, the Cistercians managed to weld the elements of the *Charter of Charity* into a coherent scheme of unique perfection, ideally suited to the web of contemporary social environment. The Charter reflected the prevalent feudal subordination, based on mutual fidelity and trust, demanding prompt obedience in time of crisis, but respecting local autonomy. Instead of purely customary relationships, however, the Cistercian constitution based itself on a carefully worded written law. Under the steadily increasing influence of the revived Roman law, in fact, both ecclesiastical and civil legislation had come to a rebirth, replacing traditional and primitive customary regulations by statutory laws, charters and constitutions. In particular, the General Chapter, an elected, representative assembly of aristocratic stamp, developed abreast of incipient feudal parliaments and the rapidly multiplying Italian and French urban communes.

The *Charter of Charity* played a dominant role not only in Cistercian development, but also in the constitution-making of other religious orders. The Premonstratensian general chapter closely followed the Cistercian pattern even to granting a special place to their own three proto-abbots. During the first half of the twelfth century, often under the personal influence of Saint Bernard, annual chapters were introduced by the Regular Canons of Saint Victor, by the Carthusians, at Grandmont, among the Gilbertines, at the Congregation of Val-des-Choux, and among many military orders and hospitallers. Cluny, too, adopted this important institution and invited four Cistercian abbots to assist them in procedural matters. Various other Benedictine congregations followed suit. The Fourth Lateran Council (1215) made general chapters compulsory in all monastic congregations which had not already adopted them and required the supervision of two Cistercian abbots closest to locality. From the outset the newly founded Franciscans and Dominicans incorporated general chapters into their constitutions.

How can Cîteaux's initial devotion to the Rule be reconciled with the legislation and constitution-making of the second and third generations? Were Cistercians as deeply and sincerely devoted to the exact observance of the Rule as some of their contemporaries thought them to be, and they themselves, perhaps, pretended to be? The *Exordium parvum* may not be an accurate and unbiased record of their beginnings, but it clearly reflects the mentality of the second Cistercian generation. Its author insisted that the founders of Cîteaux had taken "the rectitude of the Rule as the norm of conduct for their whole way of life," and that they had rejected customs which they could not find in the Rule and which they therefore considered against the Rule. They specifically repudiated recent items of monastic clothing and diet, as well as types of possession and feudal sources of income that had made monasteries active partners in contemporary social and economic life. They based their rejection on the monk's avowed intention to "stay aloof from the doings of the world" and to remain "poor as Christ was poor."

According to the same text, however, the early Cistercians began to wonder "how and with what work or occupation they should provide for themselves in this world." They answered by acquiring "landed properties which lay removed from human dwellings" for their own exclusive use, and by cultivating them through the employment of lay-brothers and hired hands, realizing that without such help "they would be unable to fulfill perfectly the precepts of the Rule day and night." As a further justification for the use of lay-brothers "they also decided that when they established granges for the practice of agriculture, the lay-brothers should manage those houses, and not the monks, whose residence, according to the Rule, should be within their cloister."

The first few lines of this short text seem to introduce a firm principle of interpretation implying that what is not in the Rule is against the Rule and therefore ought to be rejected. Within a few lines, however, the author had evidently forgotten these principles and approved lay-brotherhood, a momentous institution as foreign to the Rule as was the repudiated possession of altars and tithes. This apparent contradiction can easily be resolved if we realize that the author made reference to the Rule only for the justification of basic Cistercian ideals. The true motive for both the prohibition and the introduction of "novelties" was the monks' ardent desire to live in undisturbed solitude. Holding and administering properties in the feudal system would have forced the monks to stay in close contact with lay society and for this reason such burdens were rejected. On the other hand, lay-brotherhood was adopted, because the cultivation of extensive lands in remote locations would have drawn away the monks from the cherished solitude of their cloister.

Although the ninety-two paragraphs of the *Instituta generalis capituli* cannot be analysed here, a few observations on its obvious features will corroborate this contention. This sequence of regulations can scarcely be characterized as mere comments or explanatory notes appended to the various chapters of the Rule. The many arrangements pertaining to the annual General Chapters and to the visitation of abbeys or administration of granges are entirely outside the scope of the Rule. A conspicuously large number of prescriptions apply in a practical way the principles of poverty, simplicity and seclusion from the world. In food and clothing, fasting, abstinence and punishments, the *Instituta* go into greater detail and are considerably more restrictive than the indulgent Rule of Saint Benedict.

The most surprising regulation is the absolute exclusion of children from monastic precincts, an open defiance of a significant feature of the Rule. The justification is obvious: the presence of children could not but disturb the atmosphere of monastic solitude. A peculiar problem is posed by the insistence in the second and third paragraphs of the *Instituta* not only that absolute uniformity be maintained in the liturgical matters, but that everywhere "there must be the same food, the same clothing, the same customs in all things." Although the Rule took varieties of climate, local circumstances and customs into consideration, and opened the way to different arrangements of the *Opus Dei,* Cistercians were adamant in their insistence "that the Rule of Saint Benedict should be understood by all in the same way, followed in the same way."

How the principles laid down in the *Carta caritatis* could be harmonized with the Rule is another intriguing question. Not only is the possibility of a central control over a number of monasteries absent from the Rule, it seems to have been alien from its author's mentality. Effective external centralizing forces, such as the General Chapter and annual visitations, were to lead inevitably to the diminution of local authority and of the independence clearly assured each abbey by the Rule.

Early Cistercians were not only free from a blind devotion to the letter of the Rule, but, in fact, they handled that venerable document of monastic legislation with remarkable liberality. They invoked and applied it when it suited their purpose; they ignored or even contradicted it when it could not be fitted to their concept of monasticism, largely based on the ideals of eleventh-century reforms. In the early life of Cîteaux the Rule undoubtedly played an important role, but it was the role of instrumentality; it served as a means to the attainment of the true goal, the establishment of an austere life in poverty, simplicity and undisturbed solitude.

IV

Saint Bernard and the Expansion

 That religious vocations were plentiful in the "age of faith" is a matter of common understanding. The first half of the twelfth century stands out, even in the Middle Ages, as a unique era of devotional enthusiasm, when monasticism turned into a mass movement of unparalleled proportions. As in the case of similar other phenomena, such as the Crusades, no rational explanation can fully account for the countless thousands who were willing to leave the "world" and seek God behind the walls of institutions where everything was geared to giving ample opportunity to practice a life of heroic austerities.

Contemporaries, too, were well aware of what was happening, although, searching for reasons, they were just as baffled as we are. As the often quoted Ordericus Vitalis observed: "Though evil abounds in the world the devotion of the faithful in cloisters grows more abundant and bears fruit a hundredfold in the Lord's field. Monasteries are founded everywhere in mountain valleys and plains, observing new rites and wearing different habits; the swarm of cowled monks spreads all over the world." A source of equal amazement to the same author was the fact that it was the most austere order, the Cistercian, which fared best; the White Monks' appeal seemed to break through all social and intellectual barriers: "Many noble warriors and profound philosophers have flocked to them on account of the novelty of their practices, and have willingly embraced the unaccustomed rigor of their life, gladly singing hymns of joy to Christ as they journey along the right road." A somewhat older contemporary, Bishop Otto of Bamberg (d. 1139), who watched and promoted monastic growth, tried to rationalize it by a strangely familiar, though somewhat premature, argument: "At the beginning of the world, when there were few men, the propagation of men was necessary, and therefore they were not chaste. . . . Now, however, at the end of the world, when men have multiplied beyond measure, is the time of chastity; this was my reason, my intention in multiplying monasteries."

There is no doubt that in the circumstances Cîteaux was bound to succeed. Its ascetic program was the epitome of everything contemporaries were looking for; it was organized under an inspiring and capable

33

leadership and its constitution insured the cohesion of the movement in the event that it spread beyond the confines of Burgundy. Grandmont, Savigny, Grand Chartreuse and many similar reforms prospered with fewer potential assets than those of Cîteaux. The amazing fact that the Cistercian Order virtually exploded and by the middle of the twelfth century possessed nearly 350 houses in every country of Europe, can be explained, however, only by the dynamic character and activity of the "man of the century," Saint Bernard of Clairvaux. The often voiced notion that he was the true founder of the Order is a pardonable exaggeration, but the fact that for centuries Cistercians were widely known as "Bernardines" was not without justification.

Bernard was born in 1090, of noble Burgundian stock at Fontaines, near Dijon. After his education in the midst of his deeply religious family he was sent to Châtillon for formal studies at the school of the canons of Saint Vorles. Returning home, he lived the life of contemporary youth with his older brothers, but the silent and reserved boy soon decided that his place was at Cîteaux, already well known in the neighborhood. As soon as he became certain of his own vocation, he set about convincing all his brothers, his closest relatives and his friends to join him in his holy endeavor. This was the first occasion which proved him to be a born leader with an unwavering will and irresistible personal appeal. In the spring of 1113 he, together with his companions, asked for admission at Cîteaux. The austere religious training in the abbey did not change his character; on the contrary, Bernard found in Cîteaux the most congenial surrounding for his own spiritual temperament, and in turn, Bernard proved to be the most effective and eloquent interpreter of Cîteaux's message to the world. Abbot Stephen recognized in him a God-sent genius, and in 1115 the young man of twenty-five became the founder and abbot of Clairvaux. The trials and hardships of the founders of Cîteaux were relived during the first years of Clairvaux, but Bernard's faith and determination remained unbroken. The heroic spirit of the Abbot attracted so many recruits that in only three years Clairvaux was able to found her first daughter house at Trois-Fontaines.

On the wings of his early writings the fame of Bernard's holiness and wisdom soon spread all over France, and, although he never cared for publicity, he soon found himself in the spotlight of an era desperately searching for able and competent leadership. It was a time of political turmoil throughout Western and Central Europe. In Germany, the powerful Emperor Henry V, the last member of the Salian house, died without heir (1125) and the country was torn between the partisans of the two contesting families, the Welfs (Guelphs) and Ghibellines. Similar disturbances broke out in England after the reign of Henry I, while the boy king of France, Louis VII, was still too young and inexperienced to take over his father's role. Meanwhile in Italy, the powerful cities and the most influential families, utilizing the impotency of their northern neighbors, started anew their bloody rivalries. When, in Rome, the papacy again fell victim to the fighting parties, a perilous schism in the Church resulted. After the death of Honorius II in 1130, two opposing parties elected on the same day two popes, Innocent II and Anacletus II. The befuddled Christian world was at that moment utterly incapable of dealing with the problem; the only power able to restore order in Rome would have been Roger II of Sicily, who was, however, using the occasion to extend the territory of his new kingdom.

A convention of French clergy and nobility at Etampes committed the decision of this crucial question to Saint Bernard, who declared in favor of Innocent II. Much more difficult to solve were the political ramifications of the dual election; namely, the task of convincing the contending powers to acknowledge Innocent unanimously and driving the usurper out of his Roman stronghold. It took eight years of tedious travelings, conferences, personal meetings, and hundreds of letters to achieve the goal. During these years Saint Bernard stood literally in the center of European politics, yet he never acted merely as a diplomat. He never yielded nor used threat of force, nor did he compromise. The secret of his success was his moral superiority, his unselfish good will, and the magic of his personality. On the other hand, the fact that the whole European world obeyed the poor and humble Abbot of Clairvaux indicates an era when moral ideals still prevailed over brutal violence.

The zenith of Saint Bernard's earthly career was reached the moment when his pupil, a former monk of Clairvaux, was elected pope as Eugenius III (1145-1153). On this Pope's order, the Saint launched the Second Crusade in 1147. By his preaching, he moved hundreds of thousands of people even when they could not understand his language. His powerful words and irresistible personality worked wonders in another field of his activity, among the Manichean heretics of Germany and France. The South of France was at the edge of an open revolt against the Church; nevertheless, Saint Bernard, in his strong belief that "faith is a matter of persuasion, not of compulsion," refused to advocate violent measures against them. Though his mission had only temporary effects, his sermons and miracles left a deep impression. Not so much by his eloquence as by his penetrating mind and deep erudition, he fought victoriously against doctrinal aberrations, most notably those of Abelard, and later, Gilbert de la Porrée.

Saint Bernard's public activity was not limited to these issues of political and ecclesiastical importance. For about thirty years, he and his letters, written in a masterful Latin, were present every time peace, justice, or the interest of the Church demanded his intervention. The Cistercian Order grew and expanded with his own expanding fame and popularity. His biographers remarked that the power of his eloquence was such that "mothers hid their sons and wives their husbands" in order to keep them safe from the Saint's recruiting efforts, which brought a constantly overflowing population to his beloved Clairvaux. This abbey alone established sixty-five daughter houses during the lifetime of Bernard. Several other abbeys were almost as successful as Clairvaux, and France was soon dotted with some two hundred Cistercian establishments. Not all of these abbeys, however, were entirely new foundations. The seemingly irresistible trend drove many already existing monasteries into the Cistercian camp. Thus, for example, in 1147, of fifty-one new houses recorded, twenty-nine had belonged to the reform congregation of Savigny, while some others had been members of smaller organizations under the monasteries of Obazine and Cadouin. By this time the White Monks were well on their way in stepping across the borders of France and establishing themselves permanently in other countries of Christian Europe. Former monastic reforms, including Cluny, had largely been restricted to the countries of their origin, either because their programs were lacking universal appeal, or they were unable to control effectively a great number of distant, affiliated houses. Cîteaux, for the first time, broke through these barriers successfully, becoming the first truly international religious order in Church history.

As early as 1120 a group of monks from La Ferté crossed the Alps and founded Tiglieto in Liguria. The same La Ferté was also responsible for the establishment of Locedio (1124) in the diocese of Vercelli, and much later (1210) of Barona. Tiglieto became the "mother" of Staffarda (1135) and Casanova (1150) in the diocese of Turin. The French Morimond gave life to the Italian Morimondo Coronato (1136) in Lombardy; far more numerous were the Italian foundations of Clairvaux made in the wake of Saint Bernard's tours through that country. Chiaravalle near Milan (1135) and Chiaravalle della Colomba (1136) in the diocese of Piacensa became themselves "mothers" of numerous other Cistercian houses throughout the peninsula. The Cistercians also reformed a number of already existing monasteries, such as the ancient Saint Vincent and Anastasius in Rome, later known as Tre Fontane and offered to Saint Bernard by Innocent II. Its first Cistercian abbot (1140), Bernardo Paganelli of Pisa, the Saint's personal friend and disciple, became the first Cistercian Pope as Eugenius III (1145-1153). Another Cistercian conquest of great future significance was that of Casamari south of Rome (1140), a former Benedictine abbey and "mother" of Sambucina (1160), Matina (1180), San Galgano (1200) and Sagittario (1202). The total number of Italian Cistercian foundations eventually grew to eighty-eight.

Cistercians in the south of Italy and Sicily were much favored by Emperor Frederick II (1212-1250), but the endless turmoils following his death signalled the end of prosperity and expansion. Italy was in fact the scene of the first crack in Cîteaux's tight organization. Schism originated in Calabria, where the traditions of eremitism and oriental asceticism were particularly strong at a time when flourishing Cistercian communities no longer seemed able to satisfy those aspiring to great austerities. The originator of the movement remains one of the most colorful and enigmatic characters of medieval religious history, Joachim of Fiore (d. 1202). As a young man he had made a pilgrimage to the Holy Land and on his return had joined the Cistercian community of Sambucina and later Corazzo, where he became abbot about 1177. In the firm expectation of a new kingdom of the Holy Spirit he left the Order and in 1189 started at San Giovanni in Fiore a new community dedicated to the absolute renunciation of the world. Soon a number of other houses sprang up and the new federation was approved by Celestin III in 1196. By the middle of the thirteenth century the Congregation of Fiore, or "Florians," numbered nearly forty houses. They borrowed externals from the Cistercians, but their spirituality presaged the Franciscans. Their quick growth was followed by an equally precipitate disintegration. Eventually many abbeys, Fiore included, found their way back to the fold of Cîteaux.

The first Cistercian community in Germany was founded by monks of Morimond, who in 1123 settled Camp (Altenkamp) near Cologne. So successful was this house that its overflowing population was able to establish in rapid succession Walkenried in Brunswick (1129), Volkenrode in Thuringia (1131), Amelunxborn near Hildesheim (1135), Hardehausen in Westphalia (1140) and Michaelstein in the diocese of Halberstadt (1146). While the "family" of Morimond remained strongest in the north and northeast, Clairvaux spread its affiliations along the Rhine, in the Low Countries and in Bavaria. Monks of Clairvaux settled Eberbach in Nassau (1131), Himmerod in the electorate of Trier (1134), the great Les Dunes (Ter Duinen) in Flanders (1149) and later Klaarkamp in Friesland (1165). By the end of the twelfth century the rush of Cistercian foundations was over in the old Germanic lands, but the White Monks followed German expansion into Prussia and along the Baltic coast throughout the thirteenth century. The farthest abbey in the northeast was Falkenau in Livonia near Dorpat (1234).

The first Cistercian house in Switzerland was Bonmont (1131), originally a Benedictine monastery. Then followed Montheron (1135) and Hauterive (1137), although the largest of the altogether eight Swiss houses were the last two: Saint Urban (1195) and Wettingen (1227).

In Austria the first foundation was that of Rein (1130), populated from the Bavarian Ebrach, although a greater future was in store for Heiligenkreuz (1135), near Vienna, founded directly from Morimond. Both houses were effective in the propagation of the Order; monks of Heiligenkreuz built the first Hungarian abbey, Cikádor in 1142. The total number of Cistercian abbeys in Germanic lands amounted to about one hundred.

Waverley, the first foundation in England was settled in 1129 from the French l'Aumône; though successful, it was not particularly consequential. The establishment of Rievaulx (1132) and Fountains (1135), both in Yorkshire, created such a nationwide publicity in behalf of Cistericans, however, that for the subsequent twenty years the greatest families of the country vied with one another for the favor of having the White Monks settled on their estates.

The story of the foundation of Fountains has all the elements of tension, suspense and threat of violence that preceded the secession of dissident monks from Molesme to Cîteaux; only the names were different. In fact, recent scholarship analyzing the sources of the foundation of Fountains raised the possibility that the parallel might have been the intentional work of the author, Hugh of Kirkstall; therefore certain details of the drama (as in the case of Cîteaux) might belong more to the realm of literature than history. Be that as it may, this time the rebellion occurred at Saint Mary's Abbey in York, where some thirteen zealous monks, pointing to the example of Cistercians, demanded the tightening of a relaxed discipline. Archbishop Thurstan of York took the side of the reformers who, after a stormy confrontation with the reluctant majority, seceded under the leadership of Richard, the prior. Thurstan gave them a place to stay at Ripon, where the small band of heroic souls bivouacked under a hugh elm tree for several months during the winter of 1133-1134. They elected Richard as their abbot but they remained a community without an abbey and without any definite affiliation. Turning to Saint Bernard, who had followed their struggle with great sympathy, they were received by the Saint into the family of Clairvaux and were sent one of his most experienced monks to introduce them to Cistercian observances. With the help of generous benefactors they soon began to construct the great abbey of Fountains, which, even in ruins, has remained a glorious memorial to the faith of its builders.

Fountains attracted some of the most eminent ecclesiastics of England, but even the recruiting power of this splendid community was eclipsed by the phenomenal rise of Rievaulx. The site of the abbey near Helmsley, some thirty miles north of York, was donated by Walter Espec, an aging knight of great piety who, without surviving heirs, could afford to be generous to Cistercians; in addition to other similar projects, he also sponsored the foundation of Warden in Bedfordshire in 1135. He lived in the memory of the monks of Rievaulx as "an old man, keen of wit, huge in stature, yet with due proportion of limb; black-haired, long-bearded, with a broad forehead and large piercing eyes. . . . His voice was like a trumpet." The settlement on the river Rye was prepared with much care by Saint Bernard himself, who sent some of his most promising English disciples back to their homeland as pioneers. It was the example of Rievaulx that revolutionized Saint Mary's in York, but the abbey became a veritable magnet of irresistible power after a young man named Aelred joined the community in 1134. Born in 1110 of English parents, but brought up in the court of King David I of Scotland as a companion of the royal children, Aelred's youthful charms, eminent talents and precocious erudition opened the highest positions in Church and government to him, but a chance visit at the newly founded Rievaulx made him a prisoner of Cistercian ideals forever. Under Abbot William he served as master of novices, then in 1143 he became abbot of the newly founded Revesby in Lincolnshire and finally, in 1147, he followed Maurice of Durham as the third abbot of Rievaulx, a position he retained until his death in 1167.

Saint Aelred, justly called "the Bernard of the North," is one of the most appealing characters of monastic history. He could not match Saint Bernard's stature as a statesman and reformer, but was his equal in compassionate love and understanding for men of all walks of life. Through his writings, marked by great depth and piety, but even more through his personal contacts, he attracted countless vocations to Rievaulx. That the abbey under his administration housed 650 monks and lay-brothers was perhaps an exaggeration of his biographer, but the picture of the abbey church "packed with monks as closely as a hive with bees," must have left an unforgettable impression on visitors. As his disciple and biographer, Walter Daniel remarked, ". . . monks in need of mercy and compassion flocked to Rievaulx from foreign peoples and from the far ends of the earth, that there in very truth they might find peace and the holiness without which no man shall see God. And so those wanderers in the world to whom no house of religion gave entrance, came to Rievaulx, the mother of mercy, and found the gates open and entered them freely, giving thanks unto their Lord." By the time of Aelred's death the zenith of Cistercian expansion in England had passed, but Rievaulx had already made five foundations, Fountains eight, and each of these had generated scores of others, so that eventually England and Wales altogether possessed seventy-six abbeys, thirteen of which had originally been members of the Congregation of Savigny.

Cistercians were warmly welcomed in Wales, for they were considered French, rather than Anglo-Norman. Indeed, most of the fourteen houses in that principality were populated directly from France, although those in the border region, the "Marches," had strong English ties, as, for example, did Tintern, founded in 1131 by l'Aumône. Whitland (1140), on the other hand, sponsored by prominent Welsh nobility and populated from Clairvaux, was entirely Welsh and soon became the "mother" of the equally Welsh-populated Cwmhir (1143), Strata Florida (1164) and Strata Marcella (1170). All these abbeys were to suffer greatly during the English conquest, although Edward I (1272-1307) proved generous in offering aid for reconstruction. The recurrence of guerilla warfare and general lawlessness of the fifteenth century accounted for the depopulation and poverty of most Welsh houses on the eve of the dissolution.

In Scotland Cistercians were made popular by Saint Aelred's patron, King David I (1124-1153). In fact, the first Scottish abbey, Melrose, was settled in 1136 from Rievaulx, and headed by Aelred's boyhood friend, Saint Waldef, King David's stepson, formerly an Augustinian canon and Aelred's fellow-monk at Rievaulx. Melrose became the fertile "mother" of five new foundations and, with help from England, by the end of the thirteenth century, Scotland came to possess eleven Cistercian abbeys.

The first Irish foundation, Mellifont (1142), some five miles from Drogheda, was the fruit of the friendship between Saint Bernard and Saint Malachy, archbishop of Armagh. Although the first contingent of monks was carefully trained at Clairvaux, the traditions of Celtic monasticism proved to be too strong to be replaced by new observances. Despite this first setback, the speed and extent of Cistercian penetration in Ireland was as great as anywhere else, and the country finally boasted of forty-three abbeys, though a number of these were small, formerly Celtic, monasteries. The beginning of English penetration of the island in 1171 added another insoluble problem; the implacable hatred between the two races leading to the separation of English from Irish controlled abbeys, each group denying admission to members of the other nationality. English visitors were barred from Irish abbeys and any attempt by the General Chapter to find a practical means for the control of Irish houses proved futile. Already by the end of the twelfth century the situation was critical. In 1228, Abbot Stephen Lexington of Salley, who was charged with quelling the "Conspiracy of Mellifont," visited the country at the risk of his life. He could no longer find among the Irish even vestiges of Cistercian observances, a sad condition that failed to improve by the dissolution in the sixteenth century. The only exceptions were the two great abbeys, Mellifont and Saint Mary's Abbey in Dublin.

The chronology of Cistercian foundations in the Iberian peninsula is often problematic. According to recent research the first abbey of the Order was not Moreruela, supposedly established as early as 1130, but Fitero, sponsored in 1140 by King Alphonso VII of Castile and populated by the Gascon house l'Escale-Dieu, although it took twelve years until the monks settled on the final site of the abbey. The same French community was also responsible for five other foundations in Spain: Monsalud (1141), Sacramenia (1142), Veruela (1146), La Oliva (1150) and Bugedo (1172), all of the "family" of Morimond. Clairvaux exercised her influence principally through the French Grandselve and Fontfroide, both active in propagating the Order in Catalonia, then only newly recovered from the Moslems. Fontfroide established the great Poblet (1150), which in turn became the "mother" of four more monasteries, one of them La Real near Palma on the island of Mallorca (1236); in 1150 Grandselve populated the illustrious Santes Creus. Moreruela, mentioned above, belonged to the same filiation, but came to being only about 1158. By the end of the thirteenth century the tide of Cistercian foundations was all but over in Spain too. Since at that time the southern part of the peninsula was either under Moslem control or was considered unsafe, nearly all Cistercian houses were located in the northern half of the country. The exceptions were Saint Bernard and Valdigna, both near Valencia, and San Isidoro in Seville, all late foundations. The total number of Spanish Cistercian houses was fifty-eight, which included several formerly Benedictine monasteries.

In Portugal the first Cistercian foundation was Alcobaça (1153), situated between Lisbon and Coimbra and populated directly from Clairvaux. Alcobaça grew to be one of the greatest monastic establishments in Europe and was the "mother" of all twelve other Cistercian houses in Portugal.

The first Cistercian settlements both in Sweden and Denmark resulted largely from the efforts of Archbishop Eskil of Lund, a friend of Saint Bernard, who ended his life at Clairvaux (1181), and of his successor at Lund, Absalon. Alvastra in Sweden, near Lake Vättern, was settled in 1143 directly from Clairvaux and became the most renowned monastic shrine of the country: the burial place of the royal Sverker family, the scene of Saint Bridget's visions, and the mother of three other houses in the same country. The other great abbey in Sweden, Nydala, was another daughter of Clairvaux, born also in 1143, though it was sponsored by Bishop Gislon of Linköping.

Herisvad (Herrevad), on the southern tip of Sweden, but in the twelfth century belonging to Denmark, was another fruit of Archbishop Eskil's admiration for Cistercians. It was populated in 1144 by monks from Cîteaux. The most prosperous Danish Cistercian house proved to be Esrom, a former Benedictine abbey, which, with the blessing of the same Eskil, was incorporated into the family of Clairvaux in 1153. Esrom in turn was instrumental in the takeover of still another Benedictine monastery, Sorø, near Copenhagen (1161). Gudvala (Roma) on the island of Gotland, was the only "daughter" of Nydala (1164). Within the present political borders, Sweden possessed altogether eight Cistercian houses; Denmark had eleven, six of them originally Benedictine communities.

Medieval Norway, with its sparse population, supported only three Cistercian monasteries. The first, Lyse Kloster near Bergen, was founded in 1146 by English monks from Fountains. Hovedø, on a small island in the Bay of Oslo, was built in the same year, also by English Cistercians arriving this time from Kirkstead. The northernmost Cistercian abbey in Europe, Tutterø (Tautra) on an island in the Fiord of Trondheim, came to life in 1207, as the "daughter" of Lyse.

Bohemia was a part of the German Empire and its first three Cistercian foundations, Sedletz (1143), Plass (1145) and Nepomuk (1145), were all made by German monks and all located in the diocese of Prague, all belonged to the "family" of Morimond. Four later foundations, Ossegg (1192), Hohenfurt (1259), Goldenkron (1263) and Königsaal (1292), eventually enjoyed greater prosperity and fame. The total Cistercian houses in the kingdom, including Moravia, was thirteen; in the latter province the most notable abbey was Welehrad (1205), in the diocese of Olmütz.

Within the historical borders of Poland there were twenty-five abbeys altogether, twenty of which were directly or indirectly affiliated with Morimond. Only nine of these were established in the twelfth century, however; the rest came to life at a time when the growth of the Order had considerably abated in Western Europe. The Polish abbeys of this latter group reached their peak of expansion only in the fourteenth century, an era when the West experienced the opposite trend. But in Poland the number of monks, and particularly of lay-brothers, always remained relatively modest and in many instances abbeys founded directly from France or Germany continued to recruit their new members abroad. Sulejow, for example, populated in 1179 directly from Morimond, retained its French character throughout the Middle Ages; similarly, Lad, Lekno and Obra, all "daughters" of the German Altenberg near Cologne, were inhabited for centuries by sons of the pious burghers of Cologne. According to all indications, there was no nationalistic policy of German colonization behind such strange phenomena; the answer lies more likely in the structure of Polish society. The princes and bishops were just as generous toward Cistercians as the sponsors of the Order in the West, but in Eastern Europe the supply of vocations was problematic. According to Polish laws of inheritance all boys of a noble household had a share in the family estates; therefore younger sons had no particular incentive for joining monastic orders. The largest pool of Cistercian vocations in the West, the bourgeoisie and other professional classes, were largely absent from Slavic countries; for lay-brothers the Order in the West relied mostly on free tenant farmers, whereas peasants in Eastern Europe were unfree serfs bound to the soil, who could not normally become brothers. On the other hand, the scarcity of lay-brothers forced the Cistercian establishments in the East to abandon the idea of direct cultivation and to accept serfs and peasant villages, which opened the way for an unlimited expansion of property, unparalleled in the West.

A similar situation might be the principal reason for the modest success of the Cistercians in Hungary. The first attempt by Heiligenkreuz to introduce the Order in this country at Cikádor in 1142, proved to be inconsequential. More promising was the initiative of King Béla III (1176-1196), whose second wife, Margaret, was the sister of King Philip II Augustus of France. Through such connections a number of French monks came to the country and there followed the foundation of Egres (1179) by Pontigny, Zirc (1182) by Clairvaux, Pilis (1184) by Acey, Saint Gotthard (1184) by Trois-Fontaines, Pásztó (1190) from Pilis, and Kerc (1202) from Egres. Kerc, in distant Transylvania, marked the farthest extension of the Order in Eastern Europe. Eventually the total number of Cistercian houses in Hungary rose to about twenty, including three formerly Benedictine monasteries. Unfortunately, the Tartar invasion of the country (1241-42) wrought havoc with the fledgling institutions, and for lack of sufficient local vocations the Order continued to languish in Hungary throughout the rest of the Middle Ages.

Father Leopold Janauschek, in his still indispensable chronological listing of all Cistercian foundations for men until 1675, identified 742 monasteries. It must be remarked, however, that at any given time the total of co-existing abbeys was considerably less than that. Many foundations, for example those in the crusader states and Latin Empire, proved to be ephemeral; others were suppressed or united with other communities. In fact, the notion that all abbeys of the Order in the twelfth century had an overflowing population is certainly mistaken. In the shadows of such giants as Clairvaux, Les Dunes, Fountains or Rievaulx, there were many marginal establishments, and the General Chapter of 1189 was obliged to re-emphasize that each house must have at least twelve monks under the abbot "or else it should either be reduced to a grange, or dissolved altogether." In 1190 the Chapter ordered the Abbot of Jouy to visit Bonlieu in the diocese of Bordeaux, and authorized him to close the house if he could not insure the presence of at least twelve "regularly living" monks. In 1191 the same was decided about San Sebastiano in Rome and Lad in Poland. In 1199 it was reported at the General Chapter that, in addition to San Sebastiano, four other Italian houses (Falera, San Giusto, San Martino del Monte, and Sala) were also underpopulated. Somewhat later (1232) Roccamadore in Sicily joined this list. In spite of appropriate measures, the Chapter of 1204 still complained "that there were abbeys in the Order which, because of deficiency and small number of personnel, pose grave scandals" to the faithful. The threat of suppression was indeed carried out in 1216, when the Chapter decided to reduce San Vicente in Asturias to a grange because the house "was so poor that it could hardly provide for more than two monks."

Reliable information about actual membership at any given monastery is extremely rare for the twelfth century. While it remains true that the rapid succession of new foundations cannot be explained without an overflowing population in many great houses of the Order, some traditionally accepted figures seem to be highly inflated. Clairvaux under Saint Bernard, and even Bellevaux, used to be credited with 500 monks, Grandselve with as many as 800, Rievaulx under Saint Aelred with 600 or more. Somewhat smaller numbers, but still in the hundreds-range, have often been quoted in many instances without sufficient documentation. Equally problematic is the assessment of the relative proportion between choir monks and lay-brothers. Since, according to all available information, the lay-brothers outnumbered the monks, an average house during the twelfth century may have had about fifteen monks and twenty lay-brothers. If this is correct, one may arrive at an approximation of the total Cistercian population. Accordingly, in 1151, when the number of Cistercian foundations reached 333, the population of the Order must have been over 11,600. A century later the 647 abbeys of the Order housed well over 20,000, including lay-brothers, a figure that certainly began to decline shortly thereafter because of the steady decline of vocations for the brotherhood. For the full appreciation of such statistics these numbers

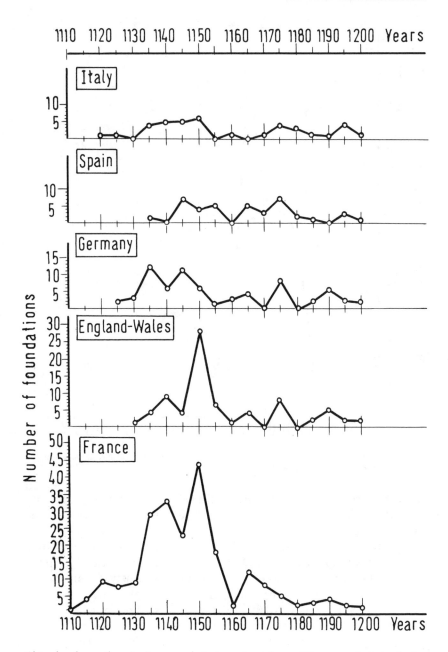

Cistercian foundations by 5 year periods throughout the twelfth century in Italy, Spain, Germany, England & Wales, and France.

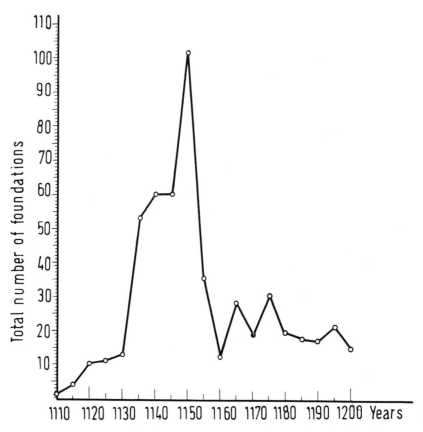

Cistercian foundations by 5 year periods throughout the twelfth century, grand totals for Europe and the Crusader States.

must be projected on the screen of twelfth- and thirteenth-century population figures, which were probably less than ten percent of the present level.

The large number of rapidly developing Cistercian foundations all over the European continent attested to the universal appeal of Cistercian ideals, which affected the whole of contemporary society; yet among the vocations, a surprisingly large number came from the intellectual elite. During the early years of Clairvaux, the famous school of Châlons was almost emptied because students, together with their professors, followed the call of the young Bernard. Similar cases repeatedly occurred wherever the Abbot happened to be preaching, particularly in Reims, Liège and Paris. According to Ernaldus, one of the first biographers of the Saint,

Clairvaux was the monastery where "men of learning, masters of rhetoric and philosophy in the schools of this world, studied the theory of divine virtues." The reason why the young scholastic generation preferred the Cistercians can scarcely be attributed to Saint Bernard's impressive personality alone, since many spent their lives in other monasteries than Clairvaux. The decisive factor in the vocation of these intellectuals must have been the appeal of Cistercian spirituality.

What the fate of Cîteaux would have been without Saint Bernard is certainly an idle question. His personal influence upon the evolution of the Order was surely a factor of paramount importance. Beyond doubt, the program of the Founding Fathers of Cîteaux was a purely contemplative one, animated by an admirable zeal for heroic asceticism. The young Bernard wholeheartedly and sincerely embraced the life of Cîteaux as it was, and under the direction of Abbot Stephen, he himself became one of the greatest contemplatives of all times. He was, however, a unique and universal genius with a providential mission for leadership. It was impossible for him to hide for long within the walls of Clairvaux; but even during his years of feverish public activity, he remained basically the same Cistercian ascetic and contemplative. The greater his faith in Cistercian ideals grew, the more devotedly he worked to propagate it. He never concealed his firm conviction that the Cistercian rule was the surest way to secure one's salvation, and he never hesitated to accept anyone into Clairvaux, from public criminals to royal princes, from fugitive monks to bishops. The prodigious increase of the Order during the first half of the twelfth century would have been impossible without Saint Bernard, and he was, therefore, though unwittingly, largely responsible for its consequences.

To this growth must be ascribed an inevitable antagonism between quality and quantity. While the twelfth century proved to be an exceptionally appropriate era to beget and foster contemplative vocations, it remained true that contemplation, according to its nature, never could concern the masses. It is therefore quite unlikely that those hundreds of new foundations all harbored true contemplative souls. To quote Ordericus Vitalis again, "voluntary poverty and true religion inspire many of them, but many hypocrites and possible counterfeiters are united with them, as tares with the wheat." The problem became even more acute when the Order reached its widest expansion, but shortly thereafter the increasingly secular spirit of the approaching Renaissance reduced the number of monastic vocations. In the meantime, the machinery of the General Chapter functioned with earnestness. The visitors reported year by year the smallest deviations from the common discipline, and the delinquents always received severe punishments. But the Chapter's desperate struggle was directed only against the symptoms, and was, of course, unable to control the real cause, the changing European mind. The Order was too large a body to resist effectively the winds of a gathering storm.

Otherwise, it is amazing how well aware the Chapter Fathers were of the dangers behind that spectacular expansion. Far from being dazzled by their own success, they proceeded with increasing caution in matters of new foundations or incorporations into the Order of already existing monasteries. An excessively reverent Cistercian posterity carefully abolished the traces of dissension among the members of the General Chapter during these glorious years. Nevertheless, there are some signs that in the matter of too hasty foundations, opinions were far from unanimous. It is indeed hard to believe that the only reason for Stephen Harding's abdication in 1133 was his old age. Other considerations certainly were ensconced in the background, since his withdrawal caused a serious crisis. His immediate successor as abbot of Cîteaux, Guido, the former abbot of Trois-Fontaines, was deposed shortly after his election and his name was even blotted from the list of abbots without any indication of a reason. Thereafter, Raynald, a monk of Clairvaux and a close friend of Saint Bernard, took over the central position in the Order. His term was an era of the most vigorous expansion. When he died in 1150, Goswin, the abbot of Bonnevaux (an affiliation of Cîteaux) succeeded him in his high office. The General Chapter turned immediately against the former policy and in 1152 categorically prohibited the foundation or incorporation of new houses in the future. Though these facts cannot safely support far-reaching conclusions, they prove sufficiently that the problem of rapid growth was well in evidence. The Chapter's decision reversed the dearly cherished ambitions of Saint Bernard who at that time lay fatally ill at Clairvaux, dying in the following year. Needless to say, the prohibition against new foundations went unheeded. At the climax of its popularity, the growth of the Order could not be stopped altogether, although the speed of expansion slowed considerably.

A natural and inevitable consequence of large-scale expansion was the increasing prestige, power and activity of the Order in the public life of the Church. Bernard was the first to answer the call of the distressed Church, and he, the great contemplative, played an unrivaled role in the direction of European politics for three long decades. His example presented an irresistible challenge to Cistercian posterity, the more so since both the highest ecclesiastical and secular authorities hopefully expected that the Order, with its immense moral potentiality, would continue to stay at their service, championing peace, justice, and order among Christian nations. The role of troubleshooters of the Church was undoubtedly far from the ideals of the founding Fathers of Cîteaux, who had sought a life of perfect silence in absolute retirement from worldly affairs. Nevertheless, to refuse the challenge and to withdraw again into solitude was just as impossible as it was to reduce the number of Cistercian abbeys to the proportion of decreasing vocations.

The incorporation of already existing monasteries, particularly that of the whole Congregation of Savigny, posed serious problems of economic and disciplinary nature. The rejection of feudal revenues was certainly one of the basic characteristics of Cistercian life. Yet, all abbeys previously under the control of Savigny were admitted into the Order without the obligation of unloading their churches, tithes, serfs and similar sources of income. These concessions encouraged other communities to reach out for hitherto forbidden possessions. By 1169 the abuse had become so widespread that Pope Alexander III addressed a strongly worded bull to the Order calling attention to the alarming deviations from the "holy institutions" of the Founding Fathers. One can hardly suppose that Saint Bernard, who was largely responsible for the fusion with Savigny, was unaware of the discrepancies between the economic basis of the newly admitted abbeys and that of the original Cistercian foundations; neither could he have failed to realize the potential effects of wholesale concessions over the rest of the Order. Why then did he promote the union? The only logical answer is that in his judgment the spiritual benefits of the arrangement outweighed the drawbacks of the compromise. But it would be unfair to blame the Saint alone for what actually followed. The General Chapter took the same lenient attitude even after his death; the consideration of local needs loomed very large in the minds of the Chapter Fathers. Preconceived principles and rigid adherence to a dogmatic position that admitted no exceptions were far from early Cistercian mentality.

In truth, the efficiency of the General Chapter was much weakened by the enormous territorial expansion of the Order. The annual Chapter was supposed to bring together all abbots of the Order. The early regulations accepted only one excuse for absence—illness. The speedy geographical expansion of the Order, however, made regular attendance difficult, if not impossible, to those in far-away lands. For reasons of great distance, expenses and dangers of travel, exceptions were soon granted. Thus, abbots of houses in Syria were required to attend the Chapter only every seventh year and others received similar concessions in proportion to their distance from Cîteaux. On the number of abbots participating in the deliberations of the Chapter during the twelfth and thirteenth centuries no figures have survived. From the constant complaints about unauthorized absences, however, one may conclude that the ordeals of travel were powerful deterrents. At any rate, the physical facilities of Cîteaux for the accommodation of the members of the Chapter were very modest. Even after the completion of the final Gothic cloister in 1193 ("Cîteaux III") the regular meeting place, the chapter hall, was a room of 17 x 18 meters in size, with a double or perhaps triple row of benches around the walls. It was estimated to hold about three hundred persons, but it remains highly doubtful that the hall was ever so well packed. A session with about a third of the abbots in attendance (250) is perhaps a more realistic assumption.

How were the absent abbots notified about the resolutions of the Chapter? On record-keeping and promulgation of statutes the twelfth-century documents are silent. The fact that until about 1180 the extant manuscripts give no information about the proceedings of single sessions seems to indicate that the consultations remained unrecorded and the resolutions of the Chapter, if there were any, were passed on orally. The matter was further complicated by the assembly's continually changing personnel from year to year, so that a considerable portion of the abbots at any given occasion was unacquainted with the discussions conducted in previous years. The frequent result was the passage of incongruous or contradictory regulations, leading to confusion and a skeptical attitude toward the validity of individual statutes. The reason for repeating important decisions year after year was, therefore, not so much deliberate noncompliance, but that by such repetitions eventually all abbots might be properly instructed.

The annual visitation of each monastery by the father-abbot became similarly impaired by the hardships of travel as well as by the excessive number of visits some abbots of numerous "daughters" were obliged to make. Cîteaux had 24 directly affiliated houses, Pontigny 16, Morimond 27 and Clairvaux over 80. Since the visitation of such a multitude of dependent establishments by these and other abbots in similar position was clearly impossible, they either delegated their powers or the visitation was delayed, but in either case the effective supervision of subordinate communities was bound to suffer.

The astounding rise of the Cistercian Order, within the lifespan of Saint Bernard, from a small community of humble hermit-monks to an international network of hundreds of abbeys, can scarcely be explained by the consideration of natural, historical factors alone. Not even the genius of the Abbot of Clairvaux can give adequate account for this unique and specifically religious phenomenon. The secret must lie in the loud and spontaneous echo Cîteaux's spirituality evoked among the congenial members of that devout generation, a spirituality exemplified to rich and poor, erudite and illiterate alike, by the austere and prayerful life of the White Monks.

But the duty of carrying on Cîteaux's exalted legacy proved to be an overwhelming burden. The momentum of growth was bound to slow down; neither could Bernard and his heroic companions be replaced by men of equal stature. Meanwhile, the constantly changing religious and social milieu posed new problems and called for new solutions. The future history of the Order proves convincingly that serious efforts were made to insure a high level of monastic discipline and to shoulder new and challenging responsibilities. The continued attempts to keep the Order abreast of a rapidly moving world, however, often demanded compromises at the expense of genuine Cistercian traditions.

V

Crusades and Missions

Throughout the twelfth century the active involvement of Rome in a multiplicity of religious and political affairs continued to expand, yet the papacy still had no adequate professional staff which could be relied upon as needs or emergencies arose. This is why Church authorities welcomed the assistance of Saint Bernard and his monks, and continued to call primarily upon Cistercians, at least until the emergence of the Mendicants early in the thirteenth century. That such a role was not easily compatible with the ideals of early Cîteaux was well evident; on the other hand, the tight organization, ubiquitous presence and overflowing membership that included some of the best and most active minds of the century predestined Cistercians to step into the vacuum and assume a variety of external duties.

The first and most spectacular of such involvements was the role of Cistercians in the organization and conduct of crusades. As early as 1124 a serious attempt was made to extend the activity of the Order toward the Holy Land. Arnold, the first abbot of Morimond, deserted his post without the authorization of the General Chapter, taking with him the best of his monks, firmly resolved to found a house in Palestine; only his early death prevented him from carrying out his plans. Although Saint Bernard vehemently opposed this adventurous idea, he encouraged the Premonstratensians in their similar endeavors. He gave his enthusiastic support to the Knights of the Temple and addressed to them his famous treatise entitled *In Praise of the New Warfare (De laude novae militiae)*.

Saint Bernard's work in launching the Second Crusade was his own personal contribution to the cause, and only a few other Cistercians are known to have assisted him in Germany. Among them were Abbot Adam of Ebrach, active in Regensburg, and Gerlach, abbot of Rein, similarly engaged in Austria. A certain French monk, Rodolphe by name, who had begun preaching without authorization and stirred up the populace against the Jews in the Rhineland, was silenced by the energetic intervention of Saint Bernard. The crusader army, however, was not accompanied by Cistercians, although two Cistercian bishops, Geoffrey of Langres and the famous historian, Otto of Freising, volunteered for the expedition. In spite of the ultimate failure of the campaign, the example of Saint Bernard remained alive and encouraged other Cistercians to take up the cross on subsequent occasions.

The fate of the Holy Land and the events of the Third and Fourth Crusades evoked a significant echo within the Order. Although the General Chapter repeatedly forbade pilgrimage to the holy places for the members of the Order, the organization of the Third Crusade (1184-1192) was largely the work of Cistercian prelates who had the moral backing of the whole Order. In Italy, the Cistercian archbishop of Ravenna, Gerard, was made papal legate and put in charge of preaching and recruiting. Henry of Marcy, cardinal bishop of Albano, a former abbot of Clairvaux, and Garnier, the actual abbot of Clairvaux, acted under a similar appointment in France and Germany, while Baldwin, archbishop of Canterbury, formerly abbot of Ford, propagandized the crusade in England. A number of abbots and monks followed the armies to the East. Archbishop Gerard fell in battle under the walls of Acre; Archbishop Baldwin and Henry, bishop of Basel, died from diseases. While King Richard I of England, the "Lionhearted," was in German captivity, two Cistercian abbots, Robert of Boxley and William of Robertsbridge, negotiated his ransom, to which the abbots of the English wool-producing houses contributed a year's clipping.

The involvement of the Order in the Fourth Crusade was even more intensive. Pressed by Innocent III (1198-1216), the General Chapter released a number of abbots and monks for the purpose and furnished substantial sums in support of the gathering armies. In Italy the most successful agent of the Pope was Abbot Luke of Sambucina, who received his commission to preach the crusade in 1198. In 1200, urged by Innocent, six more Cistercian abbots took up similar duties and in the following year several more were authorized to do the same. When the crusaders were diverted to Zara and later to Constantinople, most Cistercians echoed the Pope's warnings. It was Abbot Peter of Locedio who carried Innocent's protest to the army at Zara and Guy, abbot of Vaux-de-Cernay, who read it to the assembly of knights on the eve of their attack against the city. Some abbots, however, remained with the crusaders and followed them to the capture of Constantinople. Abbot Martin of Pairis (Alsace), although he refused to share in the general booty, enriched himself with relics found in the church of the Pantocrator and triumphantly carried the treasures back to his abbey in 1205. Peter of Locedio remained in the conquered city, participating in the election of Baldwin of Flanders as the first Latin emperor and for several years taking an active part in the pacification of conquered Greece.

As a tangible fruit of the conquest, the Order acquired or established between 1204 and 1276 twelve houses within the borders of the Empire, including two convents for nuns. Most of these monasteries had previously been inhabited by communities of the eastern rite. Few of these Cistercian foundations survived the collapse of Latin power. One of them was Daphni, a former Greek monastery between Athens and Eleusis, and there were perhaps two other houses in Crete. Daphni was affiliated with the French Bellevaux in 1217. When the Abbot of Daphni arrived at Cîteaux for the General Chapter of 1263, he created a great stir among the fathers: with him, he carried a precious relic, an arm of Saint John the Baptist, which he offered as a gift to the mother house of the Order. Then the grateful Chapter exempted him from attendance at General Chapter for the next seven years. The Turkish capture of Constantinople sealed the fate of the Cistercian community of Daphni (1458), although the Orthodox monks retook their old property and held it until the seventeenth century.

In the wake of the Crusades several Cistercian houses were established in Syria, but details of their history remain uncertain. The best known and most successful was Belmont, southeast of Tripoli in the mountains of Lebanon, populated in 1157 by monks of Morimond. A few years later the same Morimond founded another house in the same area, called Salvatio, but its exact location and subsequent history are doubtful. Belmont was responsible for two further houses, one named after Saint John (1169), another after the Holy Trinity (1187), both probably within the borders of the County of Tripoli. In 1214 the General Chapter incorporated a former Benedictine monastery, Saint George of Jubino in the Black Mountains, which was considered a "daughter" of La Ferté. Meanwhile Cistercian nuns populated two convents, one in Acre, another in Tripoli, both named after Saint Mary Magdalen. The fate of all these foundations could be no different from the fate of the crusader states: as the Moslems were closing in, all were evacuated and abandoned. Today only the ancient cloister of Belmont stands (Dayr Balamand), housing Eastern Orthodox monks. Sensing the inevitable, Belmont founded Beaulieu as a refuge in Cyprus, under the walls of Nicosia. After the fall of Tripoli in 1289, the whole community of Belmont fled to Cyprus, where they survived until the end of the fifteenth century. In 1567 the remains of Beaulieu were demolished by the Venetians, who used the stones for the fortifications of Nicosia.

While the occasional crusading and political activity of the Order concerned only the most eminent prelates and abbots, Saint Bernard's missionary bequest among the heretics of southern France developed into an organized sideline of the Cistercian vocation. The great Abbot of Clairvaux undertook his southern journey in 1145, upon the request of the papal legate, Alberic, cardinal bishop of Ostia, formerly a monk of Cluny. The tour was more spectacular than consequential, and in 1177 Count Raymond V of Toulouse turned again to the Cistercian General Chapter for assistance. No action was taken, however, until Alexander III entrusted a general mission in the South to Peter, cardinal of San Crisogono, with two Cistercians on his staff, Garin, archbishop of Bourges and former abbot of Pontigny, and Henry, abbot of Clairvaux. In 1179, the whole mission, both military and apostolic, was taken over by Abbot Henry, who at the same time was appointed cardinal bishop of Albano. He promptly organized a crusade and captured the heretic-held Lavaur in 1181. After his death in 1198, Innocent III created another Cistercian commission headed by two monks of Cîteaux, Rainier of Ponza, his own confessor, and Guy. After Rainier fell ill, the Pope replaced him by Master Peter of Castelnau, archdeacon of Maguellone, who almost immediately made his profession in the Cistercian monastery of Fontfroide near Narbonne. In 1203, Peter was appointed legate of the Holy See with the assistance of another monk of Fontfroide, Raoul. Finally, to emphasize that the undertaking was entrusted to the whole Order, in 1204 the Pope conferred the supreme direction of the Albigensian mission on Arnold Amaury, abbot of Cîteaux, who became the spiritual leader in the subsequent crusade of Simon of Montfort. After similar efforts elsewhere, in 1207, Amaury, with twelve Cistercian abbots in his entourage, held a fifteen-day debate with the heretics in Montréal and later at Pamiers, without results. One of the active participants was the already mentioned Abbot Guy of Vaux-de-Cernay, uncle of Peter, monk in the same abbey, famous chronicler of the Albigensian Crusade. The extraordinary difficulties of the undertaking among the rebellious crowds, distrustful nobility and tepid prelates seemed to exhaust Peter's energies, and he begged the Pope to allow him to retire to the solitude of Fontfroide. The permission was not granted. "Stay where you are," wrote Innocent, "at this hour, action is better than contemplation." However, this work soon called for effective help and the Pontiff instructed Diego, bishop of Osma and his young canon, Dominic Guzman, to assist the Cistercians. Before they joined them, the two Spaniards visited Cîteaux, pondered the possibility of becoming members of the Order and, though only symbolically, put on the Cistercian habit. They eventually decided against the idea, but it was in the company of the hard-working Cistercians that Dominic conceived the plan of forming an organization specifically suited for the purpose, the future Order of Preachers. By 1207 the number of Cistercians "preaching of Jesus Christ" had reached about forty, but early in the next year an ugly incident turned the peaceful mission to an armed crusade.

On January 14, 1208, Peter of Castelnau was assassinated and public opinion attributed the responsibility for the murder to Count Raymond VI of Toulouse, chief promoter of the Albigensian cause. The long and bloody war that followed (1209-1219) under Simon de Montfort cannot be detailed here, but it is certainly noteworthy that most episcopal sees in the conquered South were eventually filled with Cistercians. Arnold Amaury occupied the key metropolitan position of Narbonne from 1212 until his death in 1225; in 1205, a monk of Grandselve, the ex-troubadour Folquet of Marseille, was installed in the heart of the resistance, as bishop of Toulouse. It was the same Folquet (or Fulk) who, in 1215, was instrumental in the foundation of the first Dominican house in Toulouse and remained a lifelong promoter of the new order. In 1210, the newly retaken bishopric of Carcassone was promptly granted to yet another Cistercian, Guy, abbot of Vaux-de-Cernay.

Of the many colorful Cistercian characters of the crusade the most outstanding and, inevitably, the most controversial was Arnold Amaury. Was he a fearless champion of faith, or a typical southerner, violent, ambitious and fanatical, like many others fighting in the same war? Characteristically, his name has been linked with one of the most durable apocrypha of medieval history. It happened supposedly at the capture of Béziers (1209), a fortress of the Albigenses, that the victorious crusaders became puzzled over the condign punishment of the inhabitants, for it was impossible to tell apart the faithful from the heretics. "Kill them all," decided Amaury, "the Lord knows who are his." The words echoed the Second Epistle to Timothy (II, 19), but the story seems to have originated with the *Dialogus miraculorum* of the German Cistercian, Caesarius of Heisterbach, who composed this collection of edifying anecdotes between 1219 and 1223. The nature of the *Dialogus* should be a sufficient warning to credulous readers; moreover, the honest author himself related the incident as a pure hearsay (*fertur dixisse*); nevertheless, few historians have missed the opportunity of retelling it.

On the Iberian peninsula the Cistercian crusading spirit manifested itself in organizing or inspiring a number of orders of knights, all dedicated to the reconquest of their land from the Arabs. The first and most significant of them proved to be the Order of the Knights of Calatrava. In 1157 it was rumored that the Moors were about to attack Calatrava, a key fortress defending Toledo. The Knights of the Temple in charge of Calatrava claimed that they were unable to meet the emergency and sent a plea for help to King Sancho III of Castile. Coincidentally Abbot Raymond Serrat of the Cistercian Fitero was then visiting in Toledo. There was in his company one of his monks, Diego Velazquez, a former knight and childhood friend of King Sancho. Prompted by Diego, Abbot Raymond offered his assistance in the organization of a defense force for Calatrava, whereupon, in 1158, the King granted the fortress to him, "to possess and defend forever."

The Moorish attack failed to materialize, but a large number of willing defenders put on the Cistercian habit and submitted themselves to Abbot Raymond. After his death about 1163, the knights elected their first master, Don Garcia, who turned to the Cistercian General Chapter for a rule of life and recognition as a branch of the Cistercian Order. The Chapter of 1164 answered favorably, but the formal incorporation took place only in 1187, when the new order of knights was placed under the abbot of Morimond, the father-abbot of Fitero. His rights included annual visitation, appointment of a prior, and confirmation of the master's election. The latter, later known as "grand master," was in charge of the knights and military operations; the prior, who soon became a mitered "grand prior," was always a French Cistercian monk of the filiation of Morimond, and he was responsible for the priests and brothers, who cared for the spiritual and material needs of the knights. Calatrava was lost to the Moors in 1195, but was recovered in 1212, and from then on the knights were instrumental in the recovery of Andalusia. By the end of the fifteenth century, divided into eighty-four "commanderies," they accumulated immense land holdings, including seventy-two churches with about 200,000 people under the Order's jurisdiction. It was largely because of the wealth of the Order that it came under royal control in 1489 and in 1523 the title of the grand master of Calatrava was attached to the Spanish Crown. After the conclusion of the war of reconquest, the Order lost its military and even religious character, although the organization, as an honorary society of Spanish nobility, has been preserved.

The Knights of ·Alcantara sprang to life about the same time as Calatrava through the efforts of two brothers, Suarez and Gomez of Salamanca. In 1158 they found a sponsor in Bishop Odo of Salamanca, a former Cistercian, who himself assumed the role of the first prior of the knights. The center of their activity was the fortress of Saint Julian of Peyrero, and they themselves bore the name of that place for over six decades. Their rule, similar to that of Calatrava, was approved by Alexander III in 1177, but closer association with Cistercians began only in 1221, when the Knights of Calatrava transferred to them the defense of

Alcantara in Leon on the Tagus river, close to the Portuguese border. From this time on the two orders were closely associated and Alcantara, too, was accepted by the Cistercian General Chapter and was placed under the authority of Morimond. The eventual fate of Alcantara was the same as that of Calatrava.

The Knights of Montesa inherited the goods of the suppressed Templars (1312) in Valencia. They were organized in 1317 by members of Calatrava; thus Montesa became another member of associated orders under the authority of Morimond. A similar situation emerged in Portugal, where the Order of Christ was organized by King Denis in 1319 as a replacement for the Knights of the Temple. They too were trained in the observances of Calatrava by ten Spanish knights dispatched to Portugal for that purpose. The Order of Christ, however, came under the jurisdiction of Alcobaça. Still another Cistercian-affiliated Portuguese order of knights was that of Aviz. After obscure beginnings, they first held Evora (1176) and bore the name of this fortress; then, in 1211, they received Aviz from King Alfonso II. They followed the well-established pattern of adopting the customs of Calatrava, together with the jurisdiction of Morimond. In 1551 the Order of Christ and Aviz were united with the Portuguese crown and lost their religious character.

Another territory where a combination of missionary and crusading activity was carried out largely by Cistercians was northeastern Europe, particularly Prussia and the Baltic provinces. There, as among the Albigenses, preaching constituted only a part of the task; the conversion of hostile and warlike tribes required clever diplomacy, sometimes able military leadership. The first tentative efforts in this direction were made by Archbishop Eskil of Lund. In 1164, on one of his sojourns in France, he ordained in the cathedral of Sens and in the presence of Alexander III, the Cistercian Stephen of Alvastra as the first archbishop of Uppsala. Then, somewhat later, he also ordained Fulco, a French Cistercian monk, to be the bishop of the still pagan Estonia. Upon Fulco's request, Alexander III called for a crusade in order to subdue the Estonians, but whatever was done had no lasting results. After 1180 Fulco's name disappeared from the official records.

More successful was the mission in Livonia, headed by Saint Meinhard (d. 1196), a former Augustinian Canon and first bishop of Livonia. It was probably Meinhard who recruited that most remarkable Cistercian missionary, Dietrich (Theodoric) of Thoreida (Treiden), a monk probably of Loccum. He served faithfully not only Meinhard but also his successor, Berthold, his former abbot in Loccum, until the latter fell in battle against his reluctant converts (1198). Dietrich's real opportunity, however, came

58

with the new bishop, the zealous and capable Albert of Buxhovden (d. 1229), formerly canon of Bremen, founder of his new episcopal see, Riga. Dietrich became his most trusted advisor as well as an effective liaison with the papal court. He visited Rome at least six times, where he informed Innocent III in all matters related to the northern missions. Later, as bishop of Estonia, he was one of the participants of the Fourth Lateran Council in 1215. But much before that date there emerged the possibility of forming an independent church-state under papal auspices, governed from Riga. All resources of papal diplomacy were mobilized for the project which, though never fully realized, became the matrix of a multiplicity of crusading and missionary activities for decades to come. Unfortunately, after the death of Emperor Henry VI (1197), Germany plunged into political chaos. Effective crusades, therefore, could scarcely be organized in spite of repeated papal summons. However, the movement featured one of the most colorful characters of that turbulent era, Bernard of Lippe (d. 1224), a powerful vassal and comrade-in-arms of Henry the Lion, duke of Bavaria.

The *Chronicle* of Henry of Livonia gives a lively account of his "conversion": ". . . Count Bernard, when he was formerly in his own land, had taken part in many wars, burnings and assaults. He was punished by God and was afflicted with a debilitating disease of the feet so that, lame in both feet, he was carried in a litter for many days. He was chastened by this and received religion in the Cistercian Order. After learning letters and religion for some years, he received authority from the lord pope to preach the Word of God and to come to Livonia. As he often told it, after accepting the cross to go to the land of the Blessed Virgin, his limbs were immediately made firm and his feet became sound."

In 1185 Bernard contributed to the foundation of the Cistercian abbey of Marienfeld, and it was there that he soon became a monk himself. A few years later he put on his old armor and led a crusade, but eventually turned up as abbot of Dünamünde (1211-1218), a successful pioneering Cistercian foundation. Encouraged by Bishop Albert of Riga, the old warrior accepted another missionary post as bishop of Semgallia (in Lithuania), after he was consecrated by his own son, Bishop Otto of Utrecht. The climax of his long career came undoubtedly in 1219, when, close to eighty, he consecrated his second son, Gerhard, as archbishop of Bremen.

An enigmatic Cistercian personality emerged from obscurity when the death of Bishop Albert of Riga was followed by a disputed episcopal election (1229). The contesting parties turned to Pope Gregory IX, who dispatched Cardinal Otto to the scene. On his way to Riga the Cardinal enlisted the talents of Baldwin, a Cistercian monk of Aulne, a great abbey in lower Lorraine. While the Cardinal tarried in Denmark, Baldwin seized the initiative and, exploiting the opportunity, rekindled the idea of forming a papal vassal-state covering the whole eastern Baltic area. In 1232, after rallying some local support, he rushed to Italy and persuaded the Pope of the practical nature of the scheme, whereupon Gregory consecrated him bishop of Semgallia and Kurland and appointed him papal legate over the whole territory in question. Baldwin set up his headquarters in Riga, but his ambitious plans provoked the militant resistance of the Knights of the Sword, already in possession of much of the land claimed by Baldwin. The Bishop's hastily organized army was defeated by the Knights in the battle of Reval (1233), ending the project and discrediting its author, who also lost his papal legacy. After having spent some time in Aulne, the disappointed Baldwin joined the court of Emperor Baldwin II of Constantinople, who rewarded him with the metropolitan see of Verissa, where he died in 1243.

Of the more enduring Cistercian achievements, notable are the orders of knights, organized on a similar basis to those of the Iberian peninsula. The idea was proposed in 1202 by Dietrich of Thoreida and warmly supported by Bishop Albert of Riga. The bull of Innocent III of 1204 calling for a crusade mentioned a group of warriors "living like the Templars," and, in fact, in that year there was already a house in Riga inhabited by such men, popularly known as Knights of the Sword or "Swordbrothers" (*Fratres Militiae Christi de Livonia*). Their ranks included knights, priests and servants. Headed by a master, they lived in strict poverty, under rules similar to those of the Templars. Their name was derived from their white cloak, decorated with the image of a red sword. In 1210, Innocent III promised them one-third of the territory they might conquer from the pagans, to be held as a fief from the bishop of Riga. The knights quickly expanded their holdings in Livonia, Estonia and Kurland and by 1230 they possessed a virtually autonomous state, administered from six strategically located castles (Ascheraden, Riga, Segewold, Wenden, Fellin and Reval), each under a provincial master. The number of knights never surpassed two hundred, but with the servants and vassals the Order could mobilize an army of two thousand fighting men. Among the thirty priests of the organization many were Cistercians. After their disastrous defeat in 1236 by the Lithuanians in Kurland, the remnants of the Knights of the Sword were absorbed by the rapidly expanding Teutonic Knights.

In Prussia a similar organization emerged from a similar background. The initiation of missionary activity in that still pagan land belonged to

Abbot Godfrey of Lekno, a Cistercian monastery situated in Poland, but sheltering German personnel. With the blessing of Innocent III, he began his preaching in 1206, and was joined in 1207 by one of his monks, Philip. In 1209 still another Cistercian took up the challenge, Christian (d. 1245), whose phenomenal success justly merited him the title of "apostle of the Prussians." In 1215, in the company of two newly converted Prussian princes, he traveled to Rome, where Pope Innocent consecrated and appointed him bishop of Prussia. Soon, however, pagan reaction set in; Philip was murdered, and Christian had to provide armed defense. It was in such circumstances that Christian, following the example of Dietrich of Thoreida, founded the Order of the Knights of Dobrin, named after their fortress on the Vistula river. Invited by Christian, some members of the Order of Calatrava arrived from Spain to train the new recruits. The knights began their service after 1222, receiving strong support from another Cistercian, Bishop Brunward of Schwerin, originally a monk of Amelunxborn. The fighting force mustered by the new Order remained modest, and eventually this organization, too, was absorbed by the Teutonic Knights, although some units of the Knights of Dobrin remained active in Russia until about 1240.

Initially a number of German Cistercian abbeys bore the burden of Baltic missions, but soon a new foundation was made in the mouth of the Duna river near Riga, serving as the basis of such activities. Dünamünde, founded in 1205 by Dietrich of Thoreida, its first abbot, was populated by German monks from Marienfeld. Dietrich remained abbot until 1213, when the tireless monk finally became bishop of still pagan Estonia. In 1218, with the encouragement of Honorius III and help from King Waldemar II of Denmark, Dietrich launched a crusade against his fiercely resisting subjects, who killed him in a skirmish in 1219, mistaking the bishop, ironically, for King Waldemar.

Dünamünde, though heavily fortified, was sacked in 1228 by the pagans and its inhabitants were massacred. The fearless Cistercians rebuilt the ruins and in steady competition with the Teutonic Knights expanded their possessions in every direction. So strategic was the abbey's location, however, that the Teutonic Order could not operate successfully without it. In 1305, under mounting pressure, the Cistercians were forced to sell Dünamünde to the Knights on the condition that thirteen monks and seven servants might remain in the fortress.

Another similar foundation of Pforta was Falkenau (1234) near Dorpat, the easternmost Cistercian outpost. The abbey successfully resisted the covetous Teutonic Knights, only to be destroyed in the sixteenth century by the advancing Russians. The last foundation in

Estonia was Padis, settled in 1317 by monks forced out of Dünamünde. Although the abbey was destroyed and twenty-eight monks were killed by the Estonians in 1343, the community rose to new life and flourished for another century. The monks held possessions and fishing rights as far away as the southern coasts of Finland. Padis, a constant target of Russian and Swedish attacks, was secularized in 1559. Finally, it may be mentioned at this point, Cistercian nuns were also involved in the Order's vigorous expansion into this region. They established convents in Riga, Leal, Dorpat, Lemsal and Reval, all of which disappeared during the sixteenth century.

There is no way to give an accurate estimate of the number of Cistercians engaged in missionary or crusading activities, but the records of the General Chapter abound in restrictive and punitive measures against "vagabond" monks or unauthorized preachers. This seems to indicate that while the rank-and-file of the Order willingly responded to the new challenge, many of the abbots looked askance at any attempt to draw monks away from their cloisters. In one of his sermons Caesarius of Heisterbach expressed eloquently the perplexity of Cistercian minds: "In these days, as you know, by the order of the Pope many monks and abbots have been removed from their cells and cloisters against their intention and will in order to preach the Cross; however, since they considered their removal fruitful, they did not resist the call to gather the harvest of the Lord." It was always under papal pressure, particularly during the reign of Innocent III, that the Chapter grudgingly agreed to the release of some individuals for missionary duties. Thus, responding to papal insistence, the General Chapter of 1211 ordered the Abbot of Cîteaux to contact Innocent III and to ask him to excuse from outside commissions at least priors, subpriors and cellarers. When the Pope did not relent, the Chapter of 1212 appointed the Abbot of Morimond to investigate the situation and to work out a satisfactory compromise whereby both the Pontiff's wishes and the Order's interest could be safeguarded. As late as 1220 Honorius III was instructing the bishops of northeastern Europe to look for missionary help "among Cistercians as well as among others." It was only after the full development of the Mendicant Orders, particularly the Dominicans, that the pressure on Cistercians abated. A resolution of the Cistercian General Chapter of 1245 may be conveniently considered the end of Cistercian missions: monks of the Order were to recite the Seven Penitential Psalms and seven Our Father's for the success of Dominican and Franciscan missions.

While the importance of Cistercians in spreading the Gospel appears to be uncontested, the role of Baltic and Prussian Cistercian abbeys in the

Germanization of these regions has been often misinterpreted. It is true that many monasteries retained their German character in their new environment, preferred to admit Germans as novices and settled German peasants within their possessions, but any supposition that such practices were motivated by conscious nationalism is totally anachronistic. A far simpler and more realistic explanation can be found in their unresponsive surroundings: for lack of local vocations, the abbeys were forced to insure their survival through a continued vital link with their mother houses, and, living within an often hostile world, they sought security in surrounding themselves by friendly settlers.

The medieval respect for piety and integrity caused many prominent members of the Order, mostly abbots, to act as mediators and peace-makers in behalf of papal or royal diplomacy. In 1138, Richard, the first abbot of Fountains, joined the Cluniac Alberic, papal legate, in his tour of visitation in England. In the disputed election of a new archbishop at York in 1140, an ardent disciple of Saint Bernard, William of Rievaulx, assumed an active role, ending with the succession of the stern Cistercian ascetic, Henry Murdac. Saint Aelred of Rievaulx was called out of his abbey almost as often as Saint Bernard. He persuaded Henry II to support Alexander III against an antipope, arbitrated disputes between abbeys, attended synods, and made himself available on many similar occasions. The busiest English prelate of the next generation was certainly Baldwin, abbot of Ford. An eminent canonist and staunch supporter of Thomas Becket, he entered Ford in 1169, was elected abbot in 1175, but continued to serve as Pope Alexander's right arm in England. Baldwin was promoted to the episcopal see of Worcester in 1180 and in 1184 rose to Canterbury, but he remained available to Pope Lucius III for several delicate missions. His role in the Third Crusade and his death in Acre (1190) have already been mentioned. William, abbot of Fountains, received so many burdensome commissions from Rome that his indignant monks turned their complaints to Lucius III. The Pope, in a very charitable letter, dated 1185, expressed his sympathy for both the monks and William, and assured the latter "by witness of this document . . . that we shall take care, with the help of God, that responsibilities are not assigned to you by us . . . unless by chance some other greater problem should arise which we do not think can be settled suitably without you." Between 1170 and 1196 a number of other Cistercian abbots, among them those of Rievaulx, Vaudey, Bruern, Thame, Combe, Stoneleigh, Boxley, Buckfast, Kirkstall and Warden, served in a variety of legal matters as papal delegates in England. In the thirteenth century Cistercian abbots were invited to sit in Parliament in considerable numbers. Simon de

Montfort summoned seventeen Cistercians in 1265; during the reign of Edward I (1272-1307), forty-four Cistercian abbots received such calls. In the strife between Emperor Frederick Barbarossa and Pope Alexander III (1159-1181), Peter, Archbishop of Tarentaise, the former abbot of La Ferté, promoted the cause of the lawfully elected Alexander against Barbarossa's antipopes. During these troublesome two decades, the General Chapter and a score of the Order's most influential abbots were working on an agreement acceptable to both parties, while the final negotiations were carried out by two Cistercians, Bishop Pontius of Clermont, and Abbot Hugh of Bonnevaux. The Pope acknowledged the excellent services of the Order by the solemn canonization of Saint Bernard of Clairvaux on January 18, 1174.

The differences between pope and emperor were renewed under Frederick II (1215-1250), when three Cistercian Cardinals, Conrad of Urach, Jacob of Pecoraria, and Rainier of Viterbo served Pope Honorius III and his successor, Gregory IX. The Cistercian Order was also involved in the conflict between Pope Boniface VIII (1294-1303) and Philip the Fair, king of France. The Pope and John of Pontoise, abbot of Cîteaux, fought side by side against royal violence. As a reward, the Pope granted Abbot John the use of the white pontifical seal with his likeness in a sitting posture; the Pope explained, "you alone stood by me, so you alone are privileged to sit with me." Unfortunately, however, this time their fearless resistance did not result in anything but early death for the Pontiff and imprisonment for the Abbot.

If the number of Cistercian cardinals and bishops is a reliable witness to the Order's high standing and influence in the Church throughout the centuries, there should be no doubt about the Order's prestige: forty-four cardinals and nearly six hundred bishops can be identified in Cistercian annals.

VI

Privileges, Constitutional and Administrative Developments

 Early Cîteaux, in sharp contrast to Cluny, sought neither fiscal immunities nor exemption from episcopal jurisdiction. The founders of the New Monastery vowed to live exclusively from the fruits of their own labor and, as long as monastic observances were not affected, saw no reason for renouncing the obedience normally due diocesan bishops. Yet, within a few decades, the nascent Order was well on its way toward a fully privileged status both in financial and jurisdictional matters. The change was not precipitated by changing ideals or attitudes but by the explosive growth of the institution. The rapid sequence of new foundations and the unprecedented growth of membership taxed the material foundation of each abbey to such a degree that any financial relief was gratefully accepted. Similarly, the preservation of unity and effective administration of the ever expanding network of subordinate houses did not seem to be possible without the limitation of diocesan authority. The ease and speed with which the Order obtained immunities and exemptions clearly attest to the fact that the popes considered the granting of such favors reasonable on their own merits, as much as well-deserved rewards for the vital services the Order rendered in behalf of the papacy.

One immunity that greatly facilitated the growth of the Order, but eventually turned out to be the source of bitter jealousy and outright hostility in ecclesiastical circles, was the exemption from paying tithes, the traditional source of clerical income. Since Carolingian times it had been considered compensation for pastoral services and its total divided into three or four parts: one to the bishop, another to the lower clergy, the third to be spent for the maintenance of the church, and finally, something set aside for relief of the poor. Although, by their nature, tithes were to be collected by the secular clergy, eventually monasteries, and even lay proprietors, got hold of them. The reclamation of tithes from secular owners and monasteries was an important issue in the Gregorian Reform. During the course of the eleventh century such resolutions were passed at a number of synods, but a good deal of ambiguity remained over monastic tithes. Monastic exceptions seemed to be justifiable because priests increasingly constituted the personnel of most abbeys and some of them actually discharged pastoral duties. Monastic possessions of tithes in some cases, moreover, were based on immemorial customs or papal privileges. Nevertheless, monastic reformers of the eleventh and twelfth centuries unanimously renounced their claims on tithes and determined to exist by their own manual labor. The early regulations of Cîteaux regarding tithes merely echoed the opinion which, among many others, Abbot Odo of Saint Martin in Tournai enunciated about 1092, who "was determined to accept neither *altaria* nor churches nor tithes, but to live solely from the labor of their hands . . . [because] such revenues should be owned only by clerics, not by monks."

After the renunciation of the acceptance of tithes, Cistercians still had to deal with the other side of the same issue: whether the monks should pay tithes for their own possessions. Since many early foundations were made in "deserts," on uncultivated, virgin soil, on which no tithes had been paid for some time, the question raised no great problems. Even when donations included previously taxed lands, the manifest poverty of the Cistercians and the hardships of pioneering justified the remission of tithes. Indeed, by the testimony of twelfth-century cartularies, bishops and other collectors of tithes willingly exempted the new foundations from such burdens. In 1132 the prevailing policy received official sanction in a bull of Innocent II, who, as a token of his gratitude to Saint Bernard, declared that no one might demand tithes from abbeys of the Order. The reasonable nature of this privilege was universally acknowledged. As the foundation document of Bonnefont (1136) pointed out: " . . . since the Cistercian brothers receive no tithes or taxes, no one should demand or accept [such things] from them."

In areas where several Cistercian abbeys continued to expand simultaneously by accepting lands previously taxed, serious problems soon emerged: the amount of the tithes received by the diocesan clergy diminished considerably, rendering the maintenance of some rural churches impossible. In 1156, responding to such complaints, Adrian IV made a careful distinction between lands exploited for the first time by Cistercians (*novalia*) and other previously taxed donations. He decreed, accordingly, that while the Order might continue to enjoy the customary immunity on *novalia*, the monks were to pay tithes for their possessions in the second category.

Alexander III (1159-1181), another pope greatly indebted to the Cistercians, returned to the original, broader interpretation of this immunity, but warned the Order repeatedly "that those whose attention should be directed to heaven, should strive by all means to set a limit to their expansion on earth." A less gentle reminder came in a letter of the Englishman Peter of Blois addressed before 1180 to the General Chapter. It stated that "the prayers and tongues of all men should have risen to praise your sanctity, had you not stolen what is not yours. . . . And why should the right of another person be endangered if the lands have come into your possession. . . . If the Lord Pope as a special indulgence gave you a privilege at a time when your Order rejoiced in poverty . . . now, when your possessions have multiplied even into immensity, these privileges are regarded as instruments of ambition." The General Chapter of 1180 admitted the seriousness of the charges and "in view of the great scandals that rise everywhere day after day on account of the retention of tithes," ordered payments without delay or further resistance. The Chapter of 1190 took even more drastic action against the manifest "cupidity" of some abbots and prohibited land purchases in the future altogether. The measures obviously fell short of their intended purpose, for in 1213 new accusations reached Innocent III. The Bishop of the Hungarian Pécs complained that Cistercians in his diocese continued to expand their vineyards and, while refusing to pay tithes, sold their wine for profit. Under the impact of this and similar other charges the Fourth Lateran Council (1215) regulated the payment of tithes definitively. According to the new legislation, *novalia,* as well as properties possessed before 1215 and cultivated by the monks themselves for their own needs, remained exempt as before; but newly acquired land, regardless of the means and purpose of exploitation, was subject to taxation. Since after that date more and more Cistercian estates were turned over for cultivation to peasant tenants, Honorius III in 1224 extended the privilege to old Cistercian possessions, even though they were no longer tilled by Cistercian brothers. At the same time, gardens, orchards and fisheries were exempted. Some years later (1244), Innocent IV added to this list forests, salt mines, mills, wool, milk and sheep. By then the expansion of Cistercian estates in western Europe had come to an end. Monastic economy took a turn toward commercialization and the issue of tithes therefore lost much of its earlier sting.

Obedient to the earliest Cistercian legislation, the abbeys of the Order refused to accept tithes or similar ecclesiastical revenues as donations, and infractions of this rule remained only sporadic until 1147, the year when the Congregation of Savigny was admitted into the Order. Many of the newly joined abbeys already possessed the prohibited revenues and because of the leniency of the General Chapter, continued to enjoy them.

Their example proved to be contagious; by the end of the century most Cistercian abbeys turned out to be "tithers," collectors and users of tithes.

An equally debated, but by its nature a more complex, question was the privilege of exemption from diocesan authority. In this matter, too, the founders of Cîteaux had no intention of following the example of Cluny; therefore all early foundations were made with due respect for episcopal rights. Indeed, the enthusiastic support Cistercians received from the hierarchy in those years may be derived from the monks' submission to local bishops. The "Roman Privilege" of Paschal II in 1100 was merely a document of papal protection against undue and malicious interference in the internal life of the monks. More significant were successive bulls in approval of the *Charter of Charity,* inasmuch as sanction of the Cistercian constitution automatically eliminated episcopal supervision of abbatial elections as well as the right of visitation of individual abbeys. Saint Bernard was certainly in the position to use his influence for the extension of Cistercian privileges, but, in his *De consideratione* addressed to Eugenius III, he inveighed instead against those who entertained such ambitions. But by then Innocent II had exempted Cistercian abbots from attendance at diocesan synods (1132), and in 1152 Eugenius III permitted the continuation of Cistercian services even within territories under interdict. Alexander III, who had exhibited much good will toward the Order in the matter of tithes, in 1169 granted full recognition to Cistercian abbots even if local bishops refused them their benediction, and he prohibited bishops from coercing abbeys of the Order by threatening excommunication. All previously granted privileges were summed up and expanded in 1184 by a bull, issued by Lucius III, who freed all Cistercian abbeys from the punitive authority of bishops. This document was not the last in the process of gradual and eventually total exemption, for the increasing role of the Order in the pastoral care of laborers and villages under Cistercian seignioral rule called for further legal clarification. The right of preaching and administering the sacraments became a constant irritant, as did the rising social prestige of abbots, their use of episcopal insignia, their power to confer minor orders and their competition for precedence in various public functions. The progressive alienation of abbots from the secular hierarchy was unfortunate and detrimental for both parties. The split and even enmity among the clerical ranks facilitated secular intervention, and led to ruthless despoliation of abbeys either by confiscatory taxation or by the imposition of commendatory abbots.

With the changing posture of the Order within the Church, the Cistercian constitution was bound to undergo important modifications. One obvious reason for such adjustments was the fact that the original *Charter of Charity* could not provide for all the problems which resulted from the Order's geographical expansion. These problems can be summed up, for the sake of brevity, as the weakness of the General Chapter; the emergence of the "lines" or "affiliations" organized and firmly held by the proto-abbots; and the repeated attempts of the abbots of Cîteaux to exploit this imbalance for their own aggrandizement.

That the annual Chapter was much less than a general assembly of all abbots of the Order was well evident by the middle of the twelfth century. The dangers, expenses and time of travel kept away the majority of the abbots of houses outside of France, and it is difficult to believe that an average session was attended by more than one-third of all Cistercian abbots. As a result, the convention was poorly informed about local conditions in certain areas, and it was therefore in no position to take adequate and enforceable corrective measures. The constantly changing personnel of the Chapter rendered the pursuance of a consistent line or policy difficult, and many of its resolutions were haphazard and contradictory. Such weaknesses were only compounded by the lack of adequate record keeping and effective promulgation. The vacuum of authority was easily and naturally filled by the father-abbots, who ultimately depended on one of the five proto-abbots. These abbots (of Cîteaux, La Ferté, Pontigny, Clairvaux and Morimond) kept a close watch over the cohesion of their respective filiations and, conversely, affiliated abbots looked to them for directives. This was particularly true on the occasions of General Chapters, when the well-disciplined "family" of Clairvaux, outnumbering all other "lines," easily controlled the proceedings. Although in the original version of the *Charter of Charity* neither the "proto-abbots" nor their "affiliations" were recognized as legal entities, the final modification of this document had already granted considerable powers to the four abbots and had empowered them collectively to depose the abbot of Cîteaux and to govern the mother house during the vacancy. The growing suspicion, tension and periodic hostility between the abbots of Cîteaux and their four principal colleagues, as well as the struggle for the control of the General Chapter, were the unhappy results of legal ambiguities.

If a much later tradition can be relied upon, the first serious clash between Cîteaux and Clairvaux occurred in 1168, when the newly elected Abbot Alexander of Cîteaux visited Clairvaux, where he deposed Abbot

Geoffrey for his "reprehensible conduct." Although the Chapter supported Alexander, Geoffrey was more successful in Rome and the scandal was settled only after long and painful negotiations. In 1202 a new conflict broke out between Cîteaux and the proto-abbots, climaxed by the deposition of Abbot Guy of Clairvaux in 1213. The affair was about to come to the attention of the Fourth Lateran Council in 1215, when Innocent III intervened and upheld the position of Abbot Arnold Amaury of Cîteaux, without, however, removing the fundamental irritants. A reconciliation in 1222 was followed by another flare-up of hostilities under Abbot John of Cîteaux (1236-1238), an Englishman and formerly abbot of Boxley, who tried unsuccessfully to force the Chapter to pay the debts of Cîteaux in the amount of four thousand marks.

These incidents, although unfortunate, were only preludes to the feud between Cîteaux and Clairvaux which ran from 1263-1265 and, for the first time, put to a serious test the Order's cohesive forces. The leading characters of the drama were Abbot James of Cîteaux (1262-1266) and Abbot Philip of Clairvaux (1262-1273), both elected about the same time, both strong, unyielding and resourceful personalities, both determined to settle the long-simmering issues on their own respective terms. The hostilities began at the General Chapter of 1263, over the organization of the *definitorium*. This body had first emerged at the General Chapter of 1197 as an executive committee in charge of the preparation of the Chapter and of the formulation of its statutes. Its composition and legal authority had not been defined until 1265, and prior to this date its membership and function were matters of troublesome bargaining between Cîteaux and the proto-abbots. At the beginning of the 1263 Chapter attacks against the legality of Abbot James's election and complaints about his refusal to appoint the proto-abbots' nominees as definitors created an atmosphere explosive from the outset. News soon arrived that Abbot Philip had been elected bishop of Saint-Malo, but he, suspecting merely a maneuver to remove him from the scene, refused to accept the election and decided instead to go to Rome to present his grievances in person to Urban IV. Although Abbot James ordered him to return under pain of excommunication, he continued his journey to Rome, where the Pope not only accepted his reasons for refusing the bishopric, but on March 15, 1264, also appointed Nicolas, bishop of Troyes, Stephen, abbot of the Benedictine Marmoutier and Geoffrey of Beaulieu, the Dominican confessor of King Louis IX, to investigate the roots of the trouble. The committee was as unsuccessful as were the repeated interventions of the saintly King Louis, great friend and benefactor of the Order. Under the cloud of hatred and mistrust, and with the permission of the Pope, Abbot Philip refused to attend the Chapter of 1264, suspecting treachery, perhaps his imprisonment, at Cîteaux. The death of Urban IV further complicated the situation, although his successor, Clement IV, elected early in 1265, followed the Cistercian crisis with equal interest. He appointed a new committee for the unfinished business: the Bishop of Puy, the Benedictine Abbot of Chaise-Dieu, and Humbert of Romans, the newly retired master general of the Dominicans. On June 9, 1265, followed the publication of the bull *Parvus fons*, known in Cistercian history as the *Clementina*. Among many weighty provisions the bull intended to settle the problem of definitors by ordaining that before the annual Chapter each of the four proto-abbots present five names to the abbot of Cîteaux, who was to appoint four of them; adding his own four appointees and the proto-abbots themselves as *ex officio* members, altogether the *definitorium* was to consist of twenty-five abbots.

Who was actually responsible for the text of the bull is not entirely clear, but the fact that the papal committee was dispatched to Cîteaux to explain its contents at the General Chapter of 1265 seems to indicate that the committee, or at least the much experienced Humbert of Romans, had some influence in its formulation. As soon as the Chapter opened in mid-September, the bull and its interpretation became subjects of heated argument, for the proto-abbots charged that even the new formula gave too much arbitrary power to the abbot of Cîteaux. Fortunately, the previous abbot of Cîteaux, Guy, then cardinal priest of San Lorenzo in Lucina and papal legate, was also present, and all the participants of the Chapter submitted the problem of the selection of definitors to his arbitration. Cardinal Guy decided that each of the four proto-abbots should appoint two abbots for the *definitorium,* whom the abbot of Cîteaux might not reject; the other two were to be appointed by the abbot of Cîteaux from the remaining three names. The compromise was accepted by the Chapter and eventually by the Pope.

The other provisions of *Parvus fons* were intended to restrict the overbearing powers of father-abbots and visitors, and to bolster the authority of the General Chapter. Thus, vacant abbeys, under the temporary direction of the priors, would be free to conduct their affairs; abbatial elections would be decided exclusively by the votes of local communities; the newly elected abbot of Cîteaux would assume his duties without confirmation by the proto-abbots. Finally, the visitation of Cîteaux by the four proto-abbots was to take place annually on the feast of Saint Mary Magdalen (July 22), but the visitors either at Cîteaux or elsewhere were not empowered to depose abbots without due legal process and authorization of the General Chapter. *Ipso facto* depositions of abbots were restricted to cases of flagrant public offenses or dereliction of duty. A more businesslike functioning of the General Chapter was facilitated by the granting to a hitherto informal *definitorium* a legal status, as an executive inner council in charge of preparing an agenda and helping in the formulation of statutes. The emergence of this powerful body, however, tended to reduce the active role of other participants of the Chapter and discouraged the attendance of those abbots who had no chance of becoming definitors. Furthermore, the selection of definitors, as a prelude to the formal sessions of the Chapter, proved to be an occasion for intense politicking, which certainly did not promote much-needed concord among the proto-abbots.

The next milestone in the Order's legal history was the *Fulgens sicut stella,* an apostolic constitution issued by the Cistercian Benedict XII in 1335, and popularly referred to as the *Benedictina*. It was a document of about eight thousand words, the last third of which formed the first code of Cistercian education, to be discussed below. The major part of the constitution fitted into a general scheme of religious legislation sponsored by the Pope. Within four years he issued similar constitutions for the Black Monks, the Mendicants and the Augustinian Canons; all were conceived in a spirit of highly advanced bureaucratic centralization, whose model was the papal court itself at Avignon. These documents constituted the foundation for future medieval legislation concerning religious orders.

The *Clementina* had introduced a constitutional reform; the *Benedictina* was basically a reform of financial administration. Those years were long past when, following the Rule's prescription, one cellarer could manage alone the material needs of a monastery. The once modest Cistercian farms had become enormous feudal estates, and at the same time the evolution of European economics rendered their administration increasingly complicated. The accumulation of material wealth also increased the dangerous possibility of natural disasters, wars or illegal demands and immoderate exactions of avaricious princes, to say nothing of the impending problems of adjustments to a basically changing economic system. Despite the vast extent of their possessions, a large number of monasteries had fallen victim to unfortunate circumstances and were deeply submerged in debt. To remedy these ills the *Benedictina* restricted the unlimited power of abbots over finances by establishing a system of controls. Supervisory rights were granted to the communities or to the General Chapter and, in the most important cases, decision was reserved to the Holy See. The documents of legal transactions, if the consent of the community was required, were to be stamped by the official seal of the convent. The constitution created the office of the treasurer, whose duty it was to record the income and expenditure of the monastery, and it demanded the making of annual financial reports of all those charged with fiscal administration.

Further paragraphs emphasized the importance of General Chapters and emphatically urged regular attendance. Abbots were reminded that, despite a sharp decrease in vocations, no novice should be admitted without proper qualifications for the religious life. The Pope also insisted on simplicity in clothing and food, although in some cases a general dispensation from abstinence was granted abbots and their company. A new arrangement providing for single cells instead of the common dormitory was condemned and strictly forbidden.

In the first draft of the document there was a revolutionary innovation: the Pope proposed that besides abbots, each community should be represented at the annual Chapter by a delegate elected by a majority vote. The move was most likely inspired by the Dominican constitution; among the abbots of the Order, however, it caused a universal alarm. In a lengthy memorandum they protested against this and against other curtailments of abbatial powers, and, as a result, the idea of a conventual delegate was dropped from the final composition. The office of the treasurer was another unpopular item in the administrative reform and upon the abbots' request it was soon modified by Clement VI, Benedict's immediate successor.

It is evident from the *Benedictina* that sporadic abuses or signs of mismanagement notwithstanding, the Order as a whole still observed the high ideals of its founders, worthily enjoying the widest reputation and deserving the eloquent accolade of the Pontiff in the introductory paragraph of his Constitution. Those lofty lines also solemnly recognized the Order's active character by attributing to it the role of both Mary and Martha.

Gleaming like the morning star in the midst of a clouded sky, the Sacred Cistercian Order by its good works and edifying example shares in the combats of the Church Militant. By the sweetness of holy contemplation and the merit of a pure life, it strives with Mary to ascend the mountains of God, while by praiseworthy activities and pious ministration it seeks to imitate the busy cares of Martha. Full of zeal for the divine worship so as to secure the salvation of both its own members and outsiders, devoted to the study of Holy Scripture so as to learn therefrom the science of perfection, powerful and generous in the works of charity so as to fulfill the law of Christ, this Order has merited to propagate itself from one end of Europe to the other. It has mounted gradually to the summit of the virtues, and it abounds in the graces of the Holy Spirit, who delights to inflame humble hearts.

Among important administrative innovations which resulted from practical needs rather than from legislative action, the most significant was the creation of a "procurator general" of the Order, who was to attend to the growing volume of legal business in Rome, or, most of the time in the fourteenth century, in Avignon. As early as 1220 two secular clerics occupied themselves with such matters in Rome. Throughout the rest of the century secular canonists continued to function in a similar capacity under the direction of one or another of the Cistercian abbots in Rome or in Casamari; their salaries, twelve marks annually, were paid from funds made available by the General Chapter. Some time in the fourteenth century prominent members of the Order took over the same function but, instead of two, only one "procurator general" appeared in the documents, who most likely headed a small office with several secretaries. All abbots of the Order were to channel all their legal cases in the Curia through the procurator, who was also the watchful defender of Cistercian privileges. The first procurator general mentioned by name in 1390 was Petrus Mir, Parisian doctor of theology and later abbot of Grandselve. The role of procurators in later centuries became ever more important, particularly during the feud of observances in the seventeenth century.

It was probably under the influence of the Franciscans that Cistercians, too, looked for a "cardinal protector" in the Curia. No doubt a long line of Cistercian cardinals had in fact "protected" the Order for some time, but the title of *protector ordinis* emerged first in 1260, in reference to the Cistercian Cardinal John of Toledo, an Englishman by birth. The role of the protector was never clearly specified and appears to have been more a title of honor than an office, unless the cardinal was appointed for a specific duty either by the General Chapter or by the Curia.

A thorny problem, and one entirely unforeseen by the authors of the *Charter of Charity,* was created by the substantial expenses Cîteaux had to shoulder during the sessions of the General Chapter. In order to reduce the burdens of food and shelter, the nonessential personnel of Cîteaux were temporarily transferred to granges and other houses in the vicinity, while the attending abbots were ordered to enter Cîteaux alone, leaving behind their traveling companions and their horses at some neighboring abbey. Food for the occasion was gathered, some of it certainly donated, before the opening of the sessions. According to the records of the Chapter of 1199, fish was shipped to Cîteaux from as far away as Lausanne. In 1204, Guiard, Lord of Reynel, granted to Clairvaux fishing rights on his property for eight days before and eight days after the General Chapter. A portion of the catch was obviously destined for

Cîteaux as Clairvaux's contribution to the feeding of the assembly. The fact that donations were collected from the attending abbots is evident from the twelfth-century records, but the amount was apparently not fixed, nor was the payment compulsory. The Chapter of 1212 merely insisted that the collected donations be used in such a fashion that they benefit all participants in an equal manner. The *Parvus fons* of 1265 appointed two abbots to handle the whole operation.

Meanwhile the Order actively solicited from friends and benefactors gifts or permanent sources of revenues for the same purpose. According to Chapter records, kings, princes and members of the hierarchy often contributed substantial amounts. King Alexander II (1214-1249) of Scotland offered twenty pounds sterling annually; Béla IV (1235-1270) of Hungary donated the revenues of several churches in Transylvania. Louis IX (1226-1270) of France and Blanche of Castile, his mother, granted Cîteaux several rents to be paid in perpetuity, and their example was followed by other members of the royal family. The most memorable of all such donations was made in 1189 by King Richard I of England, just before he left for his celebrated Crusade. The rich revenues of the church of Scarborough near York were granted for the support of the General Chapter under the condition that the Order, under the supervision of the abbot of Rievaulx, maintain a vicar in charge of pastoral services. The revenues were handsome, but for this very reason the clergy of York was most unwilling to watch the flow of substantial sums to a distant French abbey. Secular as well as regular seekers of benefices used every opportunity and pretext to block the Cistercian administration of the church, which became precarious for other reasons as well, such as the Hundred Years' War (1337-1453) between France and England. The litigation over Scarborough, protracted from the end of the twelfth century to the eve of the Dissolution, holds the record for the longest lawsuit in Cistercian history.

From a legal point of view the most enduring success of the General Chapter was the systematic collection and periodic publication of its own statutes, which solved, at least partially, the problems each abbey faced in trying to apply the formidable and often incongruous volume of annual decisions. The first such collection, entitled *Book of Definitions (Libellus definitionum)*, was completed in 1202 under the auspices of Arnold Amaury, abbot of Cîteaux. The Chapter of 1204 insisted that the "book be acquired by all as soon as possible, so that none of the abbots could in the future excuse himself on grounds of ignorance." The new code featured fifteen chapters in sequence: (1) on the foundation of abbeys; (2) on the admission of novices, professions and the blessing of abbots; (3) on the Divine Office; (4) on privileges and immunities; (5) on the General Chapter; (6) on the daily chapter of faults; (7) on visitations and powers of father-abbots; (8) on monastic officials and workers; (9) on traveling monks; (10) on the reception of guests and burials within abbeys; (11) on the practice of poverty; (12) on buying and selling; (13) on food and clothing; (14) on lay-brothers; and finally, (15) a series of unclassified regulations.

Retaining the same basic structure, this code was updated in 1220, 1240 and in 1257. The publication of the *Parvus fons* in 1265 necessitated a more fundamental readjustment, which was achieved only in 1289. Neither the title nor the structure of the original collection were changed, but the first chapter included the texts of both the *Charter of Charity* in its final version and of the *Parvus fons*. As another innovation, the fourteenth chapter was followed by rules and regulations concerning Cistercian nuns.

In 1316 the General Chapter ordered a new compilation of Cistercian laws, and when it was presented to the Chapter in the following year, the convention not only accepted it but also decreed all previous collections obsolete and therefore suppressed. The title of the new code was *Book of Old Definitions (Libellus antiquarum definitionium)*. In spite of many new features, this work retained the traditional fifteen chapters. Following the publication of the *Fulgens sicut stella* in 1335, it became evident that still another substantial revision was imminent. As in the previous cases of adjustment, an abbatial committee was appointed for the arduous project which was completed four years later.

The author of the *Fulgens sicut stella*, Benedict XII, an eminent canonist, was dissatisfied with the results, however. After hearing his objections voiced at the Chapter of 1339 by his Cistercian nephew, Cardinal Guillaume le Court (Curti), the protector of the Order, the convention agreed that further study was necessary. The new text was approved and published in 1350 under the title *New Definitions (Novellae definitiones)*, but it comprised only the new material that had accumulated since 1316. In many instances the new laws modified the *Book of Old Definitions*, but the new collection was not designed to replace the old one; in actual practice the simultaneous use of both collections remained necessary.

The fusion of the two books into one code was proposed several times, notably in 1487, but the plan was never executed. Thus the "Old" and "New" definitions continued to be used as the legal handbooks of Cistercian life until the eve of the French Revolution, even though many of their provisions had been greatly modified by subsequent legislation.

VII

The Challenge of Scholasticism

The twelfth century was the most creative era in the history of medieval Christianity. The Gregorian expectations of a world governed by Christian principles failed to materialize; still, the reign of Innocent III brought the Church to a climax of unprecedented moral and political power. The attempt to form a Christian commonwealth out of the emerging nations of Europe fell short of its goal, yet the Crusades attested to the power of common ideals and to the will for united action. The growth of individual piety, the restless search for truth and beauty led to the renewal of mysticism and to matchless originality in poetry and art. The intoxicating pursuit of lofty but elusive ideals came to genial expression in the poetry of Chrêtien de Troyes (d. 1190), and created the inspiring saga of the Holy Grail, the source of new life, knowledge and heavenly bliss on earth, the allegoric epitome of all that made life worth living for that noble generation.

Among the renewed monastic orders the Cistercians offered what thousands of pious souls recognized as the most rewarding choice, a way of life leading safely to salvation. According to some students of contemporary piety and poetry, Clairvaux served Chrêtien as the model for the mystical château of the Holy Grail, and Parceval spoke the language of Saint Bernard. Be that as it may, the great Abbot spoke the language of the best of his contemporaries with irresistible authority. In 1139 he addressed an erudite audience in Paris and promised his spellbound listeners knowledge and happiness, not, like Abelard, through the powers of reason and logic, but through affectionate love. He invited them to come to Clairvaux, where they might "find the admirable shrine, where man is feeding on the bread of angels; find the paradise of delights planted by God . . . not a paradise of the senses but one of internal happiness. This is the garden that can be entered not on foot but on [the wings of] affections." As long as this was what Cistercian novices were looking for, there was no need for formal instruction within the abbeys; the appeal of Cîteaux proved strongest among those who had already been instructed in the world before their "conversion."

The arrival of the thirteenth century, however, heralded a drastic change in this rarefied cultural atmosphere. The shameful debacle of the Fourth Crusade, diverted by Venetian commercial interest from the Holy Land to Constantinople, cooled the enthusiasm of thirteenth-century warriors for similar ventures. After the premature death of Innocent III, the papacy became the instrument, and eventually the victim, of clashing political interest. Frederick II, the last of the great Hohenstaufens, was cast from an entirely different mold from that of his crusading grandfather, and he was willing to trade the Holy Roman Empire for a highly centralized Sicilian monarchy, where he lived and ruled independently of standards of Christian morality. Popular piety, particularly the fascination with poverty, turned into the dangerously antisocial and anticlerical heresy of Albigensianism. Against these formidable adversaries the weapons of Cistercian missionaries proved ineffective. Saint Dominic turned against this heresy of emotional eccentricity with the weapons of merciless logic implemented, when insufficient, by force. Armed repression of dissent and the Inquisiton were phenomena as new as "scholastic" theology, based no longer on the Neoplatonic teachings of Church Fathers, but on the recently discovered philosophy of Aristotle. The new learning turned away from the gentle mysticism and carefree informality of the twelfth century, and transformed theology into a rigidly controlled discipline of certified professionals, who, firmly entrenched in the new universities, delivered everywhere the same sort of lectures based on the same textbooks. Triumphant rationalism imprinted its mark on every field of intellectual and artistic pursuit. Everything worth knowing was gathered into systematized *summa's* or encyclopedias; music was a branch of science, architecture was dominated by engineering virtuosity, and even poetry had to put on the guise of scholarship. The commercialization of economy and the further growth of cities inhabited by a well-educated, prosperous and ambitious bourgeoisie were not directly related to changing intellectual currents, but they certainly added to the striking differences which distinguish the thirteenth century from the twelfth.

That Cistercian abbeys in their rural isolation and rustic simplicity no longer stood in the forefront of thirteenth-century developments is a matter of foregone conclusion. The Dominicans were better adapted to serve the Church as missionaries and theologians; the Franciscans more effectively conveyed the message of poverty to the urban masses; the professionally educated secular clergy or laity could easily replace Cistercians as royal or papal advisors and negotiators. More importantly, the best religious vocations joined the Mendicants rather than the old monastic orders and even lay-brothers found more rewarding employment in the city convents of the new orders than in Cistercian granges. The constitutional and administrative changes that had been executed within the Cistercian Order clearly indicated that the General Chapter was not only aware of new demands but was also willing to adopt corresponding modifications. But by the third decade of the thirteenth century it became evident that, for the first time, the old public image of the Order needed to be refurbished if it was to remain attractive enough to maintain and populate abbeys with adequate personnel. During the rest of the century the figure of the Cistercian ascetic spending his day in prayer and hard manual labor was replaced by that of the scholarly monk, dividing his working hours between school and library.

In searching for more tangible reasons for the establishment of the first Cistercian educational institutions, Matthew Paris, a well-informed contemporary witness, came to the conclusion that "Cistercians, in order to avoid the contempt of Dominicans, Franciscans and erudite seculars, particularly lawyers and canonists . . . obtained houses in Paris and elsewhere where schools flourished, then they established their own schools where they could study with more devotion theology, canon and [Roman] law, because they did not wish to look inferior to others." The chronicler had some reservations about the trend among monastic orders and reminded them that the author of their Rule, Saint Benedict, had abandoned the schools of Rome to retire to the desert. Yet, he did not blame the orders, but the corrupting influence of a world that no longer respected monastic simplicity.

Undoubtedly, the great English historian echoed the opinion of his puzzled contemporaries who believed, with good reason, that the competitive existence of the major religious orders had much to do with the pursuit of higher education. In the case of the Cistercians, however, two other factors gave an even greater urgency to the matter. One was the disappointing experience of the many abbots who had preached among the Albigenses and whose lack of theological schooling was widely recognized as one source of Cistercian failures. The other, and more decisive factor, was the appearance of an extraordinary personality, Stephen Lexington, another great Englishman in the history of the Order, who not only noticed the crying need for educated monks, but possessed the energy and zeal to launch a successful program in the teeth of considerable opposition.

Stephen Lexington was born to a prominent family of high-ranking officials serving both the English church and royal government. Stephen received an excellent education, studying first in Paris, then in Oxford, where he was a disciple of Saint Edmund Rich of Abingdon, later

79

archbishop of Canterbury. In 1214 Stephen received a prebend in the church of Southwell, but, probably under the influence of his saintly master, he soon joined the Cistercians with seven companions at Quarr Abbey on the Isle of Wight. In 1223 he became abbot of Stanley and it was in this capacity that he received from the General Chapter a commission to visit the turbulent abbeys in Ireland. His tour of visitation in 1228 turned out to be a shocking experience and the Abbot came to believe that most of the disorders stemmed from the total ignorance and backwardness of the monks, with whom he could not even communicate, for the Irish neither spoke nor understood Latin, English or French. In 1229 Stephen was elected abbot of Savigny and used his enlarged authority to improve the number and quality of vocations throughout the network of Savigny's extensive "family." He undertook a tour of visitation without delay and in each abbey ordered that after the completion of the novitiate the young monks should spend two more years in "reading, meditation, studying the laws and customs of the Order, during which time no other duties should interfere with these [studies]." In 1241 he joined the abbots of Cîteaux, Clairvaux and other houses on their journey to a Roman synod called by Gregory IX. The Genoese ships carrying the prelates were intercepted by the imperial fleet under Enzio, illegitimate son of Frederick II. Most of the abbots were captured, but Stephen escaped, thanks to the bravery of his brother, John Lexington. Late in 1243 Stephen reached the climax of his career when he was elected abbot of Clairvaux. His new position enabled him to give new direction and outlook to Cistercian vocation through opening a new road to institutionalized higher education.

The inevitability of such a move must have been clear in Stephen's mind for a long time. As abbot of Stanley, about 1227, he had written a letter to Abbot Raoul of Clairvaux warning him about "the menacing ruin and extinction of our Order for defects in personnel, and justly so . . . because we no longer have men commendable for both piety and learning, as they were during the lifetime of Saint Bernard, men who could, in this emergency, lend a helping hand to our ageing and faltering Order." The rumors of heresy spreading among Cistercians in the south added a new gravity to the issue. Writing to John, abbot of Pontigny (1233-1242), Stephen called attention to seven heretical monks in Gondon (a filiation of Pontigny), all in error because of their ignorance. "It is to be feared," he continued, "that the dire prediction of one of the leading Dominicans about us might be verified, namely, that within a decade they would be obliged to take over the direction and reform of our Order, because during the past thirteen years no prominent scholar, and particularly no theologian, has joined us, and those whom we still have are elderly and well advanced on the road of all flesh." In conclusion Abbot Stephen asked his colleague at Pontigny to mobilize his connections in Rome, so that his friends there might inform the Pope about the grave problems of the Order in the hope that the Pontiff would put pressure on the Abbot of Cîteaux and the proto-abbots and spur them to action. Stephen's concrete proposal was an abbatial convention "near Paris, so that the leaders of the Order could discuss the matter among themselves and find means to counter the danger created by the lack of learning."

Details of the immediate developments are not known, but Abbot Stephen's move must have been successful, for the General Chapter of 1237, on the request of Abbot Everard of Clairvaux (1235-1238), permitted that he, Everard, send his monks to Paris for the sake of studies, and with them another monk and two lay-brothers to provide for the students' material needs. The same was granted to other abbots as well who wished to send their students to Paris to join those of Clairvaux. In fact, Clairvaux already possessed a house in Paris acquired in 1227 near the abbey of Saint-Germain-des-Prés, and it was most likely that the first Cistercian student body was formed there.

The development of the institution took a giant step forward immediately after the election of Stephen Lexington as abbot of Clairvaux on December 6, 1243. Without wasting any time he informed Innocent IV of his intention to build a full-fledged Cistercian college in Paris, and found in the Pontiff an enthusiastic supporter. A bull issued on January 5, 1245, authorized the Abbot of Clairvaux to establish in Paris a *studium* "for the salvation and honor of the [Cistercian] Order and for the ornament and glory of the universal Church." Since Clairvaux's original property proved to be ill-suited for the purpose, Stephen first moved into a house next to the abbey of Saint Victor. Then, in 1246, he purchased a large tract of land in Chardonnet, close to the place on the left bank where the fortifications built by Philip Augustus reached the Seine. The Abbot, suspecting that his initiative might not be approved by the majority of his more conservative fellow-abbots, turned to the Pope for assistance. On the eve of the General Chapter of 1245 Innocent IV addressed a letter to the convention praising the Parisian house of studies and warmly recommending its support. This, of course, insured success, and the assembly granted its approval, although the abbots emphasized that it was done "at the order of his Lordship the Pope and at the petitions and admonitions of numerous cardinals, especially those of Lord John [of Toledo], titular of Saint Laurence in Lucina." It was equally significant that the same statute encouraged all abbots to promote studies within

81

their own monasteries and ordered that at least one abbey in each region be designated for the study of theology. Although all abbots were offered the choice of sending students either to these regional centers or to the Parisian house "already in operation," such a study was not made compulsory, and thus formal studies remained entirely voluntary.

During the next decade the new college, named after Saint Bernard, made remarkable progress. Substantial endowments brightened its financial outlook, while papal privileges enhanced its status among other colleges in Paris. The most valued document was issued by Innocent IV on January 28, 1254, which granted to the College of Saint Bernard all the rights and privileges that the colleges of the Dominicans and Franciscans had already enjoyed, a status that Cistercians achieved before any other monastic order, including Cluny. Following the established Parisian customs, the College of Saint Bernard was headed by a provisor, who enjoyed full authority over both scholastic and disciplinary matters, and who was an appointee of the abbot of Clairvaux. The first provisor was William, formerly procurator of Clairvaux, who presided over a community of twenty young scholars. A papal brief issued early in 1254 authorized the College to admit novices and lay-brothers. The arrangement was approved by the General Chapter of the same year, but the plan was never carried out, due probably to the premature retirement of Abbot Stephen.

According to the testimony of Matthew Paris, the College of Saint Bernard not only prospered, but the Cistercian students proved to be more popular with the university authorities than the Mendicants. Despite this and despite Abbot Stephen's high standing in Rome, he encountered mounting hostility among the members of the General Chapter, who were obviously perplexed about the potential influence of higher studies over the century-old Cistercian traditions and who resented the fact that the Abbot of Clairvaux in the process of the foundation had turned to the Chapter only after he had secured the full support of Roman authorities. Although the records of the General Chapter are entirely silent about the matter, the session of 1255 turned against Stephen Lexington and deposed him as abbot of Clairvaux, whereupon the worthy prelate retired to the abbey of Ourscamp. It is very likely that the Chapter's action was greatly influenced by the death in December 1254 of Innocent IV, Stephen's staunch supporter. Innocent was succeeded by Alexander IV, who was not expected to take any strong stand in the controversy. Nevertheless, the new Pope, alert to the events at Cîteaux, sided strongly with the deposed Abbot of Clairvaux. In a letter to Guy, abbot of Cîteaux, he demanded Stephen's restoration to his dignity, and when Guy refused to act, the Pope turned to Louis IX. The King, however, took the part of Cîteaux, whereupon Stephen, in order to save his Order from further embarassment, dropped the matter and remained in Ourscamp, where he died soon afterwards.

In spite of these unfavorable events, the College of Saint Bernard continued to grow and by the end of the century a group of sizeable buildings housed about thirty-five monks. The original endowment of the College proved to be insufficient to support an institution of such size and the financial burden on Clairvaux grew so heavy that in 1320 the abbey sold the College to the General Chapter, and the College was thereafter operated directly under the authority of the General Chapter for the benefit of the whole Order. The apogee of the institution coincided with the reign of the Cistercian pope, Benedict XII (1334-1342), who initiated the building of a monumental, though never entirely completed church. The Hundred Years' War and its doleful consequences greatly hampered the functioning of the College and the sorry conditions failed to improve during the turbulent decades of civil and religious wars in the sixteenth century. The seventeenth-century renewal, however, restored the institution to its medieval splendor and it remained a well-administered and well-attended college until its suppression in 1791. In the course of five centuries the College of Saint Bernard in Paris graduated about five hundred doctors of theology; few of them turned out to be original and productive thinkers or scholars, but almost all came to fill key positions in the administration of the Order, both in France and abroad.

Although the idea of higher learning met resolute resistance at the General Chapter of 1255, the trend was irresistible and after a few years the same body heaped extravagant praises upon the endeavor and did everything possible for the cultivation of studies throughout the whole Order. In 1260 Cardinal John of Toledo encouraged the abbey of Valmagne to open a college attached to the University of Montpellier. The General Chapter concurred and the institution was opened in 1265. It received the support of the abbots of southern France, although it never came close to the significance of the Parisian *studium,* and ceased to function after the Huguenots captured the city in 1567. A more important institution was the College of Saint Bernard in Toulouse, initiated by Grandselve and approved by the General Chapter of 1280. After a disastrous fire in 1533 the buildings remained vacant for several decades, but eventually instruction was resumed and continued until the middle of the eighteenth century. In 1281 the English abbeys founded a college in Oxford. A few years later the German Ebrach built a college in Würzburg, and Camp erected a similar institution in Cologne.

The *Fulgens sicut stella* of Benedict XII (1335) furnished the first charter of Cistercian higher education and as such inspired another wave of college construction. The Pope, a renowned canonist of his time, granted the rank of *studium generale* to the already existing colleges of Paris, Oxford, Toulouse and Montpellier, transferred the Spanish college of Estella in the diocese of Pamplona to Salamanca, ordered the erection of a college in Bologna for the Italians and another in Metz for the German "daughters" of Morimond. Each of the Cistercian colleges was to be supported by the abbeys of a specific area, but the Parisian college remained accessible for every Cistercian of whatever nationality. Sending students to these colleges was no longer a mere recommendation but an obligation. Abbeys with at least thirty monks had to keep one or two students in Paris, smaller communities were given a choice of sending one scholar either to Paris or to the nearest college. Houses with less than eighteen members were under no such obligation. The administration of the colleges, each under the supervision of a father-abbot, was carefully regulated, as was the amount of the *bursa* or tuition and the remuneration of the staff. The course of studies, requirements for degrees and basic principles of discipline were also delineated and the traditional prohibition against studying canon law was re-emphasized. The professors were sternly warned to abstain from "an ostentatious and noisy way of life, to lecture in humility and devotion, be content with the available food and with the services of a cleric." As in other parts of the same document, Benedict XII was much concerned with the details of fiscal administration, and for good reasons. The support of scholars in Paris or elsewhere put a tremendous strain on each community both because of the length of studies and of the expenditures of graduation. In addition to the six years spent studying the arts, the course of theology demanded six more years before the student could be promoted to the bachelor's degree; after two additional years of reading the *Sentences* of Peter Lombard, the bachelor's formal studies were over, but it took at least another year until he could become a "master" or doctor of theology. The stipulation of the *Benedictina* setting the limit of 1,000 livres of Tours for the expenditures of graduation may explain the fact that many abbots were strongly inclined to withdraw their students before the completion of the full curriculum.

The fourteenth century was not an era of Cistercian prosperity, but the vogue of scholasticism was so strong that the publication of the *Benedictina* was followed by the foundation of a number of colleges, particularly east of the Rhine. Thus, shortly after the establishment of the University of Prague in 1348 a Cistercian college was initiated in a house called "Jerusalem," donated by Emperor Charles IV. After the fashion of Paris it was organized under the supervision of the abbot of Königsaal. When the Hussite uprising in 1409 forced the monks out of the city, the Cistercian students of the area flocked to the University of Leipzig, where Altzelle sponsored a new Cistercian college, completed in 1427. According to the records of the University over three hundred Cistercians studied theology between 1428-1522 in addition to students of the arts. In Vienna, thanks to the generosity of Duke Albert III, the Cistercian College of Saint Nicolas was opened in 1385 shortly after the organization of the theological faculty at the University of Vienna. Since the old college at Würzburg had failed to attract students, the Abbot of Ebrach initiated in 1387 another and more successful institution at Heidelberg, the College of Saint James. Other German universities, such as Erfurt, Rostock and Greifswald, educated many more Cistercian students, while the University of Cracow received the Polish monks, and toward the end of the fifteenth century, a college was built there under the authority of the abbot of Mogila. The rich and populous abbeys of the Low Countries sent their students first to Paris, then, following the foundation of the University of Louvain in 1425, favored that institution, although the Cistercian scholars did not live in one college, but rather in the hospices of their respective abbeys.

Financial straits and dwindling membership rendered the support of colleges increasingly difficult, and towards the end of the fifteenth century many of them fought for their bare existence. The fate of the *studium generale* in Oxford may serve as an illustration of worsening conditions. This institution was initiated in 1280, thanks to the generosity of Edmund, earl of Cornwall. The General Chapter of 1281 approved the project and ruled that as a house of study a regular monastery be established at Oxford under the sponsorship of the abbey of Thame. Indeed, the new Rewley Abbey, settled by fifteen monks of Thame, opened its doors on December 11, 1281, and by Michaelmas (September 29) of 1282 the first students had arrived, each paying 60 shillings annually for room and board. The house was supposed to serve all abbeys of the British Isles and in 1292 it was decreed that at least one student be sent there from each community having more than twenty monks. But the institution never gained popularity with the students or support among the monasteries. Most of the young scholars drifted to various inns and hostels of Oxford, while their numbers decreased steadily; Richard II, watching a university procession in 1399 was greatly scandalized when he saw only five Cistercians marching. A subsequent convocation held in Oxford appealed for funds to improve the facilities of Rewley and a plan to collect for the

85

purpose 112 pounds annually was approved by a Cistercian national chapter in 1400. Improvements failed to materialize until, urged by a number of Cistercian abbots, Henry Chichele, archbishop of Canterbury, donated in 1438 a property on Northgate Street for the construction of a new college, to be named after Saint Bernard. The beginnings were promising and in 1446 the visiting Abbot John of Morimond issued an elaborate set of statutes for the operation of the college, but the expenses of the construction of adequate buildings remained a nagging problem. In 1482 the college was still unfinished, although pressure was put on each community having more than twelve members to send one monk to the college; monasteries with twenty-six members or more were to pay for two students. Eventually much was accomplished through the generosity of Marmaduke Huby, after he was elected abbot of Fountains in 1494. A quadrangular two-storied building took shape with a central courtyard and a conspicuous square tower over the main gate. Its chapel was consecrated in 1530 and the college was made ready to house, in addition to the provisor and staff, forty-five students. The Dissolution in 1539 ended the life of the College of Saint Bernard of Oxford which was reopened after 1557 as the College of Saint John the Baptist. At that time the statue of Saint Bernard over the entrance was reshaped to look like the new patron, Saint John.

An intriguing question is posed by the fact that while heavy pressure was put on monastic communities to promote higher learning, the study of law was placed in the same category as medicine, and strictly prohibited. The condemnation of monks engaged in such pursuits emerged among the canons of the Second Lateran Council (1139), which listed as reasons avarice and the close temptation to employ the skills of an advocate for the defense of dishonesty. The Cistercian General Chapter of 1188 singled out works on canon law, and particularly the *Decreta Gratiani,* as books to be kept out of monastic libraries "because of the various errors they may generate." The same official attitude prevailed throughout the Middle Ages but it could not dampen the fascination legal studies held over inquisitive minds. The normal procedure for bypassing such obstacles was the procurement of papal dispensations which seem, according to the available records, to have been granted liberally. In other instances Cistercian students simply took up courses in canon law outside their own colleges and without the knowledge of their superiors. Such was the case with no less than seven students at the College of Saint Bernard in Toulouse, who studied canon law clandestinely, but were caught and unceremoniously thrown out of the college at the order of the General Chapter of 1334. But even such drastic actions failed to accomplish the desired end. Monks found ample opportunity to study law in their own libraries. According to a catalogue made in 1472, the library of Clairvaux held no less than 143 codices on Roman and canon law, out of a total of 1,714 volumes. The presence of such a respectable collection of legal works could scarcely be explained without the supposition that, in disregard of prohibitions, they were much in demand and much in use.

A heavy blow to the officially negative attitude was the foundation of a college in Avignon aimed specifically at the promotion of legal studies. It was the work of Jean Casaleti, abbot of Sénanque, himself a graduate of the University of Avignon as *doctor decretorum*. In close co-operation with Cardinal Giuliano della Rovere, the future Pope Julius II, he opened the "College of Saint Bernard of Sénanque" in 1496, and only in 1499 did he turn to the General Chapter for approval, which, under the circumstances, could not be denied. The institution was planned to house twelve advanced students, who, according to the customs of Bologna, the leading law school of the day, governed themselves, electing one of their own ranks as "prior." Casaleti provided for a handsome building, adequate library and considerable endowments, but the spreading commendatory system ruined the neighboring abbeys, including Sénanque. A visitation in 1603 found only three students under a "rector," and shortly thereafter the struggling institution ceased to function, although the property remained in Cistercian hands until 1790.

The extent to which the pursuit of learning influenced the traditional routine of monastic life is a question that cannot be answered with a categorical statement. It seems certain, however, that the impact of the changing outlook was felt only gradually and sporadically. The number of university graduates always remained relatively small; poor communities could never afford to educate any of their members, unless parents or other benefactors paid the expenses. Moreover, the almost universal economic stress of the late fourteenth and fifteenth centuries reduced college attendance altogether. The organization of schools of philosophy and theology in larger abbeys was often encouraged, but the available records are silent about their actual numbers, the level of instruction, or about the number and quality of their students. On the other hand, those who returned to their abbeys after the successful completion of their studies were rewarded with honors. They enjoyed precedence over other members of the community, were preferred for visitatorial assignments, they were encouraged to continue their studies and received funds for books and writing material. In some cases they were privileged to have a cell outside of the common dormitory, as in the case of Raimund Torti, a bachelor of canon law in Boulbonne, whom the General Chapter of 1402 permitted to lock the door of his cell, "for he often must prepare his sermons and he is afraid that he would lose his books and other things belonging to the monastery." From the point of view of students the greatest compensation for the long and arduous years spent in colleges was their almost inevitable promotion to the dignities of priors and abbots. The chapter fathers of 1560 were certainly correct in remarking in retrospect that "the celebrated Parisian college of our Order, as it is commonly known, has served like the Trojan horse, from which the majority of heroes, our outstanding fathers, both of the past and the present, have stepped forward."

In regard to monastic discipline, however, the influence of college students could hardly have been always constructive. The records of the General Chapter throughout the fourteenth and fifteenth centuries are full of warnings and punitive measures against delinquent students, particularly those of the College of Saint Bernard of Paris, where the sway of city and university life was the most conspicuous. Students with rich and influential parents had their own servants and threw lavish parties for fellow-students, many of whom lived in destitution. The bachelors demanded a privileged status within the College and set a bad example for the younger students. It was reported at the Chapter of 1453 that the bachelors refused to accept the authority of the provisor, but tried to boss and abuse those below their ranks. They often neglected to attend divine services and spent the time in their own quarters eating, drinking and playing with cards or dice. Particularly difficult was the keeping of discipline at times of general merriment among university students, such as the Feast of the Three Kings on January 6. It was probably occasions such as this that Cistercian students sneaked out of the College, mingled with the revelling crowds in civilian clothes, and put on masks or painted their faces. For these excesses the Chapter of 1456 inflicted the punishment of excommunication. The traditional fraternity of freshmen, called *bejani* (*béjaunes*—yellow beaks), with its elaborate initiations, fanciful dignities, titles, ranks, and preposterous duties, was a perpetual source of fun and pranks, but also the target of repressive measures, until, in 1493, the whole organization was sternly suppressed. But there were excesses of another nature that even the authorities had to condone, that is, banquets and other entertainments at the time of graduation. The pressure of ingrained customs was such that poverty was no excuse. The young Abbot of Rigny, who graduated in 1478, treated his guests so generously that his abbey had to be dispensed for three years from the payment of taxes and contributions.

One gauge by which to measure the influence of scholasticism among Cistercians would be the rate of growth of monastic libraries. A number of figures are available, indeed, but only in the case of Clairvaux are they conclusive, although the library of this greatest of Cistercian abbeys can hardly be considered typical. Toward the end of the twelfth century Clairvaux had about 350 codices, not counting liturgical books. By the end of the fourteenth century the same number had risen to 850, increasing to 1,500 by the mid-fifteenth century and reaching 1,714 volumes in 1472. Over one thousand items of this impressive collection are still available, scattered among the libraries of the western world.

In smaller abbeys the nucleus of a library was the *armarium,* often merely a recess in the wall of the sacristy, in clear indication that initially most of the books were liturgical in nature. Since, however, the daily schedule of each community called for spiritual reading, even the earliest libraries must have contained as many books as there were monks.

As a result of scholastic studies the libraries soon became enlarged with theological and philosophical textbooks as well as with a collection of popular Latin classics. During the course of the fifteenth century the General Chapter repeatedly encouraged abbots to organize and maintain large libraries, for such collections were to be regarded as the real "treasury of monks" (1454). In 1495, the Chapter authorized the Abbot of Fountains to solicit each English house for at least eight to ten books, "good and decent ones, worthy to keep in the library," for the use of the College at Oxford.

By the end of the fifteenth century, many of the wealthier abbeys added to the traditional monastic plant a spacious library furnished with an impressive number of manuscripts. Thus, in 1480, Cîteaux owned 1,200 codices, and the building of a library was finished at the end of the century under Abbot Jean de Cirey. A fragment of this once rich collection is still available in the Municipal Library of Dijon. Himmerod's library counted over 2,000 volumes in 1453 and the building of its new library was completed at the beginning of the sixteenth century. At about the same time the library of Lehnin with 1,000 codices was considered the largest in Brandenburg. The scriptorium of Heilsbronn was regarded as one of the finest in Germany; over 600 of these carefully copied parchment volumes are now in the possession of the University of Erlangen. During the fifteenth century the abbey of Altzélle rose to be a leading center of humanistic learning in Saxony, storing a large number of Latin classics in its growing library. In addition to the usual set of liturgical books, the abbey possessed, by 1514, 960 volumes. After the suppression of Altzelle in 1540, the collection enriched the library of the University of Leipzig. In

Portugal, Alcobaça played a unique role in the cultural advancement of the country. In the thirteenth century the abbey established a college at Lisbon and actively participated in the organization of the famous University of Coimbra. The abbey's library was rated as one of the largest in the country. Although its rich collection was pillaged in 1810 and again in 1833, the catalogue of the National Library of Lisbon still contains 456 manuscripts of Alcobaça, most of them copied during the thirteenth century. Even smaller houses were proud of their respectable libraries: the Austrian Zwettl owned almost 500 books in 1451; the English Meaux had 350 volumes in 1396. In order to appreciate these figures we must remember that the richest secular libraries of the same era seldom equaled an average monastic library. The famous collection of Charles V of France in 1373 amounted only to 910 codices; that of the Medici family in Florence, almost a century later, numbered only about 800 volumes.

Shortly after its invention, printing was made use of by the Order. The first Cistercian print shop was established in Zinna, Germany, as early as 1492, and was followed in France by La Charité in 1496. In the subsequent centuries a number of the richest abbeys regularly operated their own print shops. The large output of printed material soon necessitated strong measures in order to prevent the circulation of books and pamphlets advocating Protestantism. To protect nuns, who were considered incapable of recognizing the theological tendency of their spiritual readings, the Chapter in 1531 prohibited the possession of books written in languages other than Latin, and even these required the special approval of legitimate authorities.

VIII

The End of Prosperity

 Historians of an older generation who wrote about monastic conditions before the Reformation preferred such terms as "decline," "decay," or "corruption," implying that the Orders concerned had brought upon themselves their own ruin through slothful negligence or deliberate relaxation of their initial standards of discipline. The symptoms of Cistercian decline, if this should be the word, were all too obvious. The sharp increase in, and preoccupation of the General Chapter with, disciplinary cases was by no means the most dramatic proof of grave problems. The arrest of expansion, the decline of membership and the disappearing lay-brotherhood are more tangible and more compelling factors in forming an unfavorable judgment on the condition of the Order in the fourteenth and fifteenth centuries.

Between 1250 and 1300, the Order founded fifty new houses; during the first half of the fourteenth century the number of new foundations dropped to ten; from 1350 to 1400, the records show only five new establishments. The great Les Dunes in Flanders reached the peak of its population about 1300, with 211 choir monks and over 500 lay-brothers. By the end of the fourteenth century the number of monks had dropped to sixty-one and there were no lay-brothers at all. Himmerod in the Rhineland had in the early years of the thirteenth century sixty monks and two hundred lay-brothers; in 1371, only thirteen priests came together for an abbatial election. The modest French abbey, Aiguebelle, had toward the end of the thirteenth century thirty-six inhabitants, among them eight to ten lay-brothers; in 1326 there were only sixteen monks; by 1350, the number had dropped to fourteen, by 1447 to ten. After 1418 the records of Aiguebelle no longer mention lay-brothers. A study of the clerical population of medieval England has estimated that the Cistercian Order reached its largest membership in the early years of the fourteenth century, counting 1,656 monks. By 1381 the total had dropped to 824, although late in the fifteenth century the figure began to climb again, reaching 1,000 on the eve of the Dissolution. A late recovery can be observed in other countries, too, but there should be no doubt about the dramatic decrease of monastic vocations throughout the fourteenth century.

The reasons for the decline certainly went far deeper than the neglect of certain regulations; moreover, it is very likely that the multiplication of disciplinary problems was not the cause but rather a symptom of a drastically changing social environment in which the old abbeys stood like alien bodies, relics of the past, without a meaningful message for an estranged society. A similar though lesser problem could still be successfully solved in the thirteenth century by the adoption of new educational standards, when the monks simply put their new academic robes on top of their cowls. But the late medieval civilization soon left the proud universities behind, and the once uncommonly popular Mendicants experienced an even greater crisis than the monastic orders.

The new era was by no means anti-religious; on the contrary, popular devotions and pious fraternities reached a new pitch of fervor. But, posing a strange paradox, the new piety was often anti-clerical; it put great emphasis on the role of the laity, and tried to establish an intimate and highly personal relationship between God and the believer, without the encumbrances of vows and the elaborate ritual of daily monastic activities. The result was the appearance of informal associations of devout laymen and laywomen, living in inconspicuous town houses, engaged in meditation and works of charity. The outstanding figure of the movement was Gerhard Groote (1340-1384) of Deventer, whose followers have been referred to as the "Brethren of the Common Life," although they steadfastly refused to form a new "order" under any title. The finest expression of the new spirituality, the *devotio moderna,* was the *Imitation of Christ,* a work of inimitable charm and simplicity, although its humble author, Thomas a Kempis (1380-1470), merely collected the religious wisdom of a number of his congenial predecessors.

As a purely theoretical approach to the problem, one might say that if the old orders, including the Cistercians, had wished to stay abreast of religious life, insure their popularity and the flow of vocations, they should have embraced the new spirituality and new forms of devotion. In practice, however, the adaptability of a religious order is strictly limited by its own traditions, especially the structural elements in them that cannot be continually changed without the eventual loss of the order's identity. As any unbiased reader of the records of the General Chapter may ascertain, the Cistercian Order made valiant efforts to maintain a reasonable level of discipline, while insuring the influx of vocations indispensable for survival. The Cistercians did survive the crisis, but it is undeniable that the majority of those who joined the old abbeys did so not because they found in them an opportunity to develop their own spiritual life to perfection, but because the monasteries still offered a life of respectability in relative ease and security. Those who are inclined to incriminate the Order or its leaders for the undesirable but inevitable consequences of such a situation ignore the fact that the monastic orders were integral components of the old feudal society and their destinies were shaped by the society in which they were born. As feudalism declined, so did monasticism. No religious organization as closely associated with the foundation of a society as the Cistercians could possibly thrive in a world where the ideals of that foundation had long been discarded. The bare survival of the orders at a time when all other medieval institutions fell by the wayside must be taken as a sign of exceptional vigor that saved the spiritual values of monasticism for the future when, in a more favorable social atmosphere, they could rise to a new life.

In addition to such existential problems, there were innumerable external causes that deepened the crisis in almost every monastic community. The Avignon papacy, in alliance with the French royal government, put an unbearable financial pressure on the Order at a time when the changed social and economic system had already ruined the once flourishing Cistercian agriculture. The abbeys, in perpetual financial crisis, began the wholesale incorporation of parishes as means of revenues, although earlier legislation had taken a strong stand against monks in active ministry outside of their communities. One way out of the dilemma was to hire secular priests as curates willing to work in parishes for a relatively small salary, while the bulk of the income could enrich the abbey concerned. For the same reason members of the Mendicant orders were often received into the Cistercian Order, then, after their profession, employed as pastors.

The Great Western Schism (1378-1417), isolated Cîteaux from the rest of the Order, rendering the General Chapter unworkable for a generation. The Roman Pope, Urban VI (1378-1389), as well as his successor, Boniface IX (1389-1404), forbade any contact between the houses loyal to Rome and Cîteaux which, like the rest of France, acknowledged the Avignon pope, Clement VII. Instead of holding chapters at Cîteaux, the Roman popes promoted general and national chapters elsewhere, largely as occasions for the effective collection of papal contributions from the Order. Thus, between 1382 and 1408, at least fourteen sessions of the General Chapter were held outside of France: three in Rome (1382, 1383, 1390), two in Vienna (1393, 1397), one in Nuremberg (1408), one in Worms (1384) and seven in Heilsbronn (1394, 1398, 1400, 1402, 1403, 1406, 1407). In order to substitute for the missing central administration,

Urban VI appointed an Italian as "abbot of Cîteaux," several abbots in succession as "abbots of Morimond" and kept a "vicar general" for the whole Order in Rome. Boniface IX continued the same policy: his "vicar general" was John Castiel, abbot of Brondolo, responsible for the organization of a number of the above mentioned chapters. In 1409, following the Council of Pisa, the General Chapter returned for the first time to Cîteaux, where, according to one of the participants, 228 abbots convened.

In addition to general conventions, national chapters were also held. During the Schism, English, Scottish and Irish abbots were encouraged to hold such sessions in 1381 and 1386. In 1394 and 1400 chapters were held at Saint Mary Graces in London, and in 1401 Boniface IX ordered the holding of English national chapters every third year under the presidency of the abbot of Waverley or Furness. The communication of English and Welsh abbeys with Cîteaux failed to improve even after the end of the Schism. In 1437 the abbots, referring to the continued hostilities, returned to the arrangement prevailing under Boniface IX and petitioned Pope Eugenius IV that they might hold triennial chapters among themselves, so that they "could correct and legislate, decide and ordain, as needs arise, in all things pertaining to the reputation and growth of the Order." The request was granted for three years.

The Council of Constance (1414-1418) restored the unity of Western Christendom, but the execution for heresy of a popular professor of theology in Prague, John Huss, touched off the Hussite Wars (1419-1436). The well-organized rebel armies terrorized large parts of Austria, Bohemia, Moravia and Silesia, destroying some thirty Cistercian abbeys in these provinces. The rich Silesian abbeys suffered most cruelly, for all six of the (Leubus, Heinrichau, Kamenz, Rauden, Himmelwitz, Grüssau) were thoroughly sacked several times with great loss of life. The abbeys were left vacant for many years while their total economic ruin hampered reconstruction even after the restoration of peace. Thus, at Leubus, it was only in 1448 that divine services could be resumed after the lapse of eighteen years. As the chronicler of the abbey put it: "Abbot Stephen of Leubus ordered his convent to [resume] the chanting of all canonical hours and the [office] of the dead. In his benevolence the same Lord Abbot offered to his convent each day the customary measure of the good beer that he himself used to drink." Prolonged dynastic struggle over the throne of Bohemia and the frequent recurrence of the plague made recovery precarious everywhere.

During much of the fourteenth century Germany was the scene of anarchy without legal recourse against the scourge of private warfare or widespread brigandage. Cistercian abbeys, in their rural isolation, were always tempting targets for marauding bands of robbers searching for easy prey. Under such conditions disciplined monastic life—in many cases even simple survival—became questionable. Among many tragic examples the great and prosperous Lehnin in Brandenburg can be cited as not entirely atypical. In 1319, with the obvious connivance of neighboring authorities, this abbey was captured by an armed band of ciminals, who, by terrorizing the monks, enforced the election of one of their own gang as abbot three times in succession, thus remaining ensconced in the abbey until 1339. They converted the abbey into a fortress and used it as a basis for further expeditions of plunder, while protesting monks were murdered or imprisoned.

It was in the same turbulent century that, under the pretext of "protection," the German territorial lords made attempts to force a number of Cistercian abbeys into submission. The rich Maulbronn became in the fourteenth century a bone of contention between the counts of Württemberg and the Palatinate. The monastery was heavily fortified and garrisoned either by one or by the other of the contestants, while peaceful monastic life became well-nigh impossible. Eventually, thanks to imperial intervention, the claims of the counts (later dukes) of Württemberg prevailed, who did not hesitate to extort a number of economic and jurisdictional benefits from the helpless monks, although nominally the emperor retained the title of "supreme and veritable advocate and defender" of Maulbronn. Finally, in 1504, Emperor Maximilian recognized that Maulbronn was a part of the territory of Württemberg, where all secular administration, including "high and low justice," belonged to Duke Ulrich.

A similar fate awaited Herrenalb in the diocese of Speier and Königsbronn, founded under Habsburg sponsorship in the diocese of Augsburg. Although both abbeys had originally received guarantees of freedom from feudal intervention, the rulers of Württemberg never relinquished their claim of advocacy. During the fourteenth and fifteenth centuries, through diplomacy or violence, they managed to impose their "protection" over the abbeys, for which the monks had to pay by assuming a variety of fiscal and legal obligations. The lucrative nature of advocacy is well illustrated by the fact that at one phase of the jurisdictional contests in 1353 Emperor Charles IV temporarily transferred the advocacy over Königsbronn to the Count of Helfenstein for the payment of 600 silver marks. After Duke Ulrich I (1498-1550) of Württemberg had embraced Luther's Reformation, he merely completed the process of encroachment by the secularization of Maulbronn, Herrenalb and Königsbronn.

More fortunate was the populous Swabian Salem. After the fall of the

Hohenstaufen the general disorder caused much damage, so that in 1263 Abbot Eberhard II pondered the dispersion of his community. The succession of Rudolph of Habsburg (1273), however, opened an era of recovery. Under Abbot Ulrich II (1282-1311) the annual revenues rose from 300 to 1,000 marks and by 1311 the monastery housed again 310 monks and brothers.

The double election in 1314 of Louis of Bavaria and Frederick of Habsburg unleashed the curse of civil war for another generation. Salem took the side of the Habsburgs and the papacy, thus exposing the monastic estates to repeated attacks by the opposition. Abbot Conrad of Enslingen (1311-1337) was twice kidnapped and held for ransom. The debts of the monastery rose to 8,000 florins and in 1322 the abbot asked papal approval for the incorporation of three parishes. Meanwhile the abbey paid large sums for the ineffectual military protection of the counts of Heiligenberg; in 1327 alone the abbot spent 300 pounds for this purpose.

Finally in 1348 the newly elected Charles IV of Luxembourg took away the advocacy from the Heiligenberg family and declared himself and his successors to be the sole protectors of the abbey. The imperial charter of 1354 granted the abbey extensive fiscal and judicial immunities, which were further expanded in 1485 by Emperor Frederick III. By then Salem had become an independent "imperial abbey" (*Reichsunmittelbar*), symbolized by the abbots' participation at imperial diets. Meanwhile, and in similar circumstances, the Bavarian Kaisheim and Waldsassen had also obtained the "imperial abbey" status.

After the collapse of the imperial power, Italy turned into a battlefield of perpetual war among ambitious city-states, while monastic establishments suffered the same lot as those in Germany. Thus, in 1262, San Galgano, the greatest Cistercian abbey in Tuscany, sought the protection of Siena, but, during the fourteenth century, it became the victim of incessant skirmishes between Siena and Florence. In 1365 the famed English condottiere in Florentine service, Sir John Hawkwood, captured San Galgano and set up his headquarters in the abbey. By 1397 the only inhabitant of that once popular shrine was the abbot, Lodovico di Tano, who was forced to sell bit by bit monastic property in order to pay exorbitant papal impositions.

In England and the parts of France under English rule the authority of Cîteaux was severely curtailed long before the actual outbreak of the Hundred Years' War. Visitations were rendered impossible and most abbeys became helpless victims of the rapacious fiscal policies of both countries. It was a matter of common occurrence that abbots under

English rule were prevented from attending the General Chapter or sending their contributions to Cîteaux, and the visitation of French father-abbots in England was made either impossible or ineffectual. The inevitable result was spreading and unpunished abuses. Bindon in Dorset between 1306-1337 may serve as a sad example of intolerable conditions. The abbot, John Montecute, after many years of misrule, was forced to resign in 1316, and was replaced by Roger Hornhull. But a few years later Montecute and eight other monks seceded from the community, allied themselves with their local lay-sympathizers, attacked and recaptured the cloister, carried away all valuables together with the conventual seal, and took some of the resisting monks as hostages. Since John Chidley, the abbot of Ford and "father" of Bindon, was unable or unwilling to intervene, Roger Hornhull turned for help to Edward III (1327-1377), who ordered the Earl of Devon to restore order and recover the stolen property. The fact that the same command had to be repeated four times indicates, however, that no such measure was taken, probably because the local population sided with the rebels. Finally, in 1331, Montecute was captured with some of his gang, then escaped and was again recaptured. But he was thought to be dangerous even in prison: therefore King Edward asked William, abbot of Cîteaux, to banish him to a safer place and to provide another father-abbot for Bindon, because John Chidley of Ford was suspected of having an interest in Montecute's return.

Such incidents, however, gave only a foretaste of what was to happen on a nationwide scale after the outbreak of the Hundred Years' War in 1337. Cîteaux found itself all but isolated from the rest of the world. Attendance at annual Chapters was restricted most of the time to abbeys in the immediate neighborhood of Burgundy. The records of the Chapter clearly reflect the utter frustration of the participants as they watched the ever-worsening conditions all over France, without any hope of effective remedies. The available documents, in a dreary recital of endless and wholesale destruction, leave no doubt but that virtually all communities were exposed at one time or another to the vandalism of roving armies or marauding mercenaries. Looting and arson were often aggravated by murder. The terror-stricken monks fled to fortified places leaving their monastery vacant for years. In 1364 the monks of Cîteaux were forced to seek refuge in Dijon, where the abbey had a house, named "Lamonoye." Then they petitioned Urban V that they might stay and perform the divine services there until the end of hostilities. In answering the petition the Pope granted permission to all Cistercians in France to move to a place of refuge and authorized the monks to set up portable altars anywhere in order to be able to carry on their religious duties. Monastic lands were left uncultivated and for lack of funds the abbeys were unable to care even for their much-reduced communities. Monks, driven by hunger, were often found wandering from village to village begging for food. Such was the case of the monks of Boulancourt, who, after the total destruction of the abbey in 1381, survived on charity, leaving the cloister vacant for twenty-two years.

Regular visitation came to a standstill and abuses multiplied, particularly when, by means of money or violence, an unworthy man captured the abbatial see. The General Chapter no longer had effective means of intervening, local authorities all too often proved to be accomplices, and conditions which would have been unthinkable in happier times, prevailed indefinitely. For the sake of illustration some of the better documented incidents should suffice.

Guyenne in the southwest was continually contested between the belligerents, becoming the tragic scene of the worst disorders and destruction. In Candeil, by 1372, the number of monks had sunk from sixty to twelve, but even those few could not be provided for, because an unworthy intruder had come to be abbot by means of simony. He, Bernard by name, spent his time dicing, losing hundred of florins at a time, kept three concubines, indulged in hunting, and habitually bore arms; in fact, he was charged with homicide and, according to the report, several of his monks were guilty of similar crimes. Yet, characteristic of its prevailing lack of communication and control, the General Chapter took no notice of the scandal; it was Pope Gregory XI who, after a number of futile warnings, ordered the Bishop of Albi and the Abbot of Grandselve to initiate energetic measures against the scandalous abbot. The outcome of the incident is not known, but it is highly doubtful that Grandselve was in a position to offer meaningful help. Grandselve was certainly the mightiest and most populous abbey in the area, but by 1349 it had become so impoverished that the house was unable to support its members, and even the French government ordered its tax-collectors to stay away from the abbey. In 1357 Pope Innocent VI wrote a letter to the English authorities under Edward the "Black Prince," asking consideration for Grandselve, on the brink of utter disaster. In 1364 Urban V still referred to the abbey as "the most devastated of all other monasteries of the region on account of terrible wars and pestilence." The once rich lands of the abbey became battlefields and even its urban properties were ruined: in 1367 the citizens of Bordeaux demolished two houses owned by Grandselve and used the stones for the repair of fortifications.

Visitation, even when it was ordered and carried out, was by no means an assured success. The collapse of both finances and morals at

Bonnefontaine in the diocese of Reims necessitated a visitation in 1364, called for by Abbot Guy himself. Within the abbey, however, violent opposition was fomented by a dissident monk, Jean de Hermontville, and when the Abbots of Signy, Foigny and Valroy arrived, they found the gates bolted. A second team of visitors fared even worse: they were imprisoned by the rebels, who treated their own abbot in similar fashion. This case also remained unrecorded at the General Chapter, but was well known in Avignon. Although in 1374 Gregory XI ordered the Abbot of Cîteaux to discipline the turbulent community, details of further action are missing.

The subsequent schism in the Church, which was touched off by the return of Urban VI to Rome in 1377, deepened the atmosphere of gloom and helplessness in Cîteaux. The Fathers of the poorly attended General Chapter of 1390, in trying to describe the predicament of the Order, borrowed the phrases of Christ's eschatological sermon (Matthew 24: 12): " . . . when night descends over the world, as our Lord said, 'iniquity will abound and the charity of many shall grow cold.' This is why so few escape from the shipwreck of this world by reaching out for the raft of conversion and holy religion." They recognized at the same time that it was largely for want of efficient visitation that "the monasteries and houses of our Order for both sexes have become so terribly deformed, desolate, and all but annihilated in spiritual as well as in material things, that in these days scarcely any one of them has preserved piety, sincere religion, or even the vestiges of our Order's observances. . . ."

Conditions grew even worse during the first decades of the fifteenth century, when the war expanded into a murderous civil struggle between the Armagnacs and the Burgundians. The appearance of Joan of Arc (1429) improved French fortunes, but law and order was slow to return. As late as the 1440s conditions at Aiguebelle clearly attested to the fact that the rudderless government of the Order was still floundering in the midst of unmanageable problems. A former Dominican friar, Jean d'Hostel, was admitted to that abbey illegally, then, in 1441, elected abbot while his predecessor was still in office. In the next year the General Chapter approved his admission, but declared him ineligible for abbacy. In spite of this ruling he gained firm control of the abbey and held it until 1445, when the Abbot of Morimond in visiting at Aiguebelle excommunicated him and his chief supporters and ordered him to appear before the General Chapter of the same year. The intruder, however, ignored the summons and obtained the formal resignation of his predecessor, whereupon the General Chapter of 1446 not only recognized him as legitimate abbot, but also commissioned him to visit several convents of

Cistercian nuns. But Jean d'Hostel's administration was so wasteful that he was deposed again in 1448 and his predecessor was reinstated as abbot. The restless man refused to submit and continued to create so much trouble in the abbey that the Chapter of 1450 excommunicated him anew as a "contumacious rebel and conspirator."

The election of members of other religious orders as abbots was by no means exceptional when the move promised material advantages to hard-pressed monks. Benedictines were elected at Benisson-Dieu (1419), Sept-Fons (1419), Les Pierres (1436) and Dalon (1443).

While France under Louis XI (1461-1483) started on the road toward reconstruction, England plunged into a long and bloody civil strife, the "War of Roses" (1455-1485), which weighed heavily on the much afflicted monastic establishments. Regular attendance at the sessions of the General Chapter remained impossible. The English abbots were represented in 1471 by a single individual, Lazarus of Padway, who, reporting to the Abbot of Buckfast, left behind a description of a journey full of unpleasant adventures, "encountering armed enemies, robbers, great perils, labors, fears, molestations and anxieties." Several German abbots on their way to Cîteaux were captured by brigands in Morimond, were mistreated and held for ransom in spite of their passports and escaped only with their bare lives. Lazarus dared to continue his journey to Cîteaux only because he had "a lion's heart in his bosom." Returning to England he passed through Reims, where, he wrote, "everybody was wondering about my good fortune and audacity, arriving safe and unhurt, after having passed through [a terrain infested] with marauders and highwaymen."

In addition to the endless calamities of wars, the fourteenth century abounded in natural catastrophes on an unprecedented scale. Between 1315-1317 a terrible famine ravaged the whole of Europe; then, thirty years later, the first great outbreak of bubonic plague, the "Black Death," swept across the continent, carrying away within three years at least one third of the population. Among monastic communities the toll seems to have been as high as two thirds of the inhabitants. Terror and helplessness seized millions and reduced them to a state of utter despair. The social and economic consequences to the drastically reduced population led to a wave of peasant uprisings and urban disturbances that only heightened the specter of impending doom.

At Meaux in Yorkshire the plague struck hard in 1349. As Thomas Burton (d. 1437), abbot and chronicler, tells us with wry humor, the disaster was introduced by an ominous portent. On the Friday before Palm Sunday (March 27), the monks were singing the "Magnificat" in choir when a terrible earthquake threw them out of their stalls exactly at the moment when they reached the verse: "He hath put down the mighty from their seat." At the beginning of that year the abbey had forty-three monks, including the abbot and seven lay-brothers; of these only ten monks survived the epidemic. The worst was August, when on a single day five monks and Abbot Hugh were carried away. At Newenham in Devon twenty monks and three lay-brothers died in 1348-49, and only Abbot Walter and two monks survived. In the Spanish abbey of Poblet, during 1348, two abbots in succession died, together with fifty-nine monks and thirty lay-brothers. Adwert, the great Dutch abbey, had one hundred monks and two hundred lay-brothers earlier in the century; in 1350 the plague carried away forty-four monks and one hundred twenty brothers. The population of the great Pontigny before these fatal years is not known, but in 1366 the community counted only seventeen members. A visitation held in Hungary in 1356 by Abbot Siegfried von Waldstein of Rein (1349-1367) described the conditions at eleven abbeys: one of them (Ercsi) was totally abandoned. Two others had only three monks including the abbots (Pásztó and Bélháromkút) and all the others were much underpopulated. Waldstein, reporting to King Louis I, suggested the invitation of foreign personnel and the forcible return of vagrant monks throughout the country. The tolls of the later recurrences of the plague were often equally devastating. Within two months in 1419 the French Vauclair lost eleven members.

The impact of the Black Death on monastic life reached far beyond the reduction of numbers and economic hardships. In order to maintain the minimum personnel, the General Chapter of 1349 permitted the making of profession without a full year of novitiate, as long as the candidate was at least fourteen years of age and knew the Psalms by heart. The probable reduction of moral qualifications is difficult to ascertain, but the search for vocations doubtless extended toward the lower echelons of society. During the fourteenth century the nobility practically disappeared from the ranks of the monks. At Himmerod, for example, where during the twelfth and thirteenth centuries the nobility was well represented even among the lay-brothers, the composition of the community was purely bourgeois by the middle of the fourteenth century. The last noble abbot of Himmerod, Heinrich von Randeck, died in 1330. The list of monks throughout the fourteenth and fifteenth centuries shows only four names related to local gentry families.

Far more damaging to monasticism in the long run than all other calamities combined was the gradual replacement of freely elected abbots by appointed "commendatory" abbots. The term was derived from "commendation," that is, the act of granting a benefice, such as an abbey, *in commendam,* which implied the duty of protecting or administering a vacant church property. The early medieval practices of commendation had become the just targets of reformers, and at the time of Cîteaux's foundation the problem had appeared to be a thing of the past. In the middle of the thirteenth century, however, particularly after Clement IV (1265-1268), the right of free elections was endangered anew by the doctrine of unlimited papal powers (*plenitudo potestatis*), which included the right of "provision" for all benefices. Papal appointments in distant lands remained technically impossible for a long time, but Nicholas III (1277-1280) insisted that all elections must be confirmed by the Curia. The system of actual papal appointments took a giant step forward during the Avignon decades. Under increasing financial pressure the popes converted such claims to sources of revenue, granting "bulls" of appointment or confirmations of elections for a substantial fee. John XXII (1316-1334) reserved all appointments in Italy to himself and the same policy was extended over other territories by Benedict XII and Clement VI (1342-1352). The latter, when reminded that such practices were without precedents, was said to have replied: "Our predecessors failed to realize that they were popes." During the Great Western Schism both Rome and Avignon exploited papal appointments to their utmost limits, not merely for financial reasons, but also to gain faithful partisans. The fee to be paid normally amounted to one third of the annual income of the benefice. Boniface IX ruled in 1399 that those who failed to pay the stipulated amount within two months were to lose all claims over the desired position. The chief beneficiaries of the new system were papal nephews, cardinals, and other ranking officials in the Curia, many of whom accumulated a large number of profitable sinecures. Few of these "commendatory abbots" cared to spend any time in their monasteries, for their chief interest was the collection of abbatial revenues.

The abusive nature of such arrangements was clear not only to the abbeys concerned, but also to foreign governments, resentful that absentee aliens should enjoy substantial revenues. In England, as early as 1307, the Statute of Carlisle intended to limit papal appointments and in 1351 the Statute of Provisors upheld the rights of English electors and royal privileges over matters of patronage. The issue of papal provisions and commendations was much discussed at the Council of Constance (1417), but instead of a definitive prohibition of abuses, only mild modifications were suggested. The failure of Constance merely encouraged secular governments to compete with papal ambitions in the control of benefices. Throughout the fifteenth century free abbatial elections became rare exceptions.

In France the Pragmatic Sanction of Bourges (1438) took a strong stand against papal intervention in ecclesiastical appointments, but paid only lip service to the principle of free election, for it left open the door for royal pressure in the form of "benevolent recommendations." The papacy never accepted the terms of this document and, in fact, Louis XI revoked it in 1461. From the point of view of the monks, however, it made little difference whether the king or the pope deprived them of the right to govern themselves without constant external intervention. The Parlement of Paris in a remonstrance addressed in 1467 to Louis XI justly pointed out that

> the revenues of benefices are being taken out of the country; the benefices themselves face ruin; in the monasteries all forms of regular discipline have disappeared; the divine services are performed improperly and without devotion, prejudicing the intentions of founders and diminishing the prayers due for the souls of monastic benefactors. As the material establishments are being ruined, so are the spiritual ones. Such conditions are common among the monks who, for lack of discipline, lapse into lax life and often apostatize . . . resembling errant sheep without a shepherd. Until the benefices return to regular abbots it remains impossible to reverse the ruinous trend prevailing in both the spiritual and material establishments.

The same objections for the same reasons were reiterated at the Estates General of 1483, without result.

In Spain conditions were scarcely better. In 1475 King John II of Aragon demanded from Sixtus IV the appointment of one of his grandchildren, an illegitimate boy of six, to the metropolitan see of Saragossa. The Pope temporarily denied the scandalous request, but he granted the child a pension taken out of the revenues of the cathedral. In 1511 at the Synod of Burgos the Spanish bishops raised their voices against commendatory abbots appointed by the papacy, but the deeply rooted evil continued.

The brave resolutions of the Fifth Lateran Council in 1514 called for the abolition of the *commenda,* but they were cancelled by Leo X, who, following his defeat at Marignano, submitted to Francis I of France and in the Concordat of Bologna (1516) legalized the royal control over abbatial appointments. True, in the same document the King promised to appoint to such positions only monks no less than twenty-three years of age, but in practice neither he nor his successors respected these restrictions. On the contrary, the appointment of laymen, even children, became a common occurrence. In 1517 the Pope attempted to modify the Concordat to exempt monastic orders, but the King ignored the papal brief. In 1531 Clement VII formally conceded the abolition of abbatial elections, excepting only the mother houses, in the case of the Cistercians, only the abbey of Cîteaux. Since it was well understood that the commendatory system constituted the real stumbling block in the way of any monastic reform, the Council of Trent made a final attempt at the elimination of the disastroùs abuse. The royal government, however, showed no willingness to cooperate. The canons of the Council were never promulgated in France, and the commendatory system dominated monastic life until the French Revolution. The only concession, granted in 1558 and later confirmed by the Ordonnance of Blois in 1579, was the guarantee of free elections in the principal abbeys of the Order: Cîteaux, La Ferté, Pontigny, Clairvaux and Morimond. By the end of the sixteenth century the vast majority of Cistercian abbeys in France were held *in commendam,* although occasionally the king appointed members of the Order as abbots, while sometimes well-intentioned commendators voluntarily put on the habit of the Order and then governed their monasteries as regular abbots. For this reason it is difficult to give an accurate number of abbeys under regular abbots and those under commendatory abbots. But at least a steady four-fifths of all houses in France languished permanently under commendatory abbots throughout the seventeenth century.

The Cistercian Order was alert to the dangers of the commendatory system from its beginnings, although its leadership never had adequate means to halt or even to retard the trend. Beyond recording complaints and protests, the General Chapter's only tangible achievements were the confirmation of Cistercian privileges and other paper guarantees issued generously by the Curia after the payment of equally generous fees. Thus, John XXIII solemnly promised in 1415 that he would appoint only Cistercians to vacant abbacies of the Order and would void all previous appointments given to others, except those granted to cardinals. Similar or even more promising documents were issued by Nicholas V (1447-1455), so that the General Chapter of 1458 jubilantly reported that according to "the privileges of our Order, most recently renewed and confirmed by the Supreme Pontiff, no person, not even a cardinal, may head as commendator any of our Order's monasteries."

The sad facts did not substantiate the Fathers' optimism. The earliest papal appointments for Cistercian abbeys occurred in Italy under John XXII (1316-1334), but soon similar pressure prevailed throughout the Empire, France and Spain, even though most early instances of "provisions" involved the appointment of a Cistercian. Thus, as early as 1328, the abbatial see of Ebrach was granted to Albert of Anfeld, who paid 800 florins for the favor (*servitium commune*). In 1338, the new abbot of Salem, Ulrich Sargans, was expected to send 1,650 florins to Avignon. According to the papal registers of the same era, abbots were instituted in a similar manner in Wettingen, Altzelle, Villers and Orval. During the Schism, Kaisheim, Lützel, Heilsbronn, Val-Saint-Lambert, Morimond, Georgenthal, Neuzelle, Grüssau and Kamenz followed.

Throughout the fifteenth century Cistercian abbacies were freely disposed of in Hungary by the leading noble families. Similar conditions prevailed in Ireland, while in Scotland the kings claimed the right of appointing abbots. Of the twenty Cistercian abbots and priors sitting in the Scottish Parliament in 1560, fourteen were commendators. It was only in England that the commendatory system failed to gain ground. The chief reason for England's peculiar position was the fact that effective papal interference in abbatial elections was initiated at Avignon at the time when the Hundred Years' War was about to break out. Since the English suspected that the pope acted habitually as a French agent, they strongly resisted the attempts at papal intervention in English ecclesiastical affairs.

In France, guarantees notwithstanding, one great abbey after another lost its independence. In 1470 came the turn of La Ferté, although after two years of legal arguments a Cistercian was permitted to take the abbot's office. At about the same time, among others, Balerne, Fontfroide, Bonnecombe, Ourscamp, Bonnevaux and Grandselve came under commendatory government. The thoroughly alarmed Chapter of 1473 decided to send to Rome a most impressive delegation of abbots, headed by the abbot of Cîteaux himself, Humbert of Losne (1462-1476). Pope Sixtus IV (1471-1484) and his court were said to have listened to the abbots' pleading with tears in their eyes, but the bull issued on March 11, 1475, merely reiterated the traditional limitations and promises. Thus, the commendators were prohibited from reducing the number of monks; they were to feed and decently clothe the monastic community; they were required to keep the buildings in proper repair, defend the rights and privileges of the abbey and pay all dues and taxes; they were forbidden the alienation of monastic property; and finally, the commendator, upon his appointment, was to take an oath to respect and uphold the above points. Whether this document was worth the 6,000 ducats spent by the Roman delegation was open to question.

The future proved the skeptics correct, but the successor of Abbot Humbert was not one of them. He was Jean de Cirey (1476-1501), formerly abbot of Balerne and a participant of the Roman negotiations. The new Abbot of Cîteaux was a man of good intentions, ambition and energy, but he placed too much confidence in the value of his Roman connections and in the significance of a new flow of papal bulls on the Order's behalf. He obtained thirteen such documents from Sixtus IV and sixteen others from Innocent VIII (1484-1492), spending a veritable fortune for them and leaving behind a formidable debt. The only tangible fruit of his efforts was the publication of the first printed collection of Cistercian privileges in 1491, the *Collecta quorumdam privilegiorum Ordinis Cisterciensis.*

While the Curia remained inflexible, hopes for a change in French governmental policies rose high after the death of Louis XI (1483). Indeed, in anticipation of energetic action by the young Charles VIII (1483-1498), local insurgents ousted by force a number of commendators, but the Estates General of 1484 brought further disappointment. The boy-king listened politely to the endless recital of grievances, but did nothing. The tapping of monastic wealth by both Rome and Paris had by then become so simple and rewarding that no honest effort at the improvement of the sad lot of the once great but inexorably decaying abbeys could be expected.

Cistercian abbeys fared still worse in Italy than in France. During the fifteenth century all abbeys in that peninsula, without exception, were victimized by greedy curial office holders. Available statistical evidence covers only the sixteenth century, but the tragic conditions obviously resulted from a century of total neglect.

A shocking picture of the disastrous influence of the unfortunate system was presented in a report by Nicholas Boucherat, who, as procurator general, personally visited the houses of the Order in the Papal States and in the Kingdom of Naples and Sicily in 1561. Each of the thirty-five monasteries was under a commendatory abbot. Boucherat found the buildings everywhere dilapidated, many of them in ruins. Sixteen monasteries were completely deserted; in some others a few secular priests or members of other orders were living. The total Cistercian population of all those thirty-five houses consisted altogether of eighty-six monks, subsisting in misery, without any vestiges of regular discipline or liturgical service. Another visitation in 1579 revealed similar conditions in Lombardy and Tuscany, where some seventeen monasteries were hopelessly struggling with their commendatory abbots for bare subsistence.

A measure of local improvements was made possible by contracts between the commendator and the monks. Such was perhaps the case at Tre Fontane in Rome. This abbey had been under commendatory rule since 1383, and by the sixteenth century the famous monastery and church were in so scandalous a state of neglect that in 1519 Pope Leo X had to intervene. After the resignation of Cardinal Raphael Riario, the Pope appointed his cousin, Giuliano de Medici, as the new commendator, but imposed on him a contract with Tre Fontane, issued in the form of a bull. Accordingly, the "abbot's table" (*mensa abbatialis*) was separated from the "monks' table" (*mensa conventualis*), that is, a specific amount was set aside for the community to live on, 400 gold ducats, supposedly sufficient for twelve monks. The monks were free to elect their own prior, responsible for internal administration and discipline. Although the commendator was not permitted to alter the amount of the "monks' table," substantial economic losses could permit him to reduce the number of monks proportionately.

It should be obvious from the preceding paragraphs that the material ruin of monastic establishments was by no means the only, perhaps not even the most distressing, consequence of commendatory government. In the absence of an abbot many of the traditional liturgical functions could not be performed, discipline could not be enforced with vigor, and even the social status of the community was bound to decline. When the commendatory abbot, an outsider, did attempt to interfere with the monks' daily life, conditions often became intolerable. The General Chapter always insisted, therefore, on the purely titular nature of the commendator's appointment, whose only right was the collection of his portion of monastic income. All other responsibilities were transferred to the prior, who in earlier times had often been elected, but was eventually appointed by the regular father-abbot of the community *in commendam*. The prior, however, could not discharge visitatorial duties and was not entitled to sit in the General Chapter, thus the administration of the Order was as much weakened as the system of checks and controls. Attendance at the General Chapters fell dramatically during the fifteenth century, and in the first half of the sixteenth century the number of abbots never exceeded fifty; in 1541 only eighteen abbots convened.

Furthermore, although the assurance of a fixed amount of money, the "monks' table," seemed to be advantageous on the surface, in the long run it was gravely detrimental. The arrangement always carried the stipulation of a definitive number of monks to be housed in the abbey. Since the financial interest of the commendator demanded that this number be the lowest possible, and since the monks were in no position to raise the allowance, any growth or development was out of the question. Moreover, steady inflation in the sixteenth and seventeenth centuries eroded much of the purchase value of the contracted revenue; therefore the monks themselves were often tempted to keep several places vacant in the convent, so that they could better economize their meager rations.

Needless to say, such an atmosphere of perpetual gloom hardly appealed to prospective vocations. Even with the best efforts of the monks nothing more could be hoped for than the maintenance of a marginal level in numbers, discipline and economy. A true revival remained a possibility, but only in abbeys under regular abbots, or in congregations which had successfully eliminated commendatory authority.

IX

Reforms and the Reformation

 In no other epoch of church history was so much said about reform and so little accomplished as in the fifteenth century. The abuses were as much in evidence as were the necessity and intention to correct them. The most obvious cause for the failure of all well-meaning efforts was the weakness and irresolution of the executive power. The conciliar movement was unable to coordinate the universal desire for reform, while the Renaissance papacy, bogged down in the pursuit of dynastic schemes and Italian power politics, could not reform even itself, let alone champion a meaningful renewal beyond the Alps. But a regenerated Curia and an unselfish and energetic pope would still have been powerless against the rising nationalism that broke Europe into mutually hostile and increasingly self-conscious states, each under a strong monarch and all trying to minimize papal influence over domestic affairs. The Gallicanism of France was as dedicated to forcing the clergy into submission as was the newly united Spain or the Tudor monarchy in England.

Nevertheless, the horizon was not hopelessly dark. The many brilliant representatives of a Christian Humanism proved convincingly that the new learning was by no means incompatible with traditional faith or piety, and the striking success of local or regional reforms attested to the religious enthusiasm of thousands of devout souls. In addition to such new orders as the Jesuates (1360) and Hieronymites (1373), the "observant" Franciscans came to be as successful as the even more austere Minims, founded in Calabria by Saint Francis of Paula about 1457. The Benedictines, plagued by the *commenda,* found a way to escape the evil by discarding abbatial titles and organizing themselves into congregations under firm central control and strict discipline. This highly successful policy was initiated by Abbot Ludovico Barbo (d. 1443) of Santa Giustina in Padua. The movement spread throughout Italy and, after Monte Cassino joined it (1504), became known as the Cassinese Congregation. The same movement inspired the Austrian Benedictines of Melk, who effectively propagated a similar organization throughout Bavaria and Swabia. The Spanish Benedictine Congregation of Valladolid (1492)

fought successfully against the *commenda* with the Italians' weapons, that is, by converting abbeys into priories under a superior appointed for only a short term. In Germany the best-known and most effective monastic reform was that of Bursfeld near Göttingen, which was initiated about 1433 by Abbot Johannes Dederoth. By 1530 this Congregation united ninety-four well-disciplined Benedictine abbeys throughout the country. In the Low Countries and the Rhineland, in addition to the "Brethren of the Common Life," numerous communities of "Beguines" and "Beghards" came into being. The most influential of them was the reform of Augustinian Canons in Windesheim, inspired by Gerard Groote; the Canons, in turn, exercised considerable influence over Cistercian movements in the same area.

In the second half of the fifteenth century the condition of the Cistercian Order was, in microcosm, much the same as that of the whole Church. There was certainly no shortage of reforming decrees, but by then the authority of the General Chapter had been so reduced by poor attendance and so limited by national boundaries that the success of any renewal depended more on local initiative and leadership than on ineffectual declarations emanating from Cîteaux. The abbot of Cîteaux was, in fact, among the first to exploit the vacuum created by the enfeebled Chapter. The reorganized papal monarchy and rising royal absolutism undoubtedly encouraged Cîteaux to claim firmer control over the administration of the Order, and such attempts found an approving echo in the Curia. As early as 1438 Eugenius IV addressed Jean Picart of Cîteaux as "abbot general." Later in the century similar honorific titles were featured in a number of documents, until in 1499 the General Chapter recognized Jean de Cirey as "supreme father of the Order." There was no move, however, to change the constitution of the Order, and the extraordinary measures taken by the abbot of Cîteaux were usually covered by the Chapter's authorization.

The jealous proto-abbots, particularly the abbots of Clairvaux, watched the manifest ambitions of Cîteaux with dismay. Pierre de Virey of Clairvaux (1471-1496), following the example of several of his predecessors, fought a running battle with Cîteaux and the General Chapter throughout his administration. Eventually the feud reached the Parlement of Paris and the secession of Clairvaux and its affiliated houses threatened permanent schism. In Rome the influence of Jean de Cirey prevailed, and in 1489 Innocent VIII issued a bull declaring the unification of the abbatial sees of Cîteaux and Clairvaux, both under the control of Cirey. The shocking decree was never executed. Instead, Virey resigned in 1496,

and his successor, Jean Foucault, managed to establish a better relationship with Cîteaux.

Jean de Cirey's greatest ambition was, undoubtedly, the much needed
reform of his Order. Not only had nature endowed him with a wide range
of talents and tireless energy, but he was also high in favor both in Rome
and Paris. Louis XI granted him and his successors the title of "born
councillor of the Parlement of Burgundy" and in 1484 he was privileged to
serve as a delegate at the Estates General in Tours. In 1487 Innocent VIII
entrusted to him a thoroughgoing reform of the whole Order, stressing
particularly attendance at the General Chapters, regular visitation, the
obligations of commendatory abbots and the administration of dues and
taxes within the order. It was this last issue that had poisoned the relation
between Cîteaux and Clairvaux. In anticipation of success and as a
gesture of his high esteem, in 1489 the same Pontiff bestowed on Jean de
Cirey the unique privilege of administering the minor orders, and even the
diaconate, of all Cistercians.

King Charles VIII of France heeded the papal call for religious reform
and late in 1493 sponsored a convention of bishops and heads of various
orders at Tours. Abbot Cirey played an active role during the negotiations
and pointed out that before anything else the freedom of abbatial
elections must be guaranteed, the power of commendatory abbots curbed
and the abuse of recourse to secular justice removed. He emphasized,
however, that declarations of general principles were not sufficient; if a
reform was to succeed, concrete action must be planned and executed
within each order. As to the Cistercians, Cirey stated with satisfaction
that the movement of reform, already in evidence for the past twenty or
thirty years, had born fruit, but he was determined to apply force
wherever abuses persisted.

King Charles, engaged in his ill-fated Italian expedition, failed to follow
up the project of universal religious reform, but the undeterred Cirey held
a convention of forty-five French abbots in the College of Saint Bernard
of Paris early in 1494. The result was a detailed scheme of Cistercian
reform, the "Articles of Paris," which featured sixteen paragraphs dealing
with the most important issues. In a preamble the abbots disclaimed any
intention of inaugurating radical novelties, since "reform does not mean
the introduction of newfangled devices, but rather the refashioning of
customs and regulations to the lives of the holy fathers. . . . Indeed, if we
were engaged in the introduction of new forms [of life], it would certainly
be not a reform, that is, return to the ancient way [of life], but the
foundation of a new religious order." The conferees admitted that many

of the castigated abuses were consequences of wars, pestilence, secular intervention, inept abbots or corrupt communities, but they vowed to bring about the desired renewal "in the whole as in its parts, in the members as well as in the head, as much in spiritual as in temporal matters."

The document began with regulations concerning the Divine Office, then reminded the abbots of their duties, urged the holding of chapters of faults, stressed the necessity of studies, ordered the removal of fireplaces from dormitories, prescribed regular visitations, emphasized the virtue of poverty and the elimination of all private income or property, insisted on strict enclosure, renewed the regulations of the *Benedictina* concerning fiscal administration, and even included a paragraph on the reform of Cistercian nuns. Of particular interest was the new statute on abstinence. After 1475, when Sixtus IV had permitted the General Chapter to grant dispensation from perpetual abstinence, meat courses had been authorized on Tuesdays, Thursdays and Sundays, except in Advent, Lent from Septuagesima Sunday to Easter, and days of abstinence specified as such either by the Church or by the laws of the Order. Finally, in anticipation of militant resistance, the document ordered the abbots "to build or repair good and strong prisons in their monasteries, as means of strict punishment against transgressors and those who would refuse obedience to this [charter of] holy reformation."

As an important sequel to the "Articles of Paris," a new set of regulations for the College of Saint Bernard in Paris was issued on August 11, a document of unique source value, for it throws revealing light on the internal life and organization of that great and still flourishing institution of higher learning.

The General Chapter of 1494 praised and approved the "Articles of Paris," although it delayed their enforcement until the Chapter of 1495, because of unspecified "impossibilities" of local execution. No assessment of the reform's results can be made in the light of available evidence. Since the Order was unable to remove the greatest source of evil, the commendatory system, neither France nor Italy witnessed instant renewal. In other countries, where the success of reform was well in evidence, the process had originated under local inspiration long before 1494.

Posterity must be grateful to Claude de Bronseval, secretary of Abbot Edmond de Saulieu of Clairvaux, for the few glimpses revealing the conditions of some French abbeys late in 1531. They had both set out on a tour of visitation in Spain and Portugal, but before they reached the Pyrenees they sought the hospitality of several French Cistercian monasteries. At La Prée they found a small community, "but the brethren were certainly good and pious." At Benisson-Dieu, however, the visitors came to witness the "greatest misery," brought about by "the monks who were totally ignorant of the Latin language, the divine services and of the Order's ritual, as well as the [rules of] courtesy and civility." The physical facilities of the abbey were in equally bad shape. On the other hand, the small abbey of Franquevaux was well preserved, but the visitors found in it a sole religious who styled himself prior. It turned out, however, that he had been sent there by the commendator only three months before and was, moreover, a Franciscan, who had merely put on the Cistercian habit without having spent a year in a novitiate. The good friar disclosed that two other monks had legal residence in the house, but one was away on a rabbit hunt, the other was in the meadow in search of eggs. At Valmagne, the once great abbey near Montpellier, Bronseval praised the pious commendatory abbot, but referred to the monks as unruly and ignorant. Fontfroide, in spite of long commendatory rule, was still inhabited by twenty-five monks, who were well disposed, but "alienated from the observances" of the Order; they had, for example, a dormitory partitioned into individual cells, many furnished with fireplaces. Villelongue had a community of twelve monks under a regular abbot, a fine old man, who, after forty years in office, wished to resign. Ardorel was a small but well-constructed house, where the regular abbot was "a good and zealous man."

The most forceful reform movement of the fifteenth century was initiated in Castile about 1425 by an ex-hermit, Martin Vargas. This venture, however, led to the organization of an independent congregation and it will therefore be detailed in the next chapter.

The vogue of new forms of piety in the Netherlands inspired a number of Cistercian foundations in the fourteenth and fifteenth centuries. However, this subject has been so much neglected that at this time only a conjectural picture can be presented. The first such foundation was the abbey of Eytheren in Holland, sponsored by the German Ebrach in 1342. Various disasters caused the abbey to be transferred to Ysselstein near Utrecht, to be reduced to a priory and eventually to become a house affiliated with Camp (1394). The same Camp sponsored another community in 1382, established in the abandoned Marienkroon, formerly a house of Cistercian nuns in Holland, close to the borders of Brabant. In 1386, in another vacant nunnery, the small priory of Marienhave or Warmond near Leiden rose to existence, also under the patronage of Camp. War disrupted the life of the community and it was restored only in 1412 by monks of Eytheren, known by then as Ysselstein (Ijsselstein).

Early in the fifteenth century a devout secular priest, Johannes Clemme, with several of his "simple and poor brethren," founded a small community in Sibculo, located in the inhospitable region of Overyssel,

113

not far from Deventer. In 1407 they embraced the Augustinian rule, but in 1412 they joined the Cistercians. Three years later Sibculo established a relation of mutual visitation with Ysselstein and Warmond and commonly decided to follow the narrow path of poverty, solitude and fidelity to the Rule. In style with their unpretentious existence they insisted on "a frugal diet and cheap clothing," and they renounced even the ambition of ever rising to the rank of an abbey. Their days centered on the celebration of liturgy and manual labor; moreover, in their love of solitude, they vowed never to leave the precincts of their monasteries. By strict limitation of their membership and free election of their priors they tried to fend off corrupting external influences. John of Martigny (1405-1428), abbot of Cîteaux, could not fail to notice certain "novelties" in their lives, but recognized them as a "small flock" (*pusillus grex*), not unlike the one grouped around Abbot Robert on the eve of the foundation of Cîteaux. It is more likely, however, that the inspiration behind the movement was the powerful current of spiritual renewal prevailing in that whole region, the *devotio moderna*.

This was the nucleus of a growing circle of interrelated priories, known as the "Congregation of Sibculo," flourishing under the protective wings of the great Rhenish abbey of Camp. The General Chapter had very little to do with the organization. Apart from a few casual references, such as those made at the Chapter of 1423, when the possibility of the incorporation of the two Westphalian houses, Gross- and Klein-Burlo were first mentioned, it was only toward the end of the fifteenth century that the legal existence of the Congregation was formalized.

In 1446 a momentous event in the life of the new Congregation occurred in the foundation of Saint-Sauveur (Salvatorsklooster) in Antwerp. It rose to life through the generosity of a rich and pious merchant, Pierre Pot, but was populated by eight monks and four lay-brothers from Ysselstein. Saint-Sauveur soon became a fervent center of strict asceticism and within forty years had generated four other priories, all located in the same area (Mariendonck, Hemelspoort, Marienhof and Bethleem). In 1448 Marienhave sent seven monks to Waerschoot at the request of a devout knight, Simon Utenhove, who himself entered the new house as a lay-brother. The same Marienhave founded still another priory in 1465 near Haarlem, Monnikendam.

In 1448 Camp incorporated the formerly Williamite (Hermits of Saint William of Maleval) houses, Gross-Burlo and Klein-Burlo, both in the diocese of Münster, and both joined at the same time the Congregation of Sibculo. The two houses, isolated from the rest of their order, had experienced moral as well as financial difficulties, and since they had shared already many Cistercian customs, their logical solution was fusion with the Cistercians. Both Williamite houses were small (Gross-Burlo had then only ten members), but their fusion with the Congregation of Sibculo opened for them a century of successful reform and prosperity. Both received priors from Sibculo; the new prior of Gross-Burlo, Gerlach von Kranenburg, must have been a truly saintly and dedicated monk, for contemporaries called him "a second Bernard."

In the same year of 1448 Camp took over a depopulated Cistercian convent of nuns, Bottenbroich, in the diocese of Cologne. In 1480 the monks of Bottenbroich acquired and populated Mariawald in the same diocese.

Meanwhile other forces of renewal were active in Flanders. In 1414 the great abbeys of Villers and Aulne took over the depopulated Cistercian nunnery of Moulins, where they jointly sponsored the establishment of a new community of monks under Abbot Jean de Gesves, formerly monk of Aulne. Another extinct convent of Cistercian nuns, Jardinet, was settled in 1430 by monks of Aulne and Cambron. The first abbot of this community was the outstanding Jean Eustache de Mons, formerly prior of Moulins. He must have been not only a great ascetic, but also a charismatic leader of souls. During his administration he attracted to Jardinet forty-six monks and thirty-five lay-brothers; in the year of his retirement (1477) the community numbered fifty-one members. Moulins and Jardinet jointly sponsored the establishment of three other houses: Nizelle in 1441; Boneffe, a former nunnery, in 1461; and Saint-Remy in Rochefort in 1464. The influence of Jardinet under Jean Eustache was widespread. The convent furnished abbots to several monasteries and confessors to a number of Cistercian nunneries, and had a close relationship with the Benedictines of Gembloux and Saint-Martin of Tournay. Jardinet remained in flourishing condition until the beginning of the Dutch revolt against Spanish rule about 1560.

The unusual flurry of new foundations at a time when many French and Italian abbeys fought for bare survival finally came to the attention of the General Chapter of 1489, although even then the initiative was taken by Camp, puzzled over the legal status of the large number of associated priories. The chapter fathers did not fail to notice that the way of life of these priories "was somewhat different from the customary routine of the Order, however, since the deviations were necessitated by the [different] customs of the region," they did not refuse their approval. The same Chapter passed a set of regulations in seven paragraphs for the proper administration of the "Congregation of Sibculo." Accordingly, the paternity of Camp was officially recognized; the houses were entitled to hold annual conventions and to regulate their own affairs, although their statutes were to be sent to Cîteaux for approval. The houses were permitted to remain priories and the three senior priors (those of Ysselstein, Sibculo and Marienhave) were to exercise the rights and duties of visitors. The priors were to be elected by the communities, but confirmed by the abbot of Camp. Although many of these houses were situated in or about "great cities," they were to observe strict enclosure. Finally, for some reason, the Chapter insisted that the lay-brothers of the congregation be called *donati* or *familiares.*

What were the specific circumstances surrounding these unusual foundations? What program or spirituality accounted for their success? In the absence of preliminary studies only tentative answers can be offered, to be modified by further evidence.

In the case of the "Congregation of Sibculo," it is very unlikely that Camp took the initiative and made the foundations by its own disponible personnel. The small communities were probably spontaneous groups of kindred souls, perhaps Beghards, who, often suspected and harassed by the authorities, merely sought refuge under the protective umbrella of Camp. It is to the credit of that great Rhenish abbey that, in addition to a willing sponsorship, several abandoned Cistercian nunneries were put at the communities' disposal. The urban or suburban locations, the presence of a number of laymen, distinct from the old-style lay-brothers, the preference for priories over pretentious abbeys, the standards of strict asceticism, all seem to indicate that the source of inspiration was the *devotio moderna,* and that the way of life within the houses was shaped along the patterns set by the Beghards or the "Brethren of the Common Life."

Flemish abbeys mentioned above had, apparently, a more direct role in the foundation of Moulins and Jardinet. In fact, Villers and Aulne had a close and fruitful association with Beguines, and there are other indications that the monks were well disposed toward the new spirituality, such as, for example, the maintenance of educational institutions at Moulins, Nizelle and Boneffe, operated in the spirit of Christian Humanism.

The spirit of reform was much in evidence throughout Germany. Marienrode near Hildesheim had been in a full decline during the first half of the fourteenth century, but, thanks to the beneficial intervention of the abbey of Riddagshausen, a recovery set in after 1379, promoted by a succession of able and zealous abbots. Thus, Heinrich von Berten (1426-1462), author of the remarkable *Chronicon Marienrodense,* restored the ruined economy, rebuilt the damaged church and substantially increased membership. When he took office he found only twenty-six monks in the house; during his administration he admitted thirty-six new members. He was a personal friend of Cardinal Nicolas of Cusa (who visited the abbey in 1450), worked with him for the reform of the Church in Germany, and participated in the Council of Basel (1438).

The vigor of German abbeys was made manifest by their active involvement in the reform of Hungarian monasteries. The initiative in the latter country was taken by Matthias Corvinus (1458-1490), a great humanist king, who turned to the Cistercian General Chapter for assistance in breathing new life into "the pitifully languishing and nearly extinct" communities. The Chapter of 1478 appealed to the German abbots for help; they responded with generous offers of personnel. At least twenty-two abbeys promised substantial contingents of monks to be sent to Hungary; Bebenhausen, Ebrach and Heilsbronn expressed their willingness to furnish "whole convents with an abbot," meaning at least thirteen monks. In preparation for the expedition the German abbots held two conventions at Würzburg and in 1480 over one hundred monks embarked at Regensburg for their journey on the Danube to Hungary. The records of the following decade clearly attest to the energetic work of the Germans. One of them, Jodoc Rosner, became abbot of Pilis and received from the General Chapter special authorization to visit and reform the other communities of the country. The success, however, was only ephemeral. Following the disastrous battle of Mohács (1526) the heartland of Hungary was occupied by the Turks and for the next two centuries the country was reduced to a bloody battleground. By the middle of the sixteenth century all Cistercian monasteries in Hungary had ceased to function and remained dormant until another revival early in the eighteenth century.

Meanwhile Germany became the scene of chronic violence following Luther's call for a reformed church, independent from Rome. The peasant rebellion of 1525 only introduced the intermittent civil and religious wars that raged on German soil until 1648. Many Cistercian abbeys were sacked and burned during the early stages of the fight; others, within the territories of Protestant princes, were suppressed by decree. There was no general pattern of procedure; everything depended on the disposition of the monks, the attitude of the surrounding population and the temper of the prince.

By 1503 the great Ebrach still had seventy-five members, but the new abbot, Johannes Leiterbach, did nothing to prevent the inroads of the new teaching. During the Peasant War (1525) the abbey was thoroughly sacked; the monks fled and eighteen of them failed to return. Fifteen of these were known to have become Lutherans, some even married. An

117

episcopal visitation in 1531, when Leiterbach was finally deposed, listed twenty-five monks and three lay-brothers, although four names were marked as apostates. Later in the century Ebrach not only recovered, but also became the flourishing center of Baroque art and piety.

At Bebenhausen (Württemberg), when the last Catholic abbot died in 1534, the monks themselves were divided: twenty remained Catholics, eighteen sympathized with the Lutherans. The Catholics were forced to leave, seeking refuge in the surviving monasteries of Austria and Bavaria. The fortunes of war permitted them to return in 1549, when they elected a new abbot, who was, however, deposed and replaced by a Lutheran in 1560. After the Edict of Restitution in 1629 the monks of Salem managed to re-occupy Bebenhausen, until they had to flee from the Swedes in 1632. The stubborn Cistercians returned again in 1634, although the Peace of Westphalia (1648) finally awarded the much contested abbey to the Lutherans. Similar fate awaited the monks at Heilsbronn, Herrenalb, Königsbronn and Maulbronn.

As a result of the advance of Lutheranism in Northern Germany, monks there were either expelled by force or voluntarily deserted their monasteries. In the case of Loccum (Hanover) the monks continued their community life while they all gradually accepted the new creed, thus creating a peculiar form of Lutheran monasticism. The daily schedule and liturgical life remained almost intact during the sixteenth century; moreover the Lutheran abbot delegated one of his Catholic fellow-abbots as his representative at the General Chapter in 1601. In 1658, the language of monastic liturgy was changed to German, but celibacy was not abandoned until the beginning of the eighteenth century. Abbot Gerhard Molan (1677-1722), as a leading Lutheran clergyman of the highest reputation, became a close associate of Leibnitz in the endeavor toward a unification of Christian churches. Later the abbey was transformed into a Lutheran seminary, and as such, still has a distinguished role in the spiritual and intellectual life of German Lutheranism.

Of the 104 Cistercian abbeys that existed early in the sixteenth century in German lands, forty-five fell victim to the Reformation. The others survived and many came to experience great prosperity until the final secularization of the Napoleonic era. In 1573-74 Nicolas I Boucherat, abbot of Cîteaux, visited thirty-three of the surviving German, Flemish and Swiss abbeys and found most of them in satisfactory condition. The significant number of novices in many communities was a clear indication of a happier future. In 1629, when, after the successful conclusion of the "Danish" phase of the Thirty Years' War, Emperor Ferdinand II issued his Edict of Restitution, the German Cistericans were strong enough to reclaim and reoccupy eleven formerly lost abbeys, all of which had to be abandoned again following the Protestant victory in 1648.

Elsewhere in continental Europe the Reformation secularized all Cistercian abbeys in Norway, Sweden, Denmark, later in Holland and in the Baltic states, and reduced the eight houses in Switzerland to four.

In no other country did the Reformation and dissolution of monasteries stir up so heated and so enduring a controversy as in England. Although the full scholarly review of all available source material has clarified most factual details, judgment over the motives and possible justification of the accompanying violence and destruction will remain forever a vexing question. The now peaceful valleys, as much as the collective conscience of the nation, still bear the scars. Few observers can remain silent at the sight of the melancholy ruins, but the answer always depends on the state of mind or religious persuasion of each successive generation.

That from the middle of the fourteenth century English monasticism had labored under the burdens of diminishing numbers, sagging economy, lax discipline, and adverse public opinion, is a matter of consensus among historians. The causes of the malaise have already been discussed above, although two factors, at least, seem to be peculiar to England. One is the absence of the commendatory system, the other is the relative isolation of the island from continental religious currents. The first was mainly beneficial, although the English abbots came to be regarded as owners of monastic property, while the royal government looked habitually upon the great abbeys as sources of easy income in every emergency. The insular isolation, however, underscored by the Hundred Years' War and the Great Schism, deprived the English monks of the stimulating effect of the many exciting movements of reform in Italy, Spain, the Low Countries or in the Rhineland.

The Cistercians in England, Wales, Scotland and Ireland shared the isolation of other religious institutions. Their presence at General Chapters was exceptional; the visitation of their houses was carried out by English abbots appointed for the purpose by the Chapter, therefore contacts with Cîteaux were limited to occasional correspondence and the sending of some monetary contributions. Thus, at the time of the Dissolution, the English Cistercians derived no benefits from the fact that they were still nominally members of an international organization; they had to fend for themselves the best they could.

Nevertheless, the prevalence of serious problems should not be exaggerated. While toward the end of the fourteenth century the average English Cistercian house had only fifteen members, by the early sixteenth century the figure had risen to nineteen. Among the abbots one may find a number of upright characters and on the eve of the Dissolution the morale of Cistercian communities was perhaps higher than that of other monastic orders, save the Carthusians. The outstanding example was Fountains under the long and beneficial administration of Abbot Marmaduke Huby (1494-1526). Even his jealous fellow-abbots had to admit that he was "a promoter of discipline, cultivator of religion, vigorous restorer of ruined houses in our days, and it can be safely stated that [in such matters] none of us in our country had so much experience." He stood high in favor with Henry VII and in his later years was on good terms with the powerful minister of Henry VIII, Cardinal Wolsey. He was a generous benefactor of the College of Saint Bernard in Oxford and erected, among other additions to Fountains, the still standing great tower, a worthy monument to the liberality of its builder. Still more remarkable was the growth of personnel in the abbey. When Huby became abbot there were only twenty-two monks in the house; in 1520, there were fifty-two professed members, among them forty-one priests. Lack of relevant documentation prevents us from ascertaining the level of spirituality and discipline at Fountains, but such a spectacular increase in numbers can hardly be explained without supposing a commendable degree of devotion and order.

In most other cases the evidence is also insufficient for a reliable assessment of general conditions prior to 1535, while after that date the reports of royal visitors, whose duty was to uncover widespread monastic abuses, are unreliable. It seems certain, however, that the sin of English Cistercians was not general immorality, but general mediocrity. When the end was near, one may suspect, the mute obedience with which the monks submitted to the royal will was the result not only of a lack of heroism, but also a lack of zeal and a lack of dedication to their own vocation. Generalizations, however, even on this point, might be misleading. When in 1536 the commissioners questioned the monks whether they wished to apply for dispensations from their vows or rather desired to persevere in monastic life, whole Cistercian communities opted for the latter. Such information is scarce, but this was the case at least at Garendon, Stoneleigh and Stanley, while at Netley only one monk, and at Quarr two monks, wished to depart.

Local conditions, good or bad, bore no influence on the procedure firmly controlled by the clever and unscrupulous Thomas Cromwell, King Henry's powerful minister after the break with Rome. Early in 1536 a royal act suppressed all religious houses with less than twelve members or less than £200 annual income. Twenty-two Cistercian houses, many of them in Wales, fell victim to this law. The abbots and priors received a pension, while the monks of these communities had a choice of joining the secular clergy or being transferred to one of the remaining abbeys. Since the records are only partially extant, it is impossible to determine which was the option of most Cistercian monks. From the five examples mentioned above one may assume that the majority of them preferred the transfer to other houses of the Order. In a number of cases, and after the payment of substantial sums, favored communities were permitted to stay together. Such permissions were granted to Neath, Whitland, and Strata Florida in Wales, but their respite lasted only three years. Among the pensioned superiors, Abbot Alynge of Waverley was well provided for and moved to the Cistercian College of Oxford. Abbot Austen of Rewley received the pension of £22 and moved to Cambridge in order to "study the word of God sincerely."

Was the suppression of small houses planned merely as a tactical preliminary to the total destruction of monasticism? Probably not. Wolsey had already carried out a similar project between 1524 and 1528 without such implications. The relative ease of the procedure and the lack of dangerous resistance, however, emboldened the government to go further, to where the real wealth lay.

The only manifestation of outrage against the royal government and expression of sympathy with the monks was the "Pilgrimage of Grace," a series of local uprisings from the autumn of 1536 to the spring of 1537. A number of Cistercian houses, acting willingly or under duress, were involved; a monk of Sawley was credited with the authorship of the "pilgrim's" marching song. But the rebels were ill-organized. The great nobles refused to join hands with them, and Henry VIII had no great difficulty in dealing with the movement with brutality. "All the monks and canons that be in any wise faulty . . . be tied up without further delay or ceremony, to the terrible example of others," wrote the King to his agents. In addition to a number of monks, seven Cistercian abbots were executed (Robert Hobbes of Woburn, Thomas Bolton of Sawley, William Thirsk of Fountains, Adam Sedbar of Jervaulx, Thomas Carter of Holm Cultram, John Paslew of Whalley, John Harrison of Kirkstead), while the fate of some others remains unknown.

The executed Abbot Robert Hobbes of Woburn was formerly believed to have suffered for his complicity in the Pilgrimage of Grace, but, in fact, he died for his faith. He had taken the oath required by the Act of Supremacy of 1534, but he repented and urged his monks to keep faith with Rome. After the execution of the Carthusians for this very crime, he addressed his monks in chapter: "Brethren, this is a perilous time; such a scourge was never heard of since Christ's passion," and he ordered the daily recitation of Psalm 78: "O God, the heathen have broken into thine inheritance. . . ." After a number of similar incidents he was denounced to Cromwell by an ex-friar, the curate of the parish of Woburn. Although he was an old man of broken health, he was tried and executed with two of his monks. Woburn was totally demolished, but the oak from which, according to tradition, the Abbot was hanged, stood there as a mute testimony to his martyrdom until the early decades of the nineteenth century.

Of the monks whose execution had nothing to do with the uprising and was solely the result of their religious conviction, George Lazenby of Jervaulx should be remembered. When in the middle of 1535 a preacher of the new doctrine was ordered to deliver a sermon in the abbey church against the pope, Lazenby rose and publicly challenged him. When later questioned about the incident, he "thanked God who gave him the spirit and audacity so to say." He was taken to Middleham Castle, where, in the face of death, he again defended, as the magistrate put it, "yonder same idol and blood sucker of Rome so loudly and stiffly as I never in all my days saw the like." In the course of his examination he admitted having had close relations with the equally unyielding Carthusians of Mount Grace, where he had seen a vision of the Blessed Virgin. There is no documentary evidence of his execution, but an old monk of Jervaulx, Thomas Madde, is recorded as saying that he "did take away and hide the head of one of his brethren of the same house, who had suffered death for that he would not yield to the Royal Supremacy."

The Pilgrimage of Grace, as well as the King's costly foreign ventures, justified the increasing pressure on the remaining abbeys to surrender "voluntarily" all their properties to the government. The terrorized abbots, sensing that it was their last opportunity to bargain with Cromwell, did so, one by one. By the end of 1539 monasticism had disappeared from the English church and the wholesale demolition of churches and cloisters began immediately, for the new owners wished to make it sure that even in a changed religious climate there should be no return for the monks. As one of them put it bluntly, "The nest has been destroyed lest the birds should build there again." The plate and jewels were sent to the royal treasury together with the most valuable manuscripts of the libraries. Furniture and everything else movable, from paving stones to vestments and candlesticks, were sold by auction on the spot at bargain prices. Only those buildings were spared which seemed to be of some immediate utility. Sir Arthur Darcy, in charge of the dismemberment of Jervaulx, wrote in glowing terms about the amenities of this Cistercian abbey, ideally suited to accommodate the royal stud of

122

mares. For the future use of the confiscated wealth various schemes were afloat, but eventually all monastic property wound up in the possession of the land-hungry nobility. The new owners became the most devoted supporters of Henry's ecclesiastical policy. It was this situation that rendered a monastic restoration under Queen Mary entirely hopeless.

The abbots who complied with the Dissolution were granted generous pensions. Abbot John Ripley of Kirkstall received £66 annually and was permitted to stay in the gatehouse of his monastery. The monks were less fortunate even if there were no charges against them. Their average pension was £5, barely sufficient to live on. Most of those who were still of employable age sought positions among the ranks of the secular clergy. The monks of communities where either the abbot or some other members of the house were implicated in any act of noncompliance were turned out without provision for their future. Such was the case with the twenty-five members of Whalley, although eventually most of them found some clerical appointment. At Furness thirty-three monks were left without pensions and, according to the available records, only six of them found employment. There was, of course, no provision at all for the innumerable monastic servants or farm workers.

In Scotland, firmly under the control of John Knox and his Presbyterians, the confiscation of monastic property began in 1560, but it was only in 1587 that the Scottish Parliament transferred such goods to the crown. In the sixteenth century most Cistercian houses in Scotland were under commendatory abbots and were in every respect weaker than those in England. The largest of them, Melrose, still had thirty-one members in 1534, but monastic discipline, particularly in the matter of poverty, was far from satisfactory. By the middle of the century conditions had further deteriorated. The abbey was then under the rule of a bastard of King James V. He was obliged to keep at least sixteen monks in the convent, but he refused to comply; he even embezzled the sum set aside for the repair of the dilapidated cloister.

In 1565, the commendatory abbot of the Scottish Dundrennan, Edward Maxwell, simply converted his monastery into his personal property and married, but he was willing to give pensions to his former monks. The monks of Balmerino were less fortunate: pension was promised to only those of the fifteen monks who were willing to embrace the new faith, the others were to be expelled without compensation. Under such circumstances probably the majority of the monks professed to be Presbyterians, at least for the record.

In Ireland the Dissolution could not be enforced beyond the territory under effective English control, the "Pale;" that is, Dublin and its vicinity. Unfortunately, this included Mellifont and Saint Mary's Abbey, the only houses under regular discipline. Many other communities beyond this limit subsisted, often clandestinely, until the bloody invasion of Oliver Cromwell in 1650.

In the anticipation of the dissolution a remarkable private arrangement was worked out at Holy Cross near Tipperary by its regular abbot, William Dwyer. As early as 1533 much of the abbey's possessions were leased for very long periods to people favorably disposed toward the monks. Then, in 1534, Dwyer resigned as abbot in favor of a married layman, Philip Purcell, who took the title of "provost" of Holy Cross. He not only was willing to share the abbatial revenues with Dwyer, but permitted the monks to stay in the abbey. They were forced to disperse only in 1563, shortly after Queen Elizabeth had granted the abbey to her cousin, the Earl of Ormond. Thus the abbey was never formally suppressed; in fact, the abbatial title, appended to the names of various individuals, survived until 1751.

In France, the royal government, already in firm control of Church benefices, staunchly resisted the spread of Calvinism, but during the weak administration of Catherine de Medici and her feeble sons, the Huguenots gained considerable ground. The intermittent "Wars of Religion" (1559-1598) brought destruction and misery comparable only to the devastation of the Hundred Years' War. Monasteries, always believed to be rich and full of supplies, again became the targets of unruly soldiery on both sides. But it was not only physical destruction that threatened the monks. In 1561 at the Estates General of Pontoise and the subsequent "Conference of Poissy," powerful voices were heard demanding the total secularization of monastic property in order to supply the hard-pressed government with funds for the war. Knowing what had happened in England, the terrified clergy voted huge contributions, which eventually were perpetuated in the form of annual "free gifts." Many of the already impoverished abbeys, Cistercians included, unable to pay the allotted amounts otherwise, were forced to sell valuable monastic property.

Meanwhile, the central administration of the Order came to a virtual standstill. During the war the General Chapter convened only seven times (1560, 1562, 1565, 1567, 1573, 1578, 1584) with only a few abbots in attendance; in 1560 only thirteen of them managed to arrive at Cîteaux. The motherhouse herself was in constant danger. In 1574 the army of Prince Condé, in 1589 Guillaume de Tavannes, and in 1595 the soldiers of Marshal Biron, sacked the ancient abbey. The devastation of 1589 was the worst. The Huguenots spent a full week destroying everything, breaking open even the tombs under the church. The damage amounted to 600,000 livres. The incident, as it was recorded by the magistrates of Dijon, affords a precious glimpse at that still great and populous abbey. The monastic plant was considered defensible, for a contingent of one hundred soldiers, paid by the abbey, was kept within its walls. These mercenaries, however, fled without a fight at the approach of the enemy. Most of the terrified monks followed them. The personnel of the monastery consisted then of 254 persons: sixty professed monks, twelve novices, thirty lay-brothers and a number of *familiares,* servants and laborers. The abbey proper had 158 rooms, surrounded by sixteen workshops for the various arts and crafts needed for the maintenance of the establishment. The stables sheltered 162 horses.

The looting and destruction were systematic. Some of the monks and brothers who fell into the hands of the attackers were tortured to force them to disclose the possible hiding places of valuables. The collected objects, including the bells and the lead on the roof of the church, were carted away in 300 wagons. The thirty-five altars of the church, with all their paintings and statuary, were totally demolished. The eight granges immediately surrounding the abbey were equally devastated. According to conservative estimates, at least half of the French Cistercian abbeys suffered a similar fate.

At the same time the Calvinist Dutch were fighting their own war against the Catholic Spaniards. Abbeys became the favorite targets of the new iconoclasts. The fifteenth-century monastic revival came to a sudden end. Monastic life became so precarious even in Flanders that many communities sought refuge within the walls of fortified cities. In 1566 the richest and greatest abbey of the country, Les Dunes, suffered destruction. In 1578, when reconstruction was almost completed, the Calvinists struck again. From this disaster there was no recovery. Even the stones of the house were carted away for the fortification of Dunkirk and Nieuport. The surviving monks found shelter first in one of their granges, Bogaerde, and then, in 1627, the abbey moved permanently to Bruges, where the monks occupied a building formerly owned by the already suppressed abbey of Ter Doest.

When the wars of religion finally had come to an end, the Cistercian annals closed the history of that tragic era with the necrology of 180 abbeys, helpless victims of greed and violence.

X

The Rise of the Congregations

The basic structure of Cistercian interdependence, according to the principles of the *Charter of Charity,* was that of the filiation: the founding "mother" controlled a newly established "daughter." Since ultimately every abbey depended on one of the five "proto-abbeys," medieval Cistercian history witnessed a long linear expansion of the "families" of Cîteaux, La Ferté, Pontigny, Clairvaux and Morimond. The lines of affiliation from the most prolific Clairvaux extended from Portugal to Hungary and from Sweden to Southern Italy; those of Morimond were particularly long in an east-west direction, linking establishments from Spain to the Baltic region.

As long as every abbot was willing and able to discharge his duties of visitation, the system functioned with remarkable efficiency. Eventually, however, the intrusion of commendatory abbots, the wholesale suppression of monasteries and the emergence of constantly warring national states severed the lines of communication and control. Early in the fifteenth century the General Chapter was compelled to devise a new system of visitations. The *Charter of Charity* was never repealed or officially amended; each session of the Chapter opened traditionally with the reading of that venerable document. Nevertheless, the new arrangement had little in common with the earliest concept of Cistercian government. The most conspicuous novelties were the formations of "provinces" and "congregations." The first were initiated and controlled by the General Chapter; the latter often came into existence without the concurrence of the Chapter and tended to develop into more or less independent regional or national organizations.

From the fifteenth century onward, visitors for isolated monasteries were occasionally nominated by the General Chapter. If their authority was extended to a larger territory with greater powers than normally envisaged, they were frequently called "reformers." In 1433 a special visitor was appointed for each province under the authority of a "general visitor." For such an important task the most influential abbots or even the abbot of Cîteaux, were usually appointed, but, with the concurrence of the Chapter, simple monks also acted as visitors. At the same time, for other extraordinary duties, such as arbitration or the collection of contributions, the appointee of the Chapter was called a "commissary." Once established, this office became increasingly important.

The new system of administration took a steadier and more specific shape when, during the sixteenth century, those abbeys not belonging to the newly established congregations were organized into provinces or vicariates under the direct authority of the General Chapter. When the Chapter failed to convene, its authority was exercised by the abbot of Cîteaux. These Cistercian provinces, unlike those of the Mendicants, were administrative units without autonomy or constitutional role, and territorially they corresponded to the political provinces of the various countries. The new scheme first developed in France and, during the seventeenth century, spread throughout Europe. By 1683, in addition to the congregations, there were thirty-nine provinces. Control over the monasteries of a province was exercised by the provincial vicar, who, appointed by the General Chapter, was as a rule an abbot of the same province. The regulations of this new and important office were defined by the Chapter of 1605 and further developed by subsequent General Chapters. The chief obligation of provincial vicars was the annual visitation of all monasteries under their care. They reported their findings to the abbot of Cîteaux. These appointments lasted until the next Chapter, but, since decades frequently elapsed without a regular Chapter, the vicars were nominated or relieved by the abbot of Cîteaux after he had consulted with the proto-abbots. Distinguished abbots often held the office for a lifetime. When the abbot of Cîteaux assumed the title of "abbot general," the vicars became known as vicars general. The official subordinate to the vicar general was the provincial procurator, in charge of the defense or support of the abbeys in legal cases. This office originated during the struggle against the *commendam* in the fifteenth century. The title was changed in 1565 to "syndic" or "promoter," but this office was suppressed in 1699.

The rising influence of the French court in religious matters was manifested in 1601 by the appointment of a "procurator general" who resided in the College of Saint Bernard in Paris. His role was similar to that of the procurator general in Rome. In spite of these innovations, the Chapter always encouraged the abbots to exercise their constitutional rights in cooperation with the vicars general, wherever original affiliations still existed.

The same historical factors which occasioned these administrative changes, effected also a reorganization of the education of novices and of young professed members of the Order. As a result of the disruptive circumstances analyzed above, a large number of abbeys decreased both in members and regular discipline, becoming unable or unfit to maintain properly their own novitiate. The detailed reform-scheme of the Chapter of 1601 demanded the establishment of common novitiates for certain groups of abbeys. Because this had already proved a practical means of supporting uniform discipline in many other religious congregations, the plan found warm support in Rome. Undoubtedly, such a measure vitally affected the basic rights of single monasteries, and it was therefore opposed by all those abbeys, especially in Germany, where the traditional Cistercian life still survived. As an unavoidable necessity in France and Italy, however, the common novitiate became a provincial institution. The right of individual abbeys to maintain their own novitiate was always respected, insofar as they were able to fulfill the minimum requirements for its proper management. The houses of common novitiate were usually connected with a subsequent course of theology, in which the young professed received further training in monastic discipline. Because of the great importance of these educational centers for pending reforms and the general spirit of the Order, the manner of their direction and supervision was a subject of heated debates throughout the seventeenth century, during the struggle of observances.

The origins of autonomous congregations were closely linked with movements of regional reforms. Such was the case of the short-lived congregation founded by Joachim of Fiore in Calabria early in the thirteenth century. Similarly, the forces of a spiritual renewal evoked the little-known Congregation of Sibculo in the Low Countries. A movement of far greater significance sprang up in Spain early in the fifteenth century. The Congregation of Castile, or "Regular Observance of Saint Bernard," was originated by Martin Vargas, a Hieronymite (Congregation of Hermits of Saint Jerome), who became a Cistercian monk in the abbey of Piedra. Although his activity as a reformer excited great controversy at Cîteaux, he was widely recognized as a saintly and learned man, motivated by the best intentions. After a sojourn in Italy in 1425, he came to the conclusion that the best way to remedy the fallen state of the Order in Spain, due largely to the inroads of the commendatory system, would be the adoption of measures which had proved successful in similar circumstances among the Italian Benedictines under the leadership of Ludovico Barbo (d. 1443), bishop of Treviso. With the approval of Pope Martin V, Vargas left Piedra in 1427 and with eleven companions founded Montesión near Toledo.

The General Chapter was informed about the existence of the new movement only about 1430, after the highly successful Vargas and his monks had gained control of the Cistercian abbey of Valbuena. Cîteaux protested, but in 1434 the reform received new encouragement from Pope Eugenius IV, a former associate of Ludovico Barbo. The conquest of six other abbeys followed in quick succession and an outraged General Chapter excommunicated the insubordinate Spaniard. Pope Eugenius, however, convinced that Vargas was right and Cîteaux was wrong, not only approved the new Congregation of Castile in 1437, but demanded that the General Chapter approve the organization. The Chapter of 1438 obeyed grudgingly, but in 1445 Vargas was excommunicated a second time; he died in disgrace the following year. By then, however, the Congregation had found wide acclaim and survived its founder without major difficulties.

Vargas was certainly a daring innovator. To discourage potential commendators he replaced abbots by priors elected for three years. They were re-eligible, but not for consecutive terms. He called himself "Reformer" and shared authority with eight definitors. The definitors appointed the visitors, who were responsible to a triennial congregational chapter. Within the Congregation the vow of stability was abolished and individual monks could be transferred anywhere within the organization. Eventually, some of the local superiors resumed the abbatial title, but they too served only for three years. In short, Vargas adapted from contemporary reform-congregations principles that had proved their value in Italy and were about to be introduced in Spain.

Although these arrangements could scarcely be reconciled with Cistercian traditions, what the General Chapter resented most was the practical elimination of all controls which had previously linked the Spanish abbeys with their French mother houses, ultimately with Clairvaux and Cîteaux. In 1493 Pierre de Virey, abbot of Clairvaux, made a serious effort to reassert his own and the General Chapter's authority and signed a formal treaty with the Reformer. The latter expressed his devotion to Cîteaux and promised no expansion beyond the eight houses and the initial Montesión and Valbuena, but the growth of the Congregation could not be halted. By 1532 the organization had combined twenty-five monasteries. It was in the next year that another abbot of Clairvaux, Edmond de Saulieu, undertook a tour of visitation in Spain in order to insure that at least the remaining abbeys in Spain and Portugal would stay under Cîteaux and the General Chapter. His success was only temporary. In 1559 the last Cistercian house in the old Kingdom of Leon and Castile joined the Castilian Congregation, which by then consisted of forty-five populous and well-disciplined monasteries.

In spite of Cîteaux's misgivings it cannot be denied that the constitutional changes effected in the Castilian Congregation were justified. They proved themselves to be successful and even popular. True, the relation between Castile and Cîteaux remained cool, but in view of the perpetual hostility between Bourbons and Habsburgs, it is highly doubtful that the General Chapter could have retained meaningful control over the Spanish houses of the Order even if it had enjoyed the best will of Cistercians across the Pyrenees. It remains to the credit of the Castilians, however, that when Cîteaux abandoned the ancient Cistercian liturgy in the seventeenth century the Spaniards retained it until the general monastic dissolution of 1835. Occasional personal contacts helped to keep alive at least the memory of more active relations. Castilian monks appeared periodically at Cîteaux; Edmond de la Croix, abbot of Cîteaux, toured Spain in 1604, died during his journey and was buried at Poblet.

The seventeenth century was undoubtedly the "golden age" of the Congregation of Castile. The forty-five abbeys of the organization included two colleges: one was established in 1504 at Salamanca, the other, eventually the more renowned, was founded in 1534 on the campus of the fast growing university of Alcalá de Henares. Scholarship became a great tradition in the Congregation. The eminent historian, Angelus Manrique (1577-1648), monk of Huerta and graduate of Salamanca, was only one of many members of outstanding ability.

Still another noteworthy feature of the Congregation was that it welcomed Jewish converts who, according to the testimony of Claude de Bronseval (1533), made up the majority of the monks. An unfriendly witness, he might have easily exaggerated, but his statement was not wholly unfounded. At any rate, by his day the many monks of Jewish parentage had become a source of embarassment to the Congregation and in 1534 the Reformer ordered the dismissal of all such religious within his jurisdiction.

The Cistercian abbeys of northern Italy, ravaged by the commendatory system, found toward the end of the fifteenth century a benevolent patron in the person of Ludovico Sforza (il Moro), duke of Milan (1496-1500). In 1497 he obtained a bull from Pope Alexander VI authorizing the formation of an autonomous "Congregation of Saint Bernard," which united all abbeys of the Order in Lombardy and Tuscany. This organization, like that of Castile, was formed without the consent of Cîteaux and fashioned after the model of similar contemporary movements. The new Congregation was to hold its own independent chapters under a "president general," supported by nine "definitors" and several visitors. Instead of abbots, individual houses were to have "prelates," appointed for three years.

Upon the vigorous protest of Cîteaux, Alexander VI revoked his bull and in 1500 the General Chapter seized the initiative. All abbeys of the provinces were to be visited, reformed and reorganized under the auspices of Cîteaux. The effort remained fruitless. Then, in 1511, Julius II restored the independent Congregation of Saint Bernard with a slightly modified constitution. Annual chapters were now to be held alternately in Lombardy and Tuscany, and each of the provinces was to have seven definitors. The presidency was to alternate in the same manner. Within each province the monks could be transferred from one house to another, but the exchange of personnel between the two provinces was to be exceptional.

In 1578 Gregory XIII further altered the constitution: chapters were to be held only in every third year and the "president" was to hold his position for the same term. The relationship between this Congregation and Cîteaux was never determined. During the seventeenth and eighteenth centuries a number of efforts were made by the General Chapter to assert at least some measure of control over the Congregation, but success remained elusive. Eventually the Congregation came to combine forty-five small houses. The local superiors of some of the more renowned communities resumed the abbatial title, but their tenure continued to be triennial.

Elsewhere in Italy the General Chapter itself promoted the foundation of congregations. In 1605, seven surviving abbeys in southern Italy were united in the Congregation of Calabria and Lucania. In 1633 Urban VIII approved the constitutions of the new organization, calling for triennial provincial chapters under a "president." Monastic stability was abolished despite Cîteaux's protest and even the material goods of each house went into the ownership of the Congregation. Poverty and small membership, however, continued to plague the communities. The General Chapter of 1686 still complained about the "miserable status of the Congregation of Calabria and Lucania and commissioned the procurator general in the Curia to visit and reform in head and in members every one of the monasteries of the Congregation as soon as possible." The General Chapter of 1738 issued regulations for these houses, emphasizing the need for theological instruction. For this purpose the Congregation maintained a college in the town of Cosenza, where after seven years of study a monk could obtain the doctor's degree in theology. Some of the local superiors were called abbots, others priors; all, however, were appointed for four year terms.

In 1613 the General Chapter proposed the formation of a Roman Congregation, uniting nine abbeys within the Papal States and the Kingdom of Naples. According to the constitution approved by Gregory XV in 1623, these houses held provincial chapters in every fourth year, when they appointed abbots for the duration of the same term.

It was at the same Chapter of 1613 that, yielding to the demands of

Philip III, the Congregation of Aragon was organized. It combined sixteen abbeys in Spain and Navarre not included in the Congregation of Castile. This new Congregation was to remain under the authority of the General Chapter and was to send two delegates to Cîteaux each time the Chapter convened. The Congregation was entitled to hold its own chapter in every fourth year, on which occasion the elections of a vicar general, definitors and visitors for four years were to take place. These abbots, however, were to enjoy their positions for life, although the election of abbots in each community was restricted to choosing one of the three persons presented by the vicar general.

A greatly different situation in Portugal led to the development of the independent Congregation of Alcobaça. During a visitation of Portuguese houses in 1532, Edmond de Saulieu, abbot of Clairvaux, found most monasteries in deplorable condition and could not fail to notice that the Congregation of Castile was making serious efforts to infiltrate and incorporate the impoverished communities. Saulieu was successful in neutralizing the Castilian endeavor, but he could not oust the commendatory abbot and insure free elections at Alcobaça, the abbey on which all other houses depended. The deeply pious court in Lisbon had no intention, however, of allowing reforming efforts to be thwarted. When in 1540 King John III (1521-1557) appointed his brother, Cardinal Henry, as commendatory abbot of Alcobaça, the possibility of a general reform emerged. The first step was the elimination of commendators and their replacement by priors appointed for three years. Then, in 1564, the Cardinal began to hold chapters in Alcobaça. The creation of an independent congregation was approved in 1567 by Pius V, and confirmed in 1574 by Gregory XIII, who recognized Cardinal Henry as the "general" of the new Congregation of Alcobaça. This same Cardinal Henry was soon to become King of Portugal (1578-1580), thus ensuring the prosperity of the organization.

This Portuguese Congregation combined fourteen monasteries and followed the already familiar pattern of abolishing monastic stability and adopting triennial abbots. The Congregation never clarified its relationship with Cîteaux and in fact failed to send delegates to the General Chapter. But it remains undeniable that during the seventeenth century discipline and prosperity were successfully revived and there followed a remarkable intellectual and spiritual renewal. After the foundation of a college at Coimbra (1554) still another was organized at Alcobaça, which educated a large number of eminent theologians and scholars. The unusual religious fervor in that great abbey manifested itself by the institution of the *laus perennis,* uninterrupted divine services held in the church day and night. Between 1596 and 1756 the Congregation founded two new monasteries and four convents for reformed Cistercian nuns, called "Discalced Recollects." The magnificent Baroque reconstruction and expansion of Alcobaça was only the external expression of a truly impressive reform.

One congregation which not only remained faithful to Cîteaux but also played a decisive role in the seventeenth- and eighteenth-century history of the Order was the Congregation of Upper Germany. The secularization of many Cistercian abbeys during the Reformation had broken the lines of affiliation, and the subsequent religious wars, which had made both the holding of and attendance at General Chapters impossible, amply justified such an organization.

The initiative was taken in 1595 in the Bavarian house of Fürstenfeld, where an abbatial convention was held under the presidency of Abbot General Edmond de la Croix. The decision to organize a congregation was made in principle, but the problem of membership prevented immediate action. Although the Rhenish and Bavarian abbeys were willing to cooperate, the Swiss houses preferred to have their own separate congregation. It was only in 1618 that another abbatial convention in Salem could agree upon the structure of the new Congregation of Upper Germany (*Congregatio Superioris Germaniae*).

By the terms of its newly drafted constitution, the Congregation was to remain faithful to such basic Cistercian traditions as lifetime abbacy and monastic stability. The document vowed fidelity to the General Chapter and the abbot general. The "president" of the Congregation was to be elected at a congregational chapter and he was to enjoy the rights and powers previously exercised by the appointed vicar general; he was to visit all abbeys of the Congregation annually and in every fourth year all affiliated convents of nuns. A provincial chapter was to be held at Salem one year before and in the year after the sessions of the General Chapter, or when special circumstances might demand it. The congregational chapter, the assembly of all abbots, was to elect the delegation to be sent to the General Chapter the following year. At all abbatial elections the president of the congregation, or his commissary, was to preside. There were to be a common novitiate and a common school of philosophy and theology at Salem, the most populous abbey of the Congregation. The president was also authorized to admit new abbeys to the Congregation.

Abbot Thomas Wunn of Salem (1615-1647) was elected as the first president. Abbot General Nicolas Boucherat II approved the statutes in 1619 and the foundation of the Congregation was sanctioned at the General Chapter of 1623. The continued resistance of the Swiss abbeys

133

was broken in 1624, when Urban VIII ordered all abbeys of that country to join the new Congregation. Under the presidency of Thomas Wunn the organization grew to include twenty-six abbeys divided into four provinces, and thirty-six convents of nuns.

The Congregation of Upper Germany proved to be an effective and successful organization, insuring competent leadership, exemplary discipline and general prosperity until the dissolution in the early years of the nineteenth century. In the context of Cistercian history during the Ancien Régime, the Congregation proved to be the chief ally and support of Cîteaux in its fight against the separatist endeavors of the Strict Observance and against the proto-abbots, who were forever challenging the abbot general's authority.

Whether the regional organizations in Poland, Bohemia and Austria can be classified as "congregations" has been a matter of inconclusive debates. The General Chapter never arrived at a clear legal distinction among "vicariates," "provinces" or "congregations," and such terms were often used in the acts of the Chapter indiscriminately. If the holding of provincial chapters and the production of a particular set of regulations can be admitted as distinctive marks of a "congregation," then at least Poland and Bohemia came very close to being "congregations."

The Polish Congregation was born in 1580 at an abbatial convention in Wongrowitz under the presidency of Edmond de la Croix, representing Abbot General Nicolas Boucherat I. The fruit of the session was a set of regulations published in Cracow in 1581 under the title of *Statuta Reformationis*. These were statutes of religious reform, without proposing a legal framework for an autonomous organization. The General Chapter of 1605, however, authorized the holding of provincial chapters, which were held with some regularity. This Congregation united eventually fifteen abbeys and five convents of nuns.

The origin of the "vicariate" or "congregation" of Bohemia cannot be clearly dated, but it was listed together with Austria among similar organizations in the records of the General Chapter of 1613. Three years later a Bohemian provincial chapter was held in Prague in the presence of Abbot General Nicolas Boucherat II, passed a set of regulations and agreed to meet every fourth year. The Thirty Years' War rendered all such arrangements entirely futile, but about a dozen abbeys in Bohemia and Moravia continued to operate until the Napoleonic era.

The records of the General Chapter of 1613, 1618, 1623 and 1628 referred to an Irish "vicariate," but conditions in Ireland made all organized monastic life impossible. Some vestiges of Cistercian life did, however, survive. The "vicar" named in these documents was Paul Ragett, titular abbot of Saint Mary's Abbey in Dublin, who actually spent his days in exile in France, dying there in 1633. He was succeeded by Luke Archer, who collected a few novices, moved to Holy Cross, and assumed the abbatial title, retaining it until 1637. Meanwhile, a number of refugee monks received their education either in France or in Spain, holding themselves ready to return to Ireland as soon as possible.

After the accession of King Charles I of England in 1625, expectations for a basic change in the status of Catholics in Ireland ran high. In anticipation of greater leniency Urban VIII authorized in 1626 the formation of an Irish Cistercian "Congregation of Saint Malachy and Saint Bernard." The Congregation was to remain obedient to Cîteaux, but was entitled to hold national chapters every fifth year under an elected "president." In the same year in an even more optimistic mood, the Roman Congregation for the Propagation of the Faith encouraged Irish monks to initiate lawsuits to recover monastic property confiscated by the Crown. These sanguine hopes proved groundless. Only in 1638, on the eve of the great civil war, did the Irish Cistercians hold their first and last "national chapter," electing as "president" Patrick Plunkett, the new abbot of Saint Mary's Abbey. The acts of the chapter were approved by the Holy See in 1639 and Plunkett managed to assemble a few monks in Dublin. Monastic life was resumed at several other Irish sites as well. Cromwell's bloody invasion of the island in 1650 ended the precarious existence of Irish Cistercians and no further record exists of the Congregation's survival.

A unique place in Cistercian history should be reserved for the Feuillant Congregation. Its originator was Jean de la Barrière (1544-1600), a nobleman of the French South. In 1562, as a youth of eighteen, he was appointed commendatory abbot of Feuillant, a Cistercian abbey near Toulouse, which subsisted in a state of total moral decay. For years the young man never visited the sorry house. As a student at the University of Paris, however, he experienced a timely spiritual conversion and in 1573 joined the Cistercian Order, to become father and reformer of his depraved monks. After a few false starts, he ousted most members of the reluctant community and initiated in 1577 a life of extraordinary austerity. His heroic example attracted so many novices to Feuillant that new foundations soon became necessary.

His success resulted in wide publicity and the movement found enthusiastic echo in Rome, where in 1586 Sixtus V praised the Feuillants in glowing terms. In the next year a foundation was made in Rome under papal auspices and King Henry III of France invited the Feuillants to move to Paris. Some sixty monks, led by Bernard de Montgaillard, began a month-long procession on foot from Feuillant to the French capital, where they installed themselves in a monastery erected for them by the King himself.

The Feuillants' success and their break with many Cistercian traditions were observed at Cîteaux with apprehension. In 1592 a papal bull ordered the Abbot General to stop interfering with the reform. From that point on the Feuillant Congregation lived and functioned as an independent order, although they continued to call themselves the "Congregation of Our Lady of Feuillant of the Cistercian Order." Their new relationship with their parent order was clearly reflected in a statute of the Cistercian General Chapter of 1605, which demanded a second novitiate of Feuillants desiring to return to the old fold.

The Feuillants were strictly centralized under an elected general and triennial general chapters. Abbots of individual houses were also elected for three year terms. In 1630, largely for political reasons, the Feuillants broke into two autonomous units. About twenty-four abbeys in France retained the original name, while an even larger number of Italian houses became known as the "Reformed Bernardines."

Animated by the spirit of the Counter-Reformation, the Feuillant movement brought about a resolute revival of the strictest monastic standards. The monks went about barefooted and bareheaded; they slept on planks using stones for pillows; their diet was normally restricted to bread, water and vegetables. During Lent they lived on bread and water alone. They used no furniture, placing the dishes on the bare floor and eating in a kneeling position. They engaged in strenuous manual labor, although, since they preferred to settle in cities, the monks offered the local clergy their services as preachers.

At the Feuillant General Chapter of 1592, held in Rome, internal dissension broke into the open. Jean de la Barrière was deposed and a new general was elected. By 1595, the rigid austerity was considerably relaxed. A new diet permitted eggs, fish, milk products, oil and wine, and the monks were allowed to wear sandals and sleep on mattresses. Despite relaxations, the Feuillants retained throughout the seventeenth century a high degree of asceticism and, particularly in Italy, produced a number of eminent authors and scholars, including Cardinal Giovanni Bona, liturgist, and Bishop Carlo Giuseppe Morozzo, historian. During the eighteenth century the congregation lost much of its early vitality. Toward the end of the Old Regime the French Feuillants still held twenty-four houses, but their total membership had been reduced to 162 monks. The Revolution suppressed the Feuillants, as it did all other orders. The vacant Parisian monastery became the headquarters of the famed

Feuillant Club. In Italy the end came in 1802, under pressure from the Napoleonic government. Some years later the remaining Italian Feuillants joined the Roman Congregation of Cistercians.

The first superior of the Feuillant house in Paris, Bernard de Montgaillard (1562-1628), nicknamed "the little Feuillant," was an ardent supporter of the Catholic League and could not reconcile himself with the accession of the ex-Huguenot Henry IV. Exiled from France, in 1590 the young priest found a warm welcome in the Spanish Netherlands. With the active assistance of his admirer, Archduke Albert of Habsburg, "the Pious," he was installed in 1605 as abbot of Orval in Luxembourg, much against the will of the monks. Despite their lack of enthusiasm he was successful in restoring that ancient abbey to its original splendor, thus preparing the way for Orval's eventual merger with the Cistercian Strict Observance.

The Feuillants made no efforts to sponsor a female branch of their Congregation. On her own initiative, Marguerite de Polastron (d. 1598), founded a convent for nuns in Toulouse and in 1622, upon the insistence of Queen Anne of Austria, another convent was established in Paris. These nuns were known as the "Feuillantines."

XI

The War of Observances

 Administrative necessities as well as the desire to inaugu-
rate an effective moral recovery brought about the
organization of congregations. By the end of the sixteenth
century such movements were well under way in all countries in Europe
where Cistercians survived, except in France. Yet French Cistercians were
as much in need of reform as their confreres anywhere else. During the
sixteenth century nearly all French abbeys of the Order had come under
commendatory government, while the incessant civil war and religious
strife had caused widespread physical destruction.

It was not a lack of good will or honest effort that made meaningful
revival impossible; rather the blame lay on the chaotic political and
religious conditions that prevailed in France. The spectacular success of
the Feuillants demonstrated eloquently the vigor of recovery on a limited,
local level, but a nationwide movement could not possibly be launched
before peace had been restored under the shrewd and energetic Henry IV
(1589-1610). Then, as if the country wished to recapture the lost time, the
pent-up forces of Catholic reformation swept across the nation with
elemental intensity. Often inspired by their foreign brethren, all religious
orders underwent a thoroughgoing renewal, restoring firm controls and
strict asceticism.

French Cistercians could not be left behind by other monastic orders in
the search for effective self-reform. Fortunately, the abbatial see of
Cîteaux was occupied in succession by four eminent prelates, who spared
no labor when the issues of reform demanded resolute action. In 1570
Jérôme de la Souchière (1564-1571), previously abbot of Clairvaux, a
participant at the Council of Trent and later Cardinal (1568), issued a
comprehensive reform decree, composed in the spirit of Trent. Nicolas
Boucherat I (1571-1584), another active figure at Trent, spent much time
in visitations and inspired another set of regulations, incorporated into the
statutes of the General Chapter of 1584. Edmond de la Croix (1585-1604),
a principal advisor of his predecessors, composed a veritable code of
Cistercian reform which was presented at the General Chapter of 1601.
The time, however, was not yet ripe for the execution of so ambitious a

project; therefore the Chapter of 1605 returned to the more modest project of 1584. Finally in more auspicious circumstances, under Nicolas Boucherat II (1605-1625), the forces of reform burst into the open, giving birth to the Strict Observance.

The movement did not result directly from official initiative: it arose spontaneously from a number of young monks, who had become impatient with the slowly turning wheels of central administration at Cîteaux and whose good fortune it was to find a willing sponsor in the person of the Abbot of Clairvaux.

The beginning of the Strict Observance is usually linked for the sake of convenience with the date 1598. It was in that year that a young cleric of noble Italian ancestry, Octave Arnolfini, then only nineteen years old, was by the grace of King Henry IV appointed commendatory abbot of La Charmoye, a Cistercian house in Champagne belonging to the affiliation of Clairvaux. The pious young man felt an unusual degree of responsibility for the desolate abbey, ravaged during the preceding civil wars. He soon realized that he could not initiate reforms unless he himself became a Cistercian and thus a regular abbot. Arnolfini, therefore, retired to Clairvaux, where he completed his novitiate and made his monastic profession in 1603. That great abbey, under the wise direction of the saintly Denis Largentier (1596-1624), had survived the decades of destruction without material losses and remained an authentic school of Cistercian spirituality.

Largentier made a visitation at La Charmoye in 1605. He was so pleased with the work of Arnolfini that he entrusted to his care yet another abbey, Châtillon. During the following three years Arnolfini governed both houses, but in 1608, mindful of the irregularity of holding two benefices, he moved as regular abbot to Châtillon; at La Charmoye he was succeeded by another young monk of similar reformatory zeal, but of greater energy and ambition, Étienne Maugier.

In 1606, at the College of Saint Bernard in Paris, Arnolfini and Maugier met a nephew of the Abbot of Clairvaux, a certain Abraham Largentier. There the devout trio signed a document in which they renewed their monastic profession and expressed their inflexible determination to press for reform, particularly for the observance of the Rule of Saint Benedict without any dispensation. They closed the curious pact with a veiled threat: ". . . if our superiors, after repeated supplications, should refuse to come to accord with our proposition, . . . we are determined to bear the Cross of Christ and every tribulation, rather than to abandon our resolution." The reference to practising the Rule without dispensation clearly indicated their determination to resume perpetual

139

abstinence from meat, a usage which by that time had generally come to be regarded as the distinctive mark of reformed communities. For this reason, the small band of young Cistercians soon became known as "abstinents," while they themselves referred to all others in the Order as "ancients."

Denis Largentier sympathized completely with this young generation and, as his own contribution to their cause, installed reform-minded priors at several affiliated houses of Clairvaux, such as Cheminon and Longpont. In distant Brittany still another "daughter" of Clairvaux, Prières, joined the reform. The prior, Bernard Carpentier, converted the desolated monastery into a flourishing school of strict asceticism.

The Abbot of Clairvaux, if he wished to see the movement succeed, had to proceed with caution. In view of Clairvaux's traditional antagonism with Cîteaux, he could not risk creating the impression that Clairvaux, once again, was leading a separatist endeavor. This is why, until about 1615, he made no move to introduce perpetual abstinence at Clairvaux, and when, urged by his young admirers, he finally did so, he made it a free choice of his monks. By this time abstinence had already been introduced at eight other communities, and the new discipline obviously demanded some form of official approval.

Abbot General Nicolas Boucherat II, who concurred with Largentier in the matter, willingly granted his approval, subject to the approval of the General Chapter to be convened in 1618. The Chapter praised the reform in warm words, but the convention's main concern was the preservation of uniform discipline. Instead of granting an outright approval, therefore, the Chapter proposed a compromise solution: the whole Order was to embrace the reform in all its austerity, but, instead of perpetual abstinence throughout the whole year, the convention advocated abstinence from meat dishes only from the feast of the Exaltation of the Holy Cross (September 14) to Easter.

The proposal scarcely pleased the laggard or indifferent, and it certainly antagonized the Abstinents. Protected by their powerful supporters, the Abbots of Cîteaux and Clairvaux, they decided to cling to the practice of perpetual abstinence. Their resolution became the subject of another declaration, signed by an impressive number of Abstinents in 1622 and restating their nonnegotiable program: ". . . integral observance of the Holy Rule, namely perpetual abstinence from flesh meat and from the use of linen garments, fidelity in the established laws of fasting and silence and all other [regulations] which had been followed most faithfully from ancient times by our predecessors."

Since the problem of renewal among Cistercians was also duplicated within other monastic orders, the pious court of Louis XIII (1610-1643) decided to facilitate co-ordinated efforts by asking for the appointment of an apostolic visitor, endowed with far-reaching authority. Indeed, in order to promote the reformation of French Augustinians, Benedictines, Cluniacs and Cistercians, in 1622, Gregory XV appointed as apostolic visitor for six years, Cardinal François de La Rochefoucauld, a prominent member of the French hierarchy noted for his piety and reforming zeal.

The busy Cardinal came at once under the influence of Étienne Maugier and his uncompromising confreres and it was obviously on their advice that early in 1623 La Rochefoucauld issued a startling set of reforming "articles." Clairvaux, with all her affiliated houses in France, was to form an autonomous reform-congregation, entitled to hold separate chapters and to maintain distinct common novitiates, where all new vocations were to be educated for perpetual abstinence. The actual organization of the new congregation of "Strict Observance" was entrusted to Maugier and Arnolfini.

The revolutionary document acted like an exploding bombshell in the midst of the General Chapter which convened for a new session in May 1623. Reform-congregations had already broken up the Order elsewhere; such a schism could not be permitted in France! In a burst of indignation the Chapter fathers boldly denounced and rejected the visitor's order as "leading toward division, segregation, schism and separation, which cannot be sanctioned by any legitimate means. [Therefore] whatever was enacted in that matter . . . shall be regarded as lacking validity or effect." On the other hand, the same Chapter reversed itself in the matter of abstinence and permitted the reformers to continue that practice as long as it "did not endanger charity or the basic welfare and interest of the Order." Moreover, Boucherat assured the Cardinal privately that he would continue to support the Abstinents and promote their cause. To demonstrate his sincerity, he permitted the Abstinents to form a distinct vicariate and promptly appointed Maugier as the new vicar over all reformed houses. The General went even further and encouraged the Abstinents to hold among themselves a convention where they could legislate as they saw fit.

Such a convention took place in 1624 at the reformed abbey of Vaux-de-Cernay near Versailles. Maugier and nine other reformed superiors not only agreed upon issues of discipline but also requested from Boucherat authorization to hold annual chapters, to elect priors in their houses under commendatory abbots, to maintain separate novitiates and to provide for their own visitations. They also petitioned that no Ancient monks be transferred to reformed houses, nor Abstinents to nonreformed communities.

141

With the sole exception of the jealously guarded right to appoint conventual priors, Boucherat willingly acceded to all their demands until the next session of the General Chapter could pass final judgment of the issues. Thus, what La Rochefoucauld had demanded for an autonomous congregation, Boucherat granted to a vicariate. The notable difference was, of course, that the Abstinent vicariate was to function under the General's authority, but its future growth was by no means hindered. Had Maugier been satisfied with these generous concessions, the reform could have expanded peacefully on a voluntary basis and an embarrassing chapter of the history of the Order could have remained unwritten. This, unfortunately, was not the case.

The coincidence of several tragic events in 1624-25 gave Maugier the impression that his fledgling Strict Observance was in danger. Late in 1624 Denis Largentier died on a visit to Orval, and Boucherat died in the spring of 1625. The nearly simultaneous departure of these two stalwarts of reform undoubtedly weakened the position of the Abstinents, but soon even greater disappointments followed. Elections both at Cîteaux and Clairvaux were conducted in an overheated atmosphere. At Clairvaux, Maugier contended for the succession with the deceased Abbot's nephew, Claude Largentier. Despite La Rochefoucauld's vigorous intervention in his behalf, Maugier lost his bid, whereupon Claude Largentier expelled the Abstinents from his abbey. The reform lost Clairvaux forever. At Cîteaux the Cardinal's meddling met equal rebuff and the victorious Pierre Nivelle, though a man of erudition and wide administrative experience, was certainly not a reforming enthusiast.

Due to such circumstances the Strict Observance lost some momentum, but nothing else. Nivelle voluntarily reappointed Maugier as his vicar over the Abstinents, and the General posed no obstacles to the further spread of the movement. By 1628 the Strict Observance had already controlled fourteen monasteries and the General Chapter in the same year approved the terms of the arrangement which had been made between Boucherat and Maugier in 1624. It was also in 1628 that La Rochefoucauld's appointment as visitor expired, leaving the future of the Strict Observance in the hands of its own leaders.

The unspectacular growth of the Strict Observance, however, left many of the younger monks of the second reformed generation even more impatient than Maugier had been. The leadership shifted gradually to the shoulders of Jean Jouaud, who in 1631, at the age of only twenty-nine, became abbot of Prières. The young Abbot had made influential friends during his years of study in Paris and had become close to the circle of Richelieu's advisors in matters of religious reform. By his monastic profession he should have been a contemplative, but in fact he turned out to be a man of action and imperious will, well schooled in law and wielding the pen of a formidable pamphleteer.

This formed the background of La Rochefoucauld's unexpected reappointment late in 1632 as visitor to Cistercians for another three years. The circumstances that surrounded the reappearance of the old Cardinal are unclear, but it is not impossible that, as some contemporaries suspected, the maneuver had been engineered by the Abstinents, mobilizing their influential friends both in Rome and Paris. One thing is certain, however: dramatic events began to happen in rapid succession.

After numerous consultations with the Abstinent leaders, the Cardinal issued his new decree, in the summer of 1634, entitled "Project of a sentence for the re-establishment of regular observance in the Order of Cîteaux." The radical features of the document threw the Order into an unprecedented turmoil that kept boiling for over half a century. The wounds suffered in a relentless war of words and occasional physical violence have never completely healed.

The body of the text of La Rochefoucauld's "Sentence," consisting of thirty paragraphs, aimed at the total reorganization of the administration of the Order under the exclusive control of the Strict Observance. The most revolutionary of the drastic provisions was the suspension of the jurisdictions of the abbot general and the General Chapter. Executive authority was to be exercised by a vicar general of the reform, until the Strict Observance grew strong enough to take effective control of Cîteaux and the other principal abbeys of the Order. Houses of "Ancients" were forbidden to receive novices, while the Strict Observance was authorized to take possession of any monastery which might be open to successful reform.

Nivelle and the proto-abbots immediately registered their protest at the papal court and appealed to Louis XIII. As soon as the incident became known abroad, many Cistercian abbeys, particularly the powerful Congregation of Upper Germany, threatened secession, unless the "Sentence" were rescinded. At that moment, however, the Abstinents were firmly in the saddle and in 1635, with a military escort, La Rochefoucauld entered the Parisian College of Saint Bernard, expelled the provisor and his staff, and converted the institution into the headquarters of the reform.

As a last desperate gamble the thoroughly shaken Nivelle and his colleagues turned for help to Cardinal Richelieu. The great Minister held out the possibility of his aid and protection, but he also set as the price his own election as abbot general of the Cistercian Order. Nivelle, compensated by the bishopric of Luçon, obligingly resigned, and on November

19, 1635, a farcical election awarded the abbatial title of Cîteaux to Richelieu. He, however, failed to keep his part of the bargain. He took Jean Jouaud into his secretarial staff and began to implement La Rochefoucauld's "Sentence" with greater vigor than the old Cardinal could have ever been able to summon. Maugier was reappointed as vicar for the reform and he started in all earnestness the forcible propagation of the Strict Observance. The Ancient inhabitants of Cîteaux were cast out and in 1637 a new Abstinent community installed. Elsewhere similar measures were taken and only the limited availability of Abstinent monks curbed Maugier's zeal. Even so, until the death of Richelieu in 1642, the number of houses in the possession of the Strict Observance doubled, from fifteen to thirty and boasted an estimated population of 400 monks. Most of the newly conquered abbeys preferred peaceful surrender to fighting. In the few cases of resistance, such as at Barbery or Igny, military pressure was applied.

Maugier was not to enjoy the taste of victory for long. He died prematurely in 1637 at the College of Saint Bernard. His life-long friend, Octave Arnolfini, already in failing health, succeeded him, but himself died in 1641. From this point on, holding various titles, Jean Jouaud acted as the master of the Abstinents' destiny.

There was one issue, however, which spoiled Richelieu's Cistercian generalship. Since the validity of his election was highly doubtful for a number of reasons, he was repudiated by most foreign congregations. It was even more humiliating that the Holy See steadfastly refused to grant him the dispensations necessary for the canonical validity of his formally deficient election. The Curia's negative attitude, however, was merely a symptom of the worsening relations between Paris and Rome, poisoned by the issues of Gallicanism. In subsequent decades the warring Cistercian observances continued to exploit this diplomatic tangle with pragmatic shrewdness. Jouaud, under the false assumption that government support could be perpetuated even after the departure of Richelieu, continually sought protection and tactical advantages by invoking Gallican principles and brusquely rejecting papal attempts at mediation. The Ancients, officially the "Common Observance," on the other hand, turned for comfort habitually to Rome and put on the mantle of faithful defenders of papal rights against secular intrusion into fundamentally religious matters. The position of the Common Observance was further enhanced in Rome by the advocacy of an Italian Cistercian of great influence, Hilarion Rancati (1594-1663), abbot of Santa Croce and procurator general, a much admired papal theologian and advisor. It was Rancati who, in the last days of 1635, obtained a brief from Urban VIII condemning the seizure of the Parisian College and declaring null and void all measures of La Rochefoucauld that had deprived Cîteaux of her ancient privileges. As long as Richelieu was alive the brief could not even surface, but after his death the discovered document greatly improved the morale of the dispirited Common Observance.

Richelieu was still clinging to his ebbing life when some of the outcast members of Cîteaux began to converge on their abbey. As soon as the Cardinal's death became common knowledge more came, and on January 2, 1643, twenty-one Ancients, in the midst of the loudly protesting Abstinents, elected Claude Vaussin (1608-1670) as their new abbot. The tumultuous scene was certainly far from a legitimate election, but the person was well chosen. Vaussin, a young monk of thirty-five, was not only a highly talented member of a prominent bourgeois family of Dijon, but also the protégé of the governor of Burgundy, Henri II de Bourbon, Prince de Condé.

It was the turn of Jean Jouaud to protest, charging that according to La Rochefoucauld's "Sentence" and Richelieu's regulations, members of the Common Observance should not be elected abbots. During the ensuing and extremely complicated legal hassle Vaussin stood wisely in the background. The mastermind of the eventually successful strategy was Claude Largentier, the abbot of Clairvaux, fully supported by Rancati in Rome. The final result was a decision of the royal council on April 5, 1645, which left the issue of the validity of La Rochefoucauld's "Sentence" uncontested, but restored both active and passive rights of abbatial election to the Ancients. Accordingly, amidst all the required formalities, a new election was held at Cîteaux; on May 10, Vaussin received the unanimous vote of thirty-seven members of his observance, while the sixteen Abstinents of Cîteaux cast their ballots for Jouaud. Vaussin's victory was followed by quick royal and papal approval.

The stunned Strict Observance considered for a while the possibility of accepting a compromise, that is, the idea of an autonomous reform-congregation under the nominal authority of Vaussin; but, eventually, Jouaud's militancy prevailed. On the grounds of the validity of the much-contested "Sentence," the Strict Observance challenged the legitimacy of Vaussin's election and demanded the immediate implementation of La Rochefoucauld's regulations. The lawsuit, which dragged on for a decade, eventually reached the Parlement of Paris, but in the strife the real issues became greatly obscured by considerations of international diplomacy and the emergence of Jansenism.

In this new situation Jouaud had the upper hand. Under a new Pope, Innocent X (1644-1655), Rancati's influence was considerably eclipsed, while that of Jouaud, rose to prominence in the pious entourage of the Regent, Queen Anne of Austria. The Queen became a most resolute promoter of the Strict Observance and the fight against Jansenism gave her an excellent bargaining position in Rome: if the Pope seemed reluctant to grant the demands of the Strict Observance, she would be equally reluctant to proceed against the Jansenists.

Vaussin attempted to neutralize his opponents' advantage by utilizing the eager intervention of the great German and Swiss abbeys. They carried considerable weight in Rome, but in Paris, they were powerless. Thus, the decision of the Parlement of Paris on July 3, 1660, turned the clock back to 1634: La Rochefoucauld's "Sentence" was declared valid and ordered to be enforced. Only the Strict Observance was to enjoy the rights of receiving novices, and only the Abstinents could be elected abbots. Having expected the blow for some time, a large number of French Cistercian communities decided to submit to the reform even before 1660, and the spread of the movement accelerated under legal pressure after that date. By 1664 the number of Abstinent-controlled houses had risen to fifty-five, with a total membership of about 700 monks.

Important changes on the political horizon, however, soon convinced Vaussin that while he had lost a battle, he might still win the war. For one thing, under Pope Alexander VII (1655-1667), Rancati's influence rose to a new height. Then, early in 1661, following the death of Mazarin, the young Louis XIV took personal charge of the government. Addicted to absolutism, he looked askance at any move against established authority, and to him the harsh demands of the Strict Observance amounted to a rebellion against the Abbot General. Furthermore, the friendly attitude of the great German abbeys of the Rhineland seemed worth fostering to a monarch with one eye on French expansion eastward. Well aware of the close alliance between Vaussin and his German colleagues, Louis found it politically expedient to uphold the General's authority. Finally, with the arrival of a new French regime, the pious atmosphere of the old Queen Mother vanished; no longer the regent, and in failing health, she was rapidly losing her grip on public affairs.

It was in these circumstances that Vaussin petitioned the royal Council of State to permit the transfer of the seemingly endless feud to Rome for a papal arbitration. The decision of the Council of June 18, 1661, upheld the Parlement's verdict of the previous year, but authorized the Common Observance to appeal for final judgment to the Holy See.

The outmaneuvered Jouaud turned back to the Parlement for consolation and issued a series of vitriolic pamphlets against Vaussin and papal intervention, but he was unable to prevent the General from going to Rome and pleading the cause of the Common Observance in person. Vaussin's work in the Curia (November 1661-March 1662) proved very satisfactory. He convinced the authorities that the preservation of the Order's unity and the promotion of general reform were more important than the dominion of the Strict Observance. Consequently, a new papal brief expressly invalidated La Rochefoucauld's "Sentence," appointed a special Roman congregation for Cistercian affairs and invited representatives of both observances to participate in formulating a universally binding code of Cistercian reform.

Worsening diplomatic relations between France and Alexander VII prevented the immediate application of the terms of the brief, but in 1664 Vaussin was again ready to travel to Rome for the definitive phase of the litigation between the two observances. Jouaud, anticipating the worst, was inclined to boycott the Roman negotiations, but a convention of Abstinent abbots decided in the end to send two from their ranks to Rome to defend the Strict Observance. One was Dominique George, abbot of Val-Richer, the other was Armand-Jean le Bouthillier de Rancé (1626-1700), abbot of the newly reformed La Trappe.

This was the first appearance on the troubled scene of Rancé, the much talked-about convert to monasticism. He was chosen undoubtedly for his learning, piety and eloquence, but also for his aristocratic connections. His temper, ostentatious asceticism and inflexibility, however, were not the best assets of his cause in Rome. He instinctively assumed the role of a second Saint Bernard at the Curia, and tried to give the cardinals of the special congregation lessons in monastic spirituality and reform, although he had made his own monastic profession only a few months before leaving for Rome. Nevertheless, he did prove remarkably effective in rallying the support of a number of great personages, such as the revered Feuillant Cardinal Giovanni Bona, and Paul de Gondi, Cardinal de Retz.

The outcome of the Roman arbitration was never in doubt. Late in 1665 the bull of Cistercian reform was ready for promulgation and only the dying Anne of Austria's opposition caused a delay. Early in the next year she died and the much awaited bull was issued in the form of an apostolic constitution on April 19, 1666. Known from its opening words as the *In suprema,* it served as a code of Cistercian discipline until the French Revolution.

The document was a chapter-by-chapter interpretation of the Rule of Saint Benedict, and prescribed the same discipline for both observances, save in the matter of abstinence. The Strict Observance was to maintain perpetual abstinence; the Common Osbervance was permitted meat three

147

times weekly, except during Advent and Lent, when abstinence was to be total. More significant was the regulation of the Strict Observance as a distinct legal entity within the Order. The Pope praised the Abstinents for their zeal and exemplary discipline and expressed his best wishes for the further growth of the movement, but the Strict Observance had to be satisfied with a limited autonomy under the supervision of Cîteaux and the General Chapter. The reformed houses were to be divided into two provinces, each under an Abstinent visitor. The College of Saint Bernard was to be shared by both observances under the supervision of the General Chapter. Transfer of monks from one observance to the other was permitted only exceptionally. The most startling concession granted to the Strict Observance was the right to designate from their own ranks ten delegates to the *definitorium,* the executive committee of the General Chapter. As a final note of precaution, the Pope imposed perpetual silence on those who might ever be inclined to reopen the fight.

The papal constitution was solemnly promulgated at the General Chapter of 1667, its first session since an inconsequential convention in 1651. The reading of the document had scarcely been completed when Rancé rose and declared that the bull was the result of misinformation and deceit, issued with the sole purpose of stifling the Strict Observance. He therefore reserved to himself the right of initiating further legal steps in the matter. Rancé's protest was signed by all Abstinent participants of the Chapter.

The death of Alexander VII in the same year offered the Abstinents an opportunity of turning with their grievances to the new Pope, Clement IX (1667-1669). The petition was presented in Rome by Cardinal Retz. Intimately familiar with Cistercian affairs, however, the pontiff not only rejected the appeal, but in strong language condemned Rancé's "temerarious" attitude.

Since the *In suprema* demanded triennial Chapters, Vaussin soon engaged in such preparations for 1670. His death in the midst of these activities at Dijon on February 1, 1670 was a great loss to the cause of peace, a fact that in retrospect even his adversaries admitted. He was a man of good will and practical wisdom, always more willing to accept reasonable compromise than to fight for total victory. The champion's role in a distasteful feud had been forced upon him, but his tact and deference toward the jealous proto-abbots insured, at least among the Common Observance, an era of harmony and co-operation.

Vaussin's successor was Jean Petit (1670-1692), a doctor of canon law, a man of keen intelligence, but also of unflinching dedication to his principles, one of which was his absolute mastery over the Order. Within

148

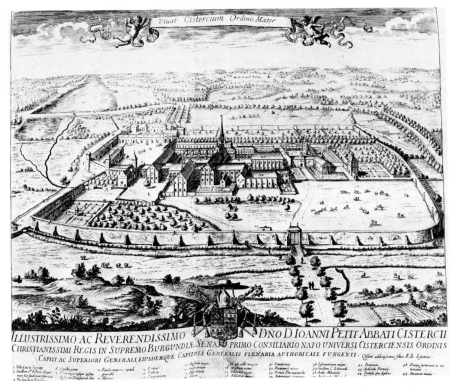

Cîteaux about 1670. Etching by P. Brissart. (Photo: H. Roger Viollet, Paris.)

A pair of windows of the church of Obazine, France. Late 12th century. (Photo: Zodiaque.)

Initial from the *Moralia in Job* (by Pope Gregory the Great) copied in Cîteaux in 1111. Original manuscript in the Municipal Library of Dijon. (Photo: Zodiaque.)

The chapter hall of Ossegg (Osek), Czechoslovakia. Late 13th century. (Photo: Vladimir Hyhlik.)

The cloister of Fontfroide, France, end of 12th century. (Photo: Caisse Nationale des Monuments Historiques, Paris.)

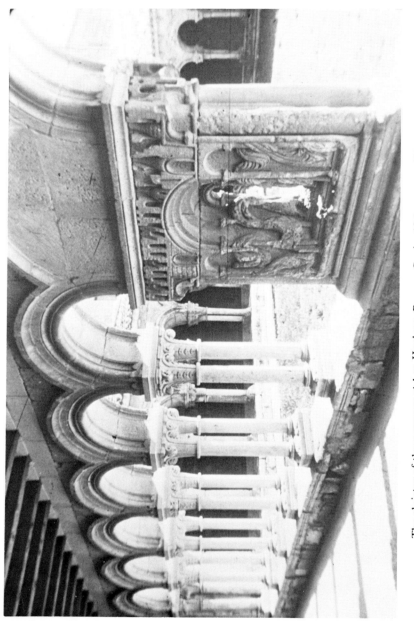

The cloister of the nunnery of Las Huelgas, Burgos, Spain. 13th century. (Photo Jürgen Eberle, Archiv P. Hermann Josef Roth.)

The refectory of Poblet, Spain. 12th century. (Photo Jürgen Eberle, Archiv P. Hermann Josef Roth.)

The monks' dormitory at Eberbach, Germany. End of 13th century.

The washing fountain at Maulbronn, Germany. 14th century.

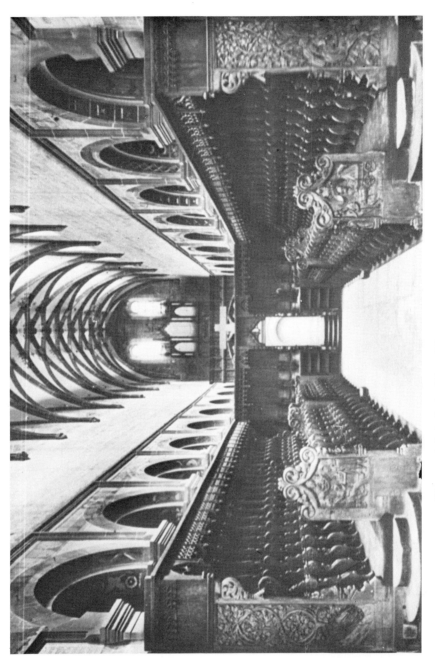

The monks' choir (stalls) at Maulbronn, Germany. 15th century.

The monumental grange barn (Lissewege) of Ter Doest, Flanders. About 1280. (Photo: Institut Belge d'Information.)

Nave of the church of Alcobaça, Portugal. 13th century. (Courtesy of Ministerio da Communicação, Lisbon.)

The ruins of the church of Rievaulx, England. 13th century. British Copyright: reproduced by permission of the Department of the Environment.

The Gothic interior of the church at Neuberg, Austria, 14th century, with Baroque
furnishings. (Photo: Kurt Woisetschlager, Archiv P. Hermann Josef Roth.)

Interior of the shrine of Vierzehnheiligen, Germany, designed by Balthasar Neumann, 1743. Erected by the abbey of Langheim. (Photo: Scala, New York-Florence.)

The interior of the new church of Mehrerau, Austria. Hans Purin, architect, 1965.
(Photo: G. Hohenems.)

one year he was engaged in combat not only with the Abstinents, but also with the proto-abbots. Although Vaussin's death had postponed the General Chapter announced for 1670, a Chapter was held in 1672. It was the stormiest ever recorded in Cistercian annals. The proto-abbots found themselves in a strange alliance with the Strict Observance, both contesting the methods by which Petit attempted to control the sessions; packing the powerful *definitorium* with his own partisans, he also reduced the ten Abstinent delegates to six. The proto-abbots and the members of the Strict Observance staged a dramatic walk-out and the Chapter broke up in disorder.

The death of Jean Jouaud in 1673 merely aggravated an already impenetrable tangle. He was undoubtedly a combative character, but his dedication to genuine Cistercian traditions could never be questioned. The leadership of the Strict Observance devolved to Rancé, whose penchant for quarrels was legendary and whose adherence to moral rigorism was a poor substitute for his lack of understanding of authentic Cistercian spirituality.

Because the Strict Observance had never enjoyed much popularity in Rome, Rancé decided late in 1673 to try another avenue for the redress of his grievances, which by then included the abortive session of the General Chapter of the previous year. He addressed an eloquent appeal to the King in person, and pledged to accept his verdict as the voice of God. His action was accompanied by the total mobilization of Rancé's numerous friends in Paris and Versailles, and by a new wave of widely circulated pamphlets. Investigation of his charges was assigned to a specially formed royal committee headed by François de Harlay de Champvallon, archbishop of Paris. Petit was in no position to match Rancé's influence in Parisian society, and a verdict in favor of the Strict Observance was expected. It was the inevitable intervention of foreign Cistercian abbeys that turned the tide and forced the King to change his mind; at this critical moment his armies were engaged in an inconclusive campaign in the Rhineland, the area of loudest protest. On April 19, 1675, the Council of State turned down the Abstinent claims, although it permitted the plaintiffs to turn to Rome if they wished to continue litigation. The Pope was now Clement X (1670-1676), the same Emilio Altieri who had served for years as head of the Roman congregation for Cistercian affairs. This alone dampened the Abstinent's hopes for success in Rome, and the issue was dropped for a time.

The Abstinents' charges and claims seemed to go on forever, but popes were only mortal. Clement was succeeded by Innocent XI (1676-1689), a saintly ascetic, who had not previously been involved in the Cistercian

149

war of observances, but who was believed to have high regard for Rancé and his much publicized success at La Trappe. After the Abbot of La Trappe had obtained several valuable briefs for his own abbey from the new Pope, the Strict Observance decided to launch a last attempt at the resuscitation of La Rochefoucauld's "Sentence." By 1677 Abstinent emissaries were hard at work in Rome. This time the authorities proved receptive and there emerged the text of a new papal bull which incorporated the major provisions of the famed "Sentence" and led the Strict Observance once again to the threshold of total victory. But papal relations with France had reached a critical stage and the Curia dared not publish the document without previously consulting Louis XIV. The papal nunciature in Paris was put in charge of the exploratory talks and by early 1679 the results were no longer secret: the King, although sympathetic toward the reform, would not permit Cîteaux's authority to be weakened by the establishment of an independent congregation. Clearly, nothing else could be done but to drop the issue completely.

Not another lawsuit, but Petit's belated wisdom eventually led to a measure of improvement in the status of the Strict Observance. After a decade of hard fighting on two fronts, he finally came to the conclusion that he could not defeat the proto-abbots without making peace with the Strict Observance. By 1683 a much delayed session of the General Chapter was imminent. In order to avoid the confrontation of 1672, Petit negotiated a reasonable settlement with the Abstinents. He assured them practical independence in the administration of their own houses, by then sixty in number, and granted to reformed abbots the right of holding annual conventions, while reserving the presidency to himself. Such conventions were to have authority over the appointment of Abstinent visitors, while complaints of whatever nature were to be turned over to a delegation of reformed abbots. Finally, Petit assured the Strict Observance that he in no way opposed the introduction of the reform where a majority of monks favored such a move.

Thus, after six decades of incessant feuding, a slowly revolving wheel returned to its original position. The accord reached between Petit and the Reform resembled very closely the agreement of 1624, negotiated between Nicolas Boucherat and Étienne Maugier. It is idle to speculate on what the fate of the movement would have been without the obstinate efforts to take Cîteaux by storm. Still, it is not entirely unwarranted to state that, had the Strict Observance applied all its material, intellectual and spiritual resources toward a peaceful penetration of the Order, rather than seeking victory through authoritarian pressure, the final results might have been more gratifying, although perhaps less spectacular.

150

Ironically, when the feuding finally came to an end, the Strict Observance was already in the process of fragmentation. The divisive factor among the ranks of the reform was chiefly Rancé's personality. During Richelieu's administration the Abstinent leadership worked out a code of reformed discipline, based largely on the "Book of Old Definitions" of 1316. This was the instrument of a remarkably well-preserved uniformity until it was challenged by Rancé and his disciples. His own regulations for La Trappe went far beyond Abstinent standards in severity, and he insisted on his right to shape the spirituality of his community any way he saw fit. After 1667 he no longer attended either the sessions of the General Chapter or the special assemblies of the Strict Observance, and he steadfastly rejected any attempt to bring his abbey into line with other reformed communities.

While Rancé's zeal and piety remain undeniable it must be pointed out that the most conspicuous characteristics of his reform at La Trappe were novelties in the history of the Order. Instead of revivifying genuine Cistercian traditions, La Trappe reflected its reformer's spiritual development and the exaggerated asceticism of seventeenth-century France. Rancé believed that monasticism was basically a form of penitential life; monasteries were like prisons, their inmates criminals, doomed to spend the rest of their lives in severe penances. The chief duty of the abbot was to create for his monks all types of humiliations and to encourage them to practice austerity even at the cost of ruining their health. The monks were never to be permitted to feel any satisfaction in their works and exercises; their proper activity was to lament their sins. The discipline of the house, menu and daily schedule were arranged accordingly. Rancé and his followers multiplied the time spent in prayers, turned to hard labor, put new emphasis on silence and banned from their table not only meat, but also fish, eggs and butter. To some extent, the heroic spirit of the first Cistercians had resurged at La Trappe, but for the wonderful vibrancy of Saint Bernard's contemplative spirit, Rancé substituted the gloom of contemporary rigorism.

The introduction of reform at Sept-Fons, another famed center of renewal, was the work of Eustache de Beaufort (1636-1709). In 1656, when he received the abbey through royal favor, he was only a youth of twenty. Somewhat reluctantly he decided to become a monk, completed his novitiate at Clairvaux, but joined the Strict Observance only in 1664, after having experienced a second "conversion." In subsequent years Beaufort was considerably influenced by Rancé, although Sept-Fons, too, developed an independent version of the Abstinent discipline.

A similar situation emerged at Tamié, where the Strict Observance was

151

introduced in 1677 by Abbot Jean-Antoine de la Forest de Somont, acting under the inspiration of Rancé. The only uncompromising disciple of Rancé among Cistercians was Charles de Bentzeradt, abbot of Orval, who sent his monks for training to La Trappe and adopted Rancé's regulations in 1674. Orval in turn managed to impose the same style of life on the communities of Conques (1697), Düsselthal (1701) and Beaupré (1710). Among all Cistercian houses only Orval and her three dependent houses gave Jansenism a firm foothold. Though Rancé enjoyed the friendship of many Jansenists, he managed to avoid involvement.

Although the Strict Observance remained until the French Revolution a principally French institution, in 1705 La Trappe revived and reformed the Italian Buonsolazzo, which in turn introduced the same observance at Casamari in 1717. The last incident of growth was the acquisition and reform by Sept-Fons of the originally Caulite (an independent contemplative congregation) Val-des-Choux in 1761. Under the new administration this ancient abbey changed its name to Val-Saint-Lieu. As happened throughout the monastic world in France during the eighteenth century, the Strict Observance lost much of its original fervor, although La Trappe and Sept-Fons remained to the end populous communities of exemplary discipline.

During the seventeenth century the Strict Observance incorporated five convents of Cistercian nuns (Maubuisson, Argensolles, Lieu-Dieu, Thorigny, Sainte-Catherine d'Angers), while the convent of Les Clairets was reformed under the tutelage of La Trappe.

Since some smaller communities changed their allegiances between the two observances several times, to give a definitive number of abbeys belonging to the Strict Observance before the Revolution is problematic. At the peak of its growth the Strict Observance included about sixty-five houses, in addition to the five nunneries.

XII

Cistercians and the Ancien Régime

 The religious fervor that animated the Strict Observance was by no means restricted to France. As soon as the century of devastating religious wars had ended with the Peace of Westphalia (1648), the spirit of Catholic renewal manifested itself throughout central and eastern Europe. This was the era of the Baroque, an era characterized by passionate pursuit of glory, grandeur and magnificence, but also by religious enthusiasm clearly expressed in the visual arts, music, mysticism, the pageantry of liturgy and popular devotion. The message of monasticism, wrapped in new forms and colors, again reached the Catholic masses. Vocations multiplied and in a number of cases the medieval cloisters became too small and confining. Most such abbeys were completely rebuilt or at least substantially remodeled. Ruined, abandoned and almost forgotten monasteries were revived and repopulated by a new generation of Cistercian pioneers.

Devastated Hungary, reconquered from the Turks, became again the homeland of four re-established abbeys within a few decades. The populous Moravian Welehrad sent new settlers first to Pástó (1702), and then to Pilis (1712). After several unsuccessful attempts, the Silesian Heinrichau acquired and rebuilt Zirc (1726), the abbey which was to become a great center of Cistercian renewal. The Austrian Heiligenkreuz took an interest in the abandoned Saint Gotthard and rekindled monastic life in its elegantly rebuilt abbey (1734).

The zeal of Polish Cistercians resulted in entirely new foundations in Lithuania. Between 1670 and 1710 three houses for monks were erected to be followed somewhat later by a convent for nuns. Several German abbeys, ruined and abandoned in the storm of the Reformation, rose to new life. Waldsassen near Regensburg was revived in 1669 by Fürstenfeld. Within a short time the reborn abbey, populated by fifty monks, became a magnificent home of Baroque art and piety.

In Flanders, under Austrian rule throughout the eighteenth century, Villers recovered completely from the wars of Louis XIV and in 1734 numbered sixty-two monks. Aulne enjoyed great prosperity in the same epoch and toward the end of the century had about eighty priests. The totally destroyed Les Dunes, resettled in Bruges, built for its large community a magnificent new abbey, today the home of the diocesan seminary.

In distant Portugal, the abbey of Alcobaça reached its apogee in the eighteenth century. Not only was the monastic plant expanded into a complex of monumental buildings, but in 1762 its population rose to 139 professed monks. The abbot enjoyed permanent membership in the Cortes and the royal council, served as the Grand Almoner of the court, and bore, among many others, the titles of "Excellency" and "Defender of the Frontiers." William Beckford (1760-1844), the noted English author and traveler, visited Alcobaça in 1794 and published a colorful description of the abbey and its surroundings. He estimated the personnel of the splendid establishment at about 400, and praised the monks' lavish hospitality, which included concerts and plays performed by the monks in the abbey's theater. But the irreverent Englishman most appreciated the exquisite cuisine, produced in a kitchen of enormous size, "the most distinguished temple of gluttony in all Europe." Alcobaça was by no means the only flourishing Cistercian center in the country: Tarouca, Salzedas and Bouro, each populated by more than fifty monks, enjoyed similar prosperity. Many abbeys in Spain, particularly the great Poblet, continued to expand throughout the eighteenth century. The Swiss Cistercian abbeys shared the success of Bavaria and the Rhineland, and only in Italy, largely for the lack of financial resources, did the process of recovery lag.

Baroque splendor and external growth were generally matched by an equally impressive moral rebirth and high degree of monastic discipline. It must be admitted, however, that the basically aristocratic civilization of the Baroque deeply penetrated the ranks of the monks. The abbots assumed, or at least emulated the social mien of neighboring princes, and the monks often succumbed to the temptation to create within the cloister the atmosphere of the château.

One of the most conspicuous manifestations of this spontaneous tendency was the passionate love of music. There were among the Cistercians a few original composers of wide reputation such as the Feuillant Lucretio Quintiani of Cremona, and Johannes Nucius (d. 1620), abbot of Himmelwitz, an accomplished follower of his Dutch contemporaries, especially Orlando di Lasso. Choir, and on some occasions even an orchestra, were regularly employed in the church, and ambitious monk-musicians found ample opportunity for displaying their talents in frequent monastic festivities. On such occasions—just as at any other aristocratic gathering—the chamber orchestra entertained the convent and invited guests during dinner. In some otherwise well-disciplined monasteries such customs prevailed without demur; elsewhere they were branded intolerable abuses. The problem was discussed at the provincial chapter of Bohemia in 1737, where the convened abbots condemned and prohibited table-music in any form on any occasion. A spokesman of this anti-musical party, the stern master of novices of Salem, Matthias Bisenberger, in 1737 wrote a scholarly study, entitled *De musica monachorum,* an extraordinary document on the subject. In describing the universal enthusiasm for music he certainly exaggerated; one bitter remark is, nevertheless, worth quoting: "At the reception of a candidate for the novitiate, he is questioned first and above all about nothing else but music. There is no allusion or inquiry regarding his education, moral qualities or studies; only, or at least principally, one question is asked: whether he knows music."

In Austria music played an important role in most Cistercian abbeys. Abbot Johann Seifried of Zwettl (1612-1625) composed and staged a successful oratorio. Later in the same century one of his successors, Caspar Bernhard (1672-1695) borrowed in his diary the words of Psalm 150: "In these days our monastery resounded with joyful and admirable music with which we praise God by choir and organ. by the merry clang of cymbals as well as by the bray of trumpets and the sound of horns." In 1768 an abbatial jubilee was the occasion of the performance of a cantata written by the monks and entitled *Applausus.* The fine work was orchestrated by the leading genius of Austrian music, Joseph Haydn.

In imitation of their aristocratic neighbors each abbey took pride in fine pieces of art and collections of historical or scientific interest. In some instances they established well-equipped physical laboratories or even astronomic observatories. A Benedictine visitor described Raitenhaslach, three years before its secularization, as a true home of arts and sciences. An art gallery included 150 paintings of famous masters. They had a richly equipped laboratory for physical experimentation, various botanical and zoological collections, and an excellent library, especially well developed in the natural sciences. Meanwhile, the guest was greatly impressed by the exemplary discipline of the forty-three monks.

At first sight this strange blend of Cistercian monastic traditions and Baroque mentality may seem grotesque or even contradictory. However, just as the Baroque taste had no objection to remodeling Gothic churches in the new style, the adjustment of monastic customs was accepted with the same natural ease and understanding. How simplicity and magnificence, poverty and munificence, discipline and relaxation could be combined in incomparable harmony at Salem, the great center of the

155

German Congregation, was ably described by Bartholomew Sedlak, secretary of the Abbot of Heinrichau. Father Bartholomew, himself a member of a rich and flourishing community, approached the abbey with prejudice and jealousy. Yet his report of 1768 accurately reflects his admiration for everything he saw and experienced. The Abbot of Salem, a highly educated and munificent patron of the arts and sciences was honored with the title of "Excellency" as the head of a territory immediately under the Emperor (*Reichsunmittelbar*). Upon his arrival the visitor was led to the refectory, where he marveled at both the splendid service and the virtuoso vocal and instrumental music played for his entertainment. Touring the magnificent building, he admired the treasury of the sacristy, especially a huge monstrance valued at 60,000 florins, the fourteen bells of the tower, and the unique collection of the library, whose librarian was well versed in seven languages. He praised the precise perfection of Gregorian chant and liturgical services, the pageantry of a solemn high mass with military parade, but he was most impressed by the edifying recollection and discipline of the monks. "There," Father Bartholomew wrote, "while I observed such an exact regular discipline, I got the impression with consolation in my heart, that I was seeing Clairvaux at the time of our Father Saint Bernard. There are seventy monks in the cloister, yet, though we passed through the corridors several times, we did not meet a single monk. This did not happen by chance; they are engrossed in their studies and the habit of solitude is ingrained in their very nature. Although the monastery is wealthy, the monks are conspicuous for great poverty. The material of their habit is cheap, they do not wear linen but only woolen under-garments. In monastic discipline they follow to the letter the reform constitution of Alexander."

The influence of the Enlightenment within German Cistercian monasteries was short-lived as well as superficial and affected only individual monks. The famous Bavarian Kaisheim furnished a chracteristic example. There, during the 1770s, the young generation of clerics came under the influence of an outstanding professor, Ulrich Mayr, a graduate of the University of Ingolstadt and an enthusiastic disciple of "enlightened" philosophy. "I am glad to be a monk," he wrote to a friend, "because I believe that his profession is to serve the ideals of Christian philosophy. He is a man living in silent solitude, far from domestic duties, surrounded by learned friends, and yet always a virtuous philanthropist; oh, how much could he contribute to the general blissfulness!" He welcomed the abolition of the Society of Jesus as well as Emperor Joseph's measures against contemplative communities, while he did his best in order to conform his monastery to "enlightened" standards. However, the opposition of the majority grew steadily and in 1785 he left Kaisheim in utter dismay for a country parish. The conservative reaction against the Enlightenment was equally strong among Cistercians throughout Bavaria; in "enlightened" circles at Würzburg they were known as "the white Jesuits."

In a survey of the history of the Order special attention must, for obvious reasons, be given to France. For one thing, half of the Cistercian abbeys that survived the Reformation were located within the borders of France. Then, too, the organs of central administration, the General Chapter and the abbot general, continued to reside at Cîteaux. There were other features as well which had set French Cistercians apart from their confreres elsewhere in Europe. The rise of the Strict Observance as a predominantly French institution has already been discussed. The persistence of the commendatory system was still another characteristic of French monastic life that had greatly reduced the beneficial results of the universal religious renewal, so spectacularly successful elsewhere. The detrimental effects of the endless feuding between the abbot general and the four proto-abbots as well as increasing government interference in the administration and legislation of the Order were felt more in France than elsewhere. Finally, the deep inroads of the Enlightenment, undermining the social position of contemplative orders, thus preparing public opinion for the events of the Revolution, were much in evidence.

Even the Strict Observance was unable to eliminate the pretensions and fiscal demands of commendatory abbots. As an eventual compromise, discipline and internal administration were entrusted to the conventual prior, appointed by monastic superiors, while the management of the abbatial estate became the right of the commendatory abbot. The crucial problem, however, had always been the division of monastic revenues. The legal usage, established early in the seventeenth century by a number of court decisions, called for a threefold partition of the net income. The first third (*mensa abbatialis*) was paid to the abbot; the second (*mensa conventualis*) was set aside for the food and clothing of a stipulated number of monks. This amount, divided among the monks, was often called "pension." The third (*tiers lot*) was reserved for the expenses of maintenance, including the repair of buildings. The terms of the division were agreed upon in a formal contract. Often, however, the abbot refused to enter into any contractual relation or he ignored its terms. In either case he continued to extract as much from the monastic estates as he could, in complete disregard of the elementary needs of the monks. Interminable litigations over such issues fill countless pages of monastic records.

157

One of the first, weightiest, and most conspicuous consequences of the commendatory system was a decline in the number of monks. In the eyes of royal appointees, who received their abbeys as material reward for a variety of services, the presence of monks had always been merely a burdensome financial liability. They did their best to reduce the number of monks to the absolute minimum; if the abbey fell victim to war or other disaster, they refused to rebuild the ruins and repopulate the convent. Even in the best case, when a contract specified the abbot's financial obligations, the number of monks and their "pensions" were set as low as possible, without any hope for growth either in membership or in economic status. The declining numbers and the fixity of personnel at a very low level by no means resulted from a general dearth of vocations, but from an unhealthy and artificial limitation, beyond the control of the Order.

Where the number of monks had already been fixed by contracts, many commendatory abbots concentrated their efforts on enforcing the admission of their own protégés to vacant places. If the candidate proved to be unacceptable to the Order, new quarrels flared up and commendators retaliated by preventing the admission of novices altogether.

In communities where "pensions" were too small, the monks themselves felt a strong inclination to keep membership low and to improve conditions from the allotments of vacant places.

In a number of houses the presence of a single monk was merely a legal formality; still more monasteries were left totally vacant, or were lost to the Order for a variety of reasons. When the General Chapter of 1667 made arrangement for the visitation of all houses in France, the list of such monasteries of both Strict and Common Observances exhibited only 149 communities, implying that about fifty houses were, for all practical purposes, vacant. By 1683 the number of monasteries to be visited had grown to 164, but the territorial growth of France was chiefly responsible for the increase.

In all justice, however, it must be pointed out that most commendators were eventually forced to contribute a portion of their revenues to the rebuilding of the physical plant, while moral recovery was effectively promoted by various agencies of the Order. In 1600, a monastery with disciplined membership, well-administered estates and fair buildings, was a rare exception; by 1700, the majority of the surviving Cistercian houses possessed at least the essentials of orderly religious life and cases of total neglect or disorder became unusual.

Where material reconstruction succeeded and the support of a sizable community was safely guaranteed, moral recovery followed almost spontaneously. Conversely, where zeal and discipline were chronically lacking, membership was generally small and poverty depressing. Because control over key economic factors lay in most cases beyond the power of the Order, uniformity was only desired but never accomplished: in the shadows of splendid abbeys of exemplary monks, small, struggling houses barely subsisted, beset by hosts of insoluble problems.

In about one-third of French houses a potent factor in the process of recovery was certainly their affiliation with the Strict Observance. The movement succeeded most spectacularly, however, in cases where the introduction of the reform was coupled with the return of regular abbots, or carried out with the full support of the commendatory abbot. The mere acquisition of a monastery by the Strict Observance rarely resulted in noticeable improvements. While it is quite possible that an "average" house of the Strict Observance stood on a higher moral and economic plain than an "average" establishment of the Common Observance, one must also consider the higher percentage of regular abbeys in the Strict Observance. At the peak of its expansion the Strict Observance united about one-third of populated French Cistercian houses, but included half the regular abbeys.

The work of restoration within the Common Observance was championed by the General Chapter and promoted by zealous visitors, but credit for its ultimate success should chiefly be given to the apostolic constitution of Alexander VII, the *In suprema* of 1666. It was on the basis of this document that, by the end of the century, a reasonable degree of regularity was achieved nearly everywhere.

Concerning matters of central administration, the recurrence of the feud between the abbots of Cîteaux and the four proto-abbots must be recognized as the key problem throughout the remainder of the Ancien Régime. When, after decades of embittered litigation, the Strict Observance was forced into submission, the proto-abbots prepared to resume their opposition to Cîteaux, only to discover that the government of Louis XIV harbored little sympathy for them. The absolutist regime could not support rebellious subjects against established authority, which, in the case of Cîteaux, entailed effective French influence over powerful foreign congregations. Thus it was that Abbot General Jean Petit (1670-1692), victorious against both the Strict Observance and his four competitors, came closest to establishing monarchical control over the Cistercian Order.

Petit's successors managed to maintain the same prominent position at the helm of the Order. Aware that the General Chapter and the *definitorium* remained the only forums where the humiliated proto-

159

abbots might air their grievances, the abbots of Cîteaux became increasingly reluctant to convene the Chapter, despite the *In suprema's* call for triennial sessions. Nicolas Larcher (1692-1712) held only one such convention in 1699. Under Edmond Perrot (1712-1727) no Chapters were held at all. Perrot, like his predecessors, leaned heavily on the support of his German colleagues in his battle against "that ancient four-headed dragon." The German spokesman, Stephan Jung (1698-1725), abbot of Salem, produced a classic expression of their stand, reviving the argument of the preceding generation. Alluding to the popular French dictum *une foi, une loi, un roi,* he wrote to Louis XV: "As we have but one God and one faith, so our Order has but one head," and added an old threat, "if no other remedy can be found in the near future, we Germans are inclined to elect a special General for Germany, a move which would gravely prejudice [the position] of the Kingdom of France."

Mounting pressure forced Andoche Pernot (1727-1748) to call a Chapter in 1738, but the crafty manipulation by which he insured the assembly's support for his policies only increased the hostility of the proto-abbots and intensified their determination to hit back at the earliest opportunity.

Meanwhile, the changing social and political climate of the eighteenth century slowly began to favor the proto-abbots. During the first half of the eighteenth century members of the French nobility, reduced by the "Sun King" to the impotent role of courtiers, staged a remarkable revival. They grasped at a larger share of political power and bolstered their ancient privileges. At the same time an increasingly popular political philosophy denounced absolutist governments and, casting an envious eye across the Channel, demanded a more representative administration with appropriate checks and balances.

As a conspicuous manifestation of such aspirations the nobility re-established its monopoly over episcopal sees and attempted to force the exempt monastic orders into submission. Exemption had been a much criticized privilege for centuries, of course, but the fact that by the eighteenth century nearly all abbots belonged to the rapidly rising, rich and influential bourgeoisie added the aspect of class war to the chronic antagonism between bishops and abbots. The substance of most assaults on the power of the abbot of Cîteaux could justly be labeled trivialities, but the obvious design of forcing the upstart commoner head of the Order back into his proper place on the social ladder rendered every clash a fight over principles.

During these quarrels, which extended over decades, the proto-abbots fought a running battle with Cîteaux over the revival and management of

160

the College of Saint Bernard of Toulouse. Larcher and his two immediate successors made repeated efforts to put new life into that decaying institution and exerted pressure upon neighboring Cistercian abbeys to support the College both morally and financially. Meanwhile, the proto-abbots never ceased to argue that the real motive behind the scheme was the General's insatiable greed for power and his selfish exploitation of monasteries.

The General Chapter of 1738 brought only a Pyrrhic victory to Abbot Pernot, for his humiliated colleagues became more determined than ever to redress their grievances. The succession to Cîteaux of François Trouvé in 1748 failed to bring reconciliation. The new General, a native of Champagne of bourgeois origin, was then a relatively young man of thirty-seven, but already doctor of the Sorbonne and prior of La Clarté-Dieu, a small monastery in the diocese of Tours. In his personality, polished manners and erudition were joined with an acute sense of his new dignity and with a firm determination to defend or even to enhance his exalted position. The new feud climaxed in a court procedure initiated by the proto-abbots before the *Grand Conseil* on March 12, 1760. During the subsequent months a flood of pamphlets and memoirs, issued by both sides, aimed at swaying the judges as well as the interested public. The proto-abbots charged that during the past forty years a "revolution," engineered by the abbots of Cîteaux, had taken place, "to cover everything by the ocean of their overwhelming power." They no longer had any use of Chapters, thus they were, in fact, "changing the form of government from an aristocratic one, based on law, into a monarchical one, where everything was in the hands of the abbot of Cîteaux." Trouvé retorted that he had repeatedly planned the convocation of a Chapter, but was either prevented by adverse circumstances, or rebuffed by the reluctant proto-abbots. Moreover, continued the General, the administration of the Order could not depend on an aristocratic "senate" convening only on rare occasions. Such an assembly, if it was to offer meaningful assistance to the abbot of Cîteaux, should be, at least potentially, always in session.

It was on March 14, 1761, that the *Grand Conseil* issued the long-awaited decision, largely in favor of the proto-abbots. It invalidated a number of decrees passed by the Chapter of 1738, together with many subsequent appointments and administrative measures made more recently by Trouvé. The same *arrêt* emphasized that all such arrangements must be made in consultation with the proto-abbots assembled in chapter. Trouvé appealed the verdict immediately, turning directly to the King, but it was obvious that the convocation of the General Chapter could not be

161

deferred much longer. In the changed circumstances, however, a Chapter offered more advantages to the proto-abbots than to Cîteaux.

After lengthy preparations the General Chapter opened on May 5, 1765, in the presence of Antoine-Jean Amelot de Chaillou, intendant of Burgundy, representative of the royal government. The session was attended by sixty voting members, almost equally divided between the two parties. Most French abbots supported the proto-abbots, while the foreigners, particularly the Germans, lined up solidly behind the General.

Before anything of substance could be discussed, however, there emerged again the problems of the composition and authority of the *definitorium*. Since the proto-abbots could easily control it, Trouvé insisted on the pre-eminence of the plenary session of the Chapter. After a few days of futile wrangling, the General Chapter broke up in disorder, much as it had in 1672.

Both contesting parties turned to the Parlement of Dijon for justification. When that court, under German pressure, decided the pending issues in favor of Trouvé, the proto-abbots appealed the case to the royal council. At this juncture (1766), however, a "Commission of Regulars" was established under royal auspices, headed by Étienne-Charles de Loménie de Brienne, archbishop of Toulouse. Henceforth all outstanding problems were to be solved through the mediation of this body of Church and state officials.

The initially stated purpose of the Commission was the reform of religious orders; its specific scope and instruments were spelled out only later in a series of royal decrees. These regulations went into great detail on the determination of the age and other qualifications of candidates, the organization of novitiates and a variety of disciplinary and administrative matters. The most significant points of the reform were the demand for the revision and new edition of monastic constitutions and the setting of a minimum membership for each house. Obviously, this last requirement could be met only by reducing the number of smaller communities; moreover, in the event that even such drastic measures failed to bring about the desired improvements, the secularization of whole orders was projected. Indeed, during the term of the Commission, more than 450 religious houses were closed and nine entire orders secularized.

Endlessly repeated solemn assurances that the Commission's sole intention was to promote a healthy reform and thus the welfare of the Church did not silence the critics and disarm active opposition. The fact that the noisiest agitators for reform turned out to be the same individuals who engineered the expulsion of the Jesuits corroborated the suspicions of those who firmly believed that the new organization was in reality an instrument of the destruction of monasticism. Unfortunately, the character and personality of Loménie de Brienne could hardly guarantee the honest execution of his Commission's purported aims. Not only was his private life much below the minimum standards set for ecclesiastics, but even his belief in the existence of God was widely questioned.

The Commission tried with remarkable flexibility to cope with the problems of each order. In the case of the Cistercian Order the tactics of the Commission were particularly refined. Brienne merely exploited the current feud between the antagonistic parties of Cîteaux and the proto-abbots. It was commonly admitted that a settlement could best be realized by a revision of the constitution of the Order. In the strict sense of the word, there was no up-to-date constitution. The document that came closest to it was the brief *In suprema* of 1666 issued by Alexander VII, which, though comprehensive in nature, concerned itself primarily with the problem of observances. A systematic collection of laws had always been planned, but never achieved. Thus, the main purpose of the Commission, constitutional reform, was not to be achieved by external force, but with the full co-operation of both parties, simply by guiding the activity of the General Chapter in this desired direction. Since individual points of the projected reform could just as easily be incorporated in the new constitution, the Order was under no pressure to comply with isolated demands; even the suppression of small communities was deferred until the final ratification of the new constitution.

The General Chapter of 1768 was dedicated entirely to the preliminaries of constitutional reform. Among the fifty-four voting members the General's party had a clear majority. The session was dominated, however, by two royal commissioners, the already mentioned Amelot de Chaillou and Jean-Armand de Roquelaure, bishop of Senlis, both acting under the instructions they received from Brienne. Since Brienne's intention was the democratization of the Order's government by granting greater influence to the proto-abbots, Trouvé's party was not destined to prevail.

The session opened on May 2, with the circulation of a questionnaire of one hundred questions prepared by the Commission of Regulars and dealing with the government of the Order. Brienne evidently anticipated a wide variety of answers, but the process merely resulted in two sets of answers split along strictly partisan lines: thirty-one favored the General's position, twenty-three that of the proto-abbots. Since no compromise could be achieved during five subsequent days of heated argument, the drafting of a preliminary text was entrusted to an abbatial committee representing both parties.

163

After three years of work the committee was predictably unable to iron out the differences and as a result not one but two proposed constitutions emerged. Debate over the conflicting texts and a possible decision in the complex matter were to be the tasks of the General Chapter of 1771, held from September 2 to October 2, the longest session ever recorded. In the body of sixty-four voting participants the General's party had again a commanding lead, thanks to the presence of twenty-three foreign abbots. In spite of Roquelaure's constant intervention, the inevitable result was a constitution representing Trouvé's views, therefore entirely unacceptable to Brienne.

The next move was the appointment of a subcommittee composed of four members of the Commission of Regulars, to be in charge of producing the elusive compromise text, which might be acceptable to all parties concerned. The task was all but impossible and, in fact, the key issues remained undecided for over a decade.

The break in the deadlock came with the tragic events in the Empire that isolated Trouvé from his faithful German supporters and gave a decisive advantage to the party of the proto-abbots. While the French campaign against the monks gradually abated, the imperial government launched a devastating attack against the rich and powerful abbeys within its sphere of influence. The wealth of "useless" monasteries presented a temptation which "enlightened" despots found hard to resist. Corresponding with foreign superiors, sending funds abroad, and attending chapters beyond the borders had been made increasingly difficult even during the last years of the deeply religious Maria Theresa; her son and successor, Joseph II, struck a mortal blow. An imperial decree of January 12, 1782, dissolved all monastic establishments which did not directly serve the public interest. During the subsequent years nearly all Cistercian abbeys within the Habsburg lands were secularized. Those few which managed to survive were paralyzed by constant fear. In such an atmosphere the issues of a new constitution or the victory of Trouvé over his opponents became suddenly irrelevant. The last two sessions of the General Chapter before the Revolution were attended almost exclusively by French abbots. They still exhibited a surprising degree of vitality, but they labored under the heavy clouds of impending doom.

Since, in the changed circumstances, the opposition of powerful foreign abbots could safely be ignored, the subcommittee produced the long-awaited text of a new consitution, deciding all issues in favor of the proto-abbots. The new document covered only the legislative and administrative organs of the Order and deferred matters of discipline and liturgy to a later date. The constitutional draft contained the following basic provisions: future General Chapters were to be held every third year and were to begin each time on the same date: the Monday of the fourth week after Easter. The General was to issue his *indictio* at least three months before the opening of the session. If he failed to do so, all persons entitled to participate were to come directly to Cîteaux even without invitation. If the General was found unable to preside, his role was to be taken by the senior abbot among those present. Titular abbots (*in partibus*) were expressly barred from active participation. In forming the *definitorium* the general was permitted to reject only one of five nominees presented by each of the four proto-abbots. Every issue not decided by unanimous vote in the Chapter was to be transferred to the *definitorium*. Over the word of that body the General Chapter was allowed only a feeble veto, which could in turn be overruled by the definitors. In the years immediately following the triennial sessions of the General Chapter, intermediate chapters were to be held with the participation of the general, the proto-abbots, visitors, heads of congregations, and the two procurators general. This body, however, could pass only emergency regulations to be accepted or rejected by the next General Chapter. The abbot general was granted direct jurisdiction only over the houses of the filiation of Cîteaux; each of the proto-abbots was to enjoy the same authority over his own daughters, without the intervention of the general. This authority included not only the right of visitation but also that of the appointment of priors and other officials in houses *in commendam*. The same document set the minimum membership for each monastery at nine monks, including the local superior. Concerning the exploitation of monastic estates, the sale of property, taxes and other financial contributions, loans and similar matters of fiscal administration, various bureaus of the royal government were to enjoy a supervisory authority which often included even a final veto.

The text of the constitution was presented at the General Chapter of 1783, dominated by five royal commissioners. The thirty-eight participants, with only four Germans among them, had no other choice than to accept the proposed text, although they did suggest a number of modifications. The General and his few faithful adherents expressed their displeasure by passive resistance.

After a number of last minute corrections the Chapter of 1786 agreed upon a final text. The legal validity of the new constitution obviously depended on royal and papal sanctions, but this momentous document of Cistercian history never received the approval of these authorities. The doomed royal government no longer had the time and interest to devote to such issues.

Was this constitution a viable piece of legislation? Its practical value was never tested. Conclusive judgment of its merits will always remain problematic; that the passing of this signal landmark coincided with the nearly total extinction of the Order in the storm of the Revolution was certainly a tragic irony of fate.

The pressure for constitutional reform was by no means the only concern of the Commission of Regulars. The search for evidence which would support plans for a comprehensive reform of all religious orders necessitated the gathering of statistical data as well as reliable information on the condition of all such institutions throughout the country. On the basis of this remarkable source material the researcher may draw a comprehensive picture of the Cistercian Order in France on the eve of the Revolution.

Within the political borders of pre-Revolutionary France there were altogether 237 Cistercian institutions, including 9 titular priories and 3 colleges. Only 35 abbeys were governed by Cistercian regular abbots, all the others were *in commendam.*

The determination of the exact number of monastic personnel is far more difficult. Such data, although plentiful, proved to be unreliable. The most likely total figure must have been between 1,800 and 1,900, which leaves, as an average, eight monks per institution. These figures remained remarkably steady throughout the eighteenth century, unchanged even by the count of the Revolutionary authorities in 1790. In many instances individual communities were too small for meaningful monastic life. The fundamental reason for this certainly deplorable situation was not the dearth of vocations, however, but diminutive revenues, which made the support of larger numbers impossible.

The real-estate value of Cistercian abbeys was certainly great, but, contrary to later Revolutionary propaganda, the expendable revenues were in most cases modest. Clairvaux was by far the wealthiest, having an income of about 100,000 *livres* annually. But Clairvaux was also the most populous, with fifty to sixty professed members to be fed and clothed. Most communities seem to have learned to live within their means, for the records are silent about unmanageable debts.

According to the same reports, nearly all abbeys were in good physical condition; many had been rebuilt or remodeled during the eighteenth century. The Baroque splendor of German monasteries, however, had very few imitators in France. The bankruptcy of Châlis, brought on by an overly ambitious building project early in the century, might have served as a deterrent. The vast additions to Cîteaux and Clairvaux, while monumental, were austere in comparison with Ebrach or Fürstenfeld.

The Commission of Regulars encouraged all French bishops to report on the moral condition of abbeys within their dioceses, but relevant comments are few. Only 67 Cistercian establishments received such episcopal attention, of which 32 were objects of unqualified praises; many others were dismissed as "useless." Only 17 houses were rebuked for alleged irregularities or scandals, but 10 of these were located in only two dioceses, whose bishops were notorious enemies of monks.

Although the voluminous records are open to varying interpretations, it remains obvious that monastic orders were unpopular with a considerable segment of the hierarchy and stood under fire by the same group of "enlightened" intellectuals who had brought about the destruction of the Jesuits. It seems, however, that charges of decay were intended merely to justify attacks, the real targets of which were not abuses, but the very existence of monasticism. In the judgment of "enlightened" critics that medieval institution was simply unfit for a society about to be radically refashioned. They were certainly correct in pointing out that many religious communities had failed to live up to their ancient ideals, but the same attackers failed to realize that their society did not offer the same congenial and sympathetic surrounding to monasticism as had that of the twelfth century. No religious organization could maintain indefinitely standards which had long been discarded by society. The impatient builders of a new world viewed even well-disciplined houses as useless relics of the past, hopelessly stagnant and unenlightened, standing in the path of progress, and therefore destined for removal.

Most French Cistercian houses in the late eighteenth century were not consumed by moral decay, but they failed to adapt themselves in time to the new ideals of a rapidly changing world. Modern authors who portray monasticism before the Revolution as an institution in a state of progressive decline suffer under the same illusion as the passenger sitting in a fast moving railroad car—watching the telegraph poles falling behind.

XIII

On the Verge of Extinction

Towards the middle of the eighteenth century religious orders found themselves in an ambiguous position. They still enjoyed the support of the tradition-bound and basically devout masses, but they were exposed to the shrill criticism of "enlightened" intellectuals, who scrutinized every institution of the past in the light of social utility. As long as anti-religious propaganda was restricted to the erudite elite, monastic orders were in no immediate danger. The threat, however, became very real when the "enlightened despots," among them Joseph II, took up the cry and turned against the monks.

The leaders of contemplative orders, Cistercians among them, took alarm and attempted to insure the survival of their organizations by engaging the monks in activities of demonstrable social significance. An increasing amount of pastoral work, shared by a large number of Cistercian abbeys, was the most natural manifestation of the trend. Those abbeys with a sufficiently instructed membership became interested in teaching, long considered a legitimate field of monastic activity.

Of the eighteenth-century educational efforts, probably the earliest but certainly the most successful was the school established at the Silesian Rauden under the inspiration of the "enlightened" government of Frederick II. In 1743, during the War of Austrian Succession, when the province was cut off from other centers of learning, the abbey opened a Latin school which soon developed into a full-scale institution of secondary education, or gymnasium. The number of students, mostly boarders, grew rapidly and by 1788 the monastery housed 243 pupils. Teaching was free; for board a small fee was charged. The school enjoyed a country-wide reputation and survived the abbey's dissolution in 1810. During the sixty-seven years of Cistercian administration this school graduated 2,000 students of whom one-fourth became priests.

The suppression of the Society of Jesus in 1773 left innumerable educational institutions unattended. The crisis presented an opportunity to a number of Cistercian communities willing to step into the breach and save the abandoned gymnasiums. Such was the case at the Bavarian

168

Gotteszell, where shortly after 1773 the monks took over the formerly Jesuit school of Burghausen. Identical circumstances persuaded the Hungarian monks of Pásztó to accept the Jesuit gymnasium of Eger in 1776. Their example was followed by the other abbeys of the country, and their reputation as a "teaching order" was firmly established.

The General Chapter of Cîteaux, prompted by demands from the Commission of Regulars, took an interest in various schemes, all designed to prove the "usefulness" of the Order. It was, however, during the General Chapter of 1786 that an impressive plan emerged aimed at a threefold objective, based on a substantial reorganization of the College of Saint Bernard in Paris. The curriculum as well as the teaching staff and student body of that institution were to be expanded; the threat of supression of depopulated houses was to be averted by the transference of their revenues to the college; and, in order to prove the social usefulness of the Order, a number of free boarding schools were to be established, staffed by teachers trained at the Parisian institution.

The proposal, made by the provisor of the College, Jacques François Frennelet, was well received and Abbot General Trouvé referred the examination of its details to a committee, appropriately named "bureau of utility." The project, however, was not entirely new. The organization of boarding schools had originally been proposed some time earlier by Antoine Chautan, abbot of Morimond, who at that same session of the General Chapter declared his readiness to open at once three such institutions within his own affiliation in France, each for twenty boys over the age of nine, chosen "from the ranks of nobility and poor but deserving commoners," who were to be educated free of charge.

In subsequent discussions Antoine Desvignes de la Cerve, abbot of La Ferté, emphasized that the courses offered at the Parisian college should include moral theology, so that monks could be made more effective in pastoral assistance when their services were requested. It was probably the same Abbot of La Ferté who also proposed that at the College of Saint Bernard in Paris fifteen scholarships be founded in perpetuity, each worth 100 *pistoles* (1 *pistole* = 10 *livres tournois*), financed from the revenues of small houses to be united with that college. The grantees were to be chosen from among members of poor monasteries, while richer houses were expected to send to Paris additional students supported from their own funds. The General not only approved the project but also disclosed that he had already singled out two houses to be united with the college in Paris, although the records of the Chapter do not contain the actual names of the monasteries. At the same time the administrators of the College were authorized to negotiate a loan of 100,000 *livres* for the

169

necessary remodeling and enlargement of the buildings, and only the events of 1789 prevented the beginnings of construction.

The repeated blows directed against contemplative communities fell first within the Habsburg possessions. In 1782 Joseph II (1780-1790) ordered the closing of all religious institutions which he considered "useless." The operation of parishes was not accepted as grounds for exception. The majority of Cistercian abbeys fell victim to the imperial decree and only those houses managed to escape where the execution of the law had not been completed before the premature death of the Emperor. Such was the case in Belgium, where fierce local resistance slowed down the impatient authorities. Thus, the fourteen abbeys and thirty-nine nunneries of the Order had their lives extended for another decade, only to be consumed in the conflagration of the Revolution. For it was in France that the forces of destruction gathered momentum, ready to strike a mortal blow at monasticism not only within the borders of that country, but everywhere else in continental Europe, along the path of Napoleon's victorious armies.

The tragic chain of events began with the changing of the rules for the election of the delegates destined to represent the "first estate," the clergy, at the Estates General of May 1789. Louis XVI, to please the secular clergy, declared that at local electoral assemblies *curés* were to cast ballots individually, whereas each monastery was entitled to only one representative and one vote. The result was inevitable: out of 296 deputies to the First Estate only twenty-three individuals represented abbeys, and even this very modest number was made up mostly by commendatory abbots whose knowledge of and interest in monastic affairs was extremely limited. Among regular delegates the only Cistercian was Claude-François Verguet, prior of Relecq, originally professed monk of Cîteaux, who represented the diocese of Saint-Pol-de-Léon. When in June the majority of parish priests decided to merge with the Third Estate, the long simmering "revolt of the *curés*" came to a climactic end, and with it disappeared the French clergy as a separate entity. In the new National Assembly religious orders had virtually no representation, very few friends and, as the Assembly continued to shift toward the left, a growing number of resolute enemies.

The frightful news of the bloody events of July 14 which led to the destruction of the Bastille reverberated throughout the country and caused the "great fear," which was followed by widespread violence against the properties and homes of the privileged classes. Many abbeys shared the fate of the châteaux of the nobility. It seems, however, that relatively few Cistercian houses were attacked, and even in those the fury of the peasant mobs was directed against the monastic archives, which were supposed to hold the documents related to feudal dues and obligations.

The Assembly, acting under the pressure of the alarming conditions throughout the country, on August 4 and the subsequent days precipitated the abolition of all privileges of the clergy and nobility, including services, rents, tithes and all other sources of income of "feudal" origin. Hope for compensation and provision for the maintenance of religious institutions was repeatedly expressed, but no such action was taken. Monasteries began to feel the results immediately. For lack of funds Sept-Fons was compelled to dismiss fifteen of thirty-six novices in August; in November another group left and by February of 1790 only two novices remained in the house.

The unabated financial crisis furnished justification for the Assembly's resolution of November 2, which declared all goods and properties of the Church in France to be "at the disposal of the Nation." Before any orderly procedure for the confiscation could be worked out, however, the peasants felt free to help themselves to whatever they could find on monastic estates. Although the forests were designated to be taken over by the state, such properties became the prime targets of despoliation, for timber could always be converted to ready cash. Meanwhile monasteries were exposed to continuous harassment and vexation by self-appointed local committees. Monks who had always had something to share with the poor of the neighborhood began to suffer hunger and extreme privations themselves. By the spring of 1790 conditions in many monasteries had become well-nigh intolerable. In March a group of abbeys in Champagne, among them Cheminon, Trois-Fontaines, Montier, Haute-Fontaine, Boulancourt and Ecurey, addressed a moving letter to the president of the Assembly, saying that if "he in his wisdom could find no means to remedy the conditions, he should set promptly a date for the evacuation of the houses, or else the religious would be forced to abandon the monasteries, just to save their lives."

The organ of the National Assembly dealing with the religious orders was the *Comité Ecclésiastique*, established in August 1789. It was made up of fifteen legislators, mostly laymen, and was dominated by the *rapporteur*, Jean-Baptiste Treilhard (1742-1810), a hard working but freethinking lawyer, a future regicide and Napoleonic count. His religious convictions became abundantly clear through his key role in the legislation against monastic orders and in his influence in the drawing up of the Civil Constitution of the Clergy.

An excuse for direct intervention in monastic affairs was furnished by thirteen disgruntled Cluniacs of the Parisian Saint-Martin-des-Champs, who on September 25 presented a letter to the Assembly offering their house to the Nation in exchange for annual pensions, and who expressed "their desire for liberty, which they wished to enjoy like other Frenchmen." On October 28 the Assembly responded by suspending monastic professions.

After the decision of November 2, it was understood that the sale of ecclesiastical property should start with the secularization of monasteries. Accordingly, the matter was referred to the Ecclesiastical Committee, where Treilhard took the initiative. On December 17, 1789, he presented a step-by-step project for the abolition of monastic orders, although a strong opposition prevented the further discussion of the matter. The decision was only postponed, however, until Treilhard managed to pack his Committee with similar minded anti-clericals. Thus on February 11- 12, 1790, after a spirited debate, the blow fell. Pleas in behalf of the Carthusians, La Trappe and Sept-Fons were brushed aside; in fact, he text of the final decree exceeded in its severity Treilhard's original propositions. According to its terms monastic professions were definitely prohibited and all monks were to be questioned on their intentions. For those who chose to leave the monasteries a pension was promised, although its amount, ranging from 700 to 1,200 *livres,* was only later determined. For those who decided to continue monastic life certain "houses of union" were to be reserved, but on this matter no further details were disclosed. In March all religious houses were ordered to report their membership by names and ages; in April inventories were taken by municipal authorities and the administration of monastic property was transmitted to the state; in May the monks' individual declarations on their plans for the future were recorded by local magistrates. Although the majority of the religious chose to accept the pensions, many others remained undecided. Therefore, in November, further interrogations were held. By then the prospects for the continuation of a meaningful monastic life had been reduced so drastically that very few volunteered to join the "houses of union." These sorry institutions did not prove to be viable. In fact, a law passed on August 4, 1792, declared that all remaining religious houses were to be closed by October 1 of the same year, with the exception of communities affiliated with hospitals and similar charitable institutions. A few days later the wearing of religious habits or uniforms was prohibited.

Unlike the dissolution of English monasticism in the sixteenth century, the suppression by the French National Assembly never attempted to proffer widespread monastic corruption as a reason for secularization. The forces that finally triumphed against the monks were in no way provoked by the misdeeds of individuals or communities; they arose out of principle and directed their fury not against abuses, but against monasticism as an ideal, as a way of life. In the eyes of "enlightened" reformers monasticism stood as a symbol of medieval darkness and hopeless immobility, and was therefore destined for removal if progress was to be achieved. During the decisive debate in the Assembly on February 12, 1790, Barnave declared with brutal frankness: "The religious orders are incompatible with the social order and public welfare: you must destroy them all, without restrictions." Pétion, speaking in the same vein, was certainly not motivated by the supposedly decaying condition of monasteries when he added the warning that "the preservation of some would prepare the rebirth of all."

The sale of monastic property began late in 1790 and was continued and completed during the course of 1791. The unfortunate monks could not even enjoy their pensions for long. Payment was soon tied to taking the oath on the Civil Constitution of the Clergy. The ex-religious who refused to obey the law not only lost their pensions but also became "suspects" exposed to an ever-intensified persecution.

The technicalities of dissolution and the sale of monastic property were carried out by local officials according to instructions received from Paris. At Cîteaux inventories were taken and the monks were questioned concerning their future plans in May 1790. The old and much troubled Abbot General, François Trouvé, bravely announced that he wanted to "live and die as religious." His example was followed by the actual and retired priors. Eleven other monks and lay-brothers made similar declarations with the restriction that their preference for monastic life referred to Cîteaux alone. Twenty-nine mostly young monks were willing to exchange monastic life for pensions; two others made their decisions conditionally.

Most monks left the abbey in September, and in January 1791, the remaining few had to depart, for the sale of the abbey was already in progress. The conventual buildings with the immediately adjacent 800 hectares of land were sold on March 24 for the total of 482,000 *livres*. Looting was so widespread both before and after that date that the worried authorities requested help from the army. Indeed, a company of artillery was finally dispatched from Auxonne to the scene under the command of a young lieutenant named Napoleon Bonaparte.

The octogenarian Abbot General Trouvé was one of the last monks to leave Cîteaux. In his last communications with foreign Cistercians he authorized his vicars in Germany and Belgium to conduct the affairs of the Order in their respective countries with full responsibility. On April 1, 1792, he delegated his powers as abbot general to the Roman procurator of the Order, Alanus Bagatti, abbot of Santa Croce. This document was already dated at Vosne, where Trouvé lived in retirement in the house of a nephew. It was at the same Vosne, near Cîteaux, that the General died in 1797.

The same procedures were carried out at about the same time in every abbey of the Order in France. The surviving documents, particularly the monks' declarations concerning their intentions of remaining monks or accepting the pensions, turned out to have great significance.

In trying to prove the generally low morale of the monks of the time, historians have pointed out again and again that in 1790 the vast majority of monks willingly exchanged cloistered life for pensions and the freedom to settle down elsewhere. Such conclusions, however, reveal a complete misunderstanding of the situation in which the monks found themselves. When in May 1790 they were forced to choose between the continuation of monastic life and pensions, the former was no longer a possibility. The dissolution of monastic orders had already been decreed. The only apparent alternative was volunteering to join the "houses of union," where the monks of various communities were to be crowded together until their extinction. At that juncture, however, neither the location, nor the rules, regulations and other details concerning these new houses had been specified, and, in fact, the monks had every reason to believe that they would resemble prisons or poorhouses more than monasteries.

Furthermore, common sense dictated the acceptance of pensions, which was by no means a breach of their vows. Monastic vows did not, in a legal sense, demand a lifelong dedication to an abstract ideal, not even adherence to a particular mode of conduct, but stability to a specific monastery and obedience to a legitimate superior. Since early in 1790 the secularization of houses and communities had already been resolved, the legal bonds between the abbeys and individual monks had also been broken, freeing the monks to choose among reasonable alternatives. If their choice was unheroic, it was not a betrayal of vows, and certainly not an apostasy.

An unbiased examination of the documents shows the picture of hundreds of deeply disturbed, confused and perplexed human beings in an anguished attempt to balance the demands of their consciences against the dictates of common sense. The carefree, who jumped at the occasion and accepted pensions without a second thought, were the exception, as were those who unconditionally decided to continue monastic life. As the fabric of the Order began to disintegrate, individuals emerged with countless problems and anxieties clearly expressed in their declarations. Most of those inclined to leave the monastery and accept the pension took pains to give reasons for their move, while the vast majority of those who chose to remain religious promised to stay only under certain circumstances. A considerable number of monks simply refused to choose at all, claiming that they could not distinctly see the alternatives. This multiplicity of answers renders generalization scarcely possible and any attempt to tabulate the substance of the declarations by reducing them to simple formulas is misleading.

Shortly after the expulsion of the monks the persecution of priests who refused to take the oath of allegiance to the Civil Constitution of the Clergy broke out everywhere with increasing cruelty. According to information given us by the Abbot of Wettingen (Switzerland), only about one-third of the former Cistercians obeyed the law. For the majority, there was no other choice but to escape abroad or to face imprisonment, deportation or even death. Exact records are not available concerning their further trials; beyond doubt, large contingents found temporary homes in Cistercian houses in the Netherlands, Germany, Switzerland and in the Papal States, but many of them died in the inhuman conditions of French prison camps or the penal colony of French Guiana.

The refugees could not count on the lasting hospitality of their foreign brethren. The victorious French troops soon invaded the surrounding countries, propagating their revolutionary doctrines by force of arms. The Netherlands, their first victim, was treated with special severity. Monasteries were visited, detailed inventories taken, abbeys arbitrarily taxed and the religious incessantly molested. Finally, the laws of 1796 decreed that all monastic goods be confiscated. Here again refusal to take the loyalty oath to the revolutionary constitution became a pretext for the persecution of priests. Moreover, in retaliation against widespread resistance, a decree of 1798 sentenced the entire Flemish clergy to deportation. The decree was only partly carried out, but hundreds fell victim to the tyranny, among them thirty-seven Cistercians.

French penetration of Italy brought destruction to most monastic establishments there. Legal procedures against the monks differed from state to state, but the French armies respected no rights or privileges. At some abbeys looting was aggravated by murder. At Casamari, six monks were killed in 1799 while trying to save the Blessed Sacrament from profanation. Between 1806 and 1808 most still surviving monasteries were suppressed by decree.

After the establishment of the French-sponsored Helvetic Republic in Switzerland (1798), monastic property came under government control and the reception of novices was prohibited. The three Cistercian abbeys, however, escaped formal suppression. Moreover, after the secularization of German abbeys in 1803, the completely isolated Wettingen, Hauterive and Saint Urban formed an independent Swiss Cistercian Congregation, which also included eleven convents for Cistercian nuns. The three abbeys alternated in leading the new organization by electing an "abbot general" for three years. Pius VII approved its Constitution in 1806, but the life of the Congregation remained precarious. After the Napoleonic wars an increasingly liberal Swiss government resumed anti-clerical legislation. In 1830 prohibiton against the reception of novices was renewed and monastic property again came under supervision. The suppression of Wettingen came in 1841, followed by the secularization of Hauterive and Saint Urban in 1848.

The prosperous Congregation of Upper Germany was consumed by the greed of German princes. The Peace of Lunéville (1801) imposed upon them by Napoleon took away their possessions on the left bank of the Rhine, but authorized them to seek compensation by absorbing ecclesiastical property. The general secularization became law in 1803, sanctioning the confiscation of all monastic goods and providing only a small pension to the ejected monks. The decree was not executed immediately in all German states, however. In Prussia the blow fell only in 1810; in Austria, where Joseph II had not left much to be secularized, the few surviving abbeys continued in existence. Within a few years, however, forty-six Cistercian monasteries and eighty-three nunneries had been expropriated throughout Germany. The fabulous wealth of the great churches, priceless objects of art and whole libraries were sold or squandered, while the buildings were either demolished or converted to secular purposes.

After the final dismemberment of Poland (1795) both the Russian and Prussian authorities suppressed the Cistercian abbeys within their respective territories and only two Polish houses survived under Austrian control.

The fortunes of the three Lithuanian monasteries revealed a rather peculiar development. After the partition of Poland, religious orders under the Russian regime became entirely isolated and in 1803 Benedictines and Cistercians formed a united Congregation which the Camaldolesians and Carthusians also later joined. The whole group consisted of eight monasteries headed by a president elected for a three-year term. In 1832, after crushing the Polish insurrection of 1830-31, the Russian government abolished the orders in Lithuania; only the Cistercian house of Kimbarowka survived, but the acceptance of novices was forbidden. This monastery, too, was suppressed in 1842; however, the monks were permitted to stay there until 1864, when in reprisal for a new Polish revolt, the Orthodox Church took over the property and the last prior and his seven monks were deported to Siberia.

The fate of monastic establishments in Spain hung in the balance of the chaotic political conditions following the French invasion in 1808. King Ferdinand VII, who had just ascended the throne through a revolution, was deposed by Napoleon and was promptly replaced by the Emperor's own brother, Joseph. The latter immediately decreed the secularization of all religious orders, but native resistance and the English-sponsored Peninsular War prevented the French from gaining full control over the country. In 1814 Ferdinand was restored to power and re-established the suppressed abbeys.

In 1820 another revolution broke out and the new liberal regime hastily renewed the ban against religious orders. In 1823 French military intervention facilitated the return of King Ferdinand, who, once more, rescinded the decree of secularization. After the death of Ferdinand in 1833, however, the country, sorely divided between liberals and conservatives, came to the brink of civil war. The King's brother, Don Carlos, became the candidate of the clerical and conservative parties (Carlists), while the anti-clerical liberals supported the claims of Ferdinand's three year old daughter, Isabella, under a regency of her mother, Maria Christina. Eventually the liberals gained the upper hand, led by Juan Alvarez Mendizabal, who proposed the confiscation of ecclesiastical property in order to finance from its spoils his war against the Carlists.

At first only monasteries with less than twelve members were suppressed (1835), then, in the French revolutionary pattern, a law of March 1836, converted all monastic property into "goods of the nation," and ousted monks from their ancient homes. The decree found within the Congregation of Castile forty-seven abbeys inhabited by 813 Cistercian monks; the Congregation of Aragon numbered eighteen houses with the total of 396 monks. The minimal and ill-paid pension failed to provide for the outcast religious, who were forced to seek employment as secular priests or else to live on the charity of their relatives. Some of the great abbeys were converted to secular purposes, others were abandoned and exposed to slow decay. Thus, the fruits of seven centuries of Cistercian work and prayer returned to the dust of the Spanish soil.

In Portugal a parallel development took place. The Peninsular War waged against the French thoroughly devastated the country; the great Alcobaça was sacked in 1811. The restoration of meaningful monastic life proved to be impossible even after the war. For the next twenty years the country became the stage for intermittent civil wars between liberal and conservative forces. Eventually, as in Spain, the liberals prevailed and a decree of May 1834 secularized all monastic property. The fate of both the monks and the buildings was the same as that in Spain.

Thus the whirlwind generated by the French Revolution demolished almost totally the monastic establishment of Europe and left behind only a few isolated communities, thoroughly demoralized by liberal and anti-clerical violence. In favorable circumstances the rubble of physical destruction could have been easily removed and replaced by new churches and cloisters, but the hostility of a world estranged from religious traditions frustrated the monks' stubborn will to survive. Even more disturbing was the fact that the disappearance of Cîteaux, the death of the last abbot general and the impossibility of holding general chapters, left the remnants of the Order disorganized and leaderless for half a century. The insular survival of individual abbeys certainly attested to the vitality of their inhabitants, but the lines of separate development failed to converge. This rendered the restoration of the "Order," as a centrally governed and organically coherent institution, extremely problematic.

XIV

The Nineteenth-Century Revival: The Trappists

 Few historical phenomena are more astounding than the regenerative powers of monastic orders. Regardless of the nature or frequency of disasters, monks have always been eager to put together the scattered pieces and start their interrupted lives in a new house of God.

The fires of the Revolution had not yet been extinguished when some heroic Cistercians were already hard at work. The communities brought together in the early years of the nineteenth century, however, should not be regarded merely as survivors or continuers of eighteenth-century monastic traditions. They salvaged much from the past, but they were willing to learn. The world after the Revolution was so drastically different from that of the Ancien Regimé that no institution of the collapsed order could be simply refitted into the new structure. In this regard the monks entertained no vain illusions. The humble place that Cistercians managed to insure for themselves in the changed conditions was a far cry from the distinction the Order had previously enjoyed, but the loss in external stature was not without attractive compensations.

The twelfth-century Cistercian reform started as a movement of spiritual renewal, but inevitably grew to be a major factor in the social, economic and even political life of medieval and early modern Europe. Then the violent storm that rumbled across the continent for over twenty years shattered the remains of feudalism and broke the protective shell of medieval abbeys. The monk who emerged from the ruins was no longer a privileged, revered and self-assured member of a great order; he was merely a poor man in search of God, surrounded by a society engaged in far different pursuits.

The Cistercian Order of the nineteenth century could no longer claim a prominent role in the new society or in its economic or political life. While even the shortest survey of medieval civilization must save a few pages for monasticism, the reader of a bulky volume of contemporary history would search in vain for any reference to monks. Repudiated by the builders of the new order, monks were forced to return to their original mission, offering assistance to the select few, striving for Christian perfection in the midst of an un-Christian world.

But it was not only the Order as an organization that had to face the challenge of uncongenial surroundings. Religious vocation as a matter of individual choice came under fire. The triple vows of poverty, chastity and obedience were pitted against the new ideals of unrestrained freedom and the relentless pursuit of wealth and pleasure. Monastic life was highly desirable in the Old Regime; it was therefore encouraged, occasionally forced upon boys by their parents or by other external factors. The desire to become a monk in the atmosphere of nineteenth-century materialism became uncommon; therefore the execution of such a wish demanded careful deliberation and firm will ready to overcome formidable obstacles. It was for such reasons that the inflated population of old abbeys had often included a number of misfits, causing chronic disciplinary problems. The new monk, on the other hand, was certainly a volunteer, tested for his idealism. His presence in the community enhanced the exemplary level of monastic standards. Thus, while Cistercians had lost their wealth, their prestigious position and overflowing membership, they managed to insure the success of a purely interior regeneration.

Nor was the climate of the early nineteenth century totally hostile toward a monastic renewal. Disillusionment over the failures of the Enlightenment gave birth to Romanticism, displacing reason by demanding a greater role for the human heart. Romanticism was primarily a literary and artistic movement, but for inspiration it turned back to the past, particularly to the formative period of the great European nations, the Middle Ages. The study of that epoch led inevitably to a greater appreciation of Christianity, which gave due credit to monks, the first teachers of the young barbarians. A widespread antiquarian interest, the resurrection of Gothic architecture, the vogue for historical novels and the reintroduction of Gregorian chant in liturgy, were all valuable dividends of the new trend. This was also the time when the "romantic" ruins of forgotten cloisters piqued the curiosity of a growing number of wanderers in European forests and inspired poets and painters, all puzzled over the mysterious frame of mind that had once animated swarms of their hooded inhabitants. How far this rekindled interest in monasticism can be credited with the success of a reborn La Trappe is difficult to gauge. Nevertheless, it remains undeniable that the early stages of Cistercian reconstruction were considerably facilitated by the sympathetic attitude of a new generation of intellectuals.

When it became evident that everything had been lost in France, the only organized effort to salvage a viable Cistercian nucleus for the future came from La Trappe. It was a group of tightly controlled and dedicated monks who, after a quarter century of trial and error, returned to their homeland and began to propagate the Order with remarkable success. The fact that all were avowed followers of Abbot Rancé, the great reformer of La Trappe, was of capital importance, bearing heavily on the future history of the Order. Before the Revolution the particular observance of La Trappe was restricted to a few communities; after 1815, the influence of Rancé became the dominant force of Cistercian revival throughout France and beyond, wherever the vigor of expansion had carried the "Trappists," the popular name that in these countries become synonymous with "Cistercians."

Extraordinary circumstances call for extraordinary personalities. The last master of novices of La Trappe, Augustin de Lestrange (1754-1827), was such an extraordinary character. Acting with the last minute authorizations of Abbot General Trouvé and Louis Marie Rocourt, abbot of Clairvaux, the father-abbot of La Trappe, Lestrange gathered some twenty-one monks of his community and fled to Switzerland. The cantonal authorities of Fribourg welcomed the exiles and granted them Valsainte, an abandoned charterhouse, where on June 1, 1791, a most remarkable chapter of Cistercian life began to unfold.

In their ardent desire to offer atonement for the crimes of the Revolutionary Terror, the monks led by the domineering Lestrange, outdid one another in introducing ever greater mortifications, until they reached the limits of human endurance. Heating was unknown at Valsainte. The monks slept on the bare floor, using only a straw-filled pillow and a single blanket. Their diet was restricted to bread, water and boiled vegetables. These new athletes of mortification slept only about six to seven hours, spent five to six hours in hard manual labor and devoted the rest of their time to prayer; on great feasts this latter activity took as much as twelve hours. In 1794 an attempt was made to introduce the *laus perennis,* that is, uninterrupted divine services in the church.

Lestrange was anxious to regulate every phase of the monks' life to the smallest details. No one was permitted to initiate anything, unless he had been instructed by the rule or the superior. The regulations amounted to a sizable book, duly published in 1794 at Fribourg. Animated by the ardent desire to create for the monks a life of hardship, these elaborate prescriptions went far beyond the Rule of Saint Benedict, beyond the early statutes of Cîteaux, and surpassed in severity even Rancé's code for the monks of La Trappe. Strangely enough, the unprecedented asceticism at Valsainte failed to deter vocations. The number of monks began to grow and Pius VI authorized the community to elect an abbot. This momentous event took place in 1794. The choice fell naturally on Augustin de Lestrange, who continued with renewed vigor a program of expansion which was forced upon him by the fact that the Fribourg Senate had limited the population of Valsainte to twenty-four.

The motto of Abbot Lestrange was "the holy will of God," and he was strongly inclined to believe that whatever occurred to him was in fact the will of God and must therefore be executed with unwavering zeal. His ceaseless efforts for new foundations were more impulsive than realistic, executed in a most unorthodox fashion. He would send out three or four monks at a time without much preliminary preparation, trusting that Providence would take care of the details. Some of these foundations were purely accidental: in 1793, after having been informed about opportunities in Canada, Lestrange promptly dispatched two monks and a lay-brother, among them Father Eugene de Laprade. But England was at war with France and the three men found themselves stranded at Amsterdam. While waiting for some opportunity, the Bishop of Antwerp encouraged them to settle down in his diocese on a farm near Westmalle. Lestrange agreed, without, however, giving up the Canadian project. In 1794 another threesome left Valsainte to cross the Atlantic. They were more fortunate than their predecessors, but could go no farther than England, where they received the offer of land for a permanent settlement at Lulworth in Dorsetshire. This, too, was accepted, although at the moment Westmalle was no longer in existence. The advancing French army had forced Laprade's colony to move to Westphalia, where in 1795 the refugees found a home at Darfeld. Meanwhile, several other haphazard foundations were made in Italy and Spain and plans were held ready for Hungary and Russia.

As a true child of his epoch, the indefatigable Lestrange wished to prove to the world that his brand of monasticism had great social utility. He gathered a number of small boys at Valsainte and opened a school for them. Some of the teachers were recruited from the ranks of those who, because of the hardships of the abbey, were unable to go on to profession; others were devout laymen informally associated with Valsainte. In 1796 Lestrange congregated refugee nuns of various orders in the Swiss canton of Valais and encouraged them to operate a similar educational institution for girls. He called the two schools with their teaching and supervisory staffs the "Third Order of La Trappe," another revolutionary innovation in Cistercian history.

The times, however, were singularly inauspicious for the launching of any enduring enterprise. In 1798 Switzerland was invaded by the victorious French armies and Lestrange had to realize that Valsainte was in mortal danger, the more so as the authorities charged, with some justification, that the abbey's overflowing population included a number of draft-dodgers and French army deserters. But the stubborn monks were in no mood simply to disband and Lestrange accepted instead the invitation of Tsar Paul I to seek haven in Russia.

With holy abandon Abbot Lestrange gave marching orders to his faithful flock which included his monks, the nuns, his "Third Order" with some sixty boys and forty girls, altogether 254 persons. They all left Valsainte during the course of 1798 to begin the famous "monastic Odyssey." For nearly two years they operated a veritable abbey-on-wheels, a logistic feat that allegedly stupefied even the great Napoleon. In order to reduce the problems of finding supplies and shelter, the strange pilgrimage moved eastward in three columns. After an eventful six months journey across Austria and Poland, they finally reached White Russia, but by then Lestrange had become greatly disillusioned with Russian hospitality and had fixed his mind on America. With this as his goal the intrepid Abbot retreated from Russia and on July 26, 1800, managed to embark with his whole motley assemblage at the port of Danzig.

The intervention of higher powers again frustrated his effort. A storm forced the ships to seek safety at Lübeck, where monks, nuns and children scattered in search of shelter. Fortunately, Napoleon's victory at Marengo was followed by a few years of relative peace. The earlier foundation at Darfeld could be revitalized without great problems; the Swiss authorities permitted the restoration of Valsainte, and finally, a small colony led by Urbain Guillet reached in 1803 the shores of America at Baltimore. Moreover, the signing of the Concordat with Pius VII changed Napoleon's attitude toward the Trappists. As freshly crowned emperor he personally supported several foundations, among them a house in the high Alps at Mont-Genèvre to serve as a resting place for wounded or sick soldiers passing between France and Italy. But the fragile peace that the Concordat seemed to assure did not last for long.

French occupation of the Papal States (1809), the excommunication of Napoleon and the subsequent arrest and exile of Pius VII exposed the fledgling Trappist foundations to new violence. Abbot Lestrange himself became a fugitive. He was arrested, but managed to escape, and after an adventurous passage across the Atlantic wound up in New York, where, hoping for a foundation, he purchased the site of the future Saint Patrick's Cathedral. Napoleon's fall (1814), however, changed Dom Augustin's mind and the plan of an American settlement was suspended. Lestrange and his monks returned to Europe firmly determined to move back to France and restore La Trappe.

None of the many foundations made during the years of exile proved enduring (although Westmalle was restored in 1814), but the return of the

183

Trappists to France in 1815 was the beginning of a truly remarkable expansion, thanks to the influx of a large number of vocations. The resettlement of La Trappe by Lestrange was followed in quick succession by Port-du-Salut, Aiguebelle, Bellefontaine, Bellevaux and Melleray. The last was restored by Antoine Saulnier de Beauregard, abbot of Lulworth, whose community was forced out of England in 1817 for a variety of reasons; one of them was the unrelenting Lestrange's refusal to permit the monks to pray for the "heretical" King, George III. The French monks of Darfeld in 1816 reoccupied the ancient Cistercian Notre-Dame-du-Gard, while the remaining German members abandoned Darfeld and moved in 1835 to Ölenberg in Alsace. The visitation of French houses by Abbot Saulnier in 1825 revealed that within a decade the prolific Trappists had managed to found or revive eleven houses for monks and five convents for Trappistine nuns, while they still maintained two establishments for the "Third Order," one for the education of boys and another for girls. The most populous was Melleray, numbering 175 professed members, followed by Port-du-Salut, Aiguebelle and Notre-Dame-du-Gard, each with about eighty monks. The majority at each house, however, were lay-brothers, engaged in extensive agriculture.

Trappist expansion continued throughout the rest of the nineteenth century, not only in France, but elsewhere in Europe as well as overseas. In 1855 the monks populated twenty-three abbeys, including four houses in Belgium, two in the United States, one in Ireland, one in England and one in Algeria. In the meantime the affiliated houses of nuns had grown to eight. By the end of the century (1894) even these impressive numbers had more than doubled, adding to Trappist-inhabited lands Germany, Italy, Austria-Hungary, Holland, Spain, Canada, Australia, Syria, Jordan, South Africa and China, fifty-six monasteries in all, sheltering a total of 3,000 monks, among them 600 priests.

The success of the American foundation remained in doubt for a long time. All early attempts for a permanent settlement were given up in 1814, when all but one of the monks returned to Europe. The sole remaining French monk, Father Vincent de Paul Merle, was left behind by an accident: while he was stopping for supplies in the Canadian port of Halifax, his ship sailed without him, leaving him stranded ashore. He lived as a missionary among the Indians for nearly a decade, until, in 1825, with the help of a small colony from Bellefontaine, he established Petit Clairvaux in Nova Scotia. The monks struggled for survival for many years, and finally, after two disastrous fires, they sought a new home near Lonsdale, Rhode Island, where in 1900 they built the monastery of Our Lady of the Valley. It was this same community that, after still another conflagration in 1949, moved to Spencer, Massachusetts, where they established Saint Joseph's Abbey.

The two ultimately successful Trappist establishments originated in the United States were Gethsemani in Kentucky and New Melleray, Iowa. The first was founded in 1848 by monks of the French Melleray; the second, a few months later, was populated by the Irish Mount Melleray. Both American houses experienced chronic difficulties for financial reasons as well as for the lack of native vocations. The Civil War brought additional problems, particularly in Gethsemani, but both houses were soon raised to the rank of abbey and continued to hold their own until the end of the century.

While Trappist leaders could find comfort and encouragement in the high moral standards, popular esteem and vigorous growth of their Order, several problems remained unsolved, creating constant, and occasionally severe, difficulties. One of these was the question of observances.

That the regulations of Lestrange as practiced at Valsainte were beyond normal human endurance and incompatible with genuine Cistercian traditions soon became evident to many Trappist refugees. The opposition centered around Eugene de Laprade (1764-1816), who at Darfeld quietly abandoned the rules of Lestrange and with papal approval returned to the regulation of Rancé, written for La Trappe. The split was further accentuated when, after 1815, both abbots became very active in the restoration of French monasteries and represented clashing points of view in matters of discipline. The result was that by 1825 six of the eleven French abbeys still kept faith with Lestrange and Valsainte, while five others had returned to Rancé's regulations. Abbot Lestrange, then in control of La Trappe, bitterly resented the challenge to his authority, but he was unable to obtain the long desired papal approval for his extremely severe monastic code.

When Lestrange died in 1827, the Roman Congregation of Bishops and Regulars appointed Abbot Saulnier of Melleray as "superior and visiting general" of all Trappist abbeys in France, in the expectation that under the new leadership a union of the two observances would be effected. This, however, was not to be the case until 1834, when a decree issued by the same authority united all French abbeys into one congregation (*Congregatio Monachorum Cisterciensium Beatae Mariae de Trappa*) and imposed upon them the "Rule of Saint Benedict and the constitutions of Abbot Rancé."

The document, however, failed to eliminate the tension between the two groups. In 1847 therefore Pius IX rescinded the decree of 1834 and agreed to the formation of two autonomous Trappist congregations, each guided by different disciplinary codes. Since a return to the observances of Valsainte was out of the question, the abbeys originally under the authority of Lestrange constituted the "New Reform," and, led by the Abbot of La Grande-Trappe, vowed allegiance to the *Charter of Charity* and the earliest usages of Cîteaux. The other group of abbeys, once the followers of Laprade, remained faithful to Rancé's regulations, accepted the leadership of Sept-Fons and called themselves the "Old Reform." In 1864 the latter included eight abbeys with a total of 483 monks; the "New Reform" had in the same year fifteen abbeys, having altogether 1,229 professed members.

The question of observances was greatly complicated by the closely related and equally thorny issues of effective central government and legal relations with the surviving and steadily multiplying communities of the old Common Observance.

To be sure, Abbot Lestrange ruled his monks with an iron hand and refused to submit either to the vicar general of the still functioning Congregation of Upper Germany or to the Roman procurator general, who assumed the duties of the abbot general after the dissolution of Cîteaux. But a new situation emerged in 1814, when Pius VII returned to Rome, and with his assistance a number of Cistercian abbeys came back to life throughout Italy. The creation of an "abbot general" did not seem to be opportune, but the Holy See granted the title of "president general" to the abbot of Santa Croce, who was considered the titular head of the Order, including both the Trappists and the Common Observance.

The intention of the Holy See was clearly expressed through the fact that the president general was granted the right to confirm abbatial elections within the whole Order, "so that its unity and indivisibility would always remain intact." Unfortunately, his other possible duties in the Order were never specified, a failure that led to many misunderstandings in matters of jurisdiction. In 1827 Abbot Saulnier was appointed Trappist visitor in France directly by the Congregation of Bishops and Regulars, and he promptly interpreted the fact as the recognition of his independence from the president general; he expected moreover that "the Reform of La Trappe will be absolutely separated from the Order of Cîteaux." The ambiguity of this relationship was not removed, however, and the decree of Trappist union in 1834 merely repeated that "the confirmation of individual abbots [was the right and duty] of the General Moderator of the Cistercian Order." The same principle was reiterated in 1836, when the Trappist abbeys in Belgium formed their own congregation. On the other hand, the decree of 1834 granted full authority to the Trappist vicar general to govern his congregation and entitled the abbots to hold annual chapters. After 1838, moreover, the Trappists maintained their own procurator general in Rome and enjoyed the distinction of having their own cardinal protector.

The undoing of the union in 1847 merely added to the legal complexities. There were again two clearly distinct observances, but four autonomous groups of abbeys: the "Old" and "New" reforms, the Belgian congregation under Westmalle, and Casamari, an eighteenth-century Trappist foundation in Italy, having no clear affiliation with any of the other three organizations.

As long as the disorganized and acquiescent Common Observance posed no challenge to the virtual independence of the Trappists, the legal tangle, confusing as it was, created no emergencies. But the necessity of a definitive solution came sharply into focus in 1869. It was in that year that Teobaldo Cesari, abbot of the Roman San Bernardo and president general, managed to convene the first General Chapter since 1786, for which, however, only abbots of the Common Observance were invited. Even more disturbing was the fact that the same General Chapter decided to elect an abbot general, but again only monks of the Common Observance were eligible for that position, which implied jurisdiction over the Trappists as well.

The other event creating a stir within the Order was the opening of the First Vatican Council in 1869. According to the rules concerning the participation of religious bodies set by the committee in charge of preparations, only general superiors and heads of independent congregations were to be invited to sit in the Council. This arrangement qualified the newly elected Cesari as the Cistercian abbot general, but disqualified the vicars of the Trappist congregations, the leaders of the more populous branch of the Order. It was only the last minute personal intervention of Piux IX that saved two places for the vicars of the "Old" and "New" Trappist congregations.

These unhappy experiences convinced the leading Trappist abbots that, unless they reconciled themselves to a subordinate role in the Order, they should heal their own internal division and move toward the formation of an entirely independent organization.

During the 1870s several Trappist chapters occupied themselves with such issues. In 1876 the chapter of Sept-Fons decided to request the papal appointment of a Trappist general. The session of 1877 moved closer to a projected union of Trappist congregations. In 1878 the plan was further advanced and preparations were made to hold a joint session in 1879 for all Trappist congregations in anticipation of the election of an independent general superior.

Although Abbot Timothée Gruyer of La Trappe expressed serious reservations concerning the wisdom of a union which would imply uniformity in observances, late in 1878 the project was submitted to the Congregation of Bishops and Regulars for final approval. The examination of the request was the duty of the Congregation's consultor, the Dominican Raimondo Bianchi. His detailed analysis pointed out the many drawbacks of a final and irreversible schism within the Cistercian Order; therefore the Congregation refused to endorse the plan. Bianchi admitted, nevertheless, that one point of the Trappist proposal was worthy of careful consideration, that is, the unification of the four distinct congregations under one vicar general and one representative in Rome, who would, however, still recognize the abbot general as the head of the whole Order. This unified organization, concluded Bianchi, did not exclude the possibility of the preservation of both basic observances, to be practised the same way as before the union. In short, the report maintained that while a Trappist union was desirable, uniformity in observances was not to be enforced, and a schism within the Cistercian Order must be avoided.

In retrospect it is difficult to dispute the wisdom of the Bianchi report, but the Trappist leaders of the time, particularly those of the Congregation of Sept-Fons, were disappointed. The drive toward the same goals continued under the leadership of Sébastien Wyart (1839-1904), an ex-officer of the papal army and decorated hero of the Franco-Prussian War. He joined the Trappists as a late vocation, was ordained priest in 1877, but was permitted to continue his studies until he obtained the doctor's degree in theology. His exceptional erudition and firmness of character were greatly enhanced by his valuable Roman connections: both Pius IX and Leo XIII held him in high personal regard. When in 1887 Wyart was elected abbot of Sept-Fons, thus becoming the vicar of the "Old Reform," the road toward Trappist independence was reopened.

After having been properly informed of the problems, Leo XIII convoked an extraordinary chapter to be held in Rome in October 1892, with the participation of the representatives of all four Trappist congregations, including even Casamari. The purpose of the assembly was threefold: a fusion of the congregations; election of a general superior; agreement on common observances. Although the three representatives of Casamari had decided to preserve their independence and remained aloof, there was a near unanimity on the first objective, and the united Trappists

188

promptly assumed a new title: "Order of Reformed Cistercians of Our Lady of La Trappe." Nor was there significant dissension over the necessity of having a general superior, although the possible relation of such a superior with the abbot general of the Common Observance caused some reflection. It was soon decided, however, that a merely autonomous congregation was not sufficient, and total independence called for an independent abbot general. In the election which followed a few days later, Wyart received twenty-eight votes out of the total of fifty-one ballots cast.

On the question of observances, however, the opinions were as divided as ever. In principle the adherence to the Rule of Saint Benedict received wide support, but certain details of the daily schedule remained open for discussion. During the fruitless debates over the relative merits of the *horaria* of Saint Benedict and of Rancé, the atmosphere grew so tense that Wyart, in order to avoid a fatally divisive vote, proposed that the issue be submitted to the Holy See for arbitration. The move was grudgingly accepted, but the Congregation declined the challenge, merely advising the general chapter to defer decision to a later date, when a carefully prepared compromise solution could be considered. Such setbacks notwithstanding, the chapter could still claim credit for establishing a totally independent branch of the Cistercian family, an achievement solemnly approved by a brief of Leo XIII issued on March 12, 1893.

On the basis of the preparatory work of a committee the general chapter of 1893, held at Sept-Fons, resumed the debate over the disputed *horarium*. The chief point of dissent involved the time, number and quality of monastic meals. Although the Rule's solution received a slight majority, eventually it was Wyart's skillful handling of the exhausted assembly that insured the prevalence of Rancé's regulations. The new constitution, featuring the basic principles of the *Charter of Charity* and the early Cistercian customs in Rancé's interpretation, could be published in 1894.

Before the close of the century a substantial donation enabled the Trappists to acquire the ruins of Cîteaux (1898) and to revive the ancient abbey. Wyart himself assumed the abbatial title. The move symbolized the sincerity of the new organization in its endeavor to return to genuine Cistercian traditions. The achievement received solemn recognition in 1902, when, in a new apostolic constitution, the Pope dropped the reference to La Trappe and called the new branch on the old tree "Order of Reformed Cistercians, or of the Strict Observance," true heirs to all Cistercian rights and privileges.

While a steady numerical growth, territorial expansion and the eventual union of Trappist houses were unmistakable signs of inner vigor, the everyday life at many communities posed nagging economic problems throughout the century.

Although the monks and the many lay-brothers of the new or revived foundations returned to the traditionally Cistercian agricultural life-style, the modest scope of their operations failed to furnish the funds needed for physical expansion or even for the safe survival of their monastic families. In the early years of the century monks were often forced to go from door to door begging for donations. As late as 1835 the chapter held at La Trappe still tolerated such practices, although admitted that "begging for alms was entirely alien from the mentality of our fathers." In 1839 it was decided that collections be made away from public view, through the services of trusted lay friends. The same approach was adopted at the chapter of 1847. Meanwhile the chapters sternly warned the abbots to admit only as many monks as they were able to provide for. New foundations were permitted only if the proposals were accompanied by proofs for sufficient funding.

In order to ease the steady financial pressure, communities were authorized to receive donations from prospective novices, including even pensions or annuities promised by well-to-do relatives. The shortage of labor on monastic farms and in workshops justified the acceptance of free help from devout laymen, although the proposal to establish for them a "third order" was declined. As "oblates," however, lay-helpers continued to be employed in some abbeys. Until about 1850 rooms or apartments in the abbeys were often rented to individuals with whom the monks had friendly relations; beyond that date, however, the accommodations of "guests" beyond two months was prohibited. Mass stipends furnished a steady and substantial source of income, although the relatively small number of priests set a limit to such services. Occasionally long-term mass foundations netted large sums. Chambarand, for example, in 1874 accepted 25,000 francs for daily masses to be said for one hundred years for the intention of a donor.

Since agriculture often proved unrewarding, many abbeys began to sell food products or other items of domestic industry. Beer, wine and alcoholic spirits were produced and sold, although not at monastic premises. The nationwide advertising of a liqueur sold by Grace-Dieu under the name of "Trappistine," however, became the source of such embarrassment that the Sept-Fons chapter of 1863 prohibited this and all similar promotional methods. Horticulture and fruit-growing were equally widespread. The production of cheese helped about a dozen French abbeys; the quality cheese at Port-du-Salut earned the monks a worldwide reputation. Together with several other abbeys, Westmalle operated a well-equipped printing shop, where all Cistercian liturgical books were published.

The maintenance of protective or educational institutions as well as pastoral ministry were generally considered incompatible with the contemplative vocation, but local circumstances often demanded compromise. Thus, the institutions of the "Third Order," initiated by Abbot Lestrange, continued to function until the middle of the century. The abbey of N.-D. des Neiges operated a short-lived (1870-71) hospice for epileptics. In 1872 the Abbot of Désert received permission for the opening of an orphanage. In 1876 the flourishing Mariastern in Bosnia was permitted to accept a large sum for a foundation in Austria, tied to the obligation to educate twelve orphans in perpetuity. Though this foundation never materialized, within twenty years Mariastern itself was caring for 132 boys. Westmalle, Mount Melleray and Gethsemani maintained grammar schools; La Trappe educated oblates; La Trappe even had two parishes under the monks' care; the South-African Mariannhill branched off into missionary activities among the natives.

Intellectual pursuits, disapproved by Rancé, were discouraged through the nineteenth century. Most Trappist monks noted for their erudition joined the Order after they had completed their academic education. The ascetic ideals of Trappist communities placed no particular emphasis on the priesthood and, in fact, priests constituted only a minority of the total membership. The priests who were ordained as Trappists received only private instruction in their own abbeys, with varying degrees of success. The chapter of 1861 held at La Trappe discussed the problem of inadequate education for the priesthood which had evidently become a source of adverse criticism. The fathers complained that they had too few priests of sufficient education who might become confessors, spiritual directors or superiors. They proposed, therefore, that seminaries be established at La Grande-Trappe and Aiguebelle, although individual houses having at least "one capable professor," were permitted to educate their own priests.

Another legacy of Rancé's spirituality, the consideration of monks primarily as "penitents," became another source of problems. The prevalent notion that Trappist abbeys were "refuges for sinners" made the screening of novices difficult. The chapter of 1843 was compelled to take a strong stand against such popular beliefs and insisted on the careful examination of vocations before their admission. For the same reason the prolongation of the year of probation became a general practice. Moreover, the chapter of 1847 held at Sept-Fons suggested that the novitiate "be extended to two years and beyond," if necessary. The cautious attitude of the chapter of 1835 toward frequent communion of novices and the fact that priest-novices were normally not permitted to say masses, were later in the century widely considered as anachronistic relics of seventeenth-century rigorism.

The reputation of Trappist abbeys for piety and asceticism was very high throughout the nineteenth century. A strictly secluded contemplative life protected them from political involvements of dubious value, although they were by no means immune to anti-clerical attacks. When in 1832 Melleray was unjustly accused of sympathy with the legitimist uprising led by the Duchess of Berry, the monks were dispersed for several years. The calamity, however, turned to blessing. It was in 1832 that members of the original Lulworth community established in Ireland Mount Melleray, and the same group re-entered England from Mount Melleray, founding in 1835 Mount Saint Bernard. Bismarck's *Kulturkampf* in the 1870s endangered the two Trappist foundations in Germany and, at least temporarily (1875-1887), the monks of Mariawald had to seek refuge in Holland. In 1880 a French anti-clerical campaign threatened the existence of several abbeys and led to the disruption of religious life at Sept-Fons for eight years. Such distressing experiences served as powerful incentives for an accelerated program of foundations in countries where the future of monasticism seemed to be more secure.

It was perhaps for reasons of political instability and because of the tenuous links the Trappists had with the Roman president general that a decree of 1834 placed the French houses under episcopal jurisdiction, and that in 1837 Gregory XVI qualified the vows taken in the same communities as "simple" instead of "solemn." The resentful monks, however, managed to have their privileges restored: solemn vows were reintroduced in 1868, while their full exemption was recognized in 1892.

XV

The Nineteenth-Century Revival: The Common Observance

 The conservative regimes which returned to power after 1815 were not unfriendly toward religion. In some countries willing co-operation with the Church came close to a new alliance between the "throne and the altar." Monastic orders, however, did not belong to the beneficiaries of official cordiality. Enlightened aversion toward "useless" abbeys remained much in evidence; then, too, the members of the recently dissolved communities could not be permitted to reorganize their ranks without endangering the new owners' possession of confiscated monastic property; and finally, in a tense atmosphere of nationalism, religious orders with international ties and foreign superiors were suspected of being disloyal, or at least unpatriotic. These were only some of the reasons why surviving Cistercian abbeys in Central Europe were unable to launch a vigorous campaign of renewal and were condemned to subsist for decades in complete isolation.

The only country where no such considerations could prevail was the Papal States. Indeed, it was in Rome and under papal auspices that the first steps were taken for the restoration not only of individual monasteries, but also of the Cistercian Order as an organization. Pope Pius VII revived Casamari as early as 1814, followed in 1817 by two ancient abbeys in Rome: Santa Croce in Gerusalemme and the formerly Feuillant house of San Bernardo alle Terme. Soon a few other monasteries rose to new life and the representatives of six houses were able to hold a chapter in 1820. Under the name of the "Italian Congregation of Saint Bernard" they adopted the constitution of the defunct Congregation of Lombardy and Tuscany, holding congregational chapters in every fifth year and electing a "president general" for five-year terms.

Particular significance must be attached to the Italian initiative because of the fact that the Holy See considered the "president general" of the Congregation the legitimate heir of the Cistercian abbot general. The first holder of this title was Raimondo Giovannini, who was followed by Sisto Benigni and Giuseppe Fontana. They all practiced the right of confirming abbatial elections even among the Trappists, and all made repeated, though unsuccessful, efforts to establish closer relations with Cistercian abbeys outside Italy. The most notable of such incidents was Fontana's approach to the Swiss Congregation in 1825, proposing the resumption of legal relations between the two Congregations. The Swiss abbots, however, declined the offer in fear of retaliation by their government. A subsequent anti-clerical drive ending Cistercian life in Switzerland amply justified the abbots' caution.

The revolution of 1830 separated Belgium from Holland, and the new Belgian government, unlike the former regime, showed much good will toward the Catholic Church. The remnants of the homeless Cistercians of Lieu-Saint-Bernard who remained organized under the successors of their last legitimate abbot, were unable to reoccupy their former abbey. In 1833 they acquired suitable facilities at Bornhem, which two years later was recognized as the legal successor of Lieu-Saint-Bernard. Monastic life was fully restored in the following year.

The last surviving monk of Val-Dieu, Bernard Klinkenberg, repurchased the ruins of his abbey in 1840, and with the help of Bornhem, was able to restore community life in 1844. The two abbeys formed the "Vicariate of Belgium" and accepted as its legal basis Alexander VII's *In suprema* of 1666. The head of the organization was a "vicar general" elected for five years. Chapters representing both communities were held in every fifth year.

After the restoration, the first Belgian novices were educated at Santa Croce in Rome, but, following their own statutes' approval by the Holy See in 1846, the abbeys remained independent.

The revival of the Common Observance in France was launched as a personal endeavor of a pious diocesan priest, Abbé Léon Barnouin, who in honor of the Immaculate Conception (defined as a dogma in 1854) restored monastic life at the ancient Cistercian abbey of Sénanque in the diocese of Avignon in 1855. Abbé Barnouin, receiving the name Marie-Bernard, finished his novitiate at Rome, and the new foundation remained for a while affiliated to the Congregation of Saint Bernard in Italy. But the flourishing community soon became independent and formed the Congregation of Sénanque in 1867. Within a short time the abbey revived three other abandoned monasteries, among them the famous center of pre-Benedictine French monasticism, Lérins (Provence), which later became the headquarters of the whole Congregation. This group was the only one in the Common Observance retaining a life of a purely contemplative character. Their discipline, however, was not as strict as that of the Trappists; therefore this Congregation was often referred to as the "middle observance" (*observantia media*).

One group of abbeys which could have initiated a movement of revival on a truly impressive scale was composed of the survivors of the disastrous reign of Emperor Joseph II. There were eight such abbeys in Austria, two in Bohemia, two in Austrian Poland, and one in Hungary, thirteen monasteries in all, most of them well populated and in possession of their ancient cloisters and a sizeable portion of their eighteenth-century estates. What prevented the monks from taking any initiative toward a meaningful Cistercian reconstruction was the official policy prevailing within the Habsburg Monarchy until 1850, the so-called Josephinism, the sorry legacy of Joseph II. It was based on the premise that the Church was a governmental department watching over the morals of obedient citizens. The eventually tolerated monastic communities had to prove themselves useful by extensive pastoral ministry, teaching or other works of charity. However, monastic exemption was abolished, any contact with the papacy or foreign superiors prohibited and, since the monks were regarded merely as auxiliaries in pastoral ministry, all abbeys came under the close supervision of diocesan bishops. Strict governmental control over clerical education, both regular and secular, insured a new generation properly indoctrinated in the spirit of Josephinism and able to carry on the priestly duties in accordance with such instructions indefinitely.

The impact of this policy on the internal life of individual communities was predictable and can be well illustrated by the example of the Hungarian Zirc, a house originally dependent on the Silesian Heinrichau. After the suppression of the latter abbey in 1810, Zirc became independent. In 1814 Emperor Francis I appointed the abbot of the already united Pilis and Pásztó as the new abbot of Zirc. Thus the three Hungarian monasteries became permanently unified under one head, the abbot of Zirc. But the price of imperial favor was the monks' assumption of the operation of two previously Jesuit gymnasiums, in addition to the one in Eger, already under the control of the monks of Pásztó. Such tasks substantially increased the already considerable burden of operating about a dozen parishes.

Since the total number of priests at the abbot's disposal was about thirty-five, practically all able-bodied monks were employed either as teachers or pastors, leaving in the abbey of Zirc only the novices and some absolutely necessary administrative personnel. Under such circumstances neither the traditional *horarium* nor the eighteenth-century statutes could be observed. The commonly recited divine office was reduced to the hours of the day and all other monastic observances suffered a similar reduction.

Zirc, unable to establish contact with higher authorities in the Order, came under the jurisdiction of the bishop of Veszprém. He held periodic visitations at the abbey and in 1817 issued a set of regulations adjusted to the new circumstances. In 1822, a Hungarian episcopal conference undertook the compilation of new statutes for the monks, but the text never received governmental approval and was soon forgotten. Thus, until the 1850s the daily lives of the monks were based purely on local customs, satisfying elementary sacerdotal requirements, but ignoring monastic traditions.

Conditions were much the same in the other twelve Austro-Hungarian abbeys. Lay-brotherhood had all but disappeared, but four or five abbeys each had about fifty priests with an adequate number of new vocations to sustain their life. But the external burdens were heavy. The Tirolese Stams had eighteen parishes under its care and the others were not far behind. In 1854 the thirteen abbeys were in charge of altogether 138 parishes in addition to forty-five other nonparochial churches and chapels served by the monks. Nearly all the parishes operated grammar schools; Neukloster and Ossegg had gymnasiums under their care and five other abbeys furnished a number of teachers for secondary schools maintained in their neighborhood. Zwettl operated a poorhouse for thirty inmates, and five other abbeys maintained similar, though smaller, institutions. Heiligen-kreuz, Zwettl and Lilienfeld organized boarding schools for choir boys. Because the total number of priests of the thirteen communities in the same year (1854) was 433, it goes without saying that after meeting their external duties the monks had neither time nor enthusiasm to fulfil their monastic obligations with zeal and devotion. In fact, it was only at Rein, Stams, Ossegg and the two Polish houses, Mogila and Szczyrzyc, that the whole divine office was commonly recited. Elsewhere such prayers were considerably reduced; at Neukloster the monks satisfied themselves only with the *pretiosa* (a part of Prime) at seven in the morning.

Extensive engagement in teaching and pastoral work necessitated an appropriate education for the monks. During the regime of Joseph II members of both the regular and secular clergy were forced to attend the newly organized "general seminaries" in order to be educated in the spirit of Josephinism. In 1790 religious communities were again permitted to provide for the education of their members independently, as long as they had government-certified professors and were willing to use the compulsory textbooks. Accordingly, a school of theology was organized at Heiligenkreuz, attended by the clerics of four other abbeys as well. Stams opened a similar institution, but the other monasteries sent their students in theology to the nearest diocesan seminaries. The course of studies lasted four years, although in the third year the clerics were permitted to take solemn vows, provided that they were twenty-one years old, the minimum age prescribed by the government. The teachers employed in the gymnasiums, in addition to the above studies, had to obtain the appropriate certificate at a government-sponsored university.

Meanwhile, the rigidly enforced government regulations not only prevented Cistercian abbeys from establishing legal relations with the Roman president general, but also made organized co-operation among the abbeys within the Habsburg Empire extremely difficult or even risky, for such an organization would have rendered them suspect in the eyes of the authorities. It was only through informal letters or news received from travelers that the Cistercian procurator in Rome could gather some information about conditions in Austria. In 1846, Alberico Amatori, the Roman procurator general, addressed a letter to the Abbot of Heiligen-kreuz in which he confessed his ignorance of the situation, even of the number of Cistercian houses in Austria, and asked for information. He also urged the Abbot to explore the possibility of a closer co-operation with Rome, giving the example of the newly organized Belgian Congregation.

The procurator received no encouraging answer from Heiligenkreuz, but the revolutions of 1848-49 shook the Monarchy at its foundation and resulted in a basic change in Church-State relations. The new constitution of 1849 recognized the autonomy of the Church in Austria and a subsequent episcopal conference in Vienna began to implement the concession. In 1850 the young Emperor Francis Joseph abolished the imperial *placet* (assent), thus opening free communications with Rome. Finally, a concordat of 1855 definitely broke with Josephinism, making the clergy of Austria again a part of the universal Church.

It was in this changed political climate that the possibility of an abbatial convention emerged in 1851. The proposed agenda included the formation of an Austrian Cistercian province; restoration of monastic exemption; establishment of relations with the Roman president general; regulations for the administration of schools and parishes and, finally, a reform of monastic discipline.

Since there had been no organization among the abbots within living memory, the initiative was taken privately by several abbots. The immediate reaction of other abbots was extremely cautious. Despite their fears of provoking episcopal anger, the abbots held their convention, in an almost clandestine fashion in Baden near Vienna, late in October 1851.

Of the numerous problems the question of exemption received particular attention, but the timid abbots merely resolved to wait until the Holy See would take the initiative in the matter. No action was taken in any other direction, except for a resolution to meet again in the near future, drafting of a provincial constitution and establishment of direct relations with Rome.

In preparation for this second meeting several abbots visited the apostolic nuncio in Vienna. It was then that the abbots heard for the first time that all questions concerning religious orders in Austria were to be decided by means of an apostolic visitation. The initiative had been taken, the abbots were informed, at the episcopal conference of 1849, when the bishops complained about the fallen state of monastic discipline throughout the Monarchy and asked the intervention of the Holy See in this highly sensitive matter.

The startling news greatly reduced the significance of the planned convention, yet the abbots met in Vienna in the middle of May 1852. They promptly decided to prepare a detailed report for the Holy See on the embarrassingly sad state of the Cistercian Order in Austria. In this very frank document the abbots readily admitted that during the past century "discipline was weakened, regularity has diminished and monastic virtues have largely disappeared," but they placed the responsibility squarely on the anti-religious policies of the government. The colorful presentation contained only three specific requests: the appointment of a cardinal protector; permission to have a Roman procurator; and the organization of an Austrian Cistercian province under the authority of the abbot general.

The document was handed over to the nuncio in Vienna, who duly forwarded it to Rome. The answer of Pius IX was addressed to the Abbot of Rein. The Pope praised the abbots' solicitude and readiness for reform, but made all concrete decisions dependent on the outcome of the apostolic visitation.

On June 25, 1852, the papal choice of a visitor fell on Friedrich Cardinal Schwarzenberg, archbishop of Prague. Within Hungary the same authority was granted to the Archbishop of Esztergom. Since, however, there was only one Cistercian abbey in Hungary, the visitation of Cistercians, including Zirc, became Schwarzenberg's responsibility. The Cardinal was a highly educated and zealous prelate who took his charge seriously, although he delegated the actual visitation of individual abbeys to Bishop Augustin Hille. It was the latter who called on Cistercian abbeys, accompanied in his journey by Salesius Mayer, a pious and erudite monk of the Bohemian Ossegg, who subsequently served as professor of moral theology and rector of the University of Prague, and ended his life (1876) as abbot of Ossegg. The nature, scope and outcome of the visitation in Cistercian abbeys was heavily influenced by the tireless Father Mayer.

In preparation for the visitation each house was required to put together a full report on every phase of its monastic life, including a copy of the statutes observed in the community. Characteristic of the prevailing conditions, Ossegg alone was able to produce its statutes. All other monasteries lived without binding regulations, following merely customs handed down by previous generations of monks.

The visitation of Cistercian abbeys took place in 1854-55, followed by the issuance of individual charters for each community. These documents were based on a declaration of principles composed by the Cardinal, but were adjusted to local conditions. As the closing act of the whole process, on August 12, 1856, Schwarzenberg dispatched to Rome a detailed report on his findings and recommendations.

The visitors, stated the Cardinal, were received everywhere "with the greatest honors and promptness of heart," and the majority of monks exhibited "love for the Order and desire for progress." However, "the strictness of discipline that once made the Order of Saint Bernard distinguished and is still practiced in the Strict Observance of the Trappists, is absent from the Austrian convents, and, considering the present monks and present conditions, cannot be introduced." Indeed, as the Cardinal observed, as long as the half or even larger percentage of the communities lived permanently outside of the abbeys as pastors or teachers, it remained all but impossible to introduce a uniform discipline. He did his best to emphasize the basic elements of monastic life, but he hoped for substantial improvements only after a sizable increase of membership and gradual reduction of external duties. The Cardinal also asserted that the first step toward improvement should be the organization of an autonomous Cistercian province. Practical details of a reform should be the subject of a provincial chapter, where, together with the new constitution, a basic book of uniform statutes could also be composed.

The much heralded and carefully planned convention was opened in Prague by Cardinal Schwarzenberg on March 30, 1859. All Cistercian monasteries were duly represented and even the two affiliated nunneries sent their chaplains as delegates; in all, twenty-eight persons attended. There appeared for the first time the prior of Mehrerau in the name of the exiled Swiss community of Wettingen, which in 1854 managed to find a new home in the Austrian Mehrerau, an abandoned Benedictine abbey.

On most issues of importance the conferees were far from unanimity. Differences of opinion on matters of monastic discipline were greatly accentuated by nationalistic pride. Ever since the bloody suppression of the revolutions of 1848-49, Poles, Czechs, and particularly Hungarians, had their own grievances and were habitually suspicious toward any move that implied Austrian domination. The fact that Cardinal Schwarzenberg's brother, Felix, as Austrian prime minister (1848-1853), had been the thoroughly hated instrument of subjugation was an unfortunate coincidence. Nevertheless, after a week of hard work the purpose of the meeting was achieved: a new book of statutes was accepted; the legal framework for an autonomous congregation was constructed; and even the first vicar general was elected.

The set of regulations, the so-called "Prague Statutes," amounted to a promptly published small booklet of forty-four pages. It was generally believed that the text was the work of Salesius Mayer, but its substance was based on the eighteenth-century statutes of the Cistercian province of Bohemia and Moravia, which, in turn, were the adaptation of the *In suprema* of Alexander VII, issued in 1666. While an honest effort to maintain the continuity of Cistercian traditions was manifest, due consideration was given to contemporary exigencies. The recitation or chanting of the whole canonical office, to be preceded by the office of the Blessed Virgin, was made absolutely compulsory in each abbey. Spiritual exercises, such as daily meditation, spiritual reading and annual retreats, were re-emphasized, and so were the rules of fasting and abstinence. Although the character of the rules was far from the strictness of those of the Trappists, the Prague Statutes, if observed, would have restored monastic discipline to a respectable level.

The provincial constitution called for a vicar general elected by all abbots for a term of six years. He was to be aided in his duties by three similarly elected assistants. The provincial chapter was to convene every third year. Similarly, visitation of each abbey by the vicar general was to take place triennially. The regulations also called for a procurator general in Rome and left the door open for a future abbot general and general chapter, both to be called back to life at a later date. The fruitful convention ended with the election of the first vicar general of the new congregation in the person of Ludwig Crophius, abbot of Rein.

Cardinal Schwarzenberg approved the new statutes on April 5, and sent them with all pertinent documentation to Rome for a final ratification by the Congregation of Bishops and Regulars. The fact that the Prague Statutes never received that sanction considerably reduced their effectiveness, but 1859 still constituted a turning point in the history of the Common Observance. A much troubled past was left behind and a path opened toward better external organization, faster growth and deeper spirituality.

Meanwhile, the changed condition of the Church in Austria encouraged the Roman president general to make another attempt at closer cooperation with his Cistercian brethren across the Alps. When Angelo Geniani, abbot of Santa Croce, was about to hold a chapter for the Italian

Congregation in 1856, he sent an invitation to both the Belgian and Austrian abbots and encouraged them to attend. Since the visitation in Austria was still in progress and it was not clear whether the call was for active participation or merely to sit in as observers, the answer was negative in both countries.

Geniani's immediate successor, Teobaldo Cesari, continued the momentum and pressed for a general chapter, using his influence at the curia in the project's behalf. He followed with great interest the progress of the Prague convention, where the office of abbot general was also discussed, although the Austrian abbots failed to follow up the matter. In 1856 he renewed his predecessor's invitation for a general chapter, but without success. In 1863 Cesari made another attempt through the services of the nuncio in Vienna, who had become an enthusiastic supporter of the idea. The plan called for a full session of the general chapter, to which even the Trappist abbots were invited. Unfortunately, the promising move received no support in Austria and was equally rejected by Stanislas Lapierre, the abbot of Sept-Fons and vicar of the "Old Reform."

The real reason for the Austrians' coolness toward Cesari's initiative is not entirely clear, but one may suspect that at least one source of their worries was the steady political tension between Italy and Austria, which erupted in open warfare in 1859 and 1866. The probability of this supposition seems to be corroborated by the fact that the undaunted Cesari made his next move through the much friendlier Hungarians. In 1865, however, he merely expressed his desire to visit informally the Austrian abbeys and asked the Abbot of Zirc to explore his colleagues' attitude concerning the matter. This time the plan was foiled by the outbreak of the Austro-Prussian War (1866) and the subsequent Italian march into Venetia. In 1867, however, Cesari went to Belgium for the visitation of the two Cistercian abbeys in that country, and on his way back to Rome he visited several Austrian communities and the Hungarian Zirc. He was very favorably impressed and became convinced that the time was ripe for holding the much delayed general chapter.

Early in 1868 Cesari turned with his plans to the Congregation of Bishops and Regulars, and the answer was prompt and favorable. On March 27 the Congregation issued a decree recognizing Cesari as the general of both the Belgian and Austrian Congregations, authorizing him to convoke "as soon as possible" a general chapter. Cesari wasted no time and invited all abbots of both Congregations to meet next September in Rome. At the request of the surprised abbots the chapter was deferred to April 6, 1869, and it was on that date that the convention was opened in the abbey of San Bernardo alle Terme.

The much heralded meeting proved to be in many ways anticlimatic.

The Congregation of Sénanque, although invited, sent no representative at all; the Polish Mogila was also unrepresented. Not counting the presiding Cesari, only four Italians appeared, who, since the discussions dealt largely with Austrian affairs, left the meeting after the third session. Considering the fact that the Trappists had not even been invited, the question was raised repeatedly whether the convention could qualify for a general chapter or was merely a special assembly of Austrian and Belgian abbots. The negative attitude toward the invitation of the Strict Observance was never officially explained. One reason was certainly the reluctance of the Trappists themselves, who had already entertained the possibility of forming their own independent organization. The other motive was the fear that a large contingent of Trappist representatives could simply overwhelm the otherwise modest assembly.

In spite of such vital problems, after ten days of intense negotiations, the chapter managed to decide at least two points on the agenda: the abbot general and the revival of the general chapter. It was resolved that the abbot general should reside in Rome; that he should be an abbot of the Common Observance, to be elected for life by all other abbots of the same observance at a special session of the general chapter. Abbot Cesari, however, was accepted as the first general, in honor of his previous appointment by the Congregation. The chief duties of the general were to be the visitation of each abbey once in every ten years, the convocation of the general chapter and presidency over the same assembly. He was to be aided by an elected procurator general, but in matters involving individual abbeys, he was to act only through the mediation of the abbot concerned.

The general chapter was to be held at Rome every tenth year, although in the case of the death of the abbot general a special session was to be called by the procurator general for the election of a new general. Membership and voting rights, however, in view of the great numerical inequality among the Congregations, constituted a grave problem. Since the conferees were unable to reach a unanimous solution, the Congregation of Bishops and Regulars was asked to arbitrate the dispute. On the extent of the chapter's jurisdiction no specific decision was made, but all agreed in principle that it had no authority to change the congregational constitutions approved by the Holy See.

The abbots decided to petition again the speedy approval of the Prague Statutes by the Congregation. On other issues, such as the uniform observance of the vow of poverty and the possibility of opening a common school of theology in Rome, no decision was made.

Neither the Austrian abbots nor the Congregation of Bishops and Regulars considered the problems that remained outstanding after the chapter vitally important. When Abbot General Cesari died in 1879, the Prague Statutes were still waiting for approval and, since the general chapter of 1880 voiced no concern in the matter, the whole issue was quietly forgotten. The only notable act of the chapter was the election of the new general in the person of Gregorio Bartolini, abbot of Santa Croce in Rome. The chapter, however, was held in Vienna, because by then both Roman abbeys of the Order had been seized by the Italian government and both had been converted into barracks. Bartolini himself had to live in a small apartment adjacent to his titular church.

The general chapter in 1891 was also held, for the same reason, in Vienna and dealt with the same emergency: Bartolini died in 1890; therefore a successor had to be elected. The distressing facts, however, were that there was no Italian abbot alive and no Roman abbey available where the new general could establish his headquarters, and these created a new problem. The Order, therefore, turned to the Holy See and petitioned that the new general, presumably a non-Italian, might live and function outside Rome. The request was granted and the choice of the chapter fell on the abbot of Hohenfurt, Leopold Wackarz, the vicar general of the Austrian Congregation, a venerable octogenarian.

More memorable events took place in 1891 in connection with the eighth centenary of the birth of Saint Bernard. The Trappists took part in a number of religious conventions and celebrations throughout France and, as a permanent memorial, re-edited the important source collection known as the *Nomasticon Cisterciense.* The Common Observance found it appropriate to honor the Saint by a number of monumental publications of great scholarly value. The most outstanding of them was certainly the *Origines Cistercienses,* a still indispensable listing of all Cistercian monasteries throughout the history of the Order, the work of a learned member of Zwettl, Leopold Janauschek. The same Janauschek edited in four volumes the *Xenia Bernardina,* which included a complete Bernardine bibliography. In 1889 the initiation of the *Cistercienser-Chronik* by Gregor Müller, turned out to be a milestone in the study of the Cistercian past. A similar French language enterprise sponsored by the Congregation of Sénanque and edited in Hautecombe, *L'Union Cistercienne,* unfortunately lived for only four years. Coincidentally with Vacandard's famous biography of Saint Bernard, Father Imre Piszter of the Hungarian Zirc published his own great *Life and Works of Saint Bernard* in two volumes. Remig Békefi, professor of history at the University of

Budapest, another distinguished member and future abbot of Zirc, began a series of multivolume monographs covering Cistercian history in Hungary.

The only shadow cast over the festive scene was the imminent split within the Order—still nominally one—between the Trappists and the Common Observance. It was not unexpected, but the editor of the *Cistercienser-Chronik* still termed the move "grave in its consequences," one which should fill the hearts of all Cistercians "with deep sorrow." The author of the short communication, Father Müller, who had worked harder than anybody else to evoke among the ranks of the Common Observance a deeper appreciation for Cistercian traditions, readily admitted that the abbot general and the general chapter of his observance had failed to give due consideration to the Trappists, but still believed that the break was unnecessary and eventually would hurt both branches of the Order.

Such thoughts were not entirely alien among the Trappist fathers either. On the eve of the eighth centenary of the foundation of Cîteaux, it was the general chapter of the Strict Observance (1896) that made a move toward a reunion of the separated branches of the Order on the basis of the newly passed Trappist constitution. The proposal was intimated through Roman channels to the general chapter of the Common Observance of 1897 held at Hohenfurt. The terms, as the abbots at Hohenfurt understood them, implied the practical absorption of the Common Observance by the Trappists, and therefore the offer could not be considered as a practical approach toward such a goal. It was politely declined.

One of the major differences that developed during the nineteenth century between the two branches of the Order was the degree and significance of uniformity and central control. Individual abbeys, as components of the Trappist congregations, were tightly supervised and were expected to follow the common statutes in rigid uniformity. The final consequence of this policy was the eventual fusion of congregations, the elimination of the variety of observances and the emergence of the united Order of the Strict Observance. In 1893 uniformity and complete domination by the Trappist general chapter were achieved with a much higher degree of effectiveness than at any other epoch of Cistercian history.

In sharp contrast, the abbeys belonging to the Common Observance, retained throughout the same century a large measure of autonomy. The prevalence of "pluralism" was most conspicuous among the ancient abbeys of Austria-Hungary. These communities had practiced the difficult art of survival for many decades and had come to be distrustful of external intervention of whatever source or nature. The return to effective controls by a congregational or general chapter did not seem to them vitally important and the observance of a uniform code of discipline appeared to them even less desirable. They did eventually create an abbot general and restored the general chapter as convenient organs of representation or publicity, but they carefully curtailed their authority while they proudly preserved their specific customs and internal organization. To judge the accomplishments of the Common Observance by measuring the degree of centralization would be entirely unrealistic and unfair as well. Progress can be assessed only by taking a closer look at other aspects of monastic life.

The most quotable evidence is numerical growth. Considering the Austrian province as a whole, the figures are not particularly impressive. In 1854 the total membership was 499, which included 433 priests. By 1898 the figures had grown to 581 for the total and to 483 for priests. Meanwhile, the Italians suffered great losses due to the secularization of their houses and the two Belgian communities merely held their own without conspicuous changes in either direction.

The Congregation of Sénanque, however, rose from the handful of founders of 1855 to a total of 157 in 1898, including 49 priests, 29 clerics, 13 novices and 66 lay-brothers, the only Congregation within the Common Observance where lay-brotherhood had significantly reappeared. Another success story was that of Mehrerau, founded by a few Swiss refugees in 1854. Within a very short time Mehrerau had not only grown to a sizable community, but by 1888 the fathers were able to revive the ancient German Marienstatt, founding with the latter community a new "Swiss-German Congregation." By 1898 the combined membership of the two abbeys had risen to 124, including 53 priests, 25 clerics, 7 novices and 39 lay-brothers.

The most spectacular growth, however, was that of the Hungarian Zirc, which increased its membership threefold and by 1898 had reached the impressive total of 138, including 103 priests. This success enabled the monks to take over in 1878 the financially burdensome Saint Gotthard from the Austrian Heiligenkreuz and to open at the same time their fourth gymnasium, adding a fifth in the early years of the next century in Budapest.

It was certainly remarkable that in 1898 the number of priests in the Common Observance was 644, higher than the corresponding figure in the statistics of the Strict Observance. The huge disparity between the two branches of the Order in total membership was caused by the fact that while the Common Observance had only 146 lay-brothers, the Trappists counted nearly 2,000 brothers.

Selfless dedication to hard work, particularly in the field of teaching and pastoral care, can also be demonstrated by statistical figures gathered in 1898. Nearly half the priests were engaged in parish work; they cared altogether for more than a quarter of a million souls. Of the remaining priests, 118 were employed as teachers in the Order's own, but public and officially accredited, gymnasiums. Most of these were eight-year institutions, offering university preparatory courses from the fifth to the twelfth grade. The tuition was minimal, but the schools were dedicated to the education of an intellectual elite and as such they were considered to be among the best, particularly those in Hungary. Most of the novices of the fast growing Zirc were recruited from the ranks of Cistercian students.

Great effort was made for the proper education of each member of the Order; intellectual ability was, therefore, required for admission. With the exception of those few who volunteered for lay-brotherhood, every professed member had to go through formal training in philosophy and theology, and those destined for teaching were expected to obtain advanced degrees in the various arts and sciences. Among them 24 monks were doctors of theology, 22 were doctors of philosophy and 3 were doctors of law. The volume of scholarly publications rose steadily throughout the century. The fact that the *Cistercienser-Chronik* was a monthly journal edited and written by and for the monks of Austria-Hungary can be cited as another proof of the prevailing love of learning.

The country where after 1860 the Order was exposed to endless vexations was the unified Italy. The anti-clerical government requisitioned monastic buildings mostly for military purposes and only the churches were spared for the sake of the parishioners. Such was the fate in 1871 of the two great Roman abbeys, both losing at the same time their priceless libraries. In order to secure their survival, in 1876 the homeless monks purchased a modest residence at Cortona, which, after 1883, began to receive novices.

In an attempt to render an account of the nineteenth-century achievements of the Common Observance, one may point out that, while monastic observances were reduced to essentials, the Order scored significantly in numbers, level of erudition, pastoral and educational services, and assured for Cistercians a high repute in all echelons of contemporary society.

XVI

Cistercians in the Twentieth Century

 A historical account of the Cistercian Order throughout the first three quarters of the twentieth century cannot be reduced to a few dominant trends. Although the new century arrived as a smooth continuation of the preceding epoch, the outbreak of the First World War introduced an era of unprecedented violence and destruction, both physical and moral, which was climaxed in the holocaust of the Second World War. After thirty years of agony the falling of bombs has subsided, but the consolidation and hoped-for peace have failed to return. It was not only the prolonged Cold War, the confrontation between the forces of Communism and democracy, that prevented the re-establishment of a condition which has survived in the memories of an older generation as "normalcy." By the middle of the century it had become evident that the ethical foundations, the values on which the old-fashioned equilibrium could be rebuilt, had been hopelessly shattered. The intense questioning of all inherited standards continued through the 1960s, without finding a basis for new consensus. What has eventually emerged is the idea of a "pluralistic society," in which various and contradictory concepts may co-exist. This seems to amount to the admission that the questions have outnumbered the possible answers and there is no longer hope of finding a new creed worth dying for. For anyone schooled in the history of institutions and civilizations, this assumption poses still other fundamental questions: can a "pluralistic Church" serve as the nucleus of a new civilization? Can any civilization be conceived without a firm set of absolute values, without a firm belief in authority?

The study of a divided religious order within a continually turbulent world, in which the chronicler himself is an unwitting participant, is fraught with pitfalls. The great abbeys of the Order which stood in the nineteenth century as islands of timeless serenity have been caught up in divisive disputes over values and principles. Since fundamental questions have yet to be answered, there is no way to view the immediate past from an unclouded vantage point. In order to minimize errors of judgment, only the bare outlines of largely external events must here suffice.

207

THE STRICT OBSERVANCE

The Cistercians of the Strict Observance entered the twentieth century in the midst of a vigorous territorial expansion, although not all of their new foundations proved to be enduring. The Trappist General Chapter habitually answered the calls of bishops for monks with unswerving generosity. In making decisions, however, the availability of personnel was more determinative than questions of climate, environment, material resources or political implications.

The first settlement in Africa, Staouéli in French Algeria, was initiated in 1843 with massive government assistance and the abbey soon became the richest in the Order. But reliance on the good will of civil authorities proved to be a dangerous liability as soon as anti-clerical elements gained the upper hand in Paris. Afraid of impending suppression, the fathers sold the place and in 1904 moved to Maguzzano in Italy on the shores of Lake Garda. An even more promising venture in South Africa, Mariannhill in Natal (1882), was soon endangered for a different reason. The monks attracted a large number of native vocations, particularly to the lay-brotherhood, but the hunger of souls for the word of God was so great that the community found itself involved in an ever more demanding missionary work. This the General Chapter could not condone and in 1909, with the concurrence of the Holy See, the community was detached from the Order to continue to function as an independent organization of missionaries. A foundation from Westmalle in the Belgian Congo had to be given up in 1925 for similar reasons.

Inhospitable climate and a strange and often hostile environment lay behind the failure of various foundations in the Pacific. A settlement on the island of New Caledonia in 1874 had to be transferred after sixteen years of futility to Australia (Beagle Bay), only to find even greater problems there, which forced the closing of the heroic enterprise in 1903. The same fate at about the same time befell a settlement in New Britain, east of New Guinea, then a German colony. A Brazilian foundation sponsored by Sept-Fons in the early years of the new century came to an end in 1927.

Canada offered a far more congenial surrounding to the enterprising monks. The highly successful Notre-Dame du Lac in the province of Quebec in 1881 was followed in 1892 by two others: Mistassini in the same province, and Our Lady of the Prairies in Manitoba. In the Far East a foundation in Japan, Phare (1896) seemed to be taking firm roots. On the other hand, political instability and the approaching war made two new ventures in the Near East precarious from the beginning.

A justification for the flurry of new overseas foundations around the turn of the century can be found in the political conditions of France, where, in the wake of the notorious "Dreyfus Affair," the reins of the government slipped into the hands of inveterate enemies of the Church. Anti-clerical laws were in the making since 1901 and within two years all religious houses were faced with the danger of immediate dissolution. Some 1,500 of them were indeed closed, but Dom Jean-Baptiste Chautard (1858-1935), abbot of Sept-Fons, successfully pleaded for the survival of Trappist monasteries, and only two smaller houses, Fontgombault and Chambarand, had to be evacuated. The latter house was eventually re-established by Trappistine nuns.

The First World War came as a severe trial to French Cistercians, for neither priests nor religious were exempt from active military duty. Many monks died in defense of their land and several abbeys, such as Ölenberg, Mont-des-Cats and Igny, suffered grave material damage. The rebuilt Igny was later transferred to Trappistine nuns. After its total devastation in the war, the Syrian foundation, Akbès, had to be given up in 1919. In the same year the new Yugoslav government evicted the predominantly German community from the Bosnian house of Mariastern.

Postwar conditions seriously endangered the position of Trappist foundations in China, which dated back to 1883. The flourishing Notre-Dame de Consolation near Peking was ravaged during the Japanese attack of 1937. Whatever could still be saved was annihilated ten years later by the Communists, who killed some thirty of the surviving monks. The younger foundation, Liesse, was more fortunate. The abbey had to be evacuated but the community managed to find refuge and a new home at Lantao within the territory of Hongkong.

In Spain, the country of vigorous Trappist expansion in the 1920s (La Oliva, Huerta, Osera), the monks soon found themselves in the midst of the bloody civil war of 1936-1939. Most houses escaped serious damage, but Viaceli near Santander was not only thoroughly sacked and bombed by the Loyalists, but lost nineteen monks murdered in cold blood by a band of anarchists in the last days of 1936.

The emergence of the Nazi government made the existence of German houses precarious. Within a few years the Second World War posed grave dangers to every Cistercian abbey throughout the belligerent countries of Europe.

Engelszell in Austria was secularized in 1939. Mariawald in the Rhineland was suppressed in 1941 and severely damaged in 1945. Ölenberg suffered nearly total devastation during the last few months of the same war. Maria-Erlösung (Marija Zvijezda) in Yugoslav Styria was expropriated by the German army in 1941 and the monks transferred to Mariastern, whose own life was soon endangered by the Tito regime, when under the pretext of agrarian reform all monastic lands were confiscated.

Many of the younger monks of French abbeys were called to arms following the declaration of war in 1939. The lightning German invasion of 1940 resulted in relatively few casualties, but a large number of monk-soldiers were taken as prisoners of war. Under German occupation all French abbeys continued to function, but those in Belgium and Holland had much to suffer. Scourmont was evacuated twice and most of its buildings were occupied by the German *Luftwaffe*. Echt and Achel were entirely expropriated by the Germans and the monks dispersed. Tegelen was almost totally destroyed in the fighting of late 1944.

The Allied invasion of Normandy brought the war back to many French abbeys, some of which, like Notre-Dame des Dombes and Timadeuc, took a more or less active part in the resistance. The latter community was eventually awarded the "Cross of Resistance." The Belgian abbey of Orval was similarly noted for offering assistance to the patriotic "Secret Army" of that country.

In Italy, Frattocchie near Rome found itself in the front line in 1943-44 and escaped only in seriously damaged condition.

Once the war was over, the work of recovery was rapid, proving again the Order's extraordinary resilience. In spite of the very considerable losses, in 1947 the Cistercian Strict Observance operated sixty-four houses with the total of about four thousand monks. Comparing these figures with those of 1894, the net gain throughout that most turbulent half century amounted to eight monasteries and about eight hundred monks.

The most spectacular gains of the century were yet to be scored, particularly during the decade of the 1950s, when a dozen new foundations were made and the number of monks approached forty-five hundred. In the United States alone, between 1944 and 1956, the number of Trappist establishments grew from three to twelve, while membership increased from about three hundred to one thousand.

Beginning in the mid-1960s the Order began to lose considerably in membership, particularly among lay-brothers, although several new foundations were made, especially in black Africa. According to the statistics of December 31, 1972, the Strict Observance controlled 84 establishments, housing 3,090 choir monks and novices, among them 1,685 priests, and 325 brothers, a grand total of 3,415.

The amazing growth and equally unexpected drop of membership within the same decade should pose an intriguing question to students of religious history. The great attraction of the monastic vocation felt among veterans of the war is an undeniable fact which may find explanation in the disillusionment of those millions forced to be instruments in the suicidal destruction of a great but basically materialistic civilization. When the idols of that generation had crumbled to heaps of ashes, the spiritual vacuum was easily filled with a new appreciation of Christianity in its most genuine and uncompromising appearance: monasticism. The search of thousands for God ended in a Cistercian abbey, where they found compassionate love, unhesitating answers, a way of doing penance for the disastrous past, and a chance to start a new life dedicated solely to divine contemplation. The monolithic structure of the Order, its liturgy and discipline, which in their never changing routine appeared ageless, must have increased in every novice the feeling of security, of having arrived at a harbor of perennial serenity, of enjoying a foretaste of heaven.

Vocations formed primarily in the experience of spiritual security were rudely shaken by the perplexing challenges raised in the wake of the Second Vatican Council. Experimentation with new forms of worship, new standards of discipline and new ideas of government inevitably divided monastic communities. Those who had left the war in order to find peace within the cloister were greatly disturbed and many of them left disillusioned. Individual motives cannot be easily classified, but the statistical figures themselves are revealing. During the two decades under examination (1951-1971), 696 solemnly professed members departed, not counting those who lived outside of their monasteries in the state of "exclaustration." During the first five year period of these twenty years, 121 monks left; in the second five year period, 151; in the third, 186; in the fourth, 232.

In all truth, the concept of the Strict Observance as a fortress and custodian of timeless monastic traditions proved mistaken. A gradual departure from the ideas of Lestrange and eventually even of Rancé, occurred during the nineteenth century and the same trend continued at a faster pace after the union of Trappist congregations in 1892. A milestone on the road leading toward the resumption of genuinely Cistercian traditions was the publication of a revised version of the Trappist *Spiritual Directory* in 1910, prepared by Dom Vital Lehodey (1857-1948), abbot of Bricquebec. It was an outgrowth of the author's deep understanding for mental prayer (*The Ways of Mental Prayer*, 1908), which in any genuine monastic life ought to take precedence over observances of external asceticism. The merits of the new *Directory* lay in a progressive liberation from a somewhat rigoristic pessimism characteristic of the nineteenth-century Trappist milieu and the breaking of a fresh path returning to the classical traditions of mysticism.

The new code of canon law promulgated in 1917 under the auspices of Benedict XV served as a powerful incentive for the modification of the old Constitution in 1925, followed by the readjustment of the Book of Usages in 1935. These undertakings were accomplished by the collaboration of a new generation of such fine scholars as Anselme Le Bail, Colomban Bock, and Joseph Canivez, all members of the Belgian abbey of Scourmont. Dom Le Bail, who eventually became the abbot of the community, as master of novices, had introduced the systematic reading and study of the early Cistercian authors, and was instrumental in 1934 in launching the first scholarly journal published by the Trappists, the *Collectanea Ordinis Cisterciensium Reformatorum.* One tireless contributor of the new magazine was Abbot Le Bail's erudite secretary, Colomban Bock, an eminent canonist and active member of the Trappist liturgical commission. His work on Cistercian law (*Les codifications du droit cistercien*) is still an indispensable introduction to the subject. The most important Cistercian scholarly undertaking of the century was undoubtedly the publication between 1933 and 1941 of the statutes of the General Chapter from the beginning to the French Revolution (*Statuta Capitulorum Generalium Ordinis Cisterciensis,*) in eight volumes. by Joseph Canivez. This work alone would have been enough to revitalize monastic studies both within and without the Order.

The growing interest in monastic studies and Cistercian traditions gave birth in 1950 to still another important journal, *Cîteaux in de Nederlanden,* later simply entitled *Cîteaux.* While the *Collectanea* continued to concentrate on spirituality, the new periodical took up the promotion of historical studies and as such attracted a number of distinguished contributors not otherwise affiliated with the Order. The promotion of professional education in the fields of philosophy and theology was the purpose of Monte Cistello, a new house of studies in Rome, established in 1958 together with the new residence of the abbot general, next to the old abbey of Tre Fontane. In the school year 1959-60 sixty-eight young monks populated the new institution, twenty-one from the United States, who were free to attend classes of any of the great universities of Rome. It was this group of the younger generation which responded enthusiastically to the call of the Second Vatican Council for religious "renewal" and the subsequent wave of revolutionary changes and continued experimentation were engineered by them, particularly by the most progressive Americans.

The rising significance of Americans within the Order cannot be explained without taking into consideration the influence of Thomas Merton (1915-1968). When he entered Gethsemani in 1941, he appeared to be only one of the many young and disillusioned intellectuals seeking God in that "desert" of Kentucky. But his best-selling autobiography (*The Seven Storey Mountain*) published in 1948 turned out to be the beginning of a prolific literary career, bringing him fame and popularity particularly among the young. He was undoubtedly the magnet which attracted hundreds to one or another of the mushrooming Trappist communities.

Although Merton—"Father Louis" to the monks of his abbey— professed to be always a contemplative, his complex character and close contact with the "world" and all its burning problems can hardly be labelled as typically Trappist. Throughout the various stages of his intellectual and spiritual journey, each amply illustrated by the constant flow of his writings, he became a guide and model to his devout readers. Since he himself possessed a highly receptive mind open to changes and a variety of new approaches to contemporary monasticism, his broad influence certainly contributed to the strength of reforming endeavors.

The demand for change, however, was far from universal within the Order. The old European abbeys preferred a slower pace. They experienced neither the vocation "boom" nor the dramatic vocational crisis of the late sixties in the same measure as did their younger confreres across the Atlantic. Many of them, therefore, remained unconvinced about the necessity for radical and immediate reforms.

The General Chapter took up the challenge and began to wrestle with a broad range of fundamental issues, on many of which the opinions have remained divided. Since it turned out that the whole spectrum of Cistercian life was to come under re-examination, the Order held in succession four special Chapters (1967, 1969, 1971, 1974), wholly dedicated to the problems of renewal. Each lasted several weeks and each produced hefty volumes of position papers, committee reports, minutes of discussions, speeches and consultations with experts on various fields under study.

The fundamental decision was taken to break away from a centralized government and uniformity in observances, in the hope of finding a "more authentic monastic life through a legitimate diversity." In fact, the chapter fathers embraced pluralism as a positive value, entirely compatible with "unity founded upon the experience of fundamental values."

The first and most conspicuous changes pertained to liturgy. The Latin and Gregorian chant were reduced to rarely retained "options," while the whole structure of the divine office was opened to experimentation. Concerning the missal, the Roman rite has prevailed, retaining only some minor Cistercian peculiarities. Certain details remain to be settled and, within given guidelines, local variants would still be permitted.

Another early and equally momentous decision concerned the lay-brotherhood. The distinction between the brothers and choir monks, both in externals and in legal status, was abolished; the brothers were granted an active vote in monastic elections and they were encouraged to participate fully in the liturgical prayers of the community. As has been pointed out, the departure from the Latin found its obvious justification in the fact that without the change to the vernacular the brothers could not fully participate in the liturgy.

A thorough revision of the old Constitution has been initiated, although the process has not reached finality and the writing of a new Constitution is probably years away. Some principles, however, have been generally adopted. Such are decentralization and the strengthening of local autonomy, coupled with the demand of broad consultation in the process of decision-making. Authority is to be exercised only after the consideration of the expressed wishes and desires of the community concerned. Only unity and not uniformity is desired, and even this in the absolute basics. In all details "pluralism will permit each community and even each monk to discover his true identity in Christ," asserted the General Chapter of 1969.

Accordingly, the General Chapter will no longer hold annual sessions. On the other hand, hitherto informal regional conferences, organized on national or linguistic bases, may become annual affairs entrusted with such important functions as the evaluation of community experiments in each abbey of the region. The traditional Definitory, with somewhat reduced authority, has been renamed Resident Council and attached to the office of the abbot general. The ideal of a representative government came to forceful expression in the newly organized General Council (*Consilium Generale*), in which the individual regions (twelve in number) would enjoy adequately balanced participation. The legislative process would no longer concern itself with details of observances, but would rather watch over the integrity of the spirit of the Rule of Saint Benedict and the principles of the *Charter of Charity*.

In the much debated matter of the abbots' term in office, the traditional term for life has been dropped and abbots, including the abbot general, will be elected for an undetermined time, or as long as they can truly serve the good of the community. How long this term should be could be decided by periodic votes of confidence. Meanwhile, as an "experiment," individual communities might elect abbots for a fixed term of six years.

In the field of customs, usages and observances the last four Chapters of renewal adopted a flexible attitude and in this process such ancient institutions as the chapter of faults have fallen into desuetude. Without weakening the spirit of penance, concessions concerning food and clothing were granted, in view of local circumstances, and even the obligation of sleeping in common dormitories has been abolished and free option has been given for building individual cells. Similarly, while silence and separation from the world have received new emphasis, many of the old restrictions on communications have been removed.

The universal scope and sweeping character of the changes that have taken place within the Cistercians of the Strict Observance, an Order justly proud of its fidelity to timeless monastic traditions, has no parallel in history beyond the past turbulent decade. Startling as they are, in the perspective of the developments sketched on the last few pages, the novelties have been well prepared by a number of gradually evolving phenomena:

The geographical extension of the Order far beyond the confines of Europe tended to decrease the firmness of control exerted by French mother-houses. In fact, the inevitability of certain adjustments of regulations in abbeys established under tropical climates has long been in evidence.

The rigidity of a daily schedule dominated by a proliferated liturgy has been challenged with increasing vigor by those in favor of an atmosphere more conducive to contemplation.

The plurality of lay-brothers, often well-educated professional people, raised the demand for their greater participation in monastic government and furnished justification for the introduction of vernacular liturgy.

Greater emphasis on scholastic studies gradually eroded the tradition of rustic simplicity and rendered the communities more receptive to contemporary currents.

And finally, the rapid numerical growth of vocations created serious problems in the strict formation of candidates, while the balance shifted in favor of the young, who, by nature, turned out to be better disposed toward changes than their tradition-bound elders.

Whether the bold new style and structure of religious life will indeed lead toward the desired spiritual renewal is a question only monks of the next generation can answer.

THE COMMON OBSERVANCE

For the Common Observance, too, the twentieth century opened a new era of both expansion and unexpected adversities. In France, to some degree, the story of Abbé Barnouin was repeated. A wealthy and devoted priest, Bernard Maréchal, formerly a member of the Congregation of the Blessed Sacrament, was searching for a community willing to sponsor his plan of founding a contemplative monastery with the special purpose of perpetual adoration of the Blessed Sacrament. Fontfroide of the Congregation of Sénanque adopted the idea. Dom Maréchal joined the Cistercians and in 1892 built a new monastery at his own expense at Pont Colbert near Versailles, becoming himself the first abbot of the new establishment. However, peaceful monastic life could not be continued for long. The persecution of religious orders between 1900 and 1904 interrupted the lives of Sénanque, Fontfroide and also Pont Colbert. Some of the monks sought refuge in Italy, and others in Spain, but the community of Pont Colbert succeeded in 1904 in founding a new monastery at Onsenoort (Marienkroon) in Holland. After World War I, the dispersed Cistercians were readmitted to France and resumed monastic life at Sénanque and Pont Colbert, while the community of Fontfroide, unable to regain its old home, settled down in 1919 in the Pyrenees at an ancient abandoned Benedictine monastery, Saint-Michel de Cuxa. Onsenoort continued its life as an affiliation of Pont Colbert until, more recently, it joined the Belgian Congregation.

In 1898 Mehrerau revived as its second daughter-house the old Cistercian abbey of Sittich (Stična) in Slovenia (founded 1135, suppressed 1784). For this flourishing community the end of World War I presented a crucial problem. Because the abbey fell within the borders of the new state of Yugoslavia, the German speaking monks of the community found it advisable to leave the country. They found a temporary home (1921-1931) in Germany at Bronnbach (Baden), a former Cistercian abbey, then the property of the family of Prince Löwenstein; later they purchased the abandoned Cistercian convent of Seligenporten (Upper Palatinate) where monastic life was resumed in 1931. Stična in 1925 revitalized the Polish monastery of Mogila, at one time a house of studies for the Polish Congregation, which after a long period *in commendam* had been greatly weakened in membership. Through the work of Slovenian monks it joined the Congregation of Mehrerau.

Similar causes brought further increase to the family of Mehrerau. Its new member was the resurgent Himmerod, one of the largest Cistercian abbeys of medieval Germany, suppressed in 1802. The German members of the Trappist monastery of Mariastern in Bosnia (Yugoslavia), unable to continue their lives under the new regime, had purchased the ruins of the ancient monastery of Himmerod in 1919. Since the Archbishop of Trier had insisted that the members of the new establishment must actively co-operate in pastoral duties—a condition unacceptable to Trappists—the monks turned to the Common Observance for assistance. Marienstatt accepted the sponsorship of the new foundation and, within a short time, a magnificent new monastery rose from the ruins. Marienstatt became the mother-abbey of another revived Cistercian house at Hardehausen (Westphalia) in 1927. When the Nazi regime confiscated their property in 1938, the monks found temporary shelter in the city of Magdeburg until the end of the war. Mehrerau also revived in 1939 the ancient Swiss abbey of Hauterive, suppressed in 1848.

With the exception of the Polish houses, the military operations of World War I had left the establishments of the Common Observance untouched. The subsequent peace treaties however, led to a regrouping of the existing Congregations. The partition of Austria-Hungary loosened the bond among the members of the Austrian Congregation. Hohenfurt and Ossegg, falling within the borders of the new Czechoslovakia, formed the Congregation of the Immaculate Heart of Mary in 1920. Zirc and its dependent houses constituted the long-desired Hungarian Congregation in 1923. Mehrerau had already gathered its own foundations into a separate Congregation since 1888, while the remaining Austrian houses were united into the Congregation of the Sacred Heart of Jesus.

More important than these administrative changes was the fusion, in 1929, of the Congregation of Casamari and its three affiliated houses with the Common Observance. This group, although originally quite close to the discipline of the Trappists, had refused to join the union of 1892, and had remained independent. In union with the Common Observance the Congregation proved its real vigor by founding eight new houses in Italy within twenty years, and by doubling its membership. The Congregation of Saint Bernard in Italy also contributed to the general expansion by the revival of the first Spanish house since the secularization. The mighty medieval Poblet in the province of Tarragona was restored in 1940. The renewal of the Breton Boquen in 1936 was the work of Dom Alexis Presse (1883-1965), formerly abbot of the Trappist Tamié, a remarkable character of an earlier monastic renewal. Dom Alexis, after his departure from Tamié, lived for some time as a hermit amidst the ruins of Boquen, then gathered a few kindred souls and began the rebuilding of the twelfth-century cloister. In 1950 his small community was received into the

Common Observance, although it remained basically contemplative. Unfortunately, Dom Alexis survived by only a few months the consecration of the expertly-restored church of Boquen in 1965.

The General Chapter, convening in every fifth year, resumed its routine work of central administration, although it was greatly impaired by the fact that neither the assembly nor the abbot general had a permanent residence, properly provided office or adequate staff. Thus, the Chapter of 1900 was held at Rome, those of 1905 and 1910 at the abbey of Stams in Austria and in 1920 it convened at Mehrerau. When, as the successor of Abbot Wackarz, Amadeus de Bie, abbot of Bornhem, was elected head of the Order in 1900, he decided to reside at Rome, temporarily as a guest of Santa Croce, later in a rented apartment. After his death in 1920, however, the new Abbot General, Cassian Haid, abbot of Wettingen-Mehrerau, accepted the election only on the condition that he might stay at his beloved Mehrerau. His wish was respected, but since the Congregation of Religious stressed anew the necessity of establishing the headquarters of the Order at Rome, Cassian Haid resigned in 1927 and an extraordinary Chapter elected Francis Janssens, abbot of Pont Colbert, who was to procure a permanent residence in Rome. In the same year the Order purchased a house on Monte Gianicolo (Villa Stolberg), which served as the residence of the Abbot general until 1950, when a new building was finished at a more convenient location, worthily housing not only the officials of the central government but also serving as a general house of study for the whole Order.

The satisfactory solution of mere technicalities did not solve another problem of vital importance—the successful function of the Order as an organic unit. The monasteries of the Order which survived the French Revolution and the secularization of the early nineteenth century lacked real cohesion. The abbeys of the Habsburg Empire and Italy, as remnants of once more or less independent Congregations each with its immemorial customs and privileges, willingly re-established the office of the abbot general and the General Chapter, but the idea of unified discipline, strict control and direction exerted from outside, lacked firm roots. The main subject of discussion at all Chapters from 1900 on was the precise definition of the power and authority of the abbot general and of the General Chapter. A patient and understanding approach to the problem by all interested parties finally brought success. After several previous attempts and after years of experimentation, the General Chapter of 1933 composed a constitution for the central government of the Order, which was approved by the Congregation of Religious in the following year. Written under the guidance of the new canon law it proved to be a skillful combination of Cistercian traditions with modern requirements.

218

An excellent proof of the efficiency of the revitalized General Chapter on one hand and of the Order's spontaneous vigor on the other was the beginning of active missionary work and through it a rapid expansion outside of the European continent. The Chapter of 1925 wholeheartedly supported the new program of extensive foreign missions sponsored by Pope Pius XI and it outlined how a monastic community could do missionary work without sacrificing its basic characteristics. Cistercians, instead of putting single monks in isolated missionary stations, were to establish properly organized communities and through their living example and educational activity promote and deepen true Christian life and culture.

This difficult task found a zealous promoter in Abbot Aloysius Wiesinger of Schlierbach, whose monastery soon became the center of the movement. At the extraordinary Chapter of 1927, the Abbot reported on the results of his investigations concerning North and South America, and the work was begun immediately. Himmerod, though itself struggling with the difficulties of an arduous beginning, sent out its pioneers to Itaporanga (São Paulo, Brazil). While the priests were engaged in pastoral duties, the brothers successfully adapted themselves to local methods of ranching and in 1939 they laid the foundations of a new monastery. Today the flourishing foundation has attained the rank of an abbey, and besides extensive parish work, the monks are engaged in agriculture.

A donation of the large estate of Jequitibá (Bahia, Brazil) became the foundation of a mission by Schlierbach in 1938. By 1945, they had finished a considerable part of their building program and besides their routine missionary activities they have been active in the field of education. In 1950 this monastery was also elevated to the rank of an abbey. A third Brazilian foundation, that of Itatinga in 1951, was made by the community of Hardehausen which had been left homeless after the abbey's suppression in 1938. In 1952 the Holy See recognized Itatinga as the legal successor of the abbey of Hardehausen. In 1961 the three Brazilian houses formed the Brazilian Congregation of the Holy Cross.

At the request of Pope Pius XI, since 1930 the Congregation of Casamari has trained in its own seminary for the monastic vocation a large number of native African boys from Eritrea, which was then an Italian colony. After finishing their studies, they were sent back to their country, where a new and flourishing Cistercian monastery came to life in 1940, near Asmara. In their liturgy they follow the Ethiopian rite, but they have remained affiliated to the Congregation of Casamari.

In French Indochina (Vietnam) in 1918 a missionary priest, Henri Denis, founded an establishment for native contemplative vocations at

Phuoc-Son. In 1933 the community applied for membership in the Cistercian Common Observance and the General Chapter of the same year granted their request. In 1935 the overflowing population of Phuoc-Son established another house in the north, Chau-Son. The civil war engulfing the country after 1945 forced the latter community to flee to the south, finding in 1953 a lasting home at Phuoc-Ly. In the same year even Phuoc-Son was forced to move to the south, re-establishing community life at Thu-Duc. In spite of the turmoil of the incessant war the Vietnamese Cistercians experienced a steady growth and formed their own congregation (1964) named after the Holy Family, uniting five communities. The final victory of Communist forces early in 1975, however, has jeopardized the very survival of Cistercian life in that long-suffering country.

Abbot General Janssens exhibited a keen interest in the expansion of the Order in North America. At his personal initiative and constant prodding, between 1928 and 1932 four properties were acquired for the purpose of foundations, two in Canada and another two in the United States. But the timing of the action was ill-chosen. The worldwide depression rendered the financial bases of the nascent institutions extremely precarious and the outbreak of the Second World War severed the vital link between Europe and America. Rougemont, one of the Canadian foundations in Quebec, survived under the sponsorship of the French Lérins and eventually proved to be a prosperous member of the Congregation of Sénanque, newly renamed Congregation of the Immaculate Conception. In 1950 Rougemont was promoted to an abbey.

In the United States, Our Lady of Spring Bank in Wisconsin was populated by Austrian monks in 1928, but the struggling monks soon found themselves in grave financial difficulties aggravated by immigration laws preventing lay-brothers from becoming permanent residents in the country. The small community did survive but its future remained uncertain for many years. The second American foundation in the state of Mississippi, named Our Lady of Gerowval (1935), was unable to rise above the level of a small residence operating a missionary parish.

During the course of the Second World War few houses of the Common Observance in Europe survived without considerable material damage and in Germany and Austria, where the monks were not exempt from active military service, scores died on the various fields of battle, while others spent years in captivity as prisoners of war. Far more tragic, however, was the postwar arrangement which assured Communist control over the countries falling behind the "Iron Curtain." The two flourishing communities in Czechoslovakia (Hohenfurt and Ossegg) were secularized and the monks dispersed. In Hungary the same policy was carried out (1948-1950), and ended the life of Zirc with all its affiliated houses and schools. Many monks, including Abbot Vendel Endrédy, were imprisoned; others were forced to find secular employment. Only a fraction of its nearly 250 members managed to flee abroad.

In Poland, although all religious institutions came under rigid governmental controls, the Order has survived. Young vocations enabled the Polish Congregation to regain and repopulate several old houses of the Order and, according to the latest count, six monasteries accommodate 110 Cistercians.

A considerable contingent of Hungarian refugee monks succeeded in finding new opportunities in the United States. At first they helped revitalize the depopulated Spring Bank in Wisconsin, then, in 1956, most of them participated in the foundation of the University of Dallas, where they soon erected their new abbey, Our Lady of Dallas, and their own college preparatory school for boys. After the Hungarians' departure, Spring Bank admitted a small group of former Trappists. In 1967 this same group founded a priory at New Ringgold, Pennsylvania, near Allentown. Meanwhile, monks of the suppressed Ossegg managed to reassemble at Rosenthal near Dresden and others of the same abbey regrouped at Langwaden near Düsseldorf. The abbey of Hohenfurt was united in 1958 with the Austrian abbey of Rein.

During the difficult postwar years the most vigorous congregation in the Common Observance proved to be the Italian Casamari which, between 1950 and 1974, not only increased the number of affiliated houses but also raised the total membership from 151 to 206. This Congregation includes Our Lady of Fatima, a small American community founded in 1967 in Moorestown, New Jersey.

The vocational crisis of the 1960s proved fatal to several European communities. In 1967 the German Seligenporten had to be suppressed for lack of vocations; in France the Congregation of the Immaculate Conception (Sénanque) was forced to give up Saint-Michel de Cuxa, Pont Colbert after a temporary transfer to Auberive, and even Sénanque, in order to insure sufficient membership for Lérins. Another severe loss was Boquen which after the death of Abbot Alexis Presse was converted to an experimental youth center of renewal, lost its monastic character and was therefore suppressed in 1973. On the other hand, in 1967, a second Spanish house was founded by monks of Poblet—Solius in the province of Gerona.

Within the Common Observance the impact of the demand for "renewal" created no revolution comparable to that which prevailed among the ranks of the Strict Observance. The idea of "pluralism," local autonomy, a positive response to the needs of the contemporary Church and a fruitful interaction between the monastery and the world, have all been long in practice in most congregations of the Common Observance.

Nevertheless, two special sessions of the General Chapter were spent in consideration of the new demands, one in 1968 in Rome, the other in 1969 at the German abbey of Marienstatt. From these conventions issued a long and detailed declaration (fifty-two printed pages) on the place of Cistercian monasticism in the modern world, and a new constitution for the supreme government of the Order.

In 109 articles the new constitution defines the "Cistercian Order" (O.Cist.) as "a union of congregations" governed by a General Chapter under the presidency of an abbot general. In addition to all abbots, the membership of the General Chapter includes delegates from each house or congregation, proportionate to the number of monks. The Chapter is to be convened every fifth year to legislate for the Order as a whole. The abbot general is to be elected by the Chapter for ten years, although he remains always re-eligible. He is to reside in Rome, and he is aided by a council of four, also elected by the Chapter. The historical *definitorium* which has been renamed "synod," is to include the abbot general, the procurator general, the presidents of each congregation and five other members elected by the General Chapter. The Synod is to meet at least every other year, and is to deal with urgent matters emerging between meetings of the General Chapter.

The regulation of monastic life on the local level is reserved to the autonomous congregations, each under an elected "abbot president" and a "congregational chapter," in which they rule on such important matters as the length of the abbots' term in office, the legal position of lay-brothers, liturgical reform and monastic observances. The primary duty of each abbot president is the triennial visitation of each house of his congregation. His own abbey is visited by the abbot general.

The General Chapter of 1974 met in the Italian Casamari with the participation, for the first time, of Cistercian abbesses as observers. The convention confirmed, with minor modifications, the work of the previous extraordinary "renewal" sessions and considered, among many other things, liturgical matters and the persisting vocational crisis.

The statistics compiled for this session of the Chapter proved that the decrease in membership during the past decade had not been precipitous in spite of the tragic and irreparable losses to the Order behind the "Iron Curtain." In 1950 the total membership was 1,724; in 1974 it was 1,547, a decrease somewhat in excess of ten percent. The number of novices did

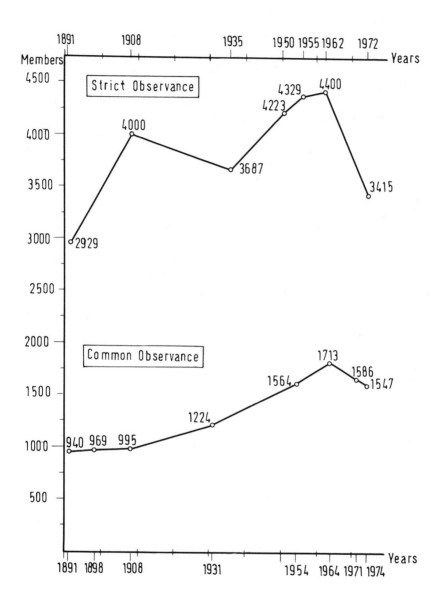

Changes in the number of personnel in both Cistercian Observances between 1891 and 1974.

not show great fluctuation. What was unusual was the high rate of attrition among novices: of 623 choir novices admitted between 1961 and 1965, only 264 survived the novitiate and the ratio of survival was even lower among novices for brotherhood. Between 1966 and 1970 fewer choir novices were admitted (525), but relatively more (247) reached first profession.

Another reason for the general decline in membership has been the number of those who left the Order after solemn profession. Between 1964 and 1968, 14 monks asked for dispensation from their vows before ordination; 20 priests were secularized; 13 received permission to live permanently outside of their monasteries; 2 priests were laicized. Between 1969 and 1974 the figures for the same categories and in the same order had grown to 20, 31, 12 and 30. The great increase in laicizations is particularly noteworthy.

Those who seek comfort in the fact that the decrease within the Order has been far lower than it has in some other institutions were warned by the Austrian abbots, who pointed out the alarming disproportion between the young and the old. In 1974, out of the total of Austrian monks and novices (329), over 18 percent were above 70 years of age and only 10 percent below 30. By far the largest age group (26.3 percent) was of those between 60 and 70. It is, indeed, only a very recent increase in the number of novices which holds out any hope for an appreciable growth of the Order in the near future.

PART II

Cistercian Life and Culture

XVII

Spirituality and Learning

The great spiritual renewal of the Gregorian Reform stimulated a general desire to return to the sources of Christianity in order to rejuvenate and purify the world in conformity with the exalted ideals of the primitive Church. Those who endeavored to free the hierarchy and secular clergy from the allurement of the world looked to the example of the Apostles; various lay-movements found new inspiration for their programs of religious and social reconstruction in the Gospel; within monastic communities the appeal of the traditions of the earliest Desert Fathers grew steadily stronger.

The movement generated a growing interest in eastern Christianity and, especially, the Holy Land, while the actual connections with the Near East elicited an intense curiosity about the fate of the great shrines of Jerusalem. The universal enthusiasm reached its climax in the First Crusade, filling Christian Society as a whole with a heroic zeal for Christ and His cause.

The monastic reform of the eleventh century, permeated by the same spirit of heroism found itself confronted with a peculiar problem: the obvious antagonism between the model of the Desert Fathers and the dominant Rule of Saint Benedict. Leading and influential authorities, such as Saint Peter Damian, did not hesitate to solve the dilemma by boldly declaring themselves in favor of the eremitic life, arguing that the Rule had been written only for beginners, whereas the imitation of the Desert Fathers was meant to lead to perfection. A number of religious communities were organized according to the new ideals, the most significant among them being Camaldoli and Vallombrosa.

North of the Alps the direct influence of Peter Damian and his followers was not decisive. In France, however, a long series of more or less successful reforms revealed similar aspirations. Stephen Muret, Bernard of Tiron, Bruno of Cologne, Robert of Arbrissel, Vitalis of Mortain and many others were unanimous in their criticism of the contemporary state of monasticism and, under the inspiration of the heroic virtues of the Desert Fathers, sought its reorganization through a return to the severe asceticism of pre-Benedictine models. Complete detachment from the world, great poverty and strict penance were the common characteristics of their programs, although in detail they varied considerably.

In this atmosphere of feverish reform activities the initiative of Saint Robert, a restless champion of monastic renewal, did not appear unusual. When he and his companions undertook the foundation of Molesme their aim was not far removed from that of their predecessors and contemporaries laboring in the same endeavor. Robert's effort was rewarded by remarkable success. As the number of monks increased, however, there emerged once again the crucial problem—the proper interpretation of the Rule of Saint Benedict. The heated debates disturbed the peace of the young community, and the Abbot and his faithful disciples were repeatedly forced to seek refuge and consolation in the solitude of neighboring hermitages. As a result of the prolonged discussions, Robert's circle reached a significant conclusion: in order to reanimate the basic ideals of monasticism, the monks must return to the letter of the Rule and disregard later interpretations or modifications of any kind. The theory put into practice, through the strictest legal interpretation of a document almost six hundred years old, led to the establishment of a life of hardships, worthy of the heroic examples of the Desert Fathers, although in its severity it undeniably surpassed Saint Benedict's genuine intention. The reformers of Molesme were scarcely aware of such a possibility; their continuous reference to the Rule constituted firm legal support for their case against any attack or opposition.

This uncompromising will to live according to the Rule, combined with an ardent desire for solitude, became the cornerstone of Cîteaux. In this skillful combination of the ascetic ideals of the popular eremitism with the traditional form of Benedictine monasticism lies the real importance of the Cistercian reform. Cîteaux provided ample opportunity for those ready to follow the heroic virtues of the Desert Fathers, while the new foundation saved both the cenobitic character of monastic life and the absolute authority of Saint Benedict and his Rule.

The consolidation of the "New Monastery" was the work of Robert's immediate successors, Alberic and Stephen. It is difficult to determine exactly what share each of them had in the formation of Cistercian spirituality. In the earliest documents of Cîteaux, poverty, simplicity and detachment from all worldly affairs seem to be the most vigorously stressed virtues. Poverty and extreme simplicity in every phase of their life was a natural consequence of the arduous circumstances. Their complete segregation from society entailed their own hard manual labor, which in other contemporary monasteries was provided by serfs. This humble and exhausting toil became another distinctive feature of the Order; a few years later it came to be shared with a growing number of lay-brothers. At the beginning, the arduous work of clearing and tilling their land aggravated the monks' already heavy burdens to such a degree that anyone intending to join the community was deterred by the "unusual and almost unheard of austerity of their lives" (*Exordium parvum*).

The written documents of the first two decades of Cîteaux's history, such as the *Exordium Cistercii* and the earliest version of the *Carta caritatis,* have been traditionally attributed to Stephen Harding, although his authorship is by no means certain. Only three short letters and the brief preface to the new Hymnal can be recognized as his authentic works. It was he, however, who contributed decisively to a spiritual and intellectual atmosphere that many of his best contemporaries found irresistible.

In spite of the prevailing spirit of uncompromising asceticism, Cîteaux became under Stephen's regime a unique center of monastic learning. It is hard to conceive how a small community in a remote monastery managed to accomplish such difficult tasks as large-scale liturgical reform, the collection of authentic hymns and Gregorian melodies, the revision of the Bible and the composition of a constitution of admirable wisdom and foresight. In carrying out these tasks, Stephen certainly relied upon his able companions. The *Exordium parvum* explicitly stated that Alberic, Stephen's predecessor, had been a man of letters, well versed in divine and human science, and, when a flood of new candidates finally reached the monastery, the same document joyfully recorded that many of them were noble and learned clerics. Abbot Stephen himself made one significant exception in his program of stern simplicity: he remained an ardent lover of beautiful books. The manuscripts copied in the early days of Cîteaux belong to the most lavishly illuminated codices of the whole century.

When giving a well-deserved credit to the genius of Stephen Harding, one must still admit that for the phenomenal success of Cîteaux Saint Bernard of Clairvaux (1091-1153) was responsible. The appeal of his character drew thousands to the Order, the depth of his spirituality enriched the growing foundations, and his masterly pen carried Cîteaux's message not only to his contemporaries, but to all future generations of western Christianity.

Bernard's formal education, acquired before his entry at Cîteaux in 1113, was not exceptional, but at Cîteaux, under the guidance of Abbot Stephen, and after 1115 as abbot of Clairvaux, inspired by such friends as William of Saint-Thierry, he had the opportunity to acquaint himself with the full range of Latin patristic tradition, particularly with Saint

Augustine, and even with some of the Greek Fathers, such as Gregory of Nyssa and Origen, whose works were available in Latin translation. Another cornerstone of his spirituality as well as his theology was his amazing knowledge of the Bible. The style, vocabulary and imagery of his writings are so saturated with Biblical references that the understanding and proper evaluation of his thought are impossible without constant recourse to the books of both New and Old Testament.

The orientation of Bernard's mind was basically conservative. He distrusted the new philosophy of the schools as represented by Abelard and Gilbert de la Porrée, and fought with all his ardor against the trend to separate reason from faith, theology from life. To him philosophy, theology, morality and personal piety were all combined into one pursuit: "to know Jesus, and Jesus the crucified."

The range of Bernard's writing was broad, but in all of them it was always the monk, the man of God, who spoke. His penetrating and deeply felt personal insights were invariably oriented toward a fuller knowledge and greater love of God.

His first major essay in chronological sequence was *On the Degrees of Humility and Pride,* a sequel to the seventh chapter of the Rule, where Saint Benedict established twelve degrees of humility through which monks were to attain perfection. Bernard, utilizing his unusual understanding of human nature, meditated on twelve degrees of pride as the chief obstacles to monastic perfection. The more famous *Apology to Abbot William,* written at the request of his friend William of Saint-Thierry, was Bernard's contribution to the debate between Cîteaux and Cluny. A spirited defense of Cistercian life and ideals, it served also as a brilliant attack against the extravagant grandeur of Cluny. Its satirical details and the paragraphs on the place of art in monastic life have been some of the most often quoted lines of Bernardine literature.

His treatise *On the Love of God* comes closest to a systematic essay on Bernard's mystical theology. Writing *On Grace and Free Will,* he echoed Saint Augustine's strong stand on the necessity of grace, which frees human nature from the bondage of sin through the saving merits of Jesus Christ. Urged by some fellow monks, Bernard returned to the problems of the interpretation of the Rule and discoursed *On Precept and Dispensation.* The last of his major treatises, *On Consideration,* addressed to the Cistercian pope Eugenius III, would by itself insure its author's immortality. It records the Saint's approach to the burning issues of his time, the nature of the Church and papacy, confronted with the problems stirred up by the Gregorian Reform and the investiture conflict.

Much of Bernard's popularity among his contemporaries rested with his collections of sermons, directed primarily to monastic audiences. Well over three hundred of these carefully composed and edited homilies have survived, each one a monument to the author's inimitable artistry and personal experience. As to their contents, however, most of them were steeped in patristic tradition. Even in his most studied Christology and Mariology, Bernard proved to be a congenial and imaginative continuator of his great predecessors rather than a bold innovator. The exceptions are eighty-six sermons on the *Song of Songs*, in which Bernard found opportunity to reveal and share his mystical experiences. Through these elaborate allegories he established his reputation as the father of medieval mysticism, and his example encouraged a long line of successors to present their own insights wrapped in the same Biblical context.

From the historians' point of view the surviving five hundred pieces of Bernard's correspondence carry particular weight, for they reflect on almost every event and issue in which the Saint was either an active participant, or at least a keen and interested observer. It is through these letters that the complexity of their author's character comes to full display, together with his matchless control of every element of literary artistry.

Saint Bernard stands at the apex of his age, the greatest religious figure of his century and one of the greatest of all times. Posterity has been lavish in paying tribute to both his doctrine and holiness of life. Pope Alexander III canonized him in 1174; Innocent III praised him as *Doctor Egregius*; Humanist scholars, referring to his honeyed eloquence, preferred to call him *Doctor Mellifluus*. Recognized as a bridge between patristic and scholastic theology, he has been venerated as "the last of the Fathers." Recent recognition of his place in history as "Doctor of the Universal Church" was granted to Bernard by Pius VIII in 1830.

Saint Bernard's congenial friend and first biographer, William of Saint-Thierry (d. 1148), must be recognized as an outstanding monastic theologian of the twelfth century, although his stature has until recently been overshadowed by that of the Abbot of Clairvaux. William, an erudite Benedictine monk, first met Bernard in 1118, and fell immediately under the spell of the somewhat younger Cistercian. But William could give as much as he was to receive. It was very likely he who introduced to the young Abbot the Greek Fathers. William, then a monk of Saint-Nicaise of Reims, wished to join Clairvaux at once. Instead he was elected abbot of Saint-Thierry in 1119, a position he retained until 1135, when he resigned and retired to the Cistercian abbey of Signy.

The intellectual and spiritual relationship between William and Bernard was so close that several of William's treatises circulated for centuries under Bernard's name. This was the fate of even his most accomplished work, a synthesis of his mystical theology addressed to Carthusian monks and later known as *The Golden Epistle.* His other essays, among them *On the Contemplation of God* and *On the Nature and Dignity of Love,* have the same theme—the ascent of the soul toward God. God, William was convinced, could be found within the human soul, which bears an indelible imprint of its Creator. In all his works William proved himself to be a profound thinker, whose doctrines differed from that of Bernard through a closer relationship with Augustine and the Greek Fathers as well as through the more pronounced Trinitarian character in its mysticism.

The third great luminary of twelfth-century Cistercian monasticism was Aelred (d. 1167), monk and later abbot of Rievaulx. Born in Northumbria, he grew up in the pious court of King David I of Scotland, and received a fine education. Aelred entered Rievaulx in 1134 as a young man of twenty-four, and soon rose in England to almost the same stature as Bernard had attained in France; in fact, his contemporaries often referred to him as "the Bernard of the North." A spiritual director of magnetic personality, Aelred came close indeed to the Abbot of Clairvaux, although as a thinker and author he was less creative. He shared his fellow monks' fascination with the nature of the soul, and wrote a dialogue on the subject, entitled *De anima,* which closely followed Augustine. His best-known work, another dialogue *On Spiritual Friendship,* treated, under the inspiration of Cicero, a subject closest to his heart. Aelred's booklet on *Jesus at the Age of Twelve* and his *Prayers* of charming piety and simplicity were his contributions to devotional literature. In addition to several sermon collections, he wrote hagiographical works and even an historical work of considerable importance, the *Genealogy of the Kings of England.* Unfortunately, only a small fraction of his extensive correspondence has survived. More than his works, however, the charm of his personality kept his memory alive among his monks, well portrayed in a biography written by one of his admiring disciples, Walter Daniel.

Treading the paths of these three giants, many Cistercian authors contributed to monastic theology, to the extent permitted by their talents and erudition. Those among them who came directly or indirectly into contact with Saint Bernard and Clairvaux constituted a school of specifically Bernardine spirituality.

232

Outstanding among them was Guerric (d. 1157), who spent fifteen years at Clairvaux but ended his life as abbot of Igny. In addition to fifty-four carefully composed liturgical sermons, he was responsible for a treatise— *The Languor of the Soul in Love,* a praise of monastic life spent in happy contemplation of the divine mysteries.

The Englishman Isaac (d. 1169), who served as abbot of the French l'Étoile (Stella), continued the Bernardine tradition in his collection of sermons dealing with various topics with greater knowledge of metaphysics than of mystical experience. More influential than these was his *Letter on the Soul,* which included a sophisticated classification of spiritual and intellectual faculties. His other authentic treatise *On the Mass (De officio missae)* is an allegorical approach to the subject. The work of Alcher of Clairvaux (d. 1165), entitled *On Spirit and Soul,* was meant to be an answer to Isaac's treatise, and for some time was commonly attributed to Augustine, although it was merely a compilation, rich in definitions and classifications, borrowed from a variety of sources.

Geoffrey of Auxerre (d. 1188), a student of Abelard, faithful secretary and biographer of Bernard and for a few years abbot of Clairvaux (1162-1165), left behind several collections of sermons, including one on the *Song of Songs.* Another secretary of the Saint, Nicolas of Clairvaux (d. 1180), enriched posterity by his sermons, notably on the Blessed Virgin, as well as by his correspondence. Hugh (d. 1151), first abbot of Pontigny, a noble relative of Bernard, penned a number of homilies designed for the various feasts of the liturgical calendar. Serlo (d. 1158), abbot of Savigny, and Amadeus (d. 1159), monk of Clairvaux, later abbot of Hautecombe and finally bishop of Lausanne, also contributed similar monastic sermons. Henry of Marcy (d. 1189), preached among the heretics of southern France and published a work on ecclesiology entitled *The Progress of the City of God (De peregrinante civitate Dei).*

Gilbert of Hoyland (d. 1172), abbot of the English Swineshead and a friend of Aelred, made another attempt at continuing Bernard's commentaries on the *Song of Songs.* Still further continuations were undertaken somewhat later by Thomas "the Cistercian" of Perseigne (d. 1190), and by two other Englishmen, John (d. 1220), abbot of Ford, and Gilbert of Stanford. This later generation of the Bernardine school also included Adam (d. 1221), abbot of Perseigne, the author of sermons and long letters to fellow monks, and the ex-troubadour Helinand (d. 1235), prior of Froidmont, an accomplished poet, who, in addition to homilies and letters, wrote treatises on self-knowledge and good government, as well as a world-chronicle. John of Limoges, a master of the University of Paris of vast erudition, joined Clairvaux some time between 1246-1270. Most of his important and widely distributed works were certainly composed during his Parisian years. As monk he was responsible for several collections of sermons, an exposition of Psalm 118, a treatise on monastic exemption and a short essay on monastic silence.

Cistercian authors outside of the school of Saint Bernard were as numerous as the subjects of their works. Regarding its true nature and purpose the most baffling was a discourse on beards (*Apologia de barbis*) by Burchard (d. 1163), first abbot of Balerne, later abbot of Bellevaux. It was a curious mixture of comic and serious passages of nearly 100 folio pages, addressed to lay-brothers, who, as a matter of distinction, were obliged to wear beards and were therefore known as *barbati.* Odo of Ourscamp (d. 1172), later cardinal, and Thomas of Froidmont addressed their works to Cistercian nuns. Garnier of Rochefort (d.c. 1200), later bishop of Langres, published a collection of sermons. Arnold of Bohéries about 1200 composed a manual of ascetic theology (*Speculum monachorum*). A similar work (*De doctrina cordis*), rich in allegories, was written by Gerard of Liège, abbot of Val-Saint-Lambert (1249-1254).

The Englishman Baldwin of Ford (d. 1190) is remembered in the history of theology for his well-reasoned essay *On the Sacrament of the Altar.* The Italian Ogerius of Locedio (d. 1214) contributed a tract to Mariology and wrote thirteen sermons on the Last Supper. The Alsatian Günther of Pairis (d.c. 1220), in addition to several historical works, discoursed *On Prayer, Fasting and Alms.* The author of a number of works of piety was Stephen (d. 1252), monk and abbot of Sawley, later abbot of Newminster and finally of Fountains. His writings include a *Mirror for Novices* and several books of meditations, among them *On the Joys of the Blessed Virgin Mary* and on psalmody. His contemporary, John Godard, first abbot of Newenham, wrote among other short works, an essay on mortification and a treatise on the corporal assumption of Mary. Odo of Morimond (d. 1161) was noted for his sermons on the sufferings of Mary under the Cross.

Twelfth- and thirteenth-century Cistercians contributed generously to the popular *exempla,* short stories exemplifying the beauty of virtues and detestability of vices. Among them were Galland of Rigny, author of *Parables* and *Proverbs,* Herbert of Mores (d. 1180), Conrad of Eberbach (d. 1221), writer of the often mentioned *Exordium magnum,* and the justly famous Caesarius of Heisterbach (d. 1245), prior and master of novices in that great Rhenish abbey and author of a huge collection of edifying stories on monks, nuns and brothers which circulated under the title of *Dialogus miraculorum.* Although the historical accuracy of many of these episodes remains highly questionable, the work must be recognized as an inexhaustible source for the study of thirteenth-century monastic customs and religious folklore.

Hagiography, the lives (*vitae*) of innumerable pious persons and visionaries, was another popular form of devotional literature, particularly in the thirteenth century. One or another of such collections was certainly among the books of any monastic library. Scores of Cistercians of both sexes found their way into the pages of these volumes, especially the mystics of Villers, Aulne, Himmerod and Heisterbach. Of particular interest are the *Chronicle of Villers* and the *Lives of the Saints of Villers,* for that abbey was for over a century a fervent center of mysticism, radiating the same spirituality in all directions and enriching a large number of convents of nuns as well as communities of Beguines. The lives of David of Himmerod, Simon of Aulne, and Abundus of Huy, together with their female counterparts, prove that Cistercian mysticism remained very much alive throughout the thirteenth century.

Although his teaching was in no way related to Cistercian traditions, notice must be taken of Joachim of Fiore (d. 1202), the great mystic of Calabria. He joined the Order after a pilgrimage to Jerusalem, became abbot of Corazzo, but left the community and spent his remaining life in contemplation, writing and preaching. His *Harmony of the Old and New Testaments, Explanation of the Apocalypse* and *Psalter of Ten Cords,* dealt with the Holy Trinity in a seemingly tritheistic way and with the coming of a new age under the reign of the Holy Spirit, the age of eternal bliss and peace. Although his trinitarian doctrine was condemned in 1215, his writings had a strong influence on the piety of the late Middle Ages, particularly among the Spiritual Franciscans.

The first topic of profane study to engage a number of Cistercian abbeys from the very beginning was history. The most outstanding among the historians of the Order and certainly the greatest in his century was Otto of Freising (d. 1158), half brother of the Emperor Conrad III and uncle of Frederick Barbarossa. Having finished his education in Paris under Abelard and Gilbert de la Porrée, he soon joined the Order, became abbot of Morimond and later bishop of Freising, and in the Emperor's company participated in the ill-fated Second Crusade. His two most important works were the *Chronicle* or *Books of Two Cities,* a world history coming down to 1146, and the *Deeds of the Emperor Frederick,* a story of the early reign of Barbarossa based on Otto's own observations. His *Chronicle* was the first medieval attempt to write a "philosophical" history, which employed the basic ideas of Augustine's *City of God.*

Cistercian monasteries were founded in some instances with the express intention of fostering learning, primarily historiography. Thus Sorø in Denmark was established in 1162 for the purpose "that therein men of prominent erudition would be boarded who would compile the annals of the kingdom and record annually for posterity events worthy of memory."

Cistercian annalists secured for themselves a distinguished place in English, Welsh and Scottish historiography. Melrose, Waverley, Coggeshall, Aberconway, Stanley, Hailes, Dore, Strata Florida, Furness, Fountains and Meaux are worth mentioning in this regard. The *Monumenta Germaniae Historica* published the chronicles of forty-eight Cistercian abbeys of great interest in German history, most of them composed during the twelfth and thirteenth centuries. Among the chroniclers known by name, the most outstanding are: Ralph of Coggeshall, (d. 1227) author of the *Chronicon Anglicanum*; Günther of Pairis, (d. 1220) poet and historian of the Fourth Crusade, author of the work known as *Historia Constantinopolitana*; Alberic of Troisfontaines, (d. 1251) the compiler of a history of his own times in the second quarter of the thirteenth century; Peter of Zittau, (d. 1339) abbot of Königsaal, whose *Chronicon Aulae Regiae* covered Bohemian history between 1305 and 1377; John, abbot of Viktring (d. 1347) whose *Liber certarum historiarum* is an indispensable source for German and Bohemian history, especially for the period 1217-1341. Vincent Kadlubek (1160-1223), bishop of Cracow, the father of Polish historiography, spent his last years in retirement in the Cistercian abbey of Andrejow. Peter of Vaux-de-Cernay, (d. 1218) accompanied his uncle Guy, abbot of Vaux-de-Cernay, on the Fourth Crusade and later followed the progress of the Albigensian Crusade as an eyewitness. His *Historia Albigensis* is a unique and indispensable, though not unbiased, source for that tragic episode of French history.

There were scarcely any houses without a book of formularies (*ars dictaminis*), assisting the less proficient in Latin in the composition of effective letters, properly written documents or charters of visitation. A work of this nature and of great popularity was compiled by "Master" Transmundus, papal notary in 1185-1186, later monk of Clairvaux (d. c. 1216).

Scholasticism brought about the first major reorientation of Cistercian spirituality, dramatized in 1245 by the foundation of the College of Saint Bernard in Paris. Thereafter the Order assumed responsibility not only for the ascetic, but also for the intellectual formation of its members; moreover, with the passage of time, the intellectual endeavor carried obvious preponderance. As has been discussed above, the causes of the change included the fear of heresy, the increasing prestige of scholarship, the Order's role in pastoral and missionary activities, and the spirit of competition with the Mendicants.

236

The zeal for formal education, however, did not remain unchallenged. The most resolute opposition came from Villers, that great and flourishing center of mysticism, whose abbot, Arnulf of Louvain (1240-1248), refused to contribute anything toward the construction of the Parisian College. Even after the successful opening of the institution conservative reaction was strong enough to force the deposition of Abbot Stephen Lexington of Clairvaux, the originator of the College. Nevertheless, a few years later, support for higher education became universal, well reflected in the ever increasing enthusiasm exhibited by the General Chapter for all matters relative to the welfare of the College.

As early as 1245, the Chapter Fathers greeted the news of papal approval for the Cistercian college with the declaration that the new school was to increase "the glory of God and of the Order, the honor and luster of the holy and universal Church, ennobling our hearts by the light of divine wisdom." In 1341 the General Chapter did not hesitate to state that "the Parisian *studium* glorifies our whole Order, since it is there that our members draw abundantly living waters from the fountains of the Savior." In 1490, when urging attendance at the same College, the Chapter assured prospective students "that the honor and glory of our Order depended mostly on the multiplication of literate and learned members."

When this last statement was made, not only Paris, but every major university in Europe had its Cistercian students and the number of graduates kept multiplying. The redounding glory of the Order, however, seemed to be forever elusive. It remains a curious fact that, while Dominicans had Saint Thomas Aquinas and Franciscans their Bonaventure and Duns Scotus, Cistercians failed to produce scholars of comparable stature. Partial and tentative explanation may be sought in the structure and external vocation of Mendicant orders. Dominicans and Franciscans encouraged their young philosophers and theologians to stay in schools and make a career out of teaching and studies; Cistercians had no such incentives and the abler graduates were often elected abbots even before their promotion to the doctorate. Needless to say, from the point of view of an ambitious young monk, abbacy was a career preferable to professorship, and after having accepted the former, administrative responsibilities precluded the pursuit of studies.

The case of Stephen Lexington, the founder of the Parisian College, may illustrate the predicament of a truly talented *magister* of Oxford turned Cistercian. As soon as he had made his profession at Quarr Abbey, he was elected abbot of Stanley, then of Savigny and finally of Clairvaux, each position more demanding than the last. Instead of writing learned treatises on currently popular theological subjects or producing a *Summa* of his own, he had to employ his brilliant mind in solving problems much closer to home. Instead of scholastic compendia, he left behind only charters of visitations and a voluminous correspondence of great historical, but of no theoretical, interest.

The first known Cistercian who received his doctorate as a student of the College of Saint Bernard was Guy, abbot of l'Aumône, who was, however, promoted to that degree not through normal procedures, but at the order of Pope Innocent IV in 1256. The first scholar to be awarded the same honor by the University authorities, in 1274, was Jean de Weerde (d. 1293), monk of Les Dunes. Of all his works only a set of quodlibet disputations have survived. About other Cistercian doctors who received their degrees shortly before or after the turn of the fourteenth century little is known and their still extant and identifiable works are hidden in archives and libraries. Such were François de Keysere (d. 1294) and Jean de Sindewint, both monks of Les Dunes; Humbert, abbot of Preuilly, Renier de Clairmarais, Jean de He of Ter Doest, Jean de Dun-le-Roi (d. 1319) and Jacques de Dijon, who graduated from Paris in 1310 and subsequently became abbot of Preuilly.

Among the early graduates of the Parisian College the most famous was undoubtedly Jacques Fournier, monk of Boulbonne, who became successively abbot of Fontfroide (1311), master of theology (1313-1314), bishop of Pamiers and Mirepoix, cardinal in 1327 and finally pope, assuming the name Benedict XII (1334-1342). His voluminous scholarly legacy includes a treatise *On the State of Souls Before the General Judgment,* a huge *Commentary on the Gospel of Matthew,* a number of works on contemporary heretics and heresy, sermons and even lives of saints. Before his election he enjoyed the reputation of being an expert on theological orthodoxy and he served for years as a successful inquisitor. As pope he proved to be a tireless reformer of monastic orders and a generous benefactor of his *alma mater,* the Parisian College. The great though unfinished college church, one of the finest examples of "flamboyant" Gothic in Paris, which was destroyed in the Revolution, was initiated under his auspices.

Another busy scholar was Jacques de Thérines (d. 1321), monk and later abbot of Châlis and, in 1318, abbot of Pontigny, who during his "regency" (1306-1309) at the College of Saint Bernard produced two volumes of *quodlibeta.* As a participant at the Council of Vienne (1311-1312) he composed a lengthy report on the moral and financial condition of the Cistercian Order, designed to facilitate a reform-decree, which, however, was issued only in 1335 by Benedict XII.

The most brilliant theologian of a younger generation at the College was Jean de Mirecourt, monk of Cîteaux, who, in preparation for his final degree, commented on the *Sentences* in 1344-1345. He was one of the many disciples of William of Ockham, but preserved considerable independence both in thought and style. He, like other members of the same school, was much concerned with epistemology, pursued the line of logic of skepticism and found absolute certainty only in evidence reduced to the principle of contradiction. But the watchful anti-nominalists found his theses incompatible with orthodoxy and in 1347 Clement VI condemned forty-one offensive propositions in Mirecourt's teaching. The young scholar defended his stand vigorously, but he suddenly disappeared from the scene in 1348, most likely carried away by the Black Death at Royaumont, where he had just been elected abbot. The wide geographical distribution of his manuscripts attests to his reputation and considerable popularity.

Mirecourt's schoolmate and close friend, a witness but survivor of the plague in Paris, Pierre Ceffons, monk of Clairvaux, was not only an outspoken defender of his condemned confrere, but outdid him in bold criticism of established authority. Although "his literary production was vast, manifold and important," he remained practically unknown until 1957, when some of his surviving manuscripts were discovered and identified in the municipal library of Troyes. Ceffons was a bachelor of theology in the College of Saint Bernard in 1348-1349 and finished his formal studies in 1353, but his further career is unknown. Most likely, he too, died prematurely.

His most voluminous work was his commentaries on the *Sentences*, which opened with a scathing denunciation of those "three foreign old witches," who were responsible for the condemnation of Mirecourt and his associates in 1347. He was cautious enough not to name them, but he clearly referred to three Italian friars active in Paris and Avignon, whom he wished to be banished from France and thrown to the bottom of hell. Ceffons's other works comprise a trilogy: *Centilogium* (100 chapters), a letter from Jesus Christ to the prelates of the time; *Epistola Luciferi,* an open letter of the "prince of darkness" to pope and bishops, urging them sardonically to be a little more loyal to Beelzebub; and *Parvum Decretum,* a dissertation on the limits of papal authority. In a remarkable manuscript entitled *Dream (Somnium),* he quarreled with the Cistercian General Chapter of 1348 for having renewed an old statute demanding that monks disclose once a year their already confessed sins to their abbots. He argued (all in his dream!) that the regulation violated the freedom of conscience and was therefore a patent abuse of authority.

Two English Cistercians were also involved in the nominalist controversies, and both were censured for their Ockhamist views. One was a certain "Henricus Anglicus," whom Benedict XII ordered to be investigated in 1340. The other was Richard of Lincoln, a monk of Louth Park, whose "phantastic" theses were condemned by Benedict XII, although he was exonerated in 1343 by Clement VI and was permitted to finish his studies in Paris.

Later in the same century two Cistercian scholars of Oxford took a strong stand against the teaching of John Wycliffe (d. 1384). Henry Crumpe, an Irish monk, preached assiduously against the erroneous doctrine, called its adherents "Lollards," and signed the act condemning Wycliffe for his doctrine on the Eucharist. The same Crumpe proved to be a resourceful controversialist both in speech and in writing and, among others, attacked the Mendicant friars for their excessive privileges.

The other defender of orthodoxy was the prior of Sawley, William Rymington (d. 1385), who during 1372-1373 served as chancellor of the University of Oxford. While attacking Wycliffe, however, he was not blind to the failings of the Church, and as chancellor he delivered two notable sermons sharply criticising the moral standards of contemporary clergy. His authorship of a book of meditations attested to his sincere piety.

Eminent students of the Parisian College late in the century included Jacob of Eltville (d. 1393), master of theology in 1373 and already abbot of Eberbach, whose four books of commentaries on the *Sentences* show some nominalist influences. Another German, Conrad of Ebrach (d. 1399) began his studies in Paris, continued them in Bologna and finally obtained the master's degree at Prague in 1375. His widely used commentaries on the *Sentences* revealed that he was close to the school of Augustinian theologians, particularly to Hugolin of Orvieto (d. 1373). Since shortly after his graduation Germans were no longer welcome in Prague, he moved to Vienna, where he co-operated in the organization of the theological faculty. Equally important was his role in organizing German Cistercians during the Great Schism on behalf of the Roman Pope Urban VI, who granted him the title "Abbot of Morimond." During the Schism Conrad also presided over several general chapters held for Cistercians outside of France.

When the Hussites gained control of the University of Prague, they expelled all Cistercians from the University, among them Matthaeus Steynhus of Königsaal (d. 1427), doctor of Prague, renowned theologian and author. He made his new home at Altzelle, where he assisted in the organization of the Cistercian college of Leipzig and participated in the Council of Constance (1414-1418).

240

By the beginning of the fifteenth century Scholasticism was in full decline everywhere. The new movement of Humanism had no relation with the old schools, and, indeed, many universities merely struggled for survival. Cistercians continued to attend their previously established colleges, but they produced no philosophers or theologians of note. Thus, the enthusiastic expectations that had accompanied the foundation of the early Cistercian colleges were never borne out. The large number of degree-holders within the Order failed to exert a beneficial influence on the prevailing moral and spiritual standards and failed even to generate a school of Cistercian theology. While most of the scholars named above seem to have belonged to the "modern way" (*via moderna*), influenced more or less by nominalism, they remained talented eclectics and did not stay in the field of teaching long enough to form a "school" of thought or organize a group of devoted disciples. The last word in the matter, however, should be postponed until thorough research warrants more articulate conclusions.

The lack of spadework that has hampered the formation of a definite judgment on the merits of Cistercian scholasticism is even more conspicuous when we turn our attention to Cistercian devotional literature of the fourteenth and fifteenth centuries. The names that follow are not necessarily those of the most accomplished authors; they are merely the ones who, for some reason, have been better remembered than the countless others who have fallen into total oblivion. Whether such works still carried elements of the once dominant Bernardine spirituality remains, for the time being, an insoluble problem, although in most cases the answer seems quite obviously negative.

An undoubtedly important person was Philip of Rathsamhausen (d. 1322), monk and abbot of the Alsatian Pairis, a student of theology in Paris and finally, in 1306, bishop of Eichstätt. In his latter capacity he advised three German rulers in succession: Albert I, Henry VII and Louis of Bavaria. He was a man of piety, an effective preacher and the author of an *Exposition of the Magnificat,* meditations on Psalm 4 and on the "Our Father," sermons and several *vitae* of popular saints.

Piety and learning blended in the works of Nicolas Vischel (d. c. 1330), monk of the Austrian Heiligenkreuz and author of the *Praises of the Blessed Virgin Mary,* a number of sermons and several treatises against heretics. Ulrich, abbot of the Austrian Lilienfeld (1345-1351), composed a colorful work entitled *Concordia veritatis,* a moralizing paraphrase of the Bible, and wrote meditations on the Psalms.

Gallus (d. 1370), abbot of the Bohemian Königsaal, had been credited with the composition of the *Malogranatum,* a handbook of ascetic and mystical theology in the dialogue form. The work was a skillful compilation and became a very popular propagator of a Bohemian version of the *devotio moderna*. After a century of circulation in manuscript it was printed in three incunabula editions and was even translated into French.

In popularity no Cistercian work could compete with the *Antidotarius animae* which, according to its subtitle, was "a book of devout meditations and prayers, offered as antidotes for the soul." The author was Nicolas Salicetus (Wydenbosch), a Swiss-born doctor of medicine who became a Cistercian and eventually abbot of the Alsatian Baumgarten (1482). The book was first printed in 1489 and by 1554 had seen at least thirty editions. As late as 1580 it was still selling so well that a French translation was published. The unusual appeal of the work lay in the fact that it offered efficacious prayers for every possible calamity of life, in much the same way as the author in his previous profession had prescribed medication for people suffering in bodily illnesses.

The genre of legends retained its popularity until the end of the Middle Ages. Moreover, the fourteenth century brought about a resurgence of Cistercian mysticism not only within convents of nuns but in monasteries as well, especially in Germany. Heilsbronn, under Abbot Conrad of Brundelsheim (1317-1321); Kaisheim, in the time of Abbot Ulrich Nubling (1340-1360), a personal friend of the great German mystic, Johannes Tauler; Waldsassen, under the leadership of Johannes Ellenbogen (1313-1325); and Königsaal, successively under Abbots Peter and Gallus, were widely renowned centers of monastic piety. All of the abbots mentioned above also wrote mystical and devotional literature. Johannes Ellenbogen, abbot of Waldsassen, collected the lives and described the mystical experiences of monks of his abbey and dedicated his work to Abbot Peter of Königsaal, where a similar collection had already been in circulation.

In 1439 and 1447 the General Chapter itself encouraged abbots to promote the collection of stories of pious monks and nuns in their own houses. The religious fermentation furnishing the background for the foundation of the "Congregation of Sibculo" and its relation with the *devotio moderna* has already been discussed above.

The life of Saint Bridget of Sweden (1302-1373), the famous mystic and prophetess, bears witness to the unbroken vigor of Cistercian spirituality in the North. After her husband had taken the habit in Alvastra she lived for years in the neighborhood of the monastery under the spiritual guidance of the monks. Her piety was characteristically Cistercian, centering on the passion of Christ and the glories of the Blessed Virgin. The Rule of the Order of Saint Savior (Bridgettines), founded by her, reflects Cistercian influence. Parts of her revelations were translated from the vernacular into Latin by the Cistercian Peter Olafsson, prior of Alvastra, the Saint's faithful secretary.

The sixteenth century, the age of the Protestant revolution and religious wars, was not conducive to literary or scholarly activity. In the countries where Cistercians remained strong, members of the Order took an active part in current religious controversies, but few of their writings proved to be of lasting value.

It was in Spain and Portugal that both the volume and level of scholarly production continued to be high, particularly in the field of history. Alcobaça alone counted seventeen historians among its 280 authors. The most important was undoubtedly Bernardo de Brito (1569-1617), whose many historical works included the *Chronica de Cister* (1602), a heavily documented history of Portuguese Cistercians. He was a monk of Alcobaça, doctor of Coimbra and court chronicler of Philip III. Unfortunately, however, his notorious lack of critical ability renders the use of his great work highly problematic. His extensive collection of documents (*De privilegiis Ordinis Cisterciensis*) remains in manuscript.

Spain, meanwhile, produced two historians whose works have remained firm cornerstones of Cistercian historical scholarship. Angel Manrique (1577-1649) was born in Burgos, entered the abbey of Huerta and finished his studies at Salamanca, where he remained for several years as provisor of the Cistercian College of Loreto. He enjoyed high esteem at the court of Philip IV where he often preached; it was through royal favor that in 1639 he became bishop of Badajoz. Among his many works of piety, theology and history the most outstanding was the *Annales Cistercienses,* published in four folio volumes. Following a rigid chronology, he lived to cover the history of the Order only until 1236.

Crisostomo Henriquez (1594-1632) enriched his short life by a research work of prodigious dimensions. He too was a professed member of Huerta, but moved to the Spanish Netherlands where he enjoyed the active support of Archduke Albert. His field of interest was Cistercian hagiology and he published all his pioneering works in Flanders, among them the *Fasciculus Sanctorum Ordinis, Lilia Cistercii* and *Menologium Cisterciense.*

In Italy the most outstanding Cistercian historian was Fernando Ughelli (1595-1670), a Florentine monk who became abbot in Settimo and finally abbot of the Roman Tre Fontane. While in Rome, he gained favor with Alexander VII and Clement IX and it was with their encouragement that he undertook the publication of his *Italia Sacra,* a still indispensable reference work of Italian church history in ten folio volumes (1642-1662). After his death a corrected and updated edition was published in Venice (1712-1722).

The Feuillants produced a number of accomplished authors. Among their historians the best known was Carlo Giuseppe Morozzo (1645-1729), abbot of Consolata in Turin and later bishop of Saluzzo. In addition to devotional works of note he published a history of the Carthusian Order, several biographies and the story of the Feuillant reform, entitled *Cistercii reflorescentis chronologica historia* (1690).

Gaspar Jongelinus, a monk of Flemish origins and abbot in succession of Disibodenberg and Eusserthal, spent his life working in the richest Cistercian archives. The fruit of his labors was the *Notitia Abbatiarum Ordinis Cisterciensis* published in 1640, in which he listed and identified 797 Cistercian abbeys. In spite of its many errors, it remained the only reference work of such a nature until Janauschek's *Origines Cistercienses* (1877). A history of the Cistercian military orders followed in 1641, and in 1644 his list of Benedictine and Cistercian bishops, cardinals and popes was printed.

Charles De Visch (d. 1666), monk and prior of Les Dunes compiled a bibliography of Cistercian authors of all countries from the beginnings to his day. His *Bibliotheca Scriptorum Sacri Ordinis Cisterciensis* in two editions (1649 and 1656) and completed by later augmentations remained for three centuries the only reference work of its kind.

Augustin Sartorius (d. 1733), professed member of the Bohemian Ossegg, published a popular two-volume history of the Order, *Cistercium Bis-tertium* (Prague, 1700). As the peculiar title indicated, he wished to contribute his work to the celebration of the sixth centenary of Cîteaux's foundation. Although the tone of the text was panegyrical, it enjoyed a wide distribution and was soon translated into German.

In France the most enduring monument of seventeenth-century Cistercian scholarship was the publication of the *Bibliotheca Patrum Cisterciensium* (1660-1669) by Bertrand Tissier (d. 1670), monk, prior, and reformer of Bonnefontaine and a graduate of the University of Pont-à-Mousson. His three folio volumes included fine editions of the works of early Cistercian authors and were printed in the abbey's own press. Claude Chalemot (d. 1667), monk of Cherlieu and abbot of La Colombe, among other works of theology, composed a much-used hagiographical compendium, *Series Sanctorum et Beatorum Ordinis Cisterciensis* (Paris, 1666). Of the many authors of monographs of individual abbeys, particular credit is due to Claude Auvry, monk of Vaux-de-Cernay and prior of Champagne and of Savigny in the 1680s, who left behind a voluminous *Histoire de la congrégation de Savigny,* which in a modern edition in three volumes (1896-1898) has remained in circulation. The same can be said about the great source collection of Julien Paris (d. 1672), abbot of Foucarmont, whose work, the often cited *Nomasticon Cisterciense,* was originally published in 1664, and still serves its original purpose in Séjalon's edition of 1892. Nicolas Cotheret, monk and archivist of Cîteaux and doctor of the Sorbonne, completed about 1738 a history of the abbey of Cîteaux. Because he took a sharply critical attitude towards most abbots, the book could not be printed, but its revealing details would justify its belated publication. On the other hand, the impressive looking nine volumes of the *Essai de l'histoire de l'Ordre de Cîteaux* (1696-1699) by Pierre Lenain (1640-1713) would disappoint modern readers. The author was a monk of La Trappe, an admirer and biographer of Rancé, but his *Essai* is merely a collection of pious biographies and miracle stories with no scholarly value.

French Cistercians throughout the seventeenth century were absorbed in the issues debated between the Strict and Common Observances. Among the hundreds of pamphlets published by both parties there were many of considerable historical and juridical value, written with as much erudition as partisanship. On the Abstinents' side the most gifted author was Jean Jouaud (d. 1673), abbot of Prières and leader of the reform, who in 1656 summarized the results of the first half century of debate in a full-length book, entitled *Défense des règlements.* This same work reappeared in 1746 in a polished and updated version as *Histoire générale de la réforme de l'ordre de Cîteaux en France,* under the name of François-Armand Gervaise (1660-1715), a member and ex-abbot of La Trappe, author of a number of popular lives of saints. It was this much-quoted work which perpetuated a grossly distorted judgment on the nature of that famed monastic feud. As an irony of fate, the most ambitious work of Gervaise, a two volume biography of Abbot Rancé, remained in manuscript until Abbé Dubois published it in 1866 under his own name, without giving credit to its original author.

On the side of the Common Observance the busiest pamphleteer was Jean Tédénat, procurator of the College of Saint Bernard in Paris, who in 1667 was rewarded for his services with the titular priorship of Grâce-Dieu.

During the late seventeenth and eighteenth centuries the feud between the abbots of Cîteaux and the proto-abbots attracted the widest attention throughout the Order. Since the issues were partly historical and partly juridical, most of those who actively participated in the war of words had to delve into monastic archives in search of documentation. In 1678 a remarkable work, supporting the standpoint of the abbot general, came to

245

light, *Le véritable gouvernement de l'Ordre de Cîteaux,* amounting to a full-scale (576 pages) constitutional history of the Order. Its learned author, Louis Meschet (d. 1715), served for many years as the provisor of the Parisian College, while bearing the sinecure title of abbot of La Charité. His most ambitious work, however, was a *bullarium,* on which he worked many years and finally published in 1713 as *Privilèges de l'Ordre de Cîteaux.* In spite of its selective nature, this work remained a source collection of great utility for a long time. A detailed criticism of it was offered a few years later by Richard Montaubon, secretary of the abbot of Clairvaux, and by the learned master of novices of the same abbey, Jean-Antoine Macusson.

The most original Cistercian talent of the seventeenth century was undoubtedly Juan Caramuel Lobkowitz (1606-1682). He was born in Madrid, joined the Cistercians at Espina, pursued academic studies at Alcalá, Salamanca and Louvain, and became abbot and bishop of several sees in succession, but held occasionally such positions as "Imperial Superintendent of Fortifications" in Bohemia, where he was credited with the conversion of 30,000 Hussites and Protestants to the Catholic faith. He was a peripatetic scholar known in academic circles throughout Catholic Europe. No field of learning escaped his attention; he spoke twenty-four languages and his published works number 250 titles. His greatest ambition was to reduce everything, even moral theology, to simple geometrical principles. In his most controversial work, *Fundamental Moral Theology* (1651), he proved himself an enemy of Jansenism and a protagonist of probabilism, although the title "prince of laxists," awarded him by Saint Alphonsus Liguori, was not entirely deserved.

At the other extreme was the character of the humble and retiring Louis Quinet (1595-1665), monk of Val-Richer and abbot of Barbery. Under the influence of Denis Largentier he embraced the Strict Observance, but stayed out of the acrid controversies. He was one of the few Cistercian mystics of the century, an accomplished spiritual director and author of a number of works of piety.

Scholarship, fame and sanctity of life summed up the character of Giovanni Bona (1609-1674), professor of theology, abbot and general of the Italian Feuillants and finally cardinal in 1669. As ascetic writer he gained much popularity, but lacked originality. In the field of liturgy, however, he pioneered a new scholarly approach to hotly debated issues. His works on the mass were long considered classics.

A scientific approach to biblical chronology made the name of Paul Yves Pezron (1639-1706) renowned. Although he served as Jouaud's secretary for years, he preferred study to controversy. A doctor of the

246

Sorbonne in 1680 and provisor of the College of Saint Bernard, Pezron was appointed abbot of La Charmoye in 1697, but he continued to publish extensively in the field of his speciality.

The fundamental work of spiritual formation within the Strict Observance was *Du premier esprit de l'Ordre de Cîteaux* by Julien Paris, published three times in rapid succession (1653, 1664, 1670). This was the book which was handed to every novice entering reformed communities. It presented an uncompromising asceticism as the primary goal of early Cîteaux and made a deep impression on Rancé, whose own spirituality gave further impetus to the same theme.

Armand-Jean Le Bouthillier de Rancé (1626-1700), a brilliant doctor of the Sorbonne, who converted to monasticism and became abbot of La Trappe, exerted a dominant influence over the spirituality of the Strict Observance for over two centuries. His remarkable erudition in patristic theology, rigid asceticism and combative temper characterized his many publications, all emphasizing his basic conviction that monastic life ought to be a life of penance. His most representative book was the two volume sequence of conferences *On Sanctity and the Duties of Monastic Life* (1683). The same doctrine was conveyed in *The Rule of Saint Benedict Translated and Explained According to its Genuine Spirit* (1689), and in his very extensive correspondence. His preference for manual labor and his negative attitude toward intellectual pursuits led to a prolonged literary debate with the great Maurist scholar, Jean Mabillon (1632-1707).

Throughout the nineteenth century the Trappists remained faithful to Rancé's spiritual bequest and discouraged studies and publication, although many members of their observance were well equipped for such tasks, amply demonstrated by the two volumes of the excellent *Annales de l'abbaye d'Aiguebelle* (1863), by Hugues Séjalon (1824-1890), formerly a member of the Society of Jesus, who joined Aiguebelle in 1857.

Meanwhile, the reborn Common Observance took a path in the opposite direction and encouraged studies and scholarly production with spectacular results, particularly in the abbeys of Austria-Hungary. Between 1814 and 1896 the community of Zirc alone accounted for 105 authors, several of them of national or even international reputation. The same trend continued on an expanding scale in the twentieth century, when the Strict Observance, too, began to contribute significantly to monastic studies. The bibliographical notes attached to the present work bear witness to the remarkable volume and quality of scholarly efforts among the contemporary membership of both Cistercian observances.

XVIII

Liturgy

 The contrast between Cistercian reform and Cluniac customs was nowhere so conspicuous as in liturgy, and Cîteaux's sharp criticism of Cluny was nowhere so justified as in that distinctive area of monastic life.

The preponderance of liturgy in the monks' daily schedule resulted from the reforming activity of Benedict of Aniane (d. 821), who abandoned manual labor and exalted the *opus Dei* as the only worthy occupation for monks. Under his influence the proportion of sacred services within the Benedictine *horarium* continued to increase until, by the middle of the eleventh century, it had consumed almost all the time of monks in communities under Cluny's rule.

As a preparation for the canonical office, monks said the *trina oratio* which consisted of three groups of psalms; for the living, for the dead, and for special intentions. The altars of the church were visited in procession while the monks sang litanies and selections from still other psalms, such as the fifteen "gradual psalms," the seven "penitential psalms," and the first and last thirty psalms of the Psalter. Besides the canonical offices, other offices filled the time between the hours. The most popular among them was the Office of the Dead; others included offices in honor of the Holy Cross, the Holy Trinity, the Holy Spirit, the Incarnation, the Holy Angels and later the Office of the Blessed Virgin. To the customary conventual mass was added another official mass, the *missa matutinalis.* Long processions, with stations and litanies, preceding the solemn high mass, became an almost daily routine.

With all these accretions the recitation of Prime took nearly as much time as did the whole canonical office as described in the Rule. The night office before greater feasts was begun on the preceding evening, since it was otherwise impossible to complete it before daybreak. According to the Rule of Saint Benedict, monks were supposed to recite the 150 psalms of the Psalter during a week's term; in the Cluniac liturgy, the community said daily about 210 psalms. Some monasteries went so far as to pledge themselves to the *laus perennis,* whereby monks and choirboys were divided into three shifts, to permit the various liturgical duties to be performed without interruption.

Naturally, such exaggerations resulted in a general weariness (*taedium prolixitatis*) brought on by the immoderately protracted services. A growing dissatisfaction began to spread even within the Cluniac Congregation, while outsiders freely expressed their skepticism of the value of such devotional practices. The Cistercian author of the *Exordium magnum* used unusually harsh words in explaining the necessity of a return to the purity of the Rule in matters of liturgy:

> Concerning the mode and order of divine services, the monks of Cîteaux decided right at the beginning to observe in everything the traditions of the Rule, cutting away entirely and rejecting all appendages to the psalms, orations and litanies, which were added [to the Office] arbitrarily by less considerate fathers. Aware of human frailty and infirmity, after sagacious consideration, they found [these additions] to be more dangerous than salutary for monks, since their multiplicity results in their entirely tepid and negligent recitation, not only by the slothful, but also by the diligent.

Although the founding fathers of Cîteaux had taken their liturgical books from Molesme, they were very anxious to return to the Rule's original scheme for the celebration of the Divine Office; the more so, because their only means of survival, manual labor in the fields, was incompatible with the Cluniac *horarium*. Except for a short Office of the Dead, they simply omitted all accretions to the canonical office added during the past two centuries and in the recitation of the remaining canonical hours they followed precisely the directions of the Rule which distributed 150 psalms equally among the days of the week. There are indications that even the Office of the Dead did not originally belong to Cîteaux's liturgy; it may have been added only about 1130.

This radical reform immediately provoked the indignant protest of the contemporary monastic world, well characterized by a letter from Abelard to Saint Bernard written between 1132-1136. It listed a number of "scandalous" innovations, among them the omission of generally accepted hymns, which had been replaced by "unknown and unusual" ones, chanted invariably all year round, without regard for the special demands of feasts and liturgical seasons. We know from other sources that those "unheard of" hymns had been adopted by Cîteaux from the ancient Ambrosian liturgy of Milan, because the Rule referred to "Ambrosian hymns." Abelard further charged the Cistercians with the omission of various prayers and commemorations of saints, including the Blessed Virgin; the drastic reduction of processions (only those of Candlemas and Palm Sunday were retained), and the omission of the Apostles' Creed before the canonical hours. Only the Creed of Saint Athanasius was said, and even that only on Sundays. In the eyes of contemporary critics, however, the most distasteful feature of their

249

liturgical reform was the celebration of Lent, during which Cistercians, wholly ignoring current practices, continued to recite the office without any change until Easter. Thus they did not cease to sing the *alleluja* after Septuagesima, they ended the psalms even during Holy Week with the Gloria, and they chanted the same hymns as usual.

A copy of the earliest Cistercian breviary from the times of Saint Stephen Harding, recovered in Berlin during the Second World War, not only verifies this list of distinctive characteristics but also contains the first authentic Cistercian calendar, another important proof of Cîteaux's conspicuous antiquarian tendencies. Although there were numerous commemorations of saints, the number of feasts with proper office was surprisingly low, totaling fifty-seven. Just as in the Rule, there is no trace of any ranking among them; all were celebrated according to the fashion of Sundays, with twelve lessons. The largest group of feasts were represented by the office of the Apostles; there were only four feasts of the Blessed Virgin (Purification, Annunciation, Assumption, Nativity) and the list of the remaining twenty-six saints bears a definite Roman character with a slight Gallic influence.

The fact that the first Cistercians drastically reduced the length of the Divine Office and that even the remaining services were made to conform to a general pattern of austere simplicity does not mean that the founding fathers of Cîteaux overlooked or belittled the importance of liturgy in monastic life. On the contrary, the painstaking efforts of Saint Stephen Harding and his brethren to restore the liturgy to its original purity, notwithstanding certainly foreseen conservative criticism, gave ample evidence of their deep appreciation of its intrinsic value. Their zeal for the perfection of liturgy went even further. In pursuit of faultless liturgical texts Stephen Harding, still prior of Cîteaux, undertook the critical correction of the whole Bible. His endeavor was not entirely unprecedented, but the surprisingly advanced method he applied in his attempt to restore the original text of the Vulgate was unequaled in his century. He had not only utilized a number of Latin manuscripts, but, concerning the Old Testament, had consulted renowned Jewish scholars in order to understand difficult Hebrew passages. After having been elected abbot in 1109, he published the wonderfully illuminated four volumes of his Bible "composed with much labor" as an official pattern for further copies and strictly prohibited any alterations in its text.

The learned Abbot's attention was also extended to the musical qualities of the adopted liturgical books. Since it was generally believed that the liturgy of Metz still preserved the original melodies of the time of Saint Gregory the Great, monks were sent there and they returned with a carefully copied Antiphonary. This and all other revised liturgical books of Cîteaux were declared official exemplars by the *Charter of Charity* and the newly founded monasteries were obliged to copy and to preserve them intact so that perfect uniformity could be maintained in all matters of liturgy and custom.

The celebration of liturgy was detailed in the most substantial portion of the "Book of Usages," the *Ecclesiastica officia*. This small book of 121 paragraphs contained not only instructions on how to perform liturgical and other ceremonial duties, but also directives on every phase of the monks' daily activity and descriptions of the duties of monastic officials.

Nothing in these regulations was strikingly original. The general plan was borrowed from Cluny, while many specifics were assimilated from Molesme and the abbey of Saint Benignus in Dijon, Cîteaux's two closest neighbors. The concise nature of the instructions and their strict adherence to a tradition that was considered genuinely Benedictine, however, was in harmony with the principles of the founders of Cîteaux.

The oldest extant copy of the *Ecclesiastica officia* was written between 1130 and 1134, although its contents probably resulted from the sessions of the General Chapter during the preceding decade. The relative speed and thoroughness with which the fathers completed the work indicated their firm desire to maintain uniformity within the fast-growing order. Like many other pieces of Cistercian legislation, the *Ecclesiastica officia* underwent a number of modifications and was updated in every subsequent century.

Saint Stephen's liturgical reform was not to live for long in its full integrity. No sooner had the great abbot passed away when a second Cistercian generation, under the leadership of Saint Bernard, quickly reviewed the whole bequest of the founding fathers, applying inexorably the principles of simplicity and perfect detachment from the world in those areas of monastic life which had escaped their predecessors' attention. Dissatisfied with the Antiphonary of Metz, the Chapter appointed a committee under the presidency of Saint Bernard himself to expurgate the liturgical chant used in the Order from all its alleged defects and superfluities. Bernard's principles in this matter were much the same as those expressed much earlier in his *Apology* regarding visual arts. The Saint's letter addressed to Abbot Guy of the Benedictine Montiéramey pointed out that "the chant, if it is employed, should be quite solemn, nothing sensuous or rustic. Its sweetness should not be frivolous. It should please the ear only that it may move the heart, taking away sorrow and mitigating wrath. It should not detract from the sense of the words, but rather make it more fruitful. It is not a little blow to spiritual profit

251

when more attention is paid for feats of voice than to the meaning of words."

Since the Abbot of Clairvaux was engaged in other and more important affairs, the work of revision was carried out by the "expert" members of the committee, among them Guy, abbot of Cherlieu. After a study of "many and diverse codices," they presented the new Antiphonary for approval some time before 1147. The corrections, however, were not made on the basis of manuscript evidence, but on theoretical principles so dear to the new generation of scholastics, who preferred to consider music a branch of science.

Such principles emphasized the modal unity of melodies and excluded particularly any mixture of "authentic" and "plagal" modes; insisted on the law of range, that is, no melody was to exceed the ambitus (interval) of a compound 10th; the B-flat was excluded; repetitions in text as well as melody were eliminated; exuberant phrases, especially in the *allelujas,* were simplified and shortened. According to modern musicologists, the revision worked much to the detriment of artistic quality, but to Saint Bernard, as he assured posterity in his Prologue to the Antiphonary, it was "irreprehensible in both music and text."

To the great disappointment of these fervent young theoreticians, their overzealous reformatory activity was considerably restricted by the vigorous protests of the still influential older generation. Consequently the new and revised Antiphonary was but a compromise which preserved some of the characteristic features of the earliest Cistercian Gregorian chant. Most of the above mentioned reformatory program reflected a tendency common to contemporary musicologists; but the last item, a conspicuous predilection for brevity and simplicity in the melodies, was certainly a Cistercian speciality advocated by Saint Bernard himself.

Cistercian Gregorian chant remained unchanged until the middle of the seventeenth century, but individual tastes could not be eliminated. Neither was it possible to keep out the impact of changing musical styles. Still in the lifetime of Saint Bernard, the General Chapter had to insist on a virile pitch of recitation (*non more femineo tinnulis*) and to banish the "theatrical" effects of falsetto (*falsis vocibus velut histrionicam imitari lasciviam*). The Chapter of 1217 protested against an attempt to introduce polyphony in singing (*triparti vel quadriparti voce more saecularium canitur*), as had crept in at Dore and Tintern. In 1302 the same body spoke against "novelties and conspicuous curiosities" in the choir. In 1320 the Chapter was much annoyed by news of such "absurd novelties" as syncopation of notes and the "hocket" (hiccup), an early contrapuntal device. Soon the introduction of musical instruments chagrined the staunchly conservative fathers. Protests and renewed prohibitions proved to be vain efforts. The movement continued to spread and finally, in 1486, the Chapter acceded to the use of the organ. During the seventeenth century the use of instrumental music was quite popular, at least on great solemnities in the larger abbeys.

Renaissance and Baroque Church music reinterpreted traditional liturgical chant according to the taste of a triumphant polyphony, with little understanding for the real nature of Gregorian plainsong. The fruit of the movement was the so-called "Medicean" edition of liturgical books published in Rome in 1614-1615: its mutilated melodies represented a drastic breach in the continuity of Gregorian traditions. A Cistercian liturgical reform advocated by Abbot General Claude Vaussin (1645-1670) resulted in the publication of a new missal and breviary, but both featured the mutilated melodies of the "Medicean."

It was only two centuries later that the Gregorian, restored to its original beauty through the efforts of the Benedictine monks of Solesmes, regained its deserved place in the liturgical life of the Church. The subsequent movement toward a general liturgical renewal inspired the Order to undertake the restoration of the Cistercian Gregorian to its twelfth-century character. This work, based on the achievements of Solesmes, was carried out by the members of the Strict Observance and its result, the new and revised Gradual, was published in 1899, and followed by the Antiphonary in 1903. The Common Observance also adopted the new editions and from that time until the 1960s both observances used identical liturgical books.

Since the Rule contained no hints for the celebration of the mass, Benedictines everywhere followed the rite of the diocese in which they were established. The Cistercians, too, made use of the general custom and the early Cistercian mass rite corresponded to that of the province of Lyons, modified by the usages of Molesme, which, on the other hand, were based upon the Ritual of Cluny. The liturgy of Lyons was a variation of the so-called Gallico-Roman rite, derived from the reforms of Charlemagne, who had conformed the ancient Gallic liturgy to the Roman rite, while still retaining a number of distinctive Gallic elements. A rather liberal procedure in forming a new liturgy was not a Cistercian privilege; similar principles were followed by the Carthusians and Premonstratensians, and later by the Dominicans and Carmelites. As a matter of fact, strict uniformity in rite was never enforced prior to the Council of Trent, and in France almost every diocese practiced a variation of the generally accepted Gallico-Roman rite.

The contribution of Cîteaux to the liturgical development of the twelfth century was largely a negative one, inasmuch as Cistercians applied consistently the principles of poverty and simplicity in sharp opposition to

Cluniac exuberance. With the exception of a wooden crucifix, any decoration of the sanctuary or the altar was strictly prohibited; the use of precious metals in sacred vessels was eliminated; vestments were made only of linen or wool without any variety of color or quality. The number of daily masses was reduced to one, which was sung after Terce. On greater feasts, later clarified as "Feasts of Two Masses," a low mass was added following Prime. On weekdays conventual high mass was celebrated with only one server, possibly a deacon. A daily mass for the deceased members of the Order and for relatives and benefactors belonged to the earliest Cistercian customs, but otherwise the daily celebration of private masses was neither commended nor prohibited. The custom of frequent private masses during the Middle Ages was far from universal; in Cistercian houses, however, an appropriate time between the canonical hours was always reserved for that purpose.

One powerful incentive for private masses was the steadily growing number of foundation masses requested by pious donors on behalf of deceased friends and benefactors. During the course of the thirteenth century such foundations came to impose a heavy burden on communities at a time when membership was already declining. As early as 1192 the General Chapter was forced to prohibit the acceptance of mass foundations without the Chapter's consent, but the immediate financial advantages of these masses were such that the practice was continued. Eventually abbots, priors and other prominent members of the Order established anniversaries for themselves, until the Chapter of 1609 annulled all such foundations as contrary to monastic poverty. In cases of inability to fulfill mass obligations, the General Chapter either distributed the anniversary masses among other communities or consented to the holding of collective anniversaries.

The medieval Cistercian mass, in comparison with the later prevailing Roman liturgy, exhibited a number of remarkable peculiarities. In our days of liturgical pluralism and experimentation, however, these differences do not appear to be so striking as they did to a previous generation. In fact, some features of the old Cistercian mass presaged several of the most recent innovations. The Cistercian altar was entirely unadorned; only two candelabra stood on either side. The Cistercian rite did not call for Psalm 42 (*Judica*) at the foot of the altar, and had only an abbreviated text of the *Confiteor*, similar to what is being used today. Up to the offertory the celebrant's main role was the singing of the oration; everything else was done by the servers and the choir. There was no pall or velum covering the chalice, which was protected by a corner of the corporal folded over it. Elevation after the consecration was prescribed only in 1210. There were fewer genuflexions than in the later Roman rite. The *Pater noster* was followed by a series of prayers called "Suffrages for Peace." The *Libera* was also sung, as is done in high masses today. Until 1261 all communicants received both the host and chalice, the latter by using a golden tube. After that date this manner of communion remained the privilege of those serving at the altar, but even this was discontinued in 1437. The mass ended with the *Ite missa est,* without adding the "Last Gospel," which was popularized only later by the Dominicans.

Ritual simplicity was another feature of the Order. During the course of the following centuries, however, it gave way to a more elaborate rite and ultimately lost almost entirely its original characteristics. This development was effectively forwarded by powerful historical factors, such as the growing reputation and influence of the Order, the accumulation of papal favors and privileges, the pontifical character of the abbatial office, the change in monastic occupation, the pastoral activities of monks, the discontinuation of agricultural labor, and, most of all, the ever-increasing influence of the Roman liturgy. The General Chapter was just as conservative in ritual changes as in any other field of changing monastic customs; its resistance slowed down somewhat the precipitate onward movement, but it could not halt the development altogether.

The most conspicuous phenomenon of this tendency was the gradual increase of the number of feasts and their elevation in rank in the Cistercian calendar. By the seventeenth century "Feasts of Sermon" had been doubled; the number of the "Feasts of Two Masses" increased from twenty to thirty-two during the period 1173-1259 and had risen to forty-one by 1300. The last date coincided with the climax of Scholasticism, and by this time the original daily schedule of Cîteaux had already undergone a number of changes and manual labor had been replaced by studies. Without these precedents the increase of liturgical services never could have been arranged, because previously the monks' intensive work in the fields made both regular studies and prolonged services impossible. Thus the gradual departure of the Order from its initial simplicity in liturgy can be regarded as an indirect result of Scholasticism. Meanwhile the General Chapter tried to re-emphasize liturgical tradition by the belated introduction of the feasts of Cistercian saints. The feast of Saint Bernard was celebrated for the first time in 1174, the year of his canonization, and that of Saint Robert in 1222; Saint Stephen Harding's feast was not introduced until 1638, while the feast of Saint Alberic was established even later, in 1738.

Some of the accretions to the daily office which had formerly been so sharply criticized also found their way back into the Cistercian *horarium.*

The Office of the Blessed Virgin was prescribed in 1157 for those traveling or staying in the granges; in 1185 it became compulsory in the infirmary, and in 1373 at the choir preceding the canonical hours, although most likely it had been said in many places much earlier. Another example of the general trend toward liturgical amplifications was the return of the procession before conventual mass. During the lifetime of Saint Bernard such a procession was introduced on the feast of the Ascension; in 1223 it was introduced on the feast of the Assumption. Already by 1441 there were processions on every "Feast of Sermon" and at the same time processions were begun in France on Sundays, a procedure which soon became imitated everywhere. During the seventeenth century, processions were further multiplied.

Enforcement of the rules of simplicity in vestments, vessels and other equipment became increasingly lax. In 1226 silk vestments were allowed if received as donations and in 1256 the permission was further extended. Some years later the use of a cope for abbots and dalmatic and tunic for deacons and sub-deacons was permitted, although formerly all had been forbidden liturgical garments. The *pontificalia*—that is, the mitre, ring and sandals—were first granted to the abbots of Santes Creus and Poblet in 1336-1337; Salem received them in 1373, Clairvaux and Les Dunes in 1376, Cîteaux in 1380. During the fifteenth century, the splendor-loving spirit of the Renaissance thoroughly permeated the monasteries and the classical simplicity of twelfth-century Cîteaux sank into oblivion.

With the danger of vanishing traditions, the maintenance of liturgical uniformity throughout the Order became one of the most difficult tasks of the General Chapter. The problem was kept well in evidence during the fourteenth and fifteenth centuries but the very fact that the same regulations were repeated many times also proved their inefficiency.

The technical difficulties of uniformity were largely solved by the extensive use of the newly discovered process of printing. The General Chapter soon realized the importance of the revolutionary technique and, by the Chapter's order, as early as 1484, the first printed Cistercian breviary was published in Basel under the care of Nicolas Salicetus, abbot of Baumgarten (Alsace). It was followed in 1487 by the first printing of the Cistercian missal at Strasbourg, with the co-operation of the same Abbot Nicolas. Further printings of the most important liturgical books at various places (Paris, Lyons, Venice, etc.) appeared in rapid succession, until the question of authenticity and proper authorization caused considerable confusion. In 1504 the General Chapter prohibited the printing and publishing of any liturgical books without the Chapter's special approval.

256

The program of universal renewal of the Church inaugurated by the Council of Trent (1545-1563) included a large-scale liturgical reform completed under Pope Pius V (1566-1572). A new Roman breviary (1568) and the missal (1570) were published with the explicit purpose of promoting complete liturgical uniformity throughout the Catholic world. The use of the same books was imposed on all religious orders having a liturgy of their own for less than 200 years. The different rites of the older religious bodies were approved, but the Pope extended to them a general invitation to abandon their ancient liturgy in favor of the Roman. Although in this manner the integrity of the ancient Cistercian liturgy seemed to have been secured, the moral pressure and the natural appeal of the masterfully revised and purified Roman liturgy rendered complete preservation of the particular rite of the Order highly problematic. As a matter of fact, with some few exceptions, all other exempt orders readily adopted the reform and even those which, referring to their legal rights, refused to abandon their traditional rites, adjusted their own liturgical texts according to the principles of the Roman reform.

As early as 1573 several abbeys, such as Wettingen and Marienstatt, adopted the new Roman rite and the spread of the movement was halted only temporarily by the energetic protest of Nicolas Boucherat I. The General Chapter of 1601 reiterated the necessity of upholding Cistercian liturgical traditions, but the Chapter of 1605 legalized a number of Roman elements. Abbot General Nicolas Boucherat II (1604-1625) was much in favor of the new liturgy. It was with his blessing that the Congregation of Lombardy and Tuscany adopted the Roman breviary and Cistercian abbeys in Prussia and Poland began to use the Roman missal.

The general attitude toward the problem was characteristically expressed by no less an authority than Saint Francis de Sales, who presiding in 1622 at the General Chapter of the Feuillants, openly urged the embracing of the reformed Roman breviary, charging that the "offensive, childish and obscure" parts in the old Cistercian books were incompatible with the dignity of the Church.

The trend seemed irreversible. The General Chapter of 1609 remarked that only a "few" houses still adhered to the old liturgy. In 1611 the same assembly permitted private masses according to Roman rubrics. And it was in the same year that the Feuillants abandoned the Cistercian breviary in favor of the "monastic" breviary approved by Pope Paul V for Benedictines. Finally, the General Chapter of 1618 ordained that "henceforth both conventual and private masses should be said by all, abbots as well as monks, according to the Roman rite and ceremonies, without

257

exception." The same Chapter also projected the reform of the Cistercian breviary.

For well-founded practical reasons the resolution concerning the mass met little opposition. The change was largely restricted to the ordinary of the missal and the Cistercian calendar was maintained along with many features of the ancient liturgy. Thus the well-known sequences of the Roman Missal (*Victimae paschali, Veni sancte, Lauda Sion, Dies irae*) were still missing from the Cistercian missal; on vigils and ember days there were fewer prophecies in the Cistercian mass than in the Roman, and the liturgy of the Holy Week also retained some of the characteristics of old Cîteaux. The Congregations of Castile and Portugal, separated from Cîteaux long before the liturgical reform, maintained the original Cistercian mass rite until their dissolution in the 1830s; the surviving Spanish Cistercian convents of nuns preserved some peculiar elements of the ancient liturgy up to the Second Vatican Council.

Because of the internal disturbances caused by the rise of the Strict Observance, the revision of the breviary could not be accomplished until the regime of Claude Vaussin. Unlike the missal, there were no solid reasons to abandon the ancient Divine Office; on the contrary, Abbot Vaussin's reform was only a sincere endeavor to maintain the original arrangement of Saint Benedict's Rule. Since the greatly increased number of feasts (when the psalms of nocturns were invariably taken from the Common of Saints) made impossible the recitation of the full Psalter during a week's term—the basic requirement of the Rule—the reform created a new type of feast, the "Feast of Three Lessons." On these occasions only the lessons of the nocturns were proper; the psalms were said according to the unbroken weekly order, an arrangement already adopted by the reformed breviary of Pius V. A number of feasts, formerly of higher rank, were reduced to "three lessons" while a group of new feasts was established in the same rank without disturbing the order of the ferial psalms. A considerable number of feasts and commemorations were simply suppressed, whereas three new votive offices of "three lessons" were introduced: one for every free Saturday in honor of the Blessed Virgin; the office of Saint Bernard on Tuesday, and another for Thursday in honor of the Blessed Sacrament. The biblical texts of the whole breviary were amended according to the new edition of the Vulgate made by Pope Sixtus V, and, satisfying a popular demand, the office of the last three days of the Holy Week was taken over in its entirety from the Roman breviary.

The new revised Cistercian breviary was published in 1656, under the authority of Abbot General Vaussin, amidst the vigorous protest of those in favor of the Roman breviary. The malcontents found a powerful ally in the person of Giovanni Bona, then the general of the Feuillants, later cardinal, a great champion of liturgical reform. In 1661 the highly respected and influential Bona succeeded in obtaining a decree from the Congregation of Rites which abrogated Vaussin's reform and prescribed for the whole Order the use of the so-called *Breviarium Romano-Monasticum,* published by Pope Paul V in 1612. Nevertheless, the decree was never put into practice because the pressure exerted by the Order through Hilarion Rancati, the Order's procurator in Rome, was strong enough to reverse the Congregation's decision. Vaussin's breviary became implicitly approved in 1666 by the *In suprema* of Alexander VII, which secured the unopposed use of the Cistercian Breviary for the next two centuries.

A further contribution to the final formation of the Cistercian liturgy was the publication of the Cistercian Ritual, a collection of detailed regulations and various usages concerning monastic life outside the mass and Divine Office. Slight differences between this and the Roman Ritual in the administration of sacraments found their explanation in the fact that all these functions were performed within a monastic community. In preparation by various committees since 1667, the Ritual was finally published in 1689, under the authority of Abbot General Jean Petit. This edition was accepted as the standard guide for all liturgical functions throughout the Order, save among the Feuillants and the Congregation of Castile. Abbot General Edmund Perrot, in an effort to conform some important items of Cistercian ceremonies to the Roman Ritual, issued in 1721 a newly revised edition of the Ritual, which was in general use until 1892, when the abbey of Lérins reprinted the 1689 text, adding as footnotes the variations of the 1721 edition and leaving the decision to the free choice of each community.

The question of the rightful use of the Cistercian breviary appeared once again rather unexpectedly during the 1860s. At that time the community of Bornhem (Belgium), in favor of the *Romano-Monasticum,* renewed Cardinal Bona's charges against the Cistercian breviary, emphasizing the fact that Vaussin's reform was never formally approved by Rome, and that the Cistercian breviary never kept pace with the liturgical development of the Church, that it ignored popular and universally celebrated feasts and failed to secure a proper place for the commemoration of recently canonized saints. The dispute was referred to the Congregation of Rites which, under the vigorous influence of the Trappists, upheld the legality of Vaussin's reform and in 1869 formally approved the Cistercian breviary in its traditional form. In satisfying just demands, however, the same decree arranged the introduction of forty new feasts universally celebrated in the Church; nine among them in the ranks of "two masses," two as "twelve lessons," and the rest of them as feasts of "three lessons," or as simple commemorations. This revision was solemnly sanctioned by Pope Pius IX in 1871, whose Brief has been reprinted ever since on the first page of every Cistercian breviary.

Until the most recent changes the liturgical books for both Observances of the Order remained identical, printed and published since 1854 under the exemplary care of the Trappists of Westmalle in Belgium.

The movement of liturgical renewal of the 1930s resulted in several attempts to restore the old Cistercian missal and breviary. This was done at the Breton house of Boquen after its revival in 1936 by Dom Alexis Presse. When the Swiss abbey of Hauterive was restored in 1938, it became a liturgical center for the Common Observance, experimenting with the pre-Tridentine Cistercian mass. The Catalan abbey of Poblet, where such traditions remained alive until the nineteenth century, made similar efforts after its repopulation in 1940.

In spite of the separation of the two Cistercian observances in 1892, their remarkably uniform liturgy constituted a powerful link between them. All this, even the very idea of uniformity, came to a sudden end by the promulgation of the "Constitution on the Sacred Liturgy" by the Second Vatican Council on December 4, 1963. Radical interpretations of this document encouraged a wide range of experimentations, eliminated at many abbeys Gregorian chant and led to the nearly total exclusion of Latin from liturgical usage. It is highly questionable if there are still elements in the prevailing practices that can be referred to as "Cistercian"; moreover, in any future effort toward the restoration of a truly Cistercian rite, vernacular languages will remain always a serious obstacle.

According to the statistics gathered at the General Chapter of the Common Observance of 1974, three monasteries and seventeen convents of nuns still continue the celebration of the Divine Office in the traditional way, without any change; seventeen monasteries and ten convents have introduced some structural changes, but use the Latin language exclusively; fifteen monasteries and twenty-three convents have a mixed, Latin and vernacular office; fourteen monasteries and twenty-two convents have adopted a purely vernacular liturgy.

A similar liturgical multiplicity prevails among the houses of the Strict Observance. The new *Roman Missal,* however, has received universal acceptance in both Cistercian observances.

XIX

Art

 The startling cultural progress of the eleventh-century Western world clearly manifested the arrival of a new civilization. Its roots may be traced to classical antiquity or even oriental sources, but the articulation of the borrowed patterns was peculiar to the emerging medieval man. The skill at self-expression soon achieved such spontaneous ease and perfection that the art of the era outgrew the period of childish imitations to become the first great medieval style, the Romanesque.

Cluny, with its extensive network of affiliated houses, where a magnificently elaborated liturgy occupied the center of monastic life, became a most zealous promoter of the new type of church architecture, aiming at the creation of worthy surroundings for the all-important and almost continuous services. Another powerful factor in the development of the new style was the increasing popularity of pilgrimages. Monasteries in possession of countless relics of widely-venerated saints attracted, year after year, thousands of devout pilgrims; the original churches, built to serve the needs of a small community, were of necessity remodeled or replaced by spacious structures capable of accommodating the crowds on festival occasions. Since the number of donations and pious foundations grew in proportion to the number of visitors, many monasteries spared no effort in providing for lavish decorations of shrines and churches with the obvious intention of attracting and delighting pilgrims. A competitive spirit swept over French monasteries, and from the middle of the eleventh century modest chapels were changed to splendid shrines guarding reliquaries of fabulous material value. Meanwhile every available space in the huge church edifice, walls, portals, columns, capitals, even floors, became richly adorned with most elaborate carved or painted figures and symbolic decoration.

The admirable monuments of the exuberant decorative spirit of French Romanesque art, as the monastic churches of Vézelay, Moissac, Charlieu or Saint-Gilles, may still excite the unbounded esteem of scholars, yet they found little appreciation among early Cistercians. Their uncompromising spirit of poverty, simplicity and seclusion, which dared to reject the liturgical pomposity of Cluny, could not accept the manifestation of the same inspiration in gold, silver and stone. Indeed, nothing was further from the mind of the founders of Cîteaux, men in love with eremitical solitude and silence, than crowds of pilgrims. They instinctively rejected the lucrative motivation behind the ostentatious display of eye-catching splendor and beauty. Even if the Cistercians had felt any temptation to imitate their wealthy Benedictine neighbors, the extreme poverty and hardships of the first two decades must certainly have taught them to be satisfied with the bare necessities of life.

Of the earliest buildings of Cîteaux nothing has remained. There is, however, no doubt that both church and monastery were built in the same spirit of stern simplicity, which, according to the testimony of the *Exordium parvum,* regulated the quality of liturgical vestments, furnishings and equipment. Nevertheless, during the administration of Stephen Harding, these regulations were only practical consequences of the Cistercian ideal of poverty and, where material value was not involved, as in Gregorian chant or the selection of liturgical hymns, the great Abbot's genius exhibited a deep appreciation of good taste and beauty. Just how far removed from the mentality of Abbots Alberic and Stephen was a contempt of art was strikingly demonstrated in the pages of the first Cistercian manuscripts, which even in their day were exceptionally rich in fine and elaborate initials and miniatures. The four volumes of Saint Stephen's Bible, completed in 1109, constitute one of the richest treasuries of contemporary French miniatures. Next to the Bible in artistic value stands a copy of the *Moralia in Job,* finished in the same *scriptorium* in 1111. The skillfully drawn caricature-like figures illustrate monks working in different circumstances, such as hewing a tree, harvesting grain, gathering grapes and weaving cloth, in addition to groups of jongleurs and mounted knights. Other manuscripts completed at Cîteaux until about 1125 are similiarly decorated.

As the learned paleographer Charles Oursel observed, the style and technique of these miniatures were greatly different from those of other French codices of the day; they rather resembled English illuminations. He even suggested the possibility of a relationship between the famed Bayeux Tapestry and the earliest Cistercian manuscripts. Could the artist have been Stephen Harding himself? Whatever the case may be, expert opinion holds these Cistercian miniatures to be "some of the primordial artistic treasures of Europe."

As in everything else, Saint Bernard's attitude toward monastic art proved to be decisive over Cistercian artistic endeavors.

The change was inaugurated by one of Bernard's earliest treatises, the *Apology (Apologia ad Guillelmum Abbatem),* a brilliant though not unprejudiced diatribe against Cluny, written in 1125. The argument of the essay surpassed by far the importance of a family quarrel, and it still belongs to the most frequently quoted and misinterpreted documents of medieval aesthetics. After rebuking the Cluniacs for their intemperance in food and clothing, Bernard sharply criticized the luxury of their buildings, ". . . the soaring heights and extravagant lengths and unnecessary widths of the churches, . . . their expensive decorations and their novel images, which catch the attention of those who go in to pray, and dry up their devotion." However, he carefully restricted his criticism to the monastic churches while admitting the significance of art elsewhere for the common people: "Bishops have a duty toward both wise and foolish. They have to make use of material ornamentation to rouse devotion in a carnal people, incapable of spiritual things. But we no longer belong to such people." For monks, whose devotion must be formed through contemplation, every external impulse was, in Bernard's mind, necessarily more distracting than inspiring.

The widely-accepted opinion that Saint Bernard was simply blind to the world with its beauty and despised art, may be refuted by a further paragraph of his *Apology*. After an ingenious though sarcastic description of the Cluniac decorative ensemble, he concludes: "All round there is such an amazing variety of shapes that one could easily prefer to take one's reading from the walls instead of from a book. One could spend the whole day gazing fascinated at these things, one by one, instead of meditating on the law of God." He who wrote these lines certainly felt the charm of art, but at the same time had the courage to repudiate it for the sake of divine contemplation.

Otto von Simson in his study on *The Gothic Cathedral* has voiced the opinion that Saint Bernard, far from being an enemy of art, contributed substantially to the spiritual foundations of the new style. The true characteristics of Gothic architecture, he asserts, lay not in carved or painted ornamentation, but in the use of light and the harmony of structural elements based on a "true measure" expressed in geometrical equations. Much of this theory was transmitted to the twelfth century through Saint Augustine's treatise *On Music,* which in turn echoed Pythagorean and Neoplatonic number-mysticism. In addition to members of the cathedral school of Chartres, Saint Bernard served as a persuasive spokesman of Augustinian doctrines.

In this light Bernard's position as expressed in his *Apology* was not motivated by his supposed puritanism, but by his conviction that the house of God and the cloister (*paradisus claustralis*) should be constructed to the likeness of the heavenly Jerusalem, and give a foretaste of its luminous harmony. According to Simson, not only Cistercian builders of the mid-twelfth century were in pursuit of a geometrical "perfect ratio." Abbot Suger, when he designed the famous prototype of Gothic architecture, the church of Saint Denis, employed the same theory, doing so under the influence of his close friend, Saint Bernard. The same seems to be true, continues Simson, of two other pioneer monuments of Gothic, the cathedral of Sens and the matchless west façade of the cathedral of Chartres. In both cases the builders, Archbishop Henry of Sens and Bishop Geoffrey of Chartres, were Bernard's faithful disciples. It is, therefore, entirely arguable that "the first Gothic was the child of Saint Bernard."

Under Bernard's increasing influence, the principles of his *Apology* became the norms of Cistercian artistic activity and, after Abbot Stephen's death, the General Chapter freely adopted them by prohibiting any transgression of the rule of rigid simplicity. Thus, after reaffirming the requirements of the *Exordium parvum* for simplicity of liturgical vestments and equipment, the Chapter prohibited illuminated initials and the use of colors in manuscripts, banned the fine bindings or costly decoration of codices and forbade stained glass windows, figurative carvings and murals, in both churches and monasteries. Sculptured portals were not allowed and the Chapter of 1157 prohibited the coloring even of simple portals or church doors. The same Chapter condemned steeples built of stone; only a modest wooden bell tower was allowed and this could accommodate no more than two bells of small size. In 1218, decorative pavements were forbidden and the Chapter of 1240 ordered the removal of all pictures attached to altars. These and a number of other prohibitions of a similar nature restricted the Cistercian masons, so that their constructions during the twelfth and thirteenth centuries everywhere exhibited the same ascetic simplicity, the main characteristic of Cistercian art. Thus the Cistercians, although having no ambition of developing a peculiar style, through the strict application of their spiritual ideals to art, and especially architecture, created a style characteristically Cistercian. Other religious orders never achieved the formation of a school of art equal to it in so conspicuous and uniform features.

The earliest Cistercian buildings had all been of wood; however, as soon as funds permitted, they were rebuilt in stone. The first wooden structures had been erected by the founders or by the monks themselves, but the permanent buildings were the works of skilled masons assisted by lay-brothers. In either case, however, the monks retained full control over the size and basic design of their abbeys. The builders of Cîteaux and its first daughter-houses simply borrowed the plainest possible elements of the current Burgundian style, which, although still basically Romanesque, displayed some features of the early Gothic, such as the pointed arches, and groined or ribbed vaulting; consequently, the style which was adopted and propagated by the Cistercians was called by many art historians the "transitional" or "proto-Gothic" style.

For the church, the traditional cruciform Benedictine plan was retained and only the rectangular apse represented a Cistercian characteristic, although the latter is of uncertain origin and was by no means universally adopted by Cistercians. There were a nave and two aisles, regularly of east-west direction, introduced by a porch and crossed by the transept which was flanked with square or rectangular chapels and used for private masses. The choir of the monks began in the transept and extended westward along the nave. Further west there were stalls for the sick and disabled, and the rest of the nave was occupied by lay-brothers. Since Cistercian churches were inaccessible to the public, there was no space reserved for them. In the sanctuary was only the high altar and a few furnishings necessary for solemn high masses. Instead of the usual chevet with radiating chapels encircling the sanctuary—a familiar arrangement in both Romanesque and Gothic churches—in many Cistercian churches the rectangular apse was surrounded by square chapels. The walls inside and outside were left bare; even the application of the potentially decorative flying buttresses was rare. In most cases only the rose (*oculus*) windows broke the monotony of the flat end walls of the façade, apse or transept, though they were usually small and of the simplest design. Since figured sculpture was not admitted, the only explicitly decorative element of the interior was in the columns, ending in corbels or in a formal capital with a plain leaf design.

Although Cistercian churches, in a deliberate protest against Cluniac splendor, lacked almost completely ornamental elements, the effect of their purely architectural features became all the more impressive. The fine lines of the wide, pointed arches, the quiet harmony of the cross vaults with powerfully emphasized ribs, the elegance of piers and the beauty of proportion in every detail of the structure characterize early Cistercian architecture. These features are not found in such purity even in the most lavishly decorated Cluniac churches.

The usual site of the cloister lay between the south wall of the church and the transept, the latter prolonged by a sacristy, chapter hall and community room. Turning west along the cloister, there was a small warming room, a spacious refectory, and the kitchen. As another Cistercian characteristic, the refectory was placed rectangularly to the cloister gallery, so that the same kitchen could serve conveniently the lay-brothers' refectory as well. The remaining section of the cloister, enclosing the square toward the southern wall of the church, included the dining room for lay-brothers and various storerooms. On the second floor above

265

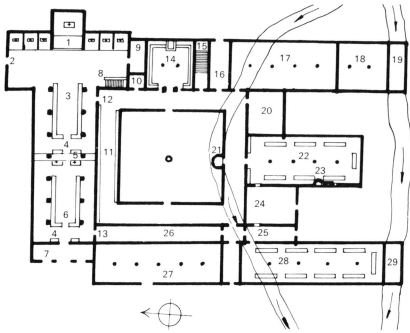

The ideal Cistercian monastery as presented by Aubert and Dimier. One of the prime requirements was a stream that could be diverted to provide water for the fountain (21) and the two latrines (19, 29). The stream also flowed through the kitchen (24). Reprinted from Braunfels, *Monasteries of Western Europe* (Thames and Hudson of London) with permission of the publisher.

1. Sanctuary
2. Lynch-gate, the door through which bodies were carried from the funeral service to the graveyard
3. Monks' choir
4. Benches for the sick
5. Rood-screen, separating the monks' choir from that of the conversi
6. Choir of the conversi, or lay-brothers
7. Narthex
8. Night-stairs from the church to the dorter
9. Sacristy
10. 'Armarium' (aumbry), where books were kept
11. Benches for reading, and for the 'maundy' ceremony of foot-washing
12. Monks' entry
13. Lay-brothers' entry
14. Chapter-house

15. Stairs from the cloister to the dorter, which extended over the whole range 14-19
16. Parlor
17. Monks' common-room
18. Room for novices
19. Latrine (used from the upper storey)
20. Calefactorium, or warming room
21. Fountain, for washing
22. Refectory
23. Pulpit, for reading during the meal
24. Kitchen
25. Cellarer's parlor
26. 'Lane' or 'alley' of the lay-brothers
27. Cellar, or store-room
28. Lay-brother's refectory. The dorter of the conversi, or lay-brothers, extended over the whole range 27-28
29. Latrines of the lay-brother's dorter

the chapter hall was located the monks' dormitory connected directly with
the church by means of a stairway. The dormitory of the lay-brothers was
above the storage room and their own dining room. Across the door from
the refectory was usually located the pavilion of the washing-fountain, a
wide flat basin with many tubular openings. The infirmary, the novitiate
and the guest-house, together with the workshops, mill and other
buildings for gardening and farming, were built somewhat apart from the
monastery. In the early Cistercian monasteries there was no library in the
proper sense of the word, because of the scarcity of books; those few
volumes absolutely necessary for liturgical services and spiritual reading
were stored in a recess on the wall of the sacristy, or in a small adjacent
chamber, called *armarium*.

The largest and most beautiful rooms in Cistercian monasteries were
always the chapter-house and the refectory. Although the rigid rules of
simplicity were strictly applied in their interiors, the skillful grouping of
columns in one or two rows and magnificent rib vaults of various design
gave them a dignity no ornamentation could supply. The inside wall of the
refectory held a balustraded pulpit in a recess with contiguous steps for
the convenience of the monk reading during meals.

Another decorative feature of Cistercian monasteries was the cloister
itself. Though much simpler than Benedictine cloisters, the gallery,
arranged in a quadrangular scheme with open arcades, always presented a
challenge to architects. The cloister was really the artery of monastic life,
connecting the vital parts of the building with one another. It was the
place where the monks performed their domestic tasks, their spiritual
reading or meditation, where they spent their free time and where
conversation was sometimes allowed; in a word, it was the monastic living
room, filled with air, light and sunshine. The arches of the arcades were
usually supported by double columns, applied alternately with massive
piers. The capitals were only modestly carved; with the spreading spirit of
the Gothic, however, the original design frequently moved toward a more
elaborate ornamentation.

The basic elements of Cistercian architecture, sober simplicity combined with good taste and excellent workmanship, characterized even
such humble buildings as forges, mills, tanneries and especially granges,
where fine vaulting was just as common as in the monasteries.

Few of the early Cistercian abbeys have survived the vicissitudes of the
centuries and even fewer have retained their original characteristics. Of
the first five establishments only the church of Pontigny stands, although
its elaborate polygonal choir-arrangement was constructed in the last
years of the twelfth century. The purest existing monument of Cistercian

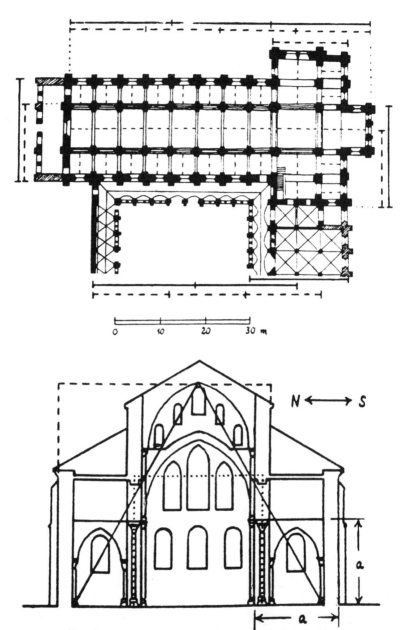

The groundplan and vertical section of the church of Fontenay (c. 1140), showing the "ideal" proportion of squares and cubes of the "Bernardine" design. After H. Hahn, *Die frühe Kirchenbaukunst der Zisterzienser* (Berlin, 1957). Courtesy of Verlag Gebr. Mann.

268

architecture is Fontenay, the second "daughter" of Clairvaux, founded in 1119, but transferred to its final location in 1130. It was there that the still standing abbey was erected, presumably under the instructions of Saint Bernard himself. At any rate, Augustine's "perfect ratio" of squares and cubes is a conspicuous feature of its design: each aisle bay is a square in plan and each square is made into a cube inasmuch as the height of the vault is the same as the width of the aisle.

Le Thoronet in Provence followed the plan of Fontenay and has been recognized as a classic example of how the simplest elements of architecture may result through careful design in a unique harmony of light and shadow and perfect acoustic effect. Among other twelfth-century abbeys which have preserved their early characteristics notable are Sénanque, Silvanès, Aiguebelle and Flaran, all in the south of France.

Despite the stubborn resistance of the General Chapter, the Cistercian severity of Saint Bernard's times was greatly mitigated during the Gothic period. However, as a proof that the decorative instinct of monks could not be suppressed entirely even during the Saint's lifetime, a peculiar technique of stained glass windows is worth mentioning. This style prevailed for about a century and involved using, instead of colors, silvery tones for geometric or floriated designs (*grisailles*).

As early as the beginning of the thirteenth century the new constructions showed conspicuous deviations from the initial simplicity. The church of Châlis (Oise), consecrated in 1219, was built with a fine interior, imitating the cathedrals of Noyon and Soissons. Royaumont (Seine-et-Oise), founded through the munificence of King Saint Louis in 1228, was as splendid as any contemporary secular church. This was the church where the King erected magnificent tombs for members of his family, while a great number of similar monuments of prominent bishops or laymen adorned other Cistercian churches. Meanwhile the popular cult of relics found an increasingly important role in Cistercian churches, and the reliquaries and shrines were always richly decorated. At Obazine (Corrèze), the tomb of the founder, Saint Stephen, exhibited a skillfully carved series of Cistercian abbots, monks, brothers and nuns in high relief, kneeling or standing before the Madonna, and on the opposite side, similar figures in the same grouping, rising from their tombs. The churches of Vaucelles and Ourscamp were as grand as that of Royaumont; in fact, the church of Vaucelles, with its 132 meter length, was the largest ever built by Cistercians.

During the fourteenth century the rigid rules became further relaxed and the Renaissance ignored them almost completely. Not only did the new foundations follow the style of the latest Gothic period with its delicate ornamentations, but the old establishments also were remodeled according to the new demands, a magnificent library usually being added as another sign of the changing times. Such expensive improvements, however, could scarcely be afforded by the growing number of monasteries under the domination of commendatory abbots, where the communities had to be content with the preservation of their ancient plant.

The early monuments of Cistercian architecture outside of France bore characteristics similar to those in the motherland, though they soon adopted and continued to develop national artistic traditions. The real significance of the Order in this respect lies in the fact that they were almost everywhere in Europe the pioneers of the highly advanced French architecture, promoting especially the development of Gothic.

Nowhere on the continent did the Cistercians leave so monumental a record in the history of medieval architecture as in England. The first foundations skillfully combined the transitional style with the local Norman elements, and during the twelfth century English monks generally abandoned the well-known sternly ascetic features and produced the finest masterpieces of the "Early English" architecture.

The part of the country richest in comparatively well-preserved Cistercian buildings is Yorkshire, where Byland, Jervaulx, Kirkstall, Roche and Sawley are all, even in their ruined state, noble witnesses of the toil, skill and taste of the White Monks. The largest and most significant monuments are undoubtedly Fountains and Rievaulx, both founded in 1132. The exterior of the church of Fountains is the most impressive example of the transitional style in the true Cistercian spirit of dignified severity. Its most prominent feature, a superb tower, which in its magnificent proportions was certainly contrary to the rule of simplicity, was erected only on the eve of the Dissolution. Large parts of the monastery are still plainly discernible. The nave of the church of Rievaulx demonstrates the usual plain transitional forms, yet the choir and transept, built about 1230, give the abbey an incomparable elegance. The capitals are exquisitely molded, the triforium and clerestory singularly graceful, though all these decorative elements were built evidently in defiance of the early traditions. On the other hand, another remarkable ruin, that of Tintern in Monmouthshire, built some three decades later, still represents the purest Cistercian Gothic in the spirit of the so-called "Geometrical" style, bare of any superfluous decoration. Even here, however, the enormous windows on the east and west walls of the church with their elaborate design, would hardly have been approved by Saint Bernard.

270

The final stage of the gradual departure from the principles established by the great Abbot of Clairvaux was marked by the rebuilt Melrose in Scotland. Founded in 1136 by Rievaulx and completely destroyed by the vengeful English army following the defeat at Bannockburn in 1314, Melrose soon began its reconstruction through a generous donation of Robert the Bruce and the work continued until the sixteenth century. The abbey, rebuilt in the "Decorated" and "Perpendicular" styles—the latest developments of English Gothic—retained only the foundations of the old plan; in every other respect it was transformed into one of the most splendid memorials of monastic architecture in Great Britain. Though the church lacks the majestic proportions of Rievaulx or Fountains, the masons applied everything they knew in decorating pier sections, arch moldings, clerestory windows, tracery and vault shafts. Even now, after the vicissitudes of four centuries, it still stands as a matchless display of the finest decorative sculpture. A "miraculous" crucifix in the choir of the lay-brothers was the work of an unnamed sculptor who received his commission from Abbot Hugh of Leven (1339-1349). According to the chronicler of Melrose, the pious artist worked on it only on Fridays, while fasting on bread and water. Public admiration was largely due to its lifelike features, made after a nude human model. So great was the fame of the crucifix that special arrangement had to be made so that even women could view it.

The dissolution of religious orders by Henry VIII brought death to countless monastic buildings of inestimable artistic value. None of the Cistercian churches or monasteries survived the era of destruction without considerable damage; most of them were entirely demolished. The still standing ruins, however, are being well preserved under the care of private owners or by the Office of Works.

The first Irish Cistercian house, Mellifont, founded in 1142, was the fruit of the intimate friendship between Saint Bernard and Saint Malachy, archbishop of Armagh. By the end of the century the number of Irish monasteries grew to twenty-five, all native foundations. With the fusion of the Congregation of Savigny and some late English foundations, the total number of Irish abbeys grew even higher. A particularly strong early nationalistic trend soon rendered Clairvaux's control over its affiliations in that country rather questionable; however, the surviving monuments of Irish Cistercian architecture, some sixteen more or less well-preserved ruins of churches, exhibit French influence. They cannot be compared in size or artistic beauty to the great English abbeys, but the flat surface decorations give them a local Irish character. During the fifteenth century a number of abbeys were partially rebuilt under English influence, with more decoration and elaborate vaulting, and with the addition of a central tower. The most impressive remains are those of Holy Cross Abbey; other notable ruins belong to Mellifont, Bective, Baltinglass, Boyle, Jerpoint and Corcomroe.

Nowhere was the influence of Cistercian architecture more decisive than in Spain, where the often simple local Romanesque was enriched by Gothic elements, especially by the ogive vaulting produced for the first time in Spain through the efforts of French Cistercian architects. The Cistercians did not arrive as apostles of a new architectural style, however, and willingly accepted and followed local artistic traditions. Although a dozen early foundations were made directly from Clairvaux, none of these churches followed strictly the "Bernardine" plan, which emerged eventually at La Espina and Santes Creus, both completed only in the first half of the thirteenth century. By the same time some Cistercian churches, such as La Oliva, Piedra and Rueda, featured the first pure Gothic in Spain. The plan of the church of Huerta was drafted in imitation of La Oliva, but the artistic fame of Huerta resulted from its refectory, one of the most elegant Gothic halls outside France.

The most prominent monument of Cistercian architecture in Spain is the royal monastery of Poblet in Catalonia, the "Escorial of Aragon," the burial place of its most generous protectors, the kings of Aragon. Its austere church is 85 meters long and the vaulting of the nave is 28 meters high. The extensive plant is completely surrounded by fortified walls and bastions while the buildings themselves, under continuous construction and remodeling until the end of the eighteenth century, may serve as an illustration for the history of architecture from the early transitional style to the Baroque. Although the Order was suppressed in the country in 1835, the monastery survived in excellent condition, so that the recently resumed monastic life could start anew without much difficulty. About half of the Spanish Cistercian foundations are still standing in fair condition, among them Moreruela in Castile, Veruela in Aragon, the famous convent of Las Huelgas in Burgos, and a close rival of Poblet, Santes Creus in Catalonia; thus Spain became probably the richest country in well-preserved Cistercian monuments of architecture. The influence of Cistercian architecture remained dominant in Spain until about the middle of the thirteenth century and extended over Premonstratensian houses, many collegiate churches and several cathedrals, particularly those of Tarragona, Lerida, Osma, Siguenza and Burgos.

Among the numerous establishments of the Order in Portugal the leading role was undoubtedly held in every respect by the mighty

Alcobaça, some sixty miles north of Lisbon. Construction was begun in 1158, but was not completed until 1252. Its church was the largest in the country (365 feet long) and of unique artistic value. Its ground plan is an exact replica of Clairvaux, but because its side aisles are vaulted practically at the same level as the nave, it represents a rarity among Cistercian churches. The internal decorations were greatly enriched with the tombs of Portugese royalty. During the course of centuries Alcobaça was also incessantly remodeled, until the dissolution of 1834, when the monastery was converted into barracks.

In Italy, too, the Gothic was introduced by the Cistercians, although it was always regarded as the style of foreigners. Indeed, the first Cistercian churches in Italy faithfully copied the patterns of the early Burgundian school of architecture with heavy, plain structure, thick walls and small windows. Among the early Cistercian monuments Fossanova is the best preserved, erected toward 1190 in the likeness of Fontenay with interesting cloister galleries. Casamari, constructed between 1203 and 1221, shows similar features. Further examples of Cistercian Gothic are Arabona in the Abruzzi, Castagnola near Ancona, San Galgano near Siena, San Martino al Cimino near Viterbo, and Colomba in the diocese of Piacenza. In this connection it is worth mentioning that late in the thirteenth century a number of lay-brothers of San Galgano participated in the construction of the *duomo* of Siena.

Although Cistercian austerity influenced Franciscan architecture remarkably, the style never became popular in Italy. Its development stalled and the later monastic buildings of the Order were much more Italian in their features than Cistercian. An interesting example of how an originally simple Cistercian church was successively transformed according to the taste of the Italian Renaissance is Chiaravalle near Milan, founded in 1135. The monastery was destroyed but the surviving church exhibits a Renaissance façade and an impressive octagonal bell tower, while the interior decoration in the same style includes the famous choir stalls of 1645, each seat with a magnificent relief representing a scene of the life of Saint Bernard. Most Cistercian abbeys in the country fell victim to the commendatory system during the fifteenth century and became so poor that they could contribute almost nothing to the further development of Cistercian art. The present possessions of the Italian congregations, in large proportion, were not originally Cistercian foundations.

In Germany, the earliest monuments of Cistercian architecture, such as Eberbach, Tennenbach and Bronnbach, made little impression upon the well-advanced German Romanesque, although during the flourishing period of Cistercian building activity in that country from 1200 to 1250, the churches of the Order represented the first purely Gothic style.

The first stage of this development toward a pure Gothic (1210-1220) was reached by Arnsberg (Hesse), Otterberg (Palatinate), Walkenried (Harz), Riddagshausen (Brunswick), by the famous porch and monastery of Maulbronn (Württemberg) which has been preserved almost in its original form, as well as by Ebrach, all following the pattern of Pontigny. The ruins of Heisterbach (consecrated in 1237) indicate yet another step forward, while the fulfillment of Gothic arrived with Marienstatt (Westerwald), begun in 1243, and Altenberg near Cologne, the foundations of which were laid in 1255. Their style marked the end of the steady Burgundian traditions in favor of the more advanced Gothic of the Ile-de-France, and also a departure from the spirit of rigid Cistercian asceticism. Their chevets with radiating chapels and ambulatory, huge windows (mostly in grisailles) and slender flying buttresses were novelties both in the Order and in Germany; nevertheless, towers were still missing and the cool and reserved simplicity of their interior still proved the active force of the original ideals.

The accomplishments of Cistercian Gothic were certainly surpassed by the great German cathedrals of the following centuries. However, as late as the second quarter of the thirteenth century, construction on the cathedral of Bamberg and the design of the church of Saint Sebaldus in Nuremberg bore the decisive influence of the monks of Ebrach. The Order's greatest pride in the eastern part of the country, where stone was scarce, the creation of a Gothic brick structure remained without rival. The ruins of Lehnin (Brandenburg) and Kolbatz (Pomerania) are fair examples of the unusual technique, but the largely intact church of Chorin (Brandenburg), with its delicate beauty, survived as one of the most outstanding monuments of Cistercian architecture.

In the northeast, German Cistercians found it necessary to fortify their monasteries, giving birth to a number of fortress-abbeys along the dangerous borders of the Baltic provinces. The most notable example of such structures was Dünamünde in the mouth of the river Düna, near Riga. The monastic plant was totally surrounded by water and a rectangular fortification. There were bastions on each corner and the only entrance led across a drawbridge. The strong walls of the abbey proper constituted a second line of defense, featuring two round towers on the north side. But even such formidable obstacles failed to discourage the fierce pagan natives, who managed to penetrate and sack the abbey in 1228 and 1263.

A similarly fortified outpost was Falkenau near Dorpat, while Neuenkamp, Bukow, Pelplin, Hiddensee on the island of Rügen, and Stolpe had also more or less developed defenses.

274

The establishments of the Order were pioneers of Gothic also in Austria, taking more liberties in the application of purely decorative elements than elsewhere in Germany. The first sample of real Gothic arrived in the country with Neuberg in Styria (1327). Similar features appeared in the choir of Heiligenkreuz and Lilienfeld but neither of them could match the artistic riches and influence of Zwettl, a treasury of art of almost every style from the twelfth century onwards.

In Belgium, the ruins of the once celebrated Orval belong to the most precious monuments of architecture in the country; however, the original church, consecrated in 1124, had no relation with the Order, since the monastery was actually taken over by the Cistercians only in 1132. Later the abbey was continually enlarged until its destruction in 1637, a victim of the Thirty Years' War. During the following century the wealthy abbey was magnificently rebuilt in Baroque, but was destroyed again by French revolutionary troops. The abbey has recently been revived by the Trappists. Aulne and Villers in Brabant, even in ruins, remain one of the finest monuments of Belgian Gothic. Of the medieval buildings of Les Dunes nothing has survived. The same fate awaited Ter Doest in Flanders. A still standing thirteenth-century farm building of this latter abbey, however, has been termed one of the "miracles" of medieval architecture. It is, in fact, a huge barn near Lissewege, one of the old granges of Ter Doest. What justify posterity's admiration are its shape and dimensions. The brick structure, featuring fine façades, dating back to about 1250, is 60 meters long and 24 meters wide, but while the side walls are only 9 meters high, the gables on both ends soar to 20 meters and are covered by an enormous steeply-slanted saddle roof. The interior is divided by two ranges of heavy oak piles supporting the wooden superstructure. The six large Gothic blind windows decorating the gables give a graceful appearance to this purely utilitarian building.

In Switzerland, the best preserved Cistercian building, still exhibiting the original features of early Gothic, is that of Kappel, now a Zwinglian parish church. The church of Hauterive bears similar characteristics, though the present monastery is a Baroque structure. Wettingen also underwent a remodeling in similar style, while the monastery of Saint Urban with its famous choir-stalls is generally regarded as one of the largest and most impressive memorials of Baroque architecture in the country.

The majority of the Hungarian abbeys were founded directly from France and represented an advanced form of transitional style. The only building which has survived in perfect condition is the church of Bélapátfalva, a faithful copy of the plain Burgundian patterns, though its interesting polychrome portal shows Italian, and its vaulting system

German, influence. Among the numerous Cistercian ruins only Kerc preserves its distinguishable French transitional forms. Kerc, situated in Transylvania, may be considered the farthest witness of Cistercian culture in southeastern Europe.

In Poland, too, Cistercians arrived as pioneers of the Gothic style. Since in that country there had been no strong architectural traditions, the uniformity and purity of Cistercian features were more pronounced than in the West, and the influence of Cistercians on later cathedrals (Cracow, Breslau) was particularly conspicuous. A number of Cistercian churches have preserved their medieval features in fair condition. The largest among them is Mogila, near Cracow. In its plan it is a classic example of Cistercian simplicity; whereas the church of Oliva near Danzig shows well-advanced forms of Gothic. Its interestingly varied vaulting system dates back to the fifteenth century. After the dissolution, this church served as the cathedral of the diocese of Danzig.

In Denmark the recently restored thirteenth-century Løgumkloster features one of the finest Gothic in brick. The remnants of the once rich Sorø are also worth mentioning. The church is a simple Romanesque brick structure; the monastery survived as a college until 1813, when it was destroyed by fire. In Norway, the Gothic was introduced by English Cistercians, but little has remained of their establishments. The oldest monasteries in Sweden were French foundations. Alvastra, the largest and richest among them, was established by Clairvaux in 1143, and its plan shows some similarity to Fontenay. A part of the original transept of Nydala, another daughter-house of Clairvaux, built in the simplest Burgundian transitional style, is used now as a parish church. In Gudvala, an affiliation of Nydala, only the nave remains, but the church of Varnhem, Alvastra's foundation, faithfully maintained its thirteenth-century form and thus became one of the most significant monuments of Swedish transitional architecture. Its interior shows German inspiration, but the plain, massive square pillars supporting the circular arches of the nave exhibit unmistakably Burgundian influence, and its circular chevet shows the influence of thirteenth-century Clairvaux.

Since the Chapter of 1157 prohibited Cistercian lay-brothers and artisans from assisting in the construction of secular buildings, the direct influence of the Order through its own trained architects was only sporadic. In those countries where Cistercians represented the only advanced style, however, their indirect influence, as models and sources of constant artistic inspiration, was considerable for centuries. Even in France, Cistercian influence prevailed until the era of the great cathedrals, especially among the newly founded or reformed religious orders. The Premonstratensians, the order of Grandmont and the Augustinian Canons copied exactly the austere Cistercian pattern in both their legislation and building activities. Through the Knights of the Temple, organized under Saint Bernard's auspices, the Cistercian artistic program invaded even the Holy Land. Moreover, when the Cistercians themselves were about to abandon their original simplicity, the Mendicants, lacking any ambition for creating a style of their own, imitated the plainest available model of the Cistercians and continued to build their churches in similar fashion until the Renaissance.

The economic crisis of the fourteenth and fifteenth centuries necessarily slowed down the building activity of the Order and the catastrophe of the Reformation and subsequent religious wars not only led to the destruction of hundreds of churches and monasteries, but also prevented the surviving abbeys from adding anything really momentous to their original plant in the new style of the Renaissance. In Italy and in Spain there are some beautiful Renaissance additions to churches and other monastic buildings, such as new façades, portals, altars and other pieces of internal decoration; however, the general poverty of these houses under commendatory abbots rendered large-scale construction utterly impossible.

From the middle of the seventeenth century until the end of the eighteenth, a period of relative peace and prosperity, the spirit of the victorious Baroque swept over the Continent. Within the Order another era of feverish building activity began, especially in central Europe. In its prolific productivity it became almost equal to the glorious medieval beginnings. Unfortunately, however, the Baroque, with its diametrically different taste, had no understanding or respect for the monuments of the past and destroyed or substantially remodeled Romanesque or Gothic buildings to the changed requirements of the new style. The fate of the thirteenth-century church of Zirc may serve as a characteristic example. Following the liberation of Hungary from the Turks, the rich Silesian abbey of Heinrichau revived the deserted Zirc in the first years of the eighteenth century. The once outstanding example of early Gothic architecture, though damaged, survived in fair condition, so that the first settlers held their services in it. Yet, instead of the obviously easy task of repairing the building, they demolished it entirely and from the same stones erected a new Baroque structure which, despite its greatness, certainly lagged far behind the original in artistic value.

Most surviving Cistercian abbeys throughout Catholic Europe from Portugal to Hungary and Poland made efforts to reconstruct, remodel or at least redecorate their ancient buildings in the new style, each according to the financial means available to it for such expensive and often quite unnecessary projects.

In France, where the vast majority of Cistercian abbeys had to share their revenues with commendatory abbots, large scale building activity was rarely possible, although the commendators often built for their own convenience elegant new residences surrounded by well-cared-for parks. In many instances the desire to build was not matched by proportionate income, and the results were incomplete projects, sometimes even financial ruin. This was the case at Châlis, where in 1736 the ambitious commendator, Duke Louis of Bourbon-Condé, decided to retain the thirteenth-century church, but to demolish the monastery in order to make room for a palatial new abbey. The plans were drawn by Jean Aubert, the great architect of the Hôtel Biron and the chateau of Chantilly, but by 1764 only one-third of the project had been accomplished, and that at the cost of heavy indebtedness. In 1770 the abbey was declared bankrupt; it closed its gates and the monks were dispersed. Only this finished portion of the plan has survived the Revolution and now houses a small museum.

The only French Cistercian abbey completely rebuilt in Baroque was Valloires in Ponthieu, which had been entirely destroyed by a conflagration in 1647. The plans for reconstruction were drawn by the architect Raoul Coignart in 1738, and were executed between 1741 and 1756, although the interior decoration was largely the work of an Austrian artist.

Similar undertakings were projected on a truly gigantic scale at Cîteaux, Clairvaux, La Ferté and Sept-Fons, but none was completed before the Revolution. At Cîteaux the ancient church was to remain intact, but the architect, Nicolas Lenoir, envisioned a wholly rebuilt abbey of enormous dimensions. The work began in 1760, but only one wing reached completion, which, since 1898, has housed the modern Trappist community.

A similar project at Clairvaux came closer to accomplishment between 1740 and 1780, a monumental complex of still largely intact buildings, used presently as a penitentiary. It was in the same era that the populous Sept-Fons was greatly expanded, largely through the physical labor of hundreds of lay-brothers.

The true homes of the Baroque, however, were the Catholic states of Germany and the domains of the Austrian Habsburgs. By this epoch the monks' living-quarters had been greatly deteriorated and the ancient water and plumbing systems could no longer be repaired. It was,

therefore, the monastery proper which was singled out for total reconstruction, providing the monks with individual cells and other conveniences demanded by the new lifestyle. The churches, on the other hand, if
they had still been standing, were piously retained, although certainly
redecorated.

The wealthy German abbeys proved to be most successful in carrying
out their extensive building programs, which resulted in monuments of
unique importance in the history of Baroque architecture. In Himmerod,
the old church was demolished and between 1735 and 1751 a splendid new
Baroque church was erected, whereas the monastery had been remodeled
even sooner. Following the conflagration of 1697, Salem was rebuilt in
the same brilliant fashion by the architect Franz Beer. In a strange
antithesis to the plain simplicity of ancient Ebrach, a new monastery was
constructed in 1716 by one of the leading geniuses of German Baroque,
Balthasar Neumann; in its gorgeous beauty it was unrivaled even among
the richest Cistercian Baroque monuments. The same architect finished in
1728 the church of Schönthal in the diocese of Wurzburg and somewhat
later, the church of Vierzehnheiligen, a favorite shrine of German pilgrims
in the valley of the Main, built under the auspices of the abbey of
Langheim. A church erected by Salem for similar purposes was Birnau on
the northern shore of Lake Constance, a real gem of late Baroque, designed
by Peter Thumb and completed between 1746 and 1750. Fürstenfeld, near
Munich, the mighty Waldsassen, Heinrichau and Grüssau in Silesia,
Königsaal and Sedletz in Bohemia, Oliva near Danzig, among many other
Cistercian abbeys of lesser importance, are all outstanding representatives
of Baroque art. The restored monastic plant of the Silesian Leubus gained
special fame for its colossal dimensions. Its old church, containing
twenty-four side altars was restored in Baroque, while the conventual
buildings were wholly rebuilt under Abbot Ludwig Bauch (1696-1729).
After their completion the abbey enjoyed the reputation of being the
greatest in Central Europe: the north-south façade measured 225 meters.

In Austria, all Cistercian establishments were more or less substantially
remodeled or completely rebuilt during the seventeenth and eighteenth
centuries representing the whole architectural development from the early
stages of Baroque to the late Classicism. In this respect the richest
treasury of art is the abbey of Zwettl; its tower and high altar are
especially admirable masterpieces. Heiligenkreuz preserved many of its
medieval characteristics, but the monks were engaged always in new
decorative projects requiring the services of famous contemporary artists,
like Giovanni Giuliani of Venice, the sculptor of the beautiful choir stalls
completed in 1707. During the same period, the young Raphael Donner,

one of the greatest sculptors of Austrian Baroque, spent the years of his apprenticeship in the monastery's workshop. In Hungary, Saint Gotthard, a monument of noble design and virtuous craftmanship, represents the best Cistercian Baroque. Zirc, rebuilt by Heinrichau, is a large though relatively simple structure with remarkable interior decoration.

It is needless to stress that the spirit of Baroque art, so eagerly adopted by the Order, entirely eliminated the tradition of stern simplicity characteristic of the early Cistercians, and only the financial status of each abbey set a limit to its sumptuous building and decorating activity. Halls, stairways, refectories and especially libraries and abbatial suites were not far behind royal palaces in rich, glittering ornamentation; they were designed by the same architects who were employed by the highest aristocracy. In interior decoration and furnishing, however, Cistercian lay-brothers rendered an important service; in some instances, as at Himmerod and at Heinrichau, their humble workshops, under expert leadership, developed into real schools of art.

The outbreak of the French Revolution (1789) was followed by a wave of wanton destruction, outdoing in callousness even the disasters of the sixteenth century. Occasionally the new owners of secularized abbeys found reasons to spare buildings of some practical utility, but churches were demolished as if they were merely eyesores blocking the proper exploitation of the property.

Of the great basilicas of Cîteaux, La Ferté, Clairvaux and Morimond, nothing remained above ground.

In 1791 Royaumont was acquired by the Marquis de Travannel, financier and Marie Antoinette's private banker. Since he was an aristocrat and suspect in the eyes of the new regime, he wished to demonstrate his republican sentiments by ordering the immediate demolition of the church. After he had indeed been accused before the Committee of Public Safety in 1793, he proudly declared in his defense that: "after I bought the property called some time ago Royaumont, I had the famous church destroyed, which had been erected by one of our ancient tyrants, whom superstition called Saint Louis, and whose children were buried there." It was evidently this heroic deed that saved his neck.

Radix de Saint-Foy, who purchased the great Ourscamp, turned out to be an enthusiastic admirer of English gardens. A fine garden he had, but how could he provide for the indispensable ruin? He found a happy solution in 1807, when he ordered the reduction of the church to a properly shaped ruin.

The new owner of Vaux-de-Cernay, General Jean-François Christophe, found for some reason that the church stood in the way of one of his projects. In 1816 he had the walls of that noble witness to six centuries of Cistercian work and prayer undermined and blown up in the presence of a number of guests invited for the unusual occasion, who, apparently, watched with great satisfaction as that magnificent monument of art fell within seconds into a formless heap of rubble.

The nineteenth century brought no new architectural glories to Cistercians, but monks of both observances deserve credit for having revived and preserved a number of ancient abbeys they inhabited. Increasing public appreciation of the Gothic resulted in an awareness of the values of medieval monuments and when most western governments took up the cause of preserving such treasures, their safe survival, often only in the form of ruins, was secured.

In some exceptional cases monastic ruins have been totally or partially restored by the efforts of architectural experts supported by public or private funds. Such works have been eminently successful at Noirlac in Berry, restored to serve as an international center of monastic studies. Similar intentions benefited the abbey of Clairmont in Maine and the charming old church of the Breton Boquen. The ruins of the Baroque Himmerod have also been totally restored largely by the diligence of the monks themselves.

American admiration for the art treasures of Europe resulted in the transplantation to the New World of whole edifices taken apart stone-by-stone and reassembled at the new location. Thus, the famous museum of medieval architecture in New York, "The Cloisters," exhibits the chapter house of Pontaut and the cloisters of the originally Benedictine Cuxa and Bonnefont. After many adversities, the Castilian Sacramenia, acquired by the late newspaper-tycoon William Randolph Hearst, and shipped to America, has been rebuilt near Miami, Florida. The same great collector purchased another Spanish Cistercian abbey, Santa Maria de Ovila. The 10,300 stones of this fine Romanesque monastery in San Francisco's Golden Gate Park still await their final destination or total disintegration.

XX

Economy

 The impressive agrarian record of twelfth-century Cistercians was not the reward of new and revolutionary techniques or economic principles; it was largely a byproduct of the organization and spiritual aspirations of the Order.

The monks' dedication to poverty and their resolution to live in total seclusion, free from secular and feudal entanglements, forced them to forgo the customary sources of ecclesiastical revenue and to seek remote and uncultivated "deserts" where the only means of survival was, of necessity, their own manual labor spent reclaiming the land at their disposal. In fact, at a time of relative rural overpopulation, they had no other choice than to accept whatever land was still available and the donors were willing to grant. The sites of most newly founded abbeys were not necessarily "places of horror and vast solitude," but they were certainly uninviting areas outside manorial boundaries, lands that no one else cared to till.

The monks' often spectacular success can be adequately explained on the grounds of three basic factors: the accumulation of extensive tracts of land; the employment of lay-brothers in large numbers; consistent planning and efficient administration.

The beginnings at each foundation were invariably hard, but ordinarily the flow of donations kept pace with the growth of the communities, while immunities from ecclesiastical taxes and royal exactions protected the monks from burdensome payments. Since Cistercians accepted neither manorial nor ecclesiastical revenues, it seemed just that they themselves be free from paying tithes and similar contributions.

PRINCIPLES AND REALITY

The position of the first Cistercian generation on these matters came to expression in the "Institutes," presented as Chapter XV of the *Exordium parvum,* paraphrasing the twenty-third paragraph of the first *Capitula,* dating back to 1119. In the wording of this earlier document, "churches, altar-revenues, burial fees, tithes or victuals furnished by the labor of others, villages, serfs, land taxes, incomes from ovens and mills and

282

similar other things contrary to monastic purity, are excluded by the rules of both religious life and our Order."

The Charter of Charity envisioned each abbey as an independent economic unit, sufficiently endowed to support its membership without taking recourse to the above listed and prohibited sources of income. Only in cases of emergencies were other abbeys of the Order to come to the aid of a needy community. The same document stressed emphatically the necessity of a uniform way of life in every abbey, a principle which served as a firm basis for the legislative activity of the General Chapter throughout the twelfth century. More or less detailed instructions issued by the Chapter referring to the maintenance and administration of property appear to be implementations of an ideal already tested and found viable at Cîteaux and the other early foundations.

While the General Chapter was wholly dedicated to the maintenance of uniform standards of life and discipline, individual abbots had to face the practical problems of everyday life and find appropriate solutions corresponding to a specific time, situation and locale. Thus each abbot of the fast-expanding Order had to shoulder a dual responsibility: fidelity to certain principles and regulations, and adequate provision for his monks.

To expect that in cases of conflict between law and local exigencies, the first always prevailed, would be an anachronistic approach to twelfth-century legal concepts, for the Middle Ages was a time when local autonomy and long established customs often outweighed the authority of a remote legislator. Since the fabric of economy and society which surrounded the early Burgundian foundations was subject to change, or had always been altogether different outside that geographic area, such conflicts became ever more frequent. When finally neither the available land nor the number of lay-brothers was sufficient for the safe survival of a large number of abbeys, even the General Chapter had to yield to compromises, leading to the eventual breakdown of the principles themselves.

Any attempt, therefore, to discourse on Cistercian economy solely on the basis of "principles" and the corresponding statutes of the General Chapter must be termed unrealistic and inadequate. A few convenient examples may illustrate the successful realization of the early articles of Cistercian economy, but the exceptions appear so numerous that generalizations, made under the assumption that the rules had been generally heeded, are entirely unwarranted.

The most conspicuous exceptions to the early rules were the monasteries, or even groups and congregations of monasteries, which joined the Order after years or decades of independent existence, notably the

Congregation of Savigny. The easy admission of such houses without forcing them to divest themselves of "unlawful" sources of income should be a clear proof of the curious fact that even the General Chapter, the chief guardian of uniformity, was willing to bend the rules, although the effects of leniency on other houses must have been well understood.

GRANTS AND FOUNDATIONS

New foundations were invariably preceded by an invitation and promise of sufficient land at a suitable location. The initiative was taken often by tenants-in-chief, members of the nobility, bishops, or occasionally, members of royal houses.

In most cases the exact size of the original donation cannot be determined. Since, however, the founding group consisted normally of twelve monks and a somewhat larger number of lay-brothers, the grant must have been modest. The holding of extensive property would have been pointless without a sufficient number of working hands.

Thanks to modern research covering the early foundations in England, that country provides the most concrete examples. Thus, Garendon in Leicestershire, one of the first foundations (1133), received about 690 acres, which was probably as much as the monks were able to cultivate. But Swineshead in Lincolnshire began its life in 1135 with only about 240 acres, while Thame in Oxfordshire experienced great difficulties, for in 1140 the founders had to be satisfied with a meager 150 acres.

The poor quality of the land was another source of grave hardships. The terrain given to the abbey of Sawley (Yorkshire) by William de Percy in 1147 was so poor that the monks found themselves "reduced to extreme want through the ill temperature of the air which permitted nothing to thrive on the ground." They were about to give up the foundation when the Countess of Warwick, daughter of the donor, came to their rescue by granting them a better piece of land. Similarly, the monks of Fountains, founding a new settlement at Haverholme (Lincolnshire) in 1137, were unable to survive on the original site and were forced to move to Louth Park, donated by the compassionate Bishop Alexander of Lincoln.

The cases when, for a variety of reasons, the original grant failed to respond to the backbreaking labor of the brethren, were numerous. In England alone at least twenty-nine original settlements, one-third of all foundations, were forced to move to more favorable locations. Some abbeys, like the Welsh Aberconway, were relocated twice before finding a satisfactory environment. According to all indications the proportion of abbeys moving from a forbidding "desert" to a more rewarding site was about the same in Germany, France and Spain. Relocations of monasteries occurred for other than economic reasons: the lack of sufficient water, troublesome neighbors, political pressure or chronic danger of war; but such considerations accounted for only a minority of cases.

The circumstances surrounding the granting of the original sites of abbeys are often obscure, therefore the retelling of an exceptionally documented case, that of Meaux, may serve as a revealing illustration.

During the late 1140s the construction of the cloister of Vaudey was directed by Adam, a monk of Fountains, who had exhibited his expertise at Kirkstead and Woburn as well. While at work at Vaudey, the highly intelligent monk made the acquaintance of the tightfisted earl of York, William "le Gros," Count of Aumale. Adam soon perceived that the Count's conscience was much troubled because in his youth he had made a vow to go on a pilgrimage to Jerusalem, "but was no longer able to do so because of his age and corpulence." The monk made the best of the opportunity and assured him that if the Count would make a generous donation for the foundation of a new abbey, he, Adam, would obtain for him a papal dispensation from his vow. The Count agreed, whereupon Adam, through the good services of Saint Bernard, obtained the dispensation from Pope Eugenius III. The much relieved Count, in a rare outburst of generosity, encouraged Adam to pick himself the most suitable grounds for the new abbey.

Adam located the place called Melsa (Meaux) in Holderness near Beverly in Yorkshire. It was, in the words of the chronicler of the future abbey, "a place shaded by groves and orchards, well-watered and surrounded by ponds, of fertile soil, [rich in all kinds] of fruits of the land. There rose a small hill named after the Blessed Mary, where now the abbey church stands. The aforesaid Adam mounted the hill, struck the staff he held in his hand forcefully into the ground and said: 'be this place called the court of the Eternal King, a heavenly vineyard, gate of life; here should be established the flock of Christ's worshippers.' "

As soon as the Count learned about the monk's choice, he became thoroughly disturbed, for he had acquired that piece of property of about 360 acres only a few days before by offering twice as much territory to its former owner. The Count wished to convert the land into a game preserve and, in fact, he had just begun its enclosure. He pleaded with the monk and told him to choose any comparable location elsewhere. Adam, however, remained adamant, and finally, mindful of their original bargain, the Count yielded.

The story seems to prove that the donor's piety, even if genuine, was not always coupled with liberality, and truly valuable land was granted only exceptionally. The monks, on the other hand, were more anxious to settle on a choice piece of property than to struggle with the reclamation of wastelands.

Since Cistercians were determined to stay out of feudal and manorial entanglements, the overwhelming majority of donations were granted as "frankalmoins," that is, free gifts, with no burdening taxes, monetary or military obligations. It is equally obvious, however, that in spite of such assurances many donors expected compensations in one form or another, which went beyond the customary appeal for the monks' prayers.

COMPENSATED DONATIONS

Burial in the abbey church and anniversary masses were often tied to grants, but obligations of other nature were also frequent, although not mentioned in the foundation documents. Granting land burdened with military obligations was not entirely unusual, nor can each incident be blamed on oversight. An inquest held in England in 1166 proved that a number of Cistercian abbeys paid "scutage," a tax in lieu of military service. It is, therefore, entirely possible that the grantor, while receiving credit for generosity, transferred an unpleasant obligation to the monks.

There were incidents of granting land for the foundation of an abbey without a hint that the property involved was of uncertain ownership. In order to avoid such complications the monks normally insisted that the charter be witnessed and signed by a number of people, including some relatives of the donor. Even so, litigation over the validity of grants could not always be avoided. Thus, in 1147, the founder of Biddlesden Abbey, Arnold de Bosco, a stewart of the Earl of Leicester, knowingly granted the monks land lacking clear title in order to save himself the trouble of litigation. Eventually the Cistercians had to buy out the rival claimant and purchase a charter of confirmation for ten marks.

A subtle yet very real compensation for grants to Cistercians was in all cases the increased reputation of the benefactor and his hope for the moral support of the popular and influential Order. These considerations alone were powerful incentives at a time of feudal anarchy, when many great barons attempted to exempt themselves from royal authority, while retaining friendly relations with the Church.

Such conditions existed in England between the death of Henry I (1135) and the accession of Henry II (1154), during the weak and steadily contested reign of King Stephen. The strength of the French monarchy scarcely extended beyond the confines of the Ile-de-France and was still further reduced by the marriage of Eleanor of Aquitaine with Henry II (1152), the future king of England, who thus became the overlord of half

286

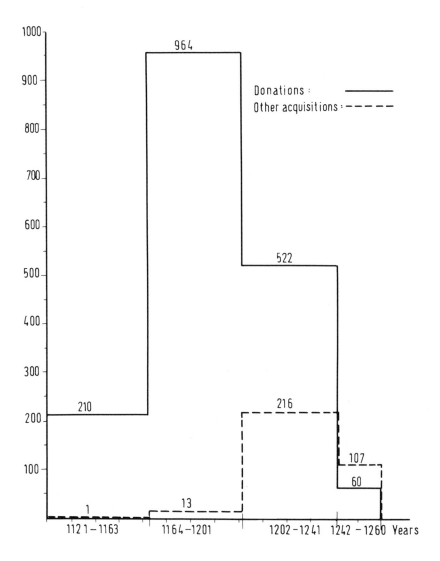

The numbers of donations and other acquisitions at Clairvaux from 1121 to 1260. According to D'Arbois de Jubainville, *Études sur l'état interieur des abbayes cisterciennes* (Paris, 1958), pp. 271-6.

of France. In Germany, Henry V (d. 1125) was followed by the powerless Lothair and Conrad III, during whose reigns much of the country was plunged into civil strife between the families and supporters of the rival claimants, the Welfs and Hohenstaufen, ending, at least temporarily, at the election of Frederick Barbarossa in 1152.

It may be pointed out at this juncture that there had been within the Empire a long-standing tradition upholding the founder's right of "advocacy" over a church or abbey (*Eigenkirche* or *Eigenkloster*); this insured the donor extensive influence over the institution in question. Although German Cistercians claimed from the beginning to be exempt from the obligation of accepting an "advocate" (*Vogtzwang*), the founders did attempt in many instances to extend their authority over abbeys, especially in judicial matters. In Germany, therefore, the foundation of abbeys, apart from moral reputation, could also add to the political power of the noble sponsor. Frederick Barbarossa's declaration shortly after his accession proclaiming himself to be the "advocate" of all Cistercian abbeys within his Empire, clearly indicated that he was well aware of the political implications of "advocacy" and intended to deprive his potential opponents of such powers by claiming them for himself.

It is certainly remarkable that the fastest growth of the Cistercian Order in France, England and Germany coincided with feudal disorders, while the stature of Saint Bernard loomed over Europe as the undisputed source of authority. The sponsorship of Cistercian abbeys became a "status symbol," a symbol of independent wealth and power, ready and willing to challenge royal authority. The fact that the nearly simultaneous return of strong monarchy in England and Germany ended the era of headlong Cistercian expansion in these countries is another indication of the close correlation between political conditions and support for the Order. The much quoted resolution of the Cistercian General Chapter of 1152 to stop new foundations altogether might have been, among other considerations, the voice of caution, trying to quell the jealousy of rulers and extricate the Order from political involvements. The effort was, of course, only partially successful. Henry II became much irritated by Cistercian support for Thomas Becket, and Barbarossa was equally resentful toward Cistercians for their rejection of his antipopes and their staunch fidelity to Alexander III. In both countries, under threat of dire retaliation, Cistercians were put under heavy pressure to conform to the royal will.

Thus came to an end in Western Europe the rush of Cistercian foundations sponsored by great noble families who, while investing land of modest agrarian value, harvested the reputation of generous benefactors of the White Monks at the peak of their popularity.

By the middle of the twelfth century most already established abbeys continued to grow in membership, and were therefore in need of a corresponding flow of donations. The number of grants remained remarkable indeed through the first third of the thirteenth century, but the nature of the gifts changed considerably. Most of the donors were no longer the men of great wealth and their generosity was clearly conditioned by modest means. Phrases in charters of more recent vintage referring to "free gifts" merely camouflaged substantial compensations, but the monks could not afford to be choosy and were compelled by economic necessity to accept land or any other sources of income if the offer seemed to be momentarily advantageous. Monastic chartularies are full of such donations, but here only a few examples should suffice.

The Danish Esrom had built up the bulk of its estate before the end of the twelfth century. Since the neighborhood was well populated and lay-brother vocations had diminished, further expansion was difficult. The not atypical problem of Cistercian abbeys in similar circumstances can be exemplified by a complicated arrangement worked out between Esrom and one of the abbey's neighbors, a certain Niels Grevesun, when he was about to join a crusader army some time after 1211. He needed money, but instead of borrowing, he transferred some pieces of his property to the monks for twenty marks of gold. The knight took along only nine marks, the rest he used for making provisions for his wife and for some charities. The transaction, however, was not a sale, for it was stipulated that the monks would enjoy only the usufruct during the knight's absence who, upon his return, intended to pay back the money and repossess his pawned property. Only if he were to die abroad would the monks become the rightful owners of the land.

The knight failed to return, whereupon King Valdemar III confirmed the monks in the quiet possession of the land in question. This, however, did not discourage Grevesun's heirs and a long lawsuit followed, at least until 1249, ending in the justification of Esrom's claims. Since by the middle of the thirteenth century land in Denmark had become ever more scarce, several similar incidents seem to indicate that what the fathers had granted to the monks, the sons often tried to take back. There must have been some truth in the phrase of a charter issued in favor of Esrom by Duke Abel of Jutland in 1249, speaking "of evil men lurking about, who were attacking and harming the innocent monks."

The English house of Vaudey experienced grave economic difficulties from the beginning and was saved by a series of such small donations as that of Geoffrey de Brachecourt, a knight in the service of the Earl of Lincoln. In return for the grant the monks were to supply him, his wife and their two servants during their lifetimes with victuals and clothing; the knight and his wife were to receive the food of the monks, the two servants were to share the table of the abbey's servants.

In 1169 a certain Raymond de l'Isle was ready to leave for a pilgrimage "overseas" and on his departure donated to the monks of the French abbey of Gimont (Gers) some poor and uncultivated land together with a church and all its revenues. But, according to the same charter, Abbot Bernard paid Raymond 200 *solidi* in compensation for his "gift," 160 *solidi* for the expenses of his trip and a mule valued at 80 *solidi*.

About 1200 the abbey of Margam in Wales received the property of a certain Geoffrey Sturmi, but the monks paid off his debts, gave gifts to each of his sons and promised him admission into the abbey's infirmary when he grew old and disabled.

Meaux under its second abbot, Philip (1160-1182), agreed with William Fossard, son of a former benefactor of the monks, that in exchange for a donation of four and a half carucates of land (about 540 acres) the abbey would take over William's debt of 1,260 marks, owed to the Jewish money-lender Aaron of Lincoln. Both the grant and the debt were substantial and the transaction led to serious consequences, but such experiences failed to discourage the monks and the chronicle of Meaux recounted a number of similar deals throughout the thirteenth century.

At the Catalan house of Poblet mortgaged land was accepted on a large scale, as a matter of policy. Through such means a debtor was able to escape the pursuing creditor and was often received into the abbey as a *donado,* that is, someone protected and cared for by the monks. In a number of cases novices entering Poblet bequeathed their mortgaged property to the abbey and after this transaction the moneylender received scarcely anything, for a royal privilege protected the monks of the abbey against such claims.

The close link between donations and admission as a choir monk or lay-brother was particularly evident in southwestern France. The chartu-lary of the already mentioned Gimont abounds in arrangements whereby a free peasant donor of a small parcel of land was either granted or promised admission whenever he wished to join the monks. The same was the policy at the neighboring Berdoues. There, in 1161, a certain Vitalis donated a piece of property to the monks, whereupon his son, Petrus Arnaldus, was promptly admitted as novice. Vitalis's sister, Martha, also donated her share of the family holding to the monks under the stipulation that her son was to be admitted as a lay-brother. At about the same time a certain Guichard Morel, upon entering the novitiate of La Ferté granted all he had to the monks. But the land was turned over immediately to one of his close kin for the annual rent of twenty sous.

290

The social benefits of all such arrangements will be detailed in a future chapter, but it is doubtful that the contractual nature of admission served the true interest of a religious community of high spiritual standards. It is entirely possible that the mounting disciplinary problems of the thirteenth century were aggravated by the presence of too many individuals lacking genuine monastic vocation. It is equally clear from the multitude of such documents that Cistercian abbeys of certain regions were founded in the immediate neighborhood of villages of free peasants; therefore the territorial expansion of these abbeys was possible only by the absorption of a number of small plots, obtained through amicable arrangements with the "donors": the abbey received the land, but it assumed the obligation of caring for the donor and his family either by admitting them to the monastic community or by providing a pension for life.

The payment of annuities to a number of small donors, such as widows, beguines, elderly ecclesiastics or sick and old people, grew to be a heavy burden on the community of Villers in Brabant. There is no doubt that throughout the thirteenth century the abbey functioned almost like a modern insurance agency. By 1272 the number of persons receiving pensions from the abbey as a compensation for previous donations had risen to 297, while the total annual value of such payments increased to 1,404 hogsheads of grain (probably more than 10,000 gallons). At about the same time the much smaller Swiss abbey of Hauterive was paying annuities to twenty benefactors and was obliged to say fifty solemn anniversary masses for deceased donors.

The changing nature of donations from truly free gifts to more or less compensated grants was a gradual process, but was already well advanced in the second half of the twelfth century. Statistics from some English abbeys indicate that between 1150 and 1200 nearly half of all donations involved monetary compensations, which eventually accumulated to large amounts constituting perilous liabilities. On the eve of the Dissolution the abbey of Kirkstall was burdened by fifty-one annuities, amounting to £58, about one sixth of the monks' total income. At about the same time Whitby paid forty-seven annuities, totalling £101, nearly one fourth of the monastic revenue; Meaux was obliged to spend similar amounts to twenty-one corrodians, altogether £25. At Clairvaux, where between 1164-1201 the number of compensated acquisitions or purchases was only thirteen, between 1202 and 1241 the chartulary of the abbey accounted for 216 such transactions.

Outright purchase of land was relatively rare in the twelfth century, but these incidents increased in direct ratio to decreasing donations. The Swiss abbey of Hauterive recorded fifty such acquisitions during the thirteenth century.

291

The most common justification for purchases was the consolidation of scattered properties, which could also be achieved by a simple exchange of land between the abbey and its neighbors. Written charters, however, tended to conceal the act of buying, for a faked "donation" was always more advantageous to both parties involved: the pretense of a "gift" protected the monks from the charge of cupidity and transformed the seller into a benefactor.

For the rapid accumulation of foundation masses as well as for the many burials in abbatial churches deathbed donations were chiefly responsible, although these practices had been frowned upon by the founders of Cîteaux. One way of bypassing the disapproval was the purely formal reception of the dying man into the monastic community. Thus, in 1170, Pierre de Polastron, fatally ill, donated a considerable portion of his estate to the monks of Gimont for the privilege of dying as a Cistercian. Similar arrangements were recorded in the same chartulary both before and after that date. A gift by the dying Raymond-Arnaud de l'Olmede in 1196 turned out to be a double transgression of rules, since he was invested and buried as a Cistercian for having donated "all his rights which he possessed over the church of Saint Justin."

In many cases of late foundations local conditions and circumstances accounted far more for the peculiar development of abbatial estates than the early "principles" and directives of the General Chapter. Beaulieu, near Southampton, in the estuary of the small Beaulieu River, was founded by King John between 1203 and 1205. But the land immediately surrounding the abbey was poor and insufficient; therefore the monks were forced to expand by any means and in every direction. Expansion was made particularly difficult by the fact that the coastline of the English Channel was well populated and had already been saturated with ecclesiastical institutions which did not exactly welcome the intruding Cistercians. In addition to several churches, a number of tithes, rents, milling and water rights, fishing privileges and saltworks, Beaulieu acquired much of its arable land through a series of purchases. Some of the land was cultivated by lay-brothers, some was immediately rented to lay tenants. Between 1205 and 1250 the chartulary of the abbey attests to at least thirty-three incidents of buying land and some urban property, amounting to a total value exceeding £734. In all likelihood this was the principal method by which Beaulieu managed, by the end of the thirteenth century, to form six granges, not counting the "great close" of the abbey itself. The better granges (Soberton, Ellingham) were at a considerable distance from Beaulieu; Faringdon was as far away as 60 miles. Meanwhile the abbey church was still under construction. By 1243, according to the estimate of King Henry III, the sum needed for its completion was 4,000 marks. How could the monks bear such financial burdens and still prosper? With the help of unrecorded pious donations? By loans? On such matters the chartulary gives no clear answers. Vocations were certainly plentiful: between 1239 and 1247 Beaulieu founded three daughter-abbeys (Netley, Hailes, Newenham).

TITHES AND CHURCHES

The acceptance of tithes, even before the admission of the Congregation of Savigny, was no rarity and found its justification in economic hardships. The same is true of the possession of serfs and whole villages, especially east of the Rhine, where lay-brother vocations were not as plentiful as in the west. According to the testimony of Franz Winter, Walkenried in Saxony received three villages at its foundation in 1129. The beginnings of Sittichenbach (also in Saxony, a daughter of Walkenried, founded in 1141) were so hard that Count Friedrich von Beichlingen, out of commiseration, donated to the monks the village of Ober-Heilingen with an income of thirty-six marks in tithes. The Polish abbey of Lekno received at its foundation (1143) the town of the same name, together with its profitable market privilege. Andreow in the same country accepted about 1149 a town and seven villages.

The number of incidents involving the donation of tithes, even whole churches with all their revenues, are past counting in every country of Cistercian settlements, although the nearly complete breakdown of restraint came only after the often mentioned fusion of the Order with Savigny in 1147. In some cases the accumulation of tithes netted the greater portion of cash revenues. The Welsh Valle Crucis drew three-fourths of all its income from tithes. At Cymmer and Aberconway in the same country such revenues accounted for one-third of their incomes; at Tintern and Dore, also in Wales, tithes amounted to one-fifth of all their revenues. The appropriation of churches in England began with the first foundation, Waverley, in 1128. By 1400 the White Monks had a share in the revenues of eighty-two churches and chapels. The holding of a single church by Sawley in Yorkshire netted the monks one hundred shillings annually. The possessions of the Rhenish Altenberg eventually included six churches with all their revenues. The Scottish Melrose owned on the eve of the Dissolution no less than twenty-nine churches. By 1244 Villers in Brabant collected tithes from as many as forty sources.

The fast rise of the Danish Sorø in Zealand exemplifies an almost total disregard of early Cistercian economic restrictions. Sorø was a daughter of Esrom, but its true founder was one of the most powerful churchmen of

293

twelfth-century Denmark, Absalon (1128-1201), bishop of Roskilde, later archbishop of Lund, primate of the country. His limitless generosity toward Sorø was imitated by his whole clan, the Hvide (White) family. The site of the abbey, a former Benedictine settlement, was occupied by Cistercians in 1161. Shortly after this date Absalon enriched the new abbey with the episcopal share of the tithes of seven villages, to which in the early years of the thirteenth century three others were added. The abbey received villages and a variety of other properties throughout the country; one of them, Tvååker on the island of Halland, was some fifty miles away. Such properties were not cultivated by monks or lay-brothers, but were mostly held until opportunities arose to exchange them for lands closer to the abbey. It was through a series of such transactions that by 1197 the monks were able to amass nine granges, in addition to countless smaller properties, industrial or commercial ventures. Sorø was grateful to Absalon and the Hvide's: many members of this great family were buried under the abbey church; the dying archbishop was taken there too to rest with his beloved monks.

What was the reaction of the General Chapter to such manifest infractions of supposedly fundamental rules? The answer in one specific case of great publicity was "yes." It involved the Roman abbey of Tre Fontane, an ancient abbey incorporated in 1140 with the blessing of Saint Bernard in spite of the fact that it already possessed a village, churches and all kinds of other customary but forbidden ecclesiastical revenues. There is no indication of subsequent efforts at giving up the "illegal" possessions. Moreover, to make sure that all was in fact permissible, Pope Eugenius III turned to the General Chapter of 1152 with a request that the abbey be permitted to retain these sources of income, arguing that "although these are strictly prohibited by the Order, their retention is imperative because of local necessities." The Pope then assured the Chapter that he would try to work out some other solution, but, for the time being, the monks could not forgo their usual sources of livelihood, or else they would be forced to go about begging for their food. The General Chapter of 1153 found the exception justifiable and readily consented.

The concession did not remain an isolated incident and was extended to the twenty-nine abbeys under Savigny and to some smaller groups of houses led by Cadouin and Obazine. The Chapter of 1157 specifically permitted the newly annexed abbeys to keep their mills until they received other instructions. Meanwhile, as could easily be anticipated, the well-publicized concessions encouraged other communities to reach out for hitherto forbidden possessions. By 1169 the abuses were so widespread that Pope Alexander III addressed a strongly worded bull to the Order calling attention to the alarming deviations from the "holy institutions" of the founding fathers.

THE GRANGES

The success of Cistercian agrarian economy and its superiority over the antiquated and decaying manors lay largely in the organization and planned exploitation of the Order's estates.

The manorial system divided the large feudal estates into isolated and virtually independent units, where the serfs, handicapped by outdated customs and innumerable dues and obligations, were left to their own primitive devices without any large-scale planning or direction: the sole interest of the absentee lord was the collection of his customary revenues. Cistercian settlers, on the contrary, worked for themselves, inspired by the fact that their life and survival depended on the success of their labors. Meanwhile, no matter how many grants they received, the exploitation of the total land-holding remained under the control of the abbot and each new acquisiton received individual attention as to the best use of its potentialities. The most successful instrument of such efforts was the organization of granges, agrarian substations, which combined the advantages of both central planning and local autonomy.

The granges, though not without antecedents, must be considered as characteristic features of early Cistercian agriculture. When the monks' estates had grown too extensive to be exploited as unbroken units, they were divided into consolidated parcels of about four to five hundred acres. Then the open fields were enclosed and a few purely utilitarian buildings were erected at the most convenient location to house a group of lay-brothers, to accommodate farm animals and to store the indispens-able equipment and harvested produce.

According to the original rules granges were not to be farther from the abbey than a day's walking distance, so that they would remain under close control and the lay-brothers could return to the abbey for religious services each Sunday. Since choir monks were not permitted to stay overnight at the granges, the day-to-day work became the responsibility of lay-brothers under the immediate supervision of the grange-master (*grangiarius*), one of the more experienced lay-brothers. He received his instructions from the cellarer or procurator of the abbey, who was in turn responsible to the abbot.

The size of each grange depended largely on local circumstances and the nature of its use. In the cases of fertile soil under intensive tillage in large tracts a grange might have been much less than 500 acres. On the other hand, if the terrain was mountainous or interspersed with woods and pastures, the granges were much larger. Thus, the grange belonging to the Welsh Aberconway, located on the slopes of Snowdon, was over 10,000 acres; two granges of Strata Florida in the same country were about 5,000 acres each.

The number of granges grew proportionately with the territorial expansion of an abbey. In well-cultivated and densely populated areas growth was limited and the number of granges seldom exceeded four or five. Elsewhere, where the flow of substantial donations continued to the end of the thirteenth century, the monks might amass huge estates, divided into fifteen or twenty granges. While the exact size of each grange often eludes the researcher, the numbers of granges can easily be determined from the carefully compiled chartularies.

The abbey of Villers (Belgium) by the end of the twelfth century already had thirteen granges; by 1276 the monks with the help of 300 lay-brothers operated twenty granges. At the same time the abbey's total possessions were estimated at about 25,000 acres. The French house of Igny eventually controlled seventeen granges, amounting altogether to about 10,000 acres. By 1348 the Irish Mellifont had accumulated about 50,000 acres, divided into sixteen granges. Clairvaux possessed in the thirteenth century twelve granges and two *celliers*, establishments specializing in viticulture.

In the case of the Spanish Poblet, founded in 1150, close to the steadily receding Moorish borders, the success of the reconquest opened practically unlimited expansion to the monks. By 1276 the abbey had been enriched by 211 donations, amounting to 55,000 acres, divided into twenty-seven granges, not including the twenty-nine villages and thirty-eight castles and other scattered acquisitions.

Cistercian foundations east of the Elbe enjoyed similar opportunities, where the German penetration of the sparsely inhabited Slavic territories facilitated a fast territorial growth. These, however, were relatively late foundations, when direct cultivation had already been greatly limited by a lack of lay-brothers; much of the land was cultivated by peasant settlers forming new villages; therefore the number of granges operated by brothers does not accurately reflect the size of total possessions. The most successful was perhaps the Silesian Leubus, founded in 1175, which eventually controlled sixty-five villages scattered over a territory of 600,000 acres. The possessions of Zinna and Paradies were not far from 100,000 acres each, while Waldsassen, a much earlier foundation near the Bohemian border, had by the end of the twelfth century as many as 150,000 acres.

296

In sharp contrast, many foundations in France had been made in the midst of well-populated areas where expansion remained always problematic and the consolidation of small and widely scattered grants was difficult. Bonnefont, near Toulouse, recorded by the end of the thirteenth century no less than 336 donations, but by 1165 the monks had formed only five granges, growing to eight by 1263. Characteristic of such conditions, one of these granges lay as far as seventy kilometers from the abbey, another was located forty kilometers away. The Swabian Salem found itself in similar circumstances. Unable to acquire sufficient land in its densely populated neighborhood, the abbey was forced to expand in a northerly direction; its farthest possessions around Esslingen (near Stuttgart) lay 125 kilometers away.

It is, however, in England that, thanks to modern research, Cistercian agrarian expansion can be demonstrated with conclusive results. The success of the White Monks was most spectacular in Yorkshire and Oxfordshire, where large tracts of land lay still thoroughly devastated as a tragic reminder of the Norman conquest. Nearly half of all Cistercian granges of this area came to existence as the result of land reclamation. The entirely wasted Vale of York witnessed the heaviest concentration of Cistercian granges. The size of these units varied, averaging from three to four hundred acres each, although one grange of Fountains (Bradley) enclosed 4,400 acres. In such cases the portion under intensive cultivation was only a fraction of the whole. The same abbey, the richest in England, possessed eventually twenty-six granges, while both Meaux and Warden had more than twenty. The granges of the heavily populated southern England were smaller and fewer in number.

During the twelfth century the normal operation of the granges depended entirely on lay-brothers, although at the time of ploughing and harvesting outside help was often employed. The multiplication of granges, however, soon outran the available supply of lay-brothers and the assistance of neighboring villagers was solicited with increasing frequency. The best cultivated was usually the "home grange," the one closest to the abbey, which could always be exploited with the greatest efficiency.

The earliest buildings on Cistercian granges did not include a chapel, for the brothers were expected to return to the abbey for religious services. When, because of greater distances, this had become impractical, chapels were erected, but daily masses could be arranged only by permission of the diocesan bishop, who, before giving his consent, made sure that the chapel would not compete with the nearest parish church. Thus, at some granges operated in the thirteenth century by Thame and

Waverley, the monks had to promise that only brothers and the abbeys' servants would be admitted to services, that no sacraments would be administered to outsiders and the masses would not be signalled by bells; occasional donations collected in the chapels were to be given to the nearest parish.

The group of grange buildings was often surrounded by walls or trenches to keep out thieves and marauders. At times of great danger the abbey's servants were armed for defense. Such arrangements were common in the north against Scottish raids. During the Hundred Years' War many French granges were also fortified. One of them, Masse, in the possession of Bonneval, even boasted a formidable keep.

RECLAMATION OF LAND

Cistercian presence was most appreciated where the monks engaged themselves in large-scale reclamation of waste land; indeed, much of the reputation of the White Monks rested on their ability to convert inhospitable deserts into rich meadows. As Gerald of Wales, one of the sharpest critics of Cistercians, put it about 1188: "Give these monks a naked moor or a wild wood; then let a few years pass away and you will find not only beautiful churches, but dwellings of men built around them."

The most famous example of successful reclamation was the often mentioned Les Dunes, founded in the midst of the forbidding sand dunes of Flanders, half-way between Saint-Omer and Bruges. By the middle of the thirteenth century, after the hard labor of an exceptionally large number of lay-brothers, the abbey was able to transform 25,000 acres of that most difficult terrain into arable land, divided into twenty-five granges.

A much-publicized feat of similar nature was achieved by the abbey of Walkenried, founded in 1127 in the midst of a wilderness of morasses in the Thuringian Basin. Within a few decades the 80 monks and about 180 brothers converted the swamps into the famous "Golden Meadows" (*Goldene Aue*) of legendary fertility, divided into eleven granges. No wonder that in 1188 Frederick Barbarossa took the abbey under imperial protection and encouraged the monks to expand their beneficial activities.

Elsewhere, however, the clearing and assarting was done as a matter of routine on a less spectacular scale. Since most abbeys were established on the fringes of populated areas, expansion often demanded the clearing of woods, although indiscriminate cutting of timber was by no means the monks' intention or interest. Timber was always easily convertible to cash, therefore was carefully preserved for emergencies. In some cases, such as at Strata Florida in Wales, a royal order enjoined the abbey in

1278 to cut down "without delay the thick coverts in woods where robberies, homicides and other enormities against the king's peace have been wont to be committed."

Meaux in Yorkshire was successful in controlling the often devastating floods in the estuary of the Humber. Some of the drainage channels were twenty feet wide, navigable by small boats. The sides of the dikes were protected against erosion by timber; locks and floodgates regulated the flow of water. Some remains of these monumental works are still visible.

The abbeys having properties in the great Fenland along The Wash, such as Kirkstead, Revesby, Swineshead, Vaudey and Sawtry, were similarly engaged in protecting their land against floods and tidal waters. The results increased the size of pastures and meadows and opened opportunities for saltworks.

DESTRUCTION OF VILLAGES

One undesirable consequence of Cistercian expansion was the occasional destruction of villages, which occurred if such settlements fell within the borders of larger tracts of land donated to the monks. At the root of these much criticized procedures lay the Cistercians' love of solitude; obedience to the prohibition against accepting villages; the exemption from the payment of tithes which could have been jeopardized by owning villages; and finally, the fact that as long as there was a sufficient labor force of brothers, the villagers merely constituted a foreign body within a consolidated monastic estate. Most known cases refer to England, where such incidents were not entirely isolated, although their exploitation by hostile propagandists, such as Walter Map and Gerald of Wales, was certainly unfair.

Three or four of Fountains' granges had originally been peasant settlements; Holmcultram, Kirkstall, Byland, Sawley and perhaps some others were equally guilty of ousting villagers, pulling down the old church and "reducing the vill to a grange." From the few detailed accounts, however, one may conclude that in most cases the demolition was pre-arranged and coupled with adequate provisions for the relocation of the inhabitants. The original site of Rufford, founded in 1146, included a village, which obviously could not remain if the monks were to accept the offer. But before any action was taken, the monks offered a generous compensation to the inhabitants both in cash and land granted them elsewhere. Moreover, it was agreed that "the monks will seek for them liberty from Gilbert de Gant and his heirs and as far as they are able, will support them against everyone by word and by prayer; and if any of them, moved by the desire to serve God or impelled by imfirmity, wishes to join the monks, they will support him as far as it seems to them expedient."

Another example, when the evacuation of a village was pre-arranged and the peasants were compensated, was the donation in 1159 of Eilfingen to the monks of Maulbronn by Bishop Günther of Speyer: "I bought with my money", said the bishop, "from all the peasants and different lords who stated they had rights in the village all that belonged or seemed to belong to them, and what I received by rightful purchase I transferred, according to custom, into the possession of the community at Maulbronn. The former inhabitants and cultivators of the whole village having been sent away, a grange was made there, and the lay-brothers alone with their own ploughs cultivated all their fields."

This might be the place to re-emphasize that in Central and Eastern Europe Cistercians often promoted new peasant settlements and that even in the West the process was to revese itself; following the virtual disappearance of lay-brotherhood most Cistercian granges were turned over to lay tenants for cultivation.

A similar development took place in Spain after the successful *Reconquista* had opened new territories to enterprising Cistercians, without, however, supplying them with sufficient lay-brother vocations. Poblet, among other abbeys, became an active colonizer and relied heavily on lay tenants in the exploitation of its vast domain. Ample land-grants, tax exemptions, loans for home construction and other privileges served as incentives in the recruiting of peasant settlers. In the Iberian Peninsula, therefore, Cistercians can justly be considered as effective agents in the repopulation and reconstruction of territories devastated by centuries of warfare.

HOSTILE PUBLIC OPINION

It was not only the occasional uprooting of villages that turned public opinion against Cistercians. Ironically, the astonishingly fast expansion and the steady increase of the Order's landed possessions became the reason, for concern, first within the jealously watching ecclesiastical society, then among governmental circles, fearful of the financial and political consequences of an all-too-powerful combine of privileged wealth and ubiquitous influence.

The actual charges voiced against Cistercians as early as the 1160s were not aimed against the expansion of the Order as such, but against the allegedly greedy and grasping abbots who could set no limits to their land-hunger, against this pervading spirit of cupidity, incompatible with the initial ideals of poverty and austerity. When the outcry of protest became

300

so loud that even such a great friend of the Cistercians as Alexander III could no longer ignore it, in 1169 he issued a sharply-worded warning addressed to the General Chapter charging that the Order had relinquished its "original institutions" and that "those who had vowed to abandon the world and clad in the garments of poverty had decided to serve God, now engage themselves in secular pursuits."

It was obvious that the Order was faced for the first time in its history with a crisis, a crisis of prosperity. Indeed, Cistercians were bound to succeed and out-distance all their competitors, not through a determined pursuit of wealth unbecoming to monks, but through hard labor, intelligent planning and efficient organization. As R. W. Southern has put it: "These puritans of the monastic life incurred the penalty of puritanism; they became rich because they renounced the glory of riches, and powerful because they invested wisely. They were blamed for being rich and powerful by those who went out for glory and invested badly."

The embattled General Chapter attempted the impossible: to silence the critics and still uphold the legitimate aspirations of the Order. After having legislated against the acquisition and retention of "illegal" sources of income, such as tithes, villages and mills, the convention of 1182 resolved to take drastic action: "In order to curb cupidity and terminate acquisitions," all already established abbeys were strictly "prohibited from the acquisition in the future of any land, cultivated or uncultivated." As a second thought, however, the abbots added that to "those poorer houses which hitherto have failed to attain a state of proper development, . . . depending on the judgment of the father abbot and two other abbots familiar with the circumstances, further expansion may be permitted." Needless to say, the decree proved to be so impractical that it was never enforced; the text, in fact, has survived only in a recently discovered manuscript.

Embarking on a less controversial course of action, the General Chapter of 1190 resolved that "beginning from the next Chapter and thenceforth in perpetuity, we refrain from the purchase of land as well as any other type of real estate," excepting communities where the possessions were insufficient for the support of thirty monks and a comparable group of lay-brothers. Free gifts, (*in puram eleemosynam*), however, could still be accepted everywhere.

Artificial limitations of a still spontaneous growth proved largely ineffectual and the critics of the Order felt justified in pressing further charges against the "avaricious" Cistercians. Impressed by such accusations, Innocent III, in a letter to the General Chapter of 1214, renewed the allegations of Alexander III and asserted that "in these and similar other matters, in defiance of the original statutes of your Order, you have relaxed [the rules] to such a degree that, unless they are soon restored to due force, one may fear of the imminent ruin of your order."

Kings, not entirely innocent of greed themselves, eagerly echoed the popes. As has been pointed out above, Henry II of England had already curbed Cistercian expansion, so that between 1154 and 1200 only six new abbeys were founded. His profligate successor, Richard I, "the Lionhearted" (1189-1199), when reproached for pride, luxury and avarice, claimed that he had delivered himself from such vices saying: "I have married my daughter pride to the Templars, luxury to the Black Friars, and avarice to the Cistercians." The Order was made to pay dearly for this notoriety. The monks in England had to contribute a year's clip of wool to King Richard's ransom when he was captured after his celebrated crusade, and on his return, the King extorted the same amount for still another year. His brother, King John (1199-1216), outdid his predecessor in brutality toward the monks. In 1210 alone he extorted from the terrorized Cistercian abbeys a sum between 25,000 and 30,000 marks. The great Fountains had its cattle and sheep seized and was forced to sell the sacred vessels of the church. The monks of Meaux, together with monks of other abbeys, were dispersed for lack of sustenance; the Abbot of Waverley, in a moment of panic, fled and kept hiding from the King's henchmen. Henry III (1216-1272) was not much better either, forcing Cistercian abbeys to pay again and again for writs of confirmation of their fiscal privileges. Thus the monks managed to hold on to their precious privileges, while the king got the money he wanted. Edward I (1272-1307) continued the same extortionist policies and sent a number of his retired or disabled servants to Cistercian abbeys for maintenance.

In 1274 Beaulieu Abbey and her three daughters (Netley, Hailes, Newenham) were forced to contribute £222 for a crusade which was never organized. In 1276 King Edward demanded from Cistercians £1,000 and in 1283 another 1,000 marks in support of his various ventures. The fact that much of the money was in fact paid attests to the general state of prosperity of English Cistercian abbeys in the late thirteenth century.

The substance of royal complaints against property in the possession of monasteries was that such lands were normally free from military obligations; that the "free alms" status deprived the king of the incidents of feudal tenure; and that there was no way to transfer the land to others; it remained perpetually under "mortmain," that is, in the "dead hand" of an ecclesiastical institution. During the course of the thirteenth century many attempts were made to restrict the expansion of land under monastic control, until in the statute *De viris religiosis* (1279), Edward I prohibited ecclesiastical acquisition of land in "free alms" altogether.

Exemptions were granted liberally, but always after substantial payment had been made, which turned the law into a new source of revenues compensating the royal exchequer for the monks' fiscal immunities.

ECONOMIC INSTABILITY

A casual visitor, looking at stately churches and monumental cloisters swarming with busy monks, then observing around the horizon the luxuriant meadows, green pastures, large herds of grazing animals, dark forests and carefully tilled fields as far as his eyes could see, scarcely escaped the impression that the Cistercians were, indeed, fabulously rich. The outward appearance of prosperity, however, covered too often serious and chronic shortcomings.

The steady growth of personnel throughout the twelfth century constituted at many abbeys a vexing financial problem. The General Chapter of 1190 stated the case with unmistakable clarity: "A number of monasteries of our Order are often overburdened by an exceeding number of personnel, thus they are forced to multiply their possessions and increase their debts." In such cases the convention ordered the suspension of admissions for three consecutive years. The 1196 session of the Chapter insisted again that admission be proportionate to revenues, and planned to set a ratio to be promulgated at the next year's meeting. At any rate, continued the decree, the abbeys should always settle for a smaller number and increase it only when additional funds would be made available. The list of fixed numbers for each abbey, if it existed, has not been preserved, but the Chapter of 1198 "strictly warned the [abbots] not to exceed the number of personnel allotted to them."

A late but eloquent illustration of the above ruling survived in the Chronicle of Meaux, from the administration of Abbot Michael Brun (1235-1249). The number of monks (*numerus taxatus*) had been set at fifty, when a certain knight, Sir John Fryboys, on entering the novitiate, made a generous donation "for the perpetual sustenance of one monk," thus raising the total to fifty-one. The subsequent donation of a mill by another knight, William of Sutton, was made specifically on behalf of a fifty-second monk.

A purely agrarian economy, however, was always unstable, in spite of precautions and the most foresighted planning. Since after the first few decades of their existence nearly all abbeys accumulated a considerable burden in the form of annuities and pensions, years of bad harvest, incidents of natural disaster, unforeseen exactions or the devastation of war might have reduced the communities to the verge of bankruptcy, unable to fulfill their financial obligations and feed their own monks.

303

An early and rather crude measure in such circumstances was the temporary dispersion of monks, who then were forced to seek hospitality at more fortunate abbeys of the Order. These occurrences were by no means limited to poorly endowed or ineptly administered monasteries. The first abbot of Meaux, Adam, a man of great ability, after ten years of success found himself in 1160 incapable of feeding and clothing his forty monks and eleven novices. In his despondency, unable to bear the odium of responsibility for the dispersion of his community, he pretended to go on a pilgrimage to Rome and resigned. The ransom payments of 1190 on behalf of King Richard again reduced the abbey to utter destitution. The monks were dismissed, and looked for hospitality "as beggars," able to return only after fifteen months. A third dispersion in 1210 followed the demand of King John for 1,000 marks, paid from the sale of valuable monastic property. That time, however, the homeless monks could find no shelter in similarly afflicted Cistercian houses, therefore some monks sought refuge in York, others fled to Scotland or survived "hiding in villages and castles." At each incident the abbot resigned.

The rich Himmerod in the Rhineland, because of sporadic violence and political disturbances endemic in the second half of the thirteenth century, faced total economic collapse in 1297. Its large community was forced to disperse for five years, in spite of the possession of twelve valuable granges. A few years later (1315) one of the wealthiest houses of the Order, Villers, had to disperse its membership, because the community was unable to meet the exorbitant impositions of the Duke of Brabant.

In 1189 the General Chapter found itself compelled to legislate about dispersion, leading to a quick succession of related regulations, passed in 1190, 1191, and 1196, a clear indication that such incidents were widespread. Accordingly, dispersal was to come only after due investigation and authorization. Host abbots were to "receive the refugees with the joy of charity," although for the duration of the emergency they were free to decline hospitality to others. On the other hand, the afflicted community was not to receive novices until safer conditions had been established.

INDEBTEDNESS

Another way of relieving a financial crisis was recourse to loans. As early as 1157 the General Chapter urged visiting father abbots to check on the material status of their charges and to take energetic measures against "abbots who had involved their houses in excessive debts." In 1175 the visitors were expected to prevent the accumulation of "immoderate debts," and to take precautions for the future. The Chapter of 1182 decreed that abbots who owed more than fifty marks should neither buy land nor initiate new construction until the debt had been paid. In 1184 the same body ordered the redemption of "enormous debts" through the sale of "movable or immovable" properties. The fathers of the Chapter of 1188 did not hesitate to state that "it is well known that on account of excessive debts many houses of our Order [are facing] the imminent danger of a disaster." Buying land and construction were again prohibited, unless such expenditures could be financed through special donations. Fire or similar emergencies could also justify exceptions. The Chapter of 1189 wisely pointed out that no house in financial trouble could ever recover through loans taken at a usurious rate of interest, which, therefore, were "absolutely prohibited," adding that "from Jews, who are enemies of the Cross of Christ, nothing may be borrowed, with or without usury."

Nevertheless, indebtedness continued to be a chronic malaise throughout the thirteenth century, although the alarmist view of the overly conservative Chapter was not entirely justified. By then European economy had clearly outgrown its purely agrarian stage and an ever quickening trade made credit an indispensable instrument of business transactions. Well-administered abbeys on their way toward a more diversified economy could pay off even substantial debts before they became unmanageable.

Stephen Lexington, as abbot of Savigny, was particularly keen on the financial status of communities under his care. His charters of visitation present a number of remarkable examples of how indebtedness was handled. In 1231 having found the abbey of Longvilliers in an "abyss of debts," he instituted detailed procedures for proper bookkeeping and fiscal administration and ordered stringent austerity measures, including the limitation of the number of monks to forty, that of the brothers to sixty. Although conditions improved somewhat, at another visitation in 1236 he still insisted on the continuation of restrictions in the monks' diet, clothing and unnecessary conveniences. Elsewhere, as at La Chaloché, the same measures were more successful: between 1230 and 1236 a large debt was reduced to forty-six *livres* of Tours. At Vaux-de-Cernay, during the same period, a debt of 2,000 Parisian *livres* was reduced to 200 *livres*.

By 1224 even the General Chapter had noted the changing economic climate, for the figure of indebtedness restricting admissions was raised from fifty to one hundred marks. Later in the same century, when substantial monastic liabilities had become more general, dispersion was freely granted as a legitimate means of liquidating debts. This was the case at the English Bruern, where in the 1290s a debt of 3,000 marks was paid

305

off by dispersion. Kirkstall owed in 1284 over £5,000, but after the monks were permitted to disperse, by 1301 the huge amount was reduced to a mere £160. Between 1280 and 1286 Meaux was able to reduce a debt of £3,678 to £1,443, largely by the means of renting several of the abbey's granges. Fountains owed in 1290 no less than £6,373, which, however, within a year went down to £1,293.

According to all indications during the thirteenth century the strict prohibitions against dealing with Jews were also relaxed or remained unenforced. In England loans were often taken from Jews in the hope that after the death of the lender the amount might be remitted by royal order. This was the case in 1186 when the famous Aaron of Lincoln died, to whom nine Cistercian houses were indebted, amounting to the total of 6,400 marks. King Richard, upon his accession in 1189, remitted the entire debt after the prompt payment of only 1,000 marks. Fiscal transactions between Jews and English Cistercians continued until the expulsion of Jews from the country in 1290.

It is difficult to determine whether a gradual diversification of Cistercian economy resulted from the recognition of a trend toward increasing commercialization, or was motivated by a search for greater financial security and the desire of netting a larger amount of regular cash income. The departure from the direct cultivation of land as the sole source of livelihood was admittedly a breach of early regulations, but from the point of view of an abbot responsible for the welfare of his monks and the safe survival of his institution, it might become a necessity. After a disastrous crop failure and forced dispersion the deeply humiliated abbot, if he remained in office at all, certainly came to realize that the economic basis of his house had been insecure. The continued acquisition of land even at scattered and distant locations was less likely the sign of insatiable greed than that of forethought for a safer future. Similarly, the already discussed acceptance of tithes, rents, mills, villages and other sources of fixed income, might find both explanation and justification in the fact that the monks themselves had to carry a mounting load of taxes, pensions and annuities. Regular payments of such nature could scarcely be made solely from the sale of surplus crops. Monetary obligations called for similar sources of income.

The logic of such arguments led the General Chapter to change its attitude, and to condone the transition from an antiquated and clearly insufficient farming operation toward a more complex but also more rewarding diversification. Contemporary critics, each for his own personal reasons, assumed a sharply censorius posture in the matter, but the willingness to change with a changing economy should redound to the credit of those Cistercians who refused to retreat into the past under the pretext of upholding wholly outdated and impractical regulations. The Church herself exemplified the virtue of flexibility when she modified the previous "doctrines" on usury and just price, which had in fact been regulated more by market conditions than by "principles." Papal understanding for Cistercian difficulties was expressed by a bull of Innocent IV in 1246, in which the pontiff permitted the collection of tithes in all parishes on Cistercian lands, including new acquisitions, so long as the rights of the previous owners were honored.

THE LEASING OF LAND

Although the ideals of the founders of Cîteaux often proved too exalted for practical execution, the characteristic feature and backbone of Cistercian economy, farming with the help of lay-brothers, was unquestionably maintained throughout the twelfth century. This is why the gradual reduction and eventual disappearance of the lay-brotherhood created a major crisis within the Order, which resulted in the leasing of most granges to lay tenants. The process, difficult as it was, did not threaten the existence of monastic communities, but demanded the sacrifice of a distinctive mark of the Cistercian heritage and the refashioning of Cistercian economy to the operational pattern of other estates of the time, lay or ecclesiastical alike.

In cases where the number of brothers failed to keep pace with territorial expansion, the renting of land had begun even before the turn of the twelfth century. Thus, the Welsh house of Margam received rent from some of its property as early as 1188. Its neighbor, Strata Florida, began leasing its possessions in 1202. The Irish Holy Cross shortly after its foundation in 1180 began leasing land. By 1208 the trend had become so widespread that the General Chapter was forced to grant permission for leasing "less useful" land. The concession, however, became a hotly debated issue among the abbots. At the convention of 1214, under conservative pressure, the decree was reversed, only to be reaffirmed in the next year, with the added qualification that newly acquired properties should be rented first. In 1224 general permission was granted for the leasing of any land, if the measure was to serve the interest of the community concerned. The final judgment in such matters was the privilege of father abbots.

The specific conditions and term of leasing of monastic land became the subject of legislation during the remainder of the thirteenth century. At first only short terms were approved, then peasant tenants were permitted to hold leases for life, and finally, in the second decade of the fourteenth century, the General Chapter recognized even the tenants' hereditary rights over originally monastic property.

The circumstances of tenure and the nature of payments varied according to local customs, but sharecropping and contributions in kind tended to give way to rents in cash, fixed by a more or less formal agreement between the parties, amounting to about four to five percent of the property's capital value. The leasing of former granges began normally with the ones farthest from the abbey, and these peasant settlers on Cistercian land increased the number of new villages, the *bastides* of the south and *villes neuves* of the north of France. On the other hand, the retention of granges closest to the abbey remained a well-guarded interest of the monks. The latter farms constituted the abbatial "demesne," cultivated either with the help of the surviving lay-brothers, or by hired labor.

In France the process had been practically completed by the early decades of the fourteenth century, about the time when the leasing of monastic land in Germany had just reached its peak. In Eastern Europe, where direct cultivation had always been limited, changes were slow to come, since the social background of the development, the emancipation of serfs, was delayed until the eighteenth century.

From the point of view of abbots, the leasing of land was not without obvious advantages. The problem of dealing with hordes of undisciplined and often rebellious lay-brothers was eliminated; the administration of monastic property was greatly simplified and was eventually reduced to the collection of fixed revenues; in a commercialized monetary economy cash payments were more desirable than the storing of surplus crops; and finally, the fixity of income seemed to insure the abbeys' fiscal stability. Indeed, by the end of the fourteenth century rents constituted the bulk of monastic revenues. In 1396 Meaux in Yorkshire netted £342 in rents, more than half the abbey's total income. The fact that monetary advantages would eventually turn against the recipients of rents on account of a slow but steady inflation was veiled from the eyes of fourteenth-century landowners.

Incidents of leasing monastic land in France were common early in the thirteenth century, although exact figures are not readily available. At any rate, in 1230, at an abbatial convention held for the filiation of Savigny, Abbot Stephen Lexington dealt extensively with the subject. He suggested to his fellow-abbots that they send out each year "two trustworthy and God-fearing monks" to all tenants of their houses in order to ascertain under oath the size and tenure of each holding together with the amount of rent "either in money or in crops," or even in labor "services, called

The façade of the church at Fontenay, France. 12th century. (Photo: Jürgen Eberle, Archiv P. Hermann Josef Roth.)

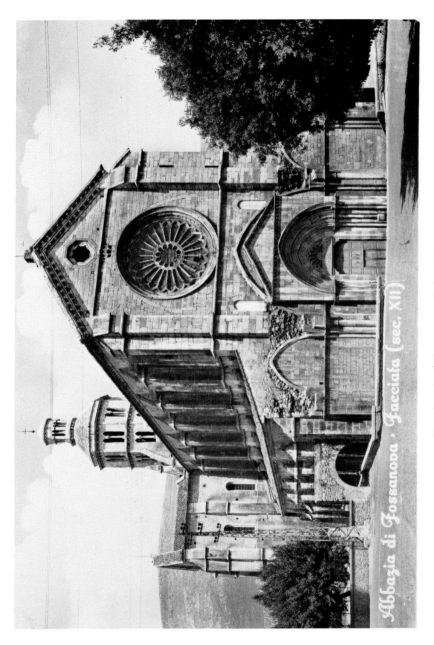

The church of Fossanova, Italy. 13th century.

The ruins of Fountains Abbey, England. 12th to 16th century. British Copyright: reproduced by permission of the Department of the Environment.

Fontfroide, France. End of 12th century. (Photo: Caisse Nationale des Monuments Historiques, Paris.)

The façade of the church of Heiligenkreuz, Austria. 12th century. (Photo: Bildarchiv d. Oest. Nationalbibliothek.)

Cloister and church of Noirlac, France. 12th–13th century. (Photo: Caisse Nationale des Monuments Historiques.)

The church of Pontigny, France. Early 13th century. (Photo: Caisse Nationale des Monuments Historiques.)

The church of Bélapátfalva, Hungary. 13th century.

The façade of Chorin, Germany. 13th century.

The church of Szczyrzyc, Poland. Originally of the late 13th century, remodeled in the 17th and 18th centuries. (Photo: Tadeusz Kazmierski.)

Western façade of the church of Altenberg, Germany. Late Gothic, 1379. (Photo:
P. Wisskirchen, Archiv P. Hermann Josef Roth.)

The south transept gable of Melrose, Scotland. 15th century. British copyright:
reproduced by permission of the Department of the Environment.

The Baroque façade of the Gothic church of Alcobaça, Portugal. (Photo: d'Almeida. Courtesy of Ministerio da Comunicação, Lisbon.)

The Baroque Himmerod, Germany. Reconstructed in the 20th century.

The old (ruins on the left) and the new Trappist Orval, Belgium. (Photo: Institut Belge d'Information.)

Two 20th century monasteries. *Above,* The Abbey of the Genesee, U.S.A., designed by Marcel Breuer. *Below,* the new church of Mehrerau, Austria; Hans Purin, architect, sculptured portal by Herbert Albrecht. (Photo: Bundesdenkmalamt, Vienna.)

corvée" (*quae corvée vocantur*). The results of the inquest were to be kept
in the monastic archives.

In England the indebtedness of the great abbeys of Yorkshire and the
urgency of repairing the damages caused by Scottish raids precipitated the
leasing of granges. By 1363 Fountains had already rented nine and
Jervaulx four granges. At Villers in Brabant the same process was well
advanced by the second half of the thirteenth century, and eventually the
persons paying rents to the monks in one form or another had swollen to
1,200. A similar process on a smaller scale took place also at Ter Doest
and Les Dunes. At Hardehausen in Westphalia the monks, before renting
their granges, had leased their mills. The first transfer of a grange to lay
tenants occurred only in 1322. At Otterberg, there were only three
incidents of land leasing before 1300, while twenty-four such agreements
were recorded between 1301 and 1350. At the Swiss Hauterive the leasing
of land began as early as 1217, but the bulk of the eleven granges was
transferred to lay tenants only during the fourteenth century. At Stams
in Tyrol, a late foundation (1273), no attempt was made to initiate direct
cultivation. Lands were given out for rent as soon as they were granted,
often to the donor himself. By 1336 the archives of the abbey had held no
fewer than 400 contracts of such nature. Only the two immediately
adjacent farms were exploited by the abbey's own personnel, which in
1333 numbered forty-one monks and ten lay-brothers. Shortly after this
date one of the two farms was also taken over by peasant tenants.

The often observable fact that the leasing of monastic land was well in
evidence while the abbey in question still commanded a sizeable force of
lay-brothers should serve as a warning against hasty conclusions and
undue generalizations. The decline of the lay-brotherhood certainly
precipitated and in many cases necessitated the renting of land, but it was
by no means the only cause of the process. It would perhaps be safer to
assume that the disappearance of the lay-brotherhood, the leasing of land
and the abbots' preference for fixed cash income were all symptoms of
those fundamental changes that led most of Europe from the decaying
feudal economy toward early capitalism.

The transfer of land to villagers, under whatever conditions, did not
cancel entirely the abbeys' responsibilities for their former possessions; in
fact the abbots came to exercise seigneurial jurisdiction over the new
settlers, adding such obligations to the duties of pastoral care. These
functions, though, were not entirely new in the Order and in some cases
preceded the leasing of granges. A number of monasteries possessed
villages and had acquired families of serfs well before the end of the
twelfth century. In England, Rievaulx, Stanley and Kirkstall had owned

serfs before 1180 and unfree workers became quite common elsewhere during the first half of the thirteenth century. Furness had even purchased serfs for an average of twenty shillings per person. As early as 1160 Villers received as a donation a family of serfs, and similar incidents followed. In 1222 a certain Jacques de Maleves granted the abbey a village with its families of serfs. According to the records of the Austrian Stams, until the beginning of the fifteenth century, the abbey frequently received serfs (*Leibeigene*) attached to the granted land.

At most early foundations the presence of hired workers can be traced back to the twelfth century and as the number of lay-brothers decreased, the monks relied more and more on secular help. The demand for laborers was occasionally so great that abbeys were forced to compete with each other for them. In 1164, some English Cistercian abbots signed an agreement with their Gilbertine neighbors insuring for each community a share in the labor supply. By the middle of the thirteenth century the number of wage earners at Kingswood Abbey had grown so high that in 1256 the monks paid £22 for hired help.

By the end of the fourteenth century not only agricultural labor but also domestic duties had often been entrusted to lay personnel. The chronicle of Meaux supplies a full list of these employees. The abbot had his own household, operated largely by lay people including his squire, chamberlain, page, cook, groom, stable boy and gardener. The monks' kitchen employed four, the bakehouse five, servants. Monastic officeholders, such as the cellarer, bursar, porter, infirmarian and sacristan, all had their lay helpers. The workshops were manned also by lay craftsmen, including the slater, tailor, maltser, carter, tanner, miller, barber, forester and dairymen. In 1393, when the number of monks was twenty-six, Meaux paid wages to at least forty domestics.

TRADE

The Rule of Saint Benedict urged monks to provide for themselves and to render their houses self-sufficient, so that there would be no excuse for trading with outsiders, creating thereby occasion for harmful distractions and temptations. At the early Cistercian establishments the warning of the Rule gained new urgency. The monks, in love with solitude, lived by choice far away from human habitations. The monks' labor in their fields became a means of survival and they themselves had to produce the tools and implements of their work, provide for their clothing and footwear, and supply material for construction, fuel for a variety of purposes, together with a number of other necessities for their simple lives.

It was equally obvious, however, that no abbey was able to achieve absolute economic independence; therefore even the earliest legislation of

310

the Order made allowance for the selling of surplus products and the buying of needed articles that the monks could not otherwise procure. As the fourteenth paragraph of the *Institutes of the General Chapter at Cîteaux* put it: "Although the frequentation of markets is dangerous and unbecoming for religious, since our poverty demands that we sell some of our products and buy necessary items, those whose duty is to provide for such necessities may go to fairs and markets, but not beyond three, or at most four days' journey; from one abbey no more than two monks or lay-brothers should go, who, however, may not cross the sea to England in order to attend fairs." The law did not deter the monks of the Irish Holy Cross from holding two fairs annually (May and September) within the precincts of the monastery. The monks collected tolls and found opportunity to sell their own products, mostly wool.

Another paragraph of the same regulations approved the establishment of depots or warehouses in neighboring towns, although it permitted no monks to stay permanently in such facilities. From a further reference to trade one may conclude that the first item of Cistercian commerce was wine, for the text insisted that it be sold only wholesale and never in taverns operated by the monks themselves. However, most such restrictions were soon replaced by liberal concessions and monastic revenues netted from trade often surpassed all other sources of income.

A major incentive behind the gradual commercialization of the Cistercian economy was undoubtedly the extensive tax-exemption of the Order, enhanced by privileges for the long-distance shipping of goods without the payment of ubiquitous tolls. Such fiscal immunities made possible the combination of low prices and high quality, making the monks formidable competitors with less privileged producers and sellers of similar commodities. Still another advantage of Cistercian production was the location of most abbeys in valleys blessed with abundant water supply. The monks eagerly harnessed the energy of fast streams and used the water not only for the operation of mills, but a number of other workshops, where a well-trained crew of lay-brothers could easily out-produce the solitary craftsmen of nearby lay settlements. A famous and often quoted description of thirteenth-century Clairvaux waxed lyrical over the blessings the river Aube brought to the monks who, forcing the rushing waters into several channels, irrigated their gardens, fed their fishponds, operated their flour and fulling mills, and furnished ample water for their kitchen, brewery and tannery.

Most other abbeys made the best of similar opportunities. A remarkable case was that of the Danish Sorø, located on an island near Sorø lake, but without running stream. Encouraged by Archbishop Anders Sunesen (d. 1228), Absalon's successor, the monks connected their own lake with

311

another lake of higher elevation through a canal, "one of the thirteenth-century Denmark's greatest engineering achievements." The fast running water of the canal provided Sorø with both power and drainage.

WOOL-TRADE

One of the earliest, and eventually the most important, items of Cistercian trade was wool, particularly in England. The wastelands of Yorkshire offered excellent pasture for large herds, although sheep-farming was also popular in Wales, Flanders, southern France and Spain. The production of wool was very attractive to Cistercians not only because of the availability of grazing land; it demanded little investment and modest personnel, yet it offered ready cash return on raw wool, sold to eager Flemish and Italian merchants.

Wool-trade had already been significant toward the end of the twelfth century and by the thirteenth century involved at least forty Cistercian abbeys in England. Many of these monasteries had export licenses and warehouses in the port cities of the country; seventeen Cistercian houses owned such depots in London alone. Some abbeys carried the wool aboard their own ships across the Channel, others sold their clip at home to traveling merchants, making regular rounds among their best clients.

The size of the flocks varied, but many abbeys owned several thousand animals, although during the thirteenth century the dreaded scab or "murrain" often wiped them out within a few months. In such cases, if the monks had already been under contract and had received advanced payment for future delivery of wool, a serious crisis ensued. High profits and grave risks both characterized this challenging business. Initially the General Chapter opposed the advanced sale of wool, but persistent infractions forced a change of heart and finally, in 1279, all restrictions were removed, provided that the netted amount was used for the liquidation of debts. Contracts binding abbeys to future delivery of a fixed quantity of wool clip ran between two and twenty years and involved huge amounts of both wool and cash. Fountains, Rievaulx and Meaux were usually at the top of the list of producers, each having toward the end of the thirteenth century 10,000-15,000 sheep and selling annually fifty or sixty sacks of wool. But the output of even smaller producers was considerable: Kirkstall's average annual sale amounted to twenty-five sacks, that of Beaulieu to seventeen sacks.

The weight of a "sack" of wool was originally the load a packhorse could carry and was eventually fixed at 364 lbs. Each sack contained about 200 fleeces; thus from the amount of wool sold one may arrive at a fairly accurate number of sheep in each abbey's possession. In 1273 the

312

average price of wool per sack was ten marks, although fine wool commanded much higher prices, poor quality lower. Cistercians had the reputation for producing some of the highest quality wool in England. In the year quoted above, Meaux received fifteen marks, Fountains sixteen marks and Pipewell as much as eighteen to twenty marks per sack. Occasionally, however, monks received wool as tithes from their tenants, or, if the abbey was unable to furnish the contracted quantity, the brothers themselves went from house to house and collected wool from small farmers to be resold to the merchants. These sacks, the so-called *collecta,* were of inferior quality and fetched only eight to nine marks.

The buying of wool for resale was not only against Cistercian regulations, but was also vehemently opposed by lay competitors. In a famous case of 1262 the city of Lincoln protested to Henry III against Cistercian *conversi,* who were busily buying up wool "to be sold to merchants of beyond seas . . . contrary to the debt of honesty of their Order and to the impoverishment of the city of Lincoln and others of the King's market towns in that county, whereby the farms and customs due to him are fraudulently withdrawn; wherefore the King commands them to desist from this kind of business, or the King will lay the hand of correction upon them not lightly." The judgment, however, failed to prevent some hard-pressed Yorkshire abbeys from repeating the same operation. Thus, in 1276, Fountains sold sixty sacks of *collecta* to Florentine merchants; Meaux sold, between 1270 and 1280, 120 sacks of wool of similar origin.

Although Cistercians were among the foremost English sheep-farmers, the total output of the Order amounted to only about three or four percent of the exported wool. In quality, however, few competitors could overtake the Cistercians. It was for this reason that the right of using common pastures was eagerly granted to Cistercians, thus creating opportunities to seculars for learning the brothers' advanced techniques and for improving the donors' flocks by cross-breeding. The sheep's droppings, a highly valued fertilizer, was another compensation for the use of the pasture. Like considerations might have motivated William de Stuteville, when he invited the *conversi* of Kirkstall to graze 840 sheep on his common pasture, but he insisted on keeping 400 of them in his sheepfold, stipulating that lambs born there belonged to him.

Wool producing abbeys often processed a portion of their clip for their own use. Between 1235 and 1249 Meaux started a workshop where wool was woven and cloth fulled for cowls and capes. Kingswood produced, in addition to cloth for the monks' habits, material for harnesses, coverlets and slippers. In 1297 Beaulieu processed in its own workshops ten sacks of wool and a comparable amount of cloth was also produced at Vaudey and

Furness. At least twenty-five Cistercian abbeys in England and Wales were known to have operated fulling mills.

English export of wool reached its highest volume between 1275 and 1325. Several abbeys maintained a considerable merchant fleet for the purpose, among them Meaux, where the monks had built a craft for 200 marks and named it "Benedictus." The outbreak of the Hundred Years' War (1337), followed by the disastrous plague of 1348-49, however, disrupted foreign connections and seriously depressed the wool-trade. Meanwhile, royal intervention in the form of granting monopolistic privileges to a group of wool-exporting merchants, later known as the "Company of Staplers," prevented Cistercians from maintaining direct contact with foreign firms, ending the Order's pre-eminence in this important business.

It is evident from the surviving documents that toward the end of the thirteenth century wool production in many abbeys was a well-organized and carefully controlled process. The account book of Beaulieu Abbey referring to the conditions of about 1270 is particularly revealing. This abbey, close to the Channel coast near the Isle of Wight, was a relatively late foundation (1203), made by King John as an act of expiation for his harsh and unjust treatment of Cistercians. Beaulieu was generously endowed indeed, and proved successful in every respect. Netley, Newenham and Hailes were founded by that populous community, all within a short few years (1239-1246). Beaulieu's book of accounts attests to the elaborate system of economic administration and professional skill in departmentalized bookkeeping. The forester, for example, was supposed to produce annually from every acre of woods, in addition to 4,000 faggots, 412 bundles of firewood, each made up of five sticks no less than three feet in length and the thickness of a lance. The trees were cut only after twenty years of growth and even the remaining stumps were used for charcoal.

The total number of sheep at Beaulieu in the year of the account was only 2,255, and half of them were soon to be lost because of murrain and other causes. The whole complex operation of sheep-farming was under the control of the "master of the sheepfolds," assisted by a number of lay-brothers and hired workers. The animals were kept in several flocks under the care of the *bercarius,* who had to provide for sufficient pasture with facilities for both men and sheep. The shearing and washing of the fleece were done at these locations, but the grading and dividing of the wool into sacks were done in the abbey. There were six distinct qualities listed (good, medium, gross, lok, warplok and grosslok), sold for prices ranging from £10 to £2 per sack. The whole amount was 17.5 sacks and, apparently, all were sold for a total of £147, 16 s., 11 d. On the other hand, the wardrobe-keeper purchased 5.5 sacks of low-quality wool for the monks' own needs.

The entire process of producing from this latter quantity of wool the many garments for the whole community of 58 monks, 7 novices and 68 lay-brothers, was done within the abbey, from carding and combing to spinning, weaving and fulling in the abbey's mill. After that the cloth was brushed and finally cleaned in detergents. From each sack of wool, four times twenty-five ells of cloth was expected, about thirty meters of strong, winter quality. For summer use a much lighter material was produced. The total length of cloth manufactured in that year was 1,100 ells, out of which a variety of useful garments were made, from twenty-eight capes to 155 pairs of slippers. Nearly everything was used up by the community, although a few articles were donated to friends or to the poor. The selling of cloth on a larger scale was made impossible by loudly protesting cloth merchants, well entrenched in neighboring cities.

No doubt, a similar process of cloth-making was followed on an even larger scale in a number of other English Cistercian abbeys.

Wool-trade in Wales was almost as important as that in Yorkshire. In 1277 Aberconway sold twenty sacks to Italian merchants and retained its high level of production until about 1340. Margam, having a flock of about 5,000 sheep, toward the end of the thirteenth century sold twenty-five sacks of wool annually, outdoing somewhat Whitland, Tintern, Basingwerk and Neath. These quantities were far behind the figures of Fountains and Rievaulx, but the quality of Welsh wool was generally higher. Tintern's wool was the best in the principality, netting the monks twenty-eight marks per sack, an annual revenue of £150 from wool alone. Late in the thirteenth century Margam's income from the same commodity rose even higher: £167.

In Ireland wool production was also significant, becoming particularly important in the years of the worst scab epidemic (1280-1290) in England. Henry III often collected his Irish taxes in wool, with which he financed his Scottish wars. Under varying degrees of economic pressure many Cistercian abbeys in Ireland were heavily indebted to Italian merchants, who advanced large payments for future deliveries. The monks of Jerpoint were burdened by a large loan accepted from merchants of Lucca, but about a dozen other Irish abbeys, among them Holy Cross, found themselves in a similar predicament.

At about the same time the monks of Cambron (Flanders) had a herd of 4,000 sheep. In 1189 Bonnefont near Toulouse possessed 1,500 sheep. In 1316 the herdsmen of the Catalan Poblet tended the flocks of 2,215 sheep and 1,500 goats.

WINE MAKING

Wine was an indispensable monastic commodity. Vineyards were planted, carefully maintained and, if possible, enlarged at every Cistercian abbey established under favorable climatic conditions. The selling of surplus wine was a subject of regulations at the earliest sessions of the General Chapter. Although the monks were not to market wine in retail, the Chapter of 1182 permitted sales if they were made through a lay middleman who would operate his shop outside monastic precincts. In the thirteenth century most such restrictions were removed, although as late as 1270 women were still barred from monastic wine shops and the opening of taverns in the city properties of Cistercian abbeys remained prohibited. It was also understood that the monks were to sell only their own products, but in cases of necessity many abbeys bought and sold wine from other sources as well.

Cîteaux became and remained the foremost producer of quality wine in France until the French Revolution. Vineyards at the best Burgundian locations enriched the abbey early in the twelfth century, including the world-famous Clos-Vougeot in the immediate vicinity of Nuits-Saint-Georges. This vineyard had grown from humble beginnings to fifty hectares (about 125 acres) entirely surrounded by walls, and equipped with presses and cellars, many of which still stand. Jealous contemporaries were always convinced that most papal and royal favors showered upon Cîteaux resulted from well-timed gifts of matchless vintage wines of Clos-Vougeot. It is a matter of documentary evidence that in the fourteenth century Cîteaux regularly furnished wine for the papal court at Avignon, for in 1364 Urban V graciously remitted the sending of the usual quota of wine in consideration of the grave financial difficulties of the abbey. In 1372, however, his successor, Gregory XI, gratefully acknowledged the receipt of thirty casks of Cistercian wine from Beaune and Gevrey-Chambertin. Undoubtedly, it was the free flow of Burgundian wines that made the annual banquets at Cîteaux in honor of neighboring bishops and clergy extremely popular. When in 1364, for the above reason, the invitations had failed to come forth, the disappointed churchmen turned with their complaints to the Pope. Urban V emphasized in his reply that these "meals of charity" had become "too sumptuous," therefore Cîteaux was justified in holding them only every fourth year.

The abbeys of the Rhine and Moselle regions, thanks to the easy transportation of wine on the rivers, grew to be major centers of the wine trade. The greatest by far was Eberbach on the Rhine, somewhat below Mainz. Less than ten acres of the famous Steinberg, one of the oldest vineyards in Germany, was donated to the monks in 1135, when most of the steep hillside was still uncultivated. The brothers terraced the difficult terrain and by 1232 the whole of the Steinberg was theirs and they had covered with precious *Reisling* vines nearly seventy-three acres. Other vineyards of similar renown in the abbey's possession were Kiedrich, Hallgarten, Hattenheim, Rüdesheim, Lorch, Ober- and Niederingelheim and Nierstein. Much of the annual production, about 60,000 gallons, was sold in Cologne, where the abbey maintained a house and cellar after 1162. Shipments were transported on the monastery's barges tax- and duty-free and were sold to retailers. Other major destinations of Eberbach wine included Mainz and Frankfurt. In 1506 the total sale involved 359 *Fuder* (about 100,000 gallons), boosting the monks' income by 6,000 gulden. The wine was stored under the lay-brothers' dormitory in a vaulted hall which was originally over 300 feet long. Still today it contains sixteen huge wine-presses made from the trunks of oak trees, some of which date back to Cistercian times. Much of the fame of the cellar was due to one gigantic cask, made in the last years of the fifteenth century. It was twenty-eight feet long, nine feet high and had the capacity of eighty-two *Stück* (about 26,000 gallons), yet it was held together by only fourteen hoops. A Bavarian humanist of the time, Vincent Obsopaeus (d. 1539), celebrated this "pool of Bacchus, from which nectar flowed day and night" in a Latin verse, comparing the wonderful cask with the "miracles" of Antiquity.

The Peasant War of 1524-1525 brought disaster to Eberbach and during the rest of the century and monks were involved in a long feud with the city of Cologne, resentful over the fiscal immunities of the abbey. The Thirty Years' War (1618-1648) introduced another era of destruction and depression, but Eberbach recovered its old prosperity in the eighteenth century and retained it until the secularization of 1803. The abbey and the Steinberg are presently in government ownership and the expertly restored buildings attract as many tourists as wine connoisseurs. The wine-auctions of Eberbach are internationally noted events attended by wholesalers and importers from far and wide.

The vineyards of Himmerod along the valley of the Moselle were second in production only to those of the elector-archbishop of Trier. The sale of wine always formed the monks' best source of cash income. While Trier and Cologne absorbed much of the abbey's surplus production, some shipments went as far as Holland. Otterberg in the Palatinate possessed a number of fine vineyards and shared in the benefits of a flourishing wine trade. Viticulture in Alsace reached back to Roman settlers and all Cistercian foundations of the province were noted wine-

317

producers, among them Lützel and Pairis in "Upper" Alsace, Baumgarten and Neuburg in "Lower" Alsace.

Beer brewing was almost as common as winemaking, particularly in the abbeys of Wales, Scotland and Scandinavia, where grapes could not be grown successfully. Beer was made in two or three qualities even at the same place: the "strong" beer or ale was the privilege of the abbot's table, or was served on special occasions. Some of the better products of the monks enjoyed wide popularity. The Welsh Margam's "strong beer" was much in demand; Strata Florida and Llantarnam in the same country operated public ale houses.

FISHERIES

One of the oldest items of monastic economy, long before the Cistercians, was pisciculture, which, because of the dietary prohibition of meat, always had a special attraction for monks. The Cistercians, experts in drainage and reclamation, had an excellent opportunity to develop fishery on an unusually large scale, since water was plentiful in reservoirs, canals and behind the dams which stored the water for milling. There was scarcely a monastery without larger or smaller fishponds, and, where the geographical formations allowed, a long chain of connected ponds served for fish breeding on a commercial basis under the direction of an expert monk, the "master of fishes." Such a territory was the Upper Palatinate in Germany with its mildly sloping Fichtel Mountains. There the abbey of Waldsassen (founded in 1133) developed its fish hatcheries from the twelfth century onwards into one of the largest known plants of its kind. Concerning its production reliable sources are available from the sixteenth century. In 1571, when the monastery had already lost a considerable part of its former territory, there were still 159 ponds in operation. The select females were kept in forty-seven smaller ponds, the yearlings in thirty ponds while the two year olds, which needed more room and food, were maintained in eighty-two ponds. In the third year, the fish were sold wholesale in the neighboring cities, especially in Eger (Bohemia). Here, as almost everywhere else, the main products were carp and in smaller amounts trout and pike.

Abbeys having access to rivers or to the sea acquired valuable fishing rights or monopolies which they often rented to others, preferring cash to fish. The Welsh Tintern operated three weirs for salmon on the Wye and had similar privileges up to the middle of the Severn. Margam and Neath were equally eager to make the best of their fishing opportunities. Irish abbeys derived a considerable portion of their revenues from the sale of fish, such as eels, salmon and pike. Holy Cross erected four weirs across

318

the Suir, for the catching of eel. Fishing for herring was carried out in coastal waters. Saint Mary's Abbey near Dublin possessed a long coastline with several small harbors, giving opportunities to the monks for collecting taxes from the users of their port facilities.

In addition to these fields of monastic economy, orchards and vegetable gardens were seldom missing from the vicinity of Cistercian houses, although their products, because of the difficulties of transportation, rarely equaled grain, wool or wine in commercial value. Nevertheless, Cistercian gardening, with its highly advanced methods and improved species, greatly influenced and forwarded horticulture among neighboring populations, especially in the northern and eastern regions of the continent. In 1273, Doberan had a glass-roofed house for purposes of plant experimentation. Fine fruits and rare vegetables were transplanted from France through the channels of monastic affiliation. The apple known in France as "gray renette" went from Morimond to Camp, and through the latter's numerous German affiliations spread eastward. In Thuringia, applegrowing and cider-making were profitable activities of monasteries; Georgental and Pforta were especially well known for their orchards. The latter possessed, besides twenty-seven vineyards, orchards in nine different locations under the care of the "master of orchards." One of the former possessions of the abbey, Borsdorf, is still famous for its apples, originally transplanted from France.

In Norway, the country's largest abbey, Lyse (founded in 1146 by Fountains), possessed in the district of Hardanger the finest orchards; this region is still famous for its fruit culture. The same monastery maintained a popular inn in the city of Bergen with the privilege of selling there its agricultural produce. The commercial connections of the abbey reached as far as England, and the goods of the two countries were exchanged in the monastery's own ships. King John "Lackland" granted these vessels the privilege of tax-free exportation in 1212. In Sweden, according to the testimony of contemporary documents, fishing was one of the most important items of monastic economy, all the more because the climate greatly limited agriculture. However, the abbey of Gudvala, situated on the island of Gotland, possessed rich lands in Estonia, and established a warehouse with a cellar in Reval. Its busy commercial activity presupposes the maintenance of a considerable fleet.

Apart from the widely fourishing sheep-farming, various other fields of stock farming contributed essentially to the Cistercian agrarian economy. Jervaulx (England) was always famous for breeding horses; the abbey of Otterberg (Germany) sold eighty wild horses to Prince Louis of the Palatinate in 1426. In the thirteenth century Clairvaux possessed 800

319

swine, apparently for commercial purposes. Milk products were important in the monks' diet and early documents testify to the great efforts made to improve the dairy stock. In the year of Saint Bernard's death (1153), lay-brothers were sent from Clairvaux to Italy to purchase animals; the brothers returned from the difficult trip across the Alps with ten fine cattle. About a century later, the same abbey possessed a herd of 900 cattle. The abbey of Kirkstall, although never one of the wealthiest in England, had at the end of the thirteenth century 216 oxen, 160 cows, 152 yearlings and bullocks, and 90 calves, in addition to 4,000 sheep. Morimond owned 700 cattle and 2,000 swine. Bee-keeping in many houses was carried on under the care of a monk called the *apiarius*. Honey during the Middle Ages was far more important than it is in our days, since honey was the principal substitute for sugar.

From frequent references to urban properties one may legitimately conclude that most prosperous abbeys of some size were anxious to acquire and maintain houses in neighboring cities to be vital links with local markets where the brothers could sell their own products and buy the necessary articles they could not produce. In important commercial centers such as in Paris, Toulouse, Cologne or Brussels a number of monasteries owned warehouses and hospices. In Boston eleven English Cistercian abbeys possessed various establishments; in London as many as twenty-one, and some abbeys had more than one house in the town.

In addition to these commercial contacts, Cistercian abbeys often obtained privileges for holding markets and even fairs on their own properties. An incentive for the marketing of goods on monastic property was the resistance of the cities toward the admission of Cistercians to their markets, for the privileged status of the Order regarding taxes and duties insured the brothers advantages which secular competitors found unfair and injurious. The fight between Eberbach and Cologne was duplicated by clashes between Waldsassen and Eger and between Bebenhausen and Ulm. In each case the abbey was forced to look for markets outside of the jurisdiction of hostile authorities. During the thirteenth century thirty-one abbeys in England and Wales possessed market and fair concessions, and many others may have held markets without written authorization. A charter generally entitled the monks to have weekly markets and an annual fair which lasted about three days. Agrarian surplus was the main attraction of these events and the monks' profit must have been substantial; in fact, some monasteries, for example Holmcultram and Jervaulx, paid large sums for market privileges.

INDUSTRY

A flourishing monastic industry, closely related to agriculture, was milling. Although originally Cistercian mills were to serve the monks exclusively, once many of the abbeys' estates had been rented to peasant families, the new tenants became the mills' principal customers; thus milling inevitably turned out to be a commercial operation. Monastic archives are full of references to the acquisition and operation of mills, which, in a manorial economy, were always items of seignorial monopoly for obviously lucrative reasons. In many instances, when direct control was not feasible, the monks leased or rented their mills to lay operators. The profitable nature of the ownership of mills is clear from the countless lawsuits over various aspects of their exploitation.

In some cases milling developed into one of the main sources of income, as happened at Zinna (Brandenburg), which in 1480 operated fourteen water-mills within its vast domain. The abbey of Foigny (France) owned the same number of mills in addition to a brewery, glassworks, fulling mill, two spinning mills, three forges and three press-sheds. In some locations in Germany milling developed into a Cistercian monopoly. During the thirteenth century Reinfeld and Doberan bought all available mills in their neighborhood, both water- and windmills. Elsewhere, if they could not control milling directly, they tried to achieve the same results indirectly, through their extensive water rights, by regulating the flow of rivers by dams.

In 1230 the Catalan Poblet attempted to monopolize the milling industry along the upper Francolí river. In 1243, after having paid 500 solidi, the monks bought off the last rival claimant, the Viscount of Bas. This threw a whole string of villages at the mercy of the Cistercians, while the latter found themselves frequent targets of vengeful violence. Fines and even excommunication of the malcontents failed to quell the disturbances. The abbey retained its precious rights, but at the cost of constant litigation and heavy loss of popularity.

Although Cistercian economy had basically an agrarian character, its practical-minded management and admirable flexibility in exploiting local possibilities to the utmost is proven in some countries by monasteries of the Order which were pioneers in mining. Stone quarries for building material were operated where circumstances allowed; large scale mining of coal, iron ore, precious metals and especially salt, was well developed in England, Scotland, Wales, Germany, Bohemia and Austria. One of the earliest Cistercian settlements in Scotland, the abbey of

Newbattle (founded in 1140), opened one of the first coal mines of the region. At the beginning they confined their work to the coal on the surface, but later followed the seams wherever the level allowed. In the same country extensive coal mines were operated by Culross (founded in 1217) in combination with a large export trade. At the neighboring port some 170 ships were engaged in transporting abroad the monastery's produce. Both abbeys also exported salt.

Fountains in England, shortly after its foundation, reopened the surrounding ancient lead mines, established smelting works, and had full mineral rights in the whole district. The greatest Cistercian producers of iron-ore in England were Furness and Flaxley. In the thirteenth century Flaxley had fourteen furnaces in operation and its income from iron surpassed that from agrarian sources. Other English abbeys involved in either mining or smelting iron-ore were Rievaulx, Kirkstall, Jervaulx, Byland, Sawley, Louth Park and Stanley.

In Wales many Cistercian abbeys received mining privileges shortly after their foundations. Neath, Margam and Llantarnam were the earliest coal producers; lead was mined at Margam, Basingwerk, Strata Florida and Strata Marcella; iron-ore was found on the properties of Margam, Tintern and Grace Dieu. Some of the same abbeys operated smelting works and forges as well.

Shortly after their foundations the Count of Champagne donated "forges to make iron" to La Crête, Clairvaux, Igny and Trois-Fontaines, indicating a growing demand for such products as well as the Cistercians' eagerness to supply them.

In the thirteenth and fourteenth centuries mining developed into a major industry at several Cistercian abbeys in Saxony and Bohemia. Walkenried operated copper mines in the Harz mountains from the end of the twelfth century. Copper mining became the speciality also of Sittichenbach, a daughter of Walkenried, established in the same mining area. Grünhain, founded by monks of Sittichenbach in the Erz mountains near the Bohemian border, continued the same tradition in iron-ore and coal mining. In one of Grünhain's mines, called *Die Kutte* (The Cowl), Cistercian brothers discovered for the first time silver deposits. Grünhain's later foundation, Ossegg in Bohemia, turned out to be another mining community. Still another "daughter" of Walkenried, Sedletz near Prague, possessed a silver mine in Kuttenberg. The abbey of Altzelle, north of Freiberg in Saxony, employed its lay-brothers in silver mining during the fourteenth century.

The first Cistercian salt mine opened in 1147 at Aussee (Austria), operated by the abbey of Rein, was also the first significant salt mine in

Styria. Northern Germany, with its vast salt deposits, presented a challenge for all Cistercian houses in those districts. During the twelfth century the saltworks of Magdeburg and Marlow were operated largely by the surrounding monasteries; moreover, the salt industry around Lüneburg developed into a strictly Cistercian enterprise of huge dimensions. From the middle of the thirteenth century Doberan and Reinfeld were mostly interested in mining, but as the plant expanded, more and more houses joined the undertaking and eventually, between 1375 and 1383, no less than thirteen abbeys participated in the apparently profitable industry.

The Polish house of Wachock in the diocese of Cracow enjoyed extensive mining rights. In 1249 the abbey received one-ninth of the salt and one-fifth of other mining products taken from its territory. In England Holmcultram, Calder, Quarr, Furness, Byland, Newminster, Jervaulx and Louth Park were involved in salt production. In 1177 Clairvaux obtained a share in the salt mining at Lons-le-Saulnier and in 1194 similar rights at Marsal. Salt was also contributed to Clairvaux in the form of rents: in 1202 Count William of Ponthieu donated to the monks 200 *muids* (hogsheads) of salt annually.

ECONOMIC CRISIS: 1350-1450

The gradual decrease of the number of lay-brothers and the wholesale leasing of monastic land to peasant tenants had undoubtedly created serious economic problems for many Cistercian abbeys, but diversification and a new emphasis on trade proved adequate compensations for losses in agrarian revenues. The century, however, extending from 1350 to 1450 brought a severe economic depression throughout Europe, afflicting particularly the owners of extensive landed estates. The symptoms of the malaise were all too evident: declining population, rising wages, falling agrarian prices and growing costs of goods in commercial circulation, abandoned villages, peasant uprisings and periodic famine. In searching for causes modern scholarship calls attention to a mysterious decline in the birth rate, to the tragic outbreaks of plague and to the general lawlessness adding to the miseries of prolonged wars. Governments, laboring under fiscal emergencies, often resorted to the debasement of currency, which only aggravated the problems caused by accelerated inflation. Landlords, including abbeys, supported largely by fixed rents, felt the stress keenly. Cistercian communities were also afflicted by mounting papal or royal exactions, demanded in spite of the Order's traditional fiscal immunities.

The alleged wealth of the Order had served as an excuse for requiring contributions for crusades and for a variety of other military ventures. As long as the papacy remained strong and independent, the Order found a measure of support in Rome, but after the fall of Boniface VIII and the move of the papal court to Avignon the General Chapter became entirely helpless against the joint economic pressure of both pope and king. In 1297 Philip IV, "the Fair," extorted from Boniface VIII a privilege granting him the right to collect tithes twice annually from all ecclesiastical benefices, including abbeys. In the case of the Cistercians this amounted to about 20,000 *livres* each year, divided among the 197 monasteries situated within the borders of France. After the ransacking of several reluctant abbeys by brutal royal tax-collectors, Cîteaux found it wise to grant the King the stipulated amount as a "voluntary gift," thus saving at least the principle of its largely meaningless tax exemption. In 1304 alone Cîteaux paid 22,000 *livres tournois* to royal agents.

ADMINISTRATIVE REFORM

The equitable distribution of such burdens among the abbeys of the Order as well as the efficient collection of contributions demanded careful planning and an elaborate bureaucratic administration. Voluntary contributions to the costs of the General Chapter had been solicited throughout the thirteenth century and eventually each house was expected to give a fixed amount adjusted to the wealth of the community, to be collected by the founding father abbots. In 1329 father abbots were to gather an inventory of goods from each house under their care, and on this basis the bursar of Cîteaux drew up in the next year a permanent list of fixed assessments for each abbey of the Order.

After the name of each monastery four figures were given: the first was "moderate;" the next, called "mediocre," was somewhat higher; the third ("double") was the double of the first figure; the last, "excessive," was the double of the second amount. It was up to the General Chapter to decide which of the four sums was to be collected in the subsequent fiscal year. The expected total of "moderate" contributions was 9,000 *livres tournois*; the "mediocre" was to net 12,000 *livres*, the "double" 18,000 *livres*, while the "excessive" 24,000 *livres*. Voluntary gifts were expected from convents of nuns as well, although after 1339 all these contributions were remitted. Most abbeys paid their taxes at the General Chapter, others preferred to pay to traveling collectors, who deposited the results of their labors at central offices in Paris, Avignon and Metz.

The collection of taxes outside France posed serious problems, partly because of the perpetual dangers and devastation caused by the Hundred Years' War, partly because foreign abbots suspected that eventually their contributions would disappear in the bottomless coffers of the papal court in Avignon or of the French king. Only about half of all Cistercian houses paid their taxes regularly; in 1342, for example, of the 700 establishments of the Order 356 houses were listed as having fulfilled their obligations. In fact, it was only in the fiscal year of 1345-1346 that the collection covered the amount required by Cîteaux and on all other occasions the balance had to be furnished from loans. That English abbeys were unable to send anything to Cîteaux, in enemy territory, was quite natural, but eventually taxes had to be discounted from Scotland and Ireland as well, while payments from the Scandinavian countries were entirely unpredictable. Concerning England, the Statute of Carlisle of 1307 strictly prohibited the payment of any taxes on behalf of foreign superiors or mother-houses, and this law was rigidly enforced.

The other reason for the chronic deficits was the rapid increase of expenditures. The costs of holding General Chapters throughout the fourteenth century amounted on each occasion to about 1,000 *livres tournois*. The fiscal demands of the Avignon papacy rose steadily and the large shipments of wine floated down on the Rhone represented only a fraction of what Cîteaux was expected to furnish. Gifts and regular pensions to cardinals, legal fees and outright bribes for various favors unremittingly drained Cistercian resources. The annual pension paid to the Cistercian Cardinal Guillaume Curti, the "protector" of the Order, amounted alone to 3,000 *livres*. The current construction and maintenance of the College of Saint Bernard in Paris also absorbed huge amounts.

After 1347 the bookkeeping of Cîteaux became disorderly and from this date on only a fraction of the assessed taxes could be collected. The Great Western Schism (1378-1414) led to a total collapse of the elaborate system of contributions, and in 1390 the indebtedness of Cîteaux amounted to 25,000 Florentine florins. The financial distress of the mother house remained unresolved throughout the fifteenth century. In 1476 Cîteaux still owed 25,448 gold florins, at a time when in France and Italy the commendatory system had already reduced many communities to utter destitution. The ambitious Abbot General Jean de Cirey (1476-1501) came under the mistaken impression that it was still possible to reverse the trend and regain by papal bulls the abbeys lost to the *commenda*. The delegation he sent to Rome in 1479 for the purpose spent 6,500 gold ducats for worthless paper guarantees. In 1489 the confirmation of Cistercian privileges cost the Order another 6,000 ducats, without adequate return.

The financial woes of the Order were often attributed by contemporaries to the monks' wasteful management and inept administration of their goods. At the Council of Vienne (1311-1312) the French hierarchy loudly demanded the reform of monastic orders, the abolition of their exemption and the restoration of their prosperity under episcopal supervision. Pope John XXII (1316-1334) reiterated the same charges of maladministration disbelieving that an order as great as the Cistercians could be unable to fulfill its financial obligations. On both occasions it was the widely respected Cistercin scholar, Jacques de Thérines, abbot of Châlis, who defended the principle of exemption and blamed the poverty of the Order on exorbitant royal exactions, cruel devastations of wars and merciless usurers.

Such was the background of the apostolic constitution *Fulgens sicut stella* issued in 1335 by the Cistercian Pope Benedict XII, aiming at a basic reorganization of the Order's fiscal administration. Accordingly, each abbot was to take an oath not to alienate monastic property without due consultation with his monks and formal permission of the General Chapter. Transactions involving entire granges, villages or major portions of monastic estates called for the approval of the Holy See. The cash revenues of each abbey were to be kept in a strong box under four different keys distributed among the abbot, prior, bursar and a senior member of the community, so that the box could be opened only in the presence of all four of them. Contracts for the renting of monastic land were to be restricted to five year terms and even these needed the approval of either the General Chapter or the Holy See, depending on the size of the property involved. The abbots' power to borrow money was limited to 100 *livres*; larger amounts needed the formal consent of the community. No legal act by the abbot alone was valid without the convent's seal. All administrators of monastic goods, specifically cellarers and bursars, were to take an oath to fulfill their duties faithfully. The bursar was to have an assistant and the two officials were obliged to present to the abbot a full account of the abbey's financial status four times annually. The abbot in turn had to prepare an annual financial report for the inspection of senior members of the community.

ECONOMIC CONDITIONS IN THE LATE MIDDLE AGES

Purely administrative measures, however, no matter how salutary, failed to bring about significant improvements and it was only in the second half of the fifteenth century that a degree of recovery became noticeable.

The depression was by no means restricted to France. Hardships at Otterberg in the diocese of Mainz forced the monks to sell monastic property and by 1362 twenty-six such incidents had been recorded. Even so, the indebtedness of the abbey increased steadily and by 1426 no less than thirty-seven creditors had to be dealt with. Loccum in Hanover experienced similar adversities. In 1426 the once populous community numbered only 20 monks and 10 lay-brothers. Abbot Ernest (1483-1492), however, managed to reverse the trend and by the end of the fifteenth century the community had grown again to 40 monks and 70 lay-brothers.

The Chronicle of Meaux presents a detailed picture of monastic economy toward the end of the fourteenth century, when the disasters of the mid-century had already been overcome and the monks were coming close to a balanced budget. In 1393-1394 the total income amounted to £614, the bulk of which was made up of rents (£338), while the once dominant sale of wool had sunk to a modest £30. The churches under the control of the abbey netted £86. The figures give an insight into the rental value of land, which, according to the quality of the soil, ranged from 6 pence to 20 pence an acre. The total expenditure in the same year was £672, of which the largest portion (£180) went to creditors. The maintenance of the churches, including the salaries of the vicars (£87) absorbed entirely the collected tithes. Hospitality cost the monks £47; pensions to be furnished for benefactors amounted to £37; the servants' wages totalled £24; £10 were paid to the lawyers of the abbey.

It appears from such details that, contrary to the often voiced charges, the monks, at least at Meaux, were very concerned with details of fiscal administration and in normal circumstances managed their estates with remarkable expertise and efficiency. The abbots were elected in succession more for their administrative abilities than for their piety and at least half the community was involved in economic management. Debts were always kept in evidence and every effort was made to reduce them. If anything should be charged against the monks, it might be their excessive devotion to economy at the expense of their spiritual obligations.

Another well-documented case was that of Villers, suffering under the extortionist dukes of Brabant, John II (1297-1312) and John III (1312-1355). The wholesale alienation of property began under Abbot Nicholas (1303-1308), but the netted 6,000 Brabantine *livres* were not enough to keep the abbey solvent. When in 1315 the monks were unwilling and unable (*non volentes nec valentes*) to meet another huge imposition, they fled to abbeys of the Order outside the reach of their rapacious prince. This, however, was by no means the end of tribulations; between 1330 and 1333, three entire granges had to be sold "for the acquittance of usurious loans."

During the fourteenth century most lands of Villers were rented under varying conditions. Only the granges closest to the abbey were cultivated by the monks, but, for lack of lay-brothers, with the help of hired laborers. The previously high rate of donations fell markedly after 1350, although during the fifteenth century the records still accounted for some twenty gifts, mostly of urban property. The second half of the fifteenth century

327

witnessed a gradual recovery. Among new purchases the monks acquired in 1483 Wilderen, the summer residence of future abbots. By the turn of the century the monks succeeded in balancing their budget and the net annual income mounted to the impressive figure of 1,000 *gross livres de Brabant* (about 4,000 *livres tournois*).

Elsewhere, when impoverished abbeys were unable to provide for their personnel, the monks often accepted regular pensions from relatives or friends. Such practices prevailed throughout the fourteenth and fifteenth centuries in spite of repeated warnings of the General chapter. According to the records of Himmerod, Heisterbach, Altenberg, Camp and Eberbach, all in the Rhineland, many monks enjoyed private revenues (*peculium*), an obvious infraction of monastic poverty, yet condoned by sympathetic visitors. At some monasteries, where the exploitation of monastic lands was no longer possible with lay-brothers, individual monks took over the cultivation of granges with full responsibility, paying a rent to the abbot, but retaining the surplus for themselves. Documents of such contracts between monks and abbots have survived, among other houses, from Himmerod and the French Jouy.

At Melrose in Scotland early in the sixteenth century many monks cultivated their private gardens and lived from private revenues. In 1533 the General Chapter dispatched to the scene Simon Patel, the abbot of Châlis, to investigate the long ingrained abuse. The monks defended themselves by charging that the commendator had refused to provide for them, therefore they requested special consideration for their plight until other means for their support could be devised. The understanding visitor was willing to tolerate this strange state of monastic economy until the General Chapter could reach a definitive judgment in the matter.

THE SEVENTEENTH AND EIGHTEENTH CENTURIES

Luther's reformation was followed by a tragic century which, from the point of view of monasticism, was merely a prolonged struggle for survival. Cistercian abbeys emerging alive from the holocaust of the wars of religion, depending on their success in reclaiming and rebuilding their estates, continued to prosper as landlords, drawing the bulk of their revenues from rents contributed by peasant tenants. Forests constituted particularly valuable assets, while animal husbandry, mining rights or industrial production furnished other sources of income. The recovery was most successful in the Catholic countries of Germany, the Austrian Netherlands (Belgium), Switzerland and Austria, where many communities invested their earnings in magnificently rebuilt churches and monasteries.

328

Among other prosperous abbeys, Rauden in Silesia operated extensive copper and iron works. The financial success of Orval in Belgium also resulted from mining and smelting iron ore. In 1759 the monks produced 700 tons of iron, worth over 100,000 florins. The abbey invested a portion of the net gain in real estate purchased in France, which by 1734 had grown to 36,484 *livres* in capital value. The wealth of the abbey attracted the curious attention of the Austrian authorities, who found in 1757 in the abbey's coffers 600,000 Luxembourgian silver florins. In order to escape a confiscatory taxation the monks initiated a great building project, which was still in progress at the time of the dissolution in 1796. In that year the income of the community amounted to 90,000 florins.

ECONOMY DURING THE ANCIEN RÉGIME

In France the seventeenth-century recovery was considerably slower, due to the fact that ninety percent of all Cistercian establishments had to share their revenues with commendatory abbots. Only a few houses can be regarded as wealthy, while the majority of Cistercian monasteries had to be satisfied with modest revenues and some bordered on destitution. Reasons for the much reduced monastic prosperity are manifold. Although the physical plants of most abbeys had been successfully restored in the seventeenth century, few managed to recover all their medieval possessions. In modern times land grants or donations of value became insignificant, while emergencies often led to repeated alienations of monastic property. Whatever remained was no longer under the direct cultivation of the monks, but was rented under various conditions to local peasantry. Some rents and some ancient feudal dues, fixed centuries before, were paid in money, but their value had been much eroded by the steady trend of inflation. Not infrequently tracts of land were given over to poorer peasants in *metayage*, that is, for the return of half of the crops, the quantity of which not only depended on the honesty and industry of the laborers, but also on weather conditions, changing from year to year.

Such incomes, modest as they were, in cases of abbeys *in commendam*, had to be shared with the commendatory abbots. This was done by the division of the revenues into three theoretically equal parts; one belonged to the commendator, another to the monks, and the third (*tiers lot*) was set aside for the costs of maintenance and repairs. In practice, however, the three amounts were rarely even, the highest being that of the abbot, the lowest the *tiers lot*. The method by which the actual apportionment was achieved differed from place to place. Where both the estates and the income were small, the monks usually remained in charge of the management of the undivided property and simply paid the abbot the annual pension fixed by contract. This was the case at Boquen, where in 1691 the abbot, Pierre-Jean Le Chapellier, a doctor of the Sorbonne, voluntarily relinquished all his claims in exchange for the annual pension of 300 *livres*. In rare instances, such as at Quincy, the opposite seems to have been true: the abbot controlled the revenues, doling out to the monks what they needed. In many other cases not the income but the estate was divided, the monks administering independently the land allotted them, while an agent of the commendatory abbot saw to the exploitation of his share.

Contracts, however, were often renegotiated, particularly if the commendatory abbot suspected that the monks' revenue was on the increase. Thus, in the case of Lanvaux, during the course of seventy years, the abbot's pension was changed four times, growing from 1,500 *livres* in 1717 to 2,400 *livres* by 1786. But even that last amount seemed too low to the commendatory abbot, claiming that the total revenue of his monastery ran as high as 12,548 *livres*. To be sure, the computation of income in terms of money always remained perplexing, for a considerable portion came in regularly in agrarian products. The two monks of the small Aubignac collected only 262 *livres*, but managed to survive and maintain the house on the sale of surplus crops.

The fact that fixed rents and feudal dues made up only a part of monastic income accounts for the fluctuation of annual revenue, which was largely influenced by the quality and quantity of harvest as well as by the actual market prices. A remarkable study on the economic conditions of the French Belloc (Beaulieu) during these crucial years may illustrate the complexity of the problem. Belloc was a small abbey in *commendam* in the diocese of Rodez (Aveyron), supporting only three to five monks, who, nevertheless, left behind a bookkeeping record of great detail and interest. Here the commendatory abbot managed his portion of the land estates independently, while the monks did the same with theirs, without any external intervention. The amount of the "abbot's portion" never figured in their accounts. We know only from other sources that the abbot's annual income was about 7,000 *livres*, indicating that he cultivated the better portion of the monastic estates.

The records of Belloc covered the years from 1766 to 1779. In 1767, for example, there was a surplus of 882 *livres* from the previous years; fixed rents amounted to over 2,000 *livres*; sale of agrarian goods netted nearly 1,000 *livres*, which, in addition to miscellaneous income, resulted in a total of 4,526 *livres*. The harvest of grain, however, the bulk of the crops, fluctuated between 213 sacks (1779) to 507 sacks (1775). This disparity explains why, in the extraordinarily good year of 1775, the monks were able to collect 9,824 *livres*. The house carried a previous loan of 3,000 *livres*, but

330

the payment of the moderate interest (150 *livres*) caused no difficulties. Ecclesiastical taxes (*décimes*) were quite high (506 *livres*), but there were no costly projects in progress and with an average income of 6,200 *livres* against 5,800 *livres* expenditures the community closed every year with a modest saving. This enabled the religious to live a quiet, comfortable life, far from the luxuries of aristocracy, but within the amenities of the prosperous bourgeoisie, to which most of them belonged. They consumed a quantity of snuff, but wasted no time in scholarly pursuits: they spent nothing for books. The presence of seven domestics spared them unpleasant physical exertions.

The thirty-five regular (noncommendatory) abbeys enjoyed the undivided amount of their monastic income, although few of them were really wealthy. Clairvaux's annual income amounted to about 100,000 *livres*; Cîteaux netted 70,000 *livres*. Thirteen regular abbeys had less than 10,000 *livres* annually. In fact these latter institutions were allowed to remain in the hands of Cistercians largely because their meager revenues did not appeal to secular seekers of sinecures.

A distressing case was that of Grace-Dieu in the diocese of Besançon, where the abbot, although always a Cistercian, was a royal appointee. The annual revenues of the abbey amounted only to about 6,000 *livres*, shared by six monks, the abbot and nine servants. Since in the eighteenth century the support of one monk, popularly referred to as "pension," demanded at least 500 *livres*, not much was left for anything else. Worst of all, the community carried a large debt, the interest of which added 3,000 *livres* to the annual expenditures. But this precarious situation was further aggravated by the fact that the last abbot, Frédéric-Léonard Rochet, had to pay 720 *livres* of annual pension to his predecessor, in addition to 1,400 *livres* due by royal order to two pensioned ecclesiastics. There was no way to balance the budget and in 1790, on the eve of secularization, the abbey was in debt for 63,566 *livres*.

A substantial financial burden on regular abbeys was the fee paid to the Roman Curia for issuing the abbot's "bull," the document of his papal confirmation. Theoretically all Church property was free from direct taxation, but in fact a considerable amount (*décimes*) was regularly collected through ecclesiastical channels in order to cover the "free gifts" periodically granted to the king. All monasteries paid these *décimes,* the richer ones more, the poorer ones less, but in most cases the tax amounted to about ten percent of their income. Contributions demanded by the Order for administrative expenses were much smaller. A surprising number of regular abbeys were afflicted with the payment of forced pensions which the monks had by royal order to furnish to individuals so favored by the Court. At Clairmarais this grew to 24,000 *livres* out of a revenue of 45,000 *livres*; Beaubec had to pay 12,000 *livres* out of 28,000; Prieres, though in chronic distress, gave away 10,000 out of a total of 26,000 *livres*. La Charmoye, Châtillon and Le Pin, quite poor themselves, had to shoulder proportionately heavy exactions of the same nature.

Eventually most houses learned to live within the limits of their income and only a few carried substantial loans, incurred through expensive building projects. But even these proved to be unmanageable only in isolated cases. Such was that of Châlis, where by the 1780s the debt had grown to an unbelievable one million *livres*. In 1785 the abbey was declared bankrupt and closed by royal order although the General Chapter of the following year launched a plan to save the house by a common effort of the whole Order. Mismanagement and internal strife lay behind financial problems at both Barbeaux and La Charmoye during the 1700s. At the latter abbey debts amounted to 139,518 *livres*, which sum, however, was soon reduced by half.

The absence of debts in most cases is a clear indication of financial stability throughout the French monasteries of the Order in the second half of the eighteenth century. Moreover, where figures of revenues covering a longer period are available, one cannot fail to notice an upward trend, proving that monastic economists had not always been inept and blind to new opportunities. Evidently after the nobility had discovered various ways for more profitably exploiting their land, the monks followed suit and scored similarly satisfying results. At Fénières, where in 1725 the monks' portion was only 1,305 *livres*, in 1766 they received 2,039 *livres*. At Fontaine-Jean in 1716 the monk's share was as little as 1,900 *livres*, which, however, had grown by 1787 to 4,671 *livres*. At Fontenay, where in 1715 the monks' "table" was 5,856 *livres*, the same came close to 10,000 in the 1770s. In consideration of a progressive inflation the seemingly general trend of growing incomes must be scaled down somewhat, but it still remains true that, at least in the field of monastic economy, the eighteenth century was by no means an era of decline, but rather one of a modest but steady prosperity.

Only a dozen Cistercian abbeys, scattered within the Austrian Empire, survived the wave of secularization. These monasteries managed to hold on to substantial pieces of their medieval patrimony and agrarian revenues covered much of their needs throughout the nineteenth century, although the majority of monks were actually engaged in teaching or pastoral work. The Trappist revival put new emphasis on agriculture and both the monks and the even larger number of lay-brothers spent their physical energies in farming. The rewards of such labors, however, were never sufficient for the adequate support of populous institutions, which relied to a large extent on wealthy donors and industrial production, such as that of the world-famous cheese of Port-du-Salut.

Comtemporary Cistercian economy defies generalization. With the secularization of Zirc in Hungary (1950) the last Cistercian *latifundium* disappeared, although some Austrian abbeys are still owners of many thousands of valuable hectares. Farming, however, has been less and less profitable and monks of both observances draw their income from a large variety of sources, from mass stipends to candy-making, from teaching and publishing to tourist guidance and giving retreats. The General Chapter and the central administration of the Order in both observances are still supported by the contributions of individual abbeys.

XXI

Lay-brotherhood

The institution of lay-brothers as a religious body under strict monastic discipline charged with the economic affairs of Cistercian establishments was in its full development certainly a distinctive feature of the Order, yet not without remarkable antecedents.

During Saint Benedict's time, the majority of monks were laymen; priests were only occasionally ordained or admitted, as the spiritual and liturgical needs of the abbeys demanded. All the monks took equal part in the necessary manual labor and if, at the harvest time, the work surpassed their capacity, laborers were hired. However, from the ninth century onward, monastic property grew enormously while the monks, by this time mostly priests and engaged in various missionary and cultural activities, were unable to fulfill the demands of their estates for manual labor. As a solution, the early medieval monasteries, including Cluny, accepted the system of manorialism and assigned agricultural work to the rural populace, thus freeing the monks' time and energy exclusively for increasing liturgical, pastoral, literary or educational activities.

This settlement, however, deeply involved the monasteries in worldly and merely political affairs; consequently, the reform movements of the eleventh century, in their zeal for solitude and strict asceticism, though unable to change the basic principles of the established social and economic system, tried at least to impose upon their lay helpers some sort of monastic discipline. Lay servants were organized by Saint Romuald at Camaldoli after 1012, followed by Saint Peter Damian at Fonte Avellana in the middle of the same century; Saint John Gualbert, the founder of Vallombrosa, called his lay helpers *conversi*, the name given lay-brothers by the Cistercians. Independently of these Italian movements, the German reform-congregation of Hirsau also gave its lay-servants a precise religious status and popularized the idea with such success that all other reformed orders or congregations, founded shortly before or after the Cistercians, adopted the institution in one form or another.

The Cistercian lay-brotherhood did not then represent an altogether revolutionary innovation, although no other order employed lay-brothers on such a large scale and with such great efficiency.

334

The early documents of Cîteaux reveal nothing about the external influences which might have led to the adoption of lay-brotherhood, nor can the date of the first appearance of this institution be easily determined. From the fact that it was during the first years of Stephen Harding's administration that Cîteaux's possessions began to multiply, one may conclude that the first lay-brothers were admitted in the second decade of the twelfth century. Abbot Stephen's familiarity with Vallombrosa offers another tempting conjecture: the admission of lay-brothers might have been inspired by the successful employment of *conversi* in that Italian abbey.

It is certain, however, that as soon as Cîteaux began to grow, some such solution became imperative. To the founders of the "New Monastery," who steadfastly rejected the traditional manorial exploitation of monastic estates and yearned for solitude, the direct cultivation of their lands remained the only choice, which, depending on the size of their estates, demanded an adequate labor force. Indeed, the unusual element in Cistercian agrarian economy was not the employment of lay-brothers, for this was merely a consequence of a far more revolutionary decision: the monks, following the Rule of Saint Benedict, felt obliged to live from the fruits of their own manual labor, from their toil on their land.

If we may give credence to the account given by Ordericus Vitalis concerning the debate between the two factions at Molesme, manual labor was a major point of disagreement. The opponents of Abbot Robert argued that "their earnest toil in the worship of God" was a worthy substitute for the abandoned physical work. It had been the well-established tradition in France, they argued, "for peasants to perform work in the fields, as is seemly, as servants to perform the duties suitable for servants. Monks, however, who have voluntarily renounced the vanities of this world for the service of the King of Kings, live peacefully in their enclosed cloisters, like the daughters of kings seeking out by study the hidden meaning of Scripture." Finally, they hoped to clinch the argument by exclaiming: "God forbid that peasants, whose true lot is continual toil, should grow useless through idleness . . . or that noble knights and gifted philosophers and learned scholars . . . should be compelled to spend their time in servile and unbecoming labors and occupations like lowborn servants in order to earn their bread."

The settlers of Cîteaux dismissed the reasoning of their opponents, although after a few years of extraordinary hardships they were forced to admit that there was some truth in the chain of thought expounded by the monks of Molesme. Cîteaux still refused to call for the help of serfs or peasants, but the recruiting of lay-brothers became inevitable. As the author of the *Exordium parvum* put it: "Since they realized that without their help they would be unable to fulfill perfectly the precepts of the Rule day and night, they decided to admit, with the permission of their bishops, bearded laymen as *conversi*, and to treat them in life and death as their own, except for [the rights reserved for] choir monks."

The compromise seemed to save Cîteaux's principles and still insure the labor force necessary for the monks' survival. As the wording of the quote clearly indicates, the decision was made as a practical solution to a practical question, without reference to the theory of what the monks' proper field of activity should be. The latter did not retreat from manual labor, nor were the *conversi* to be exploited merely as laborers; they were treated as religious, members of a monastic community, distinct from the choir monks only when it came to liturgical functions and certain legal aspects of the canonical status of monks in elections of abbots and holding other important offices.

The regulation of the brothers' daily routine of work and prayer was the duty of the General Chapter. The records of its early sessions, however, do not survive. The first extant document dealing with the brothers is the *Capitula* of 1119, then a few paragraphs in the *Instituta Generalis Capituli*, and, in a more systematic fashion, the *Usus conversorum*, part of the "book of Usages," in which regulations of different vintage were compiled about the middle of the twelfth century.

Accordingly, candidates for brotherhood were accepted like choir monks, for a one year novitiate. During that time, they were trained for their future duties and in monastic discipline, memorizing a few prayers, the *Pater, Credo* and *Miserere*, with some short responsories. The use of books or any other studies were excluded. After the year of probation they took vows promising the abbot obedience "until death." By that they became full-fledged religious, although without active or passive rights in voting for monastic officials, nor could they ever become choir monks or priests. Their habit was also distinct from that of the choir monks, being made of darker grayish or brown material. As a punishment, sometimes they even worked in civilian clothes.

The brothers' simple life was spent at the monastery in different workshops or at domestic duties, but the majority of them were put to work at the granges as farmers and herdsmen. Those staying in the monastery had living quarters similar to the choir monks', but they were separated from them, having their own weekly chapters for spiritual guidance and religious instructions. Except for Sundays and holydays they were not present at the Divine Office, but under the direction of the oldest of the group, they recited a certain number of *Pater noster's* at the time of the canonical hours wherever they happened to be working. Those living in distant granges returned to the monastery only on Sundays and on great feasts in order to take part in the solemn services; otherwise, during the week, they were all by themselves, since the choir monks were not usually permitted to stay outside the monastery. The reception of Holy Communion was compulsory only seven, later twelve, times a year. Their immediate superior was the cellarer or his subordinate, the *grangiarius*, usually a brother himself. They kept strict silence while working, but they fasted less severely and slept longer than the choir monks.

In addition to the daily routine occupations, the work of constructing and repairing buildings was also one of the important tasks of lay-brothers. They went to the market to sell surplus products and to make necessary purchases; they were employed as messengers and accompanied the abbots in official visitations. In some instances, Cistercian lay-brothers were in charge of charity organizations at royal courts as almoners, as happened at the end of the twelfth century in England. The highest office brothers ever obtained was that of papal *bullator* at Avignon, which seemed to be a privilege of Cistercians during the fourteenth century. The Curia employed them on the supposition that they, being unlettered, would keep secrecy while copying and handling papal documents, since they were unable to understand their contents.

The historical significance of Cistercian lay-brotherhood, however, lies in the fact that it was through the organized labor of unprecedented numbers of *conversi* that, at least for a century, the Order took a leading role in agrarian expansion and facilitated the unparalleled multiplication of Cistercian establishments throughout Europe. While some of the often publicized but certainly inflated numbers must be regarded with skepticism, it remains true that during the twelfth and thirteenth centuries many abbeys operated their extensive possessions with the help of several hundred lay-brothers. In most such cases the brothers outnumbered the choir monks by a ratio of 2:1 or even 3:1. Probably the largest group of lay-brothers was organized by Les Dunes in Flanders, where, about 1300, in addition to 180 choir monks, there were 350 lay-brothers, a work force easily outreaching in economic potentialities any traditionally operated feudal estate, lay or ecclesiastical. At about the same time Adwert in Holland had about 200 *conversi*; in the early years of the thirteenth century Clairvaux and the Rhenish Himmerod maintained each about 200 brothers; in 1280 Walkenried in Brunswick had 180 *conversi*; as late as 1323, the Swabian Salem had 160 brothers. In 1187 the population of the English Waverley included 120 lay-brothers, while scores of other prosperous abbeys cultivated their lands with the help of about 100 lay-brothers. According to the calculations of Knowles and Hadcock, an average English Cistercian establishment could expect to have within a few years after its foundation 36 monks and 50 brothers; the same authorities estimated the total number of Cistercian lay-brothers in England and Wales early in the thirteenth century at about 3,200.

How can the successful recruiting and holding of such armies of lay-brothers be explained? In searching for an adequate answer the economic and social conditions of Western Europe must first be considered. At the time of Cîteaux's foundation the disintegration of the traditional manorial system had already begun. A growing rural population could no longer be absorbed by those static and antiquated agrarian units. The disturbed equilibrium set a considerable portion of dependent peasantry in motion, searching for a better life and more promising employment. Such conditions drove tens of thousands into the crusading armies, lured others into the growing and prosperous cities, furnished the masses for the drive toward the east, where land was still plentiful and taxes lighter. Dissatisfaction with rural conditions might also explain the willingness of restless peasantry to join as lay-brothers the fast-multiplying Cistercian establishments.

Independent of such motivations, as many authorities have pointed out with obvious justification, the attraction of Cistercian estates lay in the fact that the monks as landlords were generally kindlier toward the peasantry and less demanding than lay-lords. The difference in some cases, as in Scotland, was so conspicuous that it alone could explain the large number of lay-brother vocations.

That the desire to escape poverty and insecurity by entering a great and prosperous abbey was a powerful incentive in a majority of applications can be supported by many witnesses. The anonymous author of the *Libellus de diversis ordinibus (Booklet on Different Orders)*, observed about 1150 that "we see many men fleeing from cruel masters and taking refuge under the lordship of churches." Abbot Conrad of Eberbach in his *Exordium magnum* quoted Saint Bernard rebuking a dying lay-brother for his presumptuous belief in his inevitable salvation: "What did you say? How could you come to such a daring audacity? Aren't you the poor and miserable man who, having nothing or almost nothing in this world, was driven to us, perhaps more by necessity than by the fear of God, obtaining admission after much supplication? We received you for God's sake as an indigent and made you equal in food and clothing with all other members of this community who have been with us, wise and noble men, and you became one of them." The historicity of this incident has, of course, no bearing on the demonstrative value of the quotation.

The Dominican Humbert of Romans (d. 1277) once preached a sermon to Cistercian lay-brothers and cited the example of one of their predecessors, prostrate before his abbot and asking for admission. When the abbot put to him the ritual question: "What do you seek?" the brother was supposed to answer: "The mercy of God and of the Order." But the good soul—real or fictional—forgot his line and in his simplicity answered: "White bread and often."

Security, more than economic pressure, must have been the motive of many who applied for admission at French abbeys, particularly, it seems, in Gascony. According to the chartulary of Gimont, during the second half of the twelfth century a large number of donations were made by small property owners under the condition that the donor or his sons would be admitted as lay-brothers. Thus, in 1175, a certain Raimond de Piamont donated to Abbot Humbert "all his rights he possessed in the parish of Causac, and for this gift the aforesaid Abbot is to receive him as lay-brother any time he wanted, also his two sons, as soon as they come to age." In 1161, at Berdoues, a certain Vitalis and his sister, Martha, donated their shares of a property to the abbey, whereupon both were assured that their sons would be received as lay-brothers.

Admission to the lay-brotherhood was by no means restricted to the lowborn or illiterate. According to the records of Himmerod, during the twelfth and thirteenth centuries, fifty nobles or knights were received as brothers. In such incidents the principal motive for joining the Order must have been religious in nature. Indeed, the just mentioned *Exordium magnum* abounds in stories featuring lay-brothers of great piety, exemplifying the appropriate virtues of humility, obedience, simplicity of heart and dedication to hard work.

It is from a more reliable source, the *Memorials of Fountains*, that the character of a truly remarkable lay-brother can be revived. His name was Sunnulphus. He lived at Fountains in the second half of the twelfth century, "a simple and illiterate man, but instructed by the Lord. Instead of books, he held on to his conscience; he had the Holy Spirit for a teacher; reading the book of experience, he grew daily in the knowledge of holy things and possessed even the spirit of revelations." It was Sunnulphus who was responsible for the conversion of the noble knight, Ralph Haget, who eventually became abbot of Fountains (1190-1203) and who recounted for the chronicler the story of his spiritual growth under the guidance of the holy brother, "sedulous in exhortation, efficacious in consolation, sweet in conversation, while always on the alert, lest his mouth would utter any idle words."

Obviously, the flourishing state of lay-brotherhood depended on the concurrence of a number of factors: quality and availability of such vocations; the attractive nature of Cistercian lay-brotherhood; the treatment of brothers within a community; the strength of religious motivation. Changes either in society, economy or religious disposition were bound to have an adverse effect on the institution, as much as would changing attitudes within the Order toward the brothers. Toward the end of the twelfth century changes on all levels were much in evidence.

The earliest signs of an altered posture of brotherhood within the Order was a statute of the General Chapter passed in 1188, demanding laconically that "noble laymen coming to our monasteries should become monks and not *conversi*." If one may attempt to discern the fathers' frame of mind from the context, the paragraph preceding this momentous decree must be of considerable significance. It was the famous passage banishing Gratian's *Decreta* from monastic libraries. Were both statutes indicative of the vanishing informality of early Cistercian life, giving way to a legalistic concept of monastic society? If that was the case, the impact of canon law was soon reinforced by the influence of Scholasticism, both tending to view life through principles, definitions and categories. Such a mentality could scarcely fit illiterate peasants and erudite noblemen into the same monastic community.

Monks became less and less concerned with the quality of soil and harvest, turning instead with much devotion to books, studies, preaching and missions. Lay-brothers, on the other hand, lived almost exclusively on the granges, rarely mingled with the monks, and they began to wonder if they were still one monastic family with them, serving under the same abbot in behalf of a common interest. Meanwhile, social theorists and critics of the early thirteenth century were having difficulties finding a proper category for lay-brothers, who were neither laymen, nor clerics, nor monks. Gautier de Coincy (d. 1236), grand-prior of Saint-Medard, found no place for them at all; the acceptance of peasant folks as lay-brothers merely turned their heads, he felt, causing them to consider themselves superior to the rest of the villagers.

Thus, the physical separation of lay-brothers from monks, accentuated by theoretical and legal considerations, reintroduced between the two groups the servant-master relationship, the very thing earlier generations had tried to avoid. In this light the rule of 1188 was entirely logical, perhaps not even necessary: a noble no longer could become a lay-brother without dishonoring his own peers.

Quickening changes in Western agrarian society were other reasons for the decrease of lay-brother vocations. By the end of the thirteenth century, serfdom had practically disappeared from Western Europe. The peasants had become free lease-holders, whose property steadily improved through intensive cultivation and the sale of agrarian produce to the ever growing cities. Poverty or uncertainty of future no longer served as major incentives for choosing the vocation of lay-brothers. The purely religious attraction of brotherhood still remained a force to reckon with, but those who felt its pull joined more likely the new and more popular mendicant orders, where the life of the brothers was easier and their social status higher.

The impact of decreasing lay-brother vocations was felt at some abbeys early in the thirteenth century. Since Cistercian economy depended entirely on them, compromises soon had to be attempted, either by lowering admission standards, or offering material benefits to the *conversi*, which amounted to the secularization of their status. Such remedies, however, touched off new and more serious problems and led to a complete breakdown of discipline and the eventual disappearance of the institution itself.

Visitors and the annual sessions of the General Chapter were beset by incidents of insubordination, while not even the harshest remedies seemed to have any beneficial effect.

In some cases, as in one recorded at the Chapter of 1262, the abbots, in order to avoid continuous difficulties disciplining the brothers, confided the granges to the *conversi* with full responsibility, the only obligation being the return of a regular rent. Thus the grange became a purely agricultural unit, the brothers lease-holders without religious character. In order to prevent a further decline in the already low quality of vocations, the Chapter of 1220 ordered a six-month period of probation (postulancy) for brothers preceding the novitiate. An attempt was made to develop the institution of *familiares*—an old form of intermediate status between hired workmen and lay-brothers—as a substitute for the missing labor. Sometimes called *donati* or *oblati*, they were in most cases devout laymen, who, for their labor, were supported by the abbey. They wore secular clothing, did not take vows, but simply promised obedience to the abbot and were treated as brothers. The General Chapters of the thirteenth century endeavored to transform them into lay-brothers without much success, but their numbers became considerable.

Meanwhile, instances of revolt among the *conversi* increased steadily. It took the form of intimidation of monks at abbatial elections, violent seizure of monastic property and even plots against the lives of abbots or other superiors. Simultaneously with these riotous incidents the wholesale apostasy of lay-brothers became a common phenomenon. Under the pressure of necessity, the Chapter agreed as early as 1237 that monasteries having no more than eight brothers might hire lay-servants for the kitchen. The permission was soon extended to all fields of monastic labor, and, as a result, ended in a complete change of economic administration. By the beginning of the fourteenth century, the once admirably efficient Cistercian direct cultivation had given way to the new rental system, in which monastic property came under the care of lease-holders who paid a regular rent; thus disappeared the distinctive character of Cistercian agrarian economy.

The problem of lay-brother vocations, however, was not a matter of equal seriousness throughout the continent. In Central and Eastern Europe the number of the *conversi* within the total monastic population was never overwhelming, and the ratio between monks and brothers remained quite stable until the fifteenth century. The explanation for the differences between East and West must be sought in the much slower economic and social development of the eastern countries, where serfdom outlived the Middle Ages, cities were fewer and smaller and commerce was slow to develop. For the same reason the influence of the lay-brotherhood on the economic life of eastern abbeys was never as decisive as it was in the West. Consequently the eventual decrease of the number of *conversi* did not create a crisis of such gravity as it did in England, France, the Rhineland and the Low Countries.

Even in Western Europe, the diminution of brothers was not necessarily precipitous and in a number of cases it reached the crisis proportion only after the great plague of 1347-1350. For lack of broad statistical evidence only some individual authorities and cases can be cited, but these seem to be significant in themselves.

Stephen Lexington, as abbot of Savigny, was much concerned with the economic condition of his filiation. Writing his instructions in the early 1230s, he ascribed many of the difficulties to the improper administration of the granges, and that, in turn, to the lack of lay-brothers. He found many granges operated by only one or two *conversi*. In order to make their burdens lighter, the Abbot gravely instructed the cellarers of these monasteries to permit the lonesome brothers to drink wine. He prohibited, however, the readmission of lay-brothers once dismissed for disciplinary reasons, and strongly opposed the transfer of granges to lay-brothers for rent.

Toward the middle of the thirteenth century the lay-brothers' discipline throughout the whole affiliation of Pontigny had become so bad that the formulary used by the abbot in composing charters of visitation offered a sample paragraph "against rebellious lay-brothers." It suggested that the visitor state that "we found the *conversi* of this house more contumacious

342

and senseless than elsewhere, insolent and notorious for constantly fighting and cursing. . . ." The formulary then advised the visitor as punishment "to take away their religious habits and reduce them to the rank of *familiares*."

The abbot of Pontigny was not alone in his blanket condemnation of lay-brotherhood. The satirical literature of the thirteenth century often took aim at the *conversi*, conveniently rhyming with *perversi*. The *Speculum stultorum* of Nigel Wireker (d.c. 1207), whose work became popular only in the fourteenth century, featured among others the malicious character of Fromond the lay-brother, whose encounter with the hero of the poem, Brunellus the donkey, ended with the brother being kicked into the Rhône.

The rise and fall of population of individual abbeys can rarely be followed through a sequence of reliable figures. A study of the monastic personnel of Ebrach in the diocese of Würzburg seems to indicate that the abbey held a steady number of lay-brothers, about half of the total population, until 1350. During the administration of Abbot Frederick (1306-1327), out of 174 names taken from various documents, 72 were lay-brothers. Under Abbot Otto (1349-1385), the total dropped to 67, which included 21 *conversi*. From this point on the number of lay-brothers continued to decline and toward the end of the fifteenth century they practically disappeared from the scene.

The population of Les Dunes suffered a similar fate. Until the middle of the fourteenth century the number of lay-brothers remained significant, but after 1354 the extant records fail to mention *conversi* at all. Most great German abbeys held on to their lay-brothers throughout the thirteenth century and only the second half of the fourteenth century showed a drastic drop in their numbers. Thus Camp, north of Cologne, had in 1280 the same number of monks and brothers: 72. In 1300, there were still 75 *conversi*, but the records of 1355 showed only 22 monks without accounting for brothers. Lay-brothers at Salem decreased between 1323-1377 from 160 to 80. In the case of Himmerod, consecutive figures are not available, but from 200 in 1200, the population of *conversi* had melted to 9 by 1450. Eberbach, which in the twelfth century had about 60 monks and 200 lay-brothers, by 1400 had increased the number of monks to 80, but the number of brothers had dropped to 50. The Silesian Heinrichau never had a large number of *conversi*, but in 1300 the abbey was still housing 50 of them; in 1336 only 30; by 1400 the figure had sunk to 20, and by 1430 only 5 brothers survived. Meanwhile, in the Spanish Poblet—if the figures can be relied upon—the opposite development took place. Throughout the fourteenth and fifteenth centuries the number of choir monks remained about the same (90), but the number of lay-brothers grew between 1311 and 1493 from 85 to 135, in spite of fearful losses (60 monks and 30 brothers) suffered in the plague of 1348.

The Cistercian population of England is somewhat better researched. Beaulieu, as late as about 1280, had 58 monks, 7 novices and 68 lay-brothers. In 1336 the Welsh Margam still housed 38 monks and 40 brothers. Meaux in 1249 accounted for 60 monks and 90 brothers, but the decrease of the latter continued throughout the thirteenth century, so that before the plague attacked in 1349, only 7 of them had remained. The records of 1393 show no brothers at all. Similarly, low numbers were given before the plague at Bordesley (34 monks, 10 brothers) and Newenham (23 monks, 3 brothers), while Vale Royal in 1336 had 21 monks, but probably no lay-brothers.

The final blow to the lay-brotherhood in England came undoubtedly from the terrible visitation of the Black Death in 1349. According to the figures of the poll tax taken between 1377 and 1381, the number of lay-brothers was everywhere smaller than that of the monks. Data from seventeen abbeys showed that the total number of monks in them was 277, but that of the brothers only 56. In 1381 there were only 3 *conversi* at the once populous Rievaulx, 2 at Jervaulx, one at Bordesley and Roche, none at Vaudey, Revesby, Saint Mary Graces and Holmcultram. Other houses recorded somewhat greater numbers: Fountains had 10 *conversi*, Furness 8, Kirkstall 6.

While smaller communities had to learn to live without lay-brothers, some great houses of the Order managed to attract a considerable number of *conversi* even after the Reformation. Cîteaux in 1589 had, in addition to 60 choir monks, 30 *conversi*. A visitation at Clairvaux in 1624 found 32 brothers. Abbot Saulieu of Clairvaux on his tour of Spain in the early 1530s found at Poblet 60 monks and 30 *conversi*; at the nearby Santes Creus 36 monks and 12 brothers; at Piedra 33 monks and 27 brothers. Santa Fé housed 29 monks and 16 *conversi*. When Abbot General Boucherat visited Germany in 1573, the only abbey where he found a substantial group of lay-brothers was Salem, but even there only 12 of them assisted the 56 priests. By 1643 Les Dunes was populated again by 44 priests and 16 brothers. As late as 1759 Villers still had 54 monks and 19 lay-brothers. Throughout the eighteenth century few Austrian abbeys had lay-brothers in significant numbers. Heiligenkreuz had the most of them; there, in 1758, 13 brothers helped 56 priests.

Elsewhere attempts were made to minimize the ill effects of missing brothers by trying to revive the semi-religious groups of *oblati* or *donati*. This was suggested in 1612 at an abbatial convention at Loos in Flanders and coupled with a decision to discontinue the admission of *conversi* altogether. The background of this move was probably another flare-up of the old debate, whether lay-brothers were truly religious tied to the Order by profession, or merely laymen linked to communities by simple promises without canonical consequences.

In attracting lay-brothers, the more successful was certainly the Strict Observance. Orval in 1757 had 49 priests and 28 brothers; Sept-Fons numbered in 1789 39 brothers, while La Trappe had in the same year 36 *conversi*. These cases, however, were the exceptions and according to all indications, beginning with the fifteenth century, Cistercian lay-brotherhood ceased to be a major factor in monastic economy, although the continued presence of the *conversi* had undoubtedly a beneficial effect on the life of these more fortunate communities.

The nineteenth-century Trappist revival featured a most remarkable upsurge of the lay-brotherhood. This movement, however, cannot be considered as the reappearance of the twelfth-century *conversi*; rather, it was an approach to lay-monasticism, much closer to the structure of the sixth-century abbeys of Saint Benedict than to Cîteaux. Accordingly, the difference between priests and brothers was de-emphasized by increased participation of priests in manual labor and by insuring to the brothers a larger part in community responsibilities.

While the admission of lay-brothers at Cîteaux emerged only as a second thought, as a matter of economic necessity, the influx of laymen to nineteenth-century Trappist houses was motivated by the belief that the full realization of monastic ideals was not dependent on holy orders; therefore it was equally attainable by the laity. The trend toward a progressive elimination of differences between the two groups within the same community has continued throughout the twentieth century and received a powerful impetus by the Second Vatican Council, stating in the decree on the renewal of religious life that "communities of men which are not exclusively lay in their character, can admit both clergy and laity on the same basis and with equal rights and duties, excepting those which result from ordination."

The renewal-sessions of the General Chapter in both Cistercian Observances dealt extensively with the implementation of this decree. The Trappists have eventually eliminated the term "lay-brother"; all members of the Order are simply "monks," enjoying equal rights, carrying equal duties and sharing similar occupations within their communities, excepting the privileges derived from the Holy Orders.

The Common Observance took the position that the fate of lay-brotherhood should be determined by each community, giving due consideration to local needs, traditions and the wishes of the membership. The retention or abolition of lay-brotherhood, therefore, remains a local option until an undisputed consensus reaches a more conclusive decision.

XXII

Cistercian Nuns

The founders of Cîteaux had no intention of establishing a new order of monks, much less of initiating an order of Cistercian nuns. Nevertheless, at a place called Tart, some ten kilometers north of Cîteaux, a foundation was made in 1125 for pious women, who were determined to imitate the austere example of the Cistercian monks.

As Cîteaux took its origin from Molesme, so Tart sprang from Jully, a nunnery sponsored about 1113 by Abbot Guy of Molesme, Saint Robert's immediate successor. It was at Jully that, under the direction of the abbot of Molesme, the wives and female relatives of the monks of Molesme congregated. The population of Jully increased considerably after Saint Bernard and his companions had joined Cîteaux, for the wives and sisters of these men, too, sought refuge at Jully. Eventually Bernard's own sister, Humbelina, was received into the same community and became prioress about 1128.

The circumstances of the foundation of Tart are not entirely clear, but the first written documents name as principal sponsors the bishop of Langres with his cathedral chapter, the ducal family of Burgundy and Stephen Harding, abbot of Cîteaux. The pioneer group of nuns came from the overflowing population of Jully, headed by Elizabeth de Vergy, who was probably the daughter of the countess by the same name, known as the generous benefactress and friend of Abbot Stephen. There is no doubt that the solicitude and moral support of the saintly abbot of Cîteaux was an important factor in the successful settlement of the nuns; on the other hand, there is no evidence that the Cistercian General Chapter took any responsibility for the move or that monks of the Order were in any way engaged in the spiritual or material care of the new community. Throughout the twelfth century the General Chapter scrupulously maintained a policy of aloofness, lest involvement in the nuns' affairs endanger the purely comtemplative character of the Order.

The negative attitude of the General Chapter did not, however, prevent the inhabitants of Tart from modeling their lives after Cîteaux, and it is not impossible that Stephen Harding gave them some guidance in this direction. The early regulations of the nuns have not survived, but there is no reason to doubt that their ascetic standards and daily *horarium* were the same as the monks'. The agricultural labor of the nuns, however, was probably not as extensive as that of the monks.

In spite of the seemingly firm principles of noninterference, the absorption of the Congregations of Savigny and Obazine in 1147 created a new problem for Cîteaux. Both groups of monasteries included affiliated nunneries and arrangements concerning the merger failed to specify the nuns' place within the new organization. In the absence of clear directives, the former relation between the newly admitted abbeys and the nuns under their care continued. After 1147 Tart, too, came to be recognized as a foundation of Cîteaux, and therefore a member of the Cistercian family.

Meanwhile, without formal involvement of the General Chapter, the multiplication of Cistercian nunneries continued, although in a number of cases such foundations received aid or encouragement from individual Cistercian abbots. It was this situation that induced the abbess of Tart to take the initiative in organizing Cistercian nunneries, at least those situated in the Duchy and County of Burgundy. Toward the end of the twelfth century the abbess of Tart held annual chapters for her eighteen affiliated houses on Michaelmas (September 29) in the presence of the abbot of Cîteaux or his representative. The nature and organization of the convention was about the same as that of the General Chapter of Cîteaux, and in order to maintain a common discipline, the abbess of Tart claimed the right to visit and correct all her "daughters." Few of the records of the chapters of Tart have survived and in all likelihood no such sessions were held after the end of the fourteenth century.

A similar organization was set up in Castile and Leon among the numerous Cistercian nunneries. In 1187, King Alfonso VIII of Castile and his wife Eleanor sponsored the foundation in Burgos of Santa Maria la Real, popularly known as Las Huelgas. In 1188, upon the request of the king, Abbot William of Cîteaux recognized Las Huelgas as the "mother" of all other Cistercian convents in the kingdom and authorized the holding of chapters like those at Tart. In 1189 the first such chapter was held in the presence of a number of bishops and Cistercian abbots, but some nunneries, such as Tulebras in Navarre and its affiliations, failed to send representatives. When King Alfonso turned to the General Chapter of Cîteaux in 1191 with the request that the Chapter put pressure on the reluctant abbesses and force them to appear at Las Huelgas, the Chapter declined to act, asserting that it had no jurisdiction over nuns. According to the extant records of the General Chapter this was the first occasion that Cistercian nuns were subjects of discussion, even in a purely negative manner.

Eventually only about a dozen abbesses attended the chapters at Las Huelgas held on Martinmas (November 11). The organization was patterned after the Charter of Charity, but the authority of the abbess of Las Huelgas was greatly enhanced by the fact that the holder of that title was ordinarily a royal princess and all other members of the populous community were recruited from the ranks of Spanish nobility. This may furnish the background to the strange custom that the abbess of Las Huelgas arrogated priestly privileges, such as blessing novices, preaching homilies and hearing nuns' confessions. The abuse was stopped only by the energetic intervention of Innocent III in 1210.

After the incident of 1191 the first reference to nuns at the General Chapter was made in 1206—a prohibition against the education of boys in the nuns' convents. Then, in 1213, the chapter fathers suddenly declared that "nuns already incorporated in the Order should not leave freely [their cloisters]" and that in the future "no [convents] should be admitted to the union with the Order, unless fully cloistered." Undoubtedly, some time between 1190 and 1210 the gates of the Order had been forced open for the admission of nuns, although the process of "incorporation" was never specified by the Chapter and of all the possible conditions for closer affiliation only strict enclosure was emphasized.

The seemingly unexpected about-face of the chapter fathers was preceded by several significant developments. One of them was certainly the spontaneous growth of female establishments, which, without the formal consent of the Order, followed the rules of Cîteaux and called themselves Cistercians. As early as about 1150 the Benedictine Herman of Tournai referred to these determined women as "striving to conquer not only the world but their own sex as well; of their own free will they embraced violently, nay joyfully, the Order of Cîteaux, which many robust men and youths fear to enter. Laying aside all linen garments and furs, they wore only woolen tunics. They did not only womens' work, such as spinning and weaving, but they went out and worked in the fields, digging, cutting down and uprooting the forest with axe and mattock, tearing up thorns and briers, laboring assiduously with their hands and seeking their food in silence. Imitating in all things the monks of Clairvaux, they proved the truth of the Lord's saying, that to the believer all things are possible."

Early in the thirteenth century another keen observer, Cardinal Jacques de Vitry, reported that "Cistercian nunneries multiplied like stars in the sky," citing the foundation of seven convents in quick succession in the

349

single diocese of Liège. The same author went even further and established a relationship between the nuns' pressure on Cîteaux and the decision of the Premonstratensian general chapter to suppress the order's double monasteries for both canons and nuns and prohibit the further incorporation of nunneries. The date of this decree, 1198, coincided with the probable date when the Cistercian General Chapter changed its forbidding attitude and came to the aid of the sisters, abandoned by their erstwhile patrons, the Premonstratensians.

Cistercian willingness to assume the hitherto declined "care of the nuns" (cura monialium) must have been significantly motivated by the informal but largely beneficial relation between monks and nuns that had already existed before the turn of the century. This is particularly demonstrable in the cases of the great Rhenish and Flemish abbeys, where the happy association with nuns began with the admiration of Saint Bernard for Saint Hildegarde of Bingen (d. 1179) and the latter's friendship with the monks of Villers in Brabant. The fascination of the community with the mystical revelations of the great Benedictine abbess generated an ever increasing interest in similar matters, turning the monks' attention toward the informal groups of devout women, known as Beguines. Throughout the thirteenth century Villers, followed by Aulne and Lieu-Saint-Bernard, took an active role in caring for Beguine communities. The monks gave them respectability, legal protection and theological guidance, while the Beguines inspired the monks with their deep spirituality and helped them to keep alive a devotional fervor at a time when other monasteries experienced the ebbing of their original zeal. At least within that geographical area, Cistercians took over the Premonstratensians' role and continued to guide the nuns until the arrival of the mendicant friars.

The principal problem that forced the General Chapter to be very circumspent in admitting nuns to the Order was enclosure. Canon law of the twelfth century was not sufficiently specific in the matter and it was the founding or "father" abbot who decided the actual limitations of the nuns' freedom to leave their cloisters. The spirit of the late eleventh-century reforms demanded strictness in the matter, consequently the abbots' responsibilities grew in proportion to the restriction of the nuns' freedom of movement. As long as the nuns were free to move in and out of the cloister and able to take care of their own needs, cultivate their estates, attend to matters of business, legal or social obligations, all they needed from the father abbot was a chaplain or confessor.

Abbots of the first Cistercian generation took a moderate position in the matter of enclosure. The nuns of Tart were free to do agricultural work outside the walls of the house. This became impossible only in 1184 through a bull of Lucius III imposing on the nuns a stricter rule of enclosure. About 1130, Abbot Hugh of Pontigny, the future bishop of Auxerre, approved a rule for nuns that permitted the sisters to leave their cloister and work in small groups on their fields. As late as 1194 a number of nuns visited Cîteaux on the feast of the dedication of the church and sang the office together with the monks. The same thing repeated itself in 1220 on a similar occasion at Savigny, where the nuns were even seated in the abbey's refectory. The General Chapter protested on both occasions, for by then the regulations of enclosure had become far more stringent and such "excesses" could no longer be tolerated.

When the point was reached that even the abbess was rarely permitted to cross the limits of the enclosure, the sponsoring abbot had to provide for all the needs of a totally enclosed, thus totally dependent, community. Abbesses were no longer permitted to visit their own foundations or to attend chapters or conventions of nuns. At that stage the respectability and good reputation of the convent depended greatly on the rigid enforcement of enclosure, and so the dilemma of the Cistercian General Chapter facing the problem was narrowed to a choice between absolute refusal or acceptance. A decision in favor of the latter involved grave and burdensome moral and material responsibilities.

The Chapter's acceptance of such liabilities in the first years of the thirteenth century opened a veritable floodgate and many abbots found themselves overwhelmed by their multifarious duties toward the nuns. In practical terms the "incorporation" benefited the nunneries by making them partakers of all Cistercian rights and privileges including exemption, but the General Chapter had to legislate for the convents, provide for each a qualified father abbot, who in turn had to furnish chaplains and confessors as well as procurators and lay-brothers in charge of the nuns' estates. The father abbot was to control admission to the convent and see to it that the number of nuns did not grow beyond their means of support. The abbot presided over professions and elections of abbesses; he was responsible for the discipline of the community through annual visitations; he was the first arbitrator in quarrels among the nuns, and he was their defender in litigations with outsiders. If a convent faced financial difficulties, the father abbot was to provide relief. If the gravity of problems suggested dispersion, translation or suppression of the convent, the General Chapter had to make the decision on the basis of the father abbot's report.

Whenever a father abbot had more than one convent under his care, his duties might easily grow to unmanageable proportions. This was the reason that as early as 1220 the General Chapter reversed itself and passed a resolution prohibiting any further incorporations of nunneries. The statute was not heeded, however, and in 1225 and 1228 the Chapter had to repeat the same decision. In 1239 the Chapter fathers claimed that the nonobservance of the law was causing grave scandals and threatened all transgressors with dire consequences. Since the nuns applying for admission often circumvented the prohibition by obtaining a papal brief supporting their desire, in 1222 the Chapter petitioned the Holy See to abstain from such interference in the future. After a number of forced admissions, the Chapter of 1251 finally obtained from Innocent IV the ultimate guaranty: the Order was free to ignore future papal briefs in the matter and to enforce a total halt to incorporations.

By the middle of the thirteenth century the big rush was over. New foundations or incorporations still occurred, but those who applied in vain at Cîteaux could easily find protection under the wings of the Dominicans and Franciscans. Over the multiplication of nunneries claiming to be Cistercian but not incorporated, and therefore remaining under diocesan authority, the General Chapter had no control and their numbers remained uncertain. At their peak the total number of convents was probably greater than that of the monasteries. In England and Wales there were only thirty-two convents, mostly priories; the numbers were even smaller in Ireland and Scandinavia. But the Low Countries had by the middle of the thirteenth century about seventy nunneries; Portugal had ten, Spain and Italy had about seventy each. In German lands, including Austria and Switzerland, there were as many as three hundred. France was somewhat behind, having about two hundred convents. According to a fifteenth-century list (Winter, III, 175-85) the total number of incorporated nunneries was 211.

The shortage of available monks during the thirteenth century demanded a rather peculiar compromise. The abbeys in charge of Cistercian convents accepted for the novitiate clerics and priests who were willing to work in nunneries, and who, after having been trained in Cistercian liturgy and spirituality, made their vows at the convent in the presence of the abbess and promised obedience to her. These priests lived permanently in the service of the sisters' community, wore the Cistercian habit, yet strictly speaking were not members of the Order because they did not belong to any monastery of men and their immediate superior was the abbess. This arrangement survived until the Council of Trent, whose canons fundamentally reformed monastic life for both sexes. According to the decisions of the Chapter of 1601, elderly members of the Order were

352

put in charge of the nuns' spiritual welfare. At the same time members of the Order or able and reliable laymen were given responsibility for the economic administration of the convent's possessions.

When the father abbot was unable to furnish for the nuns the needed lay-brother help, the convents were encouraged to admit lay-brothers themselves. Such people received some initial training with the monks, but made their profession to the abbess. They lived outside of the nuns' enclosure and were responsible for the estates and various workshops. After the virtual disappearance of lay-brotherhood the nuns were forced to rely on seculars, who, as devout laymen, might become *familiares*. In addition to the choir nuns most convents had a number of lay-sisters recruited from the lower echelons of society. Their duties were similar to those of the lay-brothers.

Because direct cultivation could never flourish on the farms of Cistercian nuns, their economic accomplishments and role in agricultural development lagged far behind the great abbeys of men, even though some of the convents were endowed with extensive possessions. The royal foundation of Las Huelgas near Burgos, for example, included the territory of sixty-four townships.

Medieval nunneries always held a prominent place in the structure of contemporary society. For widows and unmarried women of the higher classes there was scarcely any other acceptable state of life than the sisterhood; conceivably the majority of conventual personnel consisted of women for whom the religious vocation was only a second choice. Nevertheless, as long as the vigor of medieval religious ideals remained intact, such an arrangement never impaired the atmosphere of a deep and sincerely devout spirituality. This social background was also responsible for the fact that in a large number of nunneries only members of the nobility were admitted to the rank of choir sisters, while the dignity of abbess in particular was reserved for the highest aristocracy, in some instances for royal princesses. Furthermore, for girls belonging to the upper class, the convent offered for a long time the only possibility of obtaining higher education, and while Cistercian monasteries refused to admit boys, Cistercian nuns always received girls for education. Saint Mechtilde of Hackeborn entered a Cistercian convent at the age of seven, Saint Gertrude the Great at four. The curriculum was basically the same as in monastic or chapter-schools for boys, and frequently included a full course of the *trivium* and *quadrivium,* since Latin was indispensable for the daily office and spiritual reading. The higher grades of the convent-school were usually reserved for the girls who wanted to join the

353

community. The regulations of the Chapter of 1601 explicitly decreed that above the age of twelve only those girls who had religious vocation should be educated within the convents.

Cistercian convents of the thirteenth and fourteenth centuries were influential centers of the new spirituality inaugurated by Saint Bernard. Some of his congenial followers contributed essentially to the edifice of Christian mysticism and their writings have never ceased to inspire god-loving souls. Among many others, the convent of Helfta in Saxony, during the long regime of Abbess Gertrude of Hackeborn (1251-1292), developed into an important school of mystics, although the nunnery belonged to the large number of the nonincorporated houses. The abbess's sister, Mechtilde of Hackeborn, and Gertrude the Great, the latter living at the same time in the convent as a simple nun, were both well known for their revelations. Another great mystic of the era, Mechtilde of Magdeburg, also spent the last years of her life at Helfta.

This group of nuns belonged to the early promoters of the devotion to the Sacred Heart of Jesus. A circle of convents with the same type of spirituality was formed around the abbey of Villers in Brabant. Their chief glory was Saint Lutgarde of Aywières (d. 1246) whose visions of the Lord showing her His pierced heart constituted the first recorded revelation of the heart of Jesus. Other distinguished members of the same group were Blessed Ida of Louvain, who received the stigmata, and two others of the same name, both nuns of the convent of La Ramée in Brabant, a renowned center of sanctity and letters. Blessed Aleydis of Schaarbeck, a nun of La Cambre, near Brussels, suffered the martyrdom of leprosy while healing others by her simple touch. At that time there were many noble ladies who spent only their last years in a Cistercian convent, yet reached a high degree of holiness: Blessed Jeanne, daughter of Baldwin, first Latin emperor of Constantinople, who ended her days at Marquette near Lille; Saint Hedwig, the patroness of Silesia and maternal aunt of Saint Elizabeth of Hungary, who after the death of her husband, Duke Henry of Silesia, finished her life at the convent of Trebnitz, where her daughter was abbess.

Any attempt to present a comprehensive view of medieval convents should avoid generalizations as much as possible. Differences among various institutions were so great that the exceptions seem more numerous than the cases fitting into preconceived categories.

In wealth and population the French royal foundations towered over a number of small and perpetually struggling communities. The great Maubuisson, erected in 1236 in the finest Gothic by Blanche of Castile, mother of Louis IX, was lavishly endowed and ready to accommodate 140 nuns recruited from the highest nobility. Several other abbeys, such as Notre-Dame-du-Lys and Port-Royal, were founded with similar generosity. But riches and social distinction attracted to these convents too many women whose only motive for admission was the fact that they were unmarried. After the establishment of the commendatory system the abbesses were appointed at royal whims, activated by social or dynastic convenience.

The most glaring of such abuses was the appointment of Angélique d'Estrées in 1597 by Henry IV as abbess of Maubuisson. The mother of twelve children by a long string of lovers, she was also the sister of the *belle* Gabrielle, the king's influential mistress, who was responsible for the scandalous arrangement. Over the tomb of the saintly Queen Blanche the last vestiges of religious observance gave way to endless rounds of gallant social events. As long as the king was alive, however, no power could dislodge the unworthy woman. It was only in 1618 that Abbot General Nicolas Boucherat managed, with military assistance, to penetrate the convent and put the abbess to flight.

Closer to the image of an average community was the Italian Rifreddo at the foot of the Alps. After its foundation in 1220, the nuns had to wait for twenty years until they were incorporated by means of a papal brief. But the benefits of public esteem and administrative assistance did not seem to compensate the nuns for their loss of freedom. Strict enclosure forced them to abandon the management of their lands and made them entirely dependent on their new "father," the abbot of Staffarda. Since the monks never could furnish lay-brothers in sufficient numbers, Rifreddo's estates had to be leased for a fixed annual rent which allowed for the support of about twenty nuns. Disillusionment over the arrangement was followed by decades of litigation between the monks and the unhappy nuns.

The early abandonment of independent cultivation of landed estates and reliance on rents and tithes was a characteristic trait of the nuns' economy, which resulted in a rigorous limitation of membership. This was the prime object of the visitation of Stephen Lexington as abbot of Savigny, when in the 1230s he inspected the nunneries dependent on his abbey. He was much upset by the indebtedness of several convents and prohibited the taking of loans in excess of ten *livres tournois* without his permission. Conscious of the "daily increase and multiplication of malice in this world," he distrusted the nuns' ability to take care of themselves. As long as he could afford it, he was willing to furnish a small community of monks and brothers to be in charge of all administrative duties in the nunneries. At Monce, in the diocese of Tours, he found the nuns in

355

financial difficulties. He therefore reduced their numbers from thirty to twenty-eight, but gave them for their assistance four priests and two lay-brothers. Another of the problems seemed to be indiscriminate hospitality. The stern Abbot Stephen prohibited the nuns from offering shelter to "wandering students [*goliardi*] or other vagabonds pretending to be priests . . . as well as to dissolute laymen." Only the "manifestly sick and truly poor" could be received and even monks or brothers were to be told to seek hospitality at neighboring monasteries. The warning included female visitors as well. Pregnant women or persons of ill repute were to be kept out, although mothers with small children might be admitted if they were poor and their offspring were less than four years old.

Les Blanches, one of the earliest foundations of Savigny (1105), was evidently well endowed, so Stephen merely insisted that the number of nuns should not exceed fifty. But the community lacked sufficient lay-sisters and therefore had to employ a number of servants. These had to promise fidelity to the convent and chastity as long as they remained in service and were also made to vow not to disclose the secrets of the house to outsiders. No girls under twelve were to be admitted and they had to wait until nineteen before beginning their novitiate. The latter rule, however, proved to be rather flexible. At Saint-Antoine-des-Champs, on the outskirts of Paris, the abbot of Savigny agreed to the reception of girls at the "age of discretion," which was, in his judgment, eight. At Port-Royal he warned the nuns not to exceed the set number of sixty, "lest the imprudent multiplication of membership would force them, [like] the daughters of Job, to go about begging," gravely endangering their souls and seriously injuring their good reputation.

A general decline of nunneries began in the fourteenth century for the same reasons that led to the grievous problems afflicting the monks. In the midst of disasters caused by war or pestilence, nunneries were even less resistant than abbeys for men. Many of them abandoned their rural cloisters and moved permanently to fortified cities, others became so badly depopulated that they had to be suppressed. In a few cases several much reduced communities merged into one. In case of suppression the closest Cistercian abbeys inherited the estates. If the abbeys still had sufficient personnel, they converted the abandoned houses into monasteries. In such matters the General Chapter made the final decision and from 1350 to 1450 scores of drastic measures were taken. In 1393, for example, the convent of Beaufay was suppressed and its goods were incorporated by Morimond, because there were only two nuns left within the completely ruined cloister, divine services had ceased, and there was no hope for a successful revival. Financial distress became so widespread that as early as 1339 the General Chapter dispensed all Cistercian nunneries from making customary contributions to the central administration of the Order.

In the surviving communities of nuns the maintenance of discipline became an equally vexing problem. From the end of the fourteenth century the General Chapter found itself frequently engaged in disciplinary measures against convents of lax or even scandalous conduct. Luxury in clothing, food and living quarters and the violation of enclosure were the most common charges, partly resulting from the practice whereby noble ladies moved into the convents as "pensioners," followed by their maid servants, and their example was imitated by the sisters themselves. The measures applied against recalcitrant houses were more than once extremely drastic. Nevertheless, not even the severest reprisals could halt the general decline; moreover, in this process of deterioration, the male branch of the Order was not entirely blameless either. The regular visitations of father abbots became more and more rare or ceased entirely; the spiritual care of convents was neglected or assumed by priests of other orders; and the example set by the neighboring monasteries was not always an edifying one.

The climax of the general dissolution was reached in the Reformation, when in Germany the majority of Cistercian convents were secularized and the nuns dispersed. It is worth mentioning that Luther's wife, Catharine of Bora, had formerly been a Cistercian nun. A substantial number of German convents, however, survived the Reformation. In 1573-1574, a tour of visitation throughout the country by Abbot General Nicolas Boucherat I revealed that there remained seventy-one sufficiently populated communities with a total of 972 choir nuns, 389 lay-sisters, 73 novices and 68 postulants. However, the century of religious conflicts and the wars of Louis XIV made the lives of Cistercian nunneries extremely precarious. The Rhineland and Flanders, the countries having the largest still flourishing convents, were exposed to the worst disasters caused by endless warfare. Elsewhere, particularly in Spain and France, the forces of the Counter-Reformation inspired vigorous movements of moral renewal.

Efforts for a wholesome reform among the nuns were made simultaneously with similar activities among the men. The General Chapter of 1601 passed detailed legislation for convents, re-emphasizing the duties of father abbots, chaplains and confessors, regulating the nuns' daily schedule, liturgy and spiritual exercises, the admission of new members, the administration of their goods, enforcing the strict enclosure and excluding lay personnel from convents. Abbot General Nicolas Boucherat II proved himself a zealous promoter of reform among the nuns. After having supported a number of local initiatives, in 1624 he issued a decree ordering the immediate enforcement of enclosure in all convents under his jurisdiction as a condition for admission of novices and valid professions.

In Spain reform was inaugurated in 1594 with the support of the abbess of Las Huelgas. Under her tutorship a group of nuns moved in 1595 to Valladolid where they founded the convent of Saint Joachim and Saint Anne. They called themselves "Recollects," dedicated to the strict observance of the Rule of Saint Benedict. The movement spread to about a dozen other communities, which formed together the "Federation of Valladolid." The organization survived the nineteenth-century wave of secularization and in 1955 merged with the nuns of the "Spanish Federation of Regular Observance."

Savoy proved to be another country of vigorous religious reform, inspired by the great bishop of Geneva, Saint Francis de Sales (1567-1622). It was with his assistance that in 1617 a distant relative of his, Louise de Ballon, attempted to strengthen the relaxed discipline in the convent of Saint Catherine. The resistance of certain nuns, however, was so fierce that in 1622 the reformers were forced to move to Rumilly, where they made a new foundation. This convent flourished beyond expectations, and the reform spread to fifteen other nunneries, forming the congregation of the "Bernardines of the Divine Providence," no longer under Cîteaux's authority. The constitution of the new organization was patterned after that of the Visitandines, the order of nuns created under the guidance of Saint Francis de Sales, and it was approved by the Holy See in 1634. At the outbreak of the French Revolution this congregation numbered twenty-five convents.

While Mother Ballon was battling with the reluctant nuns of Saint Catherine, another devout woman, Louise de Ponçonas, went through a similar experience in the community of Ayes in the province of Dauphiné. Under the advice of the same Saint Francis, she joined the nuns of Rumilly in 1623 and became mistress of novices under Mother Ballon. But the two reformers failed to see eye to eye and soon their paths parted. The group following Mother Ponçonas, after several foundations, settled down in Paris, where they lived according to the early regulations of Cistercian nuns. The small group of only three convents adopted the name of "Bernardines of the Precious Blood"; their regulations were approved in 1661 by Jean Jouaud, vicar general of the Cistercian Strict Observance.

The reform of Tart, the first convent of Cistercian nuns, began in the early years of the seventeenth century, but became the subject of considerable publicity only after the royal appointment as abbess of

Jeanne de Courcelles de Pourlans in 1617. Nicolas Boucherat II, the father abbot of Tart, warmly supported the move, but his role was soon eclipsed by that of Sébastien Zamet, bishop of Langres. The latter was an influential prelate of great ambitions, who envisioned a reform-congregation of nuns organized under his auspices. In 1623 the community moved to Dijon and a new set of regulations of great austerity was approved by the General Chapter of the same year.

After the death of Boucherat, his successor, Pierre Nivelle, resented Zamet's meddling in the affair and tried to regain authority over the nuns. Zamet, with the full support of the nuns, reacted by obtaining a brief in Rome granting him full jurisdiction over the convent, whereupon Nivelle excommunicated the abbess and turned with his grievances to the Parlement of Dijon. Zamet not only won the case, but also secured from Louis XIII the right of electing abbesses for three-year terms. The next step in Zamet's plan was the formation of a new order of nuns dedicated to perpetual adoration under the name "Daughters of the Holy Sacrament." The members of the new organization were to be Port-Royal, Lys and Tart with her affiliated houses. The ambitious bishop spared no effort on behalf of the project, but he was unable to overcome the problems of conflicting interests and influences and the plan was abandoned.

The reform that created the greatest stir throughout France and beyond was that of Port-Royal. The story of this famed convent has been told and retold innumerable times, for it was among the nuns that the first Jansenists found shelter and enthusiastic support, and drew the whole community into that celebrated but eventually tragic controversy. The latter phase in the sequence of dramatic events occurred long after Port-Royal had left the Cistercian Order; here, therefore, only a few words about the beginnings of the movement should suffice.

Port-Royal, near Versailles, was established in 1204, and within a short time grew to be a prosperous and populous community. By the end of the sixteenth century, however, like many similar institutions, the convent had been much reduced in every respect. The twelve inhabitants lived a relaxed life without enclosure. As was not very uncommon under Henry IV, a child of seven was appointed as coadjutrix to the elderly abbess, and in 1602, the girl, by then not quite eleven, but gravely pretending she was eighteen, was invested as abbess. Her name was Angélique Arnauld, daughter of a wealthy and influential Parisian lawyer. She did not seem much different from her carefree companions, until, after having heard a sermon of a visiting Capuchin friar, she experienced a sudden conversion. Then, in a scene made unforgettable by her later admirers, she, with all the audacity of her eighteen years, shut the gate of the cloister in the face of her visiting parents and reintroduced the rule of enclosure. The date was September 25, 1609, the famous "Day of the Convent Wicket" (*Journée du Guichet*), a strange blend of drama and comedy.

From that day forward a whole galaxy of devout souls flocked around Port-Royal, all wishing to assist the young heroine and competing with one another for the distinction of championing her admirable reform. For a short while Abbot Maugier of La Charmoye seemed to have a chance of linking the community with the Cistercian Strict Observance. Then the influence of Saint Francis de Sales became prominent, broken only by his death in 1622. He was followed by Bishop Zamet, who almost succeeded in convincing Angélique of the necessity of founding a new order with Tart and Lys. The plan was only partially executed, but, as a compensation, Mother Angélique managed to reform Maubuisson after the ouster of her infamous namesake. The decisive role, however, was reserved to the Abbé de Saint-Cyran, who first guided the spellbound nuns in the direction of Jansenism.

Port-Royal's break with Cîteaux came at the same time as that of Tart, and for the same reason: Zamet convinced Mother Angélique that the new general of Cîteaux, Pierre Nivelle, was an enemy of reform, therefore she could never succeed as long as the community was under Nivelle's jurisdiction. After appropriate steps in Rome, in 1627 Urban VIII exempted Port-Royal from the general's authority and placed the autonomous convent under the jurisdiction of the archbishop of Paris. The turbulent events leading toward the suppression of Port-Royal in 1709 and the revengeful demolition of its church and cloister two years later, do not belong to Cistercian history.

There were several other local reforms of lesser publicity throughout France. Les Blanches, which in 1590 had only three nuns including the prioress, recovered under Isabelle de Saussay (1604-1631) and by 1641 the community numbered thirty choir nuns and ten lay-sisters. The ancient Savigniac convent of Villers-Canivet was reformed under Hélène de la Moricière (1593-1636), founded a new convent at Torigny, and played a very active role in the religious renewal of Normandy later in the century. In 1681 the nunnery was raised from priory to abbey and in 1705 numbered twenty-four choir nuns and nine lay-sisters.

The regulations of Torigny were approved by Abbot General Nivelle, although they called for triennially elected prioresses. The community maintained a boarding school for girls. Toward the end of the century Torigny came under the influence of the Clairets, the convent reformed by Rancé, and joined the group of nunneries belonging to the Cistercian

Strict Oservance. In 1723 Torigny had twenty-one choir nuns and seven lay-sisters.

The institution of lay-sisters was often questioned and criticized within the Order early in the seventeenth century. Much of the argument was based on a bull of Pius V (1566-1572), who demanded that the admission of lay-sisters be discontinued. Edmond de la Croix of Cîteaux and Denis Largentier of Clairvaux believed that the professions of lay-sisters, and even of lay-brothers, were only simple promises without the juridical consequences of solemn vows. The papal bull, however, made little impact on age-old practices and eventually the opinion unholding the traditional status of professions for both lay-sisters and brothers prevailed.

During the course of the eighteenth century the strict regulations of the preceding reforms were often relaxed and many nunneries, in order to prove their social usefulness, opened schools or other protective institutions for girls. The outstanding example was that of La Cambre in Flanders. There the nuns operated a school of great reputation from the sixteenth century onward. In 1787, 150 girls were boarding at the abbey, many of whom enjoyed scholarships or were instructed without charge. In the same year the convent numbered thirty choir nuns and twenty-three lay-sisters. The majority of the nuns came from bourgeois families. The community was prosperous and, apparently, maintained a reasonable level of discipline, not, however, without the sophistication of the Age of Reason. In 1759 the nuns performed in the convent Molière's farcical comedy, "The doctor in spite of himself" (*Le médicin malgré lui*), distributing both male and female roles among themselves. In order to put some old-fashioned consciences at ease, the program featured a conspicuous remark assuring the audience that all was done "with the permission of our superiors."

The abbey of Herkenrode in the province of Limbourg (Belgium) was an example of communities where all postulants had to prove their nobility before admission. Among similar institutions this was the richest in the country, without redeeming features of social utility other than accommodating in comfort a number of unmarried women. A seventeenth-century abbess chose to engrave under her coat of arms the motto: "Abundance of God." As late as the end of the eighteenth century the community still drew an annual revenue of 95,000 florins, mostly from rents and tithes. Meanwhile monastic discipline had all but disappeared and there were attempts made to convert the institution into a house of canonesses. Herkenrode remained Cistercian until its suppression in 1797, but in name only. The twenty-five or thirty nuns lived in their own apartments, where they received guests, maintained a number of servants, and were free to leave the convent and spend extended vacations with their relatives.

The French Revolution closed all convents for nuns and the same policy prevailed along the path of French victories throughout continental Europe. The actual execution of such decrees, however, was not as thorough as it was with monasteries for men, therefore the number of surviving nunneries remained considerable, particularly in Spain.

During the course of the nineteenth-century revival some convents joined the fast-growing Trappist observance and preserved their contemplative characters. More active groups of nuns chose to join the Common Observance and engaged themselves in works of charity. In 1891, a total of eighty-six convents accepted varying degrees of dependence on the Common Observance with a membership of 1,629 choir nuns and 586 lay-sisters. In the same year twenty-eight convents belonged to the Strict Observance, having altogether 559 choir nuns and 596 lay-sisters.

Until 1953 neither the number of convents nor their personnel changed very significantly. In that year the total of institutions affiliated with the Common Observance was eighty-eight, accommodating 1,739 choir nuns and 688 lay-sisters. In the same year the statistics covering the Strict Observance accounted for thirty houses, with 879 choir nuns and 700 lay-sisters.

During the rest of the 1950s, the Trappistines experienced a considerable growth, increasing the number of their convents to forty-eight, housing over two thousand nuns. Then, the "renewal" of the 1960s led to a considerable reduction of vocations. By the end of 1972 they still held all their houses, but the number of professed choir nuns was 1,450 and that of the lay-sisters only 152. During this same period the nuns belonging to the Common Observance underwent a similar experience. In 1974 they possessed eighty-six houses with the total of 1,123 choir nuns and 240 lay-sisters. During the past few years lay-sisterhood in both observances underwent the same transformation as lay-brotherhood among the monks. The prevailing trend strives for the elimination of differences which traditionally had separated lay-sisters from choir nuns.

Thanks to the "renewal," the rules of enclosure have been much relaxed, enabling the nuns to hold regional meetings, even general chapters. The various "confederations" under the sponsorship of the Common Observance have held several fruitful sessions. The nuns under the rule of the Strict Observance organized their first general chapter in 1971; in 1975, their second general chapter, held in Rome, united 91 nuns, representing 49 convents. Between these two sessions of the chapter the possibility of five new foundations has emerged, attesting to the fact that the "vocational crisis" of earlier years has eased considerably. The growth of vocations for sisterhood in Japan is one of the most remarkable signs of changing trends.

XXIII

Daily Life and Customs

 Until the current wave of *aggiornamento* the most enduring and conspicuous feature of traditional monastic life was the daily *horarium*. It was the Rule itself which delineated the monks' routine activities, based on the "sacred number of seven" hours of the Divine Office: Lauds, Prime, Terce, Sext, None, Vespers and Compline. The unusual rising at about midnight for Matins found justification, in addition to its ascetic value, in the words of Psalm 118, where the "prophet" says: "At midnight I rose to give praise to thee."

According to the same immemorial tradition, the intervals between the hours of the Office were filled with manual labor and spiritual reading. All occupations of the monastic day were to be completed between the rising and the setting of the sun. Indeed, until reliable pendulum clocks came into use in the seventeenth century, the principal timepiece the monks had was the sun. This arrangement resulted in longer hours for work in the summer and more time for rest during the long nights of winter. Since, in addition to the seasonal changes in the length of day and night, the geographical degree of latitude of the location must also be considered, it remains always difficult to reduce the medieval monastic horarium to the modern reckoning of time. Bearing in mind such problems, the following tabulation may give an idea of how the monks' day was spent toward the middle of June and middle of December:

	June A.M.	December A.M.	
Rising	1:45	1:20	
Matins	2:00	1:35	
End of Matins	3:00	2:35	
Interval			
Lauds	3:10	7:00	Began at sunrise.
Interval			Private masses and *missa matutinalis*.
Prime	4:00	8:00	
Chapter			In winter the sequence was the follow-
Work	5:00		ing: Prime, mass, Terce, Chapter.
Terce	7:45	9:20	

Mass	8:00		
Reading	8:50		
Sext	10:40	11:20	
		P.M.	
Dinner	11:00	1:35	
Siesta	P.M.		
None	2:00		In winter the None was said before
Work	2:30		dinner and the dinner was followed by
Vespers	6:00	3:30	a period of reading.
Supper	6:45		In winter there was no evening meal.
Compline	7:30	4:00	
To bed	8:00	4:30	

In addition to the time for mass the Divine Office demanded, depending on the ranks of feasts, between three to four hours of the monks' time. Manual labor came close to six hours during the summer, but was less than two hours in winter. On the other hand, during winter more time was spent in reading and meditation, particularly in the long interval between Matins and Lauds. In midsummer the night rest was somewhat less than six hours, compensated for by a siesta after the noon meal. During winter there was no need for such a rest period, for the monks enjoyed uninterrupted sleep for over eight hours. The schedule of lay brothers was entirely different. They rose after the monks had finished Matins, but spent much more time in labor, except on Sundays and holydays, when they participated in many of the monks' devotions.

Since measuring the night hours was always difficult, a variety of customs determined the exact time of rising. The General Chapter of 1429 made an attempt to establish complete uniformity by demanding that in every abbey the sacristan give the signal for rising at 2:00 A.M. throughout the whole year, and at 1:00 A.M. on all Sundays and holydays. According to the Chapter of 1601, the rising on ordinary weekdays was to be delayed until 3:00 A.M. The Chapter of 1765 granted a further concession to communities with six or fewer members, who were permitted to begin their day at 4:00 A.M. Meanwhile, at La Trappe, and later in all abbeys of the Strict Observance, the original Cistercian *horarium* was followed until the 1960s.

An important event of the abbeys' daily routine was the "chapter" (*capitulum*), held ordinarily after Prime in the chapter hall located next to the sacristy on the cloister's eastern wing. Present were all professed members of the community; novices and lay-brothers held separate chapters. The meeting was intended to be both a forum for spiritual direction and occasion for administrative decisions.

First the martyrology was read, commemorating all saints celebrated on that day. Then followed the *Pretiosa,* a short monastic "morning prayer" and the reading of a passage from the Rule of Saint Benedict with an explanation or application by the presiding abbot or prior. On Sundays and holydays the Book of Usages or the statutes of the General Chapter were read and explained.

A less formal and more dramatic part of the chapter was introduced by the superior's summons to all present to step forward and accuse themselves of their public failings and transgressions of the numerous rules and regulations of the Order. In cases of obvious reticence other monks were permitted to accuse the suspected brethren. To each delinquent a penance was given, which ordinarily consisted of acts of humiliation, fasting, demotion from office or beating, administered on the spot. For serious crimes the punishments were excommunication, expulsion or prison, but against such sentences appeal to higher authorities was often permitted.

Terms in prison, although not mentioned in the Rule, were widely practiced instruments of monastic punishment in other orders, such as Cluny, but emerged at Cîteaux only among the acts of the General Chapter of 1206, merely permitting the building of prisons in each abbey. In 1230 it was prescribed, and the statute insisted that it be made "strong and secure." Since the dates coincided with recurrences of rampant indiscipline and rebellion among lay-brothers, one may suppose that these gloomy reminders of secular justice were adopted by the monks as means to deal with crimes of violence. The records of the General Chapter furnish ample evidence that from the second half of the thirteenth century prison sentences, often for life, were meted out liberally against "incorrigible and habitual criminals, thieves, incendiaries, forgers and murderers." Because of the discussion of such subjects at the daily chapter, the monks were obliged to keep strict secrecy.

The daily chapter was also the occasion of important announcements, appointments or elections of officials, and it was then that the prior assigned the monks their particular work or duty. On more festive occasions the abbot was expected to deliver an appropriate sermon. The admission of novices, investitures and professions were also held during chapter. The session ended with the commemoration of the deceased members of the community and the recitation of Psalm 129, the *De profundis,* and its concluding prayers. As was the case with other customs, the chapter's importance and frequency were greatly reduced during the fifteenth century, but the institution was fully restored within the Strict Observance.

The burden of manual labor was largely seasonal; heavier in summer, lighter in winter. Routine chores at the granges were the duties of lay-brothers, but at times of plowing or harvesting all able-bodied monks took part in the field work for as long as it was necessary. On such days the morning mass was said at an early hour and the whole community marched out carrying various tools to the fields, where they spent the rest of the day, praying and taking their meals where they happened to work. On these occasions the laws of fasting were suspended and extra drinks were served. The *Ecclesiastica officia* mentions specifically the distribution of a pound and a half of bread and a mixture of honey and milk for drink.

With the progressive leasing of monastic land the demand for agrarian labor greatly diminished and whatever still had to be done in the gardens or orchards surrounding the abbeys was assigned to the remaining lay-brothers. The question of how choir monks should be engaged in meaningful work remained a nagging and basically unsolved problem until the French Revolution.

Quoting the Rule of Saint Benedict, both chapters and visitors were in the habit of castigating idleness mercilessly, but each failed to prescribe a truly satisfactory remedy. A return to extensive and organized agricultural labor, when most monastic lands had already been cultivated by free peasant tenants, was evidently out of the question. Pastoral activity on a significant scale ran counter to both monastic tradition and the interests of secular clergy. Intellectual work would have presupposed organization, library facilities and steady encouragement, all of which were lacking among Cistercians. When the General Chapters of the fifteenth and sixteenth centuries urged the organization of archives and maintenance of libraries it implied merely practical needs, not the desire to facilitate research. What then should the monks do when not engaged in religious duties or exercises of piety?

The nature of the rather pathetic situation was strikingly revealed when the Chapter of 1601 ordered that ". . . for the avoidance of idleness all should be occupied at certain times with honest study of letters and spiritual reading or other works of piety, and, if there should be monks unschooled and unable to study, other works must be assigned to them, such as copying, painting, weaving, mending church ornaments, binding books and other similar activities, engaging them always in something, lest the devil seeking whom he may devour, should find them idle." All this, of course, was no substitute for organized, institutional labor which had made monasticism prosperous and revered in happier centuries. Nor was it particularly helpful when the same Chapter entrusted the cleaning of the monastery on Saturdays and vigils to the junior members of the community. Eventually, manual labor was scheduled twice weekly for all monks. Undoubtedly, the sight of a line of religious, marching off for some work of maintenance or gardening, must have been an edifying one; still it is doubtful that such occupations furnished sufficient outlet for creative energies or brought the degree of satisfaction which is indispensable to a healthy religious life. The problem was, however, certainly not felt as acutely in the Old Regime as it is today, for large segments of the upper classes, including the clergy, habitually enjoyed a life of leisure, supported by pensions and sinecures.

When monastic legislators came to the point of discussing meals, due emphasis was given to the virtues of temperance and mortification. Although the Rule of Saint Benedict displays a surprising degree of moderation, from September 14 (the feast of the Exaltation of the Holy Cross) to Easter it allows eating only once a day and prescribes total and perpetual abstinence from meat all year round.

Both of these prescriptions merely followed the tradition of earlier asceticism which, through the Rule, became characteristic traits of medieval monasticism. The convictions that a mortified body increases spiritual alertness and that abstinence is an effective weapon against carnal desires were shared by an unbroken line of Christian authors from the early fathers to late scholastics. The Cistercian attitude was aptly summarized by Saint Bernard in one of his sermons (no. 66) on the Song of Songs: "I abstain from meat, because by overfeeding the body I also feed carnal desires; I strive to take even bread with moderation, lest my heavy stomach hinder me in standing up for prayer."

Saint Thomas Aquinas conveyed the same message to a later generation of greater curiosity by asserting that "the Church rations the foods which afford most pleasure and stimulate our sexual appetites. Such is the flesh of animals who browse on earth and breathe the air, and their products, such as milk from mammals and eggs from birds. These foods we find more congenial; they afford us more pleasure and greater nourishment. A greater surplus for seminal matter is produced from their consumption, and its abundance sets up a pressure for lust. Here lies a reason for the Church's ordinance that we abstain from them when fasting."

Cistercian customs, following the Rule, permitted at the main meal the serving of a generous portion of bread, two cooked vegetables and, as a third dish, fruits in season. For supper, when there was one, green vegetables and fruits were given with the remaining portion of bread. On festival occasions a "pittance," such as white bread, fish, or similar monastic delicacies was added to dinner. Foundations for anniversary

368

masses often included pittances for the community, thus such fares tended to become weekly or even more common features of the table. No pittances could be served, however, on three consecutive days, nor during the session of the General Chapter. During Advent and Lent dietary restrictions excluded the use of animal fat, cheese or eggs. On the Fridays of Lent the monks fasted on bread and water. In addition to salt, only home-grown spices could be used in the preparation of cooked dishes.

The youngest members of the community, together with some others so favored because of infirmities, were permitted to have a breakfast (*mixtum*) before or after Sext. Originally it was nothing more than some bread dipped in wine and even this was suspended during Lent. In later centuries, however, breakfast was given to everybody and in the eighteenth century many abbeys offered the familiar choice of milk, tea or coffee, adding occasionally even a bowl of soup.

Another early and widely accepted custom was the serving of a drink (*biberes*) after None, particularly in summertime. It was either a cup of wine, or, if wine was in short supply, beer or cider. Beer was commonly produced in three different qualities, with higher or lower contents of alcohol. The best beer was the privilege of the abbot's table, or was served on special occasions in the refectory.

The abbot did not eat with his community. He had his own kitchen and table, which, according to the instructions of the Rule he shared with the guests whose presence was almost a matter of course. In the case of their rare absence the abbot was free to invite two monks to his table, although otherwise the abbot, as well as his guests, were to follow the same dietary laws as the rest of the community.

The community on entering the refectory passed by a usually ornate washing-fountain spouting water continually through a number of openings, where the monks were to wash their hands. Then they took their places on the outer side of long tables arranged in a U shape. They found the food already on the tables. After a Latin blessing they sat down, but reached out for the dishes only after the presiding prior uncovered the bread.

All meals were taken in total silence while a monk read aloud selected passages from the Latin Bible. In later centuries a paragraph from the Bible was followed by the reading from a book of edification in the vernacular. The reader used a lectern placed on an elevated platform attached to the wall. The routine was the same in the abbot's dining room, although he, for the sake of the guests, could cut the reading short, opening the way to edifying conversation. The same practice was eventually adopted in the monks' refectory at many abbeys. By then

369

reading throughout the whole dinner had become a mark of particular austerity, practiced mostly in the houses of the Strict Observance.

In countries where grapes could be cultivated the drink was wine, a beverage which had been approved with some reluctance by Saint Benedict. According to his Rule a monk's daily portion of wine was a *hemina,* which is estimated by the best authorities to be 0.75 liter, something less than a quart. This, in an earthenware pitcher, was placed in front of every monk, but the same amount had to suffice even if he took breakfast and supper. In colder climates wine was replaced by beer or cider. If at all possible, the drinking of water was avoided because of the notoriously unsanitary condition of most water supplies.

The proper behavior of monks during meals was the subject of minute regulations, lending to the occasion a semi-liturgical character. Cistercian table manners demanded the monks hold drinking cups in both hands, reach out for the salt with the tip of the knife and wipe the used tablewares with a piece of bread, not with the napkin. The meals were concluded by thanksgiving, during which the whole community marched in a procession to the church, where the ceremony ended.

As happened in other areas of discipline, dietary regulations tended toward a gradual relaxation, particularly in the matter of perpetual abstinence. The process started at the monastic infirmary, where the sick were permitted to eat meat until they regained their strength. Easy admission to the infirmary under various pretexts presented an opportunity to practically anybody to enjoy the flavor of a roast. The General Chapter of 1439, in silent approval of the practice, merely insisted that at any given occasion at least two-thirds of the community should eat the regular diet in the refectory, and that no individual should be given meat more than twice a week.

Early in the fourteenth century demands of hospitality and difficulties in obtaining vegetables presented other excuses. In a number of cases papal dispensations granted to individual abbeys had weakened the law of abstinence to such an extent that even the reform bull of Benedict XII, the *Benedictina* of 1335, not only failed to enforce the original observances, but exempted from perpetual abstinence retired abbots and the company of the abbot's table.

By 1473 local practices in abstinence had become so divergent that the General Chapter decided to turn to the Holy See for new regulations. Among other and more important things, the clarification of this issue was entrusted to the oft-mentioned abbatial delegation dispatched to Rome in 1475. A bull issued by Sixtus IV on December 13, 1475, declined to grant peremptory dispensation, but empowered the General Chapter and the abbot of Cîteaux to adapt the law of abstinence to the changed circumstances. Indeed, concessions by the Chapter in favor of a number of abbeys had multiplied so fast that within a decade perpetual abstinence became a thing of the past. The terms of the permission given to the German Eberbach in 1486 served as the new standard observance: meat courses were condoned three times weekly, on Sundays, Tuesdays and Thursdays.

At the English Whalley the administration of the last abbot of tragic fate, John Paslew (1507-1537), was an era of magnificence and plenty, enjoyed by the whole community. In 1520 the monks spent about two-thirds of their annual budget on food and drink and their table featured, among other delicacies, figs, dates, sugar candy and cakes. The brethren paid substantial amounts even for entertainment, for minstrels and bear-baiting.

The return to perpetual abstinence became the basic demand of the Strict Observance in the seventeenth century. The Apostolic Constitution of Alexander VII, the *In suprema* of 1666, praised the "abstinents'" intention, but permitted meat to the rest of the Order three times weekly; that is, it approved the old and widely practiced dispensation. The reform-movement, however, reintroduced a number of earlier austerities. With frank disapproval of such mortifications, a Bohemian delegate to the General Chapter of 1667, Abbot Laurence Scipio of Ossegg, reported on the dinners at Cîteaux: "At the dining table, which was always very regular, continual reading was going on without *benedicite* [sign to stop the reading] and the whole meal was over within less than an hour; never were served more than two, or at most three, courses, all prepared in miserable Burgundian style, with practically no spices. But the wine was quite good which, if someone preferred, could be mixed with water."

Austerity was never much of a concern on occasions of professions, ordinations, first masses or graduations of university students. Only the financial means of the community involved set limits to the sumptuous quality of the banquets.

In the eighteenth century, while the Strict Observance continued to adhere to perpetual abstinence, the Common Observance adopted current bourgeois standards with only occasional traces of monastic austerity. According to the account books of the College of Saint Bernard in Toulouse, the community of a dozen monks and their guests consumed in 1755 a considerable quantity of meat of great variety: beef (176 lbs.), mutton (284 lbs.), veal (216 lbs.), game, pork (108 lbs.), hens (107 pair), pigeons (69 pair), capons (50), chicken (228), turkey (15), geese (6), and ducks (14). The fact that fish (663 lbs.) and eggs (7,422) were the two

371

largest items on the list seems to imply that the community still had a lingering preference for the traditional monastic diet. Peculiar to the locale was the easy availability of Mediterranean fruits, which the monks often found on their table: oranges, lemons, chestnuts, olives, figs and raisins. Coffee was still a rarity served only on festive occasions. On the other hand, the community drank wine in considerable quantity. In the school-year of 1753-1754, ten monks, together with their servants and occasional guests, consumed, in addition to finer bottled brands, fifteen barrels of ordinary table wine, implying more than a liter per day per person. It was, however, only on one annual occasion when the monks went into pardonable extravagance. That was the feast of Saint Bernard (August 20), which coincided with the closing of the academic year. After a splendid high mass and a panegyric delivered by a noted guest preacher, the large company, including leading members of the local clergy and laity, settled along the dining table to enjoy endless courses of appetizers, entrees, a variety of meat and fowl, each accompanied by the appropriate vintage wines of Bordeaux. Cheese, exquisite desserts, coffee and brandy served as fitting conclusions to the grand occasion.

Until the seventeenth century the Cistercian daily schedule did not include recreation. This did not prevent the monks from opening their hearts to others, particularly if conversations could be justified by spiritual motivation. Thus, the General Chapter of 1232 clearly stated that "in order to avoid illicit conversations it is decreed that when the monks receive encouragement from the "guardian of order" [a minor monastic official] to speak, the conversation be on the miracles of saints, on subjects of edification and things pertaining to the salvation of souls, excluding detractions, controversies and other vanities."

The charter of visitation issued in 1523 for the College of Saint Bernard in Paris permitted annual excursions to the countryside under strict supervision. Walks for the sake of recreation were approved by the General Chapter of 1601, when it stated that "where it is desirable to leave the monastery for the sake of getting fresh air or recreation, walks serving this purpose should not lead too far nor be of longer duration than two or three hours, and [are permitted] only when the whole community, led by the prior, would go out." Daily periods of conversation after meals appeared in the schedule of the Parisian College in the 1630s. Similar arrangements were probably quite common in other houses as well, except in those under the control of the Strict Observance.

One peculiar monastic custom, necessitated by the rule of strict silence, was the use of a sign-language. It was introduced at Cluny under Abbot

Odo (926-942) and spread among the reform-congregations of the eleventh and twelfth centuries. Cîteaux passed no compulsory rules about its use, but adopted the sign-language probably from the one practiced at Molesme. The signs, formed with fingers and arms, could not be used for carrying on conversations and were designed merely for conveying simple messages or instructions. A surviving manuscript originating at Clairvaux contains a "dictionary" of 227 signs covering the same number of Latin words or terms. Similar devices elsewhere moved within the same basic range. Various restrictive rules passed by the General Chapter seem to indicate that sign-language was often used for jesting and creating fun, instead of for promoting the spirit of silence and recollection. The gradual relaxation of the rule of strict silence eliminated the grounds for the sign-language, which was later revived by the Strict Observance.

In their sleeping quarters the monks of early Cîteaux had made a valiant effort to follow the prescriptions of the Rule of Saint Benedict. Accordingly, the monks, no matter how numerous, were to sleep in the same common dormitory and they were to go to their austere bed fully dressed. The "bed" was a simple cot furnished with a straw-filled mattress, a pillow and a blanket. An added hardship was constituted by the Cistercian prohibition against having any source of heat in dormitories. Under northern climates, where the damp, frozen air penetrated these cavernous halls late in November to be driven out only by the early spring in April, the night demanded as much of the monks' endurance as the hard day's work.

No wonder, then, that the General Chapter was soon engaged in a losing battle on two fronts: trying to fend off constant efforts to provide some heat for the sleeping quarters of the monks, and to prevent the partitioning of common dormitories into small cells, made desirable by a growing emphasis on studies and desire for privacy. As early as in 1194 the Chapter punished the abbot of Longpont for having an "irregularly" constructed dormitory. Throughout the thirteenth century irregularities grew in number, so that by 1335 the *Benedictina* had to take up the challenge and enforce the old law by papal authority. Even so, the bull took exceptions in favor of the sick in the infirmary and for an unspecified number of "officials, who could not sleep conveniently in the dormitory." Furthermore, the priors and subpriors were permitted to build individual cells within the common dormitories, although all other cells within the common dormitories were to be destroyed within three months under the pain of excommunication. According to a later interpretation of the bull, under the term "cell" a room with a door furnished with a lock was meant, therefore mere partition walls without such doors could be tolerated. At any rate, the General Chapter of 1392 permitted a monk of Boulbonne to enclose his cubicle by a door.

Meanwhile, the rapidly falling number of monks and the increasingly intellectual orientation of many communities rendered the old-fashioned common dormitories practically untenable. The Chapter of 1494 authorized the abbots to excuse from the common dormitories "for a just cause" practically anybody, although the decree still insisted that stoves be removed from common dormitories. In 1565 the abbey of Poblet received permission to partition the dormitory into private cells. The Chapter of 1573 merely tried to prevent the building of cells outside the old dormitories. The Chapter of 1601 implied that adequately furnished cells were universally available, for it permitted monks to study in their own rooms. The destruction of fireplaces was ordered for the last time in 1605, although this decree met as little compliance as countless similar demands before. Finally, the *In suprema* of 1666, "for the sake of greater modesty and honesty of life," approved moderately furnished individual cells. La Trappe and the nineteenth-century Strict Observance returned to common dormitories and in these houses, as at old Cîteaux, the only room with a fireplace was the "warming room" (*calefactorium*).

On the personal hygiene of the monks the available sources offer only scant information. There was certainly no time or opportunity for washing up before Matins and the only facility for this could be the washing-fountain at the entrance to the refectory. The *mandatum,* the washing of the monks' feet every Saturday night from Easter to September 14, had probably, apart from its liturgical character, a practical purpose. The earliest reference to it was made in the *Ecclesiastica officia,* and it is still mentioned in the statutes of the Chapter of 1601.

Originally bathing was permitted only to the sick in the infirmary. All those who dared to visit natural watering places were sharply rebuked and punished by the General Chapter. A statute of 1189 judged that those who left their monasteries seeking "warm baths," should not be readmitted. In 1202 the abbot of the Tuscan San Giusto was deposed because he ate in secular company and, as the text stated cryptically, "indulged in bathing without his habit outside of the abbey." In 1212 a monk of Hautecombe was called to account for having eaten meat and taken a bath. In 1225 the abbot of the Hungarian Pilis was charged with the crime of having entered a public bath on Holy Saturday, where he also had himself shaved.

As the first indication of a thaw in this matter, the Chapter of 1437 stated that "baths should no longer be permitted to healthy persons more

374

often than once in a month." A statute of 1439 seems to imply that by then bathing had been institutionalized. It still insisted that bathing be a matter of monthly favor, but added that it must be no occasion for "reveling or dissolute behavior" and the bathers be satisfied with the services of no more than two servants. Where was the bath arranged? Perhaps in the infirmary. Finally, the General Chapter of 1783 permitted even the frequentation of watering places, if it could be justified by medical considerations.

Shaving and cutting the monastic tonsure was arranged originally seven times annually, on the vigils of principal feasts. In 1257 the General Chapter increased the occasions to twelve and a statute of 1297 ordered shaving twice a month. This was still the prescription of the *In suprema* of 1666, although the text put more emphasis on the prohibition of wearing a fashionably trimmed beard.

A combination of medical and ascetic reasons accounted for periodic bloodletting (phlebotomy) among the monks. Every member of the monastic communities was subject to it four times annually, unless actually sick or engaged in travel or hard work. It was generally believed throughout the Middle Ages and early modern times that bloodletting, apart from its beneficial results in medical emergencies, was an indispensable prerequisite of good health and effective means against sexual appetite. Under the term *minutio* it was dealt with in the earliest Cistercian legislation and remained in practice until the nineteenth century. It was done in the *calefactorium* or in the infirmary and its victims were entitled to several days of rest, extra food and drink.

The spirit of utmost consideration prevailed in the care of the sick and aged. A spacious infirmary was an integral part of every monastic plant, constructed somewhat apart from the cloister. The main hall of the infirmary of Cîteaux was 55 meters long and 20 meters wide, divided into three aisles by two rows of slender columns supporting the elegant Gothic vaulting. The still-standing infirmary of Ourscamp serves as the local parish church. This latter structure included an upper story featuring individual cells for the gravely ill. But even smaller buildings included accommodations for the monks and brothers in charge of the sick and were equipped with a pharmacy, a kitchen and a large fireplace.

Although the sick able to walk were expected to attend services in the church, a chapel was often added to the infirmary where mass could be said and the sacraments administered. Both the patients and the service personnel were supposed to keep the rule of silence, but dietary laws were suspended to the extent of the gravity of each case. The dining room of the infirmary was often called *misericordia,* for it was there that, out of commiseration, the weak members of the community were permitted to eat meat.

Ministration to the infirm did not normally exceed home remedies and medications. If some one of the attending monks had had some experience in medicine, it was pure coincidence. It was only in the Renaissance that many populous abbeys employed a resident lay physician or surgeon, who was also in charge of the monks' regular bleeding and may have accompanied the abbot and his entourage on long trips of visitation. According to the regulations of the General Chapter of 1189, sick monks were not permitted to look for a cure outside of their abbeys and it was only much later that Cistercians were permitted to visit reputed health resorts.

When a monk was about to die, the tolling of bells called all his confreres to his bedside to witness the last sacraments and his happy departure. For these ceremonies his mattress was lifted out of the bed and placed on the floor over a layer of ashes. After he had taken his last breath the community withdrew and the body was taken to an adjacent chamber and laid on a stone slab. Then he was stripped of his garments and washed in warm water from head to toe. It was a symbolic act of immemorial Christian tradition, but could also have been a primitive autopsy revealing the visible ravages of the fatal disease and perhaps the cause of death. Inevitably, the monks had a curious eye for the marks of their departed confrere's physical mortifications, which could be recorded for posterity's edification. The stone of the death-chamber of Clairvaux on which Saint Bernard's body was washed became an object of veneration. Some pious visitors claimed to have seen the imprint of the Saint's body on the smooth stone.

If credence can be given to an unusually embellished story in the *Dialogus miraculorum* of Caesarius of Heisterbach, it was on just such an occasion that the monks of Schönau discovered that "Brother Joseph" who had died as a novice, was actually a girl. Her real name turned out to be Hildegunde, daughter of a pious burgher of Neuss am Rhein, who had taken her on a pilgrimage to the Holy Land where he died, leaving his daughter stranded in a strange country. It was after incredible hardships and miraculous adventures that Hildegunde found her way back to Germany, where the abbot of Schönau mistook her for an adolescent boy and admitted her to the novitiate. Her death occurred in 1188, and when Caesarius retold the story some thirty years later, she was well on her way to becoming "Saint Hildegunde," to be venerated as such through the remainder of the Middle Ages.

After the ceremonial washing, the body of the dead monk, clad in regular Cistercian habit and cowl, was taken in procession to the church

376

and was placed on a bier in the choir. If there was still time for the funeral mass, the burial followed on the same day. Otherwise, the monks kept vigil over the body all night and arranged the mass and interment on the following morning. After the last rites the body was carried through a door on the northern wall of the transept to the immediately adjacent cemetery. The corpse was lowered into the grave without coffin and the site was left unmarked. Only in the seventeenth century did a wooden cross with the monk's name and year of death on it come to be placed over each grave. In the cemeteries of populous abbeys, such as Clairvaux and Orval, there was always a freshly dug open grave waiting for its, perhaps unsuspecting, occupant.

Abbots were laid to rest under the cloister between the chapter hall and the church, occasionally also under the chapter hall or in a vault under the church. The locations of the abbots' bodies were marked by more or less decorated tombstones imbedded into the floor of the cloister or put on the wall.

To modern readers, a highly ritualistic, rigidly ordained monastic life, which left practically nothing to individual initiative, appears to be unnatural, even inhuman. It must be borne in mind, however, that many great abbeys harbored hundreds of individuals, each with a different temperament, level of intelligence and social background; all were to live out their lives at close quarters, without the conveniences of privacy which men of our day would consider indispensable. In such circumstances harmonious co-existence and meaningful communal creativity would certainly have been impossible without the imposition of strict regulations assigning to each individual his own limited place and role and thus reducing the possibility of continually clashing wills and colliding interests.

It was exactly through its regimentation and purposeful organization that monastic life made its indelible impact on Christian society. Even the most simple-minded onlooker must have been impressed by the monks' towering success in every field of their manifold activities. Achievements in spirituality and learning, monumental architecture, efficacy in economy and the blessings of personal security proved eloquently the superiority of a life based on the voluntary acceptance of discipline, dedication to hard work and submission to religious authority. The Western world's unshaken belief that labor, even manual labor, is ennobling, that "idleness is the enemy of the soul," therefore work is the only morally acceptable source of well-being, are all elements of the noble bequest of Cistercian monasticism.

XXIV

Monks and Society

Although twelfth-century Cistercians cherished nothing more than the solitude of their self-chosen "deserts," the sweeping success of the Order can only be explained by a fruitful interaction between those desert-abbeys and their surroundings. The monks' religious and ascetic ideals evoked a resounding echo within every segment of contemporary society. The ranks of nobility, secular clergy, scholars and burghers were as much attracted to the early Cistercian abbeys as were large numbers of peasants who swelled the population of lay-brothers. Those who had neither courage nor opportunity to join them followed the monks' heroic life vicariously and contributed materially to the growth of the Order.

A vital link between the monasteries and their secular environment was the fact that the enclosed abbeys harbored the sons (in some cases, the fathers) of those who remained outside. Acceptance as a novice was often stipulated in acts of donation, regardless of the size or value of the gift. Thus the donor and his family must have felt a sense of identity with the monks, while the monks responded with a sense of responsibility for those who helped them. The numerous later cases of compensated donations which obliged the abbey to insure the donor's livelihood by annuity, pension, food or clothing, should not be considered merely a business transaction; they reflected a pervading atmosphere of mutual trust and interdependence.

Those who needed more than financial assistance were often taken into the monastic community and provided with shelter, even with personal services. About 1200, a man who had been blinded as a hostage granted his land to the monks of the Welsh Margam, whereupon he was taken as a lay-brother into the monastery, where he "lived most securely all the days of his life." Others were received as "corrodians," like a certain John ap John Nichol, who was admitted to Margam in 1325. He donated his land to the monks, and was in turn employed as a "free sergeant," entitled to three loaves of bread, one gallon of the monks' "strong beer" daily and other benefits as long as he lived.

At the Catalan Poblet the class of small donors or benefactors, the *donados,* constituted a special group within the abbey. They lived in a separate dormitory and had access to the abbey's shops and services at a discount rate. Upon the death of their wives the *donados* could opt for lay-brotherhood. If the *donado* died first, his wife and children were provided for by the monks.

These *donati, familiares* or occasionally *oblati,* occur in so many chartularies that their numbers and role in most abbeys must have been significant. References to them in the early records of the General Chapter are somewhat ambiguous, but it is obvious from later legislation (1213, 1233) that their admission soon became an act of some solemnity. Before the abbot they renounced their right to hold property, promised obedience, and in turn were promised the same food, drink and clothing as that of the monks and were granted accommodations in a separate dormitory. They were to help the brothers in manual labor or in the management of the monastic estate. They wore a distinctive garment and even some form of tonsure.

The significance of the *familiares* grew proportionately with the disappearing lay-brotherhood. By the end of the thirteenth century their numbers had so increased that at some communities they created disciplinary problems. The General Chapter of 1293 ordered that "because of the confusion often caused by the excessive numbers of such persons . . . admission to the habit and sharing in the material goods in any way should not be granted [to *familiares*] without the special permission of the said Chapter." The institution survived the Middle Ages, although the term referring to such people was frequently changed to "prebendary."

In spite of the fact that Cistercians did not wish to play any role in the feudal establishment, it seems that in cases when it was clearly to the benefit of their peasant neighbors, some abbots did assume the responsibility of a protector or advocate. An interesting example was that of Acey in the Franche Comté, founded in 1136 and populated from Cherlieu. Soon after that date a certain Girard de Rossillon gave his house with the rest of his property to Acey, but he was merely following the example of fourteen other individuals of the same rural community, who in an apparent act of "commendation" offered all they had to Abbot Guy of Cherlieu, who promptly returned the land to the donors together with his assurances of protection. This was obviously a routine feudal procedure whereby free owners of allodial land recognized the lordship of the abbot, although neither the motive behind the move nor the actual obligations derived from the act are known. It seems certain, however, that the peasant community acted freely as an expression of preference for a monastic protector and appreciation for the newly-founded abbey.

After the virtual disappearance of lay-brotherhood and much reduction in the number of monks, the abbeys relied increasingly on the assistance of lay people, both as laborers and supervisory personnel. Surviving statistics concerning nine English Cistercian houses on the eve of the Dissolution show that while the total number of professed monks was only 108, they employed nearly 300 laymen in a variety of positions. Among the nine abbeys, Biddlesden alone had 51 servants, Stoneleigh gave work to 46 dependants. In most cases the loyalty of lay employees remained strong to the end. When the Earl of Sussex investigated the involvement of the abbey of Whalley in the "Pilgrimage of Grace," he complained that he was unable to gather evidence because of the "large number of the abbot's feed men."

As elsewhere in Europe, in late medieval England the monastic personnel was recruited from neighboring towns and the local gentry who retained a keen interest in the monks' affairs, particularly at times of abbatial elections. For example, at Furness, the last two elections before the Dissolution were decided by vigorous lay intervention. The election of Alexander Banke in 1497 was followed by decades of intrigue, the opponents trying to unseat the incumbent. At one point Abbot Banke was forced to defend his position by a private army of 300 retainers. Not surprisingly, Banke left behind a substantial debt, aggravated by pensions, annuities or manifest bribes given to a number of royal officials and local potentates.

Hospitality, a traditional monastic service, forged another link between Cistercian abbeys and society. The early legislation of the Order emphasized this virtue mostly in behalf of traveling monks and clergy, although lay travelers were offered food and lodging just as generously. Many abbeys maintained a separate hospice for visitors somewhat apart from the conventual buildings. According to the account book of the English Beaulieu, that abbey was rarely without guests. The quality and quantity of food served them was carefully specified as were the duties of the brethren who ministered to them. The monks' relatives were permitted to visit three or four times annually for two days on each occasion. The burden of providing for them must have been heavy, for it was stated that in case the guests wished to stay beyond this limit, they were expected to care for themselves.

The visits of royalty or other high ranking members of lay or ecclesiastical society were particularly burdensome. On such occasions

380

food and drink were served liberally, although, at least until the middle of the fifteenth century, the guests, whatever their status, were to observe the rule of perpetual abstinence. Upon the request of the abbot of the German Maulbronn, the General Chapter of 1493 specifically permitted the serving of meat "without scruples of conscience," because, as the Chapter stated, the abbey often hosted "guests of distinction, men of letters, nobles and magnates, who not only bring honor to the said monastery, but also to the whole Order." It is also obvious from such remarks that visitors of rank and high social status received greater attention and better accommodations than ordinary wayfarers.

Gifts or endowments for monastic hospices were granted in token of both the services and the financial sacrifices involved. In 1269 Bishop Hermann of Schwerin granted forty days indulgence to all those who donated for the support of the guest house of the abbey of Doberan, "since [the monks] carry a most heavy burden of costs and expenses on account of guests and travelers." In 1233 Saint Mary's Abbey in Dublin set aside some ecclesiastical revenues "for the use of the poor and for the sustenance of guests." The abbot of the Welsh Basingwerk excused himself in 1346 before Edward III for not having paid a demanded subsidy by referring to the location of the monastery near a heavily-traveled road, a circumstance which involved great expenditures for hospitality. On the eve of the Dissolution an appeal was made to Henry VIII on behalf of Quarr Abbey, which, according to the petition, needed to be preserved as a hospice for poor travelers and seamen. At the same time the Irish Saint Mary's Abbey was referred to as a "common resort" for all who sought hospitality, while the monks were considered "but stewards and purveyors" of benefits, helping "many poor men, scholars and orphans."

In addition to the normal services of hospitality many Cistercian abbeys maintained hospitals, particularly for the infirm poor of the neighborhood, although normally the monks did not practice medicine beyond administering ordinary household remedies. As early as 1197 the Austrian Zwettl operated a "hospital for the poor." In 1218 the establishment was moved to a large building near the gate-house of the abbey, where new accommodations included a chapel. The hospital was richly endowed, covering for the housing of thirty needy infirm under the care of ten attendants. In 1208 at the German abbey of Michaelstein, Count Siegfried of Blankenburg endowed a hospital. The General Chapter of 1218 not only approved this "hospital caring for the poor," but also insisted that it should remain under the administration of the abbey's own personnel. Himmerod maintained in 1259 a "hospital of the poor," supported by special funds and endowments. In addition to sick villagers and pilgrims some old people were taken in too, like an old soldier who about 1300 was invited by the abbot to spend the rest of his life there. According to data compiled by Franz Winter, similar institutions were operated during the thirteenth century at a number of other Cistercian abbeys in Germany, among them at Pforta, Altzelle, Chorin, Volkenrode, Camp, Reifenstein and Walderbach.

A similar number of English abbeys were engaged in caring for the destitute sick. At Beaulieu Abbey, toward the end of the thirteenth century, the account book made reference to an infirmary where the sick servants of the abbey and others were cared for. The deceased poor were buried by the monks, who also disposed of their meager belongings. At Meaux, during the abbacy of Michael Brun (1235-1249), a substantial donation was made for "the upkeep of the hospital for laymen," although the benefactor, in addition to some monetary compensation, demanded for himself the gift of a pair of white gloves every Easter. The hospital of Newminster received a number of substantial donations, some specifically "for the upkeep of that lamp which is burning in the infirmary of seculars for the convenience of the poor of Christ lying there." Other abbeys in England, such as Fountains, Furness, Holmcultram, Pipewell, Rievaulx, Robertsbridge, Sawley, Sibton and Waverley, operated similar hospitals.

In Scotland, Melrose, Cupar and Kinloss maintained hospitals, each for about eight to ten inmates. In the thirteenth century, the Welsh Strata Florida had a hospice under the care of the monks, in the "acres of the lepers." The chartulary of the French Gimont in 1187 named a monk, Arnaldus, as infirmarian in the hospice of the abbey. In 1206, another monk, Guillelmus, acted as "infirmarian of the poor." In 1222 a certain Antoine de la Crose made a donation while he lay ill "in the hospital of the abbey of Gimont." The Brabantine Villers had in the thirteenth century a well-funded "hospital of the poor," under the administration of a lay-brother.

A much later reference to a hospital is found among the statutes of the General Chapter of 1490. The Saxon abbey of Buch reported that the hospital operated by the monks was in grave financial difficulties because the funds which had been set aside "for the support of a certain number of the poor" were no longer sufficient, while curtailments caused loud complaints among the needy patients. The Chapter's answer was the appointment of three abbots of the neighborhood for the investigation of the situation, who were empowered to take whatever action they saw fit.

Eventually, the availability of improving medical care in the growing cities reduced the significance of monastic hospitals, although some abbeys continued to operate health facilities until the French Revolution.

The old infirmary of the prosperous Orval (after 1715 under Austrian rule) was replaced by a spacious structure in 1761, featuring three wards: one for professed monks, another for the lay-brothers, and the third for the many servants and lay-employees of the abbey. It had its own chapel and kitchen, while the medical care was provided by a resident physician and two orderlies. The facility was designed to serve the needs of some 120 people.

The source of reputation of Orval as a health-center, however, was its famous pharmacy under the care of the legendary Brother Antoine Périn (1738-1788). He was a professional medic trained in Paris, whose services were made available to people far beyond the confines of abbatial property. He cultivated a medicine garden where he grew himself many of the roots, herbs and flowers he needed; others he purchased chiefly in Liège. All was prepared in his own laboratory. His most popular products were potions and tinctures, among them the "water of Orval," supposedly effective against a prodigious number of maladies, both mental and physical. The Brother's reputation was greatly enhanced by his success in 1777, while fighting against a widespread epidemic of typhoid fever. The business of the pharmacy was brisk. Indeed, in 1788 alone 5,638 florins worth of medicine was sold to outsiders, while 506 florins worth of medication was provided freely to the poor.

Throughout the Middle Ages the support of the poor was the recognized duty of the Church and, according to all indications, the Cistercian Order accepted a large share in the relief of those in material need. The distribution of alms took place at the gate-house of every abbey under the watchful eye of the porter. Bread and other food items were always available for the purpose, but, according to the General Chapter of 1185, used clothing and footwear were also distributed among the needy. Even Gerald of Wales, a sharp critic of Cistercians, acknowledged the Order's generosity to the poor. The monks, he said, "although most abstemious themselves, excel all others in their over-flowing charity toward the poor and the travelers." As an example, Gerald referred to the Welsh abbey of Margam, which in 1188 sent a ship to Bristol in order to procure corn "for a very large crowd of beggars."

The thirteenth-century formulary of Pontigny, featuring samples for charters of visitation, insisted that the porter must always keep alms at hand to distribute among the poor, including discarded clothing and at least a hundred loaves of bread, delivered to him daily from the abbey's bakery. The same document demanded that in a separate building a number of beds be kept always available for the poor in need of lodging.

The late thirteenth-century account book of Beaulieu detailed the duties of the porter concerning the handling of alms. It seems that the care of the poor was well organized and the needy knew in advance not only the time but also the kind of relief they could expect. Distribution of food took place three times weekly and every night thirteen poor men were accommodated overnight in the abbey's hospice, while three others were treated as the abbot's guests. On Maundy Thursday, a penny was added to the usual benefits. During harvest time the able-bodied poor were made to work in the fields for their bread. The collection of used clothing for the needy was the duty of the abbey's wardrobe keeper.

At Meaux, during the thirteenth and fourteenth centuries, several of the abbey's workshops contributed regularly to poor relief. The master of the tannery was to furnish each year twenty ox or cow hides, properly tanned, for the shoes of the poor; eighteen shillings worth of woolen cloth fulled in the abbey's lanary was set aside for a similar purpose, while one-tenth of the cheese received from the dairy of Felsa was saved for distribution among the needy.

Although the contribution of English abbeys to the support of the poor does not seem to be exceptional, in 1535 Whalley distributed in alms the astonishing total of £122, amounting to 22% of the monks' revenues. Out of this amount £41 was spent for the maintenance of twenty-four paupers within the monastery, £63 was set aside for weekly distribution of grain, and £18 was given away on Christmas and Maundy Thursday. At about the same time Furness took care of thirteen poor men and granted weekly doles to eight poor widows; Stanley housed seven almsmen; Garendon supported six disabled persons. An undated document in the chartulary of Newminster combined a donation with the obligation that the monks distribute annually on the feast of Saint Catherine alms to one hundred poor, giving to each "two oat cakes and two herrings."

Villers was particularly noted for its generosity toward the poor, facilitated by many donations made for that specific purpose. During the thirteenth century the abbey's baker furnished weekly 2,100 loaves of bread for daily distribution among the needy gathered in large numbers around the gate-house. Many donations for anniversary masses at Villers and elsewhere included special amounts to be distributed on the same occasion among the poor. A thirteenth-century donor at the Swiss Hauterive, Humbert de Fernay, set aside forty-five livres of Lausanne, from which the monks were to purchase cheese and bread for distribution among the 366 needy persons in the town of Romont on Pentecost Monday. King Robert I (1306-1329) of Scotland bequeathed £100 annually to Melrose, partly for the improvement of the monks' diet, partly for twenty suits of clothes to be given each year at Martinmas to twenty poor men, who on the same day were to share the monks' table.

In times of famine or other emergencies the monks shared everything they had with their hard-pressed neighbors. In 1147 Morimond fed its whole neighborhood for three months, until the new harvest could be gathered. In 1153 the German Sittichenbach was said to have saved from famine 1,800 inhabitants of the region. In 1316 Riddagshausen, also in Germany, fed 400 persons daily, saving them from starvation. Some such incidents lived in posterity's memory as legendary feats of heroism, therefore the figures referring to the numbers of people supported by the monks cannot always be relied upon. This was obviously the case at Melrose in 1150, when the monks supposedly distributed food daily for three months among 4,000 starving folk, while the supplies were each time miraculously replenished.

An immemorial custom among Cistercian abbeys was the *tricenarium* of deceased brethren, which meant that the meals of the recently deceased monks were set aside for thirty consecutive days and the portions given to needy persons. A "great" *tricenarium* each year followed the closing of the annual session of the General Chapter on Saint Lambert's day (September 17), when at every abbey of the Order several poor were given meals for thirty days. The washing of the feet of twelve poor men by the abbot on Maundy Thursday was also followed by a dinner for the same poor persons.

A special occasion for large-scale alms-giving was the arrival at Cîteaux of abbots attending the annual sessions of the General Chapter. During these days the roads leading to Cîteaux were virtually clogged by the real and pretended poor beseeching the abbots for coins. By 1240 the crowd had become so unruly that the Chapter had to prohibit the distribution of alms within two miles of Cîteaux. In 1260, for the same reason, the custom was entirely discontinued. Instead, the Chapter urged the abbots to drop their donations into a box placed next to the entrance of the chapter hall.

According to all available evidence, alms-giving was a matter of course at every Cistercian abbey, although it must be emphasized that the monks were widely respected as honest distributors of relief; therefore they were the recipients of numerous gifts and foundations designed for just such purposes. For the same reason, what was given away at monastic gate-houses reflected not only on the charity of the monks, but on the generosity of monastic benefactors as well. The percentage of alms, taking monastic revenues as a whole, has always been a debated question. At times of Cistercian prosperity it might have amounted to ten percent, although a figure closer to five percent seems to be a safer estimate. During the fourteenth and fifteenth centuries, when the monks themselves experienced grave hardships, they had little to give away for charities.

Twelfth-century Cistercians steadfastly declined involvement in pastoral care of neighboring peasant communities, although the priests of the Order always administered the sacraments to lay-brothers and workers attached to monastic granges. Early and "illegal" acceptance of churches did not necessarily mean the servicing of parishes by Cistercian priests; the abbey merely became the patron of the church, obliged to hire a secular priest and pay his salary. At some foundations, however, direct involvement in pastoral care was unavoidable from the outset. San Galgano on Monte Siepi (diocese of Volterra) had been a popular shrine long before 1201 when the Cistercian foundation was made by monks of Casamari.

Due to its frontier location and jurisdiction over a number of villages the abbot of Poblet received in 1221 from Honorius III the quasi-episcopal *nullius* status, involving extensive pastoral duties. Local circumstances must have imposed pastoral duties on a number of abbeys, for in 1234 the General Chapter energetically repeated the prohibition against monks serving in parishes and ordered their immediate return to their abbeys. In the following year the same ruling was repeated, with the added stipulation that chapels already possessed by an abbey should be serviced through secular priests. In 1236 the Chapter returned again to the same subject, declaring that abbeys which had controlled chapels before they joined the Order may retain them, but that abbots should hire secular clerics for their operation. In the same statute, however, exception was granted to Les Dunes and Ter Doest, "both having chapels on several islands in the sea," where, because of their complete isolation, the faithful had to rely entirely on the monks' ministration. Accordingly, three Cistercian priests were assigned to each of the chapels to serve "the large number of lay-brothers and secular persons."

This concession was probably inspired by previous papal permissions granted to individual abbeys. In 1232, Gregory IX had permitted the monks of the Welsh Cwmhir to administer the sacraments to their servants and tenants, because at the abbey's mountainous location no secular priest could reach them. The Irish Holy Cross Abbey (settled in 1180) found several chapels on its land and from the thirteenth century on mostly the monks themselves serviced the surrounding parishes. Pastoral activity was even further expanded when, following the crusade of Richard I, relics of the Holy Cross were deposited at the abbey, transforming the modest house into one of the most popular shrines of the country.

386

At the Swiss Saint Urban, pastoral involvement began about 1280 with the acquisition of the shrine of Freibach. By the beginning of the sixteenth century the abbey had rights of patronage over ten parish churches and a number of chapels. Most of these were serviced by secular clergy, but at the four churches nearest to the abbey monks ministered the faithful.

The English Meaux under Abbot Roger (1286-1310) received a rich donation for a chantry in Ottringham. Its terms called for elaborate and perpetual services for the benefit of the deceased members of the donor's family. The abbot accepted the endowment and dispatched to the designated chapel seven monks, who established themselves at a place later called "Monkgarth." But this secluded house so often became involved in incidents of scandalous breach of discipline that the monks soon had to be recalled. Throughout the fourteenth century several Rhenish abbeys were so extensively engaged in pastoral services that the General Chapter decided to intervene. In 1393 the visiting abbot of Morimond found that many monks of Camp, Altenberg and Heisterbach lived in parishes and he ordered their immediate return to their abbeys.

In spite of the frequent protests of the Chapter, monks continued to be engaged in direct ministration to the faithful, particularly when economic necessity demanded such services. This was the case in Silesia, where all Cistercian abbeys had been so devastated during the Hussite wars that they were unable to house and feed their own members. Many monks could find a safe livelihood only in parishes. In the second half of the fifteenth century all six Silesian abbeys staffed parishes with their own personnel. Among them Leubus and Kamenz each had ten parish churches.

Finally, in 1489, even the General Chapter came to be reconciled to the unavoidable practice. Although a new statute still repeated that monks should not be engaged in the "care of souls," permission was granted to serve churches and chapels already incorporated by abbeys.

The country where pastoral services eventually absorbed the energies of a substantial number of priest-monks was Austria. Already in the thirteenth century most of the eleven abbeys of Austria possessed churches and in the fourteenth century they enjoyed full rights of patronage over them. In 1399 Boniface IX permitted Zwettl to install Cistercians as perpetual vicars in the abbey's churches. The trend continued and by the seventeenth century most Cistercian churches had been serviced by monks of the Order. In 1758, out of the 317 priests of the Austrian province, 75 were actively engaged in pastoral duties. By 1780 the number of Cistercian parishes in that country had grown to 73. Between 1780 and 1790, under pressure from the government of Joseph II, the Order had to assume the responsibility for 45 additional churches.

Besides the routine duties of pastoral care, from the thirteenth century on many Cistercian abbeys formed and conducted a variety of pious confraternities and societies. The organization began with a list of benefactors entitled to share in such spiritual benefits of the Order as anniversary masses and special offices for the deceased. Himmerod in the thirteenth century had two lists of names, one for the most prominent donors grouped in a "plenary fraternity," the other for lesser benefactors, forming a "common fraternity." At first both lists featured predominantly members of the nobility, but eventually their composition took an increasingly bourgeois character. Membership in the "plenary fraternity" implied the transfer of all the donor's property to the abbey, though he retained usufruct for life. The same individual was made to promise not to remarry after the death of his wife, or, if single, to continue life in celibacy. After 1440 there existed at Himmerod a Purgatorial Society (*Totenbruderschaft*), the members of which were promised a number of masses after their death and a share in the merits of the monks' prayers. Members held their devotions in a special chapel under the guidance of a "master," who was one of the monks. They were responsible for the decoration of altars and furnished a quantity of candles. At the same time a similar but even more populous organization was active at the abbey of Camp.

The number of anniversary masses at many abbeys grew to prodigious figures, imposing a heavy burden on the priests of the monasteries. In 1449 the General Chapter prohibited further acceptance of perpetual anniversary masses without permission of the Chapter, "lest the monasteries be overburdened or the souls of the departed be, in some way, defrauded."

In 1445 on a field owned by the Bavarian abbey of Langheim a shepherd saw a vision of fourteen individuals surrounding the infant Jesus in adoration. Three years later a shrine was erected on the site in honor of the "Fourteen Helpers-in-Need" (*Vierzehnheiligen*). The Cistercian community was soon involved in the fast-spreading devotion, which was embraced by several other communities of the Order, including Raitenhaslach, Waldsassen, Kamenz, Neuzelle, Heinrichau and Grüssau. At these abbeys, by popular demand, chapels and altars were dedicated to the fourteen saints and masses were said in their honor. Although both Langheim and Vierzehnheiligen were destroyed in the Peasant War of 1525, the shrine gained new popularity in the seventeenth century. The magnificent Baroque pilgrimage church designed by the great Balthasar Neumann and consecrated in 1772 still attests to the strength of that Cistercian-sponsored movement of piety.

388

The Swiss Saint Urban was another center of popular devotions. In 1231 the Saint Bernard Confraternity was organized for benefactors. After the acquisition of Freibach, two pious societies were centered around that popular shrine, one honoring the Blessed Virgin Mary, the other Saint Anne. At the same location a Rosary Fraternity was initiated in 1523, and in the seventeenth century a Scapular Society was founded. Freibach was also the home of a pious confraternity founded by the guilds of smiths in Emmental and Oberaargau. In the first half of the sixteenth century some seventy masters of the trade participated in annual pilgrimages to Freibach.

In 1226 Fürstenfeld, another great Bavarian abbey, received the village of Inchenhofen, and with it a shrine honoring Saint Leonard. After 1283 priests of the community were active in that church, which grew steadily in popularity during the fourteenth century. In 1401 Boniface IX authorized ten Cistercians of Fürstenfeld to hear confessions at the shrine. The same abbey erected in 1414 another shrine honoring Saint Willibald, while at a parish belonging to the abbey veneration of the Holy Cross was promoted.

In the fifteenth and sixteenth centuries the General Chapter willingly supported pious associations, which were as popular in France as in Germany. In 1491 the Chapter gave its blessing to a Saint Sebastian Confraternity sponsored by the abbot of Theuley near Besançon, promising the members a share in the merits of the monks' prayers and good works performed in every abbey of the Order. Similar benefits were granted in 1494 to a Confraternity of the Seven Joys of the Blessed Virgin organized by La Ferté. A pious society honoring Saint Margaret, Saint Anthony and Saint Leonard in the German Schönthal was equally favored in 1520.

Under Abbot Nicolas Wydenbosch (Salicetus), the Alsatian Baumgarten became a flourishing devotional center. At the request of the abbot the General Chapter of 1488 granted to all living and deceased members of a Confraternity of the Immaculate Conception a participation in the spiritual treasures of the Order. Many members of the Confraternity belonged to the circle of devout burghers of the Swiss city of Bern, the abbot's birthplace.

The seventeenth-century monastic reforms, including the Cistercian Strict Observance, looked askance at monks engaged in pastoral activity outside of their abbeys. Their disapproval was echoed by the General Chapter of 1672, which planned an appeal to the Holy See, asking the authorities not to confer to Cistercians any title or position involving active ministry. The Chapter of 1683 deliberated the same issue and proposed the recall of all Cistercians from parish work. Such duties, however, had by then become so deeply rooted in the traditions of many abbeys, particularly in German-speaking countries, that no noticeable change could have been expected.

The devotional trends of the Baroque put new emphasis on pious societies and pilgrimages, and an ever widening Cistercian pastoral activity resulted. Under Abbot Robert de Namur (1647-1652) the monks of Villers engaged themselves in the spiritual direction of thirteen affiliated nunneries. These and other types of pastoral duties demanded the services of about twenty-five monks until the end of the eighteenth century. Under the influence of the monks of the Bavarian Aldersbach the cult of the Blessed Virgin spread to four shrines, which became particularly popular in the seventeenth and eighteenth centuries (Kösslarn, Rotthalmünster, Sammerei, Frauentödling).

Within the Habsburg lands the veneration of Saint Joseph gained much popularity, because the saint was the patron of the imperial family. In 1653 under the auspices of the Austrian Lilienfeld a Saint Joseph Fraternity was founded which, until its dissolution in 1781, enjoyed the widest expansion and repute. Its membership included not only masses of humble rural folk and countless pious burghers, but also many members of the Habsburg family and leading representatives of the hierarchy. By 1755 the register of the Fraternity contained 215,000 names.

The Saint Joseph Brotherhood founded in 1669 by the Silesian Grüssau gained similar popularity. Both individuals and communities enlisted in its membership, so that by the end of the century no less than 43,000 names had been inscribed in the association's registers. The rules called for daily prayers to Saint Joseph, monthly Holy Communion and dedication to works of charity toward the sick and poor.

While the education of girls in Cistercian nunneries was a widely accepted practice, boys had been excluded from monasteries by the earliest statutes of the General Chapter. It seems, however, that the workshops of many flourishing abbeys attracted a number of children who had no intention of becoming monks, but were interested in learning from the brothers one or another of their specific trades. Such practices were tolerated even in the twelfth century and the Chapter of 1195 merely insisted that youngsters admitted as apprentices to the "workshops of weavers, tailors and tanners" be at least twelve years old.

The Chapter of 1205 inveighed against certain unnamed abbots in Friesland "who had admitted for the sake of instruction boys below fifteen. By the strict rules of the Order [these abbots] should deserve deposition, nevertheless, supposing that they failed to receive as yet the [pertinent] definitions, they are, for the time being, spared." The same warning was delivered also to the abbot of Ile-en-Barrois near Toul and repeated "irrevocably" in 1206. One of these "delinquent" abbeys might have been Adwert in western Friesland, which in the fourteenth century maintained a "Red Schoolhouse" (*Schola rubea*) for boys. Enrollment must have been considerable, for the Black Death of 1350 carried away twenty-nine students. At the time of the Reformation the same institution enjoyed a country-wide reputation. According to some indications, other monasteries of the Netherlands, such as Nizelle, Boneffe and Moulins, also maintained educational facilities before the Reformation.

In the fifteenth century the Swiss Saint Urban grew to be a renowned center of humanistic studies. Abbot Nicolas von Hollstein (1441-1480), a native of Basel, founded an "Abbey School," which reached its full development under Abbot Sebastian Seemann (1534-1557), when it employed some of the best schoolmen of the country. In 1579 the visiting Abbot General Nicolas Boucherat I found in the abbey "twelve adolescents receiving instruction in grammar."

In England before the Dissolution Furness had a grammar and singing school (*schola cantorum*) for boys who boarded within the abbey. Biddlesden housed nine boys, apparently in similar circumstances. Newminster had four such choir boys, while Woburn sheltered three boys together with their schoolmaster. At Ford Abbey a certain William Tyler, master of arts, enjoyed room and board as well as a comfortable annuity for teaching grammar to boys living in the abbey and lecturing on the Bible to the monks.

The Austrian Zwettl founded a boys' choir in the fifteenth century. This institution survived the Reformation and the religious wars and under Abbot Bernhard Link (1646-1671) the number of boys, who received free room, board and instruction, reached thirty. The tradition has been continued to the present; the "Zwettler Sängerknaben" enjoy a well-deserved international reputation for excellence.

Before the eighteenth century the maintenance of Cistercian educational institutions had always been exceptional. The generally forbidding attitude, however, changed to active interest under the impact of the utilitarian philosophy of the Enlightenment. The Silesian abbey of Rauden, under the sympathetic eyes of Frederick II, founded a seminary and a Latin school in 1744. Most students boarded in the monastery, where education for priesthood was the monks' prime concern. Before the suppression of the abbey in 1810, the registers of the school included 2,000 students of whom about 500 became priests. Similar institutions were quite common in other German Cistercian abbeys as well.

391

The abolition of the Society of Jesus in 1773 served as a powerful incentive to Cistercians to take over abandoned Jesuit schools. The Bavarian Gotteszell, which had operated a modest educational institution before that date, received the charge of the formerly Jesuit *gymnasium* of Burghausen. The same challenge induced several abbeys in the Habsburg Empire to dedicate themselves to education, which, during the nineteenth century, became the dominant occupation of the majority of their members.

A somewhat unexpected social service discharged by many medieval Cistercian abbeys was banking. The most common form of this activity was the safekeeping of money or precious objects deposited with the monks by laymen. The General Chapter registered no objections, but soon felt a need to regulate and limit the monks' responsibilities. A statute of 1183 decreed that amounts over 100 solidi be accepted only before three witnesses. Although every precaution was to be taken for the safety of the deposits, in cases of loss the monks could not be held responsible. According to another statute passed in 1195, monks or *conversi* who handled deposits in an improper fashion were to be expelled.

It was the sign of changing economic conditions that deposited sums of money were often reinvested in the form of loans, or were spent by the monks. These practices, however, were strictly prohibited by the Chapter of 1209, unless permitted by the depositor himself.

The colorful history of Welsh abbeys may furnish a few concrete examples. Dore and Margam were extensively involved in banking. In 1187 a certain Hugh de Hereford borrowed a large amount in order to secure his release from captivity. In this and similar other cases the monks demanded securities, such as jewelry, until the sum was returned. Both abbeys acted as tax-collectors in the fourteenth century, receiving and safekeeping tithes, in the name either of the clergy or of the royal exchequer. In 1328-1329 the amount collected and held by Dore was £700, spent eventually for the maintenance of Queen Isabella, mother of Edward III. On the other hand, in 1320, Margam asked to be excused from such responsibilities, for the abbey had no means of keeping the money safe.

Such services had their dangers and drawbacks. In England, under Edward II (1307-1327), the monks of Stoneleigh accepted for safekeeping large sums from the rich Despensers, a family high in royal favor. The faction of their enemies, led by the Earl of Hereford, got wind of the transactions, broke into the abbey and carried away £1,000 in coins in addition to gold and silver plate of a similar value.

The Catalan Poblet often found itself in the position of royal bankers. The abbey began to lend large amounts of money to its generous patrons, the kings of Aragon, as early as the 1170s. Such credits first financed the wars against the Moslems, but later in the thirteenth century Jaime I (1213-1276) borrowed from Poblet when he was about to attack Mallorca and Valencia. In 1285 the abbey granted 40,000 solidi of Barcelona to Pedro III for the organization of defenses aganst an expected French invasion.

For about a century, beginning in 1257, the Italian San Galgano furnished lay-brothers as controllers to the city administration of Siena. The still extant and richly illuminated account books of the city were often decorated with the cowled figures of the brothers.

As administrators of extensive tracts of land in the era of feudalism, Cistercian abbots were often burdened with duties of administering justice in cases involving their subjects. Criminal jurisdiction over monks and lay-brothers belonged always to the abbot, and the General Chapter proved to be a resolute defender of this privilege. On the other hand, the same Chapter consistently opposed the abbots' exercising jurisdiction over lay persons, even though they were employed by the abbey. The Chapter of 1206 peremptorily declared that "absolutely no [abbot] should exercise secular jurisdiction through monks or brothers, because such incidents bring great scandal to the whole Order." Presumably, it was the secular or episcopal "advocate" of the abbey who dispensed criminal justice over the lay subjects of Cistercian abbeys.

The process, however, whereby the original granges were transformed into villages inhabited by lay tenants rendered the total renunciation of abbatial jurisdiction over them problematic. The General Chapter of 1240 spoke only about cases involving capital punishment when it stated that "no [abbot] is permitted to exercise jurisdiction involving the shedding of blood through monks or brothers; we should turn to secular justice in order that we could overcome the threat of thieves and malefactors."

Eventually, and inevitably, the abbots became responsible for the maintenance of manorial courts of justice, although it was a bailiff or steward who actually presided over individual cases. The jurisdiction of some prominent abbeys, such as Pontigny, included even capital offenses, and from the fifteenth century on the death penalty was meted out liberally. The Welsh Tintern also had the rights of "gallows and judgment of life and limb." In fact, about 1200, Walter Map, attacking the abbey, repeated a gossip about a man whom the monks "hanged and buried in the sand" after he had been caught stealing their apples. The abbey of

Basingwerk exhibited a pillory, tumbrel and other instruments of punishment, although the penalty most often inflicted was a fine.

In 1348 a royal privilege confirmed the Irish Mellifont in the exercise of full criminal jurisdiction, including capital punishment, within the abbey's extensive lordship. In the same country the abbot of Holy Cross was considered to be the "earl" of the County of the Cross. King John recognized this high rank of the abbot who, in fact, was often invited to sit in Parliament. Since each county had two courts, the "king's court" took charge of criminal matters, while the "earl's court," in this case the abbot's court, possessed civil jurisdiction over all individuals within the County of the Cross. The abbot's civil jurisdiction remained unquestioned until the Dissolution under Henry VIII.

By the end of the fourteenth century the abbot of the Swabian Salem exercised judicial authority over nine villages of the neighborhood. Originally his jurisdiction covered only minor offenses, while the "four great cases," murder, robbery, arson and theft, belonged to the court of the counts of Heiligenberg. Meanwhile a few German abbeys, such as Waldsassen and Doberan, exercised the full extent of "high justice," involving capital punishment. Salem's authority was not restricted to criminal justice. The abbot was also empowered to issue orders, regulations and prohibitions for the villages under his jurisdiction, particularly in matters of trade, commerce and the holding of local markets. In 1470 Emperor Frederick III permitted the abbey to collect taxes and impositions from its subjects as well as to demand labor and military services. Salem's governmental role rested largely on its "imperial abbey" status (*Reichsabtei*) granted by Emperor Charles IV in 1354. By virtue of this privilege the abbey came under the immediate authority of the emperor and the abbot of Salem shared the rights of territorial princes. The process of administrative independence reached its fulness in 1637, when even the jurisdiction over capital crimes was transferred to the abbey.

It should be, perhaps, needless to emphasize that the correlation between Cistercian abbeys and surrounding society was not without tension and occasional hostility. Apart from the validity of specific charges, the rapid growth of the Order alone evoked the vigorous criticism of all those who found themselves threatened, or at least unfavorably affected, by the monks' success. Cistercian land acquisitions continued during the thirteenth century, though at a slower pace, and coincided with a conspicuous growth of rural population, which in turn produced an increasing land hunger. The rising value of scarce land, much of it in the firm grip of the "dead hand" of great abbeys, was bound to evoke the disapproval of contemporaries. The image of sprawling

394

monastic estates in the midst of a shrinking terrain, more than anything else, was responsible for a variety of charges leveled against Cistercians throughout the thirteenth century.

The first wave of hostility was generated by the jealousy of the Black Monks and other older religious organizations; it was joined later by bishops who objected to the ever expanding exemption and fiscal immunities of the Order. Finally, many Cistercian abbeys found themselves surrounded by great lay estates, whose powerful owners used every means to curtail the monks' further expansion.

In addition to the early antagonism between the White Monks and Cluny, as early as about 1130, a canon of the cathedral of Chartres, Payen Bolotin, directed a devastating attack against all monastic reformers, but especially against those "wearing the white habit." His work was a satirical poem, taking every liberty of that literary genre to advance sweeping denunciations of the monks' avarice, hypocrisy, boastful self-glorification and vain delight in novelties. All these vices, asserted the angry canon, had increased confusion in the Church to such a degree that one was inclined to view the new monks as apocalyptic false prophets.

Immunity from the payment of tithes coupled with the actual acquisition of churches and claims of exemption soon spoiled the originally friendly relation between Cistercian abbeys and their neighboring bishops. The vocal criticism of the hierarchy found a vigorous echo in Rome, and even such great friends of the Order as Alexander III did not hesitate to use harsh language to remind the General Chapter of its duty to watch over the observance of the early ideals of Cîteaux.

A letter of Innocent III to the General Chapter of 1214 contained the fullest catalogue of current charges against the Order: though the non-payment of tithes many parish churches had been ruined; land-grabbing abbots had made their neighbors' lives so miserable that they were forced to sell their property to the monks; the Order, despite its own laws, was engaged in buying commodities for resale at higher prices; monasteries, contrary to their professed ideals, had accepted churches and were engaged in pastoral activity; and finally, rich people were able to buy rights of burial in Cistercian churches. All these transgressions, claimed the pope, "were against your Order's initial statutes, which you have relaxed in these and other matters to such an extent that unless you restore them at once to due integrity, one may fear for your Order's imminent disaster."

The General Chapter reacted to the charges with a series of restrictive regulations, but clerical criticism could not be appeased by a mere protestation of good intentions. Nearly a century later (1284) Archbishop

John Pecham of Canterbury, a Franciscan and avowed adversary of the monks, sharply protested to Edward I against the transfer of Aberconway to Maenan, arguing that "the parson of the place, with plenty of other people, have a very great horror of the approach of the foresaid monks. For though they be good men, if God please, still they are the hardest neighbors that prelates and parsons could have. For where they plant their foot, they destroy villages, take away tithes and curtail by their privileges all the power of the prelacy."

While still in the process of vigorous expansion, the Order suffered considerable loss of prestige through the charges of clerics, low in rank but rated highly as makers of public opinion. They belonged to a new class of well-schooled and versatile propagandists, who did not hesitate to apply their literary skills, nurtured on Horace, Juvenal and Martial, to their own best advantage by attacking their real or imaginary enemies. The best known among them was certainly Gerald of Wales (d. 1223), an acerb critic of monks. Although he was a frequent guest of Welsh abbots, he became convinced that he had been slighted and in retaliation compiled damaging anecdotes about them. Five of his targets were Cistercians. Gerald was not blind to the virtues of the Order, but he eagerly repeated the charges of avarice, the familiar slur of inefficient competitors against the thrifty and hard-working monks. He thought that French Cistercians had preserved more of the intitial spirit of the Order than had their English confreres, "whose habit has become black as soot with stains that resist the fuller's art and the strength of the most mordant lye."

Gerald's contemporary and fellow-Welshman, Walter Map (d. 1210), had an intense dislike of Cistericans, largely because he had been wronged by the monks of Flaxley. He too accused the Order of shameless avarice, but his charges were made far more damaging because Walter was close to the circle of the personal entourage of Henry II. To the all-pervading sin of cupidity he added others, such as cruelty to the inhabitants of villages destroyed by the monks and the forgery of charters whereby monks encroached on other peoples' lawful properties. He remained unimpressed by the hard work and simple way of life of Cistercians and argued that upland Welshmen had a harsher and more laborious lot.

A third contemporary, Nigel Wireker (d. c. 1207), monk of Christ Church, produced a milder version of the stock criticism in his satirical *Mirror of Fools (Speculum Stultorum).* He was willing to recognize the industry and frugality of the White Monks, but he castigated them for their avarice, for tolerating no neighbors, for being never content with

396

plenty. He, like his fellow-critics, made endless fun of breechless Cistercian brothers, gratifying targets for coarse merriment.

Writing about 1205, a French counterpart of the English satirists, Guiot de Provins, lamented the limitless expansion of Cistercian estates, where herds of pigs foraged over desecrated gravesites and neighbors were driven mad by the ceaseless tinkling of cowbells. He viewed the monks as vagrant hypocrites and false hermits.

The biting criticism in itself lacked tangible consequences, yet the Order was deeply disturbed. About 1230 Abbot Stephen Lexington warned his monks against ostentatious wealth, "because in these days our Order has many sly detractors." The General Chapter of 1248 sounded the same alarm "because in these days of growing malice, our Order is exposed in many parts of the world to frequent vexations on account of our privileges and immunities; it is necessary, therefore, that our brethren support one another, so that [our Order] would survive like a strong citadel."

The reference to the Order as a fortress was, unfortunately, more than a figure of speech. The years following the Fourth Lateran Council (1215) were particularly trying for French Cistercians. Abbatial estates were constantly harassed by powerful neighbors, lay and ecclesiastical alike. Jurisdictional disputes often degenerated into armed incursions, particularly in the northeast of the country. Among other similarly afflicted monasteries, in the 1220s the abbey of Longpont was repeatedly attacked by destructive hordes hired by the Bishop of Soissons. Cîteaux itself had much to suffer from jealous neighbors and the financial distress of the abbey was largely the result of devastating raids against monastic property. Habitual recourse to papal protection brought a number of warnings, investigations and occasional excommunications of the delinquents, measures which remained largely ineffectual.

Poblet, the Catalan abbey, highly favored by Aragonese royalty and steadily supported by the papacy, had accumulated by the end of the twelfth century vast estates, but, for the same reason, aroused the jealousy of neighboring bishops and nobility, all locked in an intensive competition for the spoils of the successful *Reconquista*. Border disputes, vandalism and violence multiplied. Although the monks were mostly vindicated at royal or papal courts, paper guarantees were poor compensations for the growing number of avowed enemies. Eventually, in order to avoid bad publicity as well as expensive yet often inconclusive litigation, the monks became more and more amenable to the settlement of disputes through private negotiations; by the middle of the thirteenth century, payoffs and

397

the purchasing of rival claims had become quite common and the consolidation of scattered monastic estates was achieved by buying or exchanging land.

Meanwhile, there was no indication that the rural masses had turned against the Order. Popular disturbances affected abbeys only sporadically, mostly in connection with the outbreaks of the Black Death. In England such attacks occurred after the issuance of the Statute of Laborers in 1351, which rejected the demands for higher wages in behalf of the much reduced peasantry. The same situation was the background of agitation among the bondmen of Waghen, a hamlet of the abbey of Meaux. Under Abbot Robert Beverley (1357-1367) the villagers attempted to gain full freedom from the abbey, claiming that their ancestors had belonged to a royal manor. The abbey, after much litigation, won the case, but it was clearly at the expense of the monks' popularity. It is equally clear that the tax-collecting role of some abbots failed to improve their public image.

The Reformation jeopardized for the first time the very ideals of monasticism. The reformers' vitriolic criticism directed against monks was followed up by wholesale secularization wherever the new creed prevailed. The end of prolonged religious wars found the Cistercian Order heavily decimated, but not without a surprisingly vigorous resilience. The success of recovery must be, in a large measure, attributed to a new upsurge of popular approval, motivated either by the rekindling of strict asceticism or by an increased measure of pastoral ministry prevalent particularly in German lands.

The anti-monastic campaign of "enlightened" *philosophes* preceding the French Revolution had no widespread popular support, but it revitalized the always latent jealousy between the regular and secular clergy. The French hierarchy watched dispassionately the dismemberment of ancient monastic institutions, while the spreading wave of secularization was manipulated throughout the continent by forces of economic and political interest in disregard of the still manifest attachment to many of the great and prosperous abbeys.

Without this deep-seated and widely shared sympathy for Cistercians the nineteenth-century reconstruction of the Order could never have been achieved. Membership failed to exceed pre-revolutionary figures, but in every other respect the high standing of the Order in both observances reflected a public support which in its sincerity and disinterested spontaneity far surpassed the stale atmosphere of the Old Regime. Vocations became entirely free, yet plentiful, attracted to the Order for no other reason than fervent devotion. The encumbrances of running huge estates disappeared and monks could concentrate all their energies on the attainment of religious goals. There is no doubt that monastic discipline within the reborn Strict Observance surpassed everything the Order had experienced since the first decades of the twelfth century. The hard-working members of the Common Observance, dedicated to the selfless service of their secular environment through scholarly labors, teaching and pastoral care, insured for themselves an enviable reputation for excellence.

As long as there remains a healthy interaction between Cistercians and society, as long as the Order can exemplify an appealing ideal of Christian perfection, there will always be a new chapter added to the history of the White Monks.

Bibliographical Notes

GENERAL

1. *Bibliographies*

A practical and up-to-date guide to medieval monastic studies is Giles Constable, *Medieval Monasticism. A Select Bibliography* (Toronto: U. of Toronto Press, 1976). A previous article by the same author, "The Study of Monastic History," in *Essays on the Reconstruction of Medieval History,* ed. V. Mudroch and G. S. Couse (Montreal: McGill-Queen's U. Press, 1974), pp. 19-51, can be considered as an introduction to his *Bibliography.*

There is no comprehensive bibliography of Cistercian history. A multivolume *Repertory* of all Cistercian establishments, complete with their bibliographies, is being prepared in Hungary by Father Ferenc Hervay, but the date of publication has not been set.

A busy center of bibliographical and other reference works is the Belgian Trappist abbey of Saint-Remy in Rochefort, under the direction of Father Eugène Manning. Since 1968, under the collective title "Documentation Cistercienne," he has published several special bibliographies. These are: R. A. Donkin, *A Check List of Published Works Pertaining to the Cistercian Order as a Whole and to the Houses of the British Isles in Particular* (Doc. Cist., vol. 2, 1969). See some additions and corrections to it by Ferenc Hervay in *Analecta Cisterciensia,* 27 (1971), 310-21. Benoît Chauvin, *Bibliographie cistercienne franc-comtoise* (Doc. Cist., vol. 9, 1973). Emile Brouette and Eugène Manning, *Bibliographie de la Belgique cistercienne* (Doc. Cist., vol. 13, 1974).

There are complete bibliographies dealing with the life and works of Saint Bernard of Clairvaux. These are in chronological sequence: Leopold Janauschek, *Bibliographia Bernardina,* vol. IV of Xenia Bernardina, (Vienna: Hoelder, 1891), available also in modern reprint. Jean de la Croix Bouton, *Bibliographie bernardine,* 1891-1957 (Paris: Lethielleux, 1958). Eugène Manning, *Bibliographie bernardine,* 1957-1970 (Doc. Cist., vol. 6, 1972).

2. *Printed Collections of Sources*

Indispensable for the study of any phase of Cistercian history is Josephus-Maria Canivez, *Statuta Capitulorum Generalium Ordinis Cis-*

400

terciensis ab anno 1116 ad annum 1786, 8 vols. (Louvain: Bibliothèque de la Revue d'Histoire Ecclésiastique, 1933-1941). Since the innumerable references to the various statutes of the General Chapter will not be further identified in the text of this book, in order to help the reader to find them by their years, here is the distribution of the material by years and volumes: I, 1116-1220; II, 1221-1261; III, 1262-1400; IV, 1401-1456; V, 1457-1490; VI, 1491-1542; VII, 1546-1786; VIII, a detailed index.

The seventeenth-century work of Julien Paris, updated and republished by Hugues Séjalon, *Nomasticon Cisterciense* (Solesmes, 1892), remains a valuable collection of usages, papal documents and collections of statutes. This work, too, has an analytical index of subjects.

The latest editions of the earliest Cistercian sources are: Jean-Baptiste Van Damme, *Documenta pro cisterciensis ordinis historiae ac juris studio* (Westmalle, 1959), and the larger and better annotated Jean de la Croix Bouton and J.-B. Van Damme, *Les plus anciens textes de Cîteaux* (Achel: Saint-Remy, 1974).

For the nineteenth-century Trappist history the most important source collection is Vincent Hermans, *Actes des chapitres généraux des congrégations trappistes au XIXème siècle,* 1835-1891 (Rome, 1975: bound volume of offprints taken from *Analecta Cisterciensia,* 1971-74). References to Trappist chapters in Chapter XIV can be easily identified by their years, or with the help of indexes concluding the collection, pp. 591-663. The acts of the nineteenth- and twentieth-century sessions of the General Chapter of the Common Observance have not yet been published, although since 1953 the most important legal documents have been made available in the periodically published bulletins of the *Acta Curiae Generalis Ordinis Cisterciensis* (Rome: Curia Generalis, 1953-). The acts of the most recent Trappist chapters have been privately published and circulated.

3. *Works of Reference*

The only twentieth-century work listing all Cistercian houses, both for men and women, is Laurent H. Cottineau, *Répertoire topo-bibliographique des abbayes et prieurés,* 2 vols. (Mâcon: Protat, 1939). A third volume of indexes was published in 1970 by Grégoire Poras.

The still indispensable chronological list of all Cistercian abbeys for monks is Leopold Janauschek, *Originum Cisterciensium Tomus I* (Vienna: Hoelder, 1877), available also in a recently made reprint. Janauschek's planned "Tomus II" listing Cistercian nunneries was never completed.

Within the series "Documentation Cistercienne" a new *Dictionnaire des monastères cisterciens* in two volumes (18/I-II) is under preparation. The first volume by Maur Cocheril, *Cartes géographiques* (Doc. Cist., vol. 18/I, 1976) has already been published. The second volume, still in preparation, is intended to update Janauschek's old work, including a list of nunneries.

The beautifully printed Frédéric van der Meer, *Atlas de l'ordre cistercien* (Paris: Séquoia, 1965), is more valuable for its 878 illustrations of Cistercian architecture than for its maps or list of abbeys. Its many errors and omissions were corrected by Maur Cocheril in *Cîteaux,* 17(1966), 119-44; Edgar Krausen and Polycarpe Zakar in *Analecta Cisterciensia,* 22(1966), 279-90; Felix Vongrey and Ferenc Hervay in *Analecta Cisterciensia,* 23(1967), 115-52; Franz Schrader in *Cîteaux,* 21(1970), 265-78.

A great repertory of all French monastic institutions was initiated by Dom Beaunier and later continued by Jean-Martial Besse and others, resulting in the *Abbayes et prieurés de l'ancienne France,* 12 vols. (Paris: Picard, 1906-1941), but remains still incomplete. The volumes represent dioceses. The individual entries are particularly valuable for the full listing of archival sources. Jules de Trévillers, *Sequania monastica* (Vesoul, 1949, with a supplement added in 1955) deals only with the historical Franche-Comté, giving more historical details but less bibliography.

A work on a grand scale is the *Monasticon Belge,* initiated in 1890 by Ursmer Berlière and continued by several other scholars. Until 1973 four volumes have been published, but each features several independently published and bound "parts" (Liège: Centre Nat. de Recherches). The earlier volumes have been reprinted.

Modern scholarly repertories covering the British Isles are: David Knowles and Richard Neville Hadcock, *Medieval Religious Houses: England and Wales,* 2nd ed. (New York: St. Martin's, 1972) David E. Easson, *Medieval Religious Houses: Scotland* (London: Longmans, 1957); Aubrey O. Gwynn and R. N. Hadcock, *Medieval Religious Houses: Ireland* (London: Longmans, 1970).

A short list of all Cistercian houses for both sexes throughout the old "Holy Roman Empire" is the *Germania Monastica,* published first in the volumes of *Studien und Mitteilungen* and eventually collected in one volume (Ottobeuren, 1917, reprinted in 1967). A similar work giving the short histories of 88 Cistercian abbeys in Italy is Balduino Gustavo Bedini, *Breve prospetto delle abazie cisterciensi d'Italia* (Casamari, 1964). Sebastian Brunner, *Ein Cisterzienserbuch* (Würzburg: Woerl, 1882), gives the histories of all Cistercian abbeys of both sexes within Austria-Hungary and Switzerland.

A most useful tool of research is the *Dictionnaire d'histoire et de géographie ecclésiastiques,* ed. Alfred Baudrillart et al., 18 vols. (Paris: Letouzey, 1912-   ), but has progressed only to the letter "F." All better-known Cistercian authors are characterized in the *Dictionnaire de spiritualité,* ed. M. Viller et al., 9 vols. (Paris: Beauchesne, 1937-   ), having progressed to the letter "L." The listing of all Cistercian authors active before 1800 (altogether some two thousand) is the intention of Eugène Manning, editor of the *Dictionnaire des auteurs cisterciens* (Doc. Cist., vol. 16, 1975-   ) of which to date two bulletins have appeared, covering letters A-C. The Italian *Dizionario degli instituti de perfezione,* ed. Giancarlo Rocca et al., 6 vols. (Rome: Edizioni Paoline, 1976-) is currently in press, carrying substantial articles on Cistercians.

4. *General Surveys of Cistercian History*

The first modern attempt at a scholarly survey of Cistercian history as a whole was made by the founder and life-long editor of the *Cistercienser-Chronik,* Gregor Müller, who published the results of his research serialized in his journal. The offprints bound in one volume were published under the title *Vom Cistercienser Orden* (Bregenz, 1927). It is largely the sequence of external events in rigid chronological order. A somewhat expanded and updated French version of the same work was published by Eugène Willems, *Esquisse historique de l'ordre de Cîteaux,* 2 vols. (N.-D. du Val-Dieu, 1957-58).

Jean de la Croix Bouton, *Histoire de l'ordre de Cîteaux* (Westmalle, 1959), is a work of similar origin (published in separate bulletins as "Fiches cisterciennes" from 1955 to 1959) and similar nature, arranging the material chronologically, interspersed with various digressions. It is a rich and valuable inventory of names, dates and events, without trying to forge the material into organic units.

My first attempt at a survey, *The White Monks* (Okauchee, Wis.: Our Lady of Spring Bank, 1953) was subsequently published in French, considerably updated and enlarged; *Les moines blancs* (Paris: Seuil, 1957); the same was translated and restructured to suit German readers by Father (now abbot of Himmerod) Ambrosius Schneider, *Geschichte und Wirken der Weissen Mönche* (Cologne: Wienand, 1958).

The articles "Cîteaux" (abbey) and "Cîteaux" (Order) by J.-M. Canivez in the *Dictionnaire d'histoire et de géographie ecclésiastiques,* XII(1951), 852-997, amount to a factual survey of Cistercian history, well furnished with detailed bibliography.

The large and richly illustrated volume, edited by Abbot Ambrosius Schneider, *Die Cistercienser. Geschichte, Geist, Kunst* (Cologne: Wienand, 1974), features a number of studies by different authors, dealing mostly with the cultural and artistic achievements of the Order in Germany.

5. Scholarly Journals

The oldest and still surviving periodical dedicated to Cistercian history is the *Cistercienser-Chronik*, published by the monks of the Austrian Mehrerau since 1889. A full index in two volumes of all personal names and places for the first 75 years (ending with 1968) has been published by the Trappist monks of Achel (Belgium) in 1975. A short index of authors and titles for the first 50 volumes was printed in 1939.

The Cistercians of the Strict Observance (Trappists) are publishing the following three journals: *Collectanea Ordinis Cisterciensium Reformatorum*, edited by the monks of Scourmont (Belgium) since 1934, dedicated primarily to spirituality and liturgy. Since 1965 the title has been simplified to *Collectanea Cisterciensia*. *Cîteaux in de Nederlanden* has been published by the monks of Westmalle (Belgium) since 1950, dedicated to monastic history; its title was changed in 1959 to *Cîteaux*. The *Cistercian Studies*, edited by the nuns of Abbaye de la Paix, Chimay (Belgium) since 1966, features translations from the above two (mostly French) journals as well as original articles in English.

The leading scholarly journal of the Common Observance is the *Analecta Sacri Ordinis Cisterciensis*, published in Rome since 1945; in 1966 the title was changed to *Analecta Cisterciensia*.

There are three Benedictine periodicals carrying a number of articles of Cistercian interest. These are: *Studien und Mitteilungen zur Geschichte des Benediktiner-Ordens und seiner Zweige*, edited by the abbey of Ottobeuren (Germany) since 1880; *Revue Bénédictine*, edited by the abbey of Maredsous (Belgium) since 1884; *Studia Monastica*, edited since 1959 by the Spanish (Catalan) monks of Montserrat.

The journal with relatively few articles on Cistercians, but the richest in bibliography, is the *Revue d'Histoire Ecclésiastique*, published by the Catholic University of Louvain since 1900.

ABBREVIATIONS

AC	*Analecta Cisterciensia*, 1945-
Actes	Vincent Hermans, *Actes des chapitres généraux des congregations trappistes au XIXe siècle* (1975), bound offprints from *AC*, 1971-74
Bock	Colomban Bock, *Les codifications du droit cistercien* (Westmalle, 1966)

Bouton	Jean de la Croix Bouton, *Histoire de l'ordre de Cîteaux* (Westmalle, 1959)
Caesarius	Caesarius Heisterbacensis, *Dialogus miraculorum*, ed. J. Strange, 2 vols. (Cologne: Heberle, 1851)
Canivez	J.-M. Canivez, *L'ordre de Cîteaux en Belgique* (Forges-lez-Chimay: Scourmont, 1926)
CC	*Cistercienser-Chronik*, 1889-
Chronica	Thomas Burton, *Chronica monasterii de Melsa*, ed. E. A. Bond, Rolls Series, No. 43, 3 vols. (London: H.M. Stationary Office, 1866)
Cîteaux	*Cîteaux*, 1950-
Coll	*Collectanea Cisterciensia*, 1934-
CS	*Cistercian Studies*, 1966-
DHGE	*Dictionnaire d'histoire et de géographie ecclésiastiques*, 1912-
DS	*Dictionnaire de spiritualité*, 1937-
Exm	*Exordium magnum cisterciense*, ed. Bruno Griesser (Rome: Editiones Cistercienses, 1961)
GM	*Germania monastica* (Ottobeuren, 1917)
Janauschek	Leopold Janauschek, *Originum cisterciensium tomus I* (Vienna: Hoelder, 1877)
King	Archdale A. King, *Cîteaux and her Elder Daughters* (London: Burns & Oates, 1954)
Knowles I	David Knowles, *The Monastic Order in England*, 2nd ed. (Cambridge U. Press, 1950)
Knowles IV	D. Knowles, *The Religious Orders in England*, vol. 3 (Cambridge U. Press, 1959)
Knowles-Hadcock	D. Knowles and R. N. Hadcock, *Medieval Religious Houses: England and Wales*, 2nd ed. (New York: St. Martin's Press, 1972)
Krausen	Edgar Krausen, *Die Klöster des Zisterzienser ordens in Bayern* (Munich: Heimatforschung, 1953)
Lexington	"Registrum epistolarum Stephani de Lexinton," ed. Bruno Griesser, *AC*, 2 (1946), 1-118; 8 (1952), 181-378.
Mahn	Jean-Berthold Mahn, *L'ordre cistercien et son gouvernement des origines au milieu du XIIIe siècle* (Paris: Boccard, 1945)
Marilier	Abbé J. Marilier, *Chartes et documents concernant l'abbaye de Cîteaux, 1098-1182* (Rome: Editiones Cistercienses, 1961)
Nomasticon	*Nomasticon cisterciense*, ed. J. Paris and H. Séjalon (Solesmes, 1892)

PL	*Patrologia Latina,* ed. J.-P. Migne, 221 vols. (Paris, 1844-64)
RB	*Revue Bénédictine,* 1884-
RHE	*Revue d'Histoire Ecclésiastique,* 1900-
SM	*Studia Monastica,* 1959-
Statuta	*Statuta Capitulorum Generalium Ordinis Cisterciensis,* ed J.-M. Canivez, 8 vols. (Louvain: Bibl. de la *RHE,* 1933-41)
SuM	*Studien und Mitteilungen,* 1880-
Textes	*Les plus anciens textes de Cîteaux,* ed. Jean de la Croix Bouton and Jean-B. Van Damme (Achel: St. Remy, 1974)
White Monks	Louis J. Lekai, *The White Monks* (Okauchee, Wis.: Our Lady of Spring Bank, 1953)
Winter	Franz Winter, *Die Zisterzienser des nordöstlichen Deutschlands.* 3 vols. (Gotha: Perthes, 1868; rpt. Aalen: Scientia Verlag, 1966)

1. *The Eleventh-Century Monastic Reforms*

The body of this chapter is the adaptation of my previously published study, "Motives and Ideals of the Eleventh-Century Monastic Renewal," *The Cistercian Spirit,* ed. Basil Pennington (Spencer, Mass.: Cistercian Publications, 1970), pp. 27-47. The same came out even earlier in *CS,* 4 (1969), 3-20. See for references either of these publications. Since then the same issues have been dealt with in far greater detail by Bede Lackner, *The Eleventh-Century Background of Cîteaux* (Washington, D.C.: Cistercian Publications, 1972). A series of authoritative studies covering the same subject have been published following an international conference in Mendola (Italy) in 1968: *Il monachesimo e la riforma ecclesiastica, 1049-1122* (Milan: Univ. Cat. del Sacro Cuore, 1971). The whole problem was masterfully summarized by Jean Leclercq, "The Monastic Crisis of the Eleventh and Twelfth Centuries," *Cluniac Monasticism in the Central Middle Ages,* ed. Noreen Hunt (Hamden, Conn.: Archon Books, 1971), pp. 217-37.

For recent studies on other details see E. W. McDonnell, "The *Vita Apostolica*: Diversity or Dissent?" *Church History,* 24(1955), 15-31; Jean Leclercq, "L'érémitisme et les cisterciens," *L'eremitismo in Occidente nei secoli XI e XII* (Milan: Univ. Cat. del Sacro Cuore, 1965), pp. 573-80.

2. *From Molesme to Cîteaux*

See Saint Robert's *Vita* published by Kolumban Spahr, *Das Leben des hl. Robert von Molesme* (Freiburg [Switzerland]: Paulusdruckerei, 1944).

406

For all details on Molesme see Lackner's *The Eleventh-Century Background of Cîteaux,* pp. 217-74, with further bibliography. See for a critical survey of all known sources on Robert, J.-A. Lefèvre, "S. Robert de Molesme dans l'opinion monastique du XIIe et du XIIIe siècle," *Analecta Bollandiana,* 74 (1956), 50-83, quoting in full, among others, William of Malmesbury and Ordericus Vitalis. See the document on the abbey of Aulps in *Textes,* p. 129.

All quotations referring to the circumstances of the foundation of Cîteaux were taken from the *Exordium Cistercii* and *Exordium parvum,* both given in translation in Appendix I. See on the synod of Port-d'Anselle *Textes,* pp. 143-46. On the juridical status, location and early possessions of Cîteaux, see Abbé J. Marilier, "Les débuts de l'abbaye de Cîteaux," *Mémoires de la société pour l'histoire du droit et des institutions des anciens pays bourguignons, comtois et romands,* 15 (1953), 71-76. See the critical remarks of the *Exm* concerning Robert's behavior on p. 68. On the first three abbots of Cîteaux, see Jean-Baptiste Van Damme, *Les trois fondateurs de Cîteaux* (Westmalle, 1966). On the genuine nature of the various documents incorporated in the *Exordium parvum* see Marilier, *Chartes et documents,* pp. 34-48. See the letter of Saint-Pierre de Pothières, *ibid.,* pp. 41-46.

A critical analysis of the *Exordium parvum* and in it the *instituta* of Alberic is given in J.-A. Lefèvre, "Le vrai récit primitif des origines de Cîteaux est-il l'*Exordium parvum?*" *Le Moyen Age,* 61 (1955), 79-120, 329-61. The documents of donations and other early activities of Stephen Harding are published in Marilier, pp. 55-65. See the circumstances of the foundation of La Ferté, *ibid.,* pp. 65-66. The date of Saint Bernard's entry at Cîteaux is discussed in J. Winandy, "Les origines de Cîteaux et les travaux de M. Lefèvre," *RB,* 67 (1957), 60-63, and its further implications in A. H. Bredero, "Etudes sur la *Vita prima* de Saint Bernard," *AC,* 17 (1961), 60-62. See the bull of Callistus II of 1119 in Marilier, pp. 81-82.

3. *The Fundamentals of Cistercian Reform*

The recent developments in the research of Cistercian beginnings are conveniently summarized by David Knowles, "The Primitive Cistercian Documents," in his *Great Historical Enterprises* (London: Nelson, 1963), pp. 199-222. A more detailed article of similar nature is Polycarpe Zakar, "Die Anfänge des Zisterzienserordens," *AC,* 20 (1964), 103-38. The greatest stir was created in the 1950s by J.-A. Lefèvre, then a graduate student at Louvain, who, between 1950 and 1959, published fifteen articles on the subject in various journals and eventually established an impressive and coherent hypothesis designed to solve all related problems. See his most comprehensive "Que savons-nous du Cîteaux primitif?" *RHE,* 51 (1956),

5-41. The views expressed in this chapter on the *Exordium parvum* are based on Lefèvre's research. His theory on the development of the *Charter of Charity* has been much criticized, notably by Jean-B. Van Damme, who in turn presented another hypothesis, summarized in "Formation de la constitution cistercienne," *SM*, 4 (1962), 111-37, and "La constitution cistercienne de 1165," *AC*, 19 (1963), 51-104.

The best edition of William of Malmesbury's *Gesta* is still the one in the "Rolls Series," (No. 90) by William Stubbs, 2 vols. (London: H. M. Stationary Office, 1889). See the chapter on Cistercians in vol. 2, pp. 380-85. The *Historia ecclesiastica* of Ordericus Vitalis has a new edition and English translation by Marjorie Chibnall, *The Ecclesiastical History of Orderic Vitalis* (Oxford: Clarendon, 1973); the chapter on Cistercians is in vol. 4, pp. 312-27. The latest on the feud between Cistercians and Cluniacs are: David Knowles, "Cistercians and Cluniacs," in his *The Historian and Character* (Cambridge U. Press, 1963), pp. 50-75; and Adrian H. Bredero, "Cluny et Cîteaux au XIIe siecle: les origins de la controverse," *Studi Medievali*, 12 (1971), 135-75. On Pons de Melgueil in the context of St. Bernard's *Apologia* the latest is a debate between professors Bredero and P. Zerbi, "Sur Pons de Cluny et Pierre le Vénérable," *Aevum*, 48 (1974), 135-49, and J.-B. Van Damme, "Bernard de Clairvaux et Pons de Cluny. Controverse au sujet d'une controverse," *Cîteaux*, 25 (1974), 271-86. See St. Bernard's *Apologia* translated by Michael Casey in *The Works of Bernard of Clairvaux*, Treatises, I (Spencer, Mass.: Cistercian Publications, 1970), pp. 33-69. For the point of view of Cluny, see *The Letters of Peter the Venerable*, ed. Giles Constable, 2 vols. (Cambridge: Harvard U. Press, 1967), particularly letters No. 28 and 111. See the critical edition of the *Dialogus* by R. B. C. Huygens in *Studi Medievali*, 13 (1972), 375-470.

See the *Capitula* of 1119 translated from *Textes* in Appendix I. An early version of the *Instituta* was published by Canisius Noschitzka in *AC*, 6 (1950), 22-38, followed by the *Ecclesiastica officia*. See also J.-B. Van Damme, "Genèse des *Instituta Generalis Capituli*," *Cîteaux*, 12 (1961), 28-60. See the traditional text of the whole *Consuetudines* in *Nomasticon: Ecclesiastica officia*, pp. 84-211; *Instituta generalis capituli*, pp. 212-33; *Usus conversorum*, 234-41. See all three versions of the *Carta caritatis* in *Textes*; the *Summa cartae caritatis* and *Carta caritatis posterior* are given in translations in Appendix I.

On the influence of Vallombrosa, see D. Roger Duvernay, "Cîteaux, Vallombreuse et Étienne Harding," *AC*, 8 (1952), 379-494. See the "Accord of Molesme" in *Textes*, pp. 130-31. On the influence of the General Chapter on other orders, see Mahn, pp. 239-52. I discussed the relationship between the Rule and early Cistercian legislation in "The Rule and the Early Cistercians," *CS*, 5 (1970), 243-51; the last two pages of this chapter were taken from there.

4. *Saint Bernard and the Expansion*

All quotes from Ordericus Vitalis may be identified in the already quoted Chibnall edition, vol. 4, pp. 311-26. See the few lines from Otto of Bamberg in *Libellus de diversis ordinibus*, ed. Giles Constable and B. Smith (Oxford: Clarendon, 1972), p. XI. All references to the numbers and foundation dates of Cistercian abbeys may be verified in Janauschek.

In spite of the unabating interest in St. Bernard, there is still no adequate substitute for E. Vacandard, *Vie de Saint Bernard*, 4th ed., 2 vols. (Paris: Gabalda, 1927). English readers may turn to the dry but factually reliable Watkin Williams, *Saint Bernard of Clairvaux* (Westminster, Md.: Newman, 1952). For a genial appraisal of his works and influence, see Dom Jean Leclercq, *Saint Bernard et l'esprit cistercien* (Paris: Seuil, 1966), reprinted with updated bibliography in 1975. See the same in English translation by Claire Lavoie, *Bernard of Clairvaux and the Cistercian Revolt* (Kalamazoo: Cistercian Publications, 1976).

Concerning the Italian foundations see Gregorio Penco, *Storia del monachesimo in Italia* (Rome: Edizioni Paoline, 1961), pp. 258-71, and the above mentioned Bedini, *Breve prospetto*. That the Cistercians were warmly received in the Norman Kingdom of Sicily is clear from the quick succession of foundations. See about this Hans-Walter Klewitz, "Anfänge des Cistercienserordens in normannisch-sizilischen Königreich," *SuM*, 52 (1934), 236-51. See for German foundations for monks and nuns *GM*. On England and Wales, see the excellent Knowles-Hadcock, pp. 110-32. For a brilliant narrative of English foundations, see Knowles I, pp. 208-66. The historical reliability of the foundation-history of Fountains has been most recently questioned in a series of articles by L.G.D. Baker, "The Genesis of English Cistercian Chronicles," *AC*, 25 (1969), 14-41; 31 (1975), 179-212; a third article is still forthcoming. On Walter Espec's appearance see *Cartularium Abbathiae de Rievalle* (Edinburgh: Surtees Soc., 1889), p. XII. On Scotland and Ireland see ("Works of Reference") D. E. Easson and Gwynn-Hadcock. The more recent Geraldine Carville, "The Cistercian Settlement in Ireland," *SM*, 15 (1973), 23-41, lists fewer houses (36), all founded between 1142 and 1272. According to her the most prosperous houses were the ones built over Celtic sites. On Irish conditions in the thirteenth century see Lexington's correspondence, *AC*, 2 (1946), 1-118. For a sympathetic approach toward the Irish, see the articles by B. W. O'Dwyer, "Gaelic Monasticism and the Irish Cistercians c. 1228," *Irish Ecclesiastical Record*, 108 (1967), 19-28; *The Conspiracy of Mellifont,*

1216-1231 (Dublin: Historical Assoc., 1970); and the most detailed: "The Crisis in the Cistercian Monasteries in Ireland in the Early Thirteenth Century," *AC*, 31 (1975), 266-304, to be continued in the same journal.

On Spain and Portugal, Maur Cocheril, "L'implantation des abbayes cisterciennes dans la péninsule ibérique," *Anuario de Estudios Medievales*, 1 (1964), 217-87, has been followed. This study became a chapter in the same author's later volume: Dom Maur Cocheril, *Études sur le monachisme en Espagne et au Portugal* (Lisbon: Bertrand, 1966). The unfinished work of Edward Ortved, *Cistercieordenen og dens klostere i norden*, 2 vols. (Copenhagen: Schultz, 1927), dealing only with Sweden, could not be exploited because of language-barrier. See for some information C. A. J. France, "List of Danish Cistercian Abbots," *AC*, 20 (1964), 185-98. On Bohemia, see Franz Machilek, "Die Zisterzienser in Böhmens and Mähren," *Archiv für Kirchengeschichte von Böhmen-Mähren-Schlesien*, 3 (1973), 185-220, with good bibliography on every phase of Cistercian life in these lands. The problem of Polish foundations has been recently discussed by Jerzy Kłoczowski, "Les cisterciens en Pologne du XIIe au XIIIe siècle," *Cîteaux*, 21 (1970), 111-34. On Cistercian beginnings in Hungary, see Remigius Békefi, "Geschichte des Cistercienser-Ordens in Ungarn," *CC*, 12 (1900), 1-14.

See the quotation taken from Ernaldus's *Vita* in *PL*, vol. 185, col. 267. On the consequences of Savigny's incorporation see a revealing chapter in Bennet D. Hill, *English Cistercian Monasteries and their Patrons in the Twelfth Century* (Urbana: U. of Illinois Press, 1968), pp. 80-115. See the latest on the Savigniacs by Mary Suydam, "Origins of the Savigniac Order. Savigny's role within twelfth-century monastic reform," *RB*, 86 (1976), 94-108. On Alexander III's warning in 1169, see Jean Leclercq, "Passage supprimé dans une épître d'Alexandre III," *RB*, 62 (1952), 151. In another letter, written about the same time, Alexander III accused specifically two previously Savigniac abbeys, Swineshead and Furness, saying that although "under religious considerations you have joined the order of Cistercian brothers, contrary to what it should be befitting, you do not observe at all things which are demanded by their institutions. Namely, we have heard that you possess villages and serfs, and when you take them before your courts, you punish them by fines and, like secular lords, you claim the right of patronage when you provide for churches." J. Leclercq, "Épîtres d'Alexandre III sur les cisterciens," *RB*, 69 (1954), 73.

5. *Crusades and Missions*

See for books and articles published before 1952 my *White Monks*, p. 292. On the public activity of St. Bernard there is a series of studies

410

published in *Mélanges Saint Bernard* (Dijon: Assoc. Bourguignonne des Soc. Savantes, 1953), pp. 9-133. On the Second Crusade see André Seguin, "Bernard et la seconde croisade," in *Bernard de Clairvaux*, sponsored by the "Commission d'histoire de l'ordre de Cîteaux" (Paris: Alsatia, 1953), pp. 379-410, and Eugene Willems, "Cîteaux et la seconde croisade," *RHE*, 49 (1954), 116-51. On a leading character of the Third Crusade, see Yves Congar, "Henri de Marcy, abbé de Clairvaux, cardinal évêque d'Albano et légat pontifical," *Studia Anselmiana*, 43 (1958), 1-90. On Cistercians and the Fourth Crusade and subsequent expansion in the Latin Empire there is a comprehensive study by Elisabeth A. R. Brown, "The Cistercians in the Latin Empire of Constantinople and Greece, 1204-1276," *Traditio*, 14 (1958), 63-120. On Daphni see a substantial article by Canivez in *DHGE*, XIV (1960), cols. 78-80. See also Romain Clair, "Les filles d'Hautecombe dans l'empire latin de Constantinople," *AC*, 17 (1961), 261-77. On Cistercian foundations in the Near East see D. H. Williams, "Cistercian Settlements in the Lebanon," *Cîteaux*, 25 (1974), 61-74.

The largely controversial bibliography on the heretics of southern France is very extensive. Pierre Belperron, *La croisade contre les albigeois* (Paris: Perrin, 1967) is generally considered the best comprehensive work. In English the latest and best is Walter L. Wakefield, *Heresy, Crusade and Inquisition in Southern France, 1100-1250* (Berkeley: U. of California Press, 1974). On St. Dominic and the Cistercians, see M.-H. Vicaire, *Saint Dominic and his Times*, trans. Kathleen Pond (New York: McGraw-Hill, 1964), pp. 58-136, and in greater detail, William A. Hinnebusch, *The History of the Dominican Order* (Staten Island: Alba House, 1965), I, 39-57. See the famous quote attributed to Amaury in Caesarius, I, 302. See the English translation of the full passage in Wakefield, *op.cit.*, pp. 195-99.

On the Spanish orders of knights, see François Gutton, *L'ordre de Calatrava* (Paris: Lethielleux, 1954). More scholarly and better documented are the studies of Joseph F. O'Callaghan, *The Spanish Military Order of Calatrava and its Affiliates. Collected Studies* (London: Variorum Reprints, 1975). See the figures on the wealth of these orders in the already quoted Maur Cocheril, "L'implantation . . . ," p. 272. There is a long article on Alcántara in *DHGE*, II, cols. 6-11. See also, Fr. Gutton, "L'ordre de Montesa," *Cîteaux*, 25 (1974), 97-136. On Portugal, see Maur Cocheril, "Les ordres militaires cisterciens au Portugal," *Bulletin des études portugaises*, 28-29 (1967-68), 11-70.

For the factual details of Cistercian expansion in northeastern Germany see the century-old work of Winter. See its English summary by James Westfall Thompson, "The Cistercian Order and Colonization in

Medieval Germany," *The American Journal of Theology*, 24 (1920), 67-93. See for further details Benno Abers, "Zur päpstlichen Missionspolitik in Lettland und Estland zur Zeit Innocenz's III," *Commentationes Balticae*, 4-5 (1956-57), published in Bonn, 1958, and Wolfgang Schmidt, "Die Zisterzienser in Baltikum und in Finnland" *Suomen Kirkkohistoriallisen Seuran Vuosikirja*, 29-30 (1939-40), published in Helsinki in 1941. The last two items constitute individual bulletins with individual pagination. See also the already mentioned Ambrosius Schneider, *Die Cistercienser*, pp. 74-105. On the two orders of knights, together with a wealth of related information, see Friedrich Benninghoven, *Der Orden der Schwertbrüder* (Cologne: Böhlau Verlag, 1965). The best and most detailed work in English, covering the whole story of crusading efforts in the Baltic states, is William Urban, *The Baltic Crusade* (De Kalb: Northern Illinois U. Press, 1975). The author, exploiting *The Chronicle of Henry of Livonia*, trans. J. A. Brundage (Madison: U. of Wisconsin Press, 1961), gives full account of the activities of Theodoric (Dietrich), Bernard of Lippe, Baldwin of Aulne and the "Swordbrothers." The quote from the *Chronicle* of Henry of Livonia on Bernard of Lippe was taken from the Brundage translation, p. 113. On recent bibliography dealing with Cistercian expansion in eastern Europe, especially in Poland and Silesia, see the excellent Joseph Gottschalk, "Die Bedeutung der Zisterzienser für die Ostsiedlung, besonders in Schlesien," *Zeitschrift für Ostforschung*, 15 (1966), 67-106.

See the quote from a sermon of Caesarius of Heisterbach in Angelo Manrique, *Annales Cistercienses* (Lyons, 1642-59), IV, 25. On English abbots in papal service see Hill, *English Cistercian Monasteries,* pp. 157-61; see the quote from the letter of Lucius III, *ibid.*, p. 144. On Cistercians in Parliament, see R. A. Donkin, "Localisation, situation économique et rôle parlamentaire des abbés cisterciens anglais," *RHE*, 52 (1957), 832-41. On Cistercians and Frederick Barbarossa there is a substantial article by Sigisbert Mitterer, "Die Cistercienser im Kirchenstreit zwischen Papst Alexander III und Kaiser Friedrich I Barbarossa," *CC*, 24 (1922), 1-8, 21-27, 35-40. See for further details Martin Preiss, *Die politische Tätigkeit und Stellung der Cistercienser im Schisma von 1159-1170.* Historische Studien, Heft 248 (Berlin: Eberling, 1934). On the Cistercian popes, cardinals and bishops see the alphabetic listing with short biographies, Dominicus Willi, *Päpste, Kardinäle und Buschöfe aus dem Cistercienserorden* (Bregenz; Teutsch, 1912, a bound collection of offprints from *CC*.

6. *Privileges, Constitutional and Administrative Developments*

The whole scope of this chapter is still best covered by the works of Mahn and Bock. On tithes, the basic study is Giles Constable, *Monastic*

Tithes from their Origins to the Twelfth Century (Cambridge U. Press, 1964), dealing extensively with Cistercians: the quote by Abbot Odo may be found on p. 137; those by Peter of Blois were taken also from this work: pp. 239 and 292-3. See a closely related article by the same author, "Monastic Possessions of Churches and *Spiritualia* in the Age of Reform," published in the already mentioned *Il monachesimo e la riforma . . .*, pp. 304-31. The quote from a charter of Bonnefont was taken from Charles Samaran and Charles Higounet, *Recueil des actes de l'abbaye cistercienne de Bonnefont en Comminges* (Paris: Bibliothèque Nationale, 1970), p. 52. See the warning of Alexander III in the above mentioned article of J. Leclercq in *RB*, 62 (1952), p. 151. On further developments of the same problem see C. R. Cheney, "A Letter of Pope Innocent III and the Lateran Decree on Cistercian Tithe Paying," *Cîteaux*, 13 (1962), 146-51.

On the issue of exemption the latest is Friedrich Pfurtscheller, *Die Priviligierung des Zisterzienserordens im Rahmen der allgemeinen Schutz- und Exemtionsgeschichte vom Anfang bis zur Bulle "Parvus fons,"* (Bern: Herbert Lang, 1972). See reference to the feud of 1168 in *Statuta*, I, 75-76. The clashes between Cîteaux and the proto-abbots leading to the *Parvus fons* are covered by Bruno Griesser, "Zur Rechtsstellung des Abtes von Cîteaux. Kontroversen um Abt Johannes von Cîteaux (1236-38)," in *Festschrift zum 800. Jahrgedächtnis des Todes Bernhards von Clairvaux* (Vienna: Verlag Herold, 1953), pp. 260-97, and J.-B. Van Damme, "Les pouvoirs de l'abbé de Cîteaux au XIIe et XIIIe siècles," *AC*, 24 (1968), 47-85. See the texts of the *Parvus fons*, followed by Cardinal Guy's decision, in *Statuta*, III, 22-32, and the *Fulgens sicut stella, ibid.*, pp. 410-36. See the analysis of this latter document in J.-B. Mahn, *Le pape Benoît XII et les cisterciens* (Paris: Champion, 1949); the text of the protest of Cistercian abbots, leading to a compromise, is on pp. 85-135.

The offices of the Roman procurator and cardinal protector have not been studied in detail. See a short article by Vincent Hermans, "Notes historiques sur le procureur général de l'ordre de Cîteaux," *AC*, 24 (1968), 143-52; otherwise, all other specifics are based on *Statuta* and Mahn. The same is true about the contributions in behalf of the General Chapter. See the full story of Scarborough told by C. H. Talbot, "Cîteaux and Scarborough," *SM*, 2 (1960), 95-158. The codification of Cistercian law has been thoroughly studied by Bernard Lucet, who with J.-A. Lefèvre published "Les codifications cisterciennes aux XIIe et XIIIe siècles d'aprés les traditions manuscrites," *AC*, 15 (1959), 2-22; then, in greater detail, B. Lucet, *La codification cistercienne de 1202 et son évolution ultérieure* (Rome: Editiones Cistercienses, 1964). See a short summary by the same author in the *Festschrift* Gabriel Le Bras, *Études d'histoire du droit canonique* (Paris: Sirey, 1965), pp. 249-62.

7. *The Challenge of Scholasticism*

On the Holy Grail and Clairvaux see Leopold Grill, "Château du Graal: Clairvaux," *AC*, 17 (1961), 115-26; the quote from Bernard's sermon in Paris was taken from p. 119. On Cistercians and scholasticism see Matthew Paris, *Chronica maiora,* ed. H. R. Luard, "Rolls Series" No. 57, (London: H. M. Stationary Office, 1883), V, 79-80, and on Lexington, later in the same volume, pp. 596, 651-2. See Lexington's life in *Dictionary of National Biography* (Oxford: Clarendon Press, 1950), XI, 1083, or in the introduction to Lexington by Griesser, *AC*, 2 (1946), 4-8. See his letter to the Abbot of Clairvaux, *ibid.,* p. 48, and another to the Abbot of Pontigny on pp. 117-8. The threat of heresy is discussed by Derek Baker, "Heresy and Learning in Early Cistercianism," *Schism, Heresy and Religious Protest,* ed. D. Baker (Cambridge: Cambridge U. Press, 1972), pp. 93-107.

On all Cistercian colleges in France, with detailed bibliography on each, see my "Introduction à l'étude des collèges cisterciens en France avant la Révolution," *AC*, 25 (1969), 145-79. All other details pertaining to Paris were adapted from my two other articles: "The Cistercian College of Saint Bernard in Paris in the Fifteenth Century," *CS*, 6 (1971), 172-79, and "The College of Saint Bernard in Paris in the Sixteenth and Seventeenth Centuries," *AC*, 28 (1972), 167-218. See the *Fulgens sicut stella* on higher education in *Statuta,* III, 429-35, and its analysis by Mahn, *Le pape Benoît XII . . . ,* pp. 50-75.

On the college of Prague and Cistercian colleges in Germany, see Winter, III, 48-81; also, Sigismund Bredl, "Das Collegium Sancti Bernardi in Prag," *SuM*, 13 (1892), 493-503. On Belgium, see Albert von Iterson, "Les cisterciens et l'université de Louvain," *Cîteaux,* 21 (1970), 135-77. On the college in Oxford valuable information is in Rose Graham, "The Great Schism and the English Monasteries of the Cistercian Order," *The English Historical Review*, 44 (1929), 384-5. See its whole history in W. H. Stevenson and H. E. Salter, *The Early History of Saint John's College, Oxford* (Oxford:Clarendon Press, 1939), pp. 3-110. C. H. Talbot, "The English Cistercians and the Universities," *SM* 4 (1962), 197-220, corrects some errors in Stevenson-Salter. On all German Cistercian colleges there is a new and yet unpublished dissertation by Sr. Justina M. Grothe, *Cistercians and Higher Education in the Late Middle Ages, with a Special Reference to Heidelberg,* The Catholic University of America, Washington, D.C., Dept. of History, 1976.

On Cistercians and legal studies there is a comprehensive article by Colomban Bock, "Les cisterciens et l'étude du droit," *AC*, 7 (1951), 3-31. On legal studies in Avignon, see my article: "The Cistercian College of

Sénanque in Avignon, 1496-1795," *Cîteaux,* 22 (1971), 40-47. On the library of Clairvaux the most detailed study is André Wilmart, "L'ancien bibliothèque de Clairvaux," *Mémoires de la Société Académique,* 54 (1917), 125-90, reprinted in *Coll,* 11 (1943), 101-27, 301-19. See also, M. A. Vernet, "Note sur la bibliothèque de Clairvaux," in the commemorative volume *Bernard de Clairvaux* (Paris: Alsatia, 1953), pp. 555-6. The last few paragraphs of this chapter have been taken over from my *White Monks,* pp. 161-2.

8. *The End of Prosperity*

The older view, blaming the monks for the "decay," was represented chiefly by the prolific G. G. Coulton, particularly in his *Five Centuries of Religion,* 4 vols. (Cambridge U. Press, 1923-1950). See the problem in proper historical perspective in R. W. Southern, *Western Society and the Church in the Middle Ages.* The Pelican History of the Church, vol. 2 (Baltimore: Penguin Books, 1970), pp. 300-60. See data on Les Dunes, *ibid.,* p. 266. Further figures have been taken from Ambrosius Schneider, *Die Cistercienserabtei Himmerod im Spätmittelalter* (Speyer: Jaeger, 1954), pp. 149-50, and the chartulary compiled by the Commission d'histoire de l'ordre de Cîteaux, *Chartes et documents de l'abbaye de N.-D. d'Aiguebelle* (Paris: Centre Nat. de la Recherche Scientifique, 1953), I, 133. Josiah Cox Russell, "The Clerical Population of Medieval England," *Traditio,* 2 (1944), 194-96, takes into account only 57 of 62 houses, therefore the actual numbers must have been higher.

On General Chapters held outside of Cîteaux during the Great Schism see three articles in *CC,* bearing similar titles: "Generalkapitel ausserhalb Cîteaux," but written by three authors: B. Griesser, 62 (1955), 65-83; E. Krausen, 63 (1956), 7-11; H. Tüchle, 64 (1957), 21-22; see also Edward Ortved, "Von Generalkapiteln auf dem Festlande ausserhalb Cîteaux, während des grossen Schismas," *CC,* 38 (1926), 279-82. See also on the same and related subjects F. P. Bliemetzrieder, "Der Zisterzienserorden im grossen abendlandischen Schisma," *SuM,* 25 (1904), 62-82, and the already mentioned article by Rose Graham, "The Great Schism . . . ," in *The English Historical Review,* 44 (1929), 373-87, giving account of a disputed election at Meaux (1396-99). For similar reasons an even longer feud broke out at Fountains, detailed by E. F. Jacob, *Essays in Later Medieval History* (Manchester U. Press, 1968), pp. 79-97.

On the Hussite wars in Silesia, together with the quote referring to Leubus, see H. Grüger, "Die monastische Disziplin der schlesischen Zisterzienser vor Anbruch der Reformation," *Cîteaux,* 24 (1973), 209-49. On German conditions, see Winter, III, 1-45; the story of Lehnin, *ibid.,* 19-

20. Maulbronn, Königsbronn and Herrenalb in the clutches of the House of Württemberg are the subjects of a detailed study by Klaus Schreiner, "Altwürttembergische Klöster im Spannungsfeld landesherrlicher Territorialpolitik," *Blätter für Deutsche Landesgeschichte,* 109 (1973), 196-245. On Salem see the substantial work of Werner Rösener, *Reichsabtei Salem* (Sigmaringen: Thorbecke Verlag, 1974), pp. 57-82. See the story of San Galgano in Ferdinand Schevill, "San Galgano, a Cistercian Abbey in the Middle Ages," *American Historical Review,* 14 (1908), 22-37. The troubles of Bindon are told by L. A. Desmond, "The Statute of Carlisle and the Cistercians," *Studies in Medieval Cistercian History* (Spencer, Mass.: Cistercian Publications, 1971), pp. 154-6.

Incidents illustrating the devastation of the Hundred Years' War are given according to Heinrich Denifle, *La désolation des églises, monastères et hôpitaux en France pendant la guerre des cent ans,* 2 vols. (Paris: Picard, 1897-1899), available also in modern reprint. There is no index to this monumental work, but all Cistercian references are registered in *CC,* 18 (1906), 225-30, 267-72. See the story of Jean d'Hostel of Aiguebelle in the above quoted *Chartes et documents . . .* , I, 39-40, 134-5. The report of Lazarus of Padway has been published in full by C. H. Talbot, *Letters from the English Abbots to the Chapter at Cîteaux, 1442-1521* (London: Royal Hist. Society, 1967), pp. 46-49. See the plague in Meaux in *Chronica,* III, 37. The visitation in Hungary is described in two articles in *CC,* 7 (1895), 9-15, by Ivo Kickh, and 12 (1900), 36-40, by R. Békefi. Valuable details are given in a privately published dissertation at the University of Chicago by Peter George Mode, *The Influence of the Black Death on the English Monasteries* (1916).

The only comprehensive treatment of the commendatory system is the article "Commende" by R. Laprat in *Dictionnaire de droit canonique* (Paris: Letouzey et Ané, 1942), III, 1029-85. Data on Cistercian abbeys are available in five articles by Konrad Eubel, "Zum paepstlichen Reservations- und Provisionswesen," *Römische Quartalschrift,* 8 (1894), 169-85; "Die päpstlichen Provisionen auf deutsche Abteien während des Schismas und des Pontifikats von Martin V, 1378-1431," *SuM,* 15 (1894), on Cistercians, pp. 242-44; "Die deutsche Aebte in den *libri obligationum et solutionum* des vatikanischen Archivs während der Jahre 1295-1378," *SuM,* 16 (1895), on Cistercians on p. 95; "Die Besetzung deutscher Abteien mittels päpstliche Provision in den Jahren 1431-1503," *SuM,* 20 (1899), 234-46; "In commendam verliehene Abteien während der Jahre 1431-1503," *SuM,* 21 (1900), 3-15, 244-59. On French conditions, see E. Delaruelle, *Histoire du catholicisme en France* (Paris: Spes, 1960), II, 168-70. Concerning Hungary, there is a comprehensive study by one of the leading historians of the older generation, E. Mályusz, *Egyházi társa-dalom a középkori Magyarországon* (Ecclesiastical Society in Medieval Hungary) (Budapest: Akadémiai Kiadó, 1971), particularly pp. 239-40. On the number of Scottish abbeys *in commendam* see A. H. Christie, *The Abbey of Dundrennan* (Glasgow: Fraser, 1914), pp. 73-77. See the most revealing story of the Roman delegation of 1475 as told by a participant, in *Statuta*, V, 761-65. On the efforts of Jean de Cirey, see William J. Telesca, "The Cistercian Dilemma at the Close of the Middle Ages," published in the above mentioned *Studies in Medieval Cistercian History*, pp. 163-85. See the same subject discussed in a broader context by the same author in "Papal Reservations and Provisions of Cistercian Abbeys at the End of the Middle Ages," *Cîteaux,* 26 (1975), 129-45. Statistics on the conditions in Italy were published by Alois Postina in *CC,* 13 (1901), 193-205. The contract at Tre-Fontane was published by Dom Gabriel Monbet, *L'abbaye des Trois-Fontaines* (Lyons, 1869), pp. 99-103.

9. *Reforms and the Reformation*

On the fifteenth-century religious reform much can be found in any better Church history, such as Herbert Jedin and John Dolan, *Handbook of Church History* (New York: Herder and Herder, 1969), IV, 426-42 and 580-5. On the reform of Barbo and the Congregation of Valladolid, see Maurus Lunn, "Benedictine Reform Movements in the Later Middle Ages," *Downside Review,* 91 (1973), 274-89. On the growing power of the abbot of Cîteaux see Roger De Ganck, "Les pouvoirs de l'abbé de Cîteaux, de la bulle 'Parvus fons' (1265) à la Révolution Francaise," *AC,* 27 (1971), 3-63. On Jean Cirey, see King, pp. 62-69. See also the above quoted Telesca, "The Cistercian Dilemma . . . ," pp. 181-82. His role in 1493 at Tours was taken from Bouton, pp. 317-19. See the text of the "Articles of Paris" in *Nomasticon,* pp. 548-57. The only copy of the regulations for the College of Saint Bernard is in Michel Félibien and Guy A. Lobineau, *Histoire de la ville de Paris* (Paris, 1725), III, 168-80.

Claude de Bronseval's *Peregrinatio Hispanica* has been edited by Maur Cocheril in 2 vols. (Paris: Presses Universitaires, 1970); see the details quoted in the text in vol. I, 102-48. While Cistercian involvement in the movement of the Beguines is well known, a similar relation with Beghards remains unexplored. The coverage of this matter follows largely Canivez. The story of Sibculo and the later acquisition of Gross- and Klein-Burlo, together with the quotes, were taken from Kaspar Elm, "Die münster-ländischen Klöster Gross-Burlo und Klein-Burlo," *Westfälische For-schungen,* 18 (1965), 23-42. On the Williamites see a series of articles by the same author, "Zisterzienser und Wilhelmiten," *Cîteaux.* 15 (1964), 97-

124, 177-202, 273-311. There is some useful information in U. Berliére, "Benediktiner und Cistercienser-Reform in Belgien vor dem trienter Konzil," *SuM,* 8 (1887), 535-40, and in a long series of articles by Aloysius Nyssen, "Über einige Cistercienser Klöster in den Nederlanden vor der Reformation," *CC,* 26 (1914). See the General Chapter of 1489 on the Congregation of Sibculo in *Statuta,* V, 671-4. On the reform of Marienrode, see Augustin Steiger, "Heinrich von Bernten, Abt zu Marienrode bei Hildesheim, 1426-1462," *SuM,* 33 (1912), 236-56. See the details of the Hungarian reform in *Statuta,* under 1478, 1479 and 1480. More can be found (in Hungarian) in Remig Békefi, *A pásztói apátság története* (Budapest; Hornyánszky, 1898), I, 79-91.

On the fate of German abbeys, see *GM.* The results of Boucherat's visitation were published in *CC,* 13 (1901), 225-37, 257-76. Details concerning Ebrach were taken from Adelhard Kaspar, *Chronik der Abtei Ebrach* (Münsterschwarzach: Vier-Turme Verlag, 1971), pp. 129-42. On Bebenhausen and other abbeys in the same area see Leodegar Walter, "Die Cisterzienserklöster in Württemberg zur Zeit der Reformation," *SuM,* 38 (1917), 268-87. Loccum's bibliography is extensive; perhaps the latest is Nicolaus Heutger, *Loccum. Eine Geschichte des Klosters* (Hildesheim: Lax, 1971). See on the intellectual life of the Austrian Wilhering the dissertation of Friedrich Keplinger, *Beiträge zur Geschichte der Wissenschaftspflege im Zisterzienserstift Wilhering* (Vienna: Verlag Notring, 1969).

The narrative of the dissolution in England was adapted from Knowles IV. On Huby, see pp. 32-37; on Hobbes, pp. 373-6; on Lazenby, pp. 368-9. On the same individuals see also Sr. M. Claire Nash, "The Fate of the English Cistercian Abbots in the Reign of Henry VIII," *Cîteaux,* 16 (1965), 97-113. See on the same subject the following recent works: Geoffrey Baskerville, *English Monks and the Suppression of the Monasteries* (London: Cape, 1937); G. W. O. Woodward, *The Dissolution of the Monasteries* (New York: Walker, 1967); Christopher Haigh, *The Last Days of the Lancashire Monasteries and the Pilgrimage of Grace* (Manchester: Chetham Society, 1969); Joyce Youings, *The Dissolution of the Monasteries* (London: Allen & Unwin, 1971).

See details on Scotland in the already quoted Coulton, *Scottish Abbeys;* Christie, *The Abbey of Dundrennan,* and James Campbell, *Balmerino and its Abbey* (Edinburgh: Blackwood, 1899). On Irish Cistercians in the late 15th and early 16th centuries there is a serialized study by Father Colmcille [O'Conbhuidhe], "Decline and Attempted Reform of the Irish Cistercians," *Coll,* 18 (1956), 290-305; 19 (1957), 146-63, 371-84. Much of this material has been adopted by Brendan Bradshaw, *The Dissolution of the Religious Orders in Ireland under Henry VIII* (Cambridge U. Press, 1974). The reference to Holy Cross was taken from Geraldine Carville, *The Heritage of Holy Cross* (Belfast: Blackstaff Press, 1973), pp. 134-43.

On the French events of 1561 see James Westfall Thompson, *The Wars of Religion in France, 1559-1576* (New York: Ungar, 1909), pp. 106-10. See the calamities of Cîteaux in King, pp. 73-76. The Latin document on the pillage of the abbey in October 1589, was published by Étienne Goutagny, "Le pillage de l'abbaye de Cîteaux par Guillaume de Saulx, seigneur de Tavannes, le 16 octobre 1589," *Cîteaux*, 13(1962), 233-7.

10. *The Rise of the Congregations*

The only detailed and comprehensive study of Congregations remains the old Idesbald Eicheler, "Die Kongregationen des Zisterzienserorden," serialized in *SuM,* 49(1931), but it is restricted to legal considerations. Bock, pp. 52-87, adds to a similar coverage extensive bibliography. See also Bouton, pp. 313-33. An up-to-date history of all Cistercian Congregations is in press under "Congregazione Cisterciense" in the new *Dizionario enciclopedico dei religiosi* (Rome: Edizioni Paoline).

The most detailed account of the early history of the Congregation of Castile is in Angelo Manrique, *Annales Cistercienses,* IV, 585-742. On the Jewish question, see Bronseval, *Peregrinatio Hispanica,* I, 58-59. The organization of the Congregation of Aragon is in *Statuta,* VII, 303-07. See a letter from General Boucherat to Philip III, *ibid.,* 320-1. Bronseval's often quoted *Peregrinatio* deals extensively with the affairs of Alcobaça in both volumes.

See the beginnings of the Congregation of Upper Germany in Karl Becker, "Salem unter Abt Thomas I Wunn und die Gründung der Oberdeutschen Cist.-Kongregation," a long series of articles in *CC,* 48(1936). On the Swiss problem, see Wilhelm Wostri, "Die Schweizer Zisterzienserkongregation," *AC,* 24(1968), 168-80. The acts of the autonomous Vicariate of Bohemia were serialized by Philibert Panhölzl, *CC,* 22(1910).

See some details on the Irish Congregation in Colmcille O'Conbhuidhe, "Studies in Irish Cistercian History," *Cîteaux,* 17(1966), 17-24, and in the already quoted Carville, *The Heritage of Holy Cross,* pp. 51-56. The last "abbots" of Holy Cross were actually parish priests of the old church, without monastic community. The best summary of the Feuillant reform is in *DGHE,* XVI(1967), 1334-44, by L. Ferrando. See an article on Jean de la Barrière, *ibid.,* VI (1932), 924-26, by Canivez. On the spirituality of the movement, see *DS,* V (1964), 274-87, by Maur Standaert. All these articles carry detailed bibliographies. On Montgalliard, see N. Tillière,

Histoire de l'abbaye d'Orval, 5th ed. (Gembloux: Duculot, 1948), pp. 178-96.

11. *The War of Observances*

This chapter outlines my monograph on the same subject: *The Rise of the Cistercian Strict Observance in Seventeenth Century France* (Washington, D.C.: The Catholic U. of America Press, 1968). Some doctoral dissertations publishing much of the archival material have since been made available in print. These are: Julius D. Lelóczky, *Constitutiones et acta capitulorum Strictioris Observantiae Ordinis Cisterciensis, 1624-1687* (Rome: Editiones Cistercienses, 1967); Thomas Nguyen-Dinh-Tuyen, "Histoire des controverses à Rome entre le Commune et l'Étroite Observance de 1662 à 1666," *AC,* 26 (1970), 3-247; Bernard A. Marton, "Cardinal Jérôme Souchier, Abbot of Clairvaux and Cîteaux," *AC,* 28 (1972), 77-166. See all documents referred to until 1636 published by Polycarpe Zakar, *Histoire de la Stricte Observance de l'ordre cistercien depuis ses débuts jusqu'au généralat du Cardinal de Richelieu, 1606-1635* (Rome: Editiones Cistercienses, 1966).

On Rancé and his La Trappe much has been written, but the bibliography does not include either a reliable biography or the critical edition of his voluminous correspondence. His "standard" biography by Abbé Louis Dubois, *Histoire de l'Abbé de Rancé et de sa réforme,* 2 vols. (Paris: Bray, 1866), is nothing but the revised edition of a highly biased early eighteenth-century work authored by Armand-François Gervaise. Cf. L. J. Lekai, "The Problem of the Authorship of Rancé's 'Standard' Biography," *Coll,* 21 (1959), 157-63. The latest (and sympathetic) appraisal of Rancé's character through the analysis of his correspondence is A. J. Krailsheimer, *Armand-Jean de Rancé, Abbot of La Trappe. His Influence in the Cloister and in the World* (Oxford: Clarendon Press, 1974).

On the reform of Sept-Fons see Firmin Lamy, *L'ancien Sept-Fons* (Moulins: Crépin-Leblond, 1937), pp. 125-88, and B. Martelet, "Dom Eustache de Beaufort," *Cîteaux,* 14 (1963), 280-92. The relationship between Beaufort and Rancé is detailed in Krailsheimer, *op.cit.,* pp. 127-29. On the reform of Tamié under Somont, see Eugène Burnier, *Histoire de l'abbaye de Tamié* (Chambéry: Pouchet, 1865), pp. 101-19. On Orval and Bentzeradt see the above quoted work of Tillière, pp. 226-42; on Orval's expansion, see J. B. Kaiser, "Die Einführung der Orvalianer Observanz in Beaupré," *SuM,* 35 (1914), 114-23.

12. *Cistercians of the Ancien Régime*

On the resettlement of Cistercians in Hungary, see (in Hungarian) K. Horváth, *Zirc története* (Veszprém: Abbey of Zirc, 1930). On foundations in Lithuania there is a short notice in *CC,* 2 (1890), 17-18. The conditions in Germany are briefly sketched in Krausen. The Belgian recovery is detailed in the often quoted Canivez. On Portugal and Alcobaça see Maur Cocheril, "L'ordre de Cîteaux au Portugal," *SM,* 1 (1959), 51-95. There is on Alcobaça the colorful description of William Beckford, *Recollections of an Excursion to the Monasteries of Alcobaça and Batalha* (London, 1835), but its historical accuracy is highly doubtful.

On Nucius, there is a serial by Bernhard Widmann, "Johann Nucius, Abt von Himmelwitz," *CC,* 32 (1920). Bisenberger's *De musica monachorum* was serialized in the same *CC,* 6 (1894); see the quote on p. 90. On the musical life at Zwettl, there is a short article by Stefan Holzhauser, "Die Zwettler Sängerknaben," *CC,* 82 (1975), 129-32; this includes the quote by Abbot Bernhard. On Raitenhaslach, see Gabriel Meier, "Ein Tag in Raitenhaslach," *CC,* 30 (1918), 1-5. Sedlak's description of Salem was published by K. Horváth, serialized in *CC,* 42 (1931); see the quote on p. 89. On Ulrich Mayr, there is a serial by Luitpold Reindl, in *SuM,* 36 (1915). On the influence of the Enlightenment on German abbeys there is a substantial article by Wilhelm Foster, "Die Kirchliche Aufklärung . . . ," *SuM,* 63 (1951); see reference to "White Jesuits," *ibid.,* p. 184.

Conditions in France in the 17th and 18th centuries have been detailed in my three previously published articles, all in *AC:* "Moral and Material Status of French Cistercian Abbeys in the Seventeenth Century," 29 (1963), 199-266; "The Cistercian Order and the *Commission des réguliers,*" 23 (1967), 179-225; "Cistercian Monasteries and the French Episcopate on the Eve of the Revolution," 23 (1967), 66-116. See on the role of Salem, L. Walter, "Verdienste Salems im Kampf des Generalabtes mit den vier Primaräbten . . . ," *CC,* 67 (1960), 68-79, including the reference to the "four-headed dragon" and the letter of Jung to Louis XV in 1717.

The latest work on the Commission of Regulars is Pierre Chevallier, *Loménie de Brienne et l'ordre monastique,* 2 vols. (Paris: Vrin, 1959-60), although his evaluation of monastic conditions has not been adopted. For a detailed analysis of the work of the General Chapter and the process of constitution-making, see my above listed articles with further bibliography. See statistical tabulations covering the whole Order in France about 1770 in "Cistercian Monasteries and the French Episcopate," pp. 86-105.

13. *On the Verge of Extinction*

The school of Rauden is the subject of a long series of articles by Stefan Steffen, "Die Pflege der Wissenschaften und des Unterrichtes in der Abtei Rauden," *CC,* 32 (1920). On the educational program of the General

Chapter see my "The College of Saint Bernard in Paris on the Eve of the Revolution," *AC,* 26 (1970), 253-79. On the French Revolution and Cistercians, with further bibliography, see my article "French Cistercians and the Revolution, 1789-1791," *AC,* 24 (1968), 86-118. The last days of Cîteaux are told by Alexis Presse, "Notes et documents sur les derniers temps de l'abbaye de Cîteaux," *AC,* 10 (1954), 169-207. Concerning the transference of the general's authority, see Polycarpe Zakar, "Regelungen zur Ausübung der Rechte des Abtes von Cîteaux nach der Französischen Revolution," *AC,* 23 (1967), 226-94.

The trials of Belgian Cistercians are detailed in a long series of articles by Benedict van Doninck, "Mittheilungen über Klöster und Ordensbrüder in Belgien zu Ende des 18. Jahrhunderts," *CC,* 10-11 (1898-99). On Italy, see Gregorio Penco, *Storia del monachesimo in Italia* (Rome: Ed. Paoline, 1967), II, 141-58. On the emergence of the Swiss Congregation, see Wilhelm Wostri, "Die schweizer Zisterzienserkongregation," *AC,* 24 (1968), 161-301. On the strange case of Lithuania see the above quoted note in *CC,* 2 (1890), 17-18. The numbers of Spanish Cistercian abbeys and monks are given according to *Coll,* 1 (1934), 16-18.

Other details of the secularization of abbeys in Germany, Spain, and Portugal can be found in any handbook of Church history.

14. *The Nineteenth-Century Revival: the Trappists*

Much of what has been published on 19th-century Trappists is colored by excessive piety. There are two works, however, which still can be read with profit; Casimir Gaillardin, *Les trappistes ou l'ordre de Cîteaux au XIXe siècle,* 2 vols. (Paris: Imprimeurs-Unis, 1844), and the second volume of *Annales de l'abbaye d'Aiguebelle* (Valence: Céas, 1864), by Hugues Séjalon.

On the early years of Valsainte valuable documents were published in a long serial by G. Müller, "Briefe aus der Zeit der Niederlassung der Trappisten in der Schweiz," *CC,* 41-42 (1929-30). There is a short biography of Laprade by Bernard Martelet, "Dom Eugène de Laprade," *Coll,* 10 (1948), 199-203. The story of the administration of Lestrange has been serialized by Jérôme du Halgouët, "Pierres d'attente pour une histoire de l'ordre dans la premiere moitié du XIXe siècle," *Cîteaux,* 17-23 (1966-72) and 26 (1975), 57-81.

Of capital importance is the publication of the *Actes.* All references to Trappist chapters can be verified in this collection by looking at the place and date of the chapter. In addition to other publications by Vincent Hermans already referred to, see "Presence des Trappistes au Concile Vatican I," *Coll,* 32 (1970), 342-53. On more confidential matters, see by the same Vincent Hermans, *Supplément des actes des chapitres généraux*

de la congrégation de la Nouvelle Réforme, dite de la Trappe, 1835-1891
(Rome, 1975), privately published (mimeographed). Bouton has a detailed
chapter on 19th-century Trappist revival, pp. 405-56. See the analysis of
the Bianchi report, *ibid.,* pp. 441-4. See other documents on the same in
Actes, pp. [579-83], including the dissenting opinion of La Trappe. For
legal questions see the privately published Vincent Hermans, *Commentar-
ium cisterciense historico-practicum in Codicis canones de religiosis*
(Rome, 1961). The paragraphs on the events of 1892-93 have been adapted
from an unpublished manuscript by Dom Alexis Presse, late abbot of
Boquen, entitled *L'union des trappistes.* See for the contemporary reaction of the Common Observance *CC,* 5(1893), 26-29, 56-59. The official
records of the Trappist general chapter of October 1892 (privately printed) reached me through the courtesy of Fr. Chrysogonus Waddell of
Gethsemani. See several papal documents (those of 1794, 1847, 1868) in
Nomasticon, pp. 649-63.

15. *The Nineteenth-Century Revival: the Common Observance*

Fontana's correspondence with the Swiss abbots was published by G.
Müller, *Vom Cistercienser Orden* (Bregenz: Teutsch, 1927), pp. 263-9.
See the restoration of the two Belgian houses in Canivez, pp. 512-6. On
Sénanque, see *CC,* 6(1894), 353-5. The source of all that is said in this
chapter about Austria-Hungary until 1869 is based on the dissertation of
Nivard Konrad, *Die Entstehung der österreichisch-ungarischen Zisterzienserkongregation* (Rome: Editiones Cistercienses, 1967). All quotes
were taken from the attached documents, arranged in chronological sequence; therefore their verification should pose no problems. For the
statistical figures see pp. 80-83. On individual abbeys in Austria-Hungary,
see the still useful Sebastian Brunner, *Ein Cisterzienserbuch* (Würzburg:
Woerl, 1881).

On the constitutions of all congregations of the Common Observance
see an unsigned serial, "Ueber die Observanzen der Cistercienser," *CC,*
7(1895). On the events of 1891, see *CC,* 3(1891), 215-7. On Wackarz, see
CC, 8(1896), 226-37, and 14(1902), 41-47, 73-77. On the separation from
the Trappists, see *CC,* 4(1892), 312-5. For the statistics of 1898, see *CC,*
10 (1898), 89-91, 118-23. For all other details, see either the above work
of Müller, or Bouton.

16. *Cistercians in the Twentieth Century*

The Trappist expansion is detailed by Bouton, pp. 469-76. On the first
few decades of the century see the following three publications: Anselme
Le Bail, *L'ordre de Cîteaux,* 2nd ed. (Paris: Letouzey, 1947); Elie Maire,
Les cisterciens en France (Paris: Lethielleux, 1921); Charles Grolleau and

Guy Chastel, *L'ordre de Cîteaux. La Trappe* (Paris: Gasset, 1954). On the latest trends in both observances see Henri Daniel-Rops, *Bernard of Clairvaux,* trans. Elisabeth Abbott (New York: Hawthorn, 1964), pp. 179-210. On Dom Lehodey, see Irenée Vallery-Radot, *La mission de Dom Vital Lehodey* (Paris: Cerf, 1956). The American developments, particularly the story of Gethsemani, are told by Thomas Merton, *The Waters of Siloe* (New York: Harcourt, 1949), pp. 146-264. One of the latest of Merton is a collection of commemorative articles: *Thomas Merton,* ed. Patrick Hart (New York: Sheed & Ward, 1974). The acts of the latest renewal chapters, where all quotes are taken from, have been privately published by the Strict Observance. Those of 1974 have not yet been made available. After 1934 the best guide to individual Trappist abbeys is the regular news section of *Coll.*

The best source throughout the contemporary history of the Common Observance is *CC,* carrying in each issue (until 1941 it was a monthly journal) news on individual abbeys as well as reports on other important events. See for many official documents, records of the General Chapter and those of the *definitorium* published after 1953 as *Acta Curiae Generalis Ordinis Cisterciensis* (Rome). The rise and fall of Boquen has been a *cause célèbre* in France, widely discussed even in the popular press. For the latest statistics of the Common Observance see *Catalogus monasteriorum et personarum* (Rome: Curia Generalis, 1974). A similar publication with historical introductions to every house is *Catalogus generalis abbatiarum, prioratuum et monasteriorum et personarum S. O. Cist.* (Rome: Universitas Gregoriana, 1954). Statistics on both observances are given in Appendix II.

17. *Spirituality and Learning*

Research covering Cistercian spirituality has been very uneven. The authors of the 12th and 13th centuries have been adequately studied, but beyond that limit only the 17th century received scholarly attention. This has been the most conspicuous weakness of all studies, including the present chapter, aiming at a comprehensive presentation. For a general survey see Vincent Hermans, *Spiritualité monastique* (Rome, 1954), mimeographed, but widely distributed among Trappist monasteries. For the 12th century, the best is Jean Leclercq, *La spiritualité du moyen age,* Histoire de la spiritualité chrétienne, vol. 2 (Paris: Aubier, 1961), pp. 233-72, the chief source of the corresponding portion of the present chapter. The fullest modern list of Cistercian authors is in *Dictionnaire de théologie catholique* (Paris: Letouzey, 1905), II/2, 2538-50, by Dom J. Besse, but a disturbing number of misprints makes its use very hazardous. Spiritual authors, in a strict sense of the word, are well covered in *DS,* as far as it goes (letter "K"). The widely known Louis Bouyer, *The Cistercian Heritage,* trans. Elizabeth A. Livingstone (Westminster, Md.: Newman, 1958), deals only with St. Bernard, Wm. of Saint-Thierry, Aelred of Rievaulx, Isaac of Stella and Guerric of Igny. A somewhat similar work, but of wider range, is Robert Thomas, *Spiritualité cistercienne,* Pain de Cîteaux, 13-14 (Rochefort: Abbaye S. Remy, 1976); a topical arrangement of quotes taken from leading Cistercian authors. See the leading Cistercian figures of the 12th and 13th centuries with detailed bibligraphies in F. Vandenbroucke, *La morale monastique du XIe au XVIe siècle,* Analecta Medievalia Namurcensia, No. 20 (Louvain: Nauwelaerts, 1966), pp. 119-81.

On the spirituality of the founders of Cîteaux see bibliography listed under Chapters 2-4. The critical edition of the works of St. Bernard has just been completed in 8 vols., under the care of J. Leclercq, C. H. Talbot and H. M. Rochais, *Sancti Bernardi Opera* (Rome: Editiones Cistercienses, 1957-1976). An additional volume will feature detailed indexes.

An excellent bilingual (Latin-French) edition of many early Cistercian authors is available in the series (still in progress) *Sources chrétiennes* (Paris: Cerf). The following are presently available: Aelred of Rievaulx (Nos. 60, 76); Wm. of Saint-Thierry (Nos. 61, 82); Adam of Perseigne (No. 66); Amadeus of Lausanne (No. 72); Baldwin of Ford (Nos. 93,94); St. Gertrud (Nos. 127, 139, 143); Guerric of Igny (Nos. 166, 202), and Isaac of Stella (Nos. 130, 207). See most of the same authors in English translation, including many works of St. Bernard, in the "Cistercian Fathers Series" (Kalamazoo, Mich.: Cistercian Publications).

Of the immense, and still growing, bibliography of St. Bernard, the most authoritative studies have been published by Dom Jean Leclercq, *Recueil d'études sur St. Bernard et ses écrits,* 3 vols. (Rome: Ed. di Storia e Letteratura, 1962-69). Recent studies on other leading authors are: Jean-Marie Déchanet, *William of Saint-Thierry,* trans. R. Strachan (Spencer, Mass.: Cistercian Publications, 1972); Amédée Hallier, *The Monastic Theology of Aelred of Rievaulx,* trans. C. Heaney (Spencer, Mass.: Cistercian Publications, 1969) and Bernard McGinn, *The Golden Chain* (Washington: Cistercian Publications, 1972), on Isaac of Stella.

The identity of John of Limoges, after much controversy, has remained uncertain. See the latest by G. Raciti in *DS,* VIII (1974), 614-18. On Burchard's *Apologia de barbis* see an article by B. Griesser in *CC,* 49 (1937), 4-11, 38-50. On hagiography and mysticism in Villers, see Simone Roisin, *L'hagiograpie cistercienne dans le diocèse de Liège au XIIIe siècle* (Brussels: Ed. Universitaires, 1947). On Joachim of Fiore some of the latest are: Marjorie Reeves, *Joachim of Fiore and the Prophetic Future* (London: SPCK, 1976). See also by the same author *The Influence of Prophecy in the Later Middle Ages* (Oxford: Clarendon, 1969); M. Reeves and B. Hirsch-Reich, *The 'Figurae' of Joachim of Fiore* (Oxford: Clarendon, 1972), and the lengthy article on Joachim in *DS*, VIII (1974), 1179-2101, by Cyprien Baraut. The quote referring to the duty of the monks of Sorø to work as annalists was taken from Janauschek, p. 145. On the formulary of Transmundus, see Sheila J. Heathcote, "The Letter Collections Attributed to Master Transmundus," *AC*, 21 (1965), 35-109, 167-238. For historiography see my *White Monks*, pp. 155-6.

Cistercian scholasticism has been largely neglected by modern research. On the early doctors of Paris, with as much bibliography as available, see Palémon Glorieux, *Répertoire des maîtres en théologie de Paris au XIIIe siecle* (Paris: Vrin, 1934), II, 249-66. On English scholastics, see the sharply disapproving C. H. Talbot, "English Cistercians and Universities," *SM*, 4(1962), 197-220. On Cistercian scholars in Flanders, see A. Pelzer, "Livres de philosophie et de théologie de l'abbaye de Ter Doest," *Annales de la société d'émulation de Bruges*, 63(1913), 5-36; also, P. Glorieux, "Notices sur quelques théologiens de la fin du XIIIe siècle," *Archives d'histoire doctrinale et littéraire du moyen age*, III(1928), 201-38. On the reaction to scholasticism, particularly in Villers, se Simone Roisin, "Réflexions sur la culture intellectuelle en nos abbayes cisterciennes médievales," *Miscellanea historica in honorem Leonis van der Essen* (Brussel-Paris: Ed. Universitaires, 1947), I, 245-56.

On the three great French theologians of the 14th century, see articles in some of the recent volumes of the *Histoire littéraire de la France* (Paris: Imprimerie Nationale): 37(1938), 174-209, on Jacques Fournier by Paul Fournier; 34(1915), 179-219, on Jacques de Thérines by Nöel Valois; 40(1966), 1-52, on Jean de Mirecourt by Georges Tessier (it is an "offprint" from a yet unpublished volume). See the *Quodlibeta* I-II of J. de Thérines published by P. Glorieux in *Textes philosophiques du moyen age* (Paris: Vrin, 1958), VII, 1-321. On Mirecourt see Étienne Gilson, *History of Christian Philosophy in the Middle Ages* (New York: Random House, 1955), pp. 503-5. The latest on Mirecourt are the articles of William J. Courtenay, "John of Mirecourt and Gregory of Rimini on Whether God Can Undo the Past," *Recherches de théologie ancienne et médievale*, 39(1972), 224-56; 40(1973), 147-74. The only information on Ceffons is Damasus Trapp, "Peter Ceffons of Clairvaux," *Recherches de théologie ancienne et médievale*, 24(1957), 101-54. An important correction is offered by Robert E. Lerner, "A Note on the University Career of

Jacques Fournier, O. Cist., Later Pope Benedict XII," *AC,* 30 (1974), 66-69.

See a substantial contribution by Kassian Lauterer, "Konrad von Ebrach," distributed in 3 vols. of *AC,* 17 (1961), 151-214; 18 (1962), 60-120; 19 (1963), 3-50. See a similar series of publications by the same author on "Matthäus von Königssaal," *CC,* 71 (1964), 93-109; 73 (1966), 71-75; 74 (1967), 129-41, 170-80. Medard Barth, "Phillip von Rathsamhausen, Abt des Klosters Pairis, O. Cist. (1301-1306) und Bischof von Eichstätt (1306-1322)," *Archives de l'église d'Alsace,* 22 (1975), 79-130, appeared too late to be consulted. Other significant articles are: Severin Grill, "Nikolaus Vischel von Heiligenkreuz," *CC,* 49 (1937), 97-108; Adalrich Arnold, "Fr. Mathäus Steynhus, der Cistercienserprediger auf den Konstanzer Konzil," *CC,* 48 (1936), 226-30; B. Borucki, "Studien über die Gnadenlehre des Jakob von Eltville," *CC,* 65 (1958), 1-24; C. H. Talbot, "Two Opuscula of John Godard, First Abbot of Newenham," *AC,* 10 (1954), 208-67; R. O'Brien, "The *Stimulus peccatoris* of William Rymyngton," *Cîteaux,* 16 (1965), 278-304; and by the same author, "Two Sermons at York Synod of William Rymyngton, 1372 and 1373," *Cîteaux,* 19 (1968), 40-67; E. Mikkers, "Un traité inédit d'Étienne de Salley sur la psalmodie," *Cîteaux,* 22 (1972), 245-88; Luzian Pfleger, "Nikolaus Salicetus . . . ," *SuM,* 22 (1901), 588-99.

On 17th century spirituality in France, see my *The Rise of the Cistercian Strict Observance,* pp. 168-87. On 17th and 18th century pamphleteering, see my three articles in *AC,* 19 (1963), 105-44; 25 (1969), 107-28; 30 (1974), 188-92.

18. *Liturgy*

A comprehensive description of the Cistercian rite is given by Archdale A. King, *Liturgies of the Religious Orders* (Milwaukee: Bruce, 1955), pp. 62-156. For legislative action consult Bock, especially pp. 103-28 and pp. 163-89, with further bibliography. See the quote from *Exm,* p. 75. See Abelard's letter in *PL,* vol. 178, cols. 335-340. On other related problems, see Bede Lackner, "The Liturgy of Early Cîteaux," *Studies in Medieval Cistercian History* (Spencer, Mass.: Cistercian Publications, 1971), 1-34. See the earliest manuscript of the *Ecclesiastica officia* edited by B. Griesser, *AC,* 12 (1956), 153-288. On the highly technical problems of early Cistercian Gregorian chant see S. Marosszéki, "Les origines du chant cistercien," *AC,* 8 (1952), 1-179, and Chrysogonus Waddell, "The Origin and Early Evolution of the Early Cistercian Antiphonary," *The Cistercian Spirit,* ed. B. Pennington (Spencer, Mass.: Cistercian Publications, 1970), pp. 190-223. See St. Bernard's letter to Guy of Montiéramey in *The*

Works of Bernard of Clairvaux, Treatises I, trans. M. Cawley (Spencer, Mass.: Cistercian Publications, 1970), p. 181. See reference to the *more femineo* singing in *Statuta,* I, 30, although its date is uncertain.

On the Cistercian mass, see Eberhard Krzewitza, "Das heilige Messopfer nach dem altern Cistercienserritus," *CC,* 63 (1956), 66-72. On the multiplication of foundation masses see Jacques Laurent, "La prière pour les défunts et les obituairies dans l'ordre de Cîteaux," *Mélanges Saint Bernard* (Dijon: Assoc. Bourguignonne des Soc. Savantes, 1953), pp. 383-96. Concerning the dispute over the legitimate use of the Cistercian Breviary in the 1860s, see some important documents in *Actes,* pp. [571-77].

19. *Art*

For a delightful introduction to monastic architecture, specifically to Cistercian architecture, see Anselme Dimier, *Les moines bâtisseurs* (Paris: Fayard, 1964). Otherwise, the fundamental work is Marcel Aubert, *L'architecture cistercienne en France,* 2nd ed., 2 vols. (Paris: Vanoest, 1947). The fullest pictorial record of Cistercian architecture is Frédéric van der Meer, *Atlas de l'ordre cistercien* (Paris: Sequoia, 1965). Pictorial guides to the finest surviving monuments, enriched by photographs of extraordinary beauty, are given in two "Zodiaque" publications with explanatory notes by Anselme Dimier: *L'art cistercien. France* (Paris: 1962), and *L'art cistercien hors de France* (Paris: 1971). Works of general nature, but dealing extensively with Cistercians are: Wolfgang Braunfels, *Monasteries of Western Europe* (London: Thames & Hudson, 1972), especially pp. 67-110; Christopher Brooke, *The Monastic World* (New York: Random House, 1974), dealing with Cistercians on pp. 135-62 and 201-10.

See for a guide through the immense bibliography of monographs A. Dimier, *Recueil de plans d'églises cisterciennes* (Paris: Librairie d'art ancien et moderne, 1949) and its *Supplément* by the same author and publisher, added in 1967.

See on the early manuscripts of Cîteaux, Charles Oursel, *Miniatures cisterciennes, 1109-1134* (Macon: Protat, 1960), with 40 full-page illustrations in color. The evaluation of Bernard's *Apology* was taken from Otto von Simson, *The Gothic Cathedral,* 2nd ed. (New York: Pantheon, 1965). See the English translation of the *Apologia* by M. Casey among *The Works of Bernard of Clairvaux,* Treatises I (Spencer, Mass.: Cistercian Publications, 1970); the quotes are on pp. 63-66.

On Cistercian architecture in England see a chapter in G. H. Cook, *English Monasteries in the Middle Ages* (London: Phoenix, 1961), pp. 150-74. On Melrose, see Stewart Cruden, *Scottish Abbeys* (Edinburgh: H.

M. Stationary Office, 1960), pp. 65-71. The story of the crucifix was taken from the *Chronica,* III, p. XI. On Spain, see Elie Lambert, *L'art gothique en Espagne* (Paris: Laurens, 1931), pp. 77-133, and a substantial article by Henri-Paul Eydoux, "L'abbatiale de Moreruela et l'architecture des églises cisterciennes d'Espagne," *Cîteaux,* 5 (1954), 173-207. See also Leopoldo Torres Balbás, *Ars Hispanica* (Madrid: Plus Ultra, 1952), VII, 20-37. On Poblet (also on Fontenay, Fountains and Maulbronn) see Ian Richards, *Abbeys of Europe* (London: Hamlyn, 1968), pp. 64-110.

On San Galgano and its influence, see the already quoted article by F. Schevill in *American Historical Review,* 14 (1908), 27-29. On Germany the comprehensive work is Henri-Paul Eydoux, *L'architecture des églises cisterciennes d'Allemagne* (Paris: Presses Univérsitaires, 1952). See also Ilse Bickel, *Die Bedeutung der süddeutschen Zisterzienserbauten* (Munich: Zink, 1956), and Hanno Hahn, *Die frühe Kirchenbaukunst der Zisterzienser* (Berlin: Mann, 1957), which deals primarily with Eberbach, but has substantial chapters on early Cistercian architecture elsewhere in Europe. The latest on German Cistercian architecture is the chapter by Wolfgang Bickel in the already mentioned *Die Cistercienser,* edited by A. Schneider (pp. 193-340).

On Polish architecture there are a few pages in J. Kłoczowski, "Les cisterciens en Pologne," *Cîteaux,* 21 (1970), 124-5. On the famous grange of Ter Doest, see Dimier, *Les moines . . . ,* pp. 186-7. On the Baroque remodeling of French abbeys, see *ibid.,* pp. 192-204. On the dimensions of the Baroque Leubus see R. M. Libor, "Kloster Leubus," *Cîteaux,* 15 (1964), 221-41. On the great Cistercian Baroque churches of Germany, Austria and Bohemia, consult any history of Baroque architecture. For incidents of destruction during and after the French Revolution, see Dimier, *Les moines . . . ,* pp. 192-200.

20. *Economy*

The history of medieval economy, particularly agrarian economy, in spite of the immense scholarly efforts of the past decades, seems to raise more problems than offer possible solutions. Since the most alluring pitfall is unwarranted generalization, I tried to remain as factual as possible.

Of the old school, trying to extract economic "principles" from Cistercian legislation, noteworthy are: Eberhard Hoffmann, "Die Entwicklung der Wirtschaftsprinzipien im Zisterzienserorden während des 12. und 13. Jahrhunderts," *Historisches Jahrbuch der Görres-Gesellschaft,* 31 (1910), 699-727, and B.-J.-M. Vignes, "Les doctrines économiques et morales de Saint-Bernard," *Saint Bernard et son temps* (Dijon: Académie des sciences, 1928), I, 295-332.

BIBLIOGRAPHICAL NOTES

There is no comprehensive work on Cistercian economy, although most general manuals on medieval economic history recognize the importance of Cistercians. For orientation in all phases of medieval economy see the first three volumes of *The Cambridge Economic History of Europe*, ed. M. M. Postan et al. (Cambridge U. Press, 1941-63). Specifically for agrarian conditions Georges Duby, *Rural Economy and Country Life in the Medieval West*, trans. Cynthia Postan (Columbia: U. of S. Carolina Press, 1968) is recommended.

On the conflict between "principles" and reality, see Richard Roehl, "Plan and Reality in a Medieval Monastic Economy: the Cistercians," *Studies in Medieval and Renaissance History*, 9 (1972), 83-113, and my "Ideals and Reality in Early Cistercian Life and Legislation," in *Cistercian Studies*, ed. J. R. Sommerfeldt, (Kalamazoo: Cistercian Publications, 1977), III, in press.

On land grants and early foundations in England, see the already quoted B. D. Hill, *English Cistercian Monasteries*. On the foundation of Meaux, see the *Chronica*, I, 76-77, 82. The connection between feudal anarchy and grants to Cistercians is detailed with many examples in Hill, *op.cit.* The complicated issue of "advocacy" over Cistercians in Germany is well summarized by Werner Rösener, *Reichsabtei Salem* (Sigmaringen: Thorbecke Verlag, 1974), pp. 31-53. On Esrom, see Brian Patrick McGuire, "Property and Politics at Esrum Abbey: 1151-1251," *Medieval Scandinavia*, 6 (1973), 122-50; the final quote is taken from p. 150.

On the relationship between donation and admission, see the following: Laurence J. McCranck, "The Frontier of the Spanish Reconquest and the Land Acquisitions of the Cistercians of Poblet," *AC*, 29 (1973), 57-78; A. Clergeac, *Cartulaire de l'abbaye de Gimont* (Paris: Champion, 1905), with many obvious examples; J. H. Lynch, "Cistercians and Underaged Novices," *Cîteaux*, 24 (1973), 294-96, including Berdoues. On the admission of Morel at La Ferté, see Duby, *Rural Economy*, p. 439.

Concerning annuities in Villers, see the two outstanding monographs: Edouard de Moreau, *L'abbaye de Villers-en-Brabant au XIIe et XIIIe siècles* (Brussels: Dewit, 1909), and Th. Ploegaerts and G. Boulmont, *Histoire de l'abbaye de Villers du XIIIe siècle à la Révolution* (Nivelles: Soc. Archéologique, 1926). On the same subject (annuities) see Roman Pittet, *L'abbaye de Hauterive au moyen age* (Fribourg: Fragniére, 1934). The source of all references to Clairvaux was M. H. d'Arbois de Jubainville, *Études sur l'état interieure des abbayes cisterciennes et principalement de Clairvaux* (Paris: Durand, 1958). See references to Beaulieu in *The Beaulieu Cartulary*, ed. S. F. Hockney (Southampton: University Press, 1974); its contents are well summarized in its introduction, pp. I-

430

LXIX. On the possession of tithes and churches in Germany and Poland, see Winter. For references in similar matters see the following: David H. Williams, *The Welsh Cistercians. Aspects of their Economic History* (Pontypool: Hughes & Son, 1970); Rhŷs W. Hays, *The History of the Abbey of Aberconway, 1186-1537* (Cardiff: U. of Wales, 1963). See the story of Sorø in Brian Patrick McGuire, "Patrons, Privileges, Property. Sorø Abbey's First Half Century," *Kirkehistoriske Samlinger,* (Copenhagen, 1974), pp. 5-39. The rapid acquisition of church revenues in England is covered in detailed tabulations by Lawrence A. Desmond, "The Appropriation of Churches by the Cistercians in England to 1400," *AC*, XXXI (1975), 246-65. See the case of Tre Fontane in *Statuta,* I, 43-45, 51-52.

On granges and agrarian expansion see the following: Colin Platt, *The Monastic Grange in Medieval England* (New York: Fordham U. Press, 1969), the point of view of an archaeologist. On France, see Marguerite David-Roy, "Les granges monastiques en France aux XIIe et XIIIe siècles," *Archeologia,* 58 (1973), 52-63. Heinrich Pauen, *Die Klostergrundherrschaft Heisterbach* (Münster: Aschendorff, 1913). Meinrad Schaab, *Die Zisterzienserkloster Schönau in Odenwald* (Heidelberg: Universitätsverlag, 1963). Gerhard Kaller, *Wirtschafts- und Besitzgeschichte des Zisterzienserklosters Otterberg, 1144-1561* (Heidelberg: Universitätsverlag, 1961). Ernst Kaufmann, *Geschichte der Cisterzienserabtei St. Urban in Spätmittelalter* (Fribourg: Universitätsverlag, 1956). Coburn V. Graves, "Medieval Cistercian Granges," *Studies in Medieval Culture* (Kalamazoo, Mich.: Western Mich. U., 1966), II, 63-70. James S. Donnelly, "Changes in the Grange Economy of English and Welsh Cistercian Abbeys, 1300-1540," *Traditio,* 10 (1954), 399-458. Alfred Haidacher, *Die Entstehung- und Wirtschaftsgeschichte des Klosters Heilsbronn* (Bonn: Röhrscheid Verlag, 1955). Nikolaus Grass, *Beiträge zur Wirtschafts- und Kulturgeschichte des Zisterzienserstiftes Stams in Tirol* (Innsbruck; Universitätsverlag, 1959). On Acey, Bithaine, Theuley an Bellevaux, see the collection of studies: *Les débuts des abbayes cisterciennes dans les anciens pays bourguignons comtois et romands* (Dijon: Faculté de droit, 1953).

The work of Cistercians in England, reclamation of land and occasional destruction of villages, has been studied by R. A. Donkin: see the following three articles by him: "Settlement and Depopulation on Cistercian Estates During the 12th and 13th centuries," *Bulletin of the Institute of Historical Research* (U. of London), 33 (1960), 141-65; "Cistercian Assarting in England," *AC,* 20 (1964), 49-75; "The Cistercian Grange in England in the Twelfth and Thirteenth Centuries, with Special Reference to Yorkshire," *SM,* 6 (1964), 95-144. The "ruthless" destruction of villages has been exaggerated. The document of the acquisition of Elfingen by Maulbronn and the indemnity paid to its inhabitants is published in full by Duby, *Rural Economy*, p. 437. Poblet's role in resettlement is told by L. J. McCranck, "Cistercians of Poblet as Landlords," *Cîteaux*, 26 (1975), 274-5. On the role of the Cistercians in the foundation of new villages in southwestern France, see Charles Higounet, "Cisterciens et bastides," *Le moyen age*, 56 (1950), 69-84.

Due to the efforts of a young generation of economic historians in Germany the traditional image of Cistercians as agrarian pioneers, so successfully established by Winter, has been largely discredited. Hans Wiswe, "Grangien niedersächsischer Zisterzienserklöster," *Braunschweigisches Jahrbuch*, 34 (1953), 3-134, writing about Walkenried, Amelungsborn, Mariental, Riddagshausen, Michaelstein, Loccum and Marienrode, came to the conclusion that, contrary to previous assumptions, Cistercians moved into populated and previously cultivated territories and the novelty of Cistercian economy consisted in the acceleration of a new social mobility, capitalistic exploitation of land, manpower and surplus products (pp. 130-4). Siegfried Epperlein, "Grundungsmythos deutscher Zisterzienserklöster westlich und östlich der Elbe in hohen Mittelalter und der Bericht des Leubuser Mönches im 14. Jahrhundert," *Jahrbuch für Wirtschaftsgeschichte* (Berlin), 8 (1967), 303-35, extends the validity of Wiswe's observations to areas east of the Elbe, where, leaning on the research of Polish historians and archaeologists, he asserts that Cistercians often dislodged well-established Slavic villages and exploited native labor for their own advantage. The early Cistercian chroniclers, such as the "monk of Leubus," merely transmitted the familiar clichés on "horrible deserts" reclaimed by the labor of the monks, whereas "desert" Cistercian settlements were the rarest exceptions. How far this new appraisal of the role of Cistercians is influenced by a rekindled German and Polish nationalism and the intrusion of Marxian economic and social theories remains an unanswered question.

See Alexander III's criticism of Cistercians as published by Leclercq, *RB*, 62 (1952), 151. See the quote by Southern in his *Western Society and the Church*, p. 260. The same work deals with Les Dunes at some length, pp. 265-9. The quote attributed to Richard I on marrying his "daughter avarice" to the Cistercians was taken from Talbot, "Cîteaux and Scarborough," *SM*, 2 (1960), 96. The economic pressure on Cistercians under Richard I, John and his successors, is detailed in Coburn V. Graves, "The Economic Activities of the Cistercians in Medieval England, 1128-1307," *AC*, 13 (1957), 37-41. On the substantial amounts paid by Cistercians to Edward I see the already quoted *The Beaulieu Cartulary*, pp. 252-6. On legal efforts at curbing monastic wealth, see L. A. Desmond, "The Statute

'De viris religiosis' and the English Monks of the Cistercian Affiliation," *Cîteaux*, 25(1974), 137-55.

See the correlation of personnel and income at Meaux in the *Chronica*, II, 28-29. See the incidents of dispersion at Meaux, *ibid.*, I, 107, 178, 233, 273, 353-4. For other examples of dispersion see Schneider, *Die Cistercienserabtei Himmerod*, p. 69 and on Villers, Ploegaerts, *op.cit.*, pp. 15-18. See Lexington's observations on indebtedness in *AC*, 8 (1952), 191-268. See the same in England and the role of Jewish moneylenders in the above article of Graves, *AC*, 13(1957), 33-35, 42-45. See also Sr. James Eugene Madden, "Business Monks, Banker Monks, Bankrupt Monks. The English Cistercians in the Thirteenth Century," *The Catholic Historical Review*, 49(1963), 341-64. A commendable work on the changing attitudes of the Church in such matters is John Gilchrist, *The Church and Economic Activity in the Middle Ages* (New York: St. Martin's, 1969), particularly pp. 58-70.

Concerning the leasing of monastic land and the increasing importance of hired labor, see the above listed monographs. A formulary of rentals originated at Villers about 1384 runs for two printed pages in the collection of documents attached to Duby, *Rural Economy*, pp. 536-8. It stipulates that rents be contracted for 12 years. In the case of the extensive grange of Ostin, in addition to innumerable services, hospitality and detailed instructions on maintenance and cultivation, the contract calls annually for 100 florins and 2 old *écus* or its equivalent in other money, to be paid in two installments.

See on the exploitation of water at Clairvaux d'Arbois de Jubainville, *op.cit.*, pp. 329-38. On the still visible canal of Sorø see the already quoted McGuire, "Patrons . . . ," p. 28.

Of the extensive bibliography on Cistercian wool-trade see three recent articles by R. A. Donkin," The Disposal of Cistercian Wool in England and Wales," *Cîteaux*, 8(1957), 109-31, 181-202; "Some Aspects of Cistercian Sheep Farming in England and Wales," *Cîteaux*, 13(1962), 296-310; "The Cistercian Order in Medieval England; Some Conclusions," The Institute of British Geographers, London, *Transactions and Papers*, 33 (1963), 181-98, with many charts and maps. On other details consult Graves in *AC*, 13(1957). On Beaulieu see C. H. Talbot, "The Account Book of Beaulieu Abbey," *Cîteaux*, 9(1958), 189-210. See also D. E. Owen, *Kirkstall Abbey* (Leeds: Arnold, n.d.), particularly pp. 64-69. On some additional data concerning Rievaulx, Byland, Bruerne and Meaux see Ronald R. Bivens, "The Wool Trade and Finances of English Monasteries c. 1300," *Studies in Medieval Culture* (Kalamazoo, Mich.: The Medieval Institute of W.M.U., 1974), IV/2, pp. 330-7. On Welsh Cistercian wool the above works of Williams and Hays give valuable details. For wool and fishing in Ireland, see G. Carville, "The Economic Activities of the Cistercian Order in Medieval Ireland, 1142-1541," *Cîteaux*, 22 (1971), 278-99.

On Cîteaux's wine in Avignon, see H. Denifle, *La désolation des églises* . . . , II, 608. An outstanding study on Eberbach's wine is J. Söhn, *Geschichte des wirtschaftlichen Lebens der Abtei Eberbach in Rheingau* (Wiesbaden: Bergmann, 1914), with reference to Obsopaeus on p. 217. On Himmerod's vineyards see the often quoted Schneider, *Himmerod in Spätmittelalter,* particularly pp. 120-8. On wine in Alsace, see Luzian Pfleger, "Die Cistercienser und der Weinbau in Unteren Elsass," *SuM,* 24 (1903), 139-49. Details on German fruit growing were taken from Winter.

On urban property, markets and fairs, see two articles by R. A. Donkin, "The Urban Property of the Cistercians in Medieval England," *AC,* 15 (1959), 104-31; "The Markets and Fairs of Medieval Cistercian Monasteries in England and Wales," *CC,* 69 (1962), 1-14. On milling in Zinna, see Willy Hoppe, *Kloster Zinna* (Leipzig: Dunker & Humblot, 1914). On Poblet's involvement in mills see L. J. McCranck, "Cistercians of Poblet as Landlords," *Cîteaux,* 26 (1957), 280-1. On the forges of 4 Cistercian abbeys in Champagne, see Duby, *Rural Economy,* pp. 107-8.

In addition to the already listed works, see on German mining Karl Heinz Spiess, "Die Beziehungen einiger mitteldeutscher Zisterzienserabteien zum dortigen Bergbau." *AC,* 15 (1959), 265-83, and Georg Schreiber, *Der Bergbau in Geschichte* (Cologne: Westdeutscher Verlag, 1962), particularly pp. 12-13, 131-8. On salt mining in Germany, see Winter.

See the analysis of the economic crisis of 1350-1450 in *The Cambridge Economic History of Europe,* 2nd ed. (Cambridge U. Press, 1966), I, 660-741, and in Duby, *Rural Economy,* pp. 293-311. The oppressive taxation is the subject of Daniel S. Buczek, "Medieval Taxation: the French Crown, the Papacy and the Cistercian Order, 1190-1320," *AC,* 25 (1969), 42-106. On the method of tax-collection see H. Peter King, "Cistercian Financial Organization, 1335-1392," *The Journal of Ecclesiastical History,* 24 (1973), 127-43. On the attitude of the English Crown see L. A. Desmond, "The Statute of Carlisle and the Cistercians, 1298-1364," *Studies in Medieval Cistercian History* (Spencer, Mass.: Cistercian Publications, 1971), pp. 138-62. On the indebtedness of Cîteaux under Jean de Cirey see C. H. Talbot, *Letters of the English Abbots to the Chapter at Cîteaux, 1442-1521* (London: Royal Hist. Soc., 1967), pp. 11-12.

See the text of the *Fulgens sicut stella* in *Statuta,* III, 410-36. See the problems of Loccum in N. Heutger, *Loccum* (Hildesheim: Lax, 1971), pp.

434

29-32, 55. The financial status of Meaux is given in *Chronica*, III, pp. LX-LXVIII. The plight of Villers early in the 14th century is detailed in Moreau, *op.cit.*, pp. 257-8, continued in Ploegaerts-Boulmont, *op.cit.*, pp. 191-262. The visitation of Melrose in 1533 is told in James Campbell, *Balmerino and its Abbey* (Edinburgh: Blackwood, 1899), pp. 228-9.

On 18th century conditions see Adolf Gessner, *Abtei Rauden in Oberschlesien* (Kitzingen: Holzner-Verlag, 1952). On Orval's wealth, see Albert d'Haenens et al., *Abbayes de Belgique* (Brussels: Interentreprises, 1973), pp. 310-35. On French conditions before the Revolution see my two articles: "Moral and Material Status . . ." *AC*, 19 (1963), 199-266, and "Cistercian Monasteries and the French Episcopate . . . ," *AC*, 23 (1967), 66-114.

21. Lay-brotherhood

For a thorough study of the origins of lay-brotherhood see K. Hallinger, "Woher kommen die Laienbrüder?" *AC*, 12 (1956), 1-104. See also Jacques Dubois, "L'institution des convers au XIIe siècle," *I laici nella 'Societas Christiana' dei secoli XI et XII* (Milan: Univ. Cat. del Sacro Cuore, 1968), 183-216. See the same in English translation by C. Greenia in *CS*, 7 (1972), 161-213. Of the older studies still worth reading is Eberhardt Hoffman, *Das Konverseninstitut des Cistercienser-Ordens in seinem Ursprung und seiner Organisation* (Fribourg: Otto Geschwendt, 1905):

The quote from Ordericus Vitalis was taken from Chibnall's translation, IV, 319-21. See the translation of the *Exordium parvum* in Appendix I. The earliest version of the *Usus conversorum* was published by J.-A. Lefèvre, "Les traditions manuscrites des *Usus conversorum* de Cîteaux," *Coll*, 17 (1955), 85-97. See later texts of the same in *Nomasticon*, pp. 234-41, 352-60, 458-64. On the papal *bullatores* see an article by Florian Watzl in *CC*, 20 (1908), 193-9.

For the statistics concerning England see Knowles-Hadcock, p. 490. See the quote from the *Libellus de diversis ordinibus*, ed. G. Constable, p. 41. See the text taken from *Exm* on pp. 244-5. Humbert of Romans was quoted from Jean Leclercq, "Comment vivaient les frères convers?" *AC*, 20 (1965), 248. The connection between donations and admission is clear from the many examples quoted in *Cartulaire de l'abbaye de Gimont*; see the donation of 1175 on p. 43. See the story of Sunnulphus in the *Memorials of Fountains*, ed. J. R. Walbran (Edinburgh: Surtees Soc., 1863), p. 118. On other aspects of lay-brother vocation see Edmund Mikkers, "L'ideal religieux des frères convers . . . ," *Coll*, 26 (1962), 113-29; also, Clemens van Dijk, "L'instruction et culture des frères convers . . . ," *Coll*, 24 (1962), 243-58. It is worth mentioning that according to

Helmut Maisack, *William Langlands Verhältnis zum zisterziensischen Mönchtum* (Balingen: H. Daniel, 1953), the author of *Piers Plowman* had been for some time a Cistercian lay-brother and his spirituality was basically Cistercian.

See the views of Coincy and others, including the *Speculum stultorum,* analysed by Jean Batany, "Les convers chez quelques moralistes des XIIe et XIIIe siècles," *Cîteaux,* 20(1969), 241-59. See the decline of the institution as reflected in the decrees of the General Chapter James S. Donnelly, *The Decline of the Medieval Cistercian Laybrotherhood* (New York: Fordham U. Press, 1949). References to Lexington were taken from *AC,* 8(1952), 208-9, 232. The formulary of Pontigny was quoted from the above article of Leclercq, "Comment vivaient les frères . . . ," p. 250.

Ebrach's population was studied by J. Jaeger, "Series abbatum et religiosorum monasterii Ebracensis," serialized in *CC,* 14(1902). The figures of lay-brothers in England have been given according to J. S. Donnelly, "Changes in the Grange Economy . . . ," *Traditio,* 10(1954), pp. 452-4. On the results of Saulieu's visitation in Spain see the frequently quoted *Peregrinatio Hispanica* by Bronseval. See the results and figures of Boucherat's visitation in Germany, together with later statistics, in Appendix II.

The long and in many ways enlightening and above cited article of Jacques Dubois tries to draw a close parallel between the medieval lay-brothers and lay-monks of our days. This approach fails to take into consideration the tremendous differences between the social environments of the 12th century and ours; his theory, therefore, remains unconvincing.

22. Cistercian Nuns

On the beginnings, especially on Tart, see Jean de la Croix Bouton, "Saint Bernard et les moniales," *Mélanges Saint Bernard* (Dijon: Assoc. Bourguignonne des Soc. Savantes, 1953), pp. 225-47. On chapters organized by nuns in France and Spain, see Anselme Dimier, "Chapitres généneraux d'abbesses cisterciennes," *Cîteaux,* 11(1960), 268-73. On the question of incorporations see the substantial Ernst Krenig, "Mittelalterliche Frauenklöster nach den Konstitutionen von Cîteaux," *AC,* 10(1954), 1-105.

The quote by Herman of Tournay and references to Jacques de Vitry were taken from Ernest W. McDonnell, *The Beguines and Beghards in Medieval Culture* (New Brunswick: Rutgers U. Press, 1954), pp. 105-7. The same work gives the best appraisal of Cistercian influences on the movement of the Beguines, especially through the efforts of Villers. On the problem of enclosure, see Bouton, p. 124.

436

On the number of Cistercian nunneries, good approximations are given in the works listed under Chapter IV, but concerning France, Spain and Italy no scholarly work has been done. In addition to *GM*, another list is given in Winter, III, 175-85, and Brunner, *Ein Cistercienserbuch*, pp. 616-47. On the spirituality of Belgian nunneries, see again Canivez.

On individual abbeys the following works were utilized: O. Vergé du Taillis, *Chroniques de l'abbaye ròyale de Maubuisson* (Paris: Perrin, 1947). Catherine E. Boyd, *A Cistercian Nunnery in Medieval Italy. The Story of Rifreddo* (Cambridge, Mass.: Harvard U. Press, 1943). See Lexington's observations in *AC*, 8(1952), 235-57. The same is summarized by B. Griesser, "Stephan Lexinton, Abt von Savigny, als Visitator der ihm unterstehenden Frauenklöster," *CC*, 67(1960), 14-34. On the suppression and merger of nunneries see Bouton, p. 298. The results of Boucherat's visitation in Germany were published in *CC*, 13(1901), 225-37, 257-67. On nuns associated with the Strict Observance, see Alexis Presse, "Les moniales cisterciennes réformées," *Revue Mabillon*, 24(1934), 1-14, 81-89; 25(1935), 30-40.

On the 16th- and 17th-century reforms of nuns, with the exception of Port-Royal, no modern scholarly works are available. Recent accounts are based largely on Hippolyte Hélyot, *Histoire des ordres monastiques*, 8 vols. (Paris, 1714-19), reprinted by Migne in his *Encyclopédie Thélogique*, vols. 20-23 (Paris, 1847). On the various exploits of Zamet see Louis Prunel, *Sébastien Zamet, évêque-duc de Langres* (Paris: Picard, 1912). On the Cistercian period of Port-Royal the latest and best are by Louis Cognet, *La réforme de Port-Royal, 1591-1618* (Paris: Sulliver, 1950), and *La Mère Angélique et Saint François de Sales, 1618-1626* (Paris: Flammarion, 1951). On reforms in Normandy, there is a short article by M. Pigeon, "Les moniales cisterciennes en Basse-Normandie au XVIIe siècle," *Cîteaux*, 19(1968), 317-24. On the problems of lay-sisters, see Roger de Ganck, "The Endangered Lay Sisters in the Seventeenth Century," *Cîteaux*, 19(1968), 357-63. On the 18th century see Ryckman de Betz, *L'abbaye cistercienne de la Cambre* (Antwerp: De Nederlandsche Boekhandel, 1948). Concerning Herkenrode, see Albert d'Haenens et al., *Abbayes de Belgique* (Brussels: Clio, 1973), pp. 444-57. See the statistics of 1891 in *CC*, 3(1891), 299-320. See on the nuns of the Strict Observance the anonymously published *La Trappe in England* (London: Burns & Oates, 1937), and Yvonne Estienne, *Les trappistines* (Paris: Desclée de Brouver, 1937).

23. *Daily Life and Customs*

Among the many works on monastic life and customs the most readable is still Francis Cardinal Gasquet, *English Monastic Life*, 6th ed. (London: Methuen, 1924). Specifically on Cistercians, see Bruno Schneider, "Cîteaux und die benediktinische Tradition," *AC*, 16 (1960), 169-254; 17 (1961), 73-114. See for a similar approach Anselme Dimier, "Observances monastiques," *AC*, 11 (1955), 149-98.

The scheme of Cistercian daily schedule was adapted from Bouton, pp. 142-3. See regulations on prisons in *Nomasticon*, p. 320, including the quote on incorrigible criminals. On 17th-century conditions, see my "Moral and Material Status . . . ," *AC*, 19 (1963), 199-266. On abstinence in medieval tradition see the article in *DS*, I (1937), 112-33, containing the quote from St. Bernard. The quote from St. Thomas was taken from *Summa Theologiae* (New York: McGraw-Hill, 1968), XLIII, 115. On other aspects of Cistercian dietary rule see the index of *Nomasticon*. On the problem of perpetual abstinence see a long serial by G. Müller, "Der Fleischgenuss im Orden," *CC*, 18 (1906). On the life at Whalley under Paslew, see Haigh, *The Last Days* . . . , pp. 9-10. See the travelogue of Laurence Scipio in *CC*, 8 (1896), with the quote on p. 295. Details concerning the kitchen of the College of Toulouse were taken from my article, "The College of Saint Bernard in Toulouse, 1533-1791," *AC*, 27 (1971), 157-211. See references to the Parisian College in another article of mine, "The College of Saint Bernard in Paris in the Sixteenth and Seventeenth Centuries," *AC*, 28 (1972), 167-218.

On sign-language among Cistercians see two articles: A. Dimier, "Ars signorum Cisterciensium," *Coll*, 5 (1938), 165-86, and B. Griesser, "Ungedruckete Texte zur Zeichensprache in den Klöstern," *AC*, 3 (1947), 111-37. The latest on the same subject is Robert Barakat, *Cistercian Sign Language* (Kalamazoo, Mich.: Cistercian Publications, 1975), which includes an illustrated "dictionary" of some 400 signs.

On bloodletting, see a serial by G. Müller, "Der Aderlass," *CC*, 6 (1894). See the highly romanticised story of "Brother Joseph" in Caesarius, I, 47-53. On death and burial see again G. Müller, "Vom Sterbelager bis zum Grabe," a serial in *CC*, 27 (1915).

24. *Monks and Society*

On the charities of Margam see G. Williams, *The Welsh Cistercians*, pp. 18-19. On the *donados* of Poblet, see the article of McCranck in *AC*, 29 (1973), 66-67. The case of Acey and her 14 donors is told by J.-G. Ebersolt, "La seigneurie et la société dans les chartes de l'abbaye cistercienne d'Acey au XIIe siècle," *Les debuts des abbayes Cisterciennes dans les anciens pays bourgoignons* . . . ," pp. 107-26.

See for the numbers of lay-servants in English abbeys before the Dissolution Knowles-Hadcock, listing the houses alphabetically. The story of elections at Furness is given by Haigh, *The Last Days* . . . , pp. 14-20. See the details of the account book of Beaulieu by Talbot in *Cîteaux*, 9 (1958), 194-5, 206-10. References to Doberan and later to the hospital of Zwettl were taken from Ludwig Dolberg, "Die Liebesthätigkeit der Cistercienser im Beherbergen der Gäste und Spenden von Almosen," *SuM*, 16(1895), 243-45. On Saint Mary's in Dublin see Carville's article in *Cîteaux*, 22 (1971), 286-7. On Basingwerk, see R. W. Hays's article in *Studies in Medieval Cistercian History* (1971), p. 133.

On the hospital of Himmerod, see Schneider, *Himmerod im Spätmittelalter*, pp. 138-9, 147, 187. For hospitals elsewhere in Germany see Winter, II, 143-5. Reference to Meaux was taken from *Chronica*, II, 6. On Newminster, see *Chartularium Abbathiae de Novo Monasterio* (Edinburgh: Surtees Soc., 1876), pp. 170-72. The other English hospitals are listed in Knowles-Hadcock, pp. 119-28. The three Scottish hospitals are mentioned in Coulton, *Scottish Abbeys*, pp. 107-8. Details on the 18th-century pharmacy of Orval were adopted from *Abbayes de Belgique*, p. 322, and from a *Guide du musée pharmaceutique et du jardin des plantes médicinales de l'abbaye d'Orval* (Orval, 1975), pp. 5-17, by Dr. Jean Kelecom.

On the shipload of alms procured by Margam, see Williams, *op.cit.*, p. 21. The formulary of Pontigny was published by Jean Leclercq in *Miscellanea Populetana* (Poblet: Abadia, 1966), pp. 229-65. On the contributions of the workshops of Meaux, see the *Chronica*, II, pp. XIV-XV. On the charities of Whalley, Furness, Stanley and Garendon, see Woodward, *op.cit.*, pp. 26-7, and Haigh, *op.cit.*, pp. 53-4. The 2,100 loaves of bread for the poor of Villers was taken from Moreau, *op. cit.*, p. 265. On the charities of Hauterive see Pittet, *op.cit.*, pp. 197, 200, 215. King Robert's gift to Melrose is told by Coulton, *Scottish Abbeys*, pp. 101-2. On Morimond, Sittichenbach and Riddagshausen see Winter, II, 142. Among other charities, the *tricenarium* is detailed in a serial by G. Müller, "Almosenausteilung an der Klosterpforte," *CC*, 23(1911).

The *nullius* status of Poblet is mentioned in McCranck, "Cistercians of Poblet . . . ," *Cîteaux*, 24(1975), 267. See on the pastoral engagement of Cwmhir, Hays, *op.cit.*, p. 112. On the Irish Holy Cross as a popular shrine, see Carville, *op.cit.*, pp. 113-22. The many references to St. Urban were taken from two dissertations: Hans Wicki, *Die Geschichte der Cisterzienserabtei Sankt Urban im Zeitalter der Reformation, 1500-1550* (Fribourg: Universitätsverlag, 1945), and Ernst Kaufmann, *Geschichte der Cisterzienserabtei Sankt Urban im Spätmittelalter, 1375-1500* (Fribourg: Universitätsverlag, 1956). On the chantry of Ottringham see the *Chronica*, II, pp. XXVI-XXVII. On the visitation of the Abbot of Morimond in 1393, see Hans Mosler, *Altenberg*, Germania Sacra, NF., Erzbistum Köln, vol. 1 (Berlin: W. de Gruyter, 1965), p. 72. On the pastoral involvement of Silesian abbeys see H. Grüger, "Die monastische Disziplin der schlesischen Zisterzienser von Anbruch der Reformation," *Cîteaux,* 24(1973), 209-49. On the same concerning Austria see Bruno Schneider, "Österreichs Zisterzienserpfarren—Erbe des Josephinismus?" *SuM,* 78 (1967), 275-302. On the Benefactors' League in Himmerod, see A. Schneider, *op.cit.,* pp. 59-63. On the Bavarian pilgrim-shrines see Edgar Krausen, "Zisterziensertum und Wallfahrtskulte im bayerischen Raum," *AC,* 12 (1956), 115-29. See also: Sigmund von Pölnitz, *Vierzehnheiligen* (Weissenhorn: Konrad Verlag, 1971). Concerning St. Urban, in addition to the above dissertations, see on Freibach, Franz Schärli, "Von der Bedeutung und Wirksamkeit der einstigen Cisterzienserabtei St. Urban für die Seelsorge," *CC,* 66(1959), 35-39. See data on nuns and Villers in Ploegaerts-Boulmont, *op.cit.,* p. 154. See on the St. Joseph Fraternity of Lilienfeld N. Mussbacher, "Abt Matthäus Kolweiss von Lilienfeld (1620-1695)," *AC,* 31(1975), 114-30.

On the "Red School" of Adwert, see A. Nyssen, "Über einige Cistercienser Klöster in den Niederlanden vor der Reformation," *CC,* 26(1914), 42-45. On boys in English abbeys see (alphabetically) Knowles-Hadcock, pp. 115-28. On the choir boys of Zwettl, see Holzhauser's article in *CC,* 72(1975), 129-32. On the Latin school of Rauden, see A. Gassner, *Abtei Rauden,* pp. 5-7. On Gotteszell's school, see Krausen, pp. 18, 46.

The banking services of Cistercians in Wales are well covered in Williams, *op. cit.,* p. 22, about Dore and Margam. See the story of Stoneleigh in Baskerville, *op. cit.,* p. 34. On Poblet's loans to the kings of Aragon, see McCranck, "The Cistercians of Poblet as Landlords," *Cîteaux,* 26(1975), 257-8. The brothers of San Galgano are mentioned in Schevill's article in *American Historical Review,* 14(1908), 29.

On the relationship of criminal jurisdiction and "advocacy" see Helmut Pflüger, "Die Zisterzienser und die Vogteifrage," *Zeitschrift für württembergische Landesgeschichte,* 2(1958), 273-80. Incidents of execution in Pontigny are mentioned in King, p. 180. See Walter Map's charges against Tintern in Williams, *op. cit.,* pp. 45-46. On Mellifont, see Colmcille O'Conbhuidhe, *The Story of Mellifont,* p. 106. On the jurisdiction of Holy Cross, see Carville, *op. cit.,* pp. 57-60. On Salem's territorial autonomy see W. Rösener, *Reichsabtei Salem,* pp. 77-101.

Concerning the medieval critics of Cistercians, see the following: Jean Leclercq, "Le poème de Payen Bolotin contre les faux ermites," *RB,* 68(1958), 56-86. C. R. Cheney, "A Letter of Pope Innocent III and the Lateran Decree on Cistercian Tithe Paying," *Cîteaux,* 13(1962), 146-51. See Pecham's charges as quoted by J. S. Donnelly, "Changes in the

Grange Economy . . . ," *Traditio,* 10(1954), 409. On Gerald of Wales, Walter Map and Nigel Wireker, see Knowles I, 662-78, and by the same author, "Some Enemies of Gerald of Wales," *SM,* 1(1959), 137-41. See also Bruno Griesser, "Walther Map und die Cistercienser," *CC,* 36(1924), 137-41, 164-7. On Guiot de Provins, see J. Batany, "Les moines blancs dans les états du monde," *Cîteaux,* 15(1964), 5-25. See Lexington's remarks in *AC,* 8(1952), 302. On the large-scale devastation of Cistercian estates in France, see Daniel S. Buczek, "Pro defendendis ordinis . . . ," *Studies in Medieval Cistercian History* (1971), pp. 88-109. On Poblet's difficulties with her neighbors, see McCranck's article in *Cîteaux,* 26 (1975), 254-83. On peasant attitudes, see P. G. Mode, *The Influence of the Black Death on the English Monasteries* (U. of Chicago, 1916), pp. 50-59). The case of Waghen is given in *Chronica,* III, pp. XX-XXII.

See the bibliography covering the 18th and 19th centuries under Chapters XIII-XV.

Early Cistercian Documents in Translation

by Bede K. Lackner

The basis of the translations presented below is the collection of early
Cistercian documents published by Jean de la Croix Bouton and Jean-
Baptiste Van Damme, *Les plus anciens textes de Cîteaux* (Achel: Abbaye
Cistercienne, 1974). The reader will find the originals of the *Exordium
Cistercii, Summa cartae caritatis* and *Capitula* on pp. 107-25; the *Exor-
dium parvum* on pp. 51-86; the final version of the *Carta caritatis (poster-
ior)* on pp. 132-42.

The choice of documents to be published here was dictated partly by
limitations of space, partly by the relevance of the documents themselves.
The two *exordia* present the earliest narratives of the beginnings of
Cîteaux, documents which carry the founders' authentic message to posterity. The initial and final versions of the "Charter of Charity" give a
unique insight into monastic constitution-making. Finally, the *Capitula*
may be considered as the first fruits of the legislative activity of the
General Chapter, dealing with issues of basic importance to those who
formulated them. On the dating and analysis of these documents see
above pp. 22-30.

There is no need to dwell on the inherent difficulties the translation of
early twelfth-century Latin documents involve. The often loose syntax,
erratic grammar, and lack of punctuation of the original texts are made
more problematic by hidden biblical quotes or references, and canonical
and feudal terms of debatable meaning. A mechanical transliteration
would be as unsatisfactory as a free paraphrase of the original. The
casting of the genuine ideas of the medieval author into a smoothly
flowing English would be the ideal solution. Alas, there is no perfect
translation, therefore no translation is an entirely adequate substitute for
the original. The pages which follow represent a greater effort at textual fidelity than at stylistic excellence.

Exordium Cistercii, Summa Cartae Caritatis et Capitula

EXORDIUM CISTERCII

I. *Departure of the Cistercian Monks from Molesme*

In the diocese of Langres there lay, as is well known, a monastery by the name of Molesme; it was of great renown and outstanding in religious fervor. Within a short time of its foundation God in his goodness enriched it with the gift of his graces, raised it to honor with the presence of distinguished men, and caused it to be as great in possessions as it was resplendent in virtues. But, because possessions and virtues are not usually steady companions, several members of that holy community, men truly wise and filled with higher aspirations, decided to pursue heavenly studies rather than to be entangled in earthly affairs. Accordingly, these lovers of virtue soon came to think about that poverty which is fruitful to man. They realized that, although life in that place was a godly and upright life, they observed the Rule they had vowed to keep in a way short of their desire and intention. They spoke amongst themselves and asked one another how they were to fulfill the verse: "I will fulfill my vows to you, vows which I made with my own lips" [Ps. 65:13]. What more needs to be said? After common deliberation, together with the father of that monastery, Robert of blessed memory, twenty-one monks went out to try to carry out jointly what they had conceived with one spirit. Eventually, after many labors and extreme difficulties, which all who wish to devote their life to Christ must endure, they reached their goal. They came to Cîteaux, which was then a place of horror, a vast wilderness. Realizing that the asperity of the place accorded well with the strict design they had already conceived [in their minds], the soldiers of Christ found the place, almost as though divinely prepared, to be as alluring as their design had been dear.

II. *Beginnings of the Monastery of Cîteaux*

Thus in the year 1098 of the Incarnation of Our Lord, supported with the counsel and strengthened with the authority of the venerable Hugh, archbishop of the church of Lyons, and at the time legate of the Apostolic See, and of the God-fearing man, Walter, bishop of Chalon, and of Odo, the illustrious duke of Burgundy, these men began to transform the solitude they had found into an abbey; abbot Robert received the care of the monks and the shepherd's staff from the bishop of the diocese; and under him the others vowed stability in that place. But, after a short time it happened that the same abbot Robert was reclaimed by the monks of

Molesme, and was returned to Molesme on the order of Pope Urban II and with the permission and consent of Walter, bishop of Chalon. He was replaced by Alberic, a religious and holy man. For the sake of peace this wise agreement was made between the monasteries and confirmed by the pope: henceforth neither of them would [permanently] accept the other's monk without a proper recommendation. Through the solicitude and industry of its new father and with God's generous assistance, the New Monastery thereafter advanced in holiness, excelled in fame, and witnessed the increase of its temporal goods. The man of God, Alberic, who successfully ran his race for nine years [Phil. 2:16], obtained the crown of eternity in the tenth year. He was succeeded by the lord Stephen, an Englishman by nationality, an ardent lover of and staunch champion of religious life, poverty and regular discipline. In his days the words of Scripture came true: "The eyes of the Lord are upon the just and His ears hear their prayer" [Ps. 33: 16]. The little flock voiced its one and only complaint: that it was small in number. As I said, the "poor of Christ" came to fear and to dread almost to the point of despair one thing alone: that they might not be able to leave behind heirs to their poverty. For their neighbors applauded their holy life but abhorred its austerity and thus kept from imitating the men whose fervor they approved. Yet God, who can easily make great things from small ones and many things from a few, beyond all expectation, so aroused the hearts of many to the imitation of these monks that in the cell where the novices are tested, thirty had come to live under the same discipline: clerics as well as laymen, even nobles and men of power in the eyes of the world. Upon this so sudden and happy heavenly visitation the barren one which had no offspring began, not without reason, to rejoice; "Once forsaken, she now came to have many sons [Is. 54:1]". And God did not cease to multiply His people, and to increase their joy, so that within about twelve years the happy mother came to see twenty abbots, drawn from her own sons as well as from the sons of her sons, like olive branches around her table. Indeed she did not think it out of order to follow the example of the holy Father Benedict whose Rule she embraced. Hence, as soon as the new plantation began to produce offshoots, blessed Father Stephen in his watchful wisdom provided a document of admirable discretion; it served as a trimming knife which was to cut off the outgrowth of division which, if unchecked, could suffocate the fruit of mutual peace. Very appropriately, he wished the document to be called a Charter of Charity, for, clearly, its whole content so breathed love that almost nothing else is seen to be treated there than this: "Owe no man anything, but to love one another" [Rom. 13:8]. This charter, arranged by the same father and confirmed by the aforementioned twenty abbots, was also approved by apostolic authority. It contains in greater detail those things which we have said: here, however. we shall restrict ourselves to a brief summary.

SUMMA CARTAE CARITATIS

III. *General Statute Between Abbeys*

According to the tenor of the Charter, it was established among all abbeys of the Cistercian Order that: Mother-abbeys may not exact any temporal goods from their daughter-abbeys. A Father-Abbot visiting the monastery of an abbot-son, shall not bless that one's novice as monk, nor shall he admit an outsider for permanent stay, nor lastly, decree or ordain anything in that place against the local abbot's will, except in what relates to the care of souls. If he finds anything contrary to the Rule or to the Order in that place, he may charitably correct it, with the counsel of the local abbot. But, if by chance the local abbot is absent, he shall correct whatever he finds amiss. The abbot-son yields his place to the Father-Abbot not only in the chapter room, but everywhere else in the monastery. However, the Father-Abbot shall eat with the brethren in the refectory, for the sake of discipline, except in the absence of the local abbot. All other visiting abbots of our Order shall do likewise. But if several abbots come and the local abbot is absent, their senior shall eat in the guest-house. Further, every abbot shall visit the abbeys founded by his monastery with paternal solicitude at least once a year. Whenever an abbot-son visits his mother abbey, he shall be given due reverence as befits an abbot. He shall occupy the place of the abbot in everything pertaining to the Order, but only during the absence of the abbot of the mother-abbey. For, when that one is present, the abbot-son shall yield to him in all things, as to a father. Hence he shall not eat with the guests when the Father-Abbot is at home, but in the refectory with the brethren.

IV. *The Annual Chapter of Abbots*

The abbey of Cîteaux, the mother of all, wisely reserved to itself the prerogative that every abbot must visit it once a year at the same time, to meet one another, to tend to the affairs of the Order, to strengthen the peace and to preserve charity. At Cîteaux all shall reverently and humbly obey the lord Abbot of Cîteaux and that holy assembly when dealing with the correction of wrongs, and if they are accused, they shall seek pardon. Only abbots shall make accusations. The assembly also made this wise provision: should it come to pass that the extreme poverty of any one of the abbots become known to the assembly all shall provide for this

445

brother's relief according to the dictates of charity and [each] in the measure allowed by his own situation. Only two reasons shall justify [an abbot's] absence from the annual chapter: illness of the body, or the blessing of a novice. An abbot, to whom one of these applies, shall send his prior as his representative. But if anyone shall ever presume to stay at home for any other reason, at the next chapter he shall seek pardon for his fault and offer satisfaction according to the judgment of the abbots. And this shall be held to be a lesser fault.

V. *On the Faults of Abbots*

Should an abbot be found to scorn the Rule or the Order, or to be careless and negligent in the care entrusted to him, straightway he shall be warned by his Father-Abbot, in person or through his prior or by letter, up to four times. If he refuses to correct his ways, then, through the same Father-Abbot the wrongdoing shall be made known to the bishop and to the clergy of the diocese of the transgressor. If, perchance, the wrongdoing persists uncorrected because of their disinterest, the Father-Abbot shall summon at least two of his co-abbots and, all going to the place in question, they shall depose the incorrigible man from his office and urge the brethren to elect at an early date another who will be worthy. If they defy the visiting abbots, that is, if the abbot is unwilling to resign his office and the monks are unwilling to elect another abbot, they shall be excommunicated by the visiting abbots. Should any of these evildoers eventually regain his senses and, having pity on his soul, refuse to accept its death sentence, seek refuge in the monastery from which his own was founded, he shall be received as a son and monk of the community until he is restored to his own monastery whenever it is reformed. Further, the abbot of Cîteaux, since he is the head of all and has no abbot over himself, shall see to it that those measures, which have been decreed against other transgressors, shall be applied to himself as well. By common agreement this charge has been entrusted to the abbots of La Ferté, Pontigny and Clairvaux so that they, acting in the name of all and in behalf of all, shall zealously apply to him everything in the sequence stated above. But there is this exception: If he resigns [his office], the three abbots shall not themselves provide a new abbot nor shall they excommunicate him if he proves defiant. Instead, the prior of Cîteaux shall send three or more messengers to the abbeys of Cîteaux's direct filiation and summon as many abbots as are able to assemble within fifteen days. Then, upon the removal of the accused, they shall cause the monks to elect, in their presence, a new abbot. If the monks refuse to listen, the assembled abbots shall excommunicate both the monks and the accused abbot. If any of the monks, regaining his senses and anxious to save his soul, should at length seek refuge in one of the above mentioned abbeys—La Ferté, Pontigny or Clairvaux—he shall be received as a brother and a member of the house until he is returned to his own monastery, once it is reconciled through the mercy of God. In the meantime, however, the yearly chapter of abbots shall not be held at Cîteaux but in a place designated by the three abbots mentioned above. Let it also be known that as long as the community of Cîteaux is without an abbot, his place shall be held by the abbot of La Ferté. The election of the abbot of Cîteaux shall always be done in the manner and sequence described above. In other monasteries, however, upon the death of the abbot, the Father-Abbot of the deceased shall be summoned so that in his presence and with his advice, the brethren may hold a regular election. Whomever they elect from any Cistercian monastery they shall receive without objection. But Cistercians may not choose their abbots from other orders or release their own monks to these orders for the same purpose.

VI. *What Shall Be the Law Between Abbeys not Bound by Filiation*

Between abbeys which are not of each other's filiation this shall be the law: Every abbot shall yield his place to a visiting abbot throughout his monastery, to fulfill the Scriptures: "They give one another precedence with honor" [Rom. 12:10]. If two or more arrive, the senior of the guests will take the higher place. All shall eat in the refectory, except the local abbot. Wherever else they meet, they shall enjoy seniority according to the antiquity of their abbeys, so that the abbot of an older abbey shall take precedence. There is one exception: if one is vested in alb, then, preceding everyone else, he shall preside in everything, even if he is the junior of all. Also, after they take their places, they shall bow to each other.

VII. *No One Shall Receive a Lay-Brother Wishing to go to Another Monastery*

None of us shall dissuade any man who wishes to enter any other one of our abbeys, nor entice anyone to our own abbey; but rather each of us shall retain that one who chooses of his own accord, after a change of mind, to remain. If after arriving at the place of his choice he should regret his decision before the completion of the period of probation, he shall be free to leave if he so desires. But if he leaves after his admission, he shall not be accepted anywhere without the consent of that monastery.

VIII. *On Fugitive Monks and Lay-Brothers*

If a monk, or lay-brother, secretly flees from one of our monasteries and comes to another, let him be persuaded to return. If he refuses, he shall not be permitted to stay in that place for more than one night. If he is a monk, he shall be deprived of his habit, if he is wearing it, unless there is evidence that he had been a monk before he entered our Order.

IX. *The Founding of New Abbeys*

It has been decreed that all our monasteries must be dedicated to the Queen of Heaven and Earth. No monastery shall be constructed within cities, castles and manors. No abbot shall be sent to a new place without at least twelve monks and the following books: a psalter, a book of hymns, a book of collects, an antiphonary, a gradual, the Rule, a missal; and without the prior construction of such places as an oratory, a refectory, a dormitory, a guest-house, and a gate-keeper's cell, so that the monks may immediately serve God and live in religious discipline. No living quarters, only animal shelters, shall be constructed outside the gate of the monastery. Also, to preserve an indissoluble and lasting unity among our abbeys it has been established: first, that the Rule of blessed Father Benedict shall be interpreted and kept in one and the same way; secondly, that there shall be found the same liturgical books, the same food, the same clothing, and lastly, the same customs and usages in everything.

X. *Which Books Must not Be Dissimilar*

The missal, Gospel Book, book of epistles, book of collects, gradual, antiphonary, book of hymns, psalter, lectionary, Rule and calendar of saints shall be used everywhere in one and the same way.

XI. *On Clothing*

Clothing shall be simple and inexpensive, without underclothes, as the Rule prescribes. But this also must be observed: the outer cowls shall not be flocked with pile on the outside; and the day-shoes shall be made of cowhide.

XII. *On Food*

In addition to what the Rule prescribes about the pound of bread, the measure of drink, and the number of dishes, this must also be observed: the bread must be coarse, that is, prepared with a sieve. Where wheat is scarce, however, rye may be used. This rule shall not apply to the sick; they, and also the guests for whom it has been prescribed, shall be served wastel-bread. To those who are bled, there shall be given a pound of white bread, once, during the bleeding.

XIII. *No One May Eat Meat or* [*Food Prepared with*] *Lard in the Monastery*

In the monastery cooked dishes must always and everywhere be prepared without meat or lard; an exception is made [only] for the brethren who are seriously ill and for our hired workers.

XIV. *Days When We Eat Lenten Food*

Except for those who are ill, we fast during Lent, before Christmas [Advent], in the Septuagesima season, on all Fridays, and on the four Ember days in September. Also on the vigils of Saint John the Baptist Saints Peter and Paul, Saint Lawrence, the Assumption of Saint Mary, the apostles Matthew, Simon and Jude, All Saints, and the apostle Andrew. Nothing shall be bought for a guest, unless he is ill.

XV. *Where the Monks' Food Is to Come From*

Food for the monks of our Order ought to come from manual labor, agriculture, and the raising of animals. Hence we may possess, for our own use, streams, woodlands, vineyards, meadows, lands far removed from the dwellings of seculars, and animals, except those which tend to foster curiosity and to show themselves off rather than serve a useful purpose, such as deer, cranes, and other animals of this kind. To raise, feed, and take care of animals we may keep granges, either in the neighborhood or at a greater distance. These are to be supervised and managed by the lay-brothers.

XVI. *No Monk May Live Outside the Monastic Enclosure*

A monk whose proper home, according to the Rule, ought to be the monastery, may go to a grange as often as he is sent, but on no account may he live there for any long period of time.

XVII. *Women May Not Live in Our Houses*

At any time whatsoever—be it a time for cultivating or preserving food, or a time for washing particular objects of the monastery when this is necessary, or lastly, a time of any need whatsoever—it is absolutely forbidden for us and our lay-brothers to live under the same roof with women.

XVIII. *Women Shall not Enter Within the Monastery Gate*

Women shall not be received as guests within the courtyard of our granges, nor shall they enter within the gate of the monastery.

XIX. *There Should Be No Association with Laymen for Feeding Cattle, Cultivating Land, Giving or Receiving Shares in Crops and the Like*

In raising our animals and cultivating our lands we are not allowed to have joint dealings with laymen, such as giving or receiving shares or profits.

XX. *These Affairs Are to be Managed by Lay-Brothers*

As has been said, these affairs are to be managed by lay-brothers or by hired workers. As we do with monks, we take under our care lay-brothers with the license of the bishops, who are members of our family and helpers in our work. We hold them to be our brothers and, equally with our monks, sharers of our goods both spiritual and temporal.

XXI. *On the Probation of Lay-Brothers*

We impose a probation period of one year on those who come to us as new arrivals. At the end of that year, in chapter assembled we receive the profession of him who wishes to remain and who deserves to be retained.

XXII. *A Lay-Brother May not Become a Monk*

Once he has taken his vows, a lay-brother shall not become a monk even if he greatly desires it; but he shall remain in the vocation of his calling. If, under the influence of the devil, he shall have taken the habit of a monk or a canon regular from any bishop or abbot, he shall after that never again be admitted to any of our monasteries.

XXIII. *What Incomes We Renounce*

Our very name [of monks] and the constitution of our Order prohibit [the possession of] churches, altar revenues, burials, tithes from the labor or harvest of outsiders, manors, serfs, land-rents, oven and mill revenues, and all other incomes of the kind, as contrary to the purity of the monastic vocation.

XXIV. *Whom Do We Admit for Confession and Communion, and to Whom Do We Grant Burial*

We receive no outsider to confession or to holy communion; nor do we grant burial to any outsider unless he is a guest or one of our hired workers who dies within our monastery; nor do we accept offerings from outsiders during the conventual Mass.

XXV. *What We May or May not Have in Gold, Precious Stones and Silk*

The altar linen and the vestments of the ministers, except the stole and the maniple, must be without silk. The chasuble must be of one color. Every ornament, vessel and utensil of the monastery must be without gold, silver or precious stones, except the chalice and the communion reed. We are allowed to have these two things made of silver or of gold-plate, but never of pure gold.

XXVI. *On Sculptures, Paintings and Wooden Crosses*

We may not have sculptures anywhere; we may have paintings, but only on crosses; and we may have crosses made only of wood.

The Exordium Parvum

LETTER OF THE FIRST CISTERCIANS TO ALL THEIR SUCCESSORS

We Cistercians, the original founders of this monastery, make known to our successors through this present writing how canonically, by what authority, and by which persons, as well as at what period of time, their monastery and manner of living had its beginning. We publish the sincere truth of this matter that they may the more tenaciously love the place as well as the observance of the holy Rule therein, which we ourselves with the grace of God have only just begun; that they may pray for us who have sustained indefatigably the burden and the heat of the day; and that they may labor unto death on the strait and narrow way prescribed by the Rule, so that after they have put down the burden of the flesh they may repose happily in eternal rest. Amen.

I. *The Beginning of the Monastery of Cîteaux*

In the year 1098 of the Incarnation of our Lord, Robert of blessed memory, the first abbot of the monastery of Molesme which was founded in the diocese of Langres, and certain brethren of the same monastery appeared before the venerable Hugh, then legate of the Apostolic See and archbishop of the church of Lyons, and promised to place their lives under the custody of the holy Rule of Father Benedict. For the unhindered realization of this intention, therefore, they begged him insistently to lend them the strength of his own support and of his apostolic authority. The legate, joyfully espousing their wish, laid down the foundations of their beginning with the following letter.

II. *Letter of the Legate Hugh*

Hugh, Archbishop of Lyons and legate of the Apostolic See to Robert, Abbot of Molesme, and to the brethren who together with him desire to serve God according to the Rule of Saint Benedict. Let it be known to all who rejoice in the progress of Holy Mother Church that you and certain of your sons, brothers of the monastery of Molesme, have stood in Our presence at Lyons and stated your wish to adhere henceforth more strictly and more perfectly to the Rule of blessed Benedict, which so far you have observed poorly and neglectfully in that monastery. But, since it is obvious that in view of many obstacles this could not be accomplished in the aforementioned place, We, providing for the welfare of both parties, those departing and those remaining, have concluded that it will be expedient for you to retire to another place, which the Divine Munificence will point out to you, and there serve the Lord in a more salutary and peaceful

451

manner. To you, therefore, who had at that time presented yourselves—Abbot Robert and brothers Alberic, Odo, John, Stephen, Letald, and Peter—as well as to all others whom you shall decide to add to your company according to the Rule and by common consultation, after deliberation We gave the order that you persevere in this holy endeavor. We confirm it forever by the authority of the Apostolic See through the impression of Our seal.

III. *Departure of the Cistercian Monks from Molesme and Their Arrival at Cîteaux, and the Monastery They Founded There*

Afterwards, with the support of such great authority, the aforementioned abbot and his monks returned to Molesme and from that religious community selected like-minded associates who were devoted to the Rule, so that those who had spoken before the legate in Lyons and those who were selected from the community numbered twenty-one monks. Knit together in such a band, they eagerly set out for the solitude which was called Cîteaux. This place, situated in the diocese of Chalon, was inhabited only by wild beasts, since it was at that time unusual for men to enter there because of the density of the woods and thorny thickets. Arriving at this place the men of God found it all the more suitable for the religious life which they had already formulated in their minds and for which they had come here, the more despicable and inaccessible they realized it to be for seculars. After they had cut down and removed the dense woods and the thorny thickets, they began to construct a monastery there with the approval of the bishop of Chalon and with the consent of the territorial lord. For, inspired by the grace of God, these men, while still living in Molesme, often spoke to each other, lamented, and were saddened by the transgression of the Rule of Saint Benedict, the Father of Monks. They realized that they themselves and the other monks had promised by a solemn vow to observe this Rule, yet they had by no means kept it; and therefore they had knowingly committed the sin of perjury. For this reason they came into this solitude with the authority of the legate of the Apostolic See, as we mentioned, to fulfill their vows through the keeping of the holy Rule. Then pleased with their holy fervor and having been requested in a letter by the aforementioned legate of the holy Roman Church, Lord Odo, the duke of Burgundy, with his means completed the wooden monastery which they had begun and provided them there for a long time with every necessity and generously supported them with land as well as livestock.

IV. *How That Place Rose to an Abbey*

At the same time, the abbot who had come here, upon the command of the aforementioned legate, received from the bishop of the diocese the shepherd's staff and the care of the monks; he also caused the brethren who had come with him to undertake their stability in that place in accordance with the Rule. This is how that monastery rose to an abbey canonically and with apostolic authority.

V. *How Those from Molesme Harried the Pope in the Matter of Abbot Robert's Return*

Shortly afterwards, some monks of Molesme, charged by their abbot, lord Godfrey, who succeeded Robert, went to Rome to the lord Pope Urban. They demanded that the often mentioned Robert be restored to his former place. Moved by their importuning, the Pope ordered his legate, the venerable Hugh, to see to it that, if it could be done, the abbot should return and the monks who loved the solitude be left in peace.

VI. *Letter of the Pope Regarding the Return of the Abbot*

Bishop Urban, Servant of the Servants of God, to his venerable brother and fellow bishop Hugh, vicar of the Apostolic See: greeting and apostolic blessing. We have heard in council the great outcry of the brethren of Molesme who vehemently demanded the return of their abbot. Indeed, they have said that on account of that abbot's absence regular life in their monastery had been subverted and that they had become hateful to their lords and neighbors. Now at length, having been prevailed upon by Our brethren, We command Your Grace by indicating that it would please Us, to see to it that, if it can be done, the abbot be restored from the solitude to the monastery. But if you cannot accomplish this, let it be your concern that those who love the solitude may live in peace and those who are in the monastery observe the regular discipline.

After the legate had read this apostolic letter, he summoned a number of men of authority and piety and decided the following about the matter.

VII. *The Legate's Decision in the Whole Matter Concerning the Monks of Molesme and Cîteaux*

Hugh, Servant of the church of Lyons to his most beloved brother Robert, bishop of Langres: greeting. We have considered it necessary to let Your Fraternity know what we have decided in the meeting recently held at Port-d'Anselle regarding the matter of the monastery of Molesme.

Several monks from Molesme appeared before Us in that place with Your letter; they described to us the desolation and the ruin of their place, which the removal of the abbot Robert had brought upon them, and forcefully implored that he be given back to them as father. For, they had no hope that peace and quiet could return to the monastery of Molesme or that the full vigor of the monastic discipline could be restored to its pristine state in any other way. Present before us was also Brother Godfrey, whom You have installed as abbot of that monastery, who stated that he would gladly yield his place to the same Robert as his father if We should decide to send him back to the community of Molesme. After having considered Your request and that of the monks of Molesme and having reread the letter of the lord Pope addressed to Us in this matter, which entrusted the whole matter to Our disposition and judgment, We, upon the advice of many religious men, bishops as well as others, who were with Us in council, have at length decided to acquiesce in Your wish and theirs and return Robert to the monastery of Molesme. This shall be done in such a way that, before his return, he shall go to Chalon and surrender the staff and the care of the abbey into the hands of Our brother the bishop of Chalon, to whom he had sworn obedience as abbots customarily do. Also, he shall free and absolve the monks of the New Monastery, who made their profession and obedience to him as their abbot, from that profession and obedience. Thereupon he shall be released by that bishop from the profession of obedience he has made to him and to the diocese of Chalon.

We have also given permission to return with him to Molesme to all those brethren of the New Monastery who will follow him when he leaves it, provided that henceforth neither side will attempt to lure or receive anyone to its side, except in the manner which blessed Benedict prescribed for the admission of monks of a known monastery. After he has done all this, We release him to Your Grace, so that You may restore him as the abbot of Molesme; in such a way, however, that, if with his usual inconstancy he should again leave that same monastery, no one shall be put in his place during the lifetime of the above named abbot Godfrey, without Our and Your, as well as Godfrey's, assent. We ordain by apostolic authority that all these provisions have the force of law.

With regard to the aforementioned abbot Robert's chapel [instruments] and the other things which he took with him upon his departure from the monastery of Molesme and with which he went to the bishop of Chalon and to the New Monastery, We have ordered that everything shall remain unharmed with the brethren of the New Monastery, with the exception of a certain breviary which they may keep with the approval of the monks of

Molesme, until the feast of saint John the Baptist, so that they may copy it.

Present at this decision were the bishops Norgaud of Autun, Walter of Chalon, Beraud [Herardus] of Mâcon, Pons of Belley and the abbots Peter of Tournus, Jarente of Dijon, Gaucerand of Ainay, as well as Peter, chamberlain of the lord Pope, and many other honorable men of good character.

That abbot approved and executed all this, releasing the Cistercians from the obedience which they had promised him either at that place or in Molesme. Likewise, the lord bishop Walter of Chalon released the abbot from the care of that monastery. And so he returned with a few monks who did not find the solitude to their liking.

This is how through apostolic favor the two abbeys remained in peace and complete freedom. As a shield for his defense the returning abbot took along the following letter to his bishop.

VIII. *Commendation of Abbot Robert*

Walter, servant of the church of Chalon to His most beloved brother and fellow-bishop Robert, bishop of Langres: greeting. Be it known to You that according to the decision of the lord archbishop Hugh, We have released brother Robert, to whom We had entrusted that abbey in Our diocese which is called New Monastery, from the solemn profession made to the diocese of Chalon as well as from the obedience he promised to Us. He himself as well has released and freed those monks who have decided to remain in the aforesaid New Monastery from the obedience and the profession they had vowed to him. I enjoin you, therefore, not to fear to accept him and to treat him as a man in good standing.

IX. *About the Election of Alberic, the First Abbot of the Monastery of Cîteaux*

Deprived of its shepherd, the community of Cîteaux assembled and through a regular election elevated a certain brother by the name of Alberic to be its abbot. He was well versed in both divine and human letters, and a lover of the Rule and the brethren. For a long time he had held the office of prior in the monastery of Molesme as well as here, and he had labored much and long for the brethren to move from Molesme to this place, for which endeavor he had had to suffer many insults, prison and beatings.

X. *About the Roman Privilege*

After much resistance the aforementioned Alberic accepted the pastoral care. As a man of admirable forethought, he began to weigh what storms

455

of tribulations might at one time or another shake and disturb the house entrusted to his care. Taking precaution for the future, with the consent of the brethren he sent two monks, John and Ilbodus, to Rome. Through them he petitioned the lord Pope Paschal that, under the wings of apostolic protection, his monastery might forever remain peaceful and safe from the pressure of any ecclesiastical or lay person. The two brethren just named, supported by the sealed letters of the aforementioned arch- bishop Hugh, of John and Benedict, cardinals of the Roman church, as well as of bishop Walter of Chalon, went safely to Rome and returned before Pope Paschal had faltered in the captivity of the emperor. They brought back his apostolic privilege composed entirely according to the wishes of the abbot and his associates. We have thought it appropriate to hand down these letters as well as the Roman privilege in this little work, so that our successors might realize with how much deliberation and authority their monastery has been founded.

XI. *Letter of the Cardinals John and Benedict*

To our lord and father, Pope Paschal, to whom always and everywhere the greatest praise is due, John and Benedict, with total submission. Since it is Your office to provide for the needs of all churches and to give a helping hand to the just wishes of petitioners, and since the Christian religion must grow by leaning on the support of Your justice, we beg Your Holiness most insistently to lend a merciful hearing to the carriers of this letter who, upon our advice, have been sent to Your Paternity by certain religious brethren. In truth, they ask that the decree which they received from Your predecessor, our lord Pope Urban of blessed memory, in regard to the peace and stability of their monastic life and which, in accordance with the same decree, the archbishop of Lyons, then legate, and some of his fellow-bishops and abbots, had established between them and the abbey of Molesme, from which they had seceded in consideration of the religious life, may through the privilege of your authority forever remain undisturbed. Indeed, we ourselves have seen and vouch for the evidence of their truly religious life.

XII. *Letter of Hugh of Lyons*

To his most reverend father and lord, Pope Paschal, Hugh, servant of the church of Lyons, with total submission. The brethren bearing the present letter, journeying to the Highness of Your Paternity have passed through Our lands. Since they live in Our province, namely in the diocese of Chalon, they asked Our unworthy self for a letter of recommendation to Your Highness. You should know, then, that they come from a place which is called New Monastery. They migrated to that place, after seceding from the community of Molesme with their abbot, in order to lead a stricter and more consecrated life according to the Rule of blessed Benedict which they had resolved to keep by abandoning the usages of certain monasteries maintaining that in their weakness they were unfit to bear such a great burden. For that reason the brethren of Molesme and certain other monks of the neighborhood do not cease to attack and disturb them, thinking that in the eyes of the world they themselves are valued less and looked upon with contempt, if such exceptional and new kinds of monks are seen living in their midst. Therefore, We humbly and trustfully ask You, Beloved Father, that You receive with Your usual kindness these brothers who, after the Lord, place all their trust in You and therefore seek refuge in Your apostolic authority; also, that You free them and their place from such molestation and disturbance, and corroborate this through a privilege of Your authority. For they are the poor of Christ: they have no defense through riches or power against their enemies, but place all their hope in God's mercy and Yours.

XIII. *Letter of the Bishop of Chalon*

To his venerable Father, Pope Paschal, Walter, bishop of Chalon: greeting and due submission. As Your Holiness ardently desires the advancement of the faithful in the true religion, so must they not lack the shelter of Your protection and the encouragement of Your consolation. We therefore, humbly beg that You approve what has been done in accordance with Your predecessor's order and the decision and the rescript of the Archbishop of Lyons, then legate of the Apostolic See, as well as other bishops and abbots who had been witnesses and participants in this decision, with regard to certain brethren. Longing for a stricter life they have, upon the advice of saintly men, departed from the monastery of Molesme; Divine Mercy has placed them in Our diocese; their envoys, the bearers of this letter stand before You. We also beg You to deign to corroborate with a privilege of Your authority that that place might remain a free abbey in perpetuity, saving, however, the canonical reverence due Our person and Our successors. Also the abbot whom We have installed in that place and the other brethren ask Your Kindness most insistently for this confirmation to secure their peace.

XIV. *The Roman Privilege*

Bishop Paschal, Servant of the Servants of God, to the venerable Alberic, abbot of New Monastery, situated in the episcopate of Chalon, and to all his legitimate successors in perpetuity. An aspiration which is

457

obviously aimed at a religious purpose and the welfare of souls is to be fulfilled by the will of God without delay. Therefore, sons most beloved in the Lord, We accede to Your petition without any difficulty, because We applaud Your religious fervor with paternal affection. We decree, therefore, that the place which You have chosen in order to live in monastic tranquillity, shall be secure and free from the annoyance of all men; also, that the abbey shall exist there forever and be particularly sheltered under the protection of the Apostolic See, saving the canonical reverence due to the diocese of Chalon. By the words of this present decree We, therefore, forbid anyone whomsoever to change Your way of life or to receive monks of Your monastery, which is called New Monastery, without the recommendation demanded by the Rule, or to disturb Your community through any kind of guile or violence. The settlement of the controversy between You and the monastery of Molesme—which Our brother, the bishop of Lyons, then vicar of the Apostolic See, made together with the bishops of his province and other religious men, at the command of Our predecessor, Urban the Second of apostolic memory—We confirm as eminently reasonable. You, sons most beloved and most dear in Christ, must, therefore, remember that one part of You has left the broad roads of the world; yet another part, the paths not strait enough of a monastery too relaxed. In order that You may be considered more and more deserving of this grace, You must work to keep always in Your hearts the fear and love of God so that to the degree that you are free from the noises and pleasures of the world, by so much the more You should strive to please God with all the powers of Your mind and soul. Indeed, should any archbishop or bishop, emperor or king, prince or duke, count or viscount, judge or any other clerical or lay person whosoever knowingly dare to counteract this Our constitution, and upon two or three warnings not make amends for his wrongdoing through an adequate satisfaction, let him be deprived of the powers and honor of his dignity and let him know that he is liable to divine judgment because of the wrong he has done; and let him be excluded from the most holy Body and Blood of our God and our Lord, Jesus Christ, and undergo severe vengeance at the Last Judgment. But may the peace of our Lord Jesus Christ rest upon all those who respect the rights of this monastery so that they may receive the fruit of their good deed here on the earth and find the reward of eternal peace before the stern Judge.

XV. *The Institutes of the Cistercian Monks Who Departed from Molesme*

Thereupon the abbot and his brethren, mindful of their vows, unanimously resolved to establish and to keep the Rule of blessed Benedict in that place. They rejected what was contrary to the Rule, namely full mantles and furs, as well as shirts of fine linen, cowls and breeches, combs and blankets, mattresses, a wide variety of dishes in the refectory as well as fat and everything else which was against the purity of the Rule. Making thus the rectitude of the Rule the foremost concern of their life, they followed or conformed to the pathway of the Rule in ecclesiastical as well as in other observances. In this way, having put off the old man, they rejoiced in putting on the new.

And since they could not find either in the Rule or in the life of Saint Benedict that this teacher had possessed churches or altars, offerings or burial dues, tithes of other people, or ovens or mills or manors or serfs, and that women had ever entered his monastery or been buried there, with the exception of his sister, they renounced all these things saying: Where the blessed Father Benedict teaches that the monk must avoid worldly affairs, there he distinctly explains that these things must not have any place in the actions or in the hearts of monks who must live up to the etymology of their name by fleeing all these things. They also said that the holy Fathers, who were the instruments of the Holy Spirit and whose decisions it is a sacrilege to transgress, divided tithes into four distinct parts: namely, one part for the bishop; the second for the parish priest; the third for guests who come to the church, or else for widows and orphans or for the poor who have nothing else to live on; the fourth for the repair of churches. And since in this list they did not find mention of the monk who possesses his own lands whence he gains his livelihood by his own labor and by keeping animals, they rejected this as an unjust usurpation of the rights of others. Thus having rejected the riches of this world, the new soldiers of Christ, poor with the poor Christ, began to consult with one another as to the question of the way by which, and with what work or occupation, they should provide in this life for themselves as well as for guests who would come, rich and poor alike, whom according to the Rule they should receive as Christ.

Thereupon they decided to admit, with the permission of their bishop, bearded lay-brothers and to treat them in life and death as their equals, excepting only the status as monks; and to admit also hired workers. For they realized that without the help of these men they would be unable to observe fully the precepts of the Rule by day and by night. They also decided to accept landed properties which lay removed from the dwellings of men, as well as vineyards and meadows and woods and also streams, in order to install mills—but only for their own use—and for fishing, and horses and various cattle useful to the requirements of men. And while they established granges for the practice of agriculture in a number of places, they decreed that the aforementioned lay-brothers, and not the monks, should manage those houses, because according to the Rule the dwelling place of monks ought to be within their cloister. Since those holy men knew that blessed Benedict had built his monasteries not in towns or around fortified places or in villages, but in places removed from the traffic of men, they promised to imitate him. And since he placed twelve monks and a father abbot in new monasteries, they decided to proceed in the same manner.

XVI. *About Their Sorrow*

It caused some sorrow to the aforementioned abbot and man of God and to those with him that in those days only seldom did anyone come there in order to follow after them. For the holy men longed to hand down to their successors for the future benefit of many this treasure of virtues which had come from heaven. Yet almost all those who saw or learned about the unusual and almost unheard-of rigor of their life, instead of approaching them, hastened to avoid them in both spirit and body, nor did they cease from doubting in the ability of the monks to persevere. But the mercy of God, which inspired His own chosen ones to form this spiritual army did not cease to swell and to complete their ranks, to the profit of many, as the following will show.

XVII. *About the Death of the First Abbot and the Election of the Second and Their Institutes and Their Happiness.*

The man of the Lord, Alberic, however, after he had practiced fruitfully regular discipline in the school of Christ for nine and a half years, went home to the Lord, full of glory in his faith and virtues, and therefore deservedly to be rewarded by God with eternal life. His successor was a certain brother by the name of Stephen, an Englishman by nationality, who had also come to that place with the others from Molesme, a lover of the Rule and of the place. During his time, the brethren and this abbot prohibited the duke of that land or any other lord from keeping his court at any time in that monastery as they used in times past to do on the occasion of great feasts. Furthermore, lest anything remain in the house of God—where it was their wish to serve God devoutly day and night— that savored of pride or superfluity or that would ever corrupt poverty, the safeguard of virtues, which they had chosen of their own free will, they resolved to keep no crosses of gold or silver but only painted wooden ones; no candelabra, but only one of iron; no thuribles, but only of copper and iron; no chasubles, but of fustian or linen, without a pallium of gold or silver; no albs or amices but of linen, similarly without a pallium of gold or silver. They gave up entirely the use of all pallia and copes as well as of dalmatics and tunics. But they retained the use of chalices of silver or, where possible, of gold-plate, but not ones of pure gold; and the communion reed of silver or, where possible, of gold-plate; stoles as well as maniples of silk only, without gold and silver. Moreover they explicitly ordered that altar cloths be made of plain linen and without ornamentation and that the cruets be without gold and silver.

In those days the monastery increased in its possession of lands, vineyards, meadows and granges; but it did not decrease in religious fervor. Therefore in those days God visited that place and showed forth His deepest mercy to the brethren who implored Him, who cried out to Him, and who wept before Him, who day and night groaned long and deep, who drew near the brink of despair because they had almost no successors. For now the grace of God sent to that monastery so many literate and noble clerics and laymen who were as powerful as they were distinguished in the world that at one time thirty men eagerly entered the cell of novices, and by fighting bravely and strongly against their own vices and the temptations of evil spirits, they completed their course. Through the example of these men who were old and young, men of every age group in diverse parts of the world were encouraged, since they saw through these that what they had feared impossible in the observance of the Rule was, indeed, possible. They started to flock together there in order to place their proud necks under the sweet yoke of Christ, to love fervently the rigorous and burdensome precepts of the Rule, and they began to make that community wonderfully happy and strong.

XVIII. *About the Abbeys*

From that time forward they established abbeys in various dioceses, which under the Lord's rich and powerful blessing so prospered from day to day that within eight years among those who had gone forth from Cîteaux itself and those who in turn sprang forth from them, twelve new foundations were to be counted.

The Carta Caritatis Posterior

Before the Cistercian abbeys began to flourish, the lord abbot Stephen and his brethren, seeking to avoid any scandal between a bishop and the monks, ordained that no abbey should be founded in the diocese of any bishop before he approved and confirmed the decree enacted between the abbey of Cîteaux and its filiations. Anxious to avert a future wreck of their mutual concord, in this decree the aforementioned brethren made

461

clear, ordained and recorded for their successors by what bond, in what way, and, most importantly, by what charity their monks, scattered in body throughout abbeys in diverse parts of the world, should be indissolubly joined together in spirit. They also decided that this decree should be called a Charter of Charity, for its statutes, spurning the burden of heavy exaction, related only to charity and the welfare of souls in things human and divine.

1. Since we realize that we are servants, albeit unprofitable ones, of the one true King, our Lord and Master, we impose no exaction of temporal possessions or earthly goods on our fellow-abbots and fellow-monks and brothers whom, in diverse regions, the goodness of God has placed under the discipline of the Rule, to be cared for by us the least among men. For, wishing to be of service to them and to all the children of Holy Church, we make no provision that would burden them, that would diminish their temporal goods, lest while seeking to enrich ourselves from their poverty we ourselves should fail to avoid the evil of avarice which, according to the Apostle, is the service of idols.

2. We do wish, however, to retain the care of their souls for the sake of charity so that if they should ever attempt, even if but in a small measure, to stray from their sacred resolve and the observance of the holy Rule— which may God avert—through our solicitude they may be able to return to the right path of life.

3. Now, therefore, we will and command them to observe the Rule of blessed Benedict in every particular just as it is observed in New Monastery; not to introduce any other interpretation into the text of the Holy Rule; but to understand it and to keep it just as our ancestors, our holy fathers, namely the monks of New Monastery, understood it and kept it, and as we, ourselves, understand it and keep it today. [And because we receive all monks coming from other monasteries into ours, and they in like manner receive ours, it seems proper to us and it is, furthermore, our will that all our monasteries have usages in chanting and all the books necessary for day and night offices and the celebration of Masses similar to the usages and books in use at New Monastery; that there may be no discord in our daily actions, but that we may all live together in the bond of charity under one rule and in the practice of the same usages.]*

4. No monastery or person of our Order shall undertake to request a privilege contrary to the common regulations of the Order from anyone or, if already obtained, retain it under any pretext.

5. Whenever the Abbot of New Monastery comes to visit any one of these monasteries, in order to acknowledge that the abbey of New Monas-

*The material in brackets is from Canivez, I, 28.

tery is the mother of his abbey, the local abbot shall yield his place to the visitor, everywhere in the monastery, and the visiting abbot shall hold the place of the local abbot as long as he stays there, with one exception: he shall not eat in the guest-house but in the refectory, for the sake of preserving monastic discipline, unless the local abbot is absent. All other visiting abbots of our Order shall do likewise. But, if several abbots come and the local abbot is absent, the senior of them shall eat in the guest-house. Another exception is this: the local abbot will bless his own novices after the regular period of probation, even if a senior abbot is present.

6. The abbot of New Monastery shall also take care not to presume to treat nor to ordain anything about the affairs of the monastery he is visiting, against the wishes of the abbot and the brethren. If, however, he finds that the precepts of the Rule or of our Order are violated in that place, he shall charitably strive to correct the brethren with the advice of the local abbot. If, however, the local abbot is not present, the visitor shall nevertheless correct what he finds amiss.

7. Once a year the abbot of the mother-house shall visit all the monasteries that he himself has founded, either in person or through one of his co-abbots. And if he visits the brethren more often, then let them rejoice the more.

8. The four proto-abbots—the abbots of La Ferté, Pontigny, Clairvaux and Morimond—shall jointly visit the monastery of Cîteaux, unless one of them is prevented by grave illness, on a day appointed by them, other than when they are attending the yearly [general] chapter.

9. If any abbot of our Order comes to New Monastery due reverence shall be shown to him. If the abbot [of New Monastery] is absent, the visitor shall occupy his stall; he shall receive guests; he shall eat with them in the guest-house. But if the abbot [of New Monastery] is present, the visitor shall do none of these things; rather he shall eat in the refectory. The local prior shall manage the affairs of the monastery.

10. Between abbeys not bound by filiation this will be the law: Every abbot shall yield his place everywhere in his own monastery to a visiting fellow-abbot so that Scripture may be fulfilled: "they give one another precedence with honor" [Rom. 12:10]. If two or more abbots arrive, the senior of the guests will occupy the first place. All shall eat in the refectory, except the local abbot, just as we have said above. Wherever else they meet, seniority will be according to the antiquity of their abbeys, so that the abbot of the older house will occupy the first place. As soon as they take their seats, they shall bow to each other.

11. If by the grace of God any of our houses shall so increase that it is able to found another monastery, they too shall observe among them-

selves the agreement which we observe with our brethren, except that they shall not hold general chapters among themselves.

12. Instead, all abbots of our Order will, putting aside all excuses, meet annually in general chapter, except those who are prevented by bodily infirmity; these will depute a suitable representative through whom the reason for staying away may be reported to the chapter. Excepted also are those who live in distant regions; they shall come at intervals to be decided for them in the chapter. But if any abbot presumes to stay away from the general chapter for any other reason whatsoever, he shall ask pardon in the chapter of the following year and he shall not leave without a severe punishment.

13. In the chapter, the abbots shall discuss matters pertaining to the salvation of their souls, and ordain what is to be corrected or added in the observance of the holy Rule and [the regulations] of the Order. They shall also strengthen one another in the bond of peace and charity.

14. If any abbot is found to be less than zealous about the Rule, or too involved in secular affairs, or faulty in any matter, he shall be charitably accused at the chapter; upon his accusation, he shall ask pardon and do the penance imposed on him for his fault. Only abbots shall make such an accusation.

15. If, perchance, a controversy arises among any of the abbots, or so grievous a fault is charged against any one of them that he would deserve suspension or even deposition, whatever is decreed by the [general] chapter in this matter shall be observed without hesitation.

16. If, however, a case turns into discord because of a difference of views, then the decision of the abbot of Cîteaux and of those who appear to be of wiser counsel and more suitable character shall be observed inviolably, subject to this observation: that no one of those [abbots] who is involved specifically in the case ought to participate in the determination [of the case].

17. If any monastery incurs unbearable poverty, the abbot of that monastery shall strive to reveal this plight to the entire chapter. Then, inflamed by the fire of charity, the assembled abbots shall take quick steps to relieve the poverty of that monastery according to their ability, from the goods which God has given them.

18. If any monastery of our Order is without its own abbot, the Father Abbot of that house shall assume its administration until a new abbot is elected. When a date of election has been fixed, the abbots whom that house has sent forth—if there are any—shall be summoned, and, according to the counsel and will of the Father-Abbot, the abbots and the monks of that house shall elect an abbot.

19. Whenever Cîteaux is without her own abbot, because she is the

mother of all our monasteries, the four proto-abbots—the abbots of La Ferté, Pontigny, Clairvaux and Morimond—shall make the necessary provisions. They shall be in charge of that house until an abbot has been duly elected and confirmed.

20. At least fifteen days before a date has been appointed and announced for the election of an abbot of Cîteaux, there shall be summoned those abbots whose houses sprang from Cîteaux and other abbots whom the aforesaid abbots and brethren of Cîteaux known to be of suitable character. Then, assembled in the name of the Lord, the abbots and monks of Cîteaux shall elect an abbot.

21. Also, any mother-abbey shall be allowed freely to receive an abbot not only from the monks of her [daughter-monasteries], if it should be necessary.

22. But none of our monasteries shall elect a person of another order as its abbot, just as none of our monasteries is permitted to give an abbot to other monasteries which are not of our Order.

23. If an abbot, because of his inefficiency or timidity, asks his Father-Abbot, from whose house his own has gone forth, to be released from the burden of his abbacy, the Father-Abbot shall be careful not to consent easily and without a well-founded and compelling reason. But even if the reason is sufficiently great, the Father-Abbot shall not do anything in the matter of his own, but after having summoned other abbots of our Order he shall undertake with their counsel whatever they together judge ought to be done.

24. But if it becomes public knowledge that any abbot despises the holy Rule or sins against our Order, or acquiesces in the faults of the brethren entrusted to his care, the abbot of the mother-house shall, either in person or through the prior of his own monastery or in any other more suitable way, admonish him up to four times to correct his ways. But if he neither will be corrected in this way nor resign voluntarily, an assembly of a number of other abbots of our congregation shall remove the transgressor of the holy Rule from his office. Then, according to the counsel and the will of the abbot of the mother-abbey, a new abbot who is worthy shall be elected by the monks of that house and the abbots of its filiation, if there are any, in the manner described above.

25. If, however—which may God forbid—a deposed abbot or his monks choose to be contumacious and rebellious and altogether refuse to accept the sentence [of deposition], they shall be placed under excommunication by the abbot of the mother-house and his co-abbots; and from that time forward they shall be restrained to the extent that he is able and that he sees fit.

26. But if afterwards anyone of those evildoers, having returned to his

senses, should wish to call his dead soul back to life and to return to his mother-abbey, he shall be received as a repentant son.

27. Except for this reason—and every effort must be made that this not come about—no abbot shall retain the monk of another abbot without the latter's consent; nor shall an abbot send his own monks to live in the house of another [abbot] without the latter's consent.

28. Similarly as well—and may this never happen—if, perchance the abbots of our Order learn that Cîteaux, our mother, has grown tepid in her holy endeavor and strayed from the observance of the Rule and of our Order, the four proto-abbots—those of La Ferté, Pontigny, Clairvaux and Morimond—shall admonish the abbot of that place in the name of the other abbots, up to four times, to mend his ways and to take care to correct the conduct of his charges. In addition they shall zealously implement the other measures prescribed for abbots who prove themselves incorrigible, with this exception: If the abbot of Cîteaux refuses to resign voluntarily, they can neither depose him nor excommunicate him until they depose the unprofitable man from his office in the general chapter or, if in their judgment things cannot wait that long, in another assembly comprising the abbots of Cîteaux's filiation and certain other abbots who had been summoned. Then both the abbots and the monks of Cîteaux shall strive to elect a suitable abbot.

29. But if that abbot and the monks of Cîteaux in their pride choose to resist, the abbots shall not fear to strike them with the sword of excommunication.

30. But if afterwards any of these prevaricators, regaining his senses and anxious to save his soul, should seek refuge in any of these four houses—La Ferté, Pontigny, Clairvaux and Morimond—he shall be received in satisfaction of the Rule as a member and fellow-heir of the house, until he is restored to his own monastery upon its reconciliation, as justice demands. During this period, however, the yearly chapter of abbots will not be held at Cîteaux, but wherever the four proto-abbots shall determine.

Statistics

1. *Personnel of Some Spanish and Portuguese Abbeys in 1531-33,* after Claude de Bronseval, *Peregrinatio Hispanica.*

Spain

	Monks	Lay-brothers
Santes Creus	36	12
Poblet	60	30
Escarpe	5	
Benifazá	12	
San Bernardo	3	
S. Vincente (priory)	8	
Monsalud	13	
Ovila	16	
Espina	31	
Nogales	24	
Sobrado	6	
Piedra	33	27
Santa Fé	29	16

Portugal

	Monks	Novices	Lay-brothers
Alcobaça	11	17	
Tamarães	2		1
Ceiça	16		2
São Paulo	6		
Macenaria	16		
Alafões	3		
Salzedas	24	8	
Tarouca	16		4
Bouro	7		
Fiaẽs	5		2
São Pedro	?		
S.M. de Aguiar	4		
Estrella	2		

2. *Personnel of Cistercian abbeys in the Papal States, Naples and Sicily in 1561,* according to the visitation of Nicolas Boucherat. See *Cistercienser-Chronik,* XIII (1901), 196-203.

	Personnel
Fossanova	6
Poncio	vacant
Semprone	vacant
Real-Valle	vacant
S.Pietro della Canonica	vacant
Sagittario	10
Acquaformosa	6
Matina	2 secular priests
Sambucina	vacant
S.Angelo in Frigido	2 secular priests
Fonte Laureato	2 secular priests
Balnearia	8
S.Lucia	vacant
Corazzo	6
S.Laurentio	vacant
Altilia	secular priests
Maria Nova	2
S.Giovanni di Fiore	2
S.Angiolo in Frigido	vacant
SS.Trinità del Legno	4
S.Maria de Limachi	vacant
Galeso	vacant
S.Giovanni in Lamis	vacant
S.Maria Coronata	4 Augustinians
Ripalta	monks of other orders
Arabona	3 secular priests
Casanova	8
Ferraria	3
Altofonte	vacant
S.Spirito	Benedictines
Terrana	4
S.Maria dell'Arco	5
Roccadia	4
La Nuara	10
Roccamadore	8

3. *Personnel of Cistercian Abbeys in Switzerland, Tirol, Germany and Flanders,* according to the visitation of Nicolas Boucherat in 1573-74. See *Cistercienser-Chronik,* XIII (1901), 230-66.

	Monks	Novices	Oblates	Lay-brothers
Hauterive	22			
Saint Urban	24		12	
Wettingen	19	2		
Salem	56	4		12
Kaisheim	38	2		
Ebrach	22	5	12	1
Bildhausen	14	2		
Langheim	18	6		
Bronnbach	8	4		
Fürstenfeld	18	4		
Raitenhaslach	10	4		
Stams	16			
Aldersbach	6			
Fürstenzell	4			
Gotteszell	5			
Thennenbach	4	2		
Pairis	2			
Lützel	27	6		
Himmerod	34	3		3
Eberbach	27	3		
Marienstatt	3			
Heisterbach	13			
Walberberg	5			
Camp	20	5	4	4
Marienfeld	18	2		
Bredelar	12			
Hardehausen	14			
Altenberg	40	4		
Bottenbroich	14	1		1
Aulne	?			
Val-Saint-Lambert	22			
Saint-Rémy	19			
Orval	25	3		

4. Personnel of the Castilian Congregation in 1584

after M.Cocheril, "L'implantation des abbayes cisterciennes dans la péninsule ibérique," *Annuario de Estudios Medievales,* I (1964), p. 280.

	Number of professed monks
Montesion and Bonaval	13
Valbuena	30
Carracedo	35
Moreruela	42
Sacramenia	8
Monsalud	13
Sobrado and S.Justo	50
Melón	15
La Espina	40
Meira	24
Osera	24
Nogales	40
Huerta	45
Rioseco	18
San Prudencio	15
Montederramo	20
Castañeda	16
Armenteira	9
Benavides	12
Janqueira	9
Palazuelos	22
Sandoval	32
Valparaiso	54
Matallana	24
Herrera	25
Bugedo	8
Ovila	9
Valdeiglesias	40
Oya	13
Valdediós	13
Monfero	13
Villanueva	9
Belmonte	13
La Vega	7
San Clodio	24
Gumiel	10
Acibeiro	4
Peñamayor	4
Franqueira	3
College of Alcalá	?
Salamanca	?

5. *Personnel of the Congregation of Upper-Germany in 1595 and 1720.*
According to an anonymous booklet: *Idea chrono-topographica Congregationis Cisterciensis S. Bernardi per Superiorem Germaniam, s.l.* 1720.

	1595	1720		
	professed monks	priests	clerics	lay-brothers
Swabian province				
Kaisheim	45	50	9	8
Salem	55	49	13	10
Schöntal	22	33	3	10
Stams		23	6	3
Franconian province				
Ebrach	40	36	14	6
Langheim	37	34	7	3
Bronnbach	18	31	7	-
Bildhausen	20	36	2	4
Bavarian province				
Waldsassen		26	10	5
Waldersbach		11	5	2
Raitenhaslach	20	22	4	1
Alderspach	20	30	4	4
Fürstenfeld	20	31	11	3
Fürstenzell	13	15	3	-
Gotteszell	7	14	5	1
Swiss province				
Lützel	44	38	5	5
Neuberg	18	8	5	-
Hauterive		20	3	2
Pairis		unrecorded		
S. Urban	18	35	1	6
Tennenbach	17	19	3	5
Wettingen	20	34	3	8
Totals		595	123	79
Grand total		797		

6. *Personnel of Cistercian Abbeys in the Vicariate of Bohemia, Moravia and Lausitz in 1699 and 1780.* See *Cistercienser-Chronik,* XII (1909), 243 and XL (1928), 139.

	Priests		Clerics		Novices	Lay-brothers		Total	
	1699	1780	1699	1780	1699	1699	1780	1699	1780
Goldenkron	24	32	3	3		1	4	28	39
Hohenfurt	41	53	5	3	4	3	2	53	58
Königsaal	30	41	9	4		1		42	45
Neuzelle	21	30	7	6	3	2	2	33	38
Ossegg	35	40	9	7	2	1		47	47
Plass	44	44	11	8	6	4	5	65	57
Saar	22	50	3	6	3	1	2	29	58
Sedletz	15	20	6		3			24	20
Welehrad	29	48	17	14	4	3	2	53	64
Totals:	261	358	70	51	25	18	17	374	426

7. *Personnel of Austrian Abbeys in 1758.*

After B. Schneider, "Österreichs Zisterzienserpfarren," *Studien und Mitteilungen,* LXXVIII (1967), 293-6. (No data on Rein)

	Priests	Clerics	Lay-brothers	Total
Heiligenkreuz	56	5	13	74
Zwettl	38	9	4	51
Baumgartenberg	14	7	1	22
Wilhering	35	8	3	46
Lilienfeld	60	4	3	67
Engelszell	19	5		24
Neuberg	25	6	1	32
Säusenstein	20	2		22
Neukloster	25	3	2	30
Schlierbach	25	4	2	31
Totals:	317	53	29	399

8. *Personnel of French Cistercian Monasteries in 1790.*

For the sake of comparison, the last column gives the totals of 1770. See for further details *Analecta Cisterciensia,* XXIV (1968), 86-118. Houses of the Strict Observance are *italicized.*

MONASTERIES	CHOIR-MONKS				total of choir-monks	lay-brothers	combined total	total in 1770
	in 4 age-groups							
	below 30	30-50	50-70	above 70				
Acey	—	1	2	1	4	—	4	5
Aiguebelle	—	—	2	—	2	—	2	2
Ardorel	—	—	3	—	3	—	3	6
l'Arrivour	1	5	2	1	9	—	9	6
5 Aubepierre			no	data	given			2
Auberive	—	5	3	—	8	—	8	6
Aubignac	—	1	1	—	2	—	2	2
Aulnay	—	6	2	—	8	—	8	6
l'Aumône	—	4	1	1	6	—	6	8
10 Balerne	1	1	2	—	4	—	4	4
Barbeaux	1	6	3	1	11	—	11	10
Barbery	—	7	2	1	10	1	11	15
Barzelle	—	2	—	—	2	—	2	5
Beaubec	3	3	2	1	9	—	9	13
15 Beaugerais	—	—	1	1	2	—	2	4
Beaulieu	1	1	2	1	5	—	5	5
Beaupré (Toul)	1	7	4	—	12	3	15	14
Beaupré (Beauvais)	—	6	3	—	9	1	10	7
Bégard	—	6	2	1	9	—	9	10
20 Bellaigue	—	3	1	—	4	—	4	8
Belleau	—	—	1	—	1	—	1	1
Belleperche	—	7	2	1	10	1	11	11
Bellevaux	—	4	—	1	5	—	5	7
Belloc	—	1	3	—	4	1	5	3
25 Berdoues	—	4	1	1	6	—	6	6
Beuil	—	1	—	—	1	—	1	2
Billon	1	1	1	—	3	—	3	5
Bithaine	—	1	1	—	2	—	2	4
La Blanche	1	4	—	—	5	—	5	6
30 *Bohéries*	—	5	3	—	8	—	8	7
Bois-Grolland	—	2	1	—	3	—	3	4
La Boissière	—	2	2	—	4	—	4	3
Bonlieu or Carbon Blanc	—	3	—	—	3	—	3	2
Bonlieu (Limoges)	—	3	—	—	3	—	3	—

473

MONASTERIES	CHOIR-MONKS in 4 age-groups				total of choir-monks	lay-brothers	combined total	total in 1770
	below 30	30-50	50-70	above 70				
35 Bonlieu (Valence)	—	—	1	—	1	—	1	2
Bonneaigue	—	2	2	—	4	—	4	7
Bonnecombe	—	3	5	1	9	—	9	12
Bonnefont	2	5	2	—	9	—	9	8
Bonne-Fontaine	2	1	6	—	9	—	9	5
40 Bonneval	—	5	6	2	13	—	13	22
Bonnevaux (Poitiers)	—	1	1	—	2	—	2	5
Bonnevaux (Vienne)	—	3	—	2	5	—	5	7
Bonport	1	3	2	1	7	—	7	7
Bonrepos	—	2	1	1	4	—	4	8
45 *Boquen*	—	4	—	—	4	—	4	3
Bouchaud	—	—	1	—	1	—	1	1
Bouillas	—	3	1	1	5	—	5	9
Boulancourt	1	1	3	1	6	—	6	5
Boulbonne	3	4	4	2	13	1	14	13
50 Bouras	—	3	—	—	3	—	3	3
Breuil-Benôit	—	2	—	—	2	—	2	2
La Bussiére	1	3	3	—	7	—	7	9
Buzay	—	5	5	1	11	—	11	8
Cadouin	—	2	1	1	4	—	4	5
55 Calers	—	—	2	—	2	—	2	8
Candeil	—	2	2	—	4	—	4	5
Cercamp	3	3	6	—	12	—	12	9
Cercanceaux	—	—	1	—	1	—	1	4
La Chalade	2	5	2	—	9	—	9	7
60 Châlis	—	2	—	1	3	—	3	7
Chalivoy	1	2	1	—	4	—	4	4
Chaloché		no	data	given				6
Chambons	—	3	2	1	6	—	6	9
Champagne	2	3	1	2	8	—	8	7
65 La Charité (Langres)	—	—	1	—	1	—	1	2
La Charité (Besançon)	—	4	2	1	7	—	7	8
La Charmoye	—	2	2	—	4	2	6	9
Charon	—	2	—	—	2	—	2	4
Chassagne	—	2	3	—	5	—	5	5
70 Les Châtelliers	—	4	3	—	7	—	7	5
Châtillon	4	3	3	—	10	1	12	16
Cheminon	1	4	2	—	7	—	7	12
Cherlieu	—	1	3	2	6	—	6	10
Chéry	—	4	2	—	6	—	6	4

MONASTERIES	CHOIR-MONKS in 4 age-groups				total of choir-monks	lay-brothers	combined total	total in 1770
	below 30	30-50	50-70	above 70				
75 Chézery	—	2	2	—	4	—	4	5
Cîteaux	22	16	8	1	47	8	55	60
Clairefontaine	—	2	3	—	5	—	5	5
Clairlieu	2	3	—	3	8	—	8	7
Clairmarais	4	8	6	3	21	1	22	27
80 Clairmont	—	2	3	—	5	—	5	7
Clairvaux	2	13	6	2	23	10	33	54
La Clarté-Dieu	—	3	1	—	4	—	4	4
Coëtmaloën	—	4	—	—	4	—	4	6
La Colombe	—	1	1	1	3	—	3	3
85 La Cour-Dieu	—	2	1	1	4	—	4	9
La Crête	—	6	2	1	9	—	9	5
Dalon	1	2	1	—	4	—	4	6
Dôle	—	—	1	—	1	—	1	—
Droiteval	—	—	1	1	2	—	2	—
90 Eunes	—	5	2	—	7	—	7	4
Écurey	—	7	—	1	8	—	8	6
Élan	—	2	1	—	3	—	3	6
l'Épau	—	3	—	3	6	—	6	7
l'Escale-Dieu	—	2	4	2	8	—	8	7
95 Escharlis	1	2	1	—	4	—	4	4
l'Étoile	—	—	1	—	1	—	1	1
l'Eule	—	—	1	—	1	—	1	—
La Faise	1	2	1	1	5	—	5	7
Fénières	—	3	—	2	5	2	7	4
100 La Ferté	5	5	3	1	14	—	14	12
Flaran	—	1	2	1	4	—	4	4
Foigny	—	5	4	1	10	—	10	7
Fontaine-Daniel	—	5	1	1	7	—	7	8
Fontaine-Jean	—	2	1	—	3	—	3	3
105 Fontaines-les-Blanches	—	3	—	—	3	—	3	3
Fontenay	—	6	1	—	7	—	7	5
Fontfroide	1	6	3	—	10	—	10	10
Fontguillem	—	1	3	—	4	—	4	2
Fontmorigny	2	2	2	—	6	—	6	7
110 *Foucarmont*	4	11	1	—	16	1	17	13
Franquevaux	—	2	1	—	3	—	3	3
Freistorff	—	2	2	—	4	3	7	6
La Frénade	—	1	1	1	3	—	3	2
Froidmont	1	2	5	2	10	—	10	6

475

MONASTERIES	CHOIR-MONKS in 4 age-groups				total of choir-monks	lay-brothers	combined total	total in 1770
	below 30	30-50	50-70	above 70				
115 Le Gard	—	1	5	1	7	—	7	10
La Garde-Dieu	—	1	1	—	2	—	2	3
Gimont	—	5	2	3	10	—	10	9
Gondon	1	3	—	—	4	—	4	2
Gourdon or la Nou-velle	—		vacant					2
120 La Grâce-Dieu (Besançon)	—	1	1	—	2	—	2	5
La Grâce-Dieu (La Rochelle)	—	3	2	1	6	—	6	4
Grâce)N.-D.	—	—	1	—	1	—	1	—
Grandselve	—	7	3	2	12	4	16	15
Grosbois	—	2	1	—	3	—	3	2
125 Haute-Fontaine	2	4	2	—	8	—	8	7
Haute-Seille	—	6	3	—	9	—	9	5
Igny	2	1	1	—	4	—	4	6
Ile-en-Barrois	—	2	6	1	9	—	9	8
Jouy	1	6	4	—	11	1	12	20
130 La Joye	—	1	1	—	2	—	2	—
Landais	—	2	1	—	3	—	3	7
Langonnet	—	6	—	—	6	—	6	8
Lannoy	—	6	1	1	8	—	8	12
Lanvaux	—	2	1	—	3	—	3	3
135 Léoncel	—	2	1	—	3	—	3	5
Lieu- Croissant or Trois-rois	—	3	1	1	5	—	5	6
Lieu-Dieu	—	3	1	—	4	3	7	8
Loc-Dieu	1	3	1	—	5	—	5	5
Longpont	—	9	4	—	13	—	13	10
140 Longuay	2	3	2	—	7	—	7	3
Longvilliers	—	5	1	2	8	—	8	5
Loos	3	23	8	4	38	1	39	40
Loroux	—	1	2	2	5	—	5	5
Loroy	—	1	1	—	2	—	2	4
145 Lucelle or Lützel	4	22	14	2	42	5	47	45
Maizières	—	4	2	2	8	—	8	9
Marcilly	—	—	—	1	1	—	1	1
Mazan	—	2	4	—	6	—	6	11
Mégemont	—	2	1	—	3	—	3	4

MONASTERIES	CHOIR-MONKS in 4 age-groups				total of choir-monks	lay-brothers	combined total	total in 1770
	below 30	30-50	50-70	above 70				
150 *Melleray*	—	3	1	1	5	—	5	3
La Merci-Dieu	—	1	—	2	3	—	3	3
Miroir	—	—	3	—	3	—	3	—
Montier	1	5	5	—	11	—	11	9
Montpeyroux	—	3	1	—	4	—	4	6
155 Mont-Ste.-Marie	—	2	2	2	6	—	6	7
Moreilles	1	5	1	—	7	—	7	4
Mores	1	4	—	—	5	—	5	3
Morimond	5	6	4	1	16	9	25	30
Mortemer	—	2	3	—	5	—	5	6
160 Neubourg	—	9	6	1	16	—	16	14
Nizors	—	3	—	1	4	—	4	4
La Nöe	—	1	1	2	4	—	4	3
Noirlac	—	3	3	1	7	—	7	6
Obazine	—	1	1	—	2	—	2	6
165 Olivet	—	2	1	—	3	—	3	6
Ourscamp	2	8	6	2	18	—	18	29
Pairis	2	6	2	—	10	—	10	14
Palais N.-D.	—	1	—	—	1	—	1	4
Paris, College of S.B.	1	3	2	—	6	—	6	23
170 *Perseigne*	—	4	1	1	6	1	7	7
Peyrignac	—	1	3	—	4	—	4	2
Peyrouse	—	1	2	—	3	—	3	4
Les Pierres	3	4	3	—	10	—	10	4
La Piété-Dieu	—	4	1	—	5	—	5	5
175 *Le Pin*	—	2	2	—	4	—	4	9
Pontaut	—	—	2	1	3	—	3	4
Pontigny	1	9	1	1	12	2	14	25
Pontrond	—	2	3	—	5	—	5	6
Pré-Benoît	—	1	—	—	1	—	1	2
180 La Prée	—	4	3	—	7	—	7	5
Preuilly	—	5	3	2	10	—	10	16
Prières	1	6	8	—	15	1	16	16
Quincy	—	3	—	1	4	—	4	4
Le Reclus	2	3	1	—	6	—	6	4
185 Relecq	—	3	2	--	5	—	5	12
Rigny	—	3	1	3	7	—	7	7
Rivet	—	—	1	1	2	—	2	3
Des Roches	—	5	—	1	6	—	6	5
Rosières	—	3	—	—	3	1	4	4

477

MONASTERIES	CHOIR-MONKS in 4 age-groups				total of choir-monks	lay-brothers	combined total	total in 1770
	below 30	30-50	50-70	above 70				
190 Royaumont	—	7	3	—	10	—	10	17
Les Rozièrs	—	—	1	—	1	—	1	1
St.-André	—	4	2	—	6	—	6	7
St.-Aubin	—	5	—	—	5	—	5	6
St.-Benoît	1	1	3	—	5	—	5	8
195 St.-Lazare	—	—	2	—	2	—	2	—
St.-Léonard	1	1	—	—	2	—	2	3
St.-Marcel	—	2	1	—	3	—	3	3
St.-Maurice or Carnoet	—	—	3	—	3	—	3	7
St.-Sulpice	—	2	5	—	7	—	7	11
200 Sauvelade	—	1	2	—	3	—	3	2
Savigny	—	7	5	2	14	—	14	18
Sellieres	—	2	2	—	4	—	4	2
Sénanque	—	—	1	—	1	—	1	4
Sept-Fons	3	19	8	1	31	39	70	10
205 Signy	—	6	3	1	10	—	10	9
Silvanes	—	2	3	—	5	—	5	6
Stürzelbronn	1	5	4	1	11	—	11	12
Theuley	1	3	2	2	8	—	8	7
Thoronet	—	1	7	1	9	—	9	8
210 Tironneau	2	3	1	—	6	—	6	4
Torigny	—	3	1	1	5	—	5	4
Toulouse, College of S.B.	—	1	—	—	1	—	1	—
La Trappe	—	36	17	2	55	36	91	63
Trisay	1	3	1	—	5	—	5	3
215 Trois-Fontaines	3	6	6	1	16	—	16	10
Valasse	4	5	2	—	11	—	11	10
Val-Benoîte	—	1	2	1	4	—	4	4
Valence	—	2	1	1	4	—	4	3
Valette	—	1	1	1	3	—	3	3
220 Valloires	—	3	5	1	9	—	9	9
Valmagne	—	2	1	1	4	—	4	8
Val-Richer	1	2	3	—	6	—	6	7
Valroy	2	3	2	—	7	—	7	9
Val-Sainte	—	1	1	—	2	—	2	3
225 Val-Sainte-Lieu	1	10	7	—	18	26	44	—
Varennes	—	1	—	1	2	—	2	2
Vaucelles	7	6	15	3	31	—	31	27
Vauclair	—	9	7	1	17	—	17	24
Vauluisant or Bouchet	—	1	1	—	2	—	2	8

478

MONASTERIES	CHOIR-MONKS in 4 age-groups				total of choir-monks	lay-brothers	combined total	total in 1770
	below 30	30-50	50-70	above 70				
230 *Vauluisant*	—	6	2	1	9	—	9	16
Vaux-de-Cernay	—	3	7	1	11	—	11	11
Vaux-en-Ornois	1	2	1	—	4	—	4	6
Vaux-la-Douce	—	2	1	—	3	—	3	8
Vieuville	—	5	—	1	6	—	6	6
235 Villelongue	—	1	1	—	2	—	2	2
Villeneuve	3	5	1	—	9	—	9	11
Villers-Betnach	1	7	2	—	10	4	14	12
Totals	148	815	516	133	1612	170	1782	1843

9. *Personnel of the Congregation of La Trappe* ("*New Reform*") in 1851. After Hermans, *Actes*, p. [566].

Monasteries	Choir monks	Choir novices	Lay- brothers	Lay-b. novices	Postu- lants	Ob- lates	Fami- liars	Total
La Trappe	32	10	37	7	–	–	21	107
Melleray	39	8	57	8	5	10	33	160
Bellefontaine	24	3	36	5	1	4	3	76
N.-D. de Grâce	16	2	16	4	1	–	–	39
Mount Melleray	12	2	32	4	–	–	–	50
Mount St. Bernard	12	2	17	6	5	1	–	43
Thymadeuc	12	2	17	5	–	–	4	40
Staouëli	14	4	36	11	–	–	–	65
Gethsemani	20	5	22	3	–	–	–	50
Aiguebelle	48	13	110	29	12	8	13	233
New Melleray	18	7	20	5	–	–	–	50
Fontgombaud	6	2	10	5	–	–	–	23
Totals	253	60	410	92	24	23	74	936

Convents of Nuns	Choir nuns	Choir novices	Lay- sisters	Lay-s. novices	Pos- tulants	Don- nées	Total
N.-D. des Gardes	33	4	33	7	4	19	100
N.-D. de Vaise	20	12	20	9	5	7	73
N.-D. de Maubec	38	5	37	8	16	9	113
La Cour Pétral	14	1	16	2	2	6	41
Totals	105	22	106	26	27	41	327

10. *Personnel of Cistercian Abbeys in Austria-Hungary in 1854.* (After Konrad, *Die Entstehung der Österreichisch-Ungarischen Zisterzienserkongregation,* p. 83). The number of priests engaged in parish work is given in parentheses.

Monasteries	Priests	Clerics	Novices	Lay-Brothers	Total
Heiligenkreuz	47 (19)	6	2		55
Neukloster	21 (7)		1		22
Hohenfurt	54 (25)	3			57
Rein	29 (16)	4	1		34
Lilienfeld	40 (24)	3	3		46
Mogila	13	2			15
Ossegg	51 (15)	5	2		58
Schlierbach	17 (10)	1	1		19
Stams	38 (18)	2		3	43
Szczyrzyc	8 (1)				8
Wilhering	27 (18)	5			32
Zirc	49 (10)	7	10		66
Zwettl	39 (20)	3	1	1	44
Totals:	433 (183)	41	21	4	499

11. *Personnel of the Cistercian Strict Observance in 1972*

Monasteries	Priests	Solemn Prof.	Temp. Prof.	Novices	Postulants	Oblates	Lay-Brothers	Total
Residence of the Abbot General (Rome)	1							1
France								
1. Cîteaux	28	22	7	1		1	11	70
2. La Trappe	26	15	1	5		2	3	52
3. Melleray	26	9	1	3		5		44
4. Port-du-Salut	14	7				2		23
5. Bellefontaine	24	28	4	2		4	3	65
6. Aiguebelle	40	24	1	2		2	5	74
7. Sept-Fons	37	29	5	3			3	77
8. Oelenberg	25	10	1	1			1	38
9. Bricquebec	34	16	2				3	55
10. Mont-des-Cats	34	13	2	6		6	4	65

Personnel of the Cistercian Strict Observance in 1972

Monasteries	Priests	Solemn Prof.	Temp. Prof.	Novices	Postulants	Oblates	Lay-Brothers	Total
11. Tamié	19	2	3	5		1	3	33
12. Timadeuc	28	24	1	2	3	2	2	62
13. Neiges	29	7	3	9		2	1	51
14. Désert	18	7		2	1		1	29
15. Dombes	19	11	1	1	1		7	40
16. Acey	13	11		1		1		26
Belgium								
17. Westmalle	31	15	1		1		12	60
18. Saint-Sixte	14	6		2			7	29
19. Achel	34	18	2	2	1		4	61
20. Scourmont	34	9	2	1		1	3	50
21. Saint-Remy	16	16	3	4	1	1	1	42
22. Orval	29	9	6	2			1	47
Holland								
23. Tilburg	32	15		1			21	69
24. Echt	19	2					6	27
25. Diepenveen	25	11		2			3	41
26. Tegelen	17	12			1		11	41
27. Zundert	31	23	1	2	1			58
Spain								
28. Oliva	17	9	1	7		1	4	39
29. San Isidoro	38	39	4	1	1	1	1	85
30. Viaceli	36	21	2	2	2	3	1	67
31. Osera	13	2	1					16
32. Huerta	16	8	1					25
33. Martyrs (San Pedro)	15	11	2		3			31
34. Sobrado	5	3	3		3	1	1	16
U.S.A.								
35. Gethsemani	40	52	6	5	6	4	6	119
36. New Melleray	44	17	1	5	1		16	84
37. Spencer	44	24	4	2	2		23	99
38. Holy Spirit	35	16	4	2	2		4	63
39. Holy Trinity	26	2	1	2	3		13	47
40. Guadalupe	22	2	4	2	3		18	51
41. Mepkin	17	15		1	2	1		36
42. Berryville (Holy Cross Abbey)	14		1	1			17	33

Personnel of the Cistercian Strict Observance in 1972

Monasteries	Priests	Solemn Prof.	Temp. Prof.	Novices	Postulants	Oblates	Lay-Brothers	Total
43. Genesee	21	17		2	3	1		44
44. Ava (Assumption Monastery)	11			1	1		7	20
45. New Clairvaux	12		1	4	1		14	32
46. Snowmass	5	1	2	2	1		8	19
Canada								
47. Lac	57	35	2	4	3	1	5	107
48. Prairies	17	9	2	4	3		2	37
49. Mistassini	21	11	2	4		2		40
50. Calvaire	16	5		4				25
Great Britain								
51. Mount Saint Bernard	36	21	4	2	2		2	67
52. Caldey	20	2		3		1	2	28
53. Nunraw	17	19	1	1				38
Ireland								
54. Mount Melleray	47	47	2	1	3	3	5	108
55. Mellifont	25	16		1			5	48
56. Mount Saint Joseph	37	22	2				5	66
57. Bethlehem	23	19	2	3				47
58. Bolton Abbey	9	4					3	16
Yugoslavia								
59. Mariastern	3	1			1		1	6
60. Délivrance	7						5	12
61. Klostar Ivanic	6		1	3				10
Italy								
62. Tre Fontane	14	9	4	5		1	3	36
63. Frattocchie	14	8					2	24
Germany								
64. Mariawald	25	12	2	2			8	49
Austria								
65. Engelszell	14	2		1			8	25
Israel								
66. Latroun	17	5	2	1		1		26

Personnel of the Cistercian Strict Observance in 1972

Monasteries	Priests	Solemn Prof.	Temp. Prof.	Novices	Postulants	Oblates	Lay-Brothers	Total
Japan								
67. Phare (Shudoin)	22	22	1		3	1	4	53
Hongkong								
68. Liesse (Lantao)	10	4			1	1		16
New Caledonia								
69. N.-D. des Iles	2	2	1					5
New Zealand								
70. Kopua (Southern Star Abbey)	8	8	3	1			1	21
Australia								
71. Tarrawarra	17	2	3	3			8	33
Indonesia (Java)								
72. Rawa Seneng	12	6	4	2	5			29
Argentina								
73. Azul	8	9	1	2			1	21
Chile								
74. La Dehesa	4	5		2			1	12
Philippines								
75. O.L. of the Philippines	2	4						6
Africa								
76. Atlas (Algeria)	8						1	9
77. Koutaba (Cameroon)	2	1	3	1	2			9
78. Mokoto (Zaire)	4	4			1			9
79. Victoria (Kenya)	8	11	4	1	7		2	33
80. Kasanza (Zaire)	6	2	3	4	3	1		19
81. Maromby (Malagsay Rep.)	7		2	2			2	13
82. Bela Vista (Angola)	3	5	5		4			17
83. Bamenda (Cameroon)	6	9	4	11	5			35
84. Kokoubou (Dahomey)	2	1	1					4
Totals:	1,685	949	149	166	87	54	325	3,415

Average age of the total: 52.18

12. *Personnel of the Cistercian Order (O. Cist.) in 1974*

Monasteries	Priests	Clerics	Choir Novices	Choir Oblates	Lay-Brothers	Brother Novices	Brother Oblates	Total
Residence of the abbot general (Rome)	1				1			2
I. *Austrian Congregation*								
1. Rein-Hohenfurt	22		3		2			27
2. Heiligenkreuz	43	5			1		1	50
3. Zwettl	38							38
4. Wilhering	45				8			53
5. Lilienfeld	41	1						42
6. Schlierbach	39	2	1		12			54
	229	8	4		24		1	266
II. *Congregation of Mehrerau*								
7. Wettingen-Mehrerau (Austria)	25				16			41
8. Marienstatt (Germany)	23				4			27
9. Stična (Yugoslavia)	18				11			29
10. Stams (Austria)	16	2	3		2			23
11. Himmerod (Germany)	12				13			25
12. Hauterive (Switzerland)	11	2	2		11			26
Seligenporten (suppressed)	4							4
	109	4	5		57			175
III. *Congregation of Saint Bernard in Italy*								
13. Chiaravalle	5							5
14. S. Croce	19	2						21
15. S. Bernardo alle Terme	5							5
16. S. Maria delle Grazie	2							2
17. S. Antonio—Cortona	1							1
18. S. Maria dei Lumi	5							5
19. S. Salvatore	4							4
20. Chiaravalle Milanese	9	2	1					12
21. S. José de Rio Pardo (Brazil)	6	1	2					9
	56	5	3					64

Personnel of the Cistercian Order (O.Cist.) in 1974

Monasteries	Priests	Clerics	Choir Novices	Choir Oblates	Lay-Brothers	Brother Novices	Brother Oblates	Total
IV. *Congregation of Mary Mediatrix*								
22. Bornem (Belgium)	26			6				32
23. Val-Dieu (Belgium)	8							8
24. Marienkroon (Holland)	43			10				53
	77			16				93
V. *Congregation of the Immaculate Conception*								
25. Lérins (France)	24	1	1	1	7			34
26. Rougemont (Canada)	22	3	1					26
27. My-Ca (Vietnam)	15		7					22
	61	4	9	1	7			82
VI. *Congregation of the Immaculate Heart of Many*								
28. Ossegg (in dispersion)	9	3						12
29. Langwaden (Germany)	6			1			1	8
	15	3		1			1	20
VII. *Congregation of Zirc*								
30. Zirc (in dispersion)	87							87
31. Spring Bank (U.S.A.)	2	2			2	3		9
32. Dallas (U.S.A.)	35	2						37
	124	4			2	3		133
VIII. *Congregation of Casamari*								
33. Casamari	33	7	6		8			54
34. S. Domenico	5				1			6
35. Valvisciolo	6				1			7
36. Cotrino	5				1			6
37. Martano	5				1			6
38. Chiaravalle della Colomba	3				1			4
39. Piona	11				1			12
40. Asmara (Eritrea)	23	7	17		5			52
41. Trisulti	8				1			9
42. Claraval (Brazil)	7							7
43. Firenze	9	1			1			11
44. Mendida (Ethiopia)	8	4			4		1	17
45. Mount Laurel (O.L. of Fatima, U.S.A.)	4							4
46. Pavia	9				2			11
	136	19	23		27		1	206

485

Personnel of the Cistercian Order (O.Cist.) in 1974

Monasteries	Priests	Clerics	Choir Novices	Choir Oblates	Lay-Brothers	Brother Novices	Brother Oblates	Total
IX. *Spanish Congregation*								
47. Poblet	27	2	1		2		1	33
48. Solius	7	3	2	1				13
	34	5	3	1	2		1	46
X. *Polish Congregation*								
49. Mogila	30		1		4			35
50. Szczyrzyc	20		1		2		2	25
Oliwa	5				1			6
Henrykow	4				1			5
51. Wachock	18	1			3	1		23
52. Jedrzejow	10	1	1	1	2	1		16
	87	2	3	1	13	2	2	110
XI. *Congregation of the Holy Cross* (Brazil)								
53. Itatinga	8	3		2				13
54. Itaporanga	15	2	1		21		2	41
55. Jequitiba	10	3			4			17
	33	8	1	2	25		2	71
XII. *Congregation of the Holy Family* (Vietnam)								
56. Phuoc-Son	54	12	9		5			80
57. Chau-Son (North, dispersed)								
58. Chau-Son (South)	30	5	9					44
59. Chau-Thuy	9		3					12
60. Phuoc-Ly	26		11	2				39
	119	17	32	2	5			175
XIII. *Outside of Congregations*								
61. Borsodpuszta (dispersed)	4							4
62. New Ringgold (U.S.A.)	3		4		2			9
Boquen (suppressed)	4							4
	11		4		2			17
Totals:	1,092	79	87	10	182	2	8	1,460

486

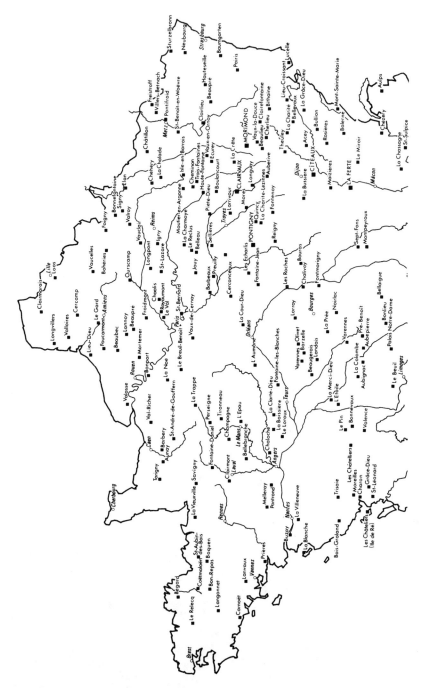

488

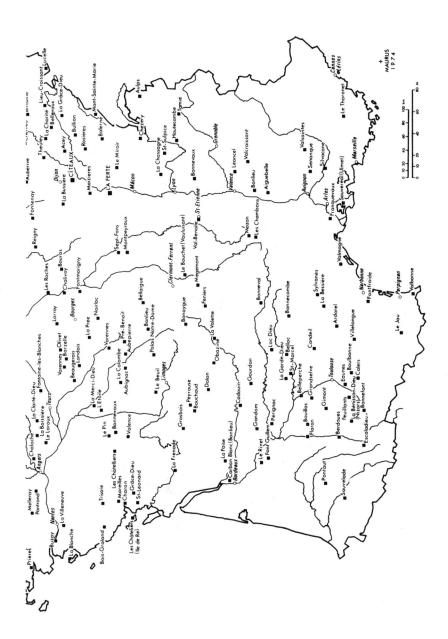

1. France

Kinloss
Deer
Aberdeen
Cupar Angus
Dundee
Balmerino
Iona
Culross
Edinburgh
Glasgow
Newbattle
Melrose
Newminster
Macosquin
Londonderry
Sweetheart
Glenluce
Dundrennan
Sadell
Assaroe
Belfast
Comber
Grey
Inch
Armagh
Calder
Rievaulx
Newry
Rushen
Jervaulx
Byland
Boyle
Furness
Fountains
Sawley
Kirkstall
Clare
Whalley
Meaux
Abbeylara
Abbeyshrule
Mellifont
Liverpool
Roche
Louth Park
Abbeyknokmoy
Bective
Kilbegan
St-Mary's Dublin
Vale Royal
Kirkstead
Corcomroe
Monasterevin
Basingwerk
Conway
Rufford
Revesby
Dieulacress
Swineshead
Baltinglass
Combermere
Croxden
Derby
Vaudey
Abbeylex
Valle Crucis
Hulton
Garendon
Kilcooly
Cymmer
Abington
Strata Marcella
Merevale
Sibton
Monasteranenagh
Holycross
Buildwass
Birmingham
Pipewell
Kilshane
Cashel
Graiguenamanagh
Cwmhir
Combe
Sawtrey
Abbeydorney
Abbeyteale
Jerpoint
Bordesley
Stoneleigh
Northampton
Fermoy
Inishlounaght
Strata Florida
Biddlesden
Warden
Woburn
Tilty
Midleton
Dunbrody
Dore
Hailes
Bruern
Coggeshall
Cork
Tintern Minor
Flaxley
Oxford
Thame
Tracton
Glangragh
Whitland
Grace Dieu
Tintern
Medmenham
Stratford
Abbeystrowley
Abbeymahon
Calder
Neath
Kingswood
London
St-Mary Grace
Margam
Llantarnam
Stanley
Boxley
BEER
Waverley
Cleeve
Robertsbridge
Dunkeswell
Forde
Netley
Newenham
Bindon
Beaulieu
Quarr
Buckfast
Buckland
+
MAURUS
1975

0   50   100 km
0   25   50   75 M

2. The British Isles

490

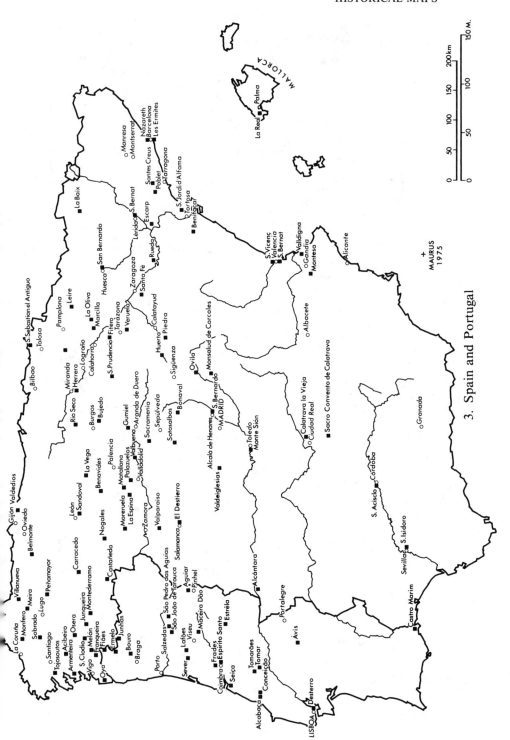

3. Spain and Portugal

MAURUS
1975

4. Germany

5. The Low Countries

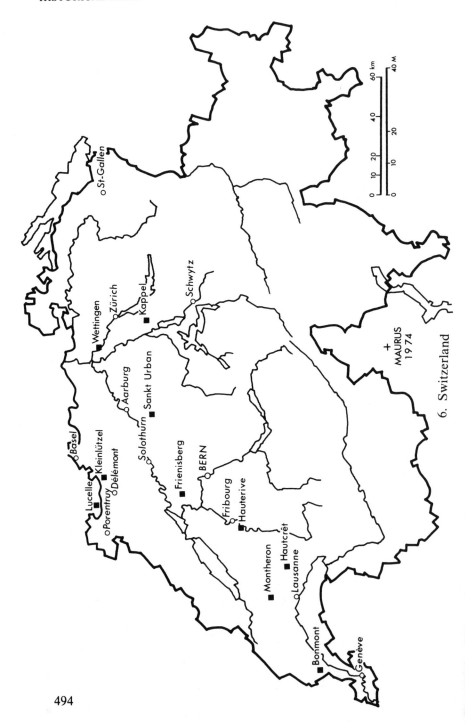

6. Switzerland

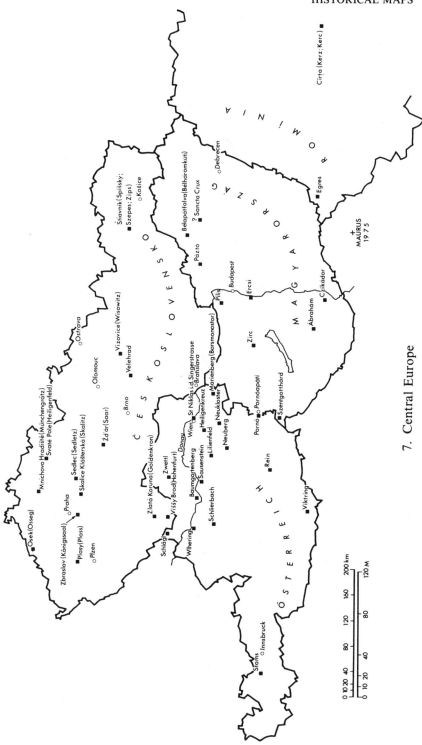

7. Central Europe

Cîrta (Kerz; Kerc) ■

R O M Í N I A

○ Debrecen

Egres ■

Bélapátfalva(Bélháromkúti)
? Sancta Crux ■

Šiavnik (Spišský;
Szepes; Zips) ○
○ Košice

M A U R U S
1975

M A G Y A R O R S Z Á G

Páztó ■

Ercsi ■
○ Budapest

Pilis ■
Csikádor ■
Ábrahám ■

Zirc ■

Vizovice (Wisowitz) ■

○ Ostrava

Velehrad ■

○ Olomouc

○ Brno

Č E S K O S L O V E N S K O

Marienberg (Borsmonostor) ■
St Niklas i.d. Singerstrasse ■
○ Bratislava

Mnichovo Hradiště (Münchengrätz) ■
Svaté Pole (Heiligenfeld) ■

Sedlec (Sedletz) ■
Skalice Klášterská (Skalitz) ■

Žďár (Saar) ■

Porná ○ Pornóapáti ■

Szentgotthárd ■

Porná ■
Neukloster ■
Neuberg ■

Wien ■
Heiligenkreuz ■
Lilienfeld ■

Zlatá Koruna (Goldenkron) ■

Zwettl ■
Vyšší Brod (Hohenfurt) ■
Danau

Baumgartenberg ■
Sausenstein ■

Rein ■

Osek (Ossegg) ■

Zbraslav (Königsaal) ■
Praha ○
Plasy (Plass) ■
○ Plzen

Schlägl ■

Wilhering ■
Schlierbach ■

Viktring ■

Ö S T E R R E I C H

Stams ■
○ Innsbruck

0 10 20 40   80   120   160   200 km

0 10 20   40   80   120 M

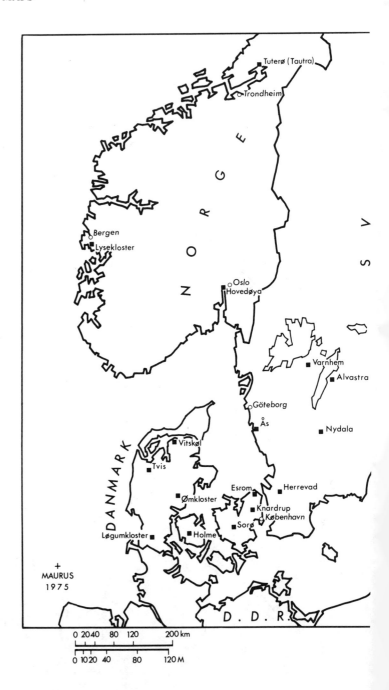

8. Scandinavia and the Baltic States

Piona
Acquafredda
Capolugo
Sanavalle
S.M. dell'Ospedale del Piave
Casalvolone
Chiaravalle di Milano
Morimondo Coronato
Milano
Lucedio
Cerreto
Torcello
Torino
Barona
S.Stefano del Corno
Venezia
Rivalta di Torino
Acqualunga
La Cava
Casanova
Quartazzola
Fontevivo
S.Trinita e S.Michele di Brondolo
Staffarda
Rivalta Scrivia
Valserena
Preallo
Parma
Chiaravalle della Colomba
Tiglieto
Strada
Sestri
Genova
Bologna
S.Severo
Mirteto
Buonsolazzo
Verruca
S.Gaudenzio
Montefavale
S.Pantaleone
Settimo
Chiaravalle d'Ancona
S.Michele a Quarto
Siena
Monte Acuto
S.Galgano
Fiastra
Monte Amiata
Sala
S.Giusto
Montalto
S.Pastore
Casanova
S.Martino al Cimino
Faleri
Ocre
Anabona
ROMA
Vittoria
S.Vito e Salvo
S.Sebastiano
S.Croce in Gerusalemme
Tre Fontane
S.Pietro di Paliano
Ripalta
Marmosoglio
Casamari
Palazzolo
Valvisciolo
Fossa Nova
Cassino
Ferraria
S.M.dell'Incoronata
Sterpeto
Zamone
Bari
Ponza
Napoli
Real Valle
Salerno
Canonica
S.M.del Galeso
Taranto
Sagittario
S.M.de Caritate
S.Spirito della Valle
Acquaformosa
Mattina
S.Trinità del Legno
Sambucina
Fiore
Corazzo
S.Angelo in Frigido
S.M. delle Paludi
S.Stefano del Bosco
Cabuabbas
S.Spirito di Palermo
S.Trinità di Palermo
Palermo
Messina
Altofonto
Roccamadore
Novara
S.M.di Spano
Catania
Roccadia
S.M.dell'Arco

0 50 100 150 200 km

0 50 100 150 M

MAURUS
1975

9. Italy

498

Buków (Bukowo)

Gdynia
Oliwa
Gdańsk (Danzig)

Pelplin

Szczecin (Stettin)
Kołbacz (Kolbatz)

Koronowo (Crone; Bessow)

Białystok

Bierzwnik (Marienwalde)

Mironice (Himmelstädt)

Łekno-Wągrowiec (Wongrowitz)
Włocławek

Wisła

Bledzew (Neu Dobrilugk; Blesen; Bleudzow)
Paradyż (Paradies)
Obra
Przemet

Ląd

WARSZAWA

Łódź

Lublin

Lubiąz (Leubus)
Wrocław (Breslau)

Sulejów

Wąchock

Krzeszów (Grüssau)

Henryków
(Heinrichau)
Kamieniece (Kamenz)

Imielnica (Himmelwitz; Chelmnick)

Jędrzejów

Koprzywnica

Rudy (Rude; Rauden)

Mogiła

Szczyrzycs

0 10 20 40   80   120   160   200 km

0 10 20   40   80   120 M

SOVETSKIJ SOJUZ

+
MAURUS
1975

10. Poland

499

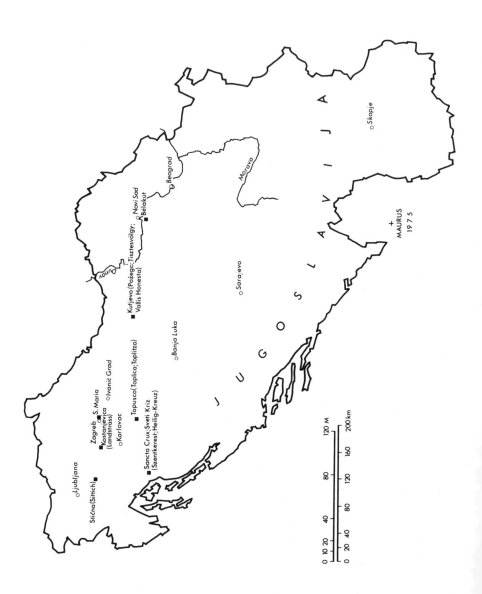

11. Yugoslavia

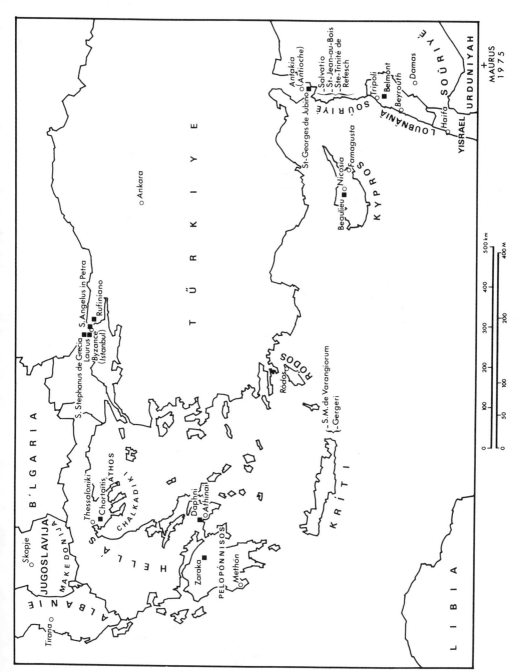

12. Greece and the Crusader States

501

Map labels:

ALBANIE
Tirana
JUGOSLAVIJA
Skopje
MAKEDONIJA
B'LGARIA
HELLAS
Thessaloniki
Chortaïtis
CHALKADIKI
ATHOS
Daphni
Athínai
PELOPÓNNISOS
Zaraka
Methón
LIBIA
KRITI
- S.M. de Varangiorum
- Gergeri
RODOS
Ródos
TÜRKIYE
Ankara
S. Stephanus de Grecia
S. Angelus in Petra
Laurus
Byzance (Istanbul)
Rufiniano
B'LGARIA
KYPROS
Beaulieu
Nicosia
Famagusta
St-Georges de Jubino
Antakia (Antioche)
- Salvatio
- St-Jean-au-Bois
- Ste-Trinité de Refesch
SOÛRIYE
Tripoli
Belmont
Beyrouth
Damas
Haifa
LOUBNANIA SOÛRIYE
YISRAEL URDUNIYAH
SOÛRIYE
+ MAURUS 1975

Scale: 0 50 100 200 300 400 500 km
400 M

INDEX

Persons active before 1500 are listed under their given names

506

Dombes, N.-D. des, abbey of, 210
Dominic, Guzman, Saint, 55, 78
Dominicans, 30, 55-6, 62, 73, 78, 79, 80, 82, 237, 352
Donati, 116, 341, 344, 379
Donations, see Economy
Donner, Raphael, sculptor, 279
Dore, abbey of, 236, 252, 293, 392
Dormitory, monastic, 73, 112, 113, 215, 373-4
Dublin, Cistercians in, 135
Dubois, Louis, biographer of Rancé, 245
Dünamünde, abbey of, 61, 62, 274
Dundrennan, abbey of, 123
Dunes, abbey of, see Les Dunes
Dunstan, Saint, 17
Düsselthal, monastery of, 152
Dwyer, William, abbot of Holy Cross, 124

Eberbach, abbey of, 37, 273, 316-7, 320, 328, 343, 371
Eberhard, abbot of Salem, 96
Ebrach, abbey of, 38, 83, 85, 104, 113, 117-8, 274, 279, 343
Ecclesiastica officia, 27, 251, 367, 374
Echt, abbey of, 210
Economy, Cistercian, 26, 282-333; changing nature of, 49, 303-10; tithes and churches in, 65-8, 293-5; decline of, 93, 323-4; under commendators, 157-8; of Trappists, 190; grants and foundations, 284-6; compensated donations, 286-93; granges, 295-8; reclamation of land, 298-9; destruction of villages, 299-300; hostile public opinion, 300-3; indebtedness, 304-7; leasing of land, 307-10; trade, 310-2; wool-trade, 312-5; wine making, 316-8; fisheries, 318-9; gardening, 310; animal husbandry, 319-20; bee-keeping, 320; urban property, 320; markets and fairs, 320; industry, 321-3; reform of, 324-6; late medieval, 326-8; of the 17th and 18th centuries, 328-9; of the *ancien régime,* 166, 329-32; contemporary, 333
Ecurey, abbey of, 171
Edmund Rich, archbishop of Canterbury, 79-80
Education of monks, 79, 80, 81, 82, 84-8, 92, 128, 131, 195, 196-7, 206; length of, 84; expenses of, 84; and Trappists, 191, 212

Edward I, king of England, 40, 64, 302, 396
Edward II, king of England, 392
Edward III, king of England, 97, 381, 392
Edward the Black Prince, 98
Eger (Bohemia), Cistercians in, 320
Eger (Hungary), Cistercians in, 169, 195
Egres, abbey of, 43
Elections, abbatial, 28
Elizabeth I, queen of England, 124
Elizabeth de Vergy, benefactress of Cîteaux, 18
Elizabeth de Vergy, foundress of Tart, 347
Endrédy, Vendel, abbot of Zirc, 221
Engelszell, abbey of, 209
England, Cistercians in, 38, 63, 75; Cistercian population of, 91, 338, 344, 380; national chapters in, 94; decline in, 97; papal provisions in, 102; free from commendatory govt., 105; dissolution in, 119-23; isolation of, 119; Trappists in, 182, 184; architecture in, 270; land grants in, 284-5; granges in, 297-8; wool-trade in, 312-5; lay servants in, 380; hospitals in, 382; distribution of alms in, 384
Enlightenment, influence of, 156-7, 164, 167, 168, 169, 193, 391, 398
Episcopal authority and Cistercians, 28-9
Ercsi, abbey of, 101
Eremitism, movement of, 6-7, 23-4, 37, 227, 228
Erfurt, university of, 85
Ernaldus, monk of Clairvaux, 46
Ernest, abbot of Loccum, 327
l'Escale-Dieu, abbey of, 41
Eskil, archbishop of Lund, 41, 42, 58
Espina, La, abbey of, 272
Esrom, abbey of, 42, 289
Estates General, of 1484, 106, 111; of 1561, 124
Estonia, Cistercians in, 319
d'Estrées, Angélique, abbess of Maubuisson, 355
Etampes, convention of, 35
Eugenius III, pope, 28, 35, 37, 68, 230, 294
Eugenius IV, pope, 94, 110, 129
Everard, abbot of Clairvaux, 81
Evora, fortress of, 58
Exemption, Cistercian, 17, 29, 68, 160, 192, 195, 197

tions in, 130-1; Feuillants in, 136-7; in the 18th cent., 154; and secularization, 175; and restoration, 193; in the 19th cent., 203, 205, 206; in the 20th cent., 221; scholarship in, 243-4; architecture in, 273
Itaporanga, abbey of, 219
Itatinga, abbey of, 219

Jacob of Eltville, abbot of Eberbach, 240
Jacob of Pecoraria, cardinal, 64
Jacques de Dijon, abbot of Preuilly, 238
Jacques Fournier, see Benedict XII
Jacques de Maleves, benefactor of Villers, 310
Jacques de Thérines, abbot of Châlis, 238, 326
Jacques de Vitry, cardinal, 349
Jaime I, king of Aragon, 393
James V, king of Scotland, 123
James, abbot of Cîteaux, 70
Janauschek, Leopold, historian, 43, 203
Jansenism, 145-6, 152, 359, 360
Janssens, Francis, abbot general, 218, 220
Japan, Trappists in, 208, 363
Jardinet, abbey of, 115, 116
Jean Casaleti, abbot of Sénanque, 87
Jean de Cirey, abbot of Cîteaux, 89, 105-6, 110-1, 325
Jean de Dun-le-Roi, scholastic, 238
Jean Eustache de Mons, abbot of Jardinet, 115
Jean de Gesves, abbot of Moulins, 115
Jean de He, scholastic, 238
Jean de Hermontville, monk of Bonnefontaine, 99
Jean d'Hostel, abbot of Aiguebelle, 99-100
Jean de Mirecourt, theologian, 239
Jean Picart, abbot of Cîteaux, 110
Jean de Sindewint, scholastic, 238
Jean de Weerde, scholastic, 238
Jeanne, nun of Marquette, Blessed, 354
Jequitibá, abbey of, 219
Jerome, Saint, 6, 18
Jerpoint, abbey of, 272, 315
Jervaulx, abbey of, 122, 270, 309, 319, 320, 322, 323, 344
Jesuates, order of, 109
Jesuits, see Society of Jesus
Jews, money-lenders, 290, 306; in Spain, 130

Joachim of Fiore, mystic, 37, 235
Jodoc Rosner, abbot of Pilis, 117
Johannes Clemme, founder of Sibculo, 113
Johannes Dederoth, reformer of Bursfeld, 110
Johannes Ellenbogen, abbot of Waldsassen, 242
Johannes Tauler, mystic, 242
John XXII, pope, 102, 104, 326
John XXIII (anti-pope), 104
John II, king of Aragon, 103
John, king of England, 292, 302, 304, 314, 319, 394
John III, king of Portugal, 132
John Cassian, ascetical writer, 23
John Castiel, abbot of Brondolo, 94
John Chidley, abbot of Ford, 97
John, abbot of Cîteaux, 70
John, monk of Cîteaux, 16
John of Fécamp, abbot, 5
John, abbot of Ford, author, 233
John Fryboys, monk of Meaux, 303
John Godard, abbot of Newenham, 234
John Gualbert of Vallombrosa, 10, 29, 334
John of Gubbio, cardinal, 16
John Hawkwood, condottiere, 96
John of Limoges, author, 233-4
John of Martigny, abbot of Cîteaux, 114
John Montecute, abbot of Bindon, 97
John, abbot of Morimond, 86
John Pecham, archbishop of Canterbury, 396
John, abbot of Pontigny, 80-1
John of Pontoise, abbot of Cîteaux, 64
John of Toledo, cardinal, 74, 81, 83
John, abbot of Viktring, 236
John Wycliffe, reformer, 240
Jongelinus, Gaspar, historian, 244
Joseph II, emperor, 156, 164, 168, 170, 176, 195, 196, 387
Joseph Bonaparte, king of Spain, 177
Josephinism, 195, 196, 197
Jouaud, Jean, abbot of Prières, 142-9, 245, 358
Jouy, abbey of, 44, 328
Julius II, pope, 87, 131
Jully, convent of, 347
Jung, Stephan, abbot of Salem, 160
Justice, abbatial courts of, 393-4

Wiesinger, Aloysius, abbot of Schlierbach, 219
William, duke of Aquitaine, 2
William, abbot of Cîteaux, 97, 348
William Fossard, benefactor of Meaux, 290
William, abbot of Fountains, 63
William of Maleval, Saint, 114
William of Malmesbury, chronicler, 12, 15, 23-24
William of Ockham, 239
William, provisor in Paris, 82
William de Percy, founder of Sawley, 284
William of Ponthieu, benefactor of Clairvaux, 323
William, abbot of Rievaulx, 39, 63
William, abbot of Robertsbridge, 53
William Rymington, scholastic, 240
William of Saint Thierry, mystic, theologian, 229-32
William de Stuteville, sheep-farmer, 313
William of Sutton, benefactor of Meaux, 303
William of Volpiano, abbot, 5
William, earl of York, founder of Meaux, 285
Williamites (hermits), 114-5

Windesheim, canons of, 110
Wine, drinking of, 370, 372; production of, see Economy
Winter, Franz, historian, 293, 352, 382
Woburn, abbey of, 122, 285, 391
Wolsey, Thomas, cardinal minister, 120, 121
Wongrowitz, abbey of, 134
Wool-trade, 53; see also Economy
Worms, general chapter in, 93
Wunn, Thomas, abbot of Salem, 133, 134
Würzburg, convention in, 117; Enlightenment in, 157
Wyart, Sébastian, Trappist abbot general, 188-9

Ysselstein, priory of, 113, 114, 116
Yugoslavia, Cistercians in, 209, 216, 217

Zamet, Sébastien, bishop of Langres, 359, 360
Zinna, abbey of, 90, 296, 321
Zirc, abbey of, 43, 153, 195-6, 198, 201, 203, 205, 206, 217, 221, 247, 277, 280, 333
Zwettl, abbey of, 90, 196, 203, 275, 279, 381, 387, 391